Food in Antiquity

Note on cover illustration

The Exeter Fish-plate

Royal Albert Memorial Museum, Exeter, England.
Reproduced courtesy of the Museum.
Photo M. Dobson

Among the more modest products of the pottery shops of the Greek mainland and the Greek settlements in Sicily and South Italy, the red-figured fish-plate enjoyed a temporary vogue in the 4th century BC. The plate has been given its name in modern times from the fish that decorate the upper surface. Some fish-plates have been found in domestic contexts, and it seems likely that the plate would have been used for fish, but it may have carried nuts, fruit and cakes besides. However, the majority of known fish-plates come from graves, and the shape was perhaps more usually made to serve as a funerary offering; in one instance, from a grave near Palermo, a quantity of fish-bones were found on the plate.

The shape of the plate consists of a broad surface that slopes down to a small depression in the centre where the juice of the fish was caught. The central depression seems also to have supported a small black bowl that held the fish-sauce. There was a deep, overhanging rim and a broad ring foot.

There are some fish-plates that carry no decoration, only the black paint, but the majority have an assortment of fish painted on the broad upper surface around the central depression. The overhanging rim may also be decorated with fish; more usually, it carries a wave pattern or vertical stripes, or is left plain black. The fish are most often perch, bream and such; sometimes shell-fish, octopus and torpedo fish are included.

The vogue for such decorated plates seems to have started in Athens around 400 BC, but by the middle of the 4th century the various areas with Greek communities in Sicily and South Italy (Campania, Paestum and Apulia), which had always been receptive to craftsmen and ideas from the Greek mainland, particularly from Athens, took up the notion of the red-figured fish-plate and made it their own. Much the largest proportion of the fish-plates that are known now (over one thousand) were made in these western localities.

The Exeter fish-plate was made in Campania, most likely in or near the town of Cumae, and comparison with other known examples suggests that it was decorated by the Bonython Painter soon after the middle of the 4th century BC. The fish depicted are two-banded and striped bream; shell-fish are also included, one large and three small white.

The plate with its central depression and its decoration underlines the importance of fish in the diet of the time.

Brian Sparkes

Bibliography

I. McPhee & A.D. Trendall 1987 *Greek Red-figured Fish-plates* (14th Supplement to *Antike Kunst*, 1987); for the Bonython Painter, see pp. 85-6 and pl. 25d-f.

J. Delorme & C. Roux 1987 *Guide illustré de la faune aquatique dans l'art grec.*

N. Kunisch 1989 *Griechische Fischteller: Natur und Bild.*

I. McPhee & A.D. Trendall 1990 'Addenda to *Greek Red-figured Fish-plates*', *Antike Kunst* 33, 31-51; for the Bony-thon Painter, see p. 40 and pl. 10,1. The Exeter fish-plate should be added as Campania IIC2i no. 56b.

FOOD IN ANTIQUITY

edited by
John Wilkins, David Harvey & Mike Dobson

Foreword by
Alan Davidson

UNIVERSITY
of
EXETER
PRESS

First published in 1995 by
University of Exeter Press
Reed Hall
Streatham Drive
Exeter EX4 4QR
UK

Designed and typeset in Caslon 10.5/13.5 by Mike Dobson,
Pallas (Computing in the Arts), University of Exeter,
Queen's Building, EX4 4QH.

Printed in Great Britain by Short Run Press Ltd. Exeter

British Library Cataloguing in Publication Data
A catalogue record of this book is available from the
British Library

ISBN 0 85989 418 5

Contents

☐

Part Two
Meat and Fish

Part Three
The Social and Religious Context
of Food and Eating

Part Six
Food and Literature

Foreword

Alan Davidson

THE concept behind this book, and behind the highly enjoyable and successful conference which it represents, is to my mind, an excellent one. It would have been unsurprising, but less felicitous, if the subject had been 'Food in Classical Greece and Rome'. The wider, almost panoramic, screen which the conference organisers and the editors of the book preferred is such that the main emphasis could be and is on Greece and Rome, quite naturally and understandably, but without leaving everyone else languishing in a sort of limbo outside the city gates.

Recalling, across five decades, my own undergraduate studies of 'Ancient History', I realise that they would have been of greater value to me if something had been done to set Greece and Rome in a wider context. I knew of course that there had been other civilisations and that while Greece and Rome flourished there were other peoples 'out there' who had to be kept at bay (or who, eventually, forced their way onto the centre of the stage and wrecked the scenery), but such peoples had little reality for me; they constituted little more than a forgotten and irrelevant past or an outer darkness which could be deemed useful because it threw into even higher relief the shining accomplishments of the two great classical civilizations.

The mild sense of wrong which I now feel when I look back at my partial studies of what should have been a wider field is echoed in a curious way by feelings which I have about much of the writing on food and cookery which confronts us on bookshop shelves. Too much of it, especially where historical aspects are involved, seems to revolve around the elite, the tiny, tiny proportion of people who could afford this or that and whose tables were almost unimaginably opulent from the point of view of the 99% of 'others' who were their contemporaries. Of course it is legitimate to write about the food of the elite if one knows and states that that is what one is doing. It can be an interesting subject, and often has the advantage that good source material survives, in literary form. But it is a different matter if one writes about the food of the elite, past or present, as though that was all there was which would interest anybody.

There is a parallel between these two feelings of mine, in that they both concern the sweeping aside of the lesser breeds or the ordinary people, *aka hoi polloi.*

The present book, as it happens, demonstrates effectively how both these failures of scope may be avoided. Part Four, 'Beyond the Greco-Roman World', by its very title dispels any notion that the first point has been overlooked; and the introductory paragraphs of Peter Reynolds' paper on Celtic Foods describe neatly how the point bears on whole nations, including the very one from which I see myself as descended. As for the second point, one need only read the papers in Part One to see that here too the spirit and practice of the contributors is absolutely as one would wish. There is a wealth of information about the food of ordinary people, indeed more that I would have dared hope for, since I had not previously known just how much information could be gleaned from a combination of archaeological and literary sources. Having been working recently on the history of cereal foods, and in the past on seafood of the Mediterranean region, I appreciate with particular warmth the new insights and data which the authors of many of the papers furnish.

Thus the paper on Byzantine porridge has a special appeal for me, dealing as it does with tracta and tarhana, two indisputably plebeian foods (whose other attributes, and even identities, may be and are disputed, as in the amiable confrontation during the early 1980s between Caroline Conran and Charles Perry). This and other essays show, also, how useful surviving food practices may be in interpreting the past. I remember the astonishment I felt, decades ago, when I read a study of Greek fish names whose author, needing to establish whether a certain species of fish existed in the Aegean in modern times, as in classical ones, cited a Greek cookery book of the mid 19th century in proof. Why, I wondered, not look in a Greek fish market? No such reproachful question could be leveled at the contributors to the present book. They show themselves well aware of the importance of the underlying continuity which makes it useful and relevant to reflect the 20th century back into the 1st or even earlier, looking for a congruence which is almost certainly there.

This continuity is at present subject to erosion on a greater scale than ever before, and extrapolation suggests that, at least in urban environments, traditional foodways may approach vanishing point during the next century. However, the continuity still exists now, and the present time may well be seen in retrospect as the ideal one for the exploration of food in antiquity – the full panoply of research tools and techniques having been brought to a condition usually referred to as 'state of the art', and the connecting threads between past and present being still, largely, intact.

Should this be so, then the already ample reasons for felicitating all who have been involved in the preparation and publication of this book will be further fortified; and so will be my hope that it proves to be the precursor of others of similar scope and quality.

I have two additional remarks, of a benedictory nature. One is highly specific. Elizabeth Craik is to be congratulated for having, near the beginning of her interesting paper on Hippokratic Diaita, laid hands on the endlessly parroted and to me somewhat irritating aphorism 'You are what you eat' and dissected it into comprehensible constituent parts – or, should I say, replaced it by significant sentences. This is exactly what Rumohr, that pioneer philosopher of food and still the most down-to-earth and unpretentious of them all, might have done, but for the circumstance that he preceded, rather than followed, the Frenchman who fed the original aphorism to the waiting parrots.

Secondly, a general point. To say that in the past there has been a chasm between classical studies as such on the one hand and food history studies on the other would be misleading. You cannot have a chasm with something on one side and nothing on the other; but food history studies, as such, have only recently come into existence. However the reader will see what I mean. And this book from Exeter, like the conference which it records, provides a clear and welcome sign that the two fields are acquiring beneficial organic connections of a kind which had only rarely been glimpsed, or dreamed of, in the past.

ABBREVIATIONS

Titles of ancient works, modern works and periodicals have been printed in full, but the usual abbreviations, listed here, have been used for standard collections of texts and works of reference. See p. 325 for abbreviations of papyrological works used in Chapter 23; p. 350 for Hippokratic treatises referred to in Chapters 25 and 26.

CIL   *Corpus Inscriptionum Latinarum*, various editors (Berlin, 1862-)

FGH   *Fragmente der griechischen Historiker* ed. F. Jacoby (Leiden, 1923-)

FHG   *Fragmenta Historicorum Graecorum* ed. C. Müller (Paris, 1841-70)

IG   *Inscriptiones Graecae*, various editors (Berlin, 1873-)

KA   *Poetae Comici Graeci* ed. R. Kassel and C. Austin (Berlin and New York, 1983-)

PG   *Patrologiae Cursus Completus*: series Graeca, ed. J.P. Migne (Paris, 1857-66)

PL   *Patrologiae Cursus Completus*: series Latina, ed. J.P. Migne (Paris, 1844-64, 1958-)

SIG   *Sylloge Inscriptionum Graecarum* ed. W. Dittenberger, 3rd edition (Leipzig, 1915-24)

ACKNOWLEDGEMENTS

We are most grateful to the following whose support of the *Food in Antiquity* conference in 1992 made the present work possible; The British Academy, J. Sainsbury plc, The Wellcome Trust, The Society for the Promotion of Hellenic Studies.

GENERAL INTRODUCTION

John Wilkins

Until recently, the production and consumption of food, that vital part of ancient life, was, apart from the occasional monograph, neglected by Classical scholars. Over the past twenty-five years, however, numerous books have appeared, particularly in Europe; in the UK, influential studies have appeared from, among others, Peter Garnsey on the food supply, K.D. White on Roman agriculture, and Robert Sallares on food and its environment in the broadest sense. Europe and Britain came together in 1990, when Oswyn Murray published *Sympotica*, an international collection of papers on the history, archaeology and cultural background of the symposium,[1] in which the significance of the reclining banquet[2] and symposium is investigated at length, together with the buildings in which they took place, and with the poetry and political discourse associated with the occasion. *Sympotica* offers little space however to the *deipnon*, the banquet that preceded the drinking session: it is given much less attention than the drinking session with all its attendant ritual and cultural significance.

In this volume we try to redress the balance. We write for a diverse public, for the general reader as well as for the Classicist, for the historian of food as well as the historian of the ancient world. We are not particularly interested in the famous moment or the famous orgy – '[Nero's] feasts now lasted from noon to midnight, with an occasional break for diving into a warm bath' (Suetonius *Nero* 27); rather, we investigate some of the ways in which food and eating shaped the lives and thoughts of the indigenous peoples, rich and poor, of the ancient Mediterranean. Our chief concern is with ideas about food and its cultural significance in the widest sense, as well as with questions of production and processing.

Food as a cultural symbol, after all, was as important in antiquity as in our own times. Take the case of meat. For us the McDonald's hamburger is not so much animal protein wrapped in plant protein as beef/slaughtered animal processed with a certain kind of fat, served without alcohol in an American-style bun in utilitarian surroundings by a global corporation.[3] Similarly, the ancient Greeks and Italians were unlikely to consume meat without associating it both with the way the animal had died – in sacrifice to a god – and with commensality, eating with their peers; they were unlikely to eat a vegetable diet without associating it with poverty or unorthodox religious groups; and when they ate foreign foods, they were likely to associate them with ideas either friendly or hostile to that place of origin.[3] This at least is what many literary sources say. In everyday life the *majority* of people probably subsisted on a largely vegetarian diet (except at times of festival) and may have had little or no contact with imported foods. It is, of course, a difficult matter to rediscover the ways in which daily routine and the symbolic intermeshed in a culture long past.

We concentrate on food and eating around the ancient Mediterranean, and in Greece and Italy in particular. There are chapters on Egypt, Palestine, Lydia and Persia, but these have frequent and strong connections with the Greek world, and are often based on Greek sources of information. Only the chapters on Babylon and Celtic Britain lie outside the Mediterranean region. There is a broad consistency of product throughout the area, exemplified most strikingly by the dominance of *alliaceae* in the recipes that are the most distant in time and place, preserved on the Babylonian tablets of 1700 BC; these are discussed by Jean Bottéro in Chapter 18. There was at the same time much regional and local variety, and great variation in the preparation and consumption of food, just as there was in government, and in social and other forms of cultural organization. Greeks shared much with Romans, Persians and Egyptians, but also differed from them fundamentally.

Trade brought exotic products from the East, such as spices, fruits, grains and varieties of fowl. With the campaigns of Alexander, the East was opened up to the Greeks and then the Romans, and in time the peach, the apricot and the citron came west.[4] Almost all movement was westerly. (It should be noted that many food products, even where correctly identified, were very different from the versions we now have. Sheep and cattle have changed a great deal; fish were perhaps the least likely to be modified.)

We range over a long period, from about 17,000 BC until 1000 AD, though most chapters focus on the 'Classical' period from about 800 BC to 400 AD. Within that period, there were important changes in food products, eating habits and their cultural context; for example, in prehistoric times, cultivated varieties of the olive, the vine and cereals were introduced into the Mediterranean world, and in the 7th or 6th century BC the Oriental style of reclining at banquets replaced sitting.[2] Over such a period, total consistency is not likely to be found, and certainly not over a range of cultures with deep regional differences, such as those of Greece and Italy.

Texts in which food plays an important part were numerous in antiquity. Homer's *Odyssey* distinguishes good men from bad and Greek from foreigner partly in terms of how and what they ate, while ethnographers from Herodotos onwards identified peoples partly in terms of their eating-customs. Athenian comedies (of which there were hundreds) celebrated eating and food production as a part of the life of the ancient city. Books on farming were composed in prose and verse, in Greek and Latin. There are the botanical and zoological works of Aristotle and his pupils which considered the natural world in exhaustive detail, though they use classifications that differ from those of modern science. Less systematic studies which nevertheless contain a great deal of valuable detail are the *Natural History* of Pliny (23-79 AD) and the *Deipnosophists* of Athenaeus (an Egyptian Greek writing in Rome in the 2nd/3rd century AD). Basing his work on the format of the banquet and symposium, Athenaeus is a valuable author since he quotes a large number of earlier works *verbatim*;

these range through literature, comedy, history, ethnography, philosophy, medicine and science. Many of those works are otherwise lost to us.

Contributors have taken a number of specific topics and studied them within a particular period and with their own methodology. The volume is designed to give as it were a number of snapshots of eating in antiquity, and to exemplify a variety of ways in which problems of sources, interpretation and understanding may be addressed. At the same time, coherence is maintained by the organization of the chapters into sections as follows: cereals and staples; meat and fish; the social and religious context of food; beyond the Greco-Roman world; food and medicine; and food and literature. These sections impose order on the wide range of topics and approaches, and also offer a clear focus on a particular area. The section on medicine for example contains four chapters which discuss the Hippokratic approach to diet, but do so from the perspectives of very different authors (Hippokrates, Galen and Oribasios) and with different approaches. It should be added that there are few accessible books which offer so extensive and concise a survey of Hippokratic dietetics.

The editors have not sought to balance Roman and Greek contributions equally. There is consequently a preponderance of Greek material, particularly in such sections as the social and religious organization of eating. In our defence (if we thought defence were needed) we would point out that while cultural specificity is in some chapters crucial, in others, broad issues on a Mediterranean-wide basis are considered. Secondly, many texts cited, such as Galen and Oribasios in the medical section and Athenaeus, who appears in many sections, were written in Greek but within the Roman system and with Roman readers in mind.

Each section of the book has its own introduction, which both explains the ancient context and offers some guidance to the secondary literature.

For information on the classical authors mentioned in this book, the reader should consult the *Oxford Classical Dictionary* (2nd ed. 1970, 3rd ed. in preparation).

Notes

1. O. Murray (ed.) *Sympotica* (Oxford, 1990); P.D.A. Garnsey *Famine and Food Supply in the Graeco-Roman World* (Cambridge, 1988); K.D. White *Roman Farming* (London, 1970); Robert Sallares *The Ecology of the Ancient Greek World* (London, 1991). Specialist studies include G. Rickman *Roman Granaries and Store Buildings* (Cambridge 1971); L. Moritz *Grain Mills and Flour in Classical Antiquity* (Oxford, 1958); J.M. Frayn *Subsistence Farming in Roman Italy* (Fontwell, 1979). Important works from France and Italy in the last twenty-five years include: M. Detienne and J-P. Vernant *The Cuisine of Sacrifice among the Greeks* (1979, Engl. trans. Chicago, 1989); M. Detienne *The Gardens of Adonis: Spices in Greek Mythology* (1972, Engl. trans. Atlantic Highlands, 1977); L. Gallo *Alimentazione e demographia della Grecia antica* (Salerno, 1984); M.-C. Amouretti *Le pain et l'huile dans la Grèce antique* (Paris, 1986); O. Longo and P. Scarpi (eds) *Homo Edens* (Verona, 1989) and most recently Pauline Schmitt-Pantel *La cité au banquet* (Paris, 1992) on ritualised eating in a social and religious context. More titles are given by Mario Lombardo at the beginning of Chapter 19.

2. For the reclining banquet see B. Fehr *Orientalische und griechische Gelage* (Bonn, 1971) and J.-M Dentzer *Le Motif du banquet couché dans le Proche Orient et le monde grec du VIIème au IVème siècle avant J.-C* (Paris, 1982).

3. Roland Barthes discusses the associations of foods in for example his *Mythologies* (1957, Engl. trans., London, 1972), in the chapters 'Wine and Milk' and 'Steak and Chips'. At the end of the latter (64) he recalls the request for chips by General de Castries when the French were leaving Indo-China. This was 'not a vulgar materialistic reflex, but an episode in the ritual of appropriating the regained French community. The General understood well our national symbolism; he knew that *la frite*, chips, are the alimentary sign of Frenchness'.

4. On fruits imported from the East see T. Braun 'Ancient Mediterranean Food', in G.A. Spiller (ed.) *The Mediterranean Diets in Health and Disease* (New York, 1991) 10-55, 40-3.

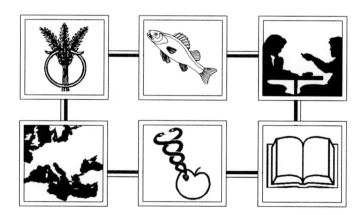

PART ONE

Cereals and Staples

Introduction cs Part One

In Book 2 of Plato's *Republic* (372a-3c), Socrates and Glaukon discuss the provision of food in the ideal city. Food is important enough to require regulation in the ideal state and is also one of the very first things that 'Socrates' discusses.

SOCRATES: First then let us consider how they will live…They will produce grain and wine and cloaks and shoes, won't they?…They will prepare their respective flours from barley and from wheat, baking bread from the wheat and kneading fine cakes from the barley, all to be placed on rushes or clean fresh leaves. They will recline on simple beds strewn with bindweed and myrtle, and will feast, they and their children, drinking their wine, garlanded, singing hymns to the gods, and living pleasantly together. They will not have children beyond their means, as a precaution against poverty or war.

GLAUKON: It seems that you are making these men have their feasts without *opsa* [strong flavours].

SOCRATES: Quite right. I forgot that they will have *opsa* – salt, of course, and olives and cheese, and that they will boil up bulbs and other vegetables, as they now do in the country. And perhaps we will serve them desserts, figs and chickpeas and beans, and they will parch myrtle-berries and acorns in the ashes, and will drink moderately with their meals. And with a peaceful and healthy life of this kind, they will no doubt reach old age and pass on a similar style of life to their offspring.

GLAUKON: If you were providing for a city of pigs, Socrates, isn't that just what you would feed them on?…They should have a normal diet. If they are not going to be uncomfortable, I think they should recline on couches and dine off tables and eat the *opsa* and desserts that they now have.

SOCRATES: Oh! I see. We are considering not just how to create a city, but how to create a *luxurious* city…The true city seems to me to be the one we described, a healthy one we might say. But if you wish, let us consider a city with inflammation. Why not? The provisions that we have described will not satisfy some people, nor will that way of life. There must be couches and tables, too, and all the other paraphernalia, and *opsa* and myrrh and incense and party girls and cakes, and each of these in great variety...So we must make a larger city, for the healthy one will no longer be big enough, but will have to be filled with a great mass of things that are not strictly necessary in cities, such as a crowd of hunters, artists..., poets...And we shall need a good many servants: tutors, nurses and wetnurses, lady's maids and barbers, and cooks and chefs, too. And we shall also need swineherds...and all the other kinds of flocks.

The community under discussion is an invented city, and Plato is by no means a typical Greek, but each of the proposals rests on assumptions which place that city firmly in the context of ancient Greek culture. Socrates at first proposes a diet for a 'true and healthy' city as opposed to a luxurious city. The foods are the staples wheat, barley and wine, to which strong flavours are added, provided by vegetables and nuts. All these (with the exception of acorns) are the products of agriculture; they are processed (by baking, kneading, boiling and parching), and then consumed in an overtly rural context. The citizens recline on rough pallets on the ground, adorned with flowers; they feast and drink and honour the gods; they do this as a group; and they balance population with the supply of food. Socrates' first proposal, then, takes the form of a self-sufficient community with no need for trade (that is, the food supply will consist of indigenous products).

Glaukon considers a vegetarian diet to be no better than pig's food, so Sokrates agrees to go a stage further, to the 'luxurious city', the one 'they now have'. This will affect both the range of foods themselves by adding meat and the work of chefs and pastry cooks, and the setting of the dinner, the furniture, the sensual element of scents, and sex. (It should be noted that the formal Greek banquet was sexually segregated, with citizen women not eating with men, though men were entertained by *hetairai*, translated above as 'party girls'. Roman wives did take part in formal meals.)

This is a literary passage, whose full interpretation would require consideration of its relation to the *Republic* as a whole, of Plato's own ideas about the simple life and the luxurious life, and of the relationship between the book he is writing and the world in which he lived. The community is based on a kind of primitivism that shows itself in the vegetarian diet and in the country life brought to town. The combination of cereal (Greek *sitos*) and strong flavour (Greek *opson*) was fundamental to a Greek approach to diet: this is discussed by James Davidson in Chapter 15. A similar approach is seen in Roman authors. The combination is similar, in the modern world, to an Italian pizza or pasta with sauce, and, in terms of current thinking, offers a good nutritional basis to the diet. Utilitarian though Socrates' proposal is, he outlines the contexts in which eating is to take place, and makes provision for ritual feasting (reclining on flower-strewn couches) and drinking in a ritualized context (indicated by garlands and song). There is no reference to eating with those outside the community, but one major form of internal contact in this society is brought about through eating and drinking, with rituals based on sharing food and drink.

Luigi Gallo,[1] taking a similar view of this passage, has suggested that the country diet, albeit modified so as to be entirely meat-free, represents the basic indigenous peasant diet of Attika (the territory controlled by Athens) while the second represents foods and processes imported into Athens: the luxury has come from somewhere else. 'Somewhere else' and 'trade' are the vital issues.

These considerations illustrate some of the ways in which the various aspects of food and eating in the ancient world may be approached by the modern scholar. Foods are not merely the plant and animal products that we eat. They either grow wild or are cultivated; they are acquired and processed for consumption, and may be eaten raw or cooked. There is more to eating than calorie intake. The preparation and consumption of food are surrounded by social rituals which are specific to each individual culture. These rituals have been investigated in, for example, an anthropological study of eating among native and immigrant American communities.[2] If we are to understand the consumption of food in antiquity then we must grasp its whole social context. Because of the distance in time, there is much we cannot know. We cannot tell, for example, how often rituals were observed, and how often (if at all) they were ignored, and by whom. A social anthropologist who studies the modern world may judge such things by empirical methods in a way that the student of the ancient world cannot.[3] To the modern observer, ancient dining appears highly formalized, with the segregation of the sexes in Greece, the diners reclining on couches, and the fixed order of eating and drinking. We might want to know how far this formality extended down the social scale. To what extent was it the practice of a relatively small proportion of the population? Did poorer people act with formality, but of a different kind from that of rich people? A famous passage of Dio Chrysostom (7.65-79) suggests that formality permeates far down the scale to the 'independent poor', at least on special occasions; here ritual is strong and the men still recline, albeit on a 'simple couch' (*stibas*) like the one described by 'Socrates'.[4]

Plato associates luxury with sensuality. Here we enter the area of sensation and pleasure associated with eating and drinking and the activities that accompanied them such as sex and games. Meat is an unexpected element in the luxurious city. Plato's definition of luxury may not be ours, but the association of certain foods with luxury is a feature of many societies.

Food and eating, then, are a complex matter, with complicated associations. In Socrates' ideal city, drinking wine and eating breads and cakes of wheat and barley are fundamental, and are conducted in a ritual way with garlands and hymns. For the cereals, the process of preparation and cooking is specified, as is the boiling of vegetables and the parching of acorns. These processes are what this section is all about, in particular the processing of staple cereals (*sitos*) or their equivalents mentioned above. Part Two then considers the supplementary proteins (*opsa*). Sarah Mason begins at first principles with the acorn, linked by the Greeks and Romans with primitivism. Early man, says Lucretius (*On the Nature of the Universe* 5.939), 'stayed his hunger among the acorn-laden oaks'. How do archaeological finds support this idea, and how is the archaeological evidence to be interpreted anyway? How were acorns eaten in the Mediterranean, and what can be learnt from comparative studies? In Chapter 2 Thomas Braun discusses two other foods unfamiliar to the modern palate, barley cakes and emmer bread. Drawing on Greek, Roman and Hebrew authors, he investigates how the grains were processed and how they were presented as breads, cakes or porridges, according to social context. K.D. White develops further related considerations, in particular the technical implications of milling – the implements and the grades of flour. While Braun and White discuss the Classical period, Stephen Hill and Anthony Bryer extend the enquiry to the Byzantine period and consider forms of porridge, cakes and bread into which processed flours were converted for consumption.

Many cereal foods were cooked (but not all – not, for example 'porridges'): in Chapter 5 Anthony Cubberley re-examines the evidence for the simple domed bread oven and suggests that this method of cooking may have been widespread. We might have known this long ago had literary sources thought it worth recording and archaeologists known what to look for among pieces of broken pottery. Grains and other foods are stored in various forms by peasant farmers. In Chapter 6, Hamish Forbes and Lin Foxhall examine strategies of food storage, with the help of comparative material from modern Greece. The section concludes with a discussion by Robert Sallares of a new technique for archaeologists, the analysis of DNA in organic remains. This technique takes further some questions raised by Sallares in *The Ecology of the Roman World* (London 1991). Where DNA has been preserved, certain identification of ancient animal and plant species will be possible. This is an area which hitherto has been fraught with uncertainty and imprecision. Readers who are unfamiliar with the molecular structures of foods will find illumination in Harold McGee, *On Food and Cooking. The Science and Lore of the Kitchen* (London 1986).

J.W.

Notes

1. 'Alimentazione urbana e alimentazione contadina nell' Atene classica', in O. Longo and P. Scarpi (eds) *Homo Edens* (Verona, 1989), 213-30 at 215.
2. M. Douglas (ed.) *Food in the Social Order: Studies of Food and Festivity in Three American Communities* (New York, 1984).
3. See for example, M. Douglas and M. Nicod, 'Taking the Biscuit: the Structure of British Meals', *New Society* 30 (1974), 744-7.
4. A. Dalby *Unequal Feasts: Food and its Social Context in Early Greece* (unpublished dissertation, Birkbeck College, London, 1993), 223-48.

❖ 1 ❖

ACORNUTOPIA? DETERMINING THE ROLE OF ACORNS IN PAST HUMAN SUBSISTENCE

Sarah Mason

Acorns: food for gods, pigs or people?

Cᴌᴀssɪᴄᴀʟ mythology and the writings of poets through the ages have often assigned the acorn a role as one of the principal foods on which people subsisted during a past 'Golden Age', when heroes and gods walked the earth, food was abundant, and there was no need for the hard labour associated with farming (see e.g. Graves 1960; Graves 1961; Hulme 1907; Loewenfeld 1957). Some have inferred that such writings represent the remnant of a folk memory from the hunter-gatherer past, and have suggested that acorns formed an important, perhaps the major, element of diet in pre-agrarian western Eurasia (Clark 1952; Frazer 1929, vol. 2, 259; Howes 1948; Loewenfeld 1957; Smith 1929; Soyer 1853). As yet, however, there is little evidence for such a hypothesis. During Classical times, and in later periods up to the present century, there are numerous documentary reports of the use of acorns as food by agrarian peoples throughout the Mediterranean basin and adjacent areas of Europe, South-West Asia and North Africa (see Mason 1992, chapter 3).

To what extent written accounts present an accurate picture of the role of acorns in western Eurasia during Classical and pre-Classical times is an important question for those interested in past diet and subsistence. Acorns are nutritionally similar to the cereals, being largely a source of carbohydrate, though some are closer to other nuts in containing considerable quantities of fats (Mason 1992, chapter 6 and appendix 1). Acorns therefore have the potential to occupy the same role in subsistence as cereals, and are known to have been an important, sometimes staple, food in other parts of the world, including California, Eastern North America and Japan. It is interesting in this context to note that the goddess Ceres of Roman mythology, better known for introducing cereals to mankind, is said to have been the first to replace their original food of leaves and grass with the acorn (Ovid *Fasti* 4.399, trans. Frazer 1929). The Greeks and Romans certainly recognised the nutritional value of acorns (e.g. Artemidoros 2.25, trans. White 1975; Borgeaud 1988, 14); and both wild and cultivated, and sweet and bitter types were known (Theophrastos *Enquiry into Plants* 3.8, trans. Hort 1916). The productivity of oak trees can also be compared favourably with that of cereals. The average yield of acorns in south-western Spain has been estimated at 5-700 kg/ha (Mazuelos Vela *et al.* 1967; Parsons 1962), in comparison with estimates made for past cereal productivity, under traditional Mediterranean systems of, at most, 650 kg/ha (Sallares 1991, 389).

Nevertheless, many of those writing, both in ancient and modern times, about western Eurasian acorn use have characterized acorns as a food fit only for animals, something which people would resort to only in times of hardship or famine, or as a food of those living in areas where agriculture was difficult (Borgeaud 1988, 14; Mason 1992, 80, 83). Documentary reports of acorn-eating often refer to people living in remote districts. Strabo, for instance, reported that in mountainous northern Spain people lived on acorn bread for much of the year (Strabo *Geography* 3.3.7, trans. Jones 1923); and the mountainous district of Arkadia in the Peloponnese, considered by the Greeks as a barbaric region where ancient customs persisted (Borgeaud 1988; Tripp 1970, 69), is closely associated with acorn-eating (Frazer 1913; Herodotos 1.66, trans. Godley 1946; Pausanias 8.4, trans. Jones 1933). As Arkadia also eventually became a model for the

'Golden Age' (Borgeaud 1988; Tripp 1970), our picture of the value put upon acorns as a food by the ancients is rather ambiguous.

The archaeology of acorns in western Eurasia: inadequacies and biases

Ideally archaeological, particularly archaeobotanical, evidence should be able to provide us with answers regarding the likely importance of acorns in the past. Acorns certainly are found at sites throughout Europe, the Mediterranean, and South-West Asia, dating from Mesolithic or Epipalaeolithic times to the medieval period (see Mason 1992, chapter 2; Vencl 1985). Finds date to at least 19,000 BP (17,000 BC) at the site of Ohalo II in Israel (Kislev *et al.* 1992). Acorns have been found at some of the early village sites of the Near East, including Çatal Hüyük, where some were found next to a fireplace 'as if they were just being roasted' (Helbaek 1964, 122). In Greece they have been recorded from early Neolithic sites, including Achilleion and Sesklo in Thessaly (Renfrew 1966), onwards. At Bronze Age Raskopanitza in Bulgaria acorns were found mixed with einkorn and barley grains on a saddle quern, and it has been suggested they were being ground into flour together (Renfrew 1973). Representations of acorns also occur as decorative items, e.g. as gold pendants from Gordion in Phrygia (7th/6th century BC: de Vries 1980, 164, fig. 4); as wreaths of gold acorns and oak leaves in the tombs of Vergina in Macedonia (4th century BC: Andronicus 1987, 75, 203, 214-5); and embossed on silver and gold bowls (*phialai*) from the Rogozen and Panagyurishté treasures of Thrace (3rd/4th century BC: Cook 1989, pl. 7B; Trustees of the British Museum 1976, 75, fig. 361).

However, there are various, largely unacknowledged, problems with interpretations of the archaeological evidence of acorn use. The number of sites in the region at which systematic techniques for the recovery of archaeobotanical remains have been used is still relatively small. The most common form in which cultural food-plant remains are preserved is as charred (sometimes termed 'carbonized') seeds, fruits, or vegetative organs (roots, tubers, etc.), in whole or fragmented form, as a result of accidental over-exposure to fire in processing, preparation for storage, or cooking, or occasionally destruction of whole settlements by fire. Such charred plant remains are protected from the usual processes of decay.

Though large charred plant organs or fragments, like large pieces of wood charcoal, are relatively easily seen and can be picked out from archaeological contexts, the use of flotation is usually necessary to separate the majority of charred plant remains from the surrounding deposits (Greig 1989).

It might be thought that the use of flotation – which can enable recovery of seeds and other plant fragments down to a size of 250μm or less – would not affect the recovery of such large and readily visible remains as acorns. Acorns have been found on many sites on which proper sampling and recovery of plant remains has not been undertaken, including sites in Europe excavated as long ago as the last century. However, in almost all cases only whole acorns or single cotyledons (half-kernels) have been recovered. In contrast, in Eastern North America, where acorns are often abundant on sites dating from *c.* 8,000 BP (*c.* 6,000 BC) until recent times, the vast majority of finds consist of fragments of acorn shell of 2 mm or less in size (Mason 1992, 30). Such fragmentary remains are not generally recovered from sites in Europe or the Near East, and it seems likely, therefore, that much of the available evidence has been overlooked.

Where acorn remains do occur in archaeological contexts it cannot necessarily be assumed that they are evidence of use as human food. Acorns have other potential uses. They may be used as tanning agents, though other parts of the oak, including the bark and the cupules of the acorns, contain higher concentrations of tannin, and are more often used in this context (cf. Jørgensen 1977; Mason 1992, appendix 2). They can also have a medicinal function, both for humans and animals (Mason 1992, 234). Dioskorides, for example, attributed healing properties to acorns (1.142, trans. Gunther 1934). They may also have been used as animal feed – their value to pigs in particular is well known (e.g. Parsons 1962; Smith 1929), and they are eaten by a wide range of domestic (as well as wild) animals (Mason 1992, chapter 3 and appendix 4). It has sometimes been suggested that the use of acorns for animal feed is unlikely to account for their presence in archaeological contexts, since it would involve much less effort to allow animals to forage for their own acorns (e.g. Jørgensen 1977; Renfrew 1973; Vencl 1985), but there is evidence from both ancient documentary sources, and from more recent times, that acorns may be collected for the stall-feeding of animals. Cato describes the collection of large quantities of acorns as feed for working oxen, and their processing to remove the astringent tannins (*On Agriculture* 54.1; 60, trans. Hooper 1934). During this century acorns have been collected for sale as pig feed on a small scale in south-western Iberia (Smith 1929). In south-eastern Turkey the collection of acorns to be fed to goats, from trees coppiced for firewood in areas from which animals are excluded, has recently been observed (Mason 1992, 93).

Generally in western Eurasia, it is difficult to obtain with certainty good direct evidence for the role of acorns in past human diet. Interpretations of past subsistence have consequently tended to reflect the ambiguity of documentary sources on acorn use. In addition, there is frequently a failure to take into account taphonomic, recovery and sampling biases which might affect the archaeobotanical record (Mason 1992, 45-46, 48, 189-95). Thus it has been possible for acorn-collecting to be considered a significant part of the economy during the Mesolithic at Grotta dell'Uzzo in Sicily (Lewthwaite 1986, 60), where the finds consist of only two charred acorn cotyledons, while in similar instances the paucity of finds in certain periods or areas has been interpreted to mean that acorn gathering could not have been an important part of the economy. In this author's opinion there is almost invariably, at present, insufficient direct archaeobotanical evidence to enable conclusions of this type to be drawn.

However, other types of information can aid the kinds of inferences that might be made about acorn use in the past. The most important of these are biological/ecological and ethnobotanical data.

Acorn availability and 'edibility'

The table on p. 18 and the map opposite give a very general picture of the present numbers and distribution of acorn species in Europe, the Mediterranean and South-West Asia. The table shows 32 species, some very widespread, and others with a much restricted distribution. In much of southern Europe and into parts of South-West Asia the number of species present is comparable with other parts of the world where acorns have been recorded ethnographically as important human food sources – e.g. California, with about 15 species, or Japan with 14. Eastern North America, which also has good archaeobotanical evidence for acorn use, has about 35 species in total. In none of these regions, nor within the regions indicated on the map overleaf, would all species necessarily be found growing together. However, in localities where several species of oak do grow in relatively close proximity this may have some significance in terms of the regular availability of acorns. Acorn production is not consistent from year to year. Both individual trees and whole local populations of one species may, for reasons that are poorly understood, go several years between producing a large crop of acorns, in what are known as 'mast' years (see Mason 1992, appendix 3). With several species present, however, it seems likely that the chance of factors adversely affecting production of all trees is likely to be reduced.

Table 1 also indicates those species for which there are data, qualitative or quantitative, on 'sweetness' or 'bitterness' of acorns. Though several

Fig. 1.1 Generalised areas of distribution of western Eurasian oaks referred to in the table on p.17. A: Northern Europe; B: South-Western Europe; C: North Africa; D: Italy and Corsica; E: South-Eastern Europe and the Black Sea coast; F: Western Turkey and the Levant; G: Central and Eastern Turkey, Iraq and Iran.

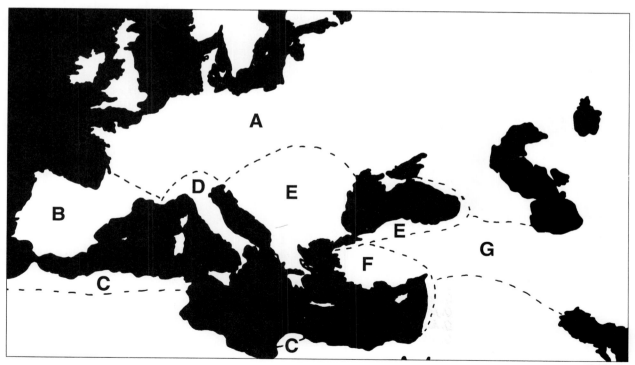

REGION	SPECIES	ENGLISH NAMES	TASTE	FOOD USE RECORDED
Throughout/ widespread (ABDEFG)	*Quercus petraea*	Sessile Oak	Bitter/Sweet	
	Q. pubescens			
	Q. robur	Pedunculate Oak	Bitter/Sweet	•
Mediterranean (BCDEF)	*Q. coccifera*	Kermes Oak	Bitter	•
	Q. ilex	Holm Oak	Sweet/Bitter	•
South-west Europe (B)	*Q. canariensis*			
	Q. congesta			
	Q. faginea			
	Q. fruticosa			
	Q. mas			
	Q. pyrenaica			
	Q. rotundifolia		Sweet	
	Q. suber	Cork Oak	Sweet	•
North Africa (C)	*Q. faginea*			
	Q. suber	Cork Oak	?Sweet	•
Italy and Corsica	*Q. cerris*	Turkey Oak		
	Q. congesta			
	Q. ithaburensis macrolepis	Valonia Oak	?Sweet	•
	Q. pyrenaica			
	Q. sicula			
	Q. suber	Cork Oak	?Sweet	•
	Q. trojana			
	Q. virgiliana			
South-east Europe and the Black Sea Coast (E)	*Q. cerris*	Turkey Oak		
	Q. dalechampii			
	Q. frainetto			
	Q. infectoria infectoria			
	Q. ithaburensis macrolepis	Valonia Oak	?Sweet	•
	Q. macranthera			
	Q. polycarpa			
	Q. pontica			
	Q. trojana			
	Q. virgiliana			
Western Turkey and the Levant (F)	*Q. alnifolia*			
	Q. aucheri		Sweet	
	Q. brantii		?Sweet	
	Q. cerris	Turkey Oak		
	Q. hartwissiana			
	Q. frainetto			
	Q. hartwissiana			
	Q. infectoria boissieri		?Bitter	

REGION	SPECIES	ENGLISH NAMES	TASTE	FOOD USE RECORDED
	Q. infectoria infectoria			
	Q. ithaburensis ithaburensis		Sweet	•
	Q. ithaburensis macrolepis	Valonia Oak	?Sweet	•
	Q. libani			
	Q. trojana			
	Q. vulcanica			
Central and Eastern Turkey, Iraq and Iran (G)	*Q. brantii*		Sweet	•
	Q. castanaeifolia			
	Q. cerris	Turkey Oak		
	Q. infectoria boissieri		Bitter	•
	Q. libani			•
	Q. macranthera			

Nomenclature and distribution follow (in order of priority) Hedge & Yaltirik (1982), Tutin et al. (1964) and Browicz (1982). See map 1 for areas of distribution. Data on taste are from Gaussen & Rouquette (1949), Hedge & Yaltirik (1982), Howes (1948), Smith (1929), Tutin et al. (1964) and the author's own observations. Records of use are from Hedrick (1972), Howes (1948), Mason (1991), Smith (1929), Townsend (1980).

Table 1.1
Oaks of western Eurasia

factors are responsible for the taste of an acorn (Mason 1992, 153-4), the most important of these is probably the tannin content. Acorns high in tannin are more astringent, and generally referred to as 'bitter'. Even 'sweet' acorns generally contain some tannin, and the term is rather subjective: in addition there may be culturally- or genetically-based variability in human perceptions of astringency (Mason 1992, 148). The acorns of the Holm Oak (*Quercus ilex*) are usually said to be sweet, but some of the most reliable authorities (Hedge and Yaltirik 1982; Tutin *et al.* 1964) report them as bitter, with their close relatives in, respectively, the eastern (*Quercus aucheri*) and the western (*Quercus rotundifolia*) Mediterranean differentiated in part by their sweet acorns. Sweet acorns are frequently referred to in the literature as 'edible' acorns. This term is misleading, as all acorns can be made edible, by leaching or otherwise removing or neutralizing the tannins. Tannin concentrations can vary considerably between trees of one oak species, a fact recognised by Theophrastos (3.8, trans. Hort 1916). Some acorns of the Holm Oak and *Quercus brantii* are palatable even when raw, and the same is said to be true of acorns from some trees of English Oak (*Quercus robur*) and Sessile Oak (*Quercus petraea*), the two species native to Britain (Mason 1992, 154).

It is not possible to assume, as some have done, that only 'sweet' acorns will be eaten (see Mason 1992, 84). The table on p. 18 shows those species which are recorded to have been utilized as food – seven of the 28 species. As the table indicates, two of these have astringent, or 'bitter', acorns, two have sweet acorns, and the remainder are variable or unknown. In North America, where acorns high in tannins tend also to have higher fat concentration, these seem to have been used at least as commonly as the sweeter species (Mason 1992, 74, 144-6, 148-9, 184). The correlation between fat and tannin does not necessarily hold with the western Eurasian species. Acorns of the Holm Oak and *Quercus brantii* are the species most commonly reported to have been used. These, both usually recorded as 'sweet' species, seem also to be slightly higher in fat than other species in their localities (Mason 1992, table 8). It may be that in some instances a high fat content, or perhaps other factors, are more important considerations in human choice than is a low concentration of tannins.

How acorns are used: ethnographic data and archaeological inference

Together with biological data, historic and ethnographic reports can aid the interpretation of archaeological data on acorn use, and enable more explicit inferences to be made about the past use of acorns. Such data can aid the understanding of factors that influence human decisions on acorns (either of particular species, or whether to use acorns at all). In addition, knowing something of the kinds of processing and preparation procedures required to make acorns palatable can aid an understanding of taphonomic processes, and thus can suggest what evidence of acorn use might, or might not, be expected in the archaeological and archaeobotanical records.

Though the sweetest acorns can be eaten after boiling or roasting like chestnuts, in all parts of the world where they have formed a major element of the diet acorns have generally been processed in more complex ways. Some form of leaching is generally required to remove the water-soluble astringent tannins from the acorns, and they are usually reduced by some means to a flour, which can then be baked into a bread- or cake-like substance, or cooked as a soup or 'mush'.

Probably the best accounts from western Eurasia of the preparation of acorn foods derive from Sardinia. Usai (1969) compiled many reports from the island, some obtained this century (see also Mason 1992, 86-7). Acorns, usually of Holm Oak, were first shelled, usually *en masse*, by being smashed in a container such as a goatskin bag. The kernels were then picked out and boiled in water for up to eight hours. This would soften them, and they would dissolve into a porridge-like mush, a process sometimes assisted by crushing with a pestle and mortar. Characteristic of the Sardinian processing sequence was the addition of red clay to the acorn mixture. Iron is present in the clay, and this has been shown to combine with the tannins in the acorns to form an insoluble compound, and thus rid the preparation of any remaining astringency (Johns and Duquette 1991). Ashes added to the cooking mixture probably assisted by raising the alkalinity and similarly neutralizing any astringent taste (Mason 1992, 187). The acorn mixture was generally cooled before eating, becoming fairly solid, and is usually described as 'bread', though it was not usually baked.

The final product of the Sardinian process in fact resembles rather closely the acorn 'mush' favoured by the Californian Indians, for many of whom, at the time of European contact, acorns formed the staple element of diet (see Mason 1992, 62-3). The particular method used in Sardinia, however, would require ready availability of fuel for such a long cooking process, as well as suitable vessels, perhaps of metal or pot. The processing sequence used most widely in California contrasts in this, and several other ways, with the Sardinian method. A great deal of detail regarding minor variations is recorded (see Mason 1992, 68-72), and the following is therefore a very generalised account.

In California acorns were invariably shelled one by one, rather than *en masse*, with tools such as a flat or cupped rock and a hammerstone. They were then pounded into very fine flour, usually with stone pestle and mortar. In some cases these were 'bedrock' mortars, made in outcrops of rock. Similar features are found in parts of South-West Asia (Hole 1979; Wright 1991). The flour was next placed in a hollow scooped in sandy soil, sometimes lined with leaves or other material. Water, cold or sometimes warmed, was repeatedly poured over the flour, a process often taking several hours, until all the tannins were leached out. This was indicated by a colour change in the flour from yellow to white. Leached flour and water were then cooked in watertight baskets, by the 'stone-boiling' method. Carefully selected stones, which would not crack with sudden temperature changes, were heated in the fire, then placed in the basket, and the mixture was stirred as it thickened to prevent burning. The 'mush' was eaten hot or cold, and when cool had a consistency firm enough to be cut into squares. Alternatively, moistened flour might be formed into large cakes which were wrapped in leaves and baked, often overnight, in a pit oven of heated stones insulated with a covering of earth.

Conclusions: preconceptions and biases

This paper has indicated something of the several types of data which can be used when investigating the role of acorns in past diet. Many of these are, however, subject to biases and it is important to recognise these. Biases affecting biological and archaeological data in particular have been discussed at length elsewhere (Mason 1992, chapters 7 and 8), and some of the problems with interpretation of archaeobotanical data have also been touched upon above. Documentary and ethnographic reports also are subject to their own biases. For instance, because of the problems of oak taxonomy and nomenclature, as well as the difficulties of translating plant names which pre-date the introduction of the Linnaean binomial system of nomenclature, to determine with certainty which species were referred to by the ancient writers, or even whether they were referring to oaks and not to other genera of food-producing tree, is virtually impossible (see e.g., Daubeny 1865; Hedrick 1972, 481; Hort 1916; Meiggs 1982; Sargeaunt 1920). Some more recent reports of acorn use give some indication of other biases. In one example, from a Mexican village, most people considered acorns to be inedible, but nevertheless believed them to be used in neighbouring mountain villages (Messer 1978), a situation reminiscent of the Greeks' view of acorn-eating in Arkadia. Similarly, one note of acorn use written by a North American as late as the middle part of this century (Hill 1952, 357) recorded that acorns currently 'furnish 25% of the food of the poorer classes in Italy and Spain in the form of acorn bread or cake', a report that is certainly not repeated in the European literature. It is a common experience among ethnobotanists that many people will not readily admit to the use of wild plants, but it also appears that wild plant-food use is commonly attributed to others, the more so the more remote they are. This does not, of course, mean that wild plant foods were not being used by these 'others', but it provides an intriguing insight into the biases that may affect such reports.

The extent to which such biases have distorted documentary reports from both ancient and more modern periods is probably unknowable. Ambiguity regarding the value of acorns as a food dates back to some of the earliest written sources, and persists to the present day in the archaeological literature. In recent times, it seems likely that it may be largely the preconception that acorns are something nasty, and even poisonous, which has prevented serious consideration of their use by many interested in past diets. A close examination of the ethnographic record indicates that such preconceptions are poorly founded. In Sardinia acorn foods were retained particularly as special foods for festivities; and in California, despite Europeans' reports of acorn mush as bland and unpalatable, acorns were an esteemed food, and the cooking of acorn products took into account subtle differences in the tastes of different species. To discover the true role of acorns as a past food source – as a last-resort famine food, as a food fit for the gods, or both – will require not only improvements in archaeobotanical and archaeological research, but an acknowledgement of both our own and past preconceptions regarding such a potentially important resource.

Acknowledgements

Many thanks to Jon Hather and Ann Butler for their comments on the paper; and to David Harvey for his many acorn-related postcards.

Bibliography

Andronicus, M. 1987 *Vergina: the Royal Tombs and the Ancient City* (Athens).

Borgeaud, P. 1988 *The Cult of Pan in Ancient Greece* (Chicago).

Clark, J.G.D. 1952 *Prehistoric Europe: the Economic Basis* (London).

Cook, B.F. (ed.) 1989 *The Rogozen Treasure: Papers of the Anglo-Bulgarian Conference, 12 March 1987* (London).

Daubeny, C. 1865 *Essay on the Trees and Shrubs of the Ancients* (Oxford & London).

de Vries, K. (ed.) 1980 *From Athens to Gordion: the Papers of a Memorial Symposium for Rodney S. Young* (Philadelphia).

Flannery, K. & Blanton, R. (eds) 1978 *Prehistory and Human*

Ecology of the Valley of Oaxaca vol. 5 pt. 2 (Ann Arbor).

Frazer, J.G. 1913 *Pausanias' Description of Greece* (London).

Frazer, J.G. 1929 *Publii Ovidii Nasonis Fastorum Libri Sex: The Fasti of Ovid* (London).

Godley, A.D. 1946 *Herodotus* (Loeb: London & Cambridge Mass.).

Graves, R. 1960 *The Greek Myths* (Harmondsworth).

Graves, R. 1961 *The White Goddess: a Historical Grammar of Poetic Myth* (London).

Greig, J. 1989 *Handbooks for Archaeologists no. 4: Archaeobotany* (Strasbourg: European Science Foundation).

Gunther, R.T. 1934 *The Greek Herbal of Dioscorides* (Oxford).

Hedrick, U.P. 1972 *Sturtevant's Edible Plants of the World* (New York).

Helbaek, H. 1964 'First impressions of the Çatal Hüyük plant husbandry', *Anatolian Studies* 14, 121-3.

Hill, A.F. 1952 *Economic Botany: a Textbook of Useful Plants and Plant Products* (New York).

Hooper, W.D. 1934 *Cato: On Agriculture; Varro: On Agriculture* (Loeb: London & Cambridge Mass.).

Hort, A. 1916 *Theophrastus: Enquiry into Plants* (Loeb: London & Cambridge Mass.).

Howes, F.N. 1948 *Nuts: their Production and Everyday Uses* (London).

Hulme, F.E. 1907 *Wild Fruits of the Countryside* (London).

Johns, T. & Duquette, M. 1991 'Traditional detoxification of acorn bread with clay', *Ecology of Food and Nutrition* 25, 221-8.

Jones, H.L. 1923 *The Geography of Strabo* (Loeb: London & Cambridge Mass.).

Jones, W.H.S. 1933 *Pausanias: Description of Greece* (Loeb: London & Cambridge Mass.).

Jørgensen, G. 1977 'Acorns as a food-source in the later Stone Age', *Acta Archaeologica* 48, 233-8.

Kislev, M.E. Nadel, D. & Carmi, I. 1992 'Epipalaeolithic (19,000 BP) cereal and fruit diet at Ohalo II, Sea of Galilee, Israel', *Review of Palaeobotany & Palynology* 73: 161-6.

Loewenfeld, C. 1957 *Britain's Wild Larder: Nuts* (London).

Mason, S.L.R. 1992 *Acorns in Human Subsistence* (unpublished Ph.D. thesis, University College, London).

Mazuelos Vela, F. Ramos Ayerbe, F. & Ros de Ursino, J.A.F. 1967 'Le fruit du chêne (*Quercus ilex*)', *Oléagineux* 22, 169-71.

Meiggs, R. 1982 *Trees and Timber in the Ancient Mediterranean World* (Oxford).

Messer, E. 1978 'Zapotec plant knowledge: classification, uses and communication about plants in Mitla, Oaxaca, Mexico', in Flannery and Blanton 1978, 1-140.

Parsons, J.J. 1962 'The acorn-hog economy of the oak woodlands of south western Spain', *Geographical Review* 52, 211-35.

Renfrew, J.M. 1966 'A report on recent finds of carbonized cereal grains and seeds from prehistoric Thessaly', *Thessalika* 5, 21-36.

Renfrew, J.M. 1973 *Palaeoethnobotany: the Prehistoric Food Plants of the Near East and Europe* (London).

Sallares, R. 1991 *The Ecology of the Ancient Greek World* (London).

Sargeaunt, J. 1920 *The Trees, Shrubs and Plants of Virgil* (Oxford).

Smith, J.R. 1929 *Tree Crops: a Permanent Agriculture* (New York).

Soyer, A. 1853 *The Pantropheon, or a History of Food and its Preparation in Ancient Times* (London).

Tripp, E. 1970 *Dictionary of Classical Mythology* (London).

Trustees of the British Museum 1976 *Thracian Treasures from Bulgaria* (London).

Tutin, T.G., Heywood, V.H., Burges, N.A., Valentine, D.H., Walters, S.M. & Webb, D.A. (eds) 1964 *Flora Europaea* (Cambridge).

Usai, A. 1969 *Il Pane di Ghiande e la Geofagia in Sardegna* (Cagliari).

Vencl, S. 1985 'Zaludy jako potravino. K poznçni vyznamu sberu pro vyzivu v praveka' ('Acorns as food. Assessing the significance of food-gathering for prehistoric dietary habits') *Archeologické Rozhledy* 37, 516-65.

Wright, K. 1991 'The origins and development of ground stone assemblages in Late Pleistocene Southwest Asia', *Paléorient* 17, 19-45.

White, R.J. 1975 *Artemidorus: Oneirocritica. The Interpretation of Dreams* (New Jersey).

❖ **2** ❖

BARLEY CAKES AND EMMER BREAD

Thomas Braun

Bᴀʀʟᴇʏ-ᴍᴇᴀʟ and wheaten flour are 'the marrow of men', says Homer (*Odyssey* 20.108). In the Mediterranean, food meant cereals first and foremost. In Hebrew and Greek the words for food in general are *lehem* and *sitos* respectively, which specifically mean grain or bread. Although wheat was always preferred for human food, the Egyptians, when speaking of both, always gave barley precedence (Währen 1965, 16). Pliny (*Natural History* 18.72) held barley to be the oldest cereal. This belief explains why it was used in the most ancient Greek sacrifices: the gods dislike innovation (Plutarch *Greek Questions* 6 = *Moralia* 292b-c).

Modern research tends to show that the cultivation of wheat and barley had begun at much the same time, in the 8th millennium BC. But barley was providing the staple diet for most people at the beginning of the first millennium, especially in Greece, and long remained a staple for those without access to scanty home-grown wheat or state-promoted wheat imports. This is because barley grows well not only on the well-drained, fertile deep soil that it likes best, but also on the thin limestone soil that is characteristic of Greece and the Judaean hills, as well as many other parts of the Mediterranean world. It is not nearly as fastidious as wheat with respect to rain supply while germinating, and takes a shorter time to

Barley

mature, so that it is less likely than wheat to suffer from disease, and can endure in regions both hotter and colder. It will consequently flourish from sea level up to nearly 5000 feet.

The *Book of Ruth* documents the predominance of barley at the outset of our period. Probably written in the 5th century BC but telling a story whose dramatic date is in the 11th, it describes how Naomi and her husband and two sons left Bethlehem for the land of Moab, east of the Dead Sea, because of a food shortage. After ten years, having lost her husband and sons, Naomi returned, destitute, with Ruth, one of her new Moabite daughters-in-law, because she had heard that God had given his people *lehem*: the word, as we have noted, means 'bread' specifically but also food in general. In accordance with the humane provisions of Jewish law, Ruth was allowed to glean after the harvesters employed by her rich kinsman, Boaz. Boaz invited her to join the reapers, to eat some *lehem* and dip a morsel into the wine (here *lehem* must literally mean bread). He gave her enough roasted grain to satisfy her hunger, and she took home an *ephah* (bushel) of barley. She went on gleaning until the end of the barley harvest and the wheat harvest. Then, in her best clothes, she crept to the threshing floor, where Boaz, after he had eaten and drunk and his heart was merry, had gone to lie down at the end of the heap of grain. Here she asked him to marry her as next of kin. To show his approval, Boaz filled her mantle with six measures of barley to bring to her mother-in-law.

The impoverished Ruth could not afford to wait with the gleaning, and the barley harvest preceded the wheat harvest. (In temperate Italy barley was reaped in June, wheat in July – Palladius 7.2, 8.1; in Palestine the harvests would be in May and June respectively). But the wheat harvest is mentioned briefly and in passing not only because it came later, but because outside certain favoured areas wheat was a scantier and riskier crop than barley. The Judaean hills will have been an even less favourable environment for wheat than Attika, the Athenian hinterland; and for Attika we have figures. An inscription recording firstfruits offered at Eleusis in 329/8 BC indicates that Attika's harvest in that year produced 11,371,420 kg of barley but only 1,082,500 kg of wheat (*IG* II² 1672, analysed by Garnsey 1988, 98). The statistics for 1931-60, the last period before modern methods transformed agriculture, show that wheat in

Attika could be expected to fail more than one year in four, but barley only one year in twenty (Garnsey 1988, 10).

Barley does not contain the necessary gluten-forming proteins to make a well-risen loaf. Barley bread, prepared with yeast and baked, is poor stuff. A chapter in Galen says so, explaining that it is made just as wheaten bread is, often out of barley of poor quality, in which case it is not nourishing (*On the strength of foods* 1.10 = 6.504 Kühn). Pliny (*Natural History* 18.74) says: 'experience has condemned barley-bread, though it was anciently much used; it is now mostly fed to animals'. Barley-bread betokened rural poverty. It was with this that Jesus miraculously fed the Five Thousand, who were humble Galileans (John 6.9). The poverty of the materials enhances the miracle. But there were better ways of making barley acceptable as human food, in the form of roasted grain, bannocks, and kneaded barley-cakes, for example. I do not discuss 'Greek' barley porridge, which was enjoyed for its own sake by Romans who could afford fine wheat flour (Pliny *Natural History* 18.72-74), barley gruel (highly valued by the physicians of the Hippokratic school) or barley beer, not drunk in wine-consuming Greece and Italy and not mentioned in the Bible, but a staple brew in Pharaonic Egypt and, under the Romans, in parts of Spain and Gaul, the Rhine frontier and Britain. Barley-meal could also be mixed into a posset to drink, or stirred with the meal of other grains and of pulses.

It is a simple matter to roast grain, before it has hardened, on a pan to make it palatable. The roasted grain that the reapers shared with Ruth during the barley-harvest must have been barley, though wheat can be treated in the same way. Roasted grain was a common article of diet in Old Testament times (cf. Leviticus 23.14; 1 Samuel 17.17, 25.18, 2 Samuel 17.28), as it still is in the Near East today. The Greeks, too, roasted barley. Every Athenian bride was required by a law of Solon (early 6th century BC) to take to her wedding a *phrygetron*, barley-roaster (Pollux *Onomastikon* 1.246). This was evidently a shallow pan with a handle in the shape of a loop into which the thumb was inserted, the fingers spreading out on the underside (Sparkes 1962, 128, plate IV 6). It would be hung up with the pots (Polyzelos fr. 6 KA). On a large scale, the general Nikias recommended transport ships carrying wheat and roasted barley to feed the Athenian expedition against Syracuse in 415 BC (Thucydides 6.22). But it does not seem that the Greeks ate the roasted grains by themselves. For them, roasting was a preliminary to making *alphita*, barley-meal: the best barley-meal, according to Galen (*On the strength of foods* 1.11 = 6.507 Kühn), was from roasted fresh barley. 'The Greeks', Pliny writes (*Natural History* 18.72), 'soak the barley-grain in water, leave it overnight to dry, and the next day roast and then grind it.'

Barley-cakes

Burns' poem about barley bannocks implies that they are strengthening:

> Bannocks o' bere meal,
> bannocks o' barley;
> here's to the Highlandman's
> bannocks o' barley!
> Wha in a brulzie
> will first cry a parley?
> Never the lads wi'
> the bannocks o' barley.
> Bannocks o' bere meal,
> bannocks o' barley;
> here's to the lads wi'
> the bannocks o' barley!
> Wha in his wae days
> were loyal to Charlie?
> Wha but the lads wi'
> the bannocks o' barley?

A bannock is a cake of unleavened and unroasted meal, fried or baked. I have eaten a fried one made of bere meal, a fine barley-flour from the Orkneys. Very good and filling it was, so much so that I am tempted to think that the Romans at one time fed some kind of bannocks to gladiators, who were known as *hordacei*, barley-men (Pliny *Natural History* 18.72). Gladiators were an investment and it would have been folly to underfeed them. The *kammata* which were served after dinner to Spartan boys were bannocks of barley-meal soaked in oil and baked and served on laurel leaves (Nikokles the Spartan, *FGH* 587 F 1, quoted by Athenaeus 4.140d).

The ancient *maza* or barley-cake was, I believe, usually just meal made from roasted barley, kneaded with water, milk or oil and then eaten straight away without baking. I have tried such a *maza*. It was tasty, but it did not keep. Wrapped in butter-paper and stored for a couple of days in the refrigerator, it went mouldy.

Galen (*On the strength of foods* 1.11 = 6.507 Kühn) says the best is made from freshly roasted barley. *Maza* derives from *masso*, 'knead', and is normally distinguished from and contrasted with the wheaten loaf, *artos*. At Skolos in Boiotia there were statues of Megalomazos and Megalartos, 'Great Barley-cake and Great Wheat-loaf (Polemon, Müller *FHG* fr. 39, from Athenaeus 3.109b). An old harvest-song, preserved among the Homeric *Epigrams* (15), shows that *maza* was thought a sign of wealth:

> Let us turn to the house of a man of great power and outstanding, lasting fortune! Plenty of Wealth will come in, and with Wealth, flourishing Joy and noble Peace. Let all bins be full, and the ...*maza* always overflow the kneading-trough!

It is surprising how appreciative the early Greeks were of barley-cakes, though they never claimed that they were better than wheaten bread. 'Next to bread, barley-cake is good too' (*Agathe kai maza met' arton*) ran the proverb (Zenobius 1.12). With few wheat-growing areas of their own, they put up cheerfully with the second-best. Hesiod, in up-country Boiotia, was a hardy farmer subsisting on his own produce, even though lowland Boiotia, one of the rare Greek wheatlands, was not far away. He describes a picnic at the height of summer. It is an idyllic one, with wine imported from Thracian Biblis to go with good home farm produce: goat's milk, veal and kid, and with it a 'milk' barley cake, *maza amolgaie* (*Works and Days* 590). The adjective *amolgaie* has puzzled commentators. Martin West's commentary (1978) is surely right in deriving it from *amolge*, milking (though a Greek farmer would smile at his supposing that 'it might be most convenient to milk a goat directly on to the flour'). It makes sense to knead barley meal or groats with milk, or for that matter with oil or honey, for an improved product. The warrior Archilochos in the mid-7th century BC, like Hesiod, washed down his *maza* with Thracian wine, the very best: 'in my spear is my kneaded *maza*, in my spear my wine of Ismaros; I drink leaning on my spear' (fr. 2 West vol. 2). The wine of Ismaros, which Odysseus gave to the Cyclops, was so wonderful that it needed to be mixed with twenty parts of water (*Odyssey* 9.196-211). *Maza*-eating went with good fare; its merit must have lain in its convenience: no trouble to prepare out of doors and on campaign, whereas fresh leavened wheaten bread required time, skill, and heat, preferably oven heat. That must be why Telemachos, a King's son, who had wheaten loaves served in the palace (*Odyssey* 17.343, 18.120) and a staff of a dozen women to prepare them (20.105f), took on board his ship not wheaten flour but twenty measures of mill-crushed *alphita* in leather bags (2.349-355), while not stinting the wine, which was to be the best sweet wine the housekeeper can supply.

In a law of the early 6th century BC, Solon ruled that those who dined at state expense at the town hall — the most signal honour Athens could provide – should receive a *maza* on ordinary days, and wheaten bread only during festivals. The barley-cakes provided at Athens' town hall were 'Achillean', from a superlative barley, according to the commentator on Aristophanes' *Knights* 819, by contrast to the coarse-ground Athenian *physte* and other kinds (Athenaeus 3.111e-f). 'We take care', says the comedy-writer Alexis in a context of banqueting with snow-cooled drink, 'that the *maza* we eat regularly should be as white as possible' (fr. 145 KA, from Athenaeus 3.124a). Lesbos' barley-meal was supreme. Archestratos, the writer on gastronomy, praises it in verse:

> The best one can get, the best of all,
> of rich barley, all cleanly sifted,
> comes from Lesbos, the wave-washed breast (i.e. hill) of Eresos,
> whiter than snow from the sky. If the gods eat barley-meal,
> then Hermes must go there and buy it for them!
> There is satisfactory barley-meal in seven-gated Thebes,
> and in Thasos and some other cities, but theirs are grape-stones
> compared to those of Lesbos. Understand this clearly!
> (Athenaeus 3.111f-112a)

The comparison with grape-stones is worth noting. When barley is prepared for human consumption today, it is often reduced to the grape-stone sized pieces called 'pearl barley'. Repeated grindings or crushings will produce meal. Barley-meal is still a dietary staple in some parts of the world: it is the present-day Tibetan *tsampa*. Barley-meal can occasionally be fine: the medical writer Erotianos (3.9) speaks of *pale* as the 'whitest and finest of barley-meal', using a word which with its variants *palemation*, *paipale*, is sometimes applied to fine barley-meal by other writers (e.g. Hippokrates *Women's Diseases* 1.64 = 8.132 Littré; Archigenes quoted by Galen 12.791 Kühn). But it is normally used of the finest wheat-flour (for example by the ancient commentator on Aristophanes, *Clouds* 262 and Pollux 6.62) and equated with wheat-flour 'dust' (Hesychios s.v. *pale*), equivalent to the Latin *pollen*; and even the finest barley-meal cannot compete with *pollen*. Moritz argued that *alphita* was the Greek word for coarse meal, and *aleura* for fine flour, regardless of what grain these were made from (Moritz 1949). True enough, the Hippokratic writers speak of coarse wheat-meal as 'wheaten *alphita*' (*Regimen in Acute Diseases* [Sp.] 53 = 1.173 Kühlewein) and of '*alphita* of beans and vetch' (*On Internal Affections* 23 = 7.226 Littré) as Galen (6.76 Kühn) notes. But these are exceptional usages. It normally makes sense to translate *alphita* as barley-meal and *aleura* as wheaten flour. Moritz, reluctant to believe that the staple food of the Homeric Greeks was barley-meal, hoped by freeing the word *alphita* from its association with barley to resolve the paradox that in Greek epic it is mentioned only as human food, whereas horses are fed with emmer as well as barley (*Iliad* 5.196, *Odyssey* 4.41) and even wheat (*Iliad* 8.188), which is also given to geese (*Odyssey* 19.536, 556). But the contrast here is between the food of ordinary folk and the fodder ascribed to the horses of mythical heroes; and the wheat-fed geese were being fattened for the royal table.

Of course there were bad barley-cakes. In the mid-6th century BC Hipponax of Ephesos describes a man who has wasted his inheritance and, unlike the Prodigal Son, cannot avoid digging: he 'eats mediocre figs and a barley cake (*kollix*), slaves' fodder' (fr. 26 West, from Athenaeus 7.304b). But this does not imply, as is often supposed, that the Greeks had already anticipated Pliny's wholesale condemnation of barley-cake. The Ephesians, with the rare advantage of the wheatlands of the Kayster valley, could afford to be more fastidious than other Greeks; and the *kollix* may have been the worst kind of *maza*, which was black, with chaff mixed in the kneading, 'prepared with a view to cheapness'. A vegetarian ascetic of the school of Pythagoras might make a meal of these low-grade barley-cakes for only an obol (Alexis fr. 223 KA, from Athenaeus 4.161b). Destitute folk would eat black *maza* with a few figs, and wild plants such as sow-thistle and mushrooms (Poliochos fr. 2 KA, and Antiphanes fr. 225 KA, both from Athenaeus 2.60b-d).

Most of the allusions to *maza* in Athenian comedy are friendly. A Megarian, starving because of Athenian depredations in the Peloponnesian War, is seen coming to Athens during the fantasy truce of Aristophanes' *Acharnians* (425 BC): he tries to sell his daughters as piglets, being tempted among other things by an Athenian *maza* (732), though figs, garlic and salt are also attractions. A *maza* steeped in sweetened wine was palatable and gave the impression of being more nourishing than it really was (Galen *On the strength of foods* 1.11 = 6.510 Kühn).

Wheat versus barley

Athenion the Aristotelian, the leader of Athens' revolt from Rome in 88 BC, was criticized during the siege for his distributions of a *choinix* of barley every four days: it was 'chicken-feed, not human food' (Poseidonios *FGH* 87 F36, from Athenaeus 4.214f). That has been taken to show that the Athenians had by this time come to reject barley altogether (Moritz 1975). But the Athenians' resentment was surely because the ration was too scanty. A *choinix* (one forty-eighth of a *medimnos*) was normally one day's allowance per person (Herodotos 7.187, Diogenes Laertius 8.18). It does not look as if the Greeks ever turned against barley on principle. But none of them will have doubted the verdict of Aristotle (*Problems* 21.2, 927a18) that wheat was more nourishing than barley, endorsed by the dietician Diphilos of Siphnos, who pronounced in the early 3rd century BC that wheaten loaves were 'superior for nourishment and digestibility and altogether better' (Athenaeus 3.115c). An unidentified quotation in Athenaeus runs (3.113a): 'we do not care for *alphita*, for the town is full of (wheaten) loaves'. That must come from an imaginary scene of feasting and merriment in a comedy. In real life in an ordinary Greek city people could not often be so choosy.

However, some wheat was grown almost everywhere, though in most places on a modest scale, with thin planting promising at best a meagre harvest. Better wheat harvests were produced in areas with rich moisture-retaining soil, such as the lacustrine plains of Thessaly, Boiotia, and upland Lykia, the volcanic region of Campania, and alluvial valleys such as those of the Po, the Maeander (adjoining Miletos), the Kaïkos (adjoining Ephesos), the Hermos (near Sardis) and the Skamander, river of Troy. Carbonised wheat was found in quantities at Troy, though barley was absent (Schliemann 1880, 320; Wittmack 1890). Especially favoured regions produced a wheat surplus: the Hauran north-west of Palestine, lowland Kilikia, the Thracian coast, Sicily, parts of Southern Italy, Sardinia and Spain, tracts of North Africa, and above all the Ukraine and Egypt. The wheat trade was the reason for Greek colonization of Olbia and other Black Sea ports from *c.* 615 BC. Xerxes saw merchant-ships carrying wheat from the Ukraine to the Peloponnese in 480 BC (Herodotos 7.147). The Ukraine was the chief source of wheat imports to classical Athens: the searoute from the Crimea through the Bosporos and Dardanelles to the Aegean was Athens' lifeline. Egypt also supplied wheat to Greece. Naukratis, the Greek treaty-port, also dates from *c.* 615 BC. Bakchylides in the first half of the 5th century BC describes how

> wheat-carrying ships over the gleaming sea
> bear from Egypt the greatest wealth.   (fr. 20B 14-16 Snell)

In 445/4 BC Psammetichos, an independent Egyptian ruler, sent Athens a gift of thirty or forty thousand *medimnoi* of wheat which were distributed among the citizens (commentator on Aristophanes *Wasps* 718, from Philochoros *FGH* 328 F130; Plutarch *Perikles* 37). Kleomenes of Naukratis, given control over Egypt after its conquest by Alexander, made gigantic profits out of his wheat monopoly, to the detriment of Athens and other Greek states (pseudo-Aristotle *Oikonomika* 2.2 1352a16-23, 1352b14-20, pseudo-Demosthenes 56.7). After Egypt was annexed to the Roman Empire in 30 BC, massive supplies of wheat were shipped to Rome.

By now, these shipments were of bread wheat; but the original grain crop of Egypt had been emmer wheat, and the same holds good for Italy. Except for the case of the *hordacei* mentioned above, it does not seem that barley was valued as human food by the Romans at any time of which we have record. Barley rations in place of wheat were a serious collective punishment in the normally well-fed Roman army as early as 214 BC (Frontinus 4.1.25, cf. Livy 24.18) and 209 BC (Livy 27.13.9; Plutarch *Marcellus* 25), and again in the 2nd century BC (Polybios 6.38.3). Antony inflicted them on his troops in 36 BC (Frontinus 4.1.37), and Octavian two years later (Cassius Dio 49.38.4); recruits were fed on barley instead of wheat if they failed in their tasks (Vegetius 1.13). *Polenta*, barley groats, are mentioned occasionally in Latin literature: the word has survived unchanged into modern times, though today's *polenta* is made from maize. But Ovid's legend of the poor old Sicilian woman who offered a drink sprinkled with roasted *polenta* (*Metamorphoses* 5.448-61) implies the direst poverty. The Romans of Pliny's day thought of barley bread as fodder for animals (*Natural History* 18.74). Even slaves were fed on wheaten bread by the exploitative Cato the Elder (*On Agriculture* 56). Columella (2.9.16) recommended a mixture of high-grade white meal from two-rowed Galatian barley with wheat to feed the slaves. Ulpian (*Digest* 33.9.3.8) mentions barley stored to feed pack-animals or slaves: when fed to slaves this, too, may have been mixed. Only in times of scarcity can we be sure that the Romans resorted to barley alone. Columella (2.9.14) concedes that when food is scarce, the six-rowed variety called *cantherinum* ('horse-barley') is better for human consumption than bad wheat.

Emmer

Emmer, the traditional Roman staple, is a hulled wheat. It was originally much valued. It was spreading over the Near East in the 7th millennium, and became the main wheat crop of Mesopotamia in the 6th, and of the Nile valley and the Mediterranean basin during the 5th and 4th. The Greeks knew it as *zeia*, with a variety *olyra* (Theophrastos *Enquiry into Plants* 8.4.1; 9.2). For Homer, fertile land is the 'emmer-bearing glebe', *zeidoros aroura*; but by Herodotus' time emmer – '*olyrai* which some call *zeiai*' (2.35.2) – as opposed to wheat and barley, was thought of as typically Egyptian. For the Romans it was typical too. In Pliny's time it was being grown from Egypt to Gaul (*Natural History* 18.81-2, 109), presumably because it had not been completely ousted by bread-wheat in Egypt, and had been introduced to Gaul by the Romans. They called it *far*: it had been their only crop for three hundred years (Verrius, from Pliny 18.63). Just as barley had been a traditional Greek sacrifice, the most ancient sacrifices of the Romans were of emmer pottage, *puls fitilla* (Pliny 18.84), or emmer grain and salt (Virgil *Aeneid* 5.745; Horace *Odes* 3.23.20; Ovid *Fasti* 2.520, 3.284). Emmer was widely grown throughout Roman Italy until at least the 4th century AD (Spurr 1986, 12-3). This was because it was more robust than naked wheat, tolerating a variety of soils, and germinating even if autumn rains were late (cf. Columella 2.8.5, 9.3; Pliny *Natural History* 18.83). Its husks gave protection from disease and insects, both when growing and in store. Modern cultivation under ancient conditions has produced a surprisingly high yield (Reynolds 1979, 60-4).

From emmer, the Romans made porridge, *puls*, their national dish. 'Porridge-eating barbarians' they called themselves in fun (Plautus *The Ghost* 828; cf. *Poenulus* 54). Moritz argued (Moritz, 1955) that emmer-porridge was eaten because toasting was essential to make the hulls brittle before they could be removed by pounding. Toasting, he thought, must have destroyed the gluten-forming proteins which would otherwise have enabled the pounded emmer-flour meal to rise when leavened. So porridge was all that emmer-flour was good for. This view has been frequently repeated, most recently by Spurr (1986, 11-12), but I have always found it hard to believe. Egyptian pharaonic leavened bread, of which examples have been found in Tutankhamun's tomb (Währen 1965, 26, fig. 14), had been emmer-bread. If the Egyptians could hull emmer without destroying its gluten-forming proteins, so, surely, could the Romans.

When a friend saw a sample of emmer bread behind glass in the museum in Abergavenny Castle, it seemed to me worth tracing to its source. The museum referred me to a retired curator; she referred me to the museum at Monmouth, where there had once been an exhibition of ancient breads; that museum referred me to a bakery in Newport, Gwent, and from there I got on to the baker of the emmer bread, Mr Fred Martin of Newport, a retired master baker in his late seventies, who is well known, not only locally but through BBC programmes, as an expert in ancient bread-making. Samples of his work, disinfected against weevil, are on show in a Belgian museum. He sent a box to the conference at which this chapter was first delivered as a paper, and would have attended had he not been convalescing from a heart attack. Mr Martin has grown emmer in his garden and made his own ancient Greek *klibanos*, baking-oven. He has parched the emmer and produced a loaf which is not as well risen as a breadwheat loaf, but is somewhat more so than barley bread, and tastes a good deal better; it is comparable to *pitta* bread.

It is not clear in any case that toasting/parching was essential for hulling. Pliny indeed says

> emmer…cannot be cleaned (i.e. hulled) unless toasted, which is why emmer grains are sown with their husks still on.
>
> (*Natural History* 18.61)

But too much, perhaps, has been built on this sentence. Peter Reynolds, who has grown emmer at the Butser Iron Age Farm in Hampshire, tells me that one can pound the hulls off untoasted emmer with an iron-capped pestle and a hollowed tree-trunk mortar, a practice known to Pliny (*Natural History* 18.105) and still common in North Africa. Jane Renfrew illustrates the big grain-drying kilns attached to Romano-British villas, 'thought to have been used for drying and parching the hulled wheats to facilitate the threshing of the grain from the spikelets'; but these are more likely to be malting floors (Reynolds and Langley 1979), which explains why there are no comparable kilns in Italy, where above all we should expect them.

Porridge from emmer-groats was, it seems, eaten by the early Romans because they liked it, and because it was simpler to prepare than bread. Moritz thought that as the taste for bread grew, bread-wheat replaced emmer; but the finds, as we have seen, may rather indicate that emmer was being grown in Italy throughout the imperial period. The Latin word for flour, *farina*, derives from *far*, emmer (Pliny *Natural History* 18.88). This surely confirms that flour could be produced from pounded emmer as well as from naked wheats. There are classical as well as Egyptian references to emmer-bread. Tryphon of Alexandria wrote of bread from *olyra* and meal-bread from *zeiai* (Athenaeus 3.109c). Dioskorides, who was an army doctor under Claudius and Nero, knows of emmer-bread, which he says is more nourishing and digestible than barley-bread though not as good as wheaten bread (2.108). Pliny says the most delicate or sweetest (*dulcissimus*) bread is made of *arinca*, which he identifies with *olyra* (*Natural History* 18.92), though the identification is not quite certain because Pliny seems confused at this point (he thinks *arinca* is naked in Italy and Egypt but not in Greece (*Natural History* 17.61, 92)). That Roman bakers were called *pistores*, 'pounders' confirms that they originally made bread from emmer rather than from naked wheat. The first *pistores* set up shop in Rome in

171-168 BC. Women before then had done the work at home (Pliny *Natural History* 18.107).

In Pliny's time plenty of bread was being consumed, but the traditional liking for porridge had continued. Pliny says little of bread-making but a good deal about *alica*, the excellent emmer-groats produced in a number of places in Italy and best of all in Campania, whose volcanic, fertile ground was sown twice a year with emmer and once with millet. Pliny notes with astonishment (*Natural History* 18.109-14) that chalk from White Earth Hill near Pozzuoli was added to it. This is not as shocking as it sounds. Present-day British law requires all except wholemeal flour to contain between 235 and 390 mg of calcium carbonate per 100 grams, in the form of *creta praeparata*. But Pliny also describes spurious *alica*, made from an inferior emmer grown in Tunisia, which had the immoderate proportion of 25% gypsum (hydrous calcium sulphate) – a reminder that, despite ancient towns having market overseers, there was little protection against adulteration of food. It is not a modern failing to adulterate food with chemicals. What is modern is the attempt at adequate consumer protection.

Bibliography

Garnsey, P. 1988 *Famine and Food Supply in the Graeco-Roman World* (Cambridge).

Moritz, L.A. 1949 'Alphita – a note', *Classical Quarterly* 48, 113-7.

Moritz, L.A. 1955 'Husked and naked grain', *Classical Quarterly* n.s. 5, 129-34.

Moritz, L.A. 1975 in *Der kleine Pauly* 2 s.v. "Gerste".

Reynolds, P. 1979 *Iron Age Farm: the Butser Experiment* (London).

Reynolds, P. & Langley, J. 1979 'Romano-British corn-drying ovens, an experiment', *Archaeological Journal* 136, 27-42.

Schliemann, H. 1880 *Ilios* (London).

Sparkes, B.A. 1962 'The Greek kitchen', *Journal of Hellenic Studies* 82, 121-37.

Spurr, M.S. 1986 Arable cultivation in Roman Italy 200 BC – *c*. AD 100, *Journal of Roman Studies Monograph* no.3 (London).

Währen, M. 1965 *Brot und Gebäck im Leben und Glauben der alten Aegypter* (Berne).

Wittmack, L. 1890 'Samen aus dem Ruinen von Hissarlik', *Verhandlungen der Berliner Gesellschaft für Anthropologie, Ethnologie und Urgeschichte*, 614-5.

❖ 3 ❖

CEREALS, BREAD AND MILLING IN THE ROMAN WORLD

K.D. White

Food in antiquity has been until recently a comparatively neglected area of enquiry; but within the last few years new techniques in prehistoric archaeology, in the analysis of food residues and especially of the stomach contents of human cadavers preserved in bogs, and more spectacularly of bone tissues, are providing long-term dietary information. Classical archaeology still lags behind in this department, and researchers still rely too heavily on literary evidence.

Cereals

In what follows I shall concentrate on the cereal components of Roman diet, noting their range and the various processes required to convert them into digestible form, along with a few comments on digestibility and nutritional values. The first point I want to make is that the diet of middle- and lower-class Romans, though heavily concentrated on cereals, as is the pasta-based diet of their Italian counterparts of today, was by no means so monotonous as is commonly assumed. First, as recent studies by Spurr[1] have demonstrated, their farmers planted a wide range of cereals, with regional variations corresponding to what they had learnt about their suitability for particular areas. Among the wheats identified from surviving seeds[2] are two varieties of naked wheats, and a third, the husked variety known to us as emmer (*far*), on which a great deal of attention has recently been focussed.[3] As Pliny points out in the following passage, emmer was in olden days the staple food-grain of the Romans:

> Emmer is the hardiest of all grains and the one that stands up best to winter conditions. It endures the coldest situations and areas that are under-cultivated or extremely hot and dry. It was the first food of the Latium of olden days... It is evident that for a long time the Romans subsisted on pottage (*puls*), not on bread (*panis*), since even nowadays foodstuffs are called porridge-stuff (*pulmentaria*), and Ennius, the oldest of our poets, describing a siege under famine conditions, recalls that fathers would snatch a morsel (*offa*) from the mouths of their crying children. Nowadays ancient sacrifices are performed with gruel-pottage (*puls fitilla*), and it seems that pottage was just as unknown to Greece as pearl-barley (*polenta*) was to Italy.
>
> (*Natural History* 18.83-4)

The hard outer coat of this useful grain could not be reduced to meal by grinding between stones: like maize, it had to be 'bashed' by pestle and mortar, as it still is in many parts of Africa; it was back-breaking work, as Pliny explains later on:

> The grain is pounded in a wooden mortar to avoid the pulverizing effect of using a stone mortar, the motive power for the pestle being provided, as is well known, by the chain-gang labour of convicts; the end of the pestle is fitted with an iron cap. After the grain has been stripped of its coats, the bared kernel is again broken up with the same instruments.
>
> (*Natural History* 18.112)

Cowell (1962, 86), who seems oblivious to the facts, writes: 'The poorer citizens... preferred wheatmeal porridge or groats to bread; porridge meal did not need grinding and would not take so long to cook'! The product of this arduous processing was a coarse meal, which was then made into a porridge, which will have resembled the 'hominy grits' of the southern United States. The other husked grain, barley (*hordeum*), also required tedious processing, that of roasting before grinding. Made by the Greeks into a 'standard' form of flat-bread called *maza*, its use was more restricted for human consumption by the Romans, who made from the flour a gruel (much used in invalid diet as a restorative) and a highly nutritious barley-water (still widely used today, with or without added lemon flavouring).

Milling

The other food-grains were ground into flour of varying degrees of fineness. The grist was further subjected to a sifting process, coarse-meshed sieves being used to remove the bran (*furfures*), finer meshes being reserved for top-grade and the best second-grade flour, from which were made the best quality cakes and pastries. The history of the grain-milling process can be traced all the way from the primitive 'up-and-down' rubber to the completely mechanized water-mill, in which the horizontal motion of the wheel was redirected into the vertical motion of the drive-shaft which was keyed into the upper of the pair of the stones by means of a crown and pinion.

The most important developments, however, took place in the sources of power. The origins of rotary motion applied to the milling process are still obscure, but it was during the Republican period that the flat surfaces of the hand-mill were replaced by the much more efficient combination of convex and concave surfaces that promoted an even continuous flow. The inventor of the 'Pompeian' hour-glass mill, operated by animal power, is unknown, but the technical link is clear. The design of the revolving upper stone is strikingly original and multi-functional, providing a receiver for the incoming grain from the hopper, a strong base for the projecting arm for the harness; more interesting still, the life of the machine could be, and was, easily extended by simple inversion of the upper stone, as may be seen on surviving donkey-mills attached to some of the large bakeries at Pompeii.

Roman engineers excelled in many branches of technology; but it was in hydraulics that their greatest and some of their most spectacular achievements were made:[4] at Barbegal near Arles on a sloping site, with ample water sources in the vicinity, they secured a head of water powerful enough to drive eight pairs of water-mills of the overshot type, estimated to have been capable of producing sufficient meal per day to feed a population some seven times the population of that city.

Leaven

Apart from the nutritious products already mentioned, the major cereal grains could be made into bread with or without a leavening agent to make the dough rise. Leavened bread cannot be made from parched grain, because of the destruction of the enzymes which cause the gluten to expand, making the dough elastic and aerated.[5]

Two important questions arise at this point: first, how much leaven did Roman bakers use? Cato distinguishes between ordinary bread (*panis*) and kneaded bread (*panis depsticius*), and his eight varieties of cakes, which were made with cheese and honey, had no leavening and only one egg to several pounds of flour.[6] Pliny the Elder's account of bread-making, written two centuries later, mentions a variety of leavens, mainly wine-based, rounding off with the first reference in baking history to the use of brewer's yeast:

> In Gaul and Spain, when they have soaked the varieties of grain I have mentioned to make beer, the froth that forms on the surface is used for leaven: the result of this process is that those peoples have a lighter kind of bread than the others.
> (*Natural History* 18.68)

Quality

The second question concerns the quality (or rather the qualities) of the various breads, and the procedures required to produce them. The only experiments that have been performed have been on handmills, and it is uncertain how many grindings will have been needed on the various machines to produce the different grades. We know that wholemeal bread (*autopyros*) was made; the few references imply that those who ate it enjoyed it; but we can only guess that it contained valuable roughage.[7] As for the milling process, we have only one piece of evidence: it comes from the *Moretum*, a short poem of the 1st century AD, falsely ascribed to Virgil, describing the first part of a day in the life of an Italian smallholder:[8]

> From there he goes away and takes his stand at the mill, and sets
> his trusty light on a little shelf. Next, after cleaning the mill-
> stones and the mortar, he sets both hands to the work, each to its
> own task, changing hands from time to time as the right hand,
> which does the actual turning, tires... Then when the task of
> turning has reached its appointed end, he transfers by hand the
> scattered meal into sieves and shakes it. The refuse stays on the
> top of the sieve, while the pure flour sinks down and, cleansed
> from impurities, filters through the holes.   (19-25, 38-42)

The poet does not spell out the number of times the tedious grinding
process was repeated to provide the day's supply of flour, but the reference
to the 'appointed end' means that after the grinding was finished the sieve
was used to separate the refuse (*purgamina*) from the flour (or meal,
depending on the fineness of the mesh). This part of the description, if
taken as reliable, confirms the findings of experiments with a similar
device. The few casual literary references include a philosophical discussion of causation illustrated by a casual encounter with a piece of grit (*lapis*)
while eating bread (Seneca *de beneficiis* 2.7.1), and a much better-known
story, Horace's delightful, if perhaps fictional, tale of a journey from Rome
to Brindisi (*Satires* 1.5.91). Reporting on various incidents that occurred
en route, the poet advises the traveller, in artful guide-book style, to pick
up the next day's ration of bread at the previous overnight stop-over before
setting out for Canossa, where the bread is 'full of grit' (*lapidosus*). Most of
the editors, with the exception of Alfred Ernout, have failed to see that
behind the facetious reference there is a serious point for technical
discussion.[9]

My fellow-contributors to this volume will doubtless open up controversial questions in profusion: none, perhaps, could be more controversial
than that of the processing of basic foodstuffs.

Notes

[1.] Spurr 1986. As in the contemporary cuisine, the ancient
Italians were able to overcome the monotony of a cereal-
based diet with a wide variety of sauces and relishes, under

the collective heading of *condimenta*, as a glance at Apicius'
cookery book will demonstrate.

[2.] Recent research on small farms in central and southern

Italy has demonstrated the variety of crops grown: see e.g. Small 1977.

3. See Braun, above Chapter 2. Emmer is one of the important food crops being grown experimentally at several British sites, including the Iron Age farm at Butser, Hampshire. Pliny's testimony to its hardiness and climactic adaptability are confirmed by experimental growers in Ontario, Canada, where I have personally observed it during the short growing season. Both emmer and millet can be made into bread; the former requires additional kneading to give it a 'roof', the term used nowadays by bakers for the crust of a well-risen loaf. The references are: Pliny *Natural History* 18.100-2 (bread and other products from millet); *ibid.* 186 (various kinds of bread made from emmer, including milk- and honey-bread).

4. See now Hodge 1992; for a summary of Roman achievements in the various branches of hydraulics, White 1984, 157-72.

5. *Aerated*: a lighter loaf, with more CO_2 in the dough, introduced to London in the late Victorian period by the *Aerated Bread Company* (ABC), proved so popular in the tea shops that the ABC competed strongly against their rivals, which had been introduced to promote Lyons' tea.

6. Cato's 'kneaded' bread: *On Agriculture* 74; his cake and pastry recipes: *ibid.* 76-82.

7. Of the half a dozen references to whole-meal bread in our sources, the majority are remedial: the digestive qualities of bread made from meal 'from which nothing has been removed' (Celsus *On Medicine* 2.18) were evidently appreciated by discriminating palates – at least if we are to place any reliance on Trimalchio's recollections of what he had offered his guests at his last banquet:

> For the first course we had a pig garlanded with sausages and served with blood-puddings and very nicely done giblets, and of course beetroot and pure wholemeal bread – which I prefer to white bread myself: it's a great tonic, and when I go to relieve myself, I'm glad of it.   (Petronius *Satyricon* 66.1)

It is worth noting that the working class in the towns, subsisting mainly on rough but nutritious emmer groats and bread with a high proportion of bran (*panis furfureus*), will have been faring better than their richer compatriots. As for the country-folk, the *rustici*, if their main food crop was emmer, which is hardy, and has now been shown to be high-yielding, they will have been doing much better than we have hitherto believed.

8. The *Moretum* has recently been edited, with translation and commentary, by Kenney (1988). For the view that the anonymous author's description of a small-holder's daily chores should be taken as authentic see White 1977.

9. Grit in the bread: for a full discussion see White 1976, 157-8.

Bibliography

Cowell, F.R. 1962 *Everyday life in Ancient Rome* (2nd edition, London).

Hodge, T. 1992 *Roman Aqueducts and Water-supply* (London).

Kenney, E.J. 1988 *The Ploughman's Lunch (Moretum)* (Cambridge).

Small, A. 1977 'Excavations at Monte Irsi', *British Archaeological Reports* 20 (Oxford).

Spurr, M.S. 1986 *Arable Farming in Roman Italy* (London).

White, K.D. 1976 'Food requirements and food supplies in classical times in relation to the diet of the various classes', *Progress in Food and Nutrition Science*, 2.4, 153-91.

White, K.D. 1977 *Country Life in Classical Times* (London).

White, K.D. 1984 *Greek and Roman Technology* (London).

❖ 4 ❖ BYZANTINE PORRIDGE
TRACTA, TRACHANÁS AND *TARHANA*

Stephen Hill and Anthony Bryer

Iɴ this contribution to the history of porridge, which explores the relationship between *tracta*, *trachanás* and *tarhana*, and traces its occurrence from classical antiquity to the present day, we make no apology for presenting again much of the material from an earlier article by Bryer which appeared in a Festschrift presented to Ralph Davis (Bryer 1985). The inclusion of further discussion, especially of the classical *tracta*, serves to strengthen Bryer's earlier conclusions concerning 'Byzantine Porridge'.

Tracta, trachanás and *tarhana*

The possible link between *tracta* and *trachanás* has been explored by others: Caroline Conran (1983) proposed a direct leap from one to the other, whilst Charles Perry (1983) has firmly suggested a Persian origin for *trachanás*. The present authors are convinced that the Greek connection is a real one, and that a Byzantine transition serves to link the classical and modern versions. This species of porridge lives on in the Balkans and northern Turkey. Arabella Boxer described it as an 'instant soup mix made by Greek peasants in late summer. It is formed from coarsely ground wheat mixed to a dough with goat's milk or yoghurt, then left in the sun for several days until as dry as powder. It is then stored, usually in the form of small rolls, and used to make a delicious and nourishing soup' (Conran (1983, 76). The present authors have encountered Greek *trachanás* and its Turkish counterpart *tarhana* in forms varying from the size of semolina granules through to more substantial lumps the size of small cakes.

The ancient form occurs as *trakton* or *trakta* in Greek or *tractum* or *tracta* in Latin. It is has often been assumed to be a Latin word, and is commonly translated as 'pastry': as such it would presumably be derived from the Latin verb *traho* (handle). Dr Smith's Latin-English dictionary presumably favours a derivation from *traho* (draw out), since it even goes so far as to translate *tracta* as 'a long piece of dough pulled out in making pastry' and adds 'hence Italian *tracciare*', the implication presumably being that *tracta* was the Roman precursor of spaghetti. The occurrence in Apicius of the term *tractogalatus*, which is at least half Greek, allows the possibility that even in a Latin cook-book *tracta* may be a term derived from a Greek original, and if 'handle' were the correct association, then it might derive from the verb *traktaïzo* (for *trakton* see Athenaeus 3.113d). Alternative possibilities are discussed at the end of this chapter; for the moment we wish to draw attention to the fact that the word *tracta* is in fact ambiguous when it appears in Roman recipes, and it should not, in any event, be translated as 'pastry'.

Cato on *tracta*

The fullest classical reference to *tracta* is found in Cato's recipe for *placenta*, a species of cake used in religious ceremonies:

> Make *placenta* this way. 2 pounds of wheat flour (*farina siliginea*) from which you make the pastry base (*solum*); 3 pounds of flour (*farina*) and 2 pounds of best husked grain flour (*alica*) for the *tracta*. Soak the *alica* in water. When it is thoroughly soft, pour into a clean mixing bowl (*mortarium*) and drain well. Then knead it by hand. When it is thoroughly worked, add the 3 pounds of flour gradually. Make this dough into *tracta*. Place them in a wicker basket where they can dry out. When they are dry,

arrange them cleanly. When you make individual *tracta*, once you have kneaded them, brush them with a cloth soaked in oil, wipe them thoroughly and oil them. When they are formed (*ubi tracta erunt*), heat up the hearth, where you will cook, and the earthenware vessel (*testum*) thoroughly. Then moisten the two pounds of wheat flour, knead them, and make a thin pastry base. Soak 14 pounds of mild, very fresh sheep's cheese in water. Macerate the cheese in the water, changing the water three times. Take the cheese out of the water gradually, squeezing it dry in the hands. When you have thoroughly dried all the cheese, knead it by hand in a clean *mortarium* and blend it together as much as possible. Then take a clean flour sieve and make the cheese pass through the sieve into the *mortarium*. Then add 4½ pounds of good honey. Mix this with the cheese very thoroughly. Then place the crust (*balteum*) on a clean board, one foot wide, over oiled bay leaves, and make the *placenta*. First place the single *tracta* over the whole pastry base, then cover it with the mixture [also *tracta*] from the *mortarium*. Add the *tracta* one at a time, and cover them up until you have used up all the cheese and honey mixture. Place the individual *tracta* on the top, and then pull over the pastry crust. Prepare the hearth [text appears corrupt here]. Then place the *placenta*, covered with a hot dish, and heap burning charcoal around and over it. See that you cook it thoroughly and gently. Uncover it for inspection two or three times. When it is cooked, remove it and spread with honey. This will make a half-modius *placenta*.[1]

(Cato *On Agriculture* 76)

The recipe draws a clear distinction between the *solum* or *balteus* (i.e. the lower and upper pastry crusts), which are made from wheat flour (*farina siliginea*), and the *tracta*, which are made from husked grain flour (*alica*). Jasny (1944) has argued clearly that *alica* and *far* are husked grain flours, most commonly emmer flour. In the context of Cato's recipe for *placenta*, the *solum* and *balteum* are clearly formed from pastry as we would understand the term, and *tracta* are equally clearly something else. It is, therefore, evidently unsatisfactory to use the English term 'pastry' as a translation for all these terms. Cato's instructions for making *tracta* involve making balls of soaked emmer flour and oil, which must be dried in the sun. The *placenta* consists of a crust of pastry which encloses alternating layers of *tracta* and a mixture of cheese and honey. But there is a problem with Cato's use of the term *tracta* in this passage since it applies both to dried balls of dough and to the kneaded cheese and honey mixture. As far as Cato is concerned the term seems to be capable of being applied to balls of emmer flour dough and to a mixture which has been kneaded. In order to distinguish the dried balls of dough from the cheese/honey mixture Cato refers to the former as the individual *tracta* (*tracta singula*). This ambiguity in Cato is of considerable assistance in understanding the use of the term when it is found in other authors; clearly the word had a range of interconnected meanings.

Apicius on *tracta*

When *tracta* are mentioned by Apicius, they are used as thickening agents. In his section on thick soups or porridges (*Pultes*) Apicius includes:

> PORRIDGE WITH *TRACTA* AND MILK: Put a *sextarius* (one-sixth of a *congius* i.e. about a pint) of milk and a little water in a new cooking-pot, and let it boil over a slow heat. Dry three balls (*orbiculos*) of *tracta*, break them up, and drop the pieces into the milk. To stop it burning, stir it up adding water. When it is cooked, pour it over lamb as it is.[2]   (Apicius 5.1.3A)

Flower and Rosenbaum (1958, 123), who translate *tracta* as 'pastry', are driven to the unhappy necessity of rendering *orbiculos* as 'slices', thus losing the clear implication of orb-like roundness and smallness which is implicit in the Latin text. In the light of our argument that *tracta* are related to later pastoral porridges, it is interesting to see that Apicius sees this particular porridge as a suitable accompaniment for lamb.

Apicius also includes a recipe for *Pullus Tractogalatus* which involves putting cooked chicken into a sauce of milk and honey thickened with crumbled *tractum*:

> …when (the chicken) is cooked, lift it from its stock and put into a new cooking-pot milk and a little salt, honey and a minimum of water. Place by a slow fire to warm, break up the *tractum* and add gradually, stir constantly, lest it burn. Put the chicken in to this, whole or cut up…[3]   (Apicius 6.9.13)

We may, then, accept that *tracta*, rather than being pastry made with wheat flour, were small balls of dried dough made from husked grain flour rolled with oil or cheese, these latter, as is clear from Cato, being the anciently available shortening agents.

Turkish *tarhana*

Emmer is still grown in northern Turkey, where it is valued for its ability to withstand the excessively damp Pontic climate, both as a growing crop and in storage. Pontic Turks still toast emmer grains and dehusk them in mortars, as was done in *mortaria* throughout the Roman Empire. This must be the kind of domestic flour production which is characteristic of peasant eating in the Roman period, and is well described in the anonymous *Moretum* (Shelton 1988, 162-63). That poem describes the morning routine of Simylus the peasant farmer who gets up at cock's crow, lights his fire with much huffing and puffing, grinds his corn in a hand-driven quern, makes his own flat bread, round with a cross cut on the top, and prepares a *moretum* of cheese, herbs, olive oil and vinegar, while his unalluring 'wife' Scybale keeps the fire going. The presence of mortars in Pompeian bakeries suggests that even there husked grain may have been used alongside finer wheaten flours (cf. White, above).

The Pontic Turks use their emmer flour to make *tarhana*. This word with its odd double consonant is peculiar in Turkish, and looks like a corrupted loan-word. Given the associations of Greek and Turkish cooking, and since the Greek letter 'chi' is regularly pronounced as a simple aspirate 'h', it seems reasonable to assume that *trachanás* (often pronounced as *trahanás*) and *tarhana* are related, whatever their origin, which is discussed further below. Turkish *tarhana* consists of balls of dough made from emmer flour plus oil, cheese, or curds which are dried in the sun on balconies and roofs. There is considerable variety in the size of the balls which range from tiny pieces the size of semolina to more substantial lumps the size of *köfte* or *keftedes*. *Tarhana* can be stored more or less indefinitely. It is used as a thickening or bulking agent in soups, and is also carried round dry by shepherds who add warm water to it to make a convenient instant meal when they are spending periods away from home in remote pastures. Other versions of our substance are found in the Balkans: it is *turkhana* in

Bulgarian and *tar(h)ana* in Serbian (Koukoules 1952, 5, 40; *Rjecnik hrvatskoja ili srpskoga Jezika* [RHISJ] 14 s.v. *tarana*).

Modern *tarhana* is also a regular ingredient of soup, appearing as tiny balls not dissimilar in effect to noodles, but it is also used as the main ingredient of a thick, sustaining, instant meal when *tarhana* is crumbled and bound with milk, *ayran*, or yoghurt to form a thick porridge. The substance bears an unmistakable resemblance to Apicius' *tractogalatus* sauce. Its consistency is formidable: a boxwood spoon will stand up in it. Its taste is unforgettable: nutty and sour from the fermented milk in which the nodules were soaked months before and in which they have been cooked again. It is a particularly refreshing way to start the day in the boundless summer pastures.

The attraction of these porridges to pastoralists is that its cooking is elementary and that it can be preserved from the lowland autumn to take up into the highland summer. Pure pastoralists have to subsist on the meat and milk of their flocks; transhumants have access to grain although they may not have fixed fields or ovens. The production of our porridges, unlike bread, requires no ovens, but they are dependent on a pastoral symbiosis with arable agriculture, which is why in the Pontos at least they are mostly the food of transhumants. Thus medieval pastoralists in various regions devised a variety of gruels as a substitute for the staff of life. *Kaskh* in the Persian epic Shâh-nâma (Levy 1967, 150), the *kishk* of the Lebanon (Perry 1983), Russian *kashi* (Davidson 1981, 134) and Spanish *gachas* (Brenan 1963, 180) are examples of a dish to which English liberal shepherds gave the grosser name of 'hasty pudding'.

Trachanás a Persian word?

Perry states that *trachanás* is a Persian word. In Persian it is spelled *tarkhâna* or *tarkhîna*; the Turks spread it through Anatolia and the Balkans (the spelling with an aspirated *t* in Armenian makes this fairly certain). In Greek the word was altered first with the inflexional endings and then by the transposition of the second and third letters, under the influence of a folk etymology connecting the foreign word with the native adjective *trachys*, 'rough'. The oldest literary reference to *tarkhâna* seems to be the

14th century Bushaq' (Fakr al-Din Ahmad b. Halladji Abu Ishak, died 1424 or 1427) (Perry 1983, 59; *Encyclopaedia of Islam* 1, 1342).

The modern Turkish *tarhana* and Greek *trachanás* may share a Persian name, but that the name was imported by the Turks and/or derived from *trachys* seems less likely since the porridge has another and older history than Bushaq.

That the Turks introduced crops and a cuisine from the Islamic world into the lands they conquered, settled and grazed in the Byzantine world is an attractive proposition, often ventured but more rarely demonstrated. That there may be something cultural about *trachanás* in particular, as the mark of the Turkish pastoralist as opposed to the diet of the Christian agriculturalist, is hinted at in a Serbian version of an Ottoman proverb:

> '*Tarhana* is Moslem food: cabbage and bacon are infidel food'. Other proverbs cited are 'Turks say: *Tarhana* is food, all *raya* are cabbage and bacon'; 'The old fame (glory, or beauty) has gone out of fashion as *tarana* when it is warmed up'; and a saying quoted by Vuk: 'My mother and his mother dried their *tarana* under the same sun'.
> (*RHISJ* s.v. *tarana*)

The Byzantine origin of *trachanas*

It is an equally attractive proposition that Anatolian Turkish names for agricultural processes and implements tend to be derived from the Greek peasants whom the Turks converted, supplanted or married, but that they brought their own terms for pastoral and transhumant activities. But such equations may not be so simple. To begin with, the Byzantine world preceded, and was in agricultural and culinary touch with, the Islamic one long before the Turks, and it was not a one-way exchange. The Byzantines wore turbans and had prayer carpets before they met the Seljuks, while '*murri* Byzantine style' (an awesome condiment made from barley dough that had been rotted for forty days) is among Byzantium's contributions to medieval Arabic cook-books (Mango 1979, 51-2; Perry 1981, 96, 98, 103 note 5). Here are some snags in the argument.

It has been proposed, for example, that Asiatic rice (which was to be a staple item in the commissariat of the Ottoman army) was introduced to

Anatolia by the Turks in the 14th century at the earliest (Beldiceanu and Beldiceanu-Steinherr 1978, 15). This does not explain why Geoffrey of Langley, Edward I's envoy to the Mongol Ilkhan of Persia, was able to buy 16 aspers'-worth of rice in Byzantine Trebizond in 1292 (Bryer 1980, 390). It is true that the Byzantines had their own words (which the Turks did not inherit) for transhumance, whereas the Turks borrowed numerous essential agricultural terms from Greek. One example of this is *dügen* (modern Greek *dókane*, Byzantine *tykane*, Latin *tribulum*) for the threshing sled which tribulates the peasant's corn (Tietze 1955, 204-257; Vryonis 1971, 476; Bryer 1975, 139-40). Similarly it is hard to envisage a Türkmen pastoralist without peering through the smoke of his dung-cake fire upon which he stirs his *tarhana*. Yet his name for the fuel, *tezek* (Curzon 1854, 110-13), is derived not from Turkic words, such as Mongol *argols* (Huc, 23), but apparently from Byzantine *zarzakon* – the fumes from which perhaps asphyxiated the Emperor Jovian in the cold Galatian highlands on the night of 16-17 February 364 (Robert 1961, 476; Foss 1977, 42 note 53). *Tarhana* is not a Turkic word, but it may be just as likely that the Turks inherited it from the Greek as the Persian.

A familiar problem is that neither Byzantine nor Islamic people wrote of the banausic things they used every day. Indeed *zarzaka*, or dung-cakes, are attested only once in the whole of Byzantine literature, and that by a desperate 10th century highland bishop who wanted to bring his plight home to his emperor, Basil II (Darrouzès 1960, 198-99). But *trachanás* is better attested, in a pre-Turkish form. The clue to its etymology lies in the way it was pronounced until recently by Greeks on Imbros (*trachanós*), Euboia (*traganós*) and in the Pontos (*tragáni*) (Koukoules 1952, 5, 40, note 3; Papadopoulos 1961 s.v. *tragáni*). Andriotes got the point by deriving it from both Turkish *tarhana* and Byzantine *traganós* (1951, s.v. *trachanás*). It may be clinched by the 10th century edition of the *Geoponica*, which claims to have been commissioned by Constantine VII Porphyrogenitus, and gives a recipe for *trágos* which echoes Arabella Boxer's description of the modern porridge (above):

> THE MAKING OF *TRÁGOS*: One must take wheat called Alexandrinos, and one must soak, separate [*sc.* in nodules] and dry it in the heat of the sun; and in doing that, discard the husks, shells and fibrous

parts of the wheat. One must dry and store the *tragós* [made] from *olyra* wheat of superior strain.

(*Geoponica* 3.8; Beckh 1895, 95. Cf. 5.30.3; 15.1.25; 17.9.)

Despite the superior strain (*eugenous olyras*) of the 'rice-wheat' here, our porridge is made from coarse wheat or spelt in most accounts. Its consistency may be the same as today, but its ancient and medieval taste and quality are irrecoverable (on this see Jasny 1944). The recipe given immediately before that for *trágos* in the *Geoponica* is for *chóndros*, or gruel. In his dream book, Artemidorus (Pack 1963, 75) equates *chóndros* with *trágos*, and there is a scattering of other references to *trágos*, or Latin *tragum*, in Galen (6.321; 12.14F) and in Dioskorides, the 1st century Cilician botanist (4.51). Tellingly, the modern Cretan for *trachanás* is *xynóchondros*. Most important, however, is that Hesychios, the 5th century Alexandrian lexicographer, defines *chóndros* gruel as *trágos* in his dictionary.

From *tracta* to *traganós*

Trachanás to *traganós*, by way of *tarhana* or not, is an easy leap. *Traganós* and *trágos* are clearly related. Greek *trágos* is a goat and that etymology leads to tragedy. But *trágos* is also spelt, the coarse ancient grain.

We are more cautious about the next leap back, which is from *traganós* and *trágos* to Latin *tracta*, because Athenaeus has the word in Greek, as *trákta*, rather than *traganós* in the 3rd century AD. In his *Deipnosophists* he writes:

> In making the so-called *artoláganon* (wheat-wafer), a little wine, pepper and milk are introduced, along with a small quantity of oil or lard. Similarly into *kapyria*, called by the Romans *trákta*, are put mixtures as into the wheat-wafer. (Athenaeus 3.113d)

Psellos makes clear that *kapyrídia* were flat dried cakes, from which Charles Perry concludes that *tracta* were dry biscuits or crackers to be eaten with wine (Perry 1983, 39). But we may be on a different track here, which might end up with *ta'amia* or *felafel*, rissoles made today from the dried white broad bean, which are claimed as an ancient Coptic dish. Claudia Roden has an enticing description of them served in her, and Athenaeus's, native Egypt (Roden 1970, 60-62). They are indeed delicious, but they are not our porridge.

The justification for a leap from Byzantine *traganós* to Latin *tracta* is, once more, in a recipe and takes us back to Apicius, whose *tracta* (sometimes mistaken as the first reference to Italian *pasta*) were evidently used to thicken sauces. They are certainly not the *tracta* rissoles of the Deipnosophists, although those might well have something to do with the kneaded mixtures which provide the alternative meaning for *tracta* in Cato. Apicius' *Pultes Tractogalatae* is much closer to modern and medieval accounts of our porridge, and is, as we have seen, appropriately, served with lamb from the pastures. Apicius's *tracta*, Byzantine *traganós*, Greek *trachanás*, Turkish *tarhana* must then be the oldest surviving form of pastoralists' packet porridge.

Notes

1. Placentam sic facito. Farinae siligineae L. II, unde solum facias, in tracta farinae L. IIII et alicae primae L. II. Alicam in aquam infundito. Ubi bene mollis erit, in mortarium purum indito siccatoque bene. Deinde manibus depsito. Ubi bene subactum erit, farinae L. III paulatim addito. Id utrumque tracta facito. In qualo, ubi arescant, conponito. Ubi arebunt, componito puriter. Cum facies singula tracta, ubi depsueris, panno oleo uncto tangito et circumtergeto unguitoque. Ubi tracta erunt, focum, ubi cocas, calfacito bene et testum. Postea farinae L. II conspargito condepsitoque. Inde facito solum tenue. Casei ovilli P. XIIII ne acidum et bene recens in aquam indito. Ibi macerato, aquam ter mutato. Inde eximito siccatoque bene paulatim manibus, siccum bene in mortarium inponito. Ubi omne caseum bene siccaveris, in mortarium purum manibus condepsito conminuitoque quam maxime. Deinde cribrum farinarium purum sumito caseumque per cribrum facito transeat in mortarium. Postea indito mellis boni P. IIII S. Id una bene conmisceto cum caseo. Postea in tabula pura, quae pateat P. I, ibi balteum ponito, folia laurea uncta supponito, placentam fingito. Tracta singula in totum solum primum ponito, deinde de mortario tracta linito, tracta addito singulatim, item linito usque adeo, donec omne caseum cum melle abusus eris. In summum tracta singula indito, postea solum contrahito ornatoque focum de ve primo temperatoque [?], tunc placentam inponito, testo caldo operito, pruna insuper et circum operito. Videto ut bene et otiose percoquas. Aperito, dum inspicias, bis aut ter. Ubi cocta erit, eximito et melle unguinito. Haec erit placenta semodialis.

2. PULTES TRACTOGALATAE: lactae sextarium et aquae modicum mittes in caccabo novo et lento igni ferveat. Tres orbiculos tractae siccas et confringis et partibus in lac summittis. Ne uratur, aquam miscendo agitabis. Cum cocta fuerit, ut est, super agninam mittis.

3. cum [pullus] coctus fuerit, levabis de iure suo et mittis in caccabum novum lac et salem modicum, mel et aquae minimum. Ponis ad ignem lentum ut tepescat, tractum confringis et mittis paulatim, assidue agitas, ne uratur. Pullum illic mittis integrum vel carptum....

Bibliography

Andriotes, N.P. 1951 *Etymologiko Lexiko tes koines Neoellenikes* (Athens).

Apicius, see Flower and Rosenbaum 1958.

Artemidorus, see Pack.

Athenaeus, see Gulick.

Beckh, H. (ed.) 1895 Cassianus Bassus Scholasticus, *Geoponica, sive De Re Rustica Eclogae* (Leipzig).

Beldiceanu, N. & Beldiceanu-Steinherr, I. 1978 'Riziculture dans l'empire ottomane XIVᶜ-XVᶜ siècle', *Turcica* 11.

Brenan, G. 1963 *South from Granada* (Harmondsworth).

Bryer, A.A.M. 1975 'Greeks and Türkmens: the Pontic Exception', *Dumbarton Oaks Papers* 29, 113-48.

Bryer, A.A.M. 1980 *The Empire of Trebizond and the Pontos* (London).

Bryer, A.A.M. 1985 'Byzantine Porridge', *Studies in Medieval History presented to R.H.C. Davis* (London), 1-6.

Charterius: Chartier R. (ed.) 1679 *Magnus Hippocrateus Cous, et Claudius Galenus, Opera* (Paris).

Conran, C. 1983 'Tracta and Trachanas', *Petits Propos Culinaires* 13, 76-7.

Curzon, R. 1854 *Armenia* (London).

Darrouzès, J. 1960 *Epistoliers byzantines* (Paris).

Davidson, A. (ed.) 1981 *National and Regional Styles of Cookery. Oxford Symposium 1981* (London).

Dioscorides 1958 Pedianus Dioscorides Anazarbeus *De Materia Medica*, 1 (Berlin).

The Encyclopaedia of Islam 1960 volume I (Leiden-London).

Flower, B. & Rosenbaum, E. 1958 *Apicius: the Roman Cookery Book* (London).

Foss, C. 1977 'Late Antique and Byzantine Ankara', *Dumbarton Oaks Papers* 31.

Galen, see Charterius.

Geoponica, see Beckh.

Gulick, C.D. (ed.) 1967 Athenaeus, *The Deipnosophists* (Loeb: London & Cambridge Mass.).

Hesychius, see Schmidt.

Huc, M. no date *Travels in Tartary, Thibet, and China during the years 1844-56* (London).

Jasny, N. 1944 *The Wheats of Classical Antiquity* (Baltimore).

Koukoules, Ph. 1952 *Byzantinon bios kai politismos* (Athens).

Levy, R. 1967 *The Epic of the Kings* (London).

Mango, C. 1981 'Discontinuity with the classical past in Byzantium', in Mullett, M. & Scott, R. (eds) *Byzantium and the Classical Tradition. University of Birmingham Thirteenth Spring Symposium of Byzantine Studies 1979*.

Pack, R.A. (ed.) 1963 Artemidorus Dablianus Daldanius *Onirocriticon libri v* (Leipzig).

Papadopoulos, A.A. 1961 *Historikon Lexikon tes Pontikes Dialektou* (Athens).

Perry, C. 1981 'Three medieval Arabic cook books', in Davidson (1981), 96-105.

Perry, C. 1982 'What was tracta?', *Petits Propos Culinaires* 12, 37-9.

Perry, C. 1983 'Tracta/Trahanas/Kishk', *Petits Propos Culinaires* 14, 58-9.

Robert, L. 1961 'Les kordakia de Nicée, le combustible de Synnada et les poissons scies. Sur les lettres d'un Métropolite de Phrygie au Xᶜ siècle. Philologie et réalités', *Journal des Savants* juillet-septembre, 117-37.

Roden, C. 1970 *A Book of Middle Eastern Food* (Harmondsworth).

Rjecnik hrvatskoja ili srpskoga Jezika (RHISJ) 1962-66 (Zagreb).

Schmidt, M. (ed.) 1862 Hesychius Alexandrinus, *Lexicon* (Halle, reprinted Amsterdam 1965).

Shelton, J-A. 1988 *As the Romans Did* (New York).

Smith, R.E.F. 1981 'Russian Diet', in Davidson (1981), 134-9.

Tietze, A. 1955 'Griechische Lehnwörter im anatolischen Türkischen', *Oriens* 8, 204-57.

Vryonis, S. 1971 *The Decline of medieval Hellenism in Asia Minor and the Process of Islamization from the Eleventh through the Fifteenth Century* (Berkeley, Los Angeles & London).

❖ 5 ❖

BREAD-BAKING IN ANCIENT ITALY
CLIBANUS AND *SUB TESTU* IN THE ROMAN WORLD: FURTHER THOUGHTS

Anthony Cubberley

Tʜᴇʀᴇ is good reason to link the *testum* and *clibanus* of the Roman writers with a highly distinctive, purpose-built, earthenware vessel which is common in Italian contexts from the late 2nd century BC. In Cubberley *et al.* (1988), John Lloyd, Paul Roberts and I presented linguistic and literary data relating to the form and function of the *testum* and *clibanus* and suggested that there was considerable overlap between the two terms, which might be, and frequently were, used to describe the same object, the simple baking-cover. We examined the archaeological record and recently-excavated finds (especially from Matrice: see Lloyd and Rathbone 1985) and, integrating these data with the literary and linguistic evidence, we proposed an archaeological identification which allows and makes necessary a reclassification of many published vessels, which we suggest should now be regarded as *clibani* or *testa*.

Clibanus and *testum*

The techniques of baking, whatever the period, can be reduced to two basic processes: first, baking directly in the hot ashes or fire, and second, baking in an enclosed heated container (Frayn 1978, Whitehouse 1978). The first technique is mentioned by Ovid;[1] the second by Cato,[2] with the author of the pseudo-Virgilian *Moretum* suggesting a stage half-way between the two.[3] Seneca[4] sees a development of the second process from the first.

From an examination of the literary evidence we found that the functions of the *testum* and the *clibanus* were almost identical, from bread-baking to roasting meat, and on to Celsus' heat-treatment of legs! This is not the place to go into detail: for this see Cubberley *et al.* (1988). The literature suggests that the *clibanus* was rounded (Cassiodorus *in Psalmos* 20.9), wider at the bottom than the top (Columella *On Agriculture* 5.1.4, *On Trees* 19.2), could have holes to regulate the heat (DiosKorides *de Materia Medica* 2.81; 2.96: this was said by Seneca about the *testum*), and that it was heated by putting a fire beneath it (Cassiodorus *in Psalmos* 20.9).

It is perhaps wrong to look for a precise meaning for the word *clibanus*. Rather, we ought to see it as having a wide semantic field which included that occupied by *testum*. I should like to propose that the Greek word *clibanus*, along with other technical and culinary words (such as *cadus*, *cyathus*, *cantharus*, *ampulla* etc.), came into Latin usage with the cultural influence that resulted from the Romans' growing contact with the Hellenistic world in the early 2nd century BC, the time when, according to Livy,[5] amongst luxuries such as soft furnishings, flute-girls, harp-girls and other forms of Greek entertainment, gastronomy was being refined into an art.

I would argue that the term *clibanus* became in fashionable circles an alternative word for a process already well known to the Romans –*sub testu* cooking. This is no different from the affected Gallicism of *gâteau* for what up to recent times has been known as cake.

It is instructive in this connection to examine the semantics of the two Latin words *testum* and *clibanus*. There is considerable evidence that *testum* and *clibanus* occupied the same semantic field. *Testum* has a large number of Romance reflexes, all with the general meaning of earthenware cook-

Fig. 5.1
Molise: Late Republican and Early Imperial baking covers.

ing-vessel (Romanian *test*, Italian *testo*, Spanish *tiesto*, Molise *test*, Lombard *test*, etc.). *Clibanus*, on the other hand, though continuing into archaizing Medieval Latin,[6] and though providing loan-words in Serbo-Croat, Old Norse and Anglo-Saxon (for which see later in this chapter), appears to have no Romance reflexes. In other words, by the time that the Romance languages were recognisably such, *sub testu* has resumed the sole occupancy of the semantic field which it covered before the intrusion of the fashionable *clibanus*.

Size, shape and fabric

Archaeological evidence suggests that the typical shape of the vessel is as in figures 5.1 and 5.2 (the examples from Matrice). The lower wall, often with an intricate or bifid foot, is straight or gently curving inwards and slopes inwards to meet the upper wall. At the junction between the upper and lower walls there is generally a projecting flange. In some of the models there is evidence of a central opening (fig. 5.2, no. 1), which is probably the heat regulator referred to by Seneca and Dioskorides.[7] Earlier versions (late Republican or Early Imperial) do not appear to show openings in the dome, but there is good evidence for holes in the side of the vessel (fig. 5.1, no. 1). The size seems to have varied considerably: the present evidence suggests a maximum diameter (Matrice) of *c.* 500 mm and a minimum (from Cosa: Dyson 1976) of less than *c.* 200 mm. If the examples from Settefinestre (Ricci 1985) are baking-covers, then some may have been less that 200 mm.

The fabric is generally among the coarsest in pottery assemblages, with temper added to the clay (quartz, grog, shell, crushed limestone etc.) in order to make the vessel more resistant to thermal shock. Important also to its identification is the burning on the foot and often on the flange. This is consistent with the vessel having been placed directly on to the hearth with embers heaped on and around it, and perhaps pre-heated as the ancient authors describe.

It is interesting to try to follow the development of this vessel into medieval and modern times, both inside and outside Italy. The continuity of both of the two types of baking mentioned at the start of this paper is well attested in Italy from the Iron Age up to the modern day. The tile

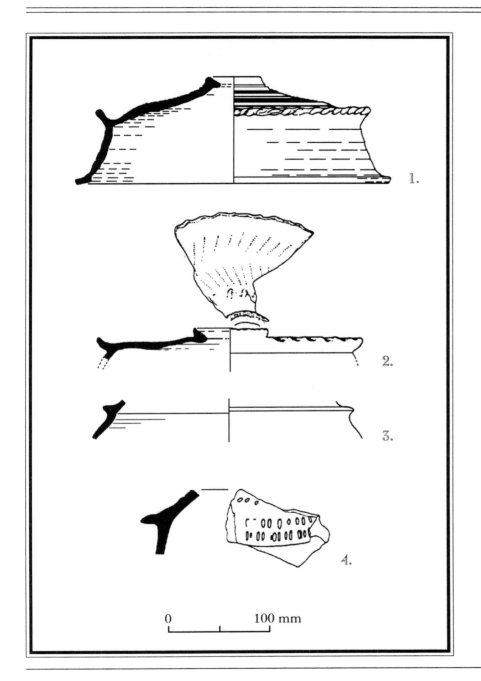

Fig. 5.2
Matrice: Mid and Late Imperial baking covers.

technique, mentioned by Ovid (note 1), is found, for example, in Liguria in the form of *testelli* (baking plates) which up to recent times were used for baking *focaccette* or chestnut-flour buns. The bun was placed on the plate and cooked in the embers (Whitehouse 1978). Similarly, in Northern Apulia, examples from the Iron Age were recognised by workmen as identical to the *piatti* which they used for making *focaccia* (thin, round hearth-cakes). The baking-cover technique is equally common. For example, *testi* are found from the 10th century at the Domusculta of Santa Cornelia just to the north of Rome. As is usual, the fabric is coarser than that of other forms on the site (see fig. 5.3 and Patterson 1991, 122-4). Similarly at Cremona, Brescia, Ravenna and Forli, to name but a few, examples are found certainly from the 15th century[8] (fig. 5.4). Documentary evidence is provided by Pietro di Crescenzi, the 13th century Bolognese agricultural writer,[9] who compares the bread baked in a *testo* unfavourably with that baked in an oven.

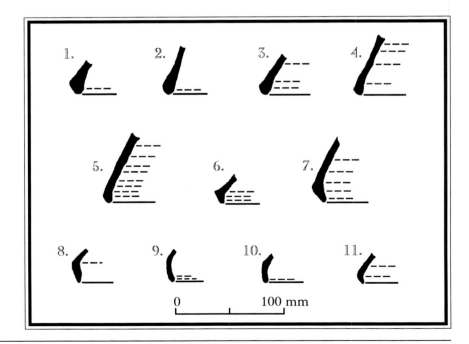

Fig. 5.3
Santa Cornelia: Early medieval and medieval kitchen wares, the testi.

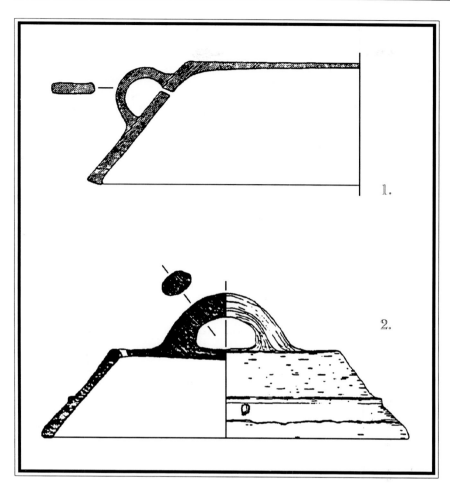

Fig. 5.4
Medieval testi *from Forli and*
Brescia. No scale.

Yugoslavia

Modern evidence is found also in Yugoslavia.[10] On the Dalmatian island of Iz various types of cooking pot are still made by hand, but the most interesting for the purpose of this discussion is that which goes under the name of *crpnja* or *cripnja*.[11] Most importantly, it represents as in Italy a continuation of a baking method attested since prehistoric times. It is very large (450-580 mm in diameter across the rim), domed and coil-built on a hand-wheel, consisting of five parts of clay to two of calcite. The method of operation is as described by the ancient literary sources. It is heated up in the hot ashes, which are then swept aside. Dough is then placed on the

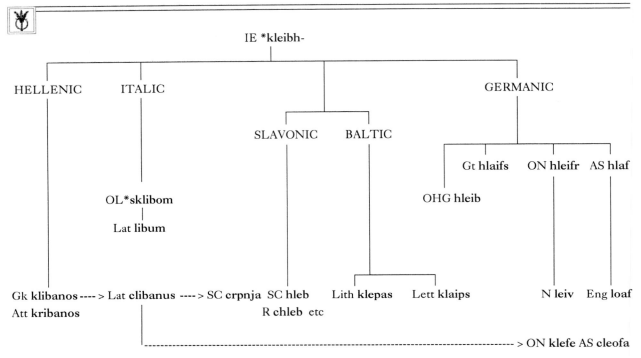

Table 5.1 *A summary of the Indo-European reflexes and loan-words in the semantic field of 'bake', 'bread' and 'oven'.*

hot surface below the fire and the *crpnja* replaced and covered with ashes. The bread rises into a lentoid shape, and has to be turned once to ensure a thick even crust. The whole baking operation takes about thirty minutes.

Linguistically, too, there is an interest. *Crpnja* probably is derived as a loan-word from the Latin *clibanus* (itself a loan-word from Greek), which would be wholly consistent with the Latin cultural influence in the area noted by Nandris (1988). The Indo-European reflexes would seem to be derived from **kleibh-*, with the possible meaning of 'to bake'. See table 5.1 for the reflexes and loan-words.

Romano-British evidence

Roman Britain ought, it is reasonable to expect, to produce examples of the *testum* or *clibanus*, and I suggest that if pottery assemblages are re-examined in the light of our original paper (Cubberley *et al.* 1988), examples will be found. A quick trial run was done on that assembled from the 1962-3 excavations at Castor, near Peterborough (Perrin and Webster 1990), and the findings, though done only from the written report, were encouraging.

Of the published assemblage, there are seven possible *testum* sherds and one possibly from a grooved plate of the type which could be used in association with the *testum* (fig. 5.5). The relevant material has been dated to the 2nd century AD and is as follows.

1: Greyware, *c.* 150 mm in diameter. ?*testum*.

2: Lower Nene Valley greyware, *c.* 180 mm in diameter. ?plate to fit *testum* (e.g. no. 7)

4: Shell gritted ware, *c.* 200 mm in diameter (of which *c.* 140 mm is usable for baking). It is burnt internally and externally up to *c.* 250 mm from the rim. ?very small *testum*.

5: Shell gritted ware, *c.* 200 mm in diameter. ?*testum*.

7: Shell gritted ware, *c.* 180 mm in diameter and shaped most like the examples from Matrice. Burnt internally.

The writers of this report were sensitive that there was something strange about pieces 4, 5 and 7: they say that they are 'unusual forms', suggesting elsewhere that they are 'kiln furniture'. Despite this, I should like, on the evidence of the shape, the presence and location of internal burning and the shell-tempered fabric of at least four of them, to put forward the tentative suggestion that they are sherds of *testa* and that the plate (piece 2) is provided with a groove to receive the bifid lip of a *testum*. Could this be the *thermospodium* with heat 'above and below' as Apicius (4.2.33) describes it?

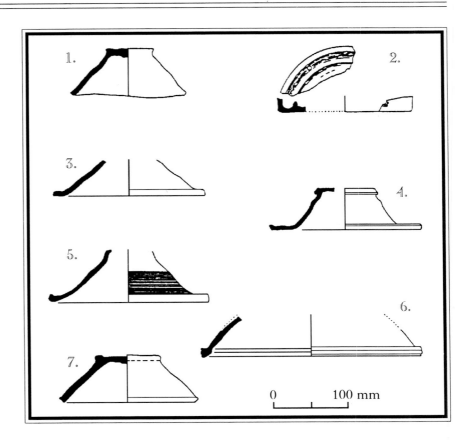

Fig. 5.5
Possible sherds of Romano-British testa *or* clibani *from Castor, near Peterborough.*

Medieval examples

Since the publication of our original paper (Cubberley *et al.* 1988), reports are showing more sensitivity to the identification of *testa* and *clibani*. Williams and Evans (1991) note the presence of what could be such a vessel in the pottery from Catterick and, very significantly, that there is nothing in the fabric to suggest that it was not manufactured locally.

If these Romano-British examples are in fact *testa*, though the identification is by no means sure, then we should perhaps look for examples also in medieval contexts in Britain. The medieval 'curfew', a vessel which preserves the fire overnight, is frequently of the same form and gritted fabric as the medieval Italian *testo*. Examples from King's Lynn can be seen in figures 5.6 and 5.7 (see Clarke and Carter 1977). The vessel was widespread in medieval England and is invariably identified as the

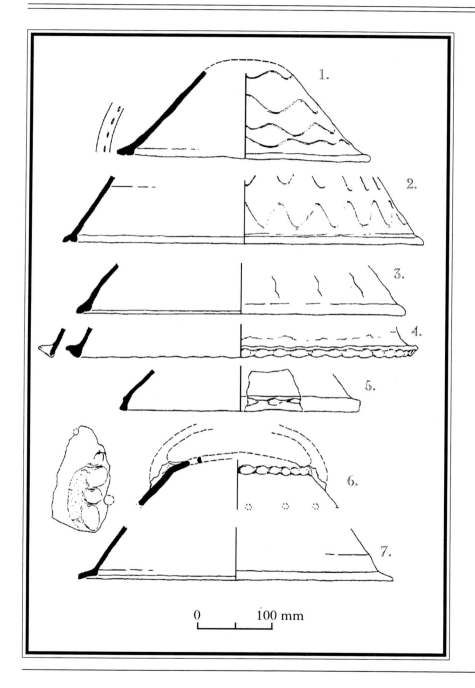

Fig. 5.6
Medieval curfews from
King's Lynn.

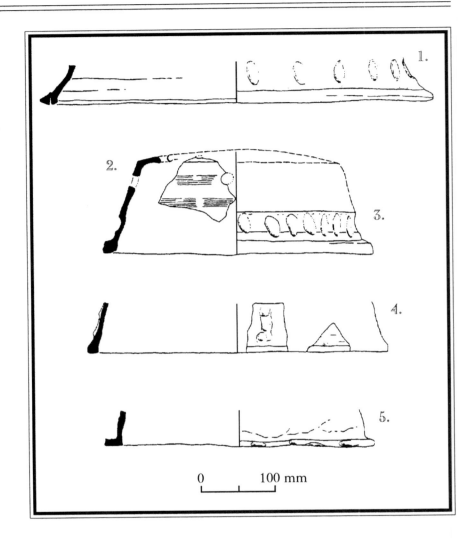

*Fig. 5.7
Medieval curfews from
King's Lynn.*

curfew. There is a variety of shape of the curfew and it is possible that some vessels given the function of curfew could have had a different use. The suggestion has been made by Moorhouse (1983) that some are fish-smokers. This is not to deny the use of the vessel as curfew, but in view of their fabric and form there is the possibility (and nothing more than that)

that they could have functioned, or at least doubled, as *testi*. Perhaps further assessment of pottery assemblages from earlier excavations will bear fruit.

If these speculative suggestions prove to be well-founded, then this simple way of cooking and the vessels relevant to this process must be more widespread than was thought. More examples ought to be identified, especially from the materials from previous excavations, where in the past coarse wares have received less than due attention. Moreover, in the wider context of domestic pottery there is need for more work both on the function of vessels, a study hitherto subordinate to other aspects, and on the links between the literary, linguistic and material evidence.

In addition, three questions pose themselves: [1] What was the *modus operandi* of these vessels? [2] What was the nature of the food so produced? [3] What are the socio-economic implications in the variations in size at different periods and in different areas? The first two of these could be illuminated by some experimental archaeology.

Conclusion

Notes

1. Ovid *Fasti* 6.315-6, talking of the Festival of Vesta (the protectress of bakers), says that 'the hearth itself baked the bread which was put under the ashes, and a broken tile had been lain on the hot floor' (suppositum cineri panem focus ipse parabat | strataque erat tepido tegula quassa solo).

2. Cato *On Agriculture* 74: 'Recipe for kneaded bread: wash your hands and a bowl well. Put flour into a bowl, add water gradually, knead thoroughly. When it has been well kneaded, mould and bake under a *testum*' (panem depsticium sic facito. manus mortariumque bene lavato. farinam in mortarium indito, aquae paulatim addito subigitoque pulchre. ubi bene subegeris, defingito coquitoque sub testu).

3. *Moretum* 50-1, where the author talks of Simylus who, after the dough has been made, marks it out on top into equal divisions, and then 'puts it on to the hearth (Scybale had first cleaned the place and made it fitting), covers it with tiles and heaps the fire on top' (infert inde foco (Scybale

mundaverat aptum | ante locum) testisque tegit, super aggerat ignis).

4. Seneca *Epistulae Morales* 90.23, tells how the wise man, by imitating the processes of nature, 'baked bread first in hot ashes or in an earthenware vessel burning hot; later ovens were gradually invented along with other devices, whose heat could be subject to regulation' (...quem [panem] primo cinis calidus et fervens testa percoxit, deinde furni paulatim reperti et alia genera, quorum fervor serviret arbitrio).

5. Livy 39.6: 'banquets began to be prepared with greater care and expense. The cook, whom ancients regarded and treated as the lowest form of slave, was rising in value, and what had been a servile task began to be considered as a fine art' (epulae quoque ipsae et cura et sumptu maiore apparari coeptae. tum coquus, vilissimum antiquis mancipium et aestimatione et usu, in pretio esse, et quod ministerium fuerat, ars haberi coepta).

[6.] Gregory of Tours *Vita Patrum* 2.4; Alexander Neckham *de Naturis Rerum* 2.107; Hariulf of S. Riquier, *Chronicon Liber* 3.32, etc.

[7.] Seneca *Epistulae* 90.3; Dioscorides *de materia medica* 2.81; 2.96.

[8.] Mannoni (1965, 1970, 1975); *La Ceramica medievale* (1986).

[9.] Pietro di Crescenzi *Liber commodorum ruralium*, who tells us that 'bread baked in an oven is better, because it cooks evenly; that cooked in *testi* is not as good' (migliore e quel [pane] che e cotto nel forno, imperocche tutto egualmente si cuoce; ma quello che e cotto in testi e piggiore).

[10.] This section relies heavily on the work of R. Carlton (1988) and J. Nandris (1988).

[11.] In 1987 71% of all pots made in the area were of this type, though the number of vessels made was rapidly decreasing.

Bibliography

Carandini, A. (ed.) 1985 *Settefinestre – una villa schiavistica nell' Emilia Romagna*, 3 vols (Modena).

Carlton, R. 1988 'An Ethnoarchaeological Study of Pottery Production. The Dalmatian island of Iz', in Chapman *et al.* (1988), 101-23.

La Ceramica medievale del Mediterraneo Occidentale (1986) (Florence), 293-316, 529-44.

Chapman, J.C., Bintliff, J., Gaffney, V. & Slapsak, B. 1988 *Recent Developments in Yugoslav Archaeology* British Archaeological Reports International Series, S431 (Oxford).

Christie, N. (ed.) 1991 *Three South Etrurian Churches* (British School at Rome, London).

Clarke, H. & Carter, A. 1977 *Excavations in King Lynn 1963-1970* (Society for Medieval Archaeology Monograph Series 7), 306-9.

Cubberley, A.L., Lloyd, J.A. & Roberts, P.C. 1988 '*Testa* and *Clibani*: the Baking Covers of Classical Italy', *Papers of the British School at Rome* 56, 98-119.

Dyson, S.L. 1976 'Cosa – the utilitarian pottery', *Memoirs of the American Academy at Rome* 33.

Frayn, J. 1978 'Home Baking in Roman Italy', *Antiquity* 52, 28-33.

Lloyd, J. A. & Rathbone, D.W. 1985 'La villa romana a Matrice', *Conoscenze* 1, 216-19.

Mannoni, T. 1965 'Il testo e la sua diffusione nella Liguria del Levante', *Bollettino Ligustico* 17, 49-64.

Mannoni, T. 1970 'La ceramica di uso comune in Liguria prima del XIX secolo', *Atti del convegno internazionale della ceramica Albisola* 3, 297-319.

Mannoni, T. 1975 *La ceramica medievale a Genova e nella Liguria* (Bordighera and Genova).

Moorhouse, S. 1983 'A Semi-circular Firecover from the Tyler Hill Kilns, Canterbury', *Medieval Ceramics* 7, 101-7.

Patterson, H. 1991 'Early medieval and medieval pottery', in Christie (1991), 120-4.

Nandris, J. 1988 'Ethnoarchaeology and Latinity in the Mountains of the Southern Velebit', in Chapman *et al.* (1988), 125-43.

Perrin, J.R. & Webster, G. 1990 'Roman Pottery from Excavations in Normangate Field, Castor, Peterborough, 1962-3', *Journal of Roman Pottery Studies* 3, 35-62.

Ricci, A. 1985 'Settefinestre III - la villa e i suoi reperti', in Carandini (1985), 246.

Whitehouse, D.B. 1978 'Home baking in Roman Italy: a footnote', *Antiquity* 52, 146-7.

Williams, D. & Evans, J. 1991 'A fragment from a probable Roman *clibanus* from Catterick, North Yorkshire', *Journal of Roman Pottery Studies* 4, 51-5.

❖ 6 ❖

ETHNOARCHAEOLOGY AND STORAGE IN THE ANCIENT MEDITERRANEAN
BEYOND RISK AND SURVIVAL[1]

Hamish Forbes and Lin Foxhall

Introduction

STORAGE facilities (e.g. grain bins, pits, large storage jars – *pithoi*) are common finds in archaeology, and the importance of storage – including such invisibles as 'social storage', on which see e.g. O'Shea (1981) – has been widely considered by archaeologists. On the other hand, very little attention has been paid to the subject of food storage in the broad sense in ancient history.[1] One problem here is that storage is not directly considered by the ancient agricultural writers; nor is the removal of commodities from storage for sale. The fact that the ancient agricultural writers are largely (though not completely) silent on this point is important, and will be discussed later.

Our major aim is to emphasize the large numbers of decisions (both conscious and unconscious) which storage of commodities involves, and to indicate that storage considerations have important ramifications at several different behavioural levels. Above all it is our intention to emphasize that storage is *the crucial* point which separates considerations of agricultural *production* from considerations of *distribution* and/or *consumption*. Storage by producers also gives them a great deal of control over how they deal with the agents of distribution. Given the fact that both agricultural production and distribution have greatly interested archaeologists and historians of the Mediterranean world for a long time, it is perhaps surprising that this intermediary aspect of storage has been so little considered.

Food storage is part of a much larger universe of storage strategies which include such items as money, works of art, cloth and clothing, water in cisterns (Columella *On Agriculture* 1.5.1-2), outstanding loans (of money or goods), and even a good reputation (social storage again). In concentrating on food, we are therefore investigating only one section of a much wider phenomenon. Furthermore, we do not consider in detail the issue of Roman state-controlled storage as evidenced by the widespread finds of large civil and military granaries, discussed for example by Rickman (1971). These are more accurately described as warehouses for relatively short-term storage. Those at Ostia may well have been for the short-term housing of grain in sacks awaiting shipment up the Tiber (Rickman 1971, 86). In Rome, the primary function of the large civil grain warehouses is likely to have been for amassing adequate supplies to feed the population over the winter months when grain shipping was too dangerous (Rickman 1980, 128). An examination of the part played by storage in the political organization of the Roman empire comparable to recent studies of this topic concerning the Inca empire (e.g. Earle and D'Altroy 1982) is long overdue, but is not our concern here.

A word of caution is necessary about our ethnoarchaeological data. These derive from small-scale agrarian ('peasant') households. Although it is generally assumed that the ancient societies of the Mediterranean were firmly founded on a peasant base[2], most of our sources (archaeological and historical) derive from the upper strata of society. Even such archetypal 'rustics' as Aristophanes' Acharnians are portrayed largely as a political (not agrarian) type – and of course, charcoal-burning, their characteristic occupation, is portrayed as a non-agrarian one. And, despite the rusticity of his aphorisms (Millett 1989, 19), Hesiod gives every indication of belonging to the wealthier end of the socio-economic spectrum.

The lack of clear ancient references to peasants has of course not, until recently, been considered reason to deny the existence of a free peasantry in ancient Greece and Rome – particularly not in the Athenian state. Detailed discussion is not desirable here, but we are not prepared simply to assume, as does Gallant (1991, 4), the existence of a numerically (still less politically) significant peasantry in Greece. For a similar argument with regard to the situation in Roman Italy, the reader is referred to Foxhall (1990a). Still less are we prepared to accept Finley's (1985, 19, 144-7) view that rich Greek and Roman households functioned in much the same way as peasant households. It is our belief that, despite the emphasis on self-sufficiency (*autarkia*) among rich Greeks in antiquity, households of the seriously rich had quite different economic aims and strategies from those of the peasants which provide ancient historians with their modern comparanda (Foxhall 1990b, 22-8). Hence major differences must be accepted, both in social standing and in economic behaviour, between the modern villagers documented here and our ancient sources. Nevertheless, the ethnoarchaeological data are highly relevant for understanding the ancient sources, for two main reasons.

i) The modern data emphasize that virtually all storage decision-making occurs at the household level – or at the level of the farm unit in the ancient documents. Different households make different decisions based on the exigencies of their specific circumstances. This is an important counterbalance to much archaeological and historical thinking, which tends to view agrarian decision-making as a unified, community-based, averaged-out activity (see e.g. Gallant (1991) for a recent, but by no means extreme, example). Nevertheless certain underlying 'rules' inform or guide households in their storage decisions.

ii) The data indicate the complexity of the competing considerations in storage decision-making found in 'real-life' situations of people making a living from farming in the Mediterranean zone. Trade-offs between natural environmental factors and those in the economic and political spheres need to be considered even by peasants. It is only to be expected that storage decision-making among the great and the good – the focus of our ancient data – would have been even more complicated because of the increased importance and complexity of economic and political considerations.

Ethnographic background

The peninsula of Methana, from which our modern data are drawn (Forbes 1982), is a largely volcanic peninsula in the eastern Peloponnese. It lies in the driest zone of Greece: average rainfall is under 40 cm per year, with a high interannual variability. As a result of these factors, it is estimated that near-complete crop failure occurs on average once every five years on Methana.

Farm work is done primarily by households' own labour-forces with their own animals. At the time of the main period of field-work in the early 1970s, the main aim of most households was subsistence: the value of the three main food staples consumed by farm families was generally greater than the cash receipts from crops grown specifically for sale. Surpluses of crops grown primarily for household consumption were also frequently sold, and were sometimes an important source of cash. But the main aim of households was production by the household's own labour for its direct consumption (Forbes 1982, 158-99; Forbes 1989, 88).

In the village of Kosona where fieldwork was concentrated, the traditional family house was usually a two-storey structure. Living accommodation consisted of two rooms on the upper floor, with one or two terraces provided by the flat roofs of single-storey extensions to the main structure. The lower floor of the main structure and often both single-storey extensions were employed for storage, although some households' animals were housed in part of this area. By no means all of the storage area was devoted to food storage. Much space was needed for all the multifarious items of equipment necessary to run a farm – sieves, digging tools, harness, pack-baskets, seed for fodder crops, etc. A similar array of equipment can be found in the Attic *stelae* (see below), where the contents of what seem to be rural outbuildings were sold off (e.g. *IG* I³ 422 col. 2. 115-66). On Methana animal fodder – primarily hay and straw – was generally not stored here, but in separate storage structures.

That the area devoted to storage on these small farms is greater than the living area may come as a surprise to many, but much the same situation can be seen in the traditional layouts of small English farms. Comparable observations on storage have been made in ethnographic studies in Switzerland, where the Alpine subsistence economy has been described as a 'storage culture' (Netting 1981, 34).

In her review of the strategies developed by self-reliant societies to cope with bad-weather induced shortages, the anthropologist Elizabeth Colson (1979, 21) stated: 'from the ethnographic literature, it is possible to distinguish five devices commonly adopted to lessen vulnerability to such risks…Storage of foodstuffs may be the least important emergency measure of the lot.' This may often be the case in regions of the tropics where staples frequently take the form of root crops. And even where cereal staples are grown in the tropics it is frequently stated that they are readily susceptible to destruction by fungi and insects. Thus in a study in Ghana, the loss rate of maize in store was measured at 30% per year. However, other studies have shown that introduced 'modern' storage methods and new (and less pest-resistant) crop varieties (especially maize) are responsible for some of the very high storage losses reported. Traditional crop varieties and storage techniques are considered to have much lower loss rates (D'Altroy and Earle 1985, 191; Sigaut 1988, 15). This is doubtless why, among the Diola of Senegal (in basically the same West African tropical zone as Ghana) individual granaries can hold ten tons or more of rice. Since each co-wife in a household must have her own granary, and the household head also has his own separate grain store, very large amounts of grain can be found in a single household. Fires are burned in these granaries specifically to combat insects (Linares 1984, 427).

This brief digression into tropical food storage emphasizes the impact that particular crop varieties and quite minor differences in storage practices can have on the lives of stored products, even in environments not conducive to crop storage. The worst problems with crop storage losses in many parts of the world seem to stem from ignoring indigenous cultivars and technologies developed over a long period. In the ancient Mediterra-

Decision-making in food storage behaviour: factors involving environmental hazards

nean it is clear from the Roman agricultural writers and Greek sources (e.g. Gallant 1991, 98) that there was a well-developed body of knowledge concerning storage of agricultural produce and the kinds of conditions to be avoided[3].

For these reasons, we believe that Gallant's (1991, 97-8) estimates of losses in storage are much too high, and furthermore they do not take account of some of the recent literature on the subject. In any case the portion of any crop damaged by pests is not completely lost if it can be fed to animals. And, as Columella (*On Agriculture* 1.6.17) makes clear, pests frequently do not destroy more than a small portion of a stored crop. We will return to the importance of the finite storage life of food products in due course.

On Methana, the high interannual variability of the climate has a major effect on storage decision-making because of the villagers' strategy of average overproduction. Most villagers produce more than enough of a crop – especially cereals – under 'average' climatic conditions so that even in rather poor years there will still be an adequate crop – a strategy widely documented elsewhere (Halstead 1989, 69-70; Garnsey 1988, 54). To cope with this policy of overproduction for subsistence purposes combined with the inevitable occasional bumper crops in good years, households must maintain a storage capacity greatly in excess of that necessary simply for their own consumption. Hence it is to be expected that a considerable proportion of a household's storage capacity would lie empty in most years, as can be seen from Hesiod's comments (*Works and Days* 473-8; cf. Garnsey 1988, 54) on cleaning cobwebs from storage jars in a bumper harvest.

So far we have considered storage decisions from the point of view of a single year's crop. Yet, as noted earlier, a household can expect a shortfall in wheat approximately twice in a decade, despite a long-term policy of overproduction. Households on Methana cope with this problem by attempting to maintain an extra year's grain *over and above* that needed for the current year (Forbes 1989, 93-4). In this way they still have a full year's grain supply to fall back on, despite partial or complete crop failure. With olive oil, the situation is still more extreme, since olives only crop in alternate years, and synchronize their fruiting. Methanites therefore need to maintain *four* years' olive oil in storage in case the following harvest fails.

All these considerations result in a very large amount of storage capacity in family farms in Methana – far larger than is necessary for feeding the household for a year, despite the fact that decisions on crop production are geared primarily to households' consumption needs. However, this capacity still represents what might be considered a minimum for short-term subsistence. Since many households maintain even greater amounts of grain in store because they wish to hold on to surplus grain from previous years until an appropriate time for a sale, still further amounts of storage capacity are necessary. These are factors which need to be considered by archaeologists when they evaluate evidence of storage facilities found on their sites.

The extent to which Methanites are regularly able to maintain extra years' supplies of staples has recently been questioned, as has the efficacy of storage alone as a risk-buffering mechanism (Gallant 1991, 94). It has been made clear elsewhere (Forbes 1982, 377-91) that the coyness of Methana householders over divulging amounts of stored produce makes absolute pronouncements impossible, but all the evidence points to the maintenance of extra years' supplies of staples as a normal practice, not simply an aspiration. It is even more obvious that in Methana storage strategies are but one vital item in a panoply of risk-buffering mechanisms (e.g. Forbes 1982, 312-435; Forbes 1989). We must therefore be cautious in too readily accepting Gallant's (1991, 97-8) recent pronouncements on the relative unimportance of storage as a hazard-response mechanism in antiquity.

Under the circumstances discussed so far, Methana households usually have supplies of foodstuffs greatly in excess of their consumption needs, even though they only *plan* for self-sufficiency. Surplus grain, even small surpluses of wheat, may be fed to animals. Other households sell their surplus wheat, even though they believe that the cash return does not cover the overheads – after all, they need to get rid of it somehow if it is surplus to requirements. The ideal is to keep storable and potentially saleable food products such as olive oil, wheat and almonds in storage until

Decision-making in food storage behaviour: factors involving economic considerations

a specific large purchase is needed (a mule, for example, or house repairs or payment of wedding expenses). But farmers also know that produce in storage will in due course deteriorate, through the combined effects of rodents, fungus, and above all insects. This is an especially important consideration when grains are naked, as all wheat is in modern Methana. Nevertheless, naked grains can still be kept for several years before they become valueless. Theophrastos (*Inquiry into Plants* 8.11) notes that wheat kept for three years was infertile, but still edible (cf. Sigaut 1988, 12-13). Other products, especially olive oil, also have finite storage lives, although relatively long ones. The quality of olive oil drops over time, and so also does the value. Hence the farmer is constrained to sell produce periodically simply to ensure that it is not entirely lost because of deterioration in storage.

Farmers may therefore occasionally find themselves in a position where they must sell stored produce before it becomes unsaleable, yet there may be nothing available at that time which is suitable for them to invest in. In such circumstances, they may make 'illogical' or 'uneconomic' purchases rather than keep their proceeds in the form of cash. In the context of the great and the good illuminated by our ancient sources, it is by no means impossible that comparable 'uneconomic' spending, though different in scale and possibly intent, may have followed sale of large amounts of steadily deteriorating stored foodstuffs.

In antiquity, however, hulled grains – especially emmer, spelt and hulled barley – were widely grown for human consumption. These needed considerably more processing before they were considered edible, and had a lower economic (and social) value. Nevertheless, the hard outer glumes of hulled grains stored in the spikelet stage mean that such grains in storage are much better protected from attack by insects and other pests than are naked grains (cf. Jones, Wardle, Halstead and Wardle 1986, 99-102). Hulled grains in antiquity therefore represented a trade-off between lower value of the crop and reduced risks of storage losses over a period of years. They also represent one of the traditional cultivars, grown with an eye to their storability, which were mentioned above.

In this context, the 'bewildering variety of opinion' (Rickman 1971, 295) in the ancient agricultural writers on how to make grain storage facilities pest-proof comes to mind (e.g. Columella *On Agriculture* 1.6.9-17 on storage facilities, especially for grain in the ideal villa). Notwithstanding the comments about traditional storage techniques made previously, the mere fact that there was so much discussion among ancient authors on how to store grain strongly suggests that no storage method was considered completely effective. Grain-storage instructions frequently involve the use of *amurca* (bitter lees from olive-pressing), sometimes boiled down, and it is possible that there may be toxins in this product which inhibit insect attack – the main concern of the ancient writers. However, a major underlying theme of the agricultural writers is not to waste time or resources. We must therefore be careful in assuming that *amurca* was genuinely effective in combatting grain storage losses. An alternative explanation is that these instructions to use *amurca* for treating storage facilities should be seen as something that can be done with a by-product generated in large quantities on agricultural estates, which had little obvious alternative use. It is widely recommended in numerous other contexts besides grain storage (e.g. as a medicine for sick cattle), and gives the impression of having much the same status as the administration of chicken soup to invalids in our society: it cannot do any harm and might occasionally do some good. In any event, Columella (*On Agriculture* 1.6.16-17) makes it clear that the recommended pest-proofing is often not fully effective.

There is an important corollary to what has been noted above about maintaining produce in store until a specific purchase is needed. Decisions on taking produce out of storage are as much a part of storage behaviour as decisions on putting produce into store. This is particularly the case with farmers who are growing storable produce primarily for the market, as were wealthy estate owners in the Greek and Roman world. Given the uncertainties of fluctuations in commodity prices on the one hand, and the steady decline in the quality of foodstuffs in store on the other, it is often not easy for the producer to decide the optimal – or even a good – time to sell. It is therefore surprising that none of the ancient authors who write about agricultural *production* say anything very specific about *sale* of agricultural produce. Hesiod briefly comments on the possibility – though the undesirability – of taking produce for sale on shipboard (*Works and Days* 631-2, 643-5, 689-90), but there are only hints in the sources of how Greek and Roman estate owners organized the sale of their major products: wheat, olive oil and wine.

On Methana in the past, villagers sold their surplus wheat and olive oil to the captains of small coasting vessels who would visit at irregular intervals. It would seem that the number of opportunities for the sale of agricultural produce was quite limited. Hence, rather than always needing to gauge the optimal time to sell, Methana farmers seem often to have been on the look-out for any opportunity for a sale. Nowadays both the economic and transportation structures of the region are very different. Merchants still occasionally visit villages speculatively, hoping to find farmers ready to sell produce, especially olive oil. But for olive oil sales, most villagers make arrangements with urban relatives, either selling to them directly, or using them as go-betweens for sales to other urbanites. Even now, however, villagers are often avid for news of a potential buyer.

Probably because of the very high *symbolic* importance of olive oil in modern Greece, these transactions involve much more than a straightforward economic 'deal'. Although wine in Methana also has a high symbolic importance, it is generally not sold and thus there is no comparability to the situation with olive oil. Nevertheless, given the high symbolic value particularly of fine wines but also of olive oil in antiquity, we might expect that ancient business transactions involving these commodities would likewise involve a high degree of social ritual.

The only work on the management of an ancient Greek agricultural estate is Xenophon's *Oikonomikos*, which is more moral than practical in tone, and barely credible as an insight into the running of a wealthy Athenian household. Yet while Ischomachos, the main speaker in the dialogue, leaves much of the domestic organization of his estate under the eye of his wife, he makes no specific statements about the maintenance or disposal of stored foodstuffs. The closest he comes is a comment about the wife's duty to keep grain in good condition for making food (7.36), but he seems to indicate that the wife's responsibility for stored food supplies does not extend beyond an amount specifically set aside for a year's consumption.

The Roman agricultural writers seem to have considered that responsibility for storage on estates lay with the bailiff's wife: Columella (*On Agri-*

culture 12.1-2) in particular indicates a large number of storage-related activities which were her responsibility. Even here there is little in the way of instructions on storage – or the maintenance while in store – of the estate's basic stock of commodities for sale. Instead, most of the instructions to the bailiff's wife involve the preparation and storage of materials related to the running of the villa household. Hence in neither Greek nor Roman documents do we find extensive discussions of the details of managing stored foodstuffs destined for the market.

The best indication of how sales were arranged on Roman estates comes from Cato (*On Agriculture* 2.5-7) and Columella (*On Agriculture* 1.8.13) in their instructions for dealing with the estate bailiff. 'The master should have the selling habit, not the buying habit' says Cato (2.7). But the actual instructions are vague: 'sell your oil if the price is satisfactory, and sell the surplus of your wine and grain' (2.7). The actual organisation of marketing arrangements seems to have been left to the bailiff: '[with the bailiff] run over the wine accounts, the oil accounts – what has been sold, what collected, balance due, and what is left that is saleable' (2.5). Columella specifically acknowledges Cato's and Xenophon's advice on dealing with bailiffs (11.1.4-5). He reiterates and elaborates much of Cato's advice that the bailiff should mind the estate owner's business, not his own (11.1.13; cf. 1.2.2). In particular he notes that the bailiff should only visit the town or the market (*nundina*) for the sale or purchase of something necessary, nor should he send his master's slaves off on his own errands (11.1.23). He should receive visits from strangers only if they are the master's friends (11.1.23). And he should not use his master's money for doing his own deals in cattle or anything else: for this diverts him from his duties as a bailiff and makes him a trader (*negotiator*) rather than a farmer and makes it impossible to balance accounts with his master; but when a reckoning up in money is being held, goods are displayed instead of cash (11.1.24).

It sounds almost as though Roman bailiffs were more comfortable dealing in commodities than in cash, like modern Methanites, though some of their reasons were probably different. Fraud and personal profit must have played an important part in bailiffs' private enterprises with their masters' money, but a lack of faith in cash might also have been a factor.

For the Roman estate owner, the ideal seems to have been that the basic organization of making business transactions for the sale of the estate's produce was largely beneath his social position. Vitruvius (6.5.2) advises that the urban houses of estate owners should have shops and *tabernae* as well as good, practical (not simply ornamental) storerooms so that their country produce can be sold, but he does not suggest that estate owners were personally involved in the day-to-day decision-making of storage and marketing. And despite the very different scale of operations, Athenian estate owners may well also have left these matters to subordinates. The obverse of this is that the position of the bailiff or estate manager, who had this responsibility, was extremely important (Parkins 1992; Foxhall 1990a, 103).

We must assume that bailiffs were enmeshed in very complex networks involving social interactions which had both commercial and non-commercial aspects. That the farm manager should be responsible for transactions involving sale of the estate's produce makes sense if the owner had estates which were widely separated geographically and thus did not have the local network of mercantile contacts which a bailiff could develop. But this state of affairs also suggests that bailiffs differed little, if at all, in social standing from the merchants with whom they dealt (cf. Parkins 1992): otherwise they would have been at too great a disadvantage to negotiate deals successfully.

By leaving the business transactions for sale of the estate's produce to the bailiff, the Roman agricultural writers have given us very little idea of the working of the vast commercial network of traded agricultural produce. Its existence is tangentially indicated in literary works by references to fine wines from distant places, and more materially by finds of amphorae in the archaeological record, but we have no idea how estates articulated with such a network. Instead we are left with Cato's general comments about desirable estate locations: near to a flourishing town, or the sea, or a navigable river, or a good and much travelled road (*On Agriculture* 1.3). Columella (*On Agriculture* 1.2.3) similarly suggests that a location close to a navigable stream or the sea is desirable to transport farm produce (*quo deportari fructus*). But interestingly, although he finds a location not far from a highway acceptable, he warns against being too close to a military road (1.5.6-7), because of passing travellers, who help themselves to the farm's produce or request accommodation.

Decision-making in food storage behaviour: political considerations

Although it is often hard to separate economic from political considerations, it is important to recognize that some decisions in storage behaviour are more closely related to the latter than the former. It has already been briefly noted above that Methana farmers and Roman bailiffs often prefer to keep wealth in form of stored produce.

Methanites do not trust ordinary paper currency because over the last half-century several different political events have caused rapid and sometimes catastrophic devaluation of the drachma. And gold, though considered a more reliable form of currency, is hard to get hold of and can be easily stolen – as happened during the operations of communist partisans during the last war. Mainly for this reason, Methanites prefer to keep commodities in storage until a major purchase is needed, even though some deterioration in value may be entailed, rather than sell immediately and bank the proceeds. An indication of their lack of confidence in the ability of the state to maintain a stable currency – or even political stability – is their use of an olive oil standard by which to gauge the 'true' worth of money. Agricultural produce – especially olive oil – is less prone to problems of devaluation due to inflation than ordinary currency. And bulk agricultural commodities are far more difficult to move about – hence to steal – than cash or gold.

Very much this situation can be seen with the Attic *stelae*, accounts issued by the state 'sellers' (*poletai*) as inscriptions listing the confiscated property (which was to be sold) of wealthy citizens who had fled Attika after being accused of impiety (Pritchett 1956). The bulk of the items seem to be the contents of store rooms on agricultural estates, and most of these items are of very low value (e.g. old doors, jars – *pithoi* – in all states of repair, a 'weasel-trap'), or else bulky items, particularly agricultural produce and textiles. The only remaining high-value items were slaves, who would have been recognizable as belonging to their owners. The high-value, portable items which might have been expected in the store rooms of wealthy estates are largely missing. They could have been squirrelled away by their owners prior to their flight, or handed over to relatives for safekeeping (as in Demosthenes 29 and 30), or they may have been pilfered by others between the time of the owners' escape and the arrival of those who drew up the lists. In either case, the fact remains that bulky agricultural produce remained in the stores along with items of equipment of little value, presumably simply because it was difficult to move them about.

In the past on Methana, when political instability was very great, and included problems with bandits and pirates, much of a household's foodstuffs was not stored anywhere close to the house. Instead, food not needed for immediate consumption was kept in storehouses hidden on the mountain-sides at considerable distances from the village. In this way, when raiders visited villages, there was little of worth to be found in houses. This situation may also have helped villagers to cut down on the more rapacious demands of tax-collectors.

A more recent scenario helps to emphasize another political aspect of storage. During the early 1970s, when Greece was run by a military dictatorship, there was a period of runaway inflation. The government tried to keep the price of wheat stable by not raising support prices, in order to maintain favour with the urban population. However, economic instability in Greece, coupled with political instability in the Middle East, led to unfocussed fears of a possible war in Greece. The combination of not only low and unchanged support prices during a period of rapid inflation but also fears of war meant that farmers throughout Greece kept their wheat in store, refusing to sell it. Not even the muscle of a military dictatorship could get the wheat away from the farmers. The result was a serious shortage of bread in Athens, leading to bread riots and a dramatic drop in the government's popularity among the urban population. It was to try to counter the deep unpopularity brought about in no small part by these shortages that the military government made its disastrous attempt to take over Cyprus. The failure of this adventure led to the fall of the dictatorship.

The refusal of producers to remove staples from store for sale is one manifestation of the fact (with which we started) that, especially for those producers who are primarily geared for the market, storage decisions belong to the economic and political realm of the household. For both modern and ancient governments in the European Mediterranean region, food supply policies must therefore focus on the aggregate of household decisions about storage which have been made beyond their control and authority. It is in this context that the concern with food supply visible in the city of Rome, in Athenian sources from the 5th century BC onwards, and in other Greek city-states in the Hellenistic and Roman periods, should be understood.

It has been argued (Gallant 1991; Garnsey and Morris 1989; Garnsey, Gallant and Rathbone 1984; cf. Jongman and Dekker 1989) that because economic behaviour was embedded in social relations, food crises were generally countered by various kinds of *ad hoc* measures on a community level. Although food supply was monitored, rarely were there permanent institutional structures to ensure grain supplies. Ancient city-states in the Graeco-Roman world had to resort to liturgies (compulsory contributions by the wealthy) and private beneficence (especially in Hellenistic Greece) or state purchase and distribution of grain (as in the Roman corn dole, or the famous 'corn law' of 3rd century BC Samos, *SIG*³ 976) to avert food crises. We would not disagree with the conclusions of Garnsey and Morris (1989) and Gallant (1991) that much of the documented euergetism in Hellenistic cities indicates the dominance of a small group of élites over all aspects of life, and that this fact was important in times of food crisis. But we do not feel that this alone explains why state institutional structures to secure food supplies at community level were not developed in these Greek city-states.

In democratic Athens the élite did not have the kind of power that they did in Hellenistic cities. Nevertheless, a broadly similar situation vis-à-vis food supply at community level (i.e. monitoring without permanent institutional control) existed. On at least one occasion Athens' food supply was secured by the euergetistic intervention of a foreign ruler (p.33 above). Garnsey and Morris (1989), in attempting to explain why Athens does not fit the Hellenistic model, blame the unbureaucratized nature of

Athenian democratic government (and the economy founded in social relations). But this fails to explain the phenomenon completely just as the stranglehold of the élite fails as an answer in the Hellenistic case.

'Raw substantivism' does not provide an adequate theoretical framework for explaining the nature of community regulation of food supply. Rather, we maintain that in both ancient and modern economies, different types and levels of economic decisions are confined to different politico-economic contexts. Even in the modern world of powerful and politically intrusive nation-states and 'hyperstates', there are areas of economic behaviour which central political authorities are virtually powerless to control. In present-day recession-hit Britain, the aggregate of individual decisions of households and consumers presents a pattern of saving (storing, if you like) money in a time of uncertainty and recession. Despite the increased incomes of those in employment, the government has been unable to persuade households to spend their own money in order to bring the country out of recession.

Similarly in antiquity, decisions surrounding food supply were largely the responsibility of households, inasmuch as they were decisions taken about storage. Even under the Roman Empire many of the largest grain- and other food-producing estates in areas like North Africa were owned by the Emperor. To what extent then, could it be argued that the food supply of the capital was dependent upon decisions about storage and distribution of food taken by the largest and most important household in the Empire?

We argue then, that food supply – founded in storage decisions and strategies – was a household, not a community matter, and thus provides an over-arching explanation which covers all the cases (ancient and modern) we have discussed. This is not simply to retreat to another substantivist position, which explains such economic behaviour entirely in terms of 'economically irrational' social relations, characteristic of societies other than our own. Rather, we would argue that the household, in a large number of both modern and ancient societies, constitutes an arena of economic decision-making which is out of reach of the state in most circumstances.

Notes

1. The inspiration for this paper derives from the work of K.D. White. We have gained much from his published work on all aspects of ancient agriculture, as well from discussions with him. We also greatly value his descriptions of life in Liverpool during his boyhood, and share with him his love of that city.

2. Although we cannot discuss the whole issue of ancient peasantries here, it should be noted that attempts by anthropologists and historians over several decades to define what is meant by a 'peasant' have not been conclusive. It is probably unwise to assume that the ancient Graeco-Roman countryside was largely populated by the class of people found in these same areas today.

3. For example, Columella advises against locating a villa close to marsh-land, because the damp air not only played havoc with farm equipment but also spoiled both stored and unstored produce (*On Agriculture* 1.5.6).

Bibliography

Colson, E. 1979 'In good years and in bad: food strategies of self-reliant societies', *Journal of Anthropological Research* 35.1, 18-29.

D'Altroy, T.N. & Earle, T.K. 1985 'Staple finance, wealth finance, and storage in the Inka political economy', *Current Anthropology* 26, 187-206.

Earle, T.K., & D'Altroy, T.N. 1982 'Storage facilities and state finance in the Upper Mantaro valley, Peru', in Ericson and Earle (1982), 265-91.

Ericson, J.E. & Earle, T.K. (eds) 1982 *Contexts for Prehistoric Exchange* (New York and London).

Finley, M.I. 1985 *The Ancient Economy* 2nd ed. (London).

Forbes, H.A. 1982 *Strategies and Soils: Technology, Production and Environment in the Peninsula of Methana, Greece* (Ann Arbor, Michigan: University Microfilms International).

Forbes, H.A. 1989 'Of grandfathers and grand theories: the hierarchised ordering of responses to hazard in a Greek rural community', in Halstead and O'Shea (1989), 87-97.

Foxhall, L. 1990a 'The dependent tenant: land leasing and labour in Italy and Greece', *Journal of Roman Studies* 80, 97-114.

Foxhall, L. 1990b *Olive Cultivation within Greek and Roman Agriculture: the Ancient Economy Revisited* (Ph.D. thesis, University of Liverpool).

Gallant, T.W. 1991 *Risk and Survival in Ancient Greece. Reconstructing the Rural Domestic Economy* (Cambridge).

Garnsey, P.D.A. 1988 *Famine and Food Supply in the Graeco-Roman World: Responses to Risk and Crisis* (Cambridge).

Garnsey, P.D.A., Gallant, T.W., & Rathbone, D. 1984 'Thessaly and the grain supply of Rome during the second century BC', *Journal of Roman Studies* 74, 30-44.

Garnsey, P.D.A., & Morris, I. 1989 'Risk and the polis: the evolution of institutionalised responses to food supply problems in the ancient Greek state', in Halstead and O'Shea (1989), 98-105.

Halstead, P. 1989 'The economy has a normal surplus: economic stability and social change among early farming communities of Thessaly, Greece', in Halstead and O'Shea (1989), 68-80.

Halstead, P. & O'Shea, J. (eds) 1989 *Bad Year Economics: Cultural Responses to Risk and Uncertainty* (Cambridge).

Jones, G., Wardle, K., Halstead, P., & Wardle, D. 1986 'Crop storage at Assiros', *Scientific American* 254.3, 96-103.

Jongman, W. & Dekker, R. 1989 'Public intervention in the food supply in pre-industrial Europe', in Halstead and O'Shea (1989), 114-22.

Linares, O.F. 1984 'Households among the Diola of Senegal: should norms enter by the front or the back door?', in Netting, Wilk and Arnould (1984), 407-45.

Millett, P. 1989 'Patronage and its avoidance in classical Athens', in Wallace-Hadrill (1989), 15-48.

Netting, R.McC. 1981 *Balancing on an Alp. Ecological Change and Continuity in a Swiss Mountain Community* (Cambridge).

Netting, R.McC., Wilk, R.R. & Arnould, E.J. (eds) 1984 *Households. Comparative and Historical Studies of the Domestic Group* (Berkeley and Los Angeles).

O'Shea J. 1981 'Coping with scarcity: exchange and social storage', in Sheridan and Bailey (1981), 167-83.

Parkins, H. 1992 'Tabernae, topography and trade: the Roman market in Pompeii' (unpublished paper presented at the University of Reading).

Pritchett, W.K. 1956 'The Attic Stelai', *Hesperia* 25, 178-317.

Rickman, G. 1971 *Roman Granaries and Store Buildings* (Cambridge).

Rickman, G. 1980 *The Corn Supply of Ancient Rome* (Oxford).

Sheridan, A. & Bailey, G.N. (eds) 1981 *Economic Archaeology* British Archaeological Reports International Series, S96 (Oxford).

Sigaut, F. 1988 'A method for identifying grain storage techniques and its application for European agricultural history', *Tools and Tillage* 6.1, 3-32.

Wallace-Hadrill, A. (ed.) 1989 *Patronage in Ancient Society* (London and New York).

❖ 7 ❖ MOLECULAR ARCHAEOLOGY AND ANCIENT HISTORY

Robert Sallares

THIS chapter considers the relevance and implications for ancient history of work in progress in a strange new subject which promises to add to our knowledge of the plants and animals which provided the food eaten by humans in antiquity. Since the new subject of molecular archaeology is probably rather unfamiliar to most readers, I am first going to describe the methods used and the types of results which workers in the field hope to obtain. Then I shall describe some work on wheat and bread in antiquity which is currently being carried out by a team of archaeologists and biologists at UMIST led by Terry Brown.

DNA, an acronym for deoxyribonucleic acid, the chemical compound which carries the genetic code in most living organisms (except retroviruses like HIV), is a very hardy molecule. It must be able to resist the wear and tear of life. DNA has been shown to survive in macrofossil remains in a fragmentary state in very small quantities, but nevertheless quite widely, long after the death of the plant or animal to which it belonged. This opens up the possibility of studying the genetics of organisms that lived in the past, even of extinct species. For example DNA has been recovered from remains of the extinct woolly mammoth, marsupial wolf and quagga.

The study of ancient DNA

Recent research has successfully recovered DNA from fossils, preserved in amber, of termites, and of a species of bee which lived in the West Indies as far back as 25-40 million years ago. Ancient DNA has also been recovered from remains of cypress, magnolia and oak trees dating to the Miocene period, about twenty million years ago.[1]

Consequently it should not be difficult in principle to find DNA which we may be able to study dating within the last few thousand years. For periods of geological time, given the fragmentary nature of the fossil record, often only isolated specimens will be available for study, although such data can still in principle yield important information concerning the course of evolution. For historical times and recent periods of prehistory, on the other hand, it is likely that enough material will eventually be available to carry out population studies, for example examining patterns of genetic variation in historical human populations. This new approach promises to yield information about human population history in antiquity which could never be obtained from the available, fragmentary literary and documentary sources.

Methods and techniques

Some preliminary words are necessary on the methods and techniques employed. Firstly, some practical advice for archaeologists. How should archaeologists go about excavating molecules? In principle any type of organic material, from any plant or animal, could contain ancient DNA. As far as humans are concerned, ancient DNA has already been recovered from fossilized bones, mummies, and corpses in bogs, in several parts of the world, dating as far back as seven to eight thousand years ago.[2] Carbonized material may also contain ancient DNA in a reasonable state of preservation. It will be seen later that this is important where cereals such as wheat are concerned. As far as possible the excavator should avoid direct contact with the material; in other words he or she should wear gloves, rather than handling ancient organic materials with bare hands. If possible, excavators should even avoid breathing on ancient organic material, by wearing surgical face masks. The reason for it is that there is a great danger of contaminating ancient DNA with modern DNA. This must be avoided at all costs.

DNA may be better preserved under dry than wet conditions. There is a widespread perception that organic materials are well preserved in water-logged sites. This is true of most types of organic material, but unfortunately it is not always true for DNA. Most bogs are either strongly acid or strongly alkaline. Both sets of conditions can destroy DNA. The corpses in bogs which I mentioned earlier as having yielded ancient DNA came from a very special bog in Florida with a peculiar chemistry. DNA will only be preserved in waterlogged conditions if the acidity-alkalinity level (pH) is roughly neutral. It is better to keep ancient organic material intended for the purpose of research into ancient DNA as dry as possible. Fortunately for us, there are plenty of dry sites in the Mediterranean.[3]

The next step is to consider briefly what happens to the archaeological finds when they arrive in a laboratory. In the case of wheat, the grains are reduced to powder with a mortar and pestle. Water-soluble components are dissolved in a salt solution with cetyl trimethyl ammonium bromide (CTAB), which dissolves plant DNA in the presence of salt. After the proteins have been removed, by extraction with a mixture of chloroform and isoamyl alcohol, DNA is precipitated from the solution by adding more CTAB, this time without any salt. Gel electrophoresis and ultra-centrifugation are two techniques that can be used to sort the DNA fragments according to size. Hybridization analysis is employed to assess the quantity of DNA present in quantitative terms. The presence of DNA can also be confirmed by ultraviolet spectroscopy. Until a few years ago it was virtually impossible to study ancient DNA because the quantities preserved were too small to be amplified by the normal laboratory method of cloning in bacterial cells.

This situation was transformed by the discovery of the polymerase chain reaction (PCR), in which enzymes are used to replicate precisely the DNA in a very small sample many times over, until there is enough for research to proceed.[4] The discovery of this process created the possibility of molecular archaeology. Much of the process is now automated. This point in the procedure is where prior contamination could have disastrous results, because the thermal cycler would amplify the well-preserved modern DNA in preference to the fragmentary ancient DNA. It is possible to design primers based on the modern DNA in genes of interest for the research topic in question. These primers will hybridize with and so identify similar, but not necessarily identical, genetic sequences, if there is any related DNA in the archaeological sample. So that is basically how ancient DNA from the specific genes in which a modern researcher is interested can be recovered from the fragmentary material in small archaeological samples. Finally, there are standard techniques available for establishing the exact sequence, or genetic code, of samples of DNA.

It is important to note that the actual biological function of any protein whose code is carried by any segment of DNA can only be determined by experiments on the living organism as it is today. In other words it is impossible to tell the function of a piece of ancient DNA simply by looking at its sequence, if the function of the corresponding modern gene remains unknown. It is also perhaps worth noting that the degree of precision that can be achieved with ancient DNA in a fragmentary condition is less than is produced by genetic fingerprinting as used by forensic scientists, for which purpose DNA in a perfect condition is required.

DNA as evidence for human relationships

What use can be made of the results of these laboratory procedures? In general the information that can be derived from simply looking at human bones and animal and plant macrofossils from antiquity is limited. Just to take one example, it is difficult to sex human skeletons if they are in a fragmentary condition. This problem will probably be tackled soon on a routine basis, because DNA from the Y chromosome, the male sex chromosome, has already been recovered from ancient bones. Keri Brown at UMIST is currently working on a PCR-based method of sex determination intended for application to archaeological material. It will, we hope, be useful even for cremations.[5]

However, the main potential of molecular archaeology lies in another direction. Little can be said by looking at a skeleton about that individual's relationship to other people buried in the same or adjacent cemeteries or to the members of other human populations. Nevertheless, by studying the DNA, the units of heredity, preserved within ancient human bones, it will be possible to study the relationships between individuals and between populations in antiquity in a way which is completely independent of documentary sources and which will, I think, eventually take us a long way beyond the fragmentary extant literary and documentary evidence.

The types of questions which I have in mind relate to the origins of human populations, to questions of descent, marriage, inbreeding and outbreeding, and population homogeneity or heterogeneity. Probably the simplest way to illustrate the potential of the field in relation to ancient history is to list a few of the problems where molecular archaeology can make a major contribution. When did Indo-European or Proto-Indo-European peoples arrive in Greece? Was it *c.* 6000 BC at the start of the Neolithic period, as Renfrew asserts, or *c.* 2200 BC at the end of the Early Helladic II period, perhaps the most popular theory, or right at the start of the Mycenaean period, *c.* 1600 BC, as Robert Drews has argued recently?[6] To what extent were the people of classical Greece descended from the Mycenaeans? Were the Dorians invaders from the north, or alternatively were they always present in the Peloponnese as a lower class, as Chadwick (1986) claims? Do burial plots in archaic Greek cemeteries represent exclusive kinship groups, as some current hypotheses about early Greek history maintain? Hammond (1992) has drawn attention recently to a series of poor graves at Epidamnos, in one of which the skeleton still bore the ankle chain of slavery, and to the cemetery at Pithekoussai, where inhumations of adults without offerings occur alongside cremations of adults with offerings and inhumations of children without offerings. Buchner (1982) argued that the adult inhumations without offerings belonged to slaves who were buried alongside their masters in the same grave plot. Hammond himself argued that the pit-burials in the second mound at Marathon were the graves of Plataians and liberated slaves who died in the battle, while the dead Athenians were cremated in the first mound. The methods of molecular archaeology provide a way of testing ideas such as these.[7]

There are many other important questions which can be investigated in this way. To give a few more examples: were the Athenians autochthonous, as the legend elaborated in the 5th century BC claims? During Greek colonization in the 8th century BC onwards, did the Greek colonists bring wives with them from home, or alternatively marry indigenous women in the areas that were colonized? Did endogamy or exogamy prevail in local communities in Greece such as Athenian demes, with implications for kinship systems? How exclusive was the citizen body of the various Greek *poleis* and indeed of other states in antiquity? Were the Macedonians Greeks, a question of current political interest? Is there any reality behind ancient stories about human migrations in antiquity? For example, what was the origin of the Etruscans? Did the formative process of the Etruscan nation take place in Italy, as those archaeologists who follow Massimo Pallottino believe, or did they migrate from Asia Minor, as ancient legend preserved by Herodotos suggests?[8] Can we trace the assimilation of the Etruscans and the other peoples of Italy into the expanding Roman state? Can we trace in detail the Celtic migration into Spain and their partial displacement of the non-Indo-European ancestors of the modern Basques? During the collapse of the western Roman empire, did the Anglo-Saxons totally displace the native inhabitants in Britain, or co-exist but remain separate as a ruling caste, or intermarry with the indigenous Romano-British inhabitants?

These are a few examples of the kinds of questions about the origins and interactions of human populations in antiquity to which molecular archaeology will start to yield answers over the next few years. The procedure for answering all these questions will require the accumulation of a large database about ancient DNA that will permit the construction of a family tree ultimately linking together all historical and modern populations in Europe. The basic principle behind the genetic family tree is that various parts of the human genome develop mutations at a more or less constant rate. Consequently the degree of genetic divergence between human lineages is a measure of the evolutionary and historical distance between them. The family tree may even turn out to contain its own built-in chronology, although there is a big controversy at the moment about the reliability of molecular clocks based on mutation rates. This controversy will probably be resolved over the next few years.

It is important to stress that a substantial body of research in population genetics has shown recently that differences in the frequencies of various genetic markers between modern European populations do correlate very closely in most cases with the boundaries between language and ethnic groups in Europe today. Consequently there is every reason for believing that genetic evidence does correlate reasonably well with conclusions reached by historians relying on the more conventional types of evidence generally exploited in historical research. Extrapolating backwards into the past, it is a reasonable hypothesis that the methods of molecular archaeology will be able to trace the origins, movements and interactions of human populations in Europe in the distant past in situations where there are no extant documentary or literary sources to guide archaeologists and historians.[9]

There is no reason of course to stop the family tree after the last few thousand years. In principle it should be possible to take the family tree all the way back to the origin of *Homo sapiens* and beyond. So far discussion of the 'Eve hypothesis' has rested mainly on the statistical interpretation of attempts to extrapolate backwards from the genetic patterns of modern populations. That stage in the scholarly debate is likely to be superseded soon by the actual study of hard evidence from the distant past. This method offers the prospect of an eventual resolution of the current controversy about the emergence of man.[10]

DNA and man's adaptation to the environment

So far I have considered using the units of heredity as evidence for patterns of descent. However the study of ancient DNA can also give us some information about man's adaptation to the external environment. A lot of medical literature is extant from antiquity, for example the Hippokratic corpus, many volumes of Galen, and other authors as well. However it is notoriously difficult to identify the diseases described in ancient authors. Moreover different diseases often produce similar symptoms on bones. Consequently it is often also very difficult to identify diseases by superficial examination of human remains, even under a microscope. The application of the techniques of molecular archaeology will make it possible to identify the diseases that were active in antiquity and also investigate human resistance to those diseases. For example van der Kuyl *et al.* (1992) are looking for retroviruses related to the HIV virus in mummified monkeys and humans from ancient Egypt.

Genetics can also potentially yield information about man's adaptation to the environment in antiquity in relation to nutrition. One example of the possibilities would be research on the feasibility of milk consumption in antiquity. Many individuals in some human populations lack the ability to digest lactose in milk in adulthood, a common state of affairs in many parts of the world, including southern Italy and Greece. By studying ancient DNA it may be possible to trace the spread of the acquisition of this capability in antiquity and relate it to other evidence for the development of pastoralism and animal husbandry. To give one more example of the possibilities in relation to food, Richards *et al.* (1992) have identified DNA from pig ribs recovered from Henry VIII's sunken warship *Mary Rose*, which should make it possible to identify the breed of pig that was eaten by the unfortunate sailors.[11]

DNA and cereals

I turn now to some of the work that is going on in Manchester at the moment insofar as it relates to wheat and bread in antiquity. K.D. White in this volume rightly emphasizes what a laborious process it was to prepare food from raw cereals in antiquity. However, before we even get to the stage of considering food technology, there are two prior stages to consider, upon which I am going to focus now. In order to know what kinds of bread could have been made by the Greeks and Romans, we need to know first, what types of wheat were cultivated in antiquity, and secondly, the genetic characteristics of those varieties in relation to bread-making quality.

Identifying types of wheat

The superficial examination of ancient wheat grains from archaeological sites is often unrewarding because the grains are usually sufficiently distorted by the processes of carbonization and humification to make it difficult to identify species and varieties solely on the basis of external morphology and dimensions. The tetraploid hulled emmer (*Triticum dicoccum*) and hexaploid hulled spelt wheat (*Triticum spelta*) can be differentiated reliably if complete spikelets are preserved. The problem of identification is much more difficult with respect to the 'naked' wheats, the tetraploid durum wheat (*Triticum durum*) and the hexaploid bread wheat (*Triticum aestivum*), which are the types of wheat most suitable for bread production and consequently most important in European agriculture from the classical period onwards. It is still a matter of debate whether the ancient Greeks and Romans cultivated mainly the durum wheat, from which pasta is now made, or the bread wheat generally used to make bread today.[12] Complete spikelets of these wheats are rarely found.

However, the study of DNA preserved in ancient wheat grains is proving extremely rewarding. The first major discovery that has been made is that grains that are carbonized on the exterior often contain pockets of uncarbonized material inside. The discussion that followed Thomas Braun's paper to the *Food in Antiquity* conference brought up the topic of emmer bread. The question arose of how bread can be made from emmer after parching and pounding it to remove the glumes. The answer to the conundrum is that the grain is not parched right through. If some DNA can survive carbonization, then probably some of the gluten survives as well. That explains how bread can be made from parched emmer. Grains of bread wheat do not become carbonized at all below about 250°C. Above that level the extent of carbonization depends on the temperature and the duration of heating, according to Bowman (1966). The carbonized exterior of ancient grains from archaeological sites actually helps to protect uncarbonized material inside, because carbon is chemically rather inert and is not decomposed by micro-organisms.

I am currently working with my colleagues Robin Allaby and Terry Brown to sort out the laboratory techniques required to study DNA from ancient wheat.[13] Ancient DNA has been detected in samples of spelt wheat from the Iron Age hillfort of Danebury in England, and emmer from the Late Bronze Age site of Assiros Toumba in Macedonia, dating to *c.* 1300 BC. The preserved fragments of DNA molecules may be up to about 500 base pairs in length, which could code for a chain of over 150 amino acids in a protein. Robin Allaby has sequenced a 246 base pair sequence immediately upstream of the glutenin genes, which are very important in bread-making, from the Danebury and Assiros wheats and shown that the ancient sequences differ from each other and from the modern wheats in the laboratory, excluding contamination. At the moment we are designing a series of experiments designed to differentiate the three wheat genomes (A,B,D) as a means of categorically identifying archaeological specimens, followed by studies of genome evolution in wheat, some in relation to evolution of breadmaking quality.[13]

To make progress towards solving the problem of identification it is necessary to work on highly variable regions which show significant differences between the different species and varieties of wheat. For this purpose it is convenient to focus on intergenic spacer regions, which do not carry any significant biological information but merely serve to separate genes on chromosomes. Because most of these spacer regions have no function that depends on their precise sequence they accumulate mutations, deletions and insertions in their sequences very rapidly and so are hypervariable, making them very useful for identification purposes. Genetic fingerprinting as used by forensic scientists works on the same principle. However, because forensic scientists wish to be able to identify individuals who have committed criminal acts they have to establish the exact sequence, a laborious process. For archaeological work of this kind, where it is often only necessary to identify species and varieties, not individuals, it will often be sufficient merely to measure the length of a sequence, without bothering to ascertain its exact sequence, because this parameter alone differentiates species and varieties of wheat. We are evaluating the suitability for this purpose of the alpha-amylase gene family, the alpha/beta-type gliadin genes, and mitochondrial DNA.

One locus that is definitely suitable for this task has already been identified in the form of the non-transcribed spacer region of the hexaploid **Nor-D3** and tetraploid **Nor-B2** loci, upstream of the 18S r(ibosomal)RNA transcription start site, in respect of which durum wheat and bread wheat are significantly different. It has already been shown that there is a considerable amount of variation at this locus in modern populations of *Triticum tauschii*, the donor of the D genome to hexaploid bread wheat.[14] At the moment I am working to optimize the experimental conditions for the application of a pair of primers specific to the **Nor** loci to PCR-based analysis of ancient wheat. Such procedures should permit the definite identification of specimens of wheat from archaeological sites and tell us what kinds of wheat were cultivated in each area of the ancient world. It will then be possible to go on and investigate various aspects of the evolution of wheat under domestication in antiquity (and of course later on to apply similar techniques to other crop plants, and domesticated animals as well). Here the one experiment currently in progress which is directly relevant to the topic of food will be briefly described. It relates to the evolution of breadmaking quality.

Bread-making quality

The seed proteins which mainly influence breadmaking qualities are a class of water-insoluble proteins called the High Molecular Weight (HMW) glutenins. The HMW glutenins comprise about 10% of the total wheat-endosperm proteins, but they are crucial to breadmaking because they confer the visco-elastic properties associated with the formation of dough. The elasticity of dough appears to increase as the complexity of the disulphide cross-linking of the glutenin matrix increases. Flavell *et al.* (1989) suggested that one glutenin subunit has a higher proportion of repeating amino acid units than another subunit under study, producing a more regular pattern of repetitive turns in the protein, which helps to make it more elastic. It has been shown that there is an ideal genotype to maximize the volume of the loaf.

There is currently a lot of interest among biotechnologists in the possibility of applying genetic engineering to the breadmaking qualities of wheat, because of its importance for consumers. The tetraploid durum wheat contains eight genes for the glutenin proteins, and the hexaploid bread wheat contains four more, making a total of twelve. These genes are located on the long arm of the group 1 homoeologous chromosomes. Two of these genes are always silent and different genes may be identical in each one of the A, B and D genomes. However there is a considerable amount of variety. For example sixteen different alleles are represented in forty-seven modern European bread wheat varieties. Modern wild emmer (*Triticum dicoccoides*) in Israel displays a greater degree of genetic polymorphism with respect to the glutenin genes than modern varieties of domesticated wheat. This finding of Felsenburg *et al.* (1991) is very important because it shows that there was a lot of variety in breadmaking quality available in the wheat used by the earliest farmers. It is interesting that in the modern wild wheat there are correlations between specific HMW genotypes and characteristics of the natural environment such as altitude, rainfall, and temperature. These effects of natural selection probably indicate either close linkage between HMW glutenin alleles and adaptive genes, or that some of the HMW allele combinations directly enhance fitness in particular environments. In any case, the exact combination of alleles for the glutenins at these twelve genetic loci determines the breadmaking quality of each variety of wheat. However, we should not forget that the characteristics that make plants and animals suitable for human consumption are purely incidental as far as the plants and animals are concerned. Those characteristics originally evolved to serve quite different purposes.[15]

It is possible to design glutenin-specific primers that are characteristic for each of the twelve glutenin genes, in order to isolate relevant DNA fragments from samples of ancient wheat, and then to sequence these units by standard procedures. The only problem anticipated is that there could conceivably be a shortage of relevant DNA fragments in archaeological samples to track, because, unlike the intergenic spacers, the glutenin genes only exist in small numbers in each wheat cell. However, this problem will probably not be insuperable because ancient DNA appears to be well preserved in wheat grains from archaeological sites dating to the 1st and 2nd millennia BC. Consequently it should be possible for us to determine eventually exactly what kind of bread could have been produced from the wheat varieties available in various parts of the classical world.

Acknowledgement

I wish to thank the Royal Society for financial support for my part in the Manchester project.

Notes

1. Johnson *et al.* (1985); Thomas *et al.* (1989); Higuchi *et al.* (1987); DeSalle *et al.* (1991); Cano *et al.* (1992); Golenberg (1991); Soltis *et al.* (1991).
2. Hagelberg and Clegg (1991); Lawlor *et al.* (1991); Pääbo (1985a) and (1985b); Pääbo *et al.* (1988); Thuesen and Ingberg (1990).
3. Hughes *et al.* (1986); Lawlor *et al.* (1991).
4. Mullis (1990).
5. Hummel and Herrmann (1991); Nakahori *et al.* (1991).
6. Drews (1988); Gamkrelidze and Ivanov (1990); Renfrew (1987) and (1992); Mallory (1989) gives the most convincing account.
7. Hammond (1992, 149 and note 42); Buchner (1982, 279); Khader and Soren (1987, 229-30) mention a female slave prostitute in North Africa buried with an inscribed lead collar around her neck, so clearly there are various ways in

which slave burials can be identified.

[8.] Pallottino (1975); Francalacci and Warburton (1992) describe the first attempts to study DNA from Etruscan skeletons.

[9.] Barbujani and Sokal (1990); Sokal *et al.* (1989).

[10.] Wilson and Cann (1992); *contra* Thorne and Wolpoff (1992); cf. Groves (1989).

[11.] Flatz (1987); Simoons (1979).

[12.] Zohary and Hopf (1988, 46-7) on the problem of identifica-

tion; Sallares (1991, chapter 3) on ancient wheat.

[13.] Brown and Brown (1992) and Ross (1992) provide recent surveys of molecular archaeology; Jones *et al.* (1986) on Assiros Toumba.

[14.] Barker *et al.* (1988); Lagudah *et al.* (1991); Lubbers *et al.* (1991).

[15.] Anderson and Greene (1989); Dong *et al.* (1991); Krattiger (1988); Payne (1987).

Bibliography

Anderson, O.D. & Greene, F.C. 1989 'The characterisation and comparative analysis of HMW glutenin genes from genomes A and B of a hexaploid bread wheat', *Theoretical and Applied Genetics* 77, 689-700.

Barbujani, G. & Sokal, R.R. 1990 'Zones of sharp genetic change in Europe are also linguistic boundaries', *Proceedings National Academy Sciences USA* 87, 1816-19.

Barker, R.F., Harberd, N.P., Jarvis, M.G. & Flavell, R.B. 1988 'Structure and evolution of the intergenic region in a ribosomal DNA repeat unit of wheat', *Journal of Molecular Biology* 201, 1-17.

Bowman, A.R.A. 1966 Studies on the heat induced carbonisation of cereal grains (BSc. dissertation, Dept. of Agr. Botany, Univ. of Reading).

Brown, T.A. & Brown, K.A. 1992 'Ancient DNA and the archaeologist', *Antiquity* 62, 10-23.

Buchner, G. 1982 'Articolazione sociale, differenze di rituale e composizione dei corredi nella necropoli di Pithecusa', in Gnoli and Vernant (1982), 275-87.

Cano, R.J., Poinar, H.N., Roubik, D. & Poinar, G.O. 1992 'Enzymatic amplification and nucleotide sequencing of portions of the 18s rRNA gene of the bee *Proplebeia dominicana* isolated from 25-40 million year old amber', *Medical Science Research* 20, 619-22.

Chadwick, J. 1986 'I Dori e la creazione dei dialetti Greci', in Musti (1986), 3-12.

DeSalle, R., Gatesy, J., Wheeler, W. & Grimaldi, D. 1991 'DNA sequences from a fossil termite in Oligo-Miocene amber and their phylogenetic implications', *Science* 257, 1933-36.

Dong, H., Cox, T.S., Sears, R.G. & Lookhart, G.L. 1991 'High molecular weight glutenin genes: effects on quality in wheat', *Crop Science* 31, 974-9.

Drews, R. 1988 *The Coming of the Greeks: Indo-European Conquests in the Aegean and Near East* (Princeton).

Felsenburg, T., Levy, A.A., Galili, G. & Feldman, M. 1991 'Polymorphism of HMW glutenins in wild tetraploid wheat: spatial and temporal variation in a native site', *Israel Journal of Botany* 40, 451-79.

Flatz, G. 1987 'Genetics of lactose tolerance in humans', *Annals of Human Genetics* 16, 1-77.

Flavell, R.B., Goldsbrough, A.P., Robert, L.S., Schnick, D. & Thompson, R.D. 1989 'Genetic variation in wheat HMW glutenin subunits and the molecular basis of bread-making quality', *Biotechnology* 7, 1281-5.

Francalacci, P. & Warburton, P.E. 1992 'Pre-amplification without primers (pre-PCR): a method to extend ancient molecules', *Ancient DNA Newsletter* 1.2, 10-11.

Gamkrelidze, T.V. & Ivanov, V.V. 1990 'The early history of Indo-European languages', *Scientific American* 262.3, 82-9.

Gnoli, G. & Vernant, J.-P. (eds) (1982) *La mort, les morts dans les sociétés anciennes* (Paris).

Golenberg, E.M. 1991 'Amplification and analysis of Miocene plant fossil DNA', *Philosophical Transactions Royal Society London* B 333, 419-27.

Groves, C.P. 1989 *A Theory of Human and Primate Evolution* (Oxford).

Hagelberg, E. & Clegg, J.B. 1991 'Isolation and characterization of DNA from archaeological bone', *Proceedings Royal Society London* B 244, 45-50.

Hammond, N.G.L. 1992 'Plataea's relations with Thebes, Sparta and Athens', *Journal of Hellenic Studies* 112, 143-50.

Higuchi, R.G., Wriscknik, L.A., Oakes, E., George, M., Tong, B. & Wilson, A.C. 1987 'Mitochondrial DNA of the extinct quagga: relatedness and extent of postmortem changes', *Journal of Molecular Evolution* 25, 283-7.

Hughes, M.A., Jones, D.S. & Connolly, R.C. 1986 'Body in the bog but no DNA', *Nature* 323, 208.

Hummel, S. & Herrmann, B. 1991 'Y chromosome-specific DNA amplified in ancient human bone', *Naturwissenschaften* 78, 266-7.

Johnson, P.H., Olson, C.B. & Goodman, M. 1985 'Prospects for the molecular biological reconstruction of the woolly mammoth's evolutionary history: isolation and characterization of deoxyribonucleic acid from the tissue of *Mammuthus primigenius*', *Acta Zoologica Fennica* 170, 225-31.

Khader, A.B.A.B. & Soren, D. 1987 *Carthage: a mosaic of ancient Tunisia* (London).

Krattiger, A.F. 1988 The genetics and biochemistry of breadmaking quality in wheat (*Triticum aestivum* L.) (PhD. Univ. of Cambridge).

Lagudah, E.S., Appels, R. & McNeil, D. 1991 'The **Nor-D3** locus of *Triticum tauschii*: natural variation and genetic linkage to markers in chromosome 5', *Genome* 34, 387-95.

Lawlor, D.A., Dickel, C.D., Hauswirth, W.W. & Parham, P. 1991 'Ancient HLA genes from 7500-year old archaeological remains', *Nature* 349, 785-8.

Lubbers, E.L., Gill, K.S., Cox, T.S. & Gill, B.S. 1991 'Variation of molecular markers among geographically diverse accessions of *Triticum tauschii*', *Genome* 34, 354-61.

Mallory, J.P. 1989 *In search of the Indo-Europeans: language, archaeology and myth* (London).

Mullis, K.B. 1990 'The unusual origin of the polymerase chain reaction', *Scientific American* 262.4, 36-43.

Musti, D. (ed.) 1986 *Le origini dei Greci: Dori e mondo egeo* (Rome).

Nakahori, Y., Hamano, K., Iwaya, M. & Nakagome, Y. 1991 'Sex identification by PCR using X-Y homologous primer', *American Journal of Medical Genetics* 39, 472-3.

Pääbo, S. 1985a 'Molecular cloning of ancient Egyptian mummy DNA', *Nature* 314, 644-5.

Pääbo, S. 1985b 'Preservation of DNA in ancient Egyptian mummies', *Journal of Archaeological Science* 12, 411-17.

Pääbo, S., Gifford, J.A. & Wilson, A.C. 1988 'Mitochondrial DNA sequences from a 7000 year old brain', *Nucleic Acids Research* 16, 9775-87.

Pallottino, M. 1975 *The Etruscans* (6th edition) (London).

Renfrew, A.C. 1987 *Archaeology and Language: the Puzzle of Indo-European Origins* (London).

Renfrew, A.C. 1992 'Archaeology, genetics and linguistic diversity', *Man* 27, 445-78.

Richards, M., Smalley, K., Hedges, R. & Sykes, B. 1992 'Henry VIII's pork chop strikes again...', *Ancient DNA Newsletter* 1.1, 17.

Ross, P.E. 1992 'Eloquent remains', *Scientific American* 266.5, 72-81.

Sallares, J.R. 1991 *The Ecology of the Ancient Greek World* (London).

Simoons, F.J. 1979 'Dairying, milk use and lactose malabsorption in Eurasia: a problem in culture history', *Anthropos* 74, 61-80.

Sokal, R.R., Oden, N.L., Legendre, P., Fortin, M.-J., Kim, J. & Vaudor, A. 1989 'Genetic differences among language families in Europe', *American Journal of Physical Anthropology* 79, 489-502.

Soltis, P.S., Soltis, D.E. & Smiley, C.J. 1992 'An rbcL sequence from a Miocene Taxodium (bald cypress)', *Proceedings National Academy Sciences, USA* 89, 449-51.

Thomas, R.H., Schaffner, W., Wilson, A.C. & Pääbo, S. 1989 'DNA phylogeny of the extinct marsupial wolf', *Nature* 340, 465-7.

Thorne, A.G. & Wolpoff, M.H. 1992 'The multiregional evolution of humans', *Scientific American* 266.4, 28-33.

Thuesen, I. & Engberg, J. 1990 'Recovery and analysis of human genetic material from mummified tissue and bone', *Journal of Archaeological Science* 17, 679-89.

van der Kuyl, A.C., Dekker, J., Clutton-Brock, J., Perizonius, W.R.K. & Goudsmit, J. 1992 'Sequence analysis of mitochondrial DNA fragments from mummified Egyptian monkey tissue', *Ancient DNA Newsletter* 1.1, 17-18.

Wilson, A.C. & Cann, R.L. 1992 'The recent African genesis of humans', *Scientific American* 266.4, 22-7.

Zohary, D. & Hopf, M. 1988 *Domestication of Plants in the Old World* (Oxford).

PART TWO

Meat and Fish

Introduction ∽ Part Two

In his *On Agriculture* (2.4.3), Varro, the prolific scholar of the 1st century BC, has one of the company in the dialogue, Scrofa, say:

> I am the seventh man in succession in my family to bear praetorian rank. All the same, I will not try to get out of saying what I know about pig-herding. I have studied agriculture from my youth, and there is a certain common interest in pig-herding for me and for you big cattle-herders. For which of our people runs a farm without any pigs, and who has not heard our fathers say that it is an idle and luxurious man who hangs up in his rafters a side of bacon that has come from the butcher (*lanius*) rather than from the family farm?

There is some humour in this passage. Scrofa's name means 'breeding-sow', hence his suitability for the subject-matter.[1] He is also suitable because he is Roman and not 'semi-Greek' like the other speakers (2.1.2; 2.4.1): the passage reflects the idea that pig-breeding is particularly Italian. This is borne out philologically: Greek borrows from Latin the term for the most commonly preserved meat, ham (*perna*). Preserved meat is not in general part of Greek life; in Italy things are different. On the other hand, pigs are not a high-status topic for conversation: from the point of view of a man from an eminent background, Scrofa is unwilling to discourse on so humble a subject. His thinking appears to be that agriculture is a topic worthy of consideration by a gentleman, but the case of pigs is not so clear-cut. Nearly all ancient literature was written by men of the upper classes and is infused in this way with their values.

Two further important points emerge: (1) all of 'our' farmers are said to have pigs; (2) animals raised at home are better than foods bought at market.

By 'our people' Varro probably means comparatively well-to-do country people. It is unlikely that he is talking about the poorer peasant farmers or mountain dwellers. It may be that every subsistence farmer in Italy kept one or more pigs and slaughtered them in late autumn to keep the family in winter hams, but that is unlikely. Poetic texts are little help on this subject, though we may note that the peasant farmer in the *Moretum* (a Latin poem falsely attributed to Virgil) subsists on cheeses, not meat.

The second point recalls the modern interest in food fresh from the farm, which is now heavily promoted by modern advertisers of processed foods. Britons have a need for an emphasis on farm produce, living as we do in a country with a heavily industrialised food-producing industry. The Romans also had a firm moral belief in the traditional values of a simple country life and allied this to philosophical notions of self-sufficiency. Clearly such ideas are a counterbalance both to the lives of country people who focused their farming on the markets of Italy's country towns,[2] and to the merchant ships of the Empire which brought grain and exotica from all the corners of the known world. These associations are widespread in Latin poetry: it is interesting to find them in a more technical treatise, such as Varro's, albeit one dressed up as an intellectual conversation.

This section considers the role of meat and fish in antiquity. These were classified as *opsa* by the Greeks (the strong flavours introduced by Socrates and Glaukon in Part One to complement the cereal staples). Many foods could be classified as *opsa*: this covered the range of additional nutrients, flavours to make the cereal staple (*sitos*) palatable, and desirable titbits. The Roman equivalent terms were *puls* (spelt porridge) and *pulmentum/pulmentarium* (the strong flavour). Many of these *opsa* were readily available and widely eaten but of little interest for the literary record. Galen records, among many others, two of these, basil and snails. 'Many people use basil as an *opson*, blending it with oil and *garum* (fermented fish sauce)' (*On the Qualities of Foods* 6.640 Kühn); 'all the Greeks eat snails every day' (6.669 Kühn). Galen may or may not be right when he says that these were widely consumed. If foods are locally available, people are likely to eat them – unless there is some cultural objection, as in the case of the British and the consumption of squid. Among possible *opsa*, there was animal and plant protein (cheeses, olives, vegetables), but it was meat and fish that were particularly valued by the Greeks and Romans.

The killing of animals is an activity that is of central importance in many societies but at the same time gives rise to profound anxiety (for Athens, see most strikingly Porphyry *De Abstinentia* 2.39-40). There are many rituals attendant on the slaughter of animals, and often special features for the presentation of the meat (so it is nearly always men who are butchers;

and in this country it is traditionally men who are more likely to carve meat than to cook or present any other food).[3] The ancient Mediterranean sustained fewer domesticated animals than northern Europe: meat was accordingly less plentiful but highly prized.[4]

More meat appears to have been raised and preserved in ancient Italy than Greece, but we should still think of peasants in both countries as eating meat only on special occasions. That is meat derived from domesticated animals. Meat from wild animals, fish and birds was not classified as sacrificial; thus small birds, hares and fish often appear as tasty additions to the bland peasant diet. (Hares and birds also served as love-gifts.) Larger game, like larger fish, were reserved for the rich, who wrote various treatises on the skills of hunting.

Animal sacrifice is discussed in the introduction to Part Three. Greek and Roman sacrificial practices seem to have been broadly similar, though the greater production of meat in Italy may imply that sacrifice was a less universal system of meat consumption there. The Italian evidence is examined by Joan Frayn in Chapter 8. The position was certainly very different in the Christian period.

The majority of chapters in this section (and Chapter 15 in the next) are on fish. Fish are part of the strange world of the sea, a world explored by Nicholas Purcell in Chapter 10. His chapter should be read for an introduction to the place of the fish in ancient thought. They were not normally offered in sacrifice to the gods. They were wrested from the sea by one of the poorest social groups: 'in all sorts of ways, men who are poor live a wretched life', sing the fishermen in Plautus' *Rope* (290). Once landed, however, fish might gain tremendous value and be sold at high cost. In many passages of Athenian literature (as James Davidson explains in Chapter 15) fish is considered a luxurious food whose consumption may show a person to be socially or politically undesirable. We have to be clear about what we are dealing with. The fish does not have this significance in itself; it is added to the fish because of the expense, rarity or other desirability of the food. If texts give fish this significance, that does not necessarily tell us much about the fish outside those texts. If people lived by the sea they were likely to eat fish, small fish or shellfish if they were poor, larger and more succulent fish if rich. If texts refer predominantly to the larger, then that tells us something about the ancient texts. Nobody can claim a high price for whitebait in antiquity.

One text where fish-eating is almost non-existent is in the poems of Homer.[5] Here, an artificial diet is constructed in which the heroes dine almost exclusively on roast meat. Is this because the Greeks behave as an army of occupation? Or because the heroes are closer to the gods than ordinary mortals and eat highly-esteemed sacrificial beef? Are all the fish of the Hellespont unsuitable for heroic consumption? Is fish insufficiently frugal fare? Athenaeus, in moralising vein, considers the dangers of in-flaming the passions of the heroes. Whatever the reasons may be, these canonical texts, which abound in scenes of feasting, construct a special diet that does not for the most part reflect what people ate in the prehistoric Aegean as far as we understand it from archaeology.

At all events fish were not just fish. The same is true in Rome: fish were somehow not Roman, suitable only for the gross epicure, unknown to Rome's early divinities. Ovid exemplifies the idea in his book on the Roman calendar:

> You ask why fat bacon is eaten on those Kalends [June], and beans are mixed with hot spelt? She [Carna] is an ancient goddess and feeds on the foods she used to eat. She seeks no luxurious foreign foods. Fish swam with no fear of being snared by the people of those days, and oysters were safe in their shells.
> (*Fasti* 6.169-74)

If these ideas were true of Rome, they were not true of Italy as a whole, the southern part of which was Greek and fish-eating.[6] Even if Romans at an early date did not eat sea fish, they ate river fish. In what quantity, of course, we cannot say.

Tom Gallant has recently claimed that less fish was eaten in Greece than is usually thought.[7] His argument centres on exports from the Black Sea; even if his case is accepted, he does not convince at a local level. Communities ate the cheap fish caught off shore and sold any valuable items. Most Greek states had a coastline; those of Athens and Sparta were unusually lengthy. Gallant has attempted to bring statistical methods to bear on the problem, drawing on comparative material from this century.

In this book, similarly, new perspectives are drawn on the fascinating world of our ancient sources and what their approaches were. Nicholas Purcell sets out the paradoxical ways in which fish were thought about in the cultures of Greece and Rome, and at the same time weighs in to the quantitative debate stirred up by Gallant. In Chapter 12, David Braund takes on both ancients and moderns in their assumptions about Byzantium, which he demonstrates to be shorthand for any city in the Black Sea, and about the fishing 'industry' there which could only be so called in a limited way.

Literature is not the only artistic form that is ambiguous and difficult to interpret. In Chapter 11, Brian Sparkes, after surveying a series of images of fish on painted vases, argues against a recent claim that one vase portrays a fish being sacrificed. Whatever rituals the vase reflects, sacrifice is not one of them.

In Chapter 9, Jon Solomon surveys the sauces of 'Apicius', the compilation of cookery books from late antiquity which carries the name of a number of earlier gourmets. For many modern readers, Apicius is the doyen of Roman chefs. Some of the book, though, derives from Greek manuals, and, furthermore, these sauces in their combination of pungent flavours are not characteristic of ancient cookery books. Like fish, sauces were viewed with suspicion by moralists: in this case the objection was to the sauce deceptively concealing the main element of the dish.[8]

J.W.

Notes

[1.] The Romans had many such surnames: Cicero = chickpea, Balbus = stutterer.

[2.] On Italian markets see Joan M. Frayn *Markets and Fairs in Roman Italy* (Oxford, 1993).

[3.] On the treatment of meat in more modern periods see N. Fiddes *Meat: a Natural Symbol* (London, 1991) and M. Visser *The Rituals of Dining* (London 1993).

[4.] On the raising of animals see C.R. Whittaker (ed.) *Pastoral Economies in Classical Antiquity* (Cambridge, 1988)

[5.] Athenaeus comments on this in various ways at 8e-25e (a fragmentary part of the *Deipnosophists*). The variety and internal contradictions of his essay make it clear that he is synthesizing his account from a wide range of earlier discussions. One such discussion is to be found in Plato's *Republic* (404).

[6.] See, for example, John Wilkins and Shaun Hill *Archestratus: The Life of Luxury* (Totnes, 1994).

[7.] *A Fisherman's Tale* (Gent, 1985)

[8.] Much of such comment is similar to English views on French sauces: see Stephen Mennell *All Manners of Foods* (Oxford, 1985).

❖ 8 ❖

THE ROMAN MEAT TRADE

Joan Frayn

THE slaughter of animals for food and the sale of meat in ancient Rome and throughout Italy were in the hands of *lanii, macellarii* (see below for these terms), the landowners and farmers, and various wholesale merchants, *negotiatores*. There were *collegia* or associations of *lanii* in Rome and Praeneste, and probably elsewhere, from the time of the late Republic, and their officers (*magistri*) were slaves or freedmen (Waltzing 1895-1900, 26, 82).

To some extent through the sale of animals which had been sacrificed, the *victimarii* (see below) were also involved, and in Pliny *Natural History* 7.12.54, perhaps a *victimarius negotiator*. But what part did each of these play in the trade in meat and meat products?

The *lanius* and the *macellarius*

The distinction between the *lanius* and the *macellarius* seems to be generally accepted now, although until recently *macellarius* has been regularly translated as 'butcher' rather than 'market trader'. Even if *macellarius* in the classical period had been the regular word for 'butcher', there would have had to be an earlier expression, since the *macellum* (market), from which it is derived, seems only to have come into being in the 3rd century BC. Some of the *macellarii* were butchers, in that they sold meat over the counter, as did Julius Vitalis who in the relief on his tombstone (Reinach 1912, 3.154, fig. 2) is shown chopping up a pig's head. Joints and butchery equipment are hanging on the wall nearby. The difference between the *lanius* and the *macellarius* comes out clearly in the anecdote told by Varro (*On Agriculture* 3.2.11), where Merula asks whether Axius gets more from the *lanius* for the boars raised on his farm than Seius does from the *macellarius* for the wild boars from his estate.[1] The reason for using *lanius* in the first case and *macellarius* in the second is that the pigs produced on the farm have to be slaughtered by the *lanius*, but the wild boars are killed in the hunt, or at any rate on the estate, and merely have to be prepared and sold in the market by the *macellarius*.

Premises

The *lanius*, who even according to our ancient sources, was a slaughterer of animals (from *laniare*, to cut up meat), must have had, in addition to a shop, sufficient space somewhere in which to keep the animals before slaughter and to slaughter them. We hear of *lanienae* and *tabernae lanienae* – premises for *lanii* (*CIL* VI.9501, 9685). The latter shows a woman described by the editor of the volume as a *negotiatrix carnis ferinae* – a game dealer. The relief includes two wild boars, four geese and a hare (cf. Reinach 1912, 3.346 fig. 1). In this instance the game may have been delivered from the country already killed, as in the passage of Varro just mentioned. In both these examples the *lanienae* may only be stalls or shops, but Livy 44.16.10[2] suggests that *laniena* can be more specifically used for a slaughterhouse. In this passage we are told that Tiberius Sempronius bought up some buildings in Rome near the statue of Vortumnus and these included slaughterhouses and the shops adjacent to them. He wanted the site for a basilica. The shops need not have been butchers' establishments, and the *lanienae* could have sold meat as well as slaughtered the animals, but a distinction is being made between them. In Roman towns in general it is difficult to locate either slaughterhouses or butchers' shops with open areas beside them which could be used in this way. Such premises do not readily appear in the rows of shops attached to *macella* or forming part of residential blocks, as shown on the *Forma Urbis* for Rome. A butcher's shop is conjectured in Pompeii at houses 7.9.45 and 46 (Gassner 1986, 147), but this is in the *macellum* area and is adjacent to other shops.

The kind of fold for animals awaiting slaughter may be suggested by the example shown in De Ruyt's drawing of the market at Pompeii (1983, 142). She describes an enclosure 4.75 m x 93 cm, surrounded by a wall 2.10 m high in the NE corner of the portico in the *macellum* at Pompeii. Its only entrance opened into the large NE room, which was thought to have some religious use. In the enclosure were found complete skeletons of sheep, probably intended for sacrifice and then for sale. This confirms what common sense suggests, that where livestock are to be kept prior to sale or sacrifice, there must be something akin to a fold to put them in. This seems to be the only example in which it has survived clearly enough to be recognized. But below the *macellum* at Dougga in Tunisia, there are two rooms with holes for tethering rings, which might have been used for stabling or an abattoir. They are reached by steps from the southern end of the market, but are on the level of some small houses outside. These rooms do not appear in Poinssot's report (1983), though the steps leading down to them are shown. They are mentioned by De Ruyt (1983, 216; cf. Romanelli 1970).

The *laniena*, if it was being used as an abattoir, might well have been situated on the outskirts of a town or beyond its boundaries, as were tanneries and other trades regarded as unsuitable for residential areas. The tannery would be using the by-products of the butcher's trade. In the case of Rome, we have epigraphic evidence for a butcher near the temple of Libitina, probably on the Esquiline, where there was an important market (*CIL* VI.33870). According to Plautus *Pseudolus* 326-31 there were butchers who slaughtered animals outside the gate, *extra portam*.[3] According to Ruggiero (1886-, s.v. *lanius*) this was a reference to the Porta Capena in the Servian Wall of Rome, by which the city could be entered from the Appian Way (*Pseudolus* 331). The *lanii piscinenses* (butchers by the pool) of *CIL* VI.167(i) were probably near the *piscina publica* (public pool), which gave its name to the 12th region of Rome under Augustus. This is in the same part of the city as the Porta Capena.

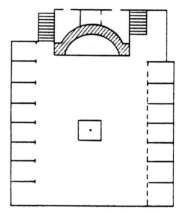

Fig. 8.1 *The* macellum *at Dougga, Tunisia (28 x 42 m).*

An interesting article by Guarducci (1989-90) discusses the grave monument of a *bublarius* or *bubularius* (beef-vendor) who is described in the inscription as '*de Sacra Via*', that is the street leading up to the Capitol through the Roman Forum. This was the route followed by religious processions on important national occasions, but the lower part of it was also notable for expensive shops. Inscriptions from these indicate that they included jewellers, perfumiers and goldsmiths. If the *bublarius* dealt in oxen or other bovines and animal products, he seems strange company for the other traders, in what must have been the Ponte Vecchio or the Bond Street of ancient Rome. Guarducci suggests that he may have sold expensive joints of beef and some medicinal products derived from bovines. She cites Pliny *Natural History* 28.184-7 for the remedies, and there are indeed many such products mentioned there. The usual vendor of such remedies was a *pharmacopola* (pharmacist) or *medicamentarius* (apothecary) and most of these strange prescriptions needed some skilled preparation, which they seem more likely to have received in the establishment of a pharmacist than a butcher. On the other hand some of these were traditional remedies used on the farms in the countryside where the ingredients were readily available. Possibly this *bublarius* took orders for whole carcases for banquets, or supplied sacrificial animals appropriate to the religious requirements. He might even have been a *negotiator* rather than a working butcher.

Cuts and joints

Both the *lanius* and the *macellarius* had the task of cutting up meat into the joints and pieces required by customers, though a large part of the trade was in whole carcases *cum intestinis omnibus*, 'together with all the innards'. This phrase is used humorously by Plautus in *Pseudolus* 343, when Ballio the brothel-keeper is talking about a girl and says that he sold her *sine ornamentis - cum intestinis omnibus*, 'without any adornments – together with all her innards', but it really belongs to the butchery trade. Also in this passage Pseudolus says that he will send for two *lanii*, with bells, to perform a sacrifice. So he is here equating the *lanii* with the *victimarii*. One of the reasons why sheep and pigs were frequently roasted whole was that they were smaller than those we rear today, and therefore for a dinner party a whole animal would be required. Much of the trade was for celebratory meals held by *collegia* and for meals intended to impress, like Trimalchio's feast, and these are also reasons why whole carcases would be used. The art of carving was highly developed during the period of *luxuria* in the early Empire, and we have some descriptions of the *scissor* or the *carptor* (carvers) at work.

Seneca, who in *Letter* 47 is deploring in general the way in which the Romans treated their slaves, wrote:

> another carves the costly game birds, slicing off choice pieces with the unerring strokes of a trained hand – unhappy man, to exist for the one and only purpose of carving a fat bird in the proper style.   (47.6; trans. Campbell)

In Juvenal 5.120-3 we find even more detail of what went on at a fashionable dinner party:

> You may watch the carver caper and posture, with knife whizzing around till he performs the whole dance his master prepared.   (trans. Creekmore)

Information regarding the joints of meat and the particular cuts favoured by the Romans can be found in reliefs showing butchers' shops, in literary descriptions of meals and in the work of Apicius. It appears from Apicius 4.14 (Teubner) that the manuscript which concerned complete dishes included some illustrations. If these were still extant we might have another source of information about cuts of meat. As it is, we can appreciate the names he gives to them, especially when they are interpreted by André (1974) in the light of French cuisine. *Ofellae* is a name which frequently occurs for small pieces of meat served as individual portions. They were however sold as larger pieces and marked out (*designare*) before cooking. This may have been because it was not easy to control the heat of a Roman cooking stove. André tells us (note on Apicius para. 278) that *copadia* were thin slices of meat, aiguillettes when referring to chicken, escalopes when referring to pork, lamb or kid. There has been some discussion about the exact meaning of the Latin terms *perna* and *petaso*, which apply to cuts of pork. It used to be thought that *perna* was salted and *petaso* was fresh. But in Varro *On Agriculture* 2.4.10 *petasones* are said to be imported from Gaul to Rome, so they could not be fresh.

Athenaeus 657e-58a makes no distinction between them. André therefore suggests that *perna* is ham in the strict sense, that is, the hind leg of the pig; *petaso* is the front leg, i.e. the shoulder.

Sacrificial meat

Among the personnel connected with the meat trade, there must have been some who provided the sacrificial animals for religious festivals and for private offerings. An inscription in memory of a butcher (Dessau 1892-1916, 7473) shows a *culter*, a *bucranium* and a *patera* (knife, ox-head and dish), all items connected with sacrifices. Were they there purely for decoration or did he sell meat for this purpose? Alternatively did he sell meat which had been sacrificed? The *bucranium* is familiar on monuments such as the Ara Pacis, where it is accompanied by garlands of the type that were draped around the victim for the ceremony. It represents the head of the ox, picked clean and dried by the sun, the trophy hung up to commemorate the sacrifice.

There were three attendants who officiated at public sacrifices, the *popa* who wielded the mallet to stun the animal, the *cultrarius* who cut its throat with a *culter*, and the *victimarius* whose role is less clear, but who is probably the person with the axe over his shoulder in the procession depicted on the Ara Pacis. The story is told by Suetonius that the Emperor Caligula, who evidently had not a very straight aim, when wielding the mallet as an attendant at a sacrifice, killed the *cultrarius* instead of the victim. It is probable that the method of stunning the animal first with a mallet, then cutting its throat, would also be used in the abattoir. The purpose of the axe would seem to be to cut off the head of the ox or other large animal. We know for example from *CIL* VI.1770 (4th century AD) that different parts of the animal were assigned in commercial transactions to the butcher and the vendor respectively. If Pliny *Natural History* 7.12.54 really does read *victimarius negotiator* (*victimarius*/tradesman), and not *suarius* (tradesman in pork), this lends support to the idea that the *victimarius* may have played some part in the purchase of the victim or the disposal of the meat. Valerius Maximus 9.14.3 has been regarded as supporting this interpretation, but it is not explicit. However this may be, someone must have acted as a liaison between the farms, the butchers and the local officials or private individuals who wished to obtain a sacrificial animal.

What happened to the meat after the sacrifice is of equal interest: some of it of course was burned on the altar, and some was assigned to the priests. In different cults and different parts of the Roman Empire the disposal of the residue varied. It appears from the New Testament, *I Corinthians* 8 and 10, that in Corinth, as probably in other parts of the eastern Mediterranean region, it was sold in shops and markets and served for meals in private homes. 'Well then, about eating this consecrated meat...', as *I Corinthians* 8.4 begins in the *Revised English Bible*. In the Greek environment this custom existed much earlier, and it is from there that some interesting comparative material originates. In the *Life of Aesop*, the famous Greek slave who wrote the fables, we find that Xanthos, Aesop's master, was going to entertain some philosophers to dinner. He asked the slave to go to the market and buy some food. Aesop wanted to do this job well and make a good impression, so he bought the tongues of some 'sacrificed pigs'. The guests were delighted with their meal and complimented their host and said to him: 'congratulations, Xanthos, you have given us a meal full of philosophy'. This incident and the New Testament passage are discussed by Isenberg (1975), where the question is raised as to whether sacrificial meat was of a better quality or differed in price from non-sacrificial meat. It seems from the story in the *Aesopica* that it was thought to be of better quality. In view of the fact that the animal was given by the worshipper or the worshipping community, it should also have been cheaper, but this does not necessarily follow. The more important question, at least to the Corinthian Christians, must have been: 'how did you know whether the meat had been sacrificed or not?'. In a world where it did not matter to anybody else, it might have been embarrassing to have to ask the shopkeeper about this. The problem is solved in *I Corinthians* 10.25-7, where we are told that it is all right to eat anything sold in the market, but that if anyone says: 'this food has been offered in sacrifice', then you must not eat it.

Quality of meat

The question of quality of meat in the Roman period in Italy is an interesting one. The strong preference for young animals, and especially sucklings, suggests that other meat could be very tough. The difficulty of hanging meat for any length of time before using it must have contributed to this problem. As regards flavour, Roman gentry seem to have preferred wild boar to the meat of the domesticated pig, even if they had to rear the wild species in special enclosures on their estates. Wild boars, says Appius in Varro's *On Agriculture* (3.13.1), can be kept in the hare-warren (*leporarium*) easily, and those that are born there become quite fat. The popularity of mince (*isicia*) and sausages suggests that the cheaper cuts of meat could be rather tough. The amount of spices and flavourings used in some of Apicius' recipes, and the preference for exotica such as peacocks, may imply that the meat of the common domestic animals was rather tasteless. With the exception of pigs, they were probably not primarily bred for eating. In fact the conclusion of our study of the Roman meat trade may well be that the Romans preferred fish!

Notes

1. *Et num pluris tu e villa illic natos verres lanio vendis, quam hinc apros macellario Seius?*

2. *... Ti. Sempronius ex ea pecunia quae ipsi attributa erat aedes P. Africani pone Veteres ad Vortumni signum, lanienasque et tabernas coniunctas in publicum emit, basilicam faciendam curavit, quae postea Sempronia appellata est.*

3. Calidorus *propera, quid stas? i arcesse agnos: audin quid ait Iuppiter?*
Pseudolus *iam hic ero: verum extra portam mi etiam currendumst prius.*
Calidorus *quid eo?* Pseudolus *lanios inde arcessam duo cum tintinnabulis.*

Bibliography

André, J. 1974 *Apicius, l'art culinaire* (Paris).

Dessau, H. 1892-1916 *Inscriptiones Latinae Selectae* (Berlin).

Gassner, V. 1986 *Die Kaufläden in Pompeii* (Vienna).

Guarducci, M. 1989-90 'Il cippo sepolcrale di un *bublarius de Sacra Via*', *Bolletino della Commissione Archeologica di Roma*, 93, 325-8.

Isenberg, M. 1975 'The sale of sacrificial meat', *Classical Philology* 70, 271-3.

Perry, B.E. (ed.) 1952 *Aesopica* (Urbana).

Poinssot, C. 1983 *Les Ruines de Dougga* (Tunis).

Reinach, S. 1912 *Répertoire de reliefs grecs et romains* (Paris).

Romanelli, P. 1970 'Topografia e archeologica dell' Africa romana', *Enciclopedia Classica* (3.10.7), 146-52.

Ruggiero, E. de 1886- *Dizionario epigrafico di antichità romana* (Rome).

De Ruyt, C. 1983 *Macellum* (Louvain).

Waltzing, J.P. 1895-1900 *Etude historique sur les corporations professionelles chez les Romains* (Louvain).

❖ 9 ❖   THE APICIAN SAUCE
IUS APICIANUM

Jon Solomon

No aspect of ancient Roman culinary art was more fundamental than the sauce. Even allowing for those exotic ingredients and fabulous, sculpted or utterly transformed presentations, it was still the sauce that was the trademark of the ancient Roman chef. In the corpus collected under the name of the 1st century gourmand and chef, Apicius, of the approximately 500 entries in the *De re coquinaria* and *Excerpta*, over 400 detail to some extent the ingredients and preparation of a sauce for that recipe, and nearly half of these 400 are in fact devoted entirely to the preparation of a sauce.[1]

And yet modern scholarship has produced few attempts at investigating the general technique of sauce-making in ancient Rome. The purpose of this paper is to employ the internal evidence presented in the corpus, which contains our only synthesized collection of Roman (and provincial) recipes[2] and techniques, to investigate the broad spectrum of Roman sauce preparation. In doing so, I do not and cannot imply that every sauce was to be prepared in the same way, for the best Roman cooks were creative and idiosyncratic artists who used their skills, experience, and personal preferences to prepare unique dishes. After all, the *De re coquinaria* was surely not compiled for the novice.

Pulverizing the herbs

The preparation of a sauce began not with fat but with the dry ingredients.[3] Spices and herbs were placed in a mortar and pulverized (8.7.8:*ut fit pulvis*, to make a powder). The effect of this pounding, which may have had its origins in the pounding of medicinal concoctions, was threefold: the powdered spice or herb gave more flavour than the whole; the whole unpounded spice (or dried herb) had an undesirable rough or seed-like texture;[4] and through pulverization the individual herbs and spices lost their identity. The last effect was desirable because of the Roman preference for eating disguised foods; there is for instance, an Apician entrée which was shaped like a fish, tasted like a fish, but was in reality well-salted liver.[5]

The Roman chef seems to have had access to a tremendous variety of herbs and spices. Apicius, for instance, calls for three species of cumin – Ethiopian, Syrian, and Libyan – in addition to the whiter *ammi*,[6] and regional varieties of asafoetida (*laser, silphium, laserpitum*), from Cyrenaica and the Persian hinterlands;[7] and Pliny[8] reports on the many varieties of herbs and spices available in Rome. Even without these regional varieties of herbs and spices the Roman chef still had almost all of the herbs and spices we use today in Western cooking – anise, basil, bay leaf, capers, caraway, cardamon, cassia, celery seed, cinnamon, coriander seed, cumin, dill, fennel, garlic, ginger, horse-radish, juniper berry, lovage, mint, mustard seed, onion, parsley, pepper (white and black), poppy seed, rosemary, rue, saffron, savory, sesame seed, shallot, thyme and turmeric. Most of these are indigenous to Europe or the Mediterranean area, but not all.[9] There were also such exotic items as asafoetida, mountain cat-mint, hazelwort, pennyroyal, hyssop, mastic, rocket and pyrethrum. Some of the smaller seeds, such as sesame or cumin, could be grilled or toasted before the pounding.[10]

While the market rarely offered pre-ground combinations of ingredients,[11] some of these spices and herbs were frequently used in combination. Pepper, of course, became almost a *sine qua non* for the Apician sauce, but it was often combined with cumin;[12] the two are the most frequently used spices in Apicius, and their combined flavours must have been familiar to the Roman gourmet. Other combinations include the various seeds – caraway, coriander (grilled), dill, and celery (8.1.7), pepper and lovage

(8.2.1-4, 6, 8; 8.3.1, 10.1.8), the fragrant herbs, thyme and oregano (7.12.2-3) or thyme and savory (1.31.2).[13]

In many recipes it is difficult to distinguish in which state or which part of an herb or spice is called for – whether fresh, dried, leaf or seed. This is particularly true of coriander, fennel and dill, of which the seminal and folial forms have entirely different flavouring and textures. Recipe 3.11.1, for beets, presents one example of this type of difficulty. The text reads *concides porrum, coriandrum, cuminum* (chop leeks, coriander, cumin), which means that the leeks are certainly to be chopped; but doubt remains in the case of the cumin: undoubtedly in seed form, but is it to be pounded? Equal uncertainty surrounds the pounding or chopping of the coriander and also whether to use coriander seeds or leaves. Apicius does not always specify *semen* (seed) or *viride* (green leaf) where he might;[14] similarly, one is at a loss whether to use fresh mint (3.4.8) or dried mint (9.10.4) in those recipes in which Apicius indicates simply mint (*menta* 10.1.12).

The number of herbs and spices added to a sauce varies greatly, though it is generally not a small number. The Apician corpus usually calls for a simple sauce to be prepared for vegetables; that given for tree fungi (7.15.2) calls for only pepper, and that for mushrooms (7.15.6) for only pepper and lovage. On the other hand, fish sauces tend to be quite elaborate, having five, six, or more herbs and spices (10.2.5 [for boiled *murena*] contains pepper, lovage, caraway, celery seed, coriander, dried mint and rue). Most sauce recipes in the Apician corpus call for a minimum of three specified spices or herbs.

Larger solids

Once the herbs and spices are pulverized, other and larger solids are then added to the mortar to be pounded. These other solids consist of two basic types – raw or toasted nuts (filberts [9.10.8], almonds [6.5.2],[15] pine-nuts [6.9.11] and perhaps walnuts [6.5.3]),[16] and fruits (plums [6.2.2; 7.6.6], dates [6.2.4 – *dactyli*; 7.6.10 – *caryotae*] and raisins [10.1.3]).

There is a problem in distinguishing when these ingredients are actually to be pulverized. Generally speaking, Apician recipes, although they sometimes differ in form of presentation, often list first the ingredients to be pounded and then follow these with the liquids.[17] Usually the fruits and nuts are listed between the poundable and the pourable ingredients, so it is not clear to us whether the chef was to put the fruits and nuts into the mortar with the poundable herbs and spices to pound them, or whether he was to add them later to the sauce along with the liquids and merely mix them in.

Again, the internal evidence of the recipes themselves reveals contradictory data which prohibit us from discerning the more common means of proceeding with the sauce. There are several recipes in which the nuts or fruits were to be added whole or merely chopped, and the recipes clearly specified this with the insertion of a second verb (10.1.1 *teres piper…adicies caryotam, mel*: pound pepper…add date, honey) – a rarity amidst mostly laconic instructions. On the other hand, there are also several recipes which call unambiguously for pounded fruits and nuts.[18] The order of the listed ingredients might help the reader to identify the process through which these ingredients must be prepared for incorporation into the sauce. The fruits and nuts are almost always listed after the herbs and spices, but it does not necessarily follow that this order of listing them was to separate the fruits and nuts from the poundables, even if several recipes certainly do call for unpounded fruits or nuts.[19] The reason that the fruits and nuts, particularly the fruits, are listed after the poundable spices and herbs may be nothing more than the very size, texture, and consistency of the fruits and nuts. To pound pepper and cumin seeds with dates or to pound fennel seeds with almonds is to invite tooth-jarring disaster; the weight and friction of the mortar would not be able to penetrate satisfactorily the viscous, gummy paste which would be permeated with tiny seeds, and although we know that strainers were used by Roman chefs, there is no evidence that they were used for sauces;[20] it is also doubtful that a cloth strainer, let alone a bronze *colum*, could have been used effectively or efficiently to strain out from a thickened fruit sauce such miniscule materials as cumin seeds or the like. In addition, the pitting of fruits, which is regularly called for (6.5.1 *uvam passam enucleatam*, pitted raisins),[21] renders them suitable for the mortar. Neither the Apician corpus nor any other passage in ancient literature offers a clear solution to this problem, for the methodology in solving culinary enigmas in the Apician corpus must inevitably differ from that used in attacking most philological or technical problems. The readers of the Apician corpus had to be capable of making their own decisions based on their own preferences and experiences, and no doubt an ancient Roman cook would have had the experience to do so. In general, however, the majority of Apician recipes list the pounded herbs and spices first and then, without distinction, the fruits and nuts which probably in more cases than not were pounded to paste in the mortar.

Liquids

The liquids are added to the pulverized herbs and spices and (pounded) fruits and nuts, directly, to the mortar (4.2.3 or 6.5.2). A Roman might add stock, water, honey, oil, milk, mustard (8.5.4), *liquamen* (fermented fish sauce), its mixtures *oxygarum* (fish sauce with vinegar), *oenogarum* (fish sauce with wine), *hydrogarum* (fish sauce with water), *piperatum* (pepper sauce) or *cuminatum* (cumin sauce), or any one of the various grape-derivatives – wine, vinegar, *caroenum* (wine boiled down by a third), *defrutum* (must boiled down),[22] *passum* (raisin wine), and a honey-wine, *mulsum*. The variety of liquids available to the Roman chef and the number of liquids poured into the typical Roman sauce recipe seems little short of astounding until one realizes that the Roman had to use honey (not sugar) for sweetness, *liquamen* (not salt) for salting, and oil (not butter or oleomargarine) for adding fat.

Rarely does a recipe call for 'stock', but when it does, as in 6.9.11, this *ius* is made by boiling the main ingredient (chicken) in another collection of liquids (*liquamen*, oil and wine) flavoured with a bouquet (of leek, coriander and savory). Varro (quoted by Apicius at 3.2.6) calls for beet (broth) cooked in water, oil and salt, although *melius…si in eo pullus sit decoctus* (it is better if a chicken has been cooked down in it first) means essentially a chicken stock, bland as it may have been. Water, as opposed to stock, is not a common ingredient in Apician sauces, suggesting either that Apician sauces were to be thick and strong[23] or that it was assumed that the chef would add water without any specific instructions to do so. The latter assumption is probably not correct. Where Apicius calls for water it is usually in particularly limited quantities, as in 2.2.1 (*hydrogarum*) and 1.30.1 (only for dissolving silphium),[24] or the water is drained off from the boiled material before its sauce is to be made, as in 7.13.1 and 3.10.1.

Moreover, there are few, if any, recipes in which *liquamen* and pepper are omitted from the list of ingredients where they are nonetheless supposed to be added by the chef, and *liquamen* and pepper are by far the most common ingredients in all of Apicius' sauces. If any ingredients were to be added without instruction from the recipe, it would be these.

Apicius calls for honey in numerous sauces, and it is usually to be balanced by the addition of vinegar (among other liquids) to create a sweet and sour effect.[25] Occasionally, however, honey is not combined with vinegar but with non-sour liquids such as wine and *liquamen* (8.7.6), *liquamen*, *passum*, *caroenum* and oil (8.2.5), or wine, *liquamen* and oil (10.2.12). Since the appropriate amount of sweetness in any recipe is a matter of individual taste, the recipes here and there allow for the optional addition of honey, as in 10.1.13 (*si vis, et mel addes*). Similarly, because excessive sweetness could ruin certain dishes, restraint is sometimes requested, as in 6.5.2 (*mel modicum*, a little honey). Honey can be omitted from a sweet and sour sauce where the honey-derived *mulsum* is used, as in 10.1.9, or where a sweet fruit has already been added to the mortar, as in 6.6.1 (with dates and vinegar).

Olive oil in all its grades was apparently the only oil used in Apician recipes. Many different fruits, nuts, berries, and flowers were pressed to extract oil in antiquity,[26] but Apicius makes no mention of any specific type of oil. Once he specifies *oleum Spanum* (6.8.15),[27] and there are specifications for *oleo puro* (3.21.2) and *olei floris* (2.2.3), but other than these specifications for quality and pressing we assume the chef used his normal supply of olive oil. More often than not, only a little oil is to be added to the sauce, and when the main ingredient of a dish has already been fried in oil, more oil need not be added to a sauce.[28]

Milk is used in four Apician recipes[29] – 8.6.6, 8.6.7, 8.6.11, and 1.10 – the first three of which are for lamb or kid sauce, the last for boiling salt meat. The type of milk is not specified, and whereas cow's milk seems the obvious choice to modern chefs, goat's or sheep's or donkey's milk was more likely in antiquity; human milk was not an impossibility.[30]

Prepared mustard already contained vinegar and pounded nuts, or honey, Spanish oil and vinegar.[31] Its addition to Apician sauces produced a powerful combination, for often (but not always) the mustard is to be added to a sweet and sour sauce.[32] Apicius usually specifies where ground (not prepared) mustard is to be used, as in 6.5.3, *sinapi trito*.

Liquamen (*garum*) with its murky colour, salty taste and pungent aroma, finds its way into almost every Apician recipe. Again, quality and taste can vary, for there were expensive and inexpensive *liquamina*,[33] and there were factory-made and home-made varieties.[34] The addition of *liquamen* served two purposes. The first was to add salt to the sauce. Rarely was salt added to Apician recipes; other than for curing or cooking meat (1.9 and 7.5.3), preserving vegetables (1.24.2), and the like, salt is added to only three of some 400 Apician sauces: 2.2.9 (rissoles), 3.4.3 (squash), and 5.8.1 (beans).[35] Only once is salt offered as a substitute for *liquamen* (9.10.10 *liquamen aut salem*). This suggests the second reason for the addition of *liquamen*: enhancing the flavour of a sauce. Judging by the omnipresence of *liquamen* in the Apician corpus, it not only gave the sauce a flavour loved by the Romans, but perhaps it was the flavour and aroma most distinguishably 'Roman' in Roman food.[36] Consequently, where there was only one liquid present in a Roman sauce, this liquid would inevitably be *liquamen*, as, for example, 3.14 and 7.21.3 (sterile sow's womb in *liquamen*, flavoured with pepper and asafoetida).

The *liquamen* mixtures – *oxygarum* (8.4.2), *oenogarum* (2.5.4), *hydrogarum*, *piperatum* (3.14) and *cuminatum* (3.21.3) – are used only occasionally (these terms are translated above). Recipes which call for their use include 1.34.1-2;[37] 2.2.2; 2.2.5 (seven parts water to one part *garum*); 1.31.1-2; and the two recipes already cited for *piperatum* and *cuminatum* (pepper-*liquamen* and cumin-*liquamen* sauces). Like plain *liquamen*, *oenogarum*, *piperatum* and *cuminatum* could serve as sauces in themselves (7.12.4), and they are used more commonly than *hydrogarum* and *oxygarum*.

Of wine there was a tremendous variety available from Italy alone, not to mention the Greek wines.[38] The long lists of products from the more famous Italian vineyards – Caecuban, Sabine, Marsic, Tarentine, Spoletine, Falernian, and the others – were of little use to the Roman chef, who, if he consulted Apicius, was generally instructed to add merely *vinum*.[39] No distinction is made between red or white, sweet or dry, though at least grape-wine can be assumed; only recipe 6.5.1 calls for *vino myrteo* (myrtle wine). Only in a few recipes (for example 4.2.29 and 8.7.13) is spiced wine (*conditum* 1.1.1) added to a sauce (even if another wine is already present). The reason for this lack of specificity is that the Roman chef had wine substitutes of different sweetnesses and strengths available to him other than his regular *vinum*. For acidic wine he had vinegar, for sweet he had raisin wine (*passum*).[40] For a strong additive he had *caroenum*, and for a mild additive he had *defrutum* (must boiled down into a slightly thick consistency).[41] Finally, for a gummy, even sweeter taste he had *mulsum*, a concoction made from wine and honey (usually drunk early in the meal).[42] Modern conceptions of a delightfully sweet and light mead will probably have to be abandoned in the case of *mulsum*, for Columella (*On Agriculture* 12.41) makes *mulsum* by adding ten pounds of honey to only three gallons of must. After sitting for a month, however, the must is strained (and smoked), and perhaps this straining removed some of the heaviness.

The combinations of wine, vinegar, *passum*, *mulsum*, *defrutum* and *caroenum* used in Apician sauces undergo numerous permutations. Sauce can be made with *caroenum* (4.2.3), *passum* (4.3.6), vinegar (6.5.3), *defrutum* (6.5.6), wine (6.9.5), wine and vinegar (6.5.2), wine or vinegar (7.14.6), *caroenum* and *passum* (8.1.1 – sweet and thick for wild boar), wine and *passum* (8.1.9), wine, vinegar and *passum* (8.4.1 – where the *passum* is merely *ad colorem* (for colour), wine, vinegar and *defrutum* (9.10.2 – where Apicius specifies *vinum modice*, a little wine), vinegar and *passum* (10.1.3), *mulsum*, vinegar and *defrutum* (10.1.6 – a typically purplish, sweet and sour *ius Alexandrinum*, Alexandrian sauce) and so on, the various combinations rendering a sauce sweeter (*mulsum* and *passum*), thicker (*caroenum*, *mulsum*), darker (*passum*), stronger, more sour (vinegar and perhaps *caroenum*), or more sweet and sour.

Proportions

When all the ingredients have been assembled, their proportions have to be determined. With a few exceptions, this was a matter of memory, personal preference, and rough estimation. Exact proportions are rarely found, and two chefs could undoubtedly make two different sauces out of the same ingredients; one *hemina* of wine with one *acetabulum* [1 *hemina* =

½ pint = 4 *acetabula*] each of vinegar and honey would make a very different sauce from one *hemina* of vinegar and one *acetabulum* each of wine and honey. Nonetheless, the exact proportions which fill modern cookbooks are for the unprofessional chef, and throughout history and still in most kitchens today cooking is a matter of vague or learned proportions which may or may not produce the exact taste twice in succession.

At times the typical Apician recipe seems to offer at least a clue to the proportions expected, for the ingredients to be used most lavishly are probably listed first in their respective groups of spices and liquids.[43] An Alexandrian sauce for grilled fish (10.1.8), for instance, includes these ingredients in the following order: pepper, lovage, fresh coriander, onion and plums; and *passum*, *liquamen*, vinegar and oil. Allowing for the Romans' excessive love for black pepper[44] – and pepper is usually the first ingredient listed – one would assume that the dominant flavouring here would be the pepper and lovage, with a sprinkling of fresh coriander and onions.[45] No doubt plums – apparently pounded – would abound, and then this typical Alexandrian sauce would be liquefied with much *passum* for colour and sweetness, less *liquamen* for salt and flavour, less vinegar to offset the *passum*, and a little oil for fat.[46] But the liquid listed first in order is not always necessarily the one to be used in the greatest amount.[47]

It must be remembered that Apicius' cookbook was hardly compiled for the novice; it was more for the experienced chef who wanted suggestions for and a catalogue of various sauces and techniques. The chef (slave or gourmet) who worked from this book had cooked many meals in his lifetime, and this knowledgeable artisan would know how to mix his ingredients. He would know his (or his master's) taste and his guests' tastes and he would prepare the sauces accordingly. Ultimately, Encolpius (in the *Satyricon* of Petronius) and Horace find fault in the banquets of Trimalchio and Nasidienus not because one sauce or another is too full of leeks or too peppery or sour – there were many dishes from which to choose, and the diners ate only what they preferred to eat – but because the food was too elaborate and too carefully prepared.

A few sauce recipes offer precise proportions, and others give partially specific instructions. An example of the former type of recipe (2.2.4) describes a sauce for chicken rissoles consisting of 31 peppercorns,[48] one cup each of good *liquamen*, *caroenum*, and 11 of water. The very next recipe (2.2.5) calls for an *acetabulum* of *liquamen* and three-and-one-half of water and one *coclear* ('teaspoon') of ground pepper, but it then becomes vague by demanding *modicum apii viridis* (a little green celery).[49] None of the legume, vegetable, or fish recipes (Books 3, 5, 9, 10) have proportions, and only a few of the sauces for birds and quadrupeds (Books 6 and 8) do so; surprisingly, also omitting proportions are those recipes which were, one would think, reserved only for special feasts: 6.6.1 for flamingo (or parrot substitute) and 6.1.1 for ostrich. Even when the proportions are given they can be less than scientific in their exactitude, as is 6.9.3 *liquaminis acetabulum minus ... porri fasciculum* (a scant ⅛ pint of *liquamen* and a bunch of leeks). The method of measurement often varies. Spices and liquids are measured by the piece or weight or quantity or not at all.[50] Sometimes the sauce ingredients are carefully measured, but that on to which the sauce is to be poured is curiously not. A case in point is 8.6.7, which calls for ⅛ pint each of *liquamen* and honey, eight dates (pounded) and half a pint of (good) wine, to be poured over a nondescript boned lamb or kid, the size of which might vary by ten pounds.[51]

Cooking time

Cooking time is another mystery, but again any experienced chef would know when a roast or a carrot was 'cooked'; individual preference would be important, for some like meat well done, others rare. When Apicius does suggest cooking time, it is in vague phrases such as 'make it boil until thoroughly cooked' (4.3.6), 'when it has boiled thoroughly' (7.9.3), 'when it boils' (9.4.4), 'put the stuffed cuttlefish in the boiling pot so that the stuffing can come together' (9.4.2), or 'when it has boiled' (9.4.4). Much of this mystery, of course, is due to the Roman chef's lack of a clock or thermometer, but even if he had had these devices he would rarely have used them; he had measuring devices yet rarely measured his ingredients. Regulation of heat was not an easy matter in cumbersome wood- or charcoal-burning ovens, and cooking time would necessarily have depended on the heat of the flame. Apicius several times specifies cooking over a low fire,[52] but only for cooking soup or stews, not for cooking sauces.

Methods

So far as one can tell, the regular method for the preparation of an Apician sauce is glimpsed in 10.1.1, a herb sauce (*ius diabotanon*) for fish, where we are instructed to pound the spices, pour in the liquids, mix (*temperabis*), pour (*refundes*) into a pot, and bring to a boil (*facies ut ferveant*). When it has boiled (*cum ferbuerit*), we are to pour it (*perfundes*) on to the fish. Clearly the sauce is brought to a boil, but is it merely brought to the boil or is it kept boiling (or simmering) until one of its properties – texture, taste, or volume – has changed? The answer is probably the former; only if whole dates are to thicken the sauce would the boiling take some ten or fifteen minutes, but if the dates were first pounded in the mortar, they would thicken the boiling sauce very quickly. There is no need to 'boil down' the wine since the *defrutum* is already concentrated. The honey would dissolve and blend with the rest long before it reached the boiling point, and since all the solids were already pounded, excessive boiling would not be necessary for them.[53]

Apicius may not specify other cooking instructions such as whether to cover the pot or how high to make the fire, but in three subtle recipes (7.6.6-8) he instructs us to stir a (meat) sauce with sprigs of thyme and oregano, savory, and savory and leek.

Thickening

The ultimate product is almost ready to be served, but to many sauces a thickening agent is now added. These agents include raw egg yolk (6.4.1), hard-boiled egg yolk (10.1.9), beaten egg white (6.9.11),[54] whole raw egg (4.2.14), steeped and pounded rice (2.2.9), water in which rice has boiled (2.2.8), wheat starch (*amulum* – 6.9.4),[55] crumbled *tracta* (pastry – 5.1.3)[56] and pounded dates (8.6.9).[57] By far the most common thickening agent is wheat starch. The percentage of thickened sauces is not overwhelming; approximately a quarter of the total number of Apician sauces are thickened, fifty of these with wheat starch. Occasionally two thickeners will be added to the same recipe (egg yolk and wheat starch),[58] and 8.6.7 (dates and wheat starch). The latter example would already be reasonably thickened by boiling the eight pounded dates with the *liquamen*, honey and wine, so Apicius specifies 'a little wheat starch'.[59]

Lastly, Apicius never describes the degree of thickness, nor does he describe the desired colour of the sauce, once again matters for personal preference and experience.[60] He does, however, make several recommendations for improving or varying or adding to the sauce, for instance, by serving the sauce boiling (8.6.6), by adding optional raisins or mustard or vinegar (9.2.2), or bay-leaf and malobathrum (9.7), or adding slices of boiled cucumber or taro or pig's trotters or chicken livers (6.5.2) or honey (10.1.13: 'add honey if desired' – to a dish which already contains sweet *passum* and raisins) or to 'season to taste' (9.4.3 – *condies ut voles*). He also adds such serving suggestions as sprinkling fish with vinegar before serving (10.1.5),[61] transferring the end product to a serving dish (*lanx* 10.2.8, *patina* 8.8.3, or *discus* 8.8.12), sprinkling with (more) pepper (10.1.1) or pounded celery seed (8.7.8), or garnishing with chopped hard-boiled eggs (9.10.4). Once (5.8.2) he even suggests that the chef should serve beans without a sauce (*simpliciter*).

Temperature

The Romans served their sauces both hot and cold. In Apicius the chef is normally instructed to boil the sauce, as we have seen, but it is not impossible that he could have let this hot sauce cool before serving. Several recipes actually specify the desired temperature. A few sauces were cold or at least room temperature; at 6.9.1 Apicius instructs the chef to prepare a *ius crudum* (uncooked sauce) for boiled chicken, but the temperature of the chicken is not specified; at 6.8 he mentions a cold sauce (*ius frigidum*) to be poured over a hot goose: 'dry off the hot boiled goose, pour on the sauce and carry it to the table'. The opposite was also possible, to pour a hot sauce over a cold chicken (6.9.7). Other than the sauces which the chef is told to boil and thus change the flavour or texture, several times Apicius wants the sauce merely heated for the purpose of temperature change (6.3.3; 7.14.4-5). Twice he makes the temperature of the sauce optional, for in 9.2.2 and 10.1.2 he gives the choice of warming the sauce.[62]

Names

Many of the sauces do not have names. Apicius simply refers to them as 'sauce for X', sometimes specifying whether the meat has been boiled, fried, roasted, or grilled, and sometimes omitting 'sauce', as at 9.8.1.

Several provincial dishes have acquired geographical names, such as Alexandrian sauce (10.1.6-7), and others are named after their taste (cumin sauce), temperature (cold sauce 8.8.1), colour (white sauce 6.5.3 and green sauce 6.5.4) or ingredient (chicken with milk and pastry 6.8.13). The last example is representative of a number of dishes (but not specifically the sauce) which have names: Parthian chicken (6.8.2), chicken with a sauce piquante (6.8.3) and Numidian chicken (6.8.4).

Conclusion

In conclusion, it would not be advantageous, even if it were possible, to categorize or catalogue these sauces, though one observes the predominance of sweet sauce for game, sweet and sour for fish, or *liquamen* sauce for sterile sow's womb. Although such a categorization would be helpful to modern scholarship in understanding the taste of the ancient Roman gourmets, it would be entirely misleading and un-Apician. The purpose of the Apician sauce was to make one's meat, fish, fowl, or vegetable as varied as possible. To disguise, to enhance, to colour, to discolour, to sweeten, sour, thicken, and liquefy, were some of the many purposes of the hundreds of Apician sauces. To cite just one category, there are almost a dozen different sauces for lamb (or kid), and these range from simple bread and oil sauce or simple *liquamen*, asafoetida and pepper sauce (8.6.1), to a thick onion, herb, and wine sauce (8.6.2), to a thick milk sauce (8.6.6), to a sweet milk and date sauce (8.6.7), to a vinegar and plum sauce (8.6.10), to a *defrutum*, milk-stock sauce (8.6.11). Moreover, if five different chefs made any one of these recipes, the result would be five different sauces because of personal preference, taste, experience, and the availability of supplies and ingredients. Considering the variety of spices and herbs available to the chef, the number of liquid additives, the various (pounded or chopped, roasted or raw) nuts and fruits, the various methods (and tastes) of thickening, the optional additives, the temperatures, colours and textures of the Roman sauce, it is little wonder that there are hundreds of different sauce recipes in the Apician corpus. In fact, one can be sure that the Apician corpus does not include all the options.[63]

Notes

1. In book 10 (Fish), twelve of the recipes describe sauces for fish, as in 10.1.1 'sauce for fried fish' and 10.1.2 'sauce for boiled fish'.

2. Apicius was the cognomen of several gourmets, the most famous of whom, M. Gavius, lived under the principates of Augustus and Tiberius. The *De re coquinaria* is actually a compilation of recipes from the first to late fourth or early fifth centuries. See Edward Brandt, *Untersuchungen zu röm- ischen Kochbüchern: Versuch einer Lösung der Apicius-Frage* (Leipzig, 1927). The best edition is by Mary Ella Milham (Leipzig, 1969), followed by Jacques André (Paris, 1974), and Aldo Marsili (Pisa 1957). English translations, com- ments, and cooking suggestions are available in Barbara Flower and Elizabeth Rosenbaum, *Apicius: The Roman Cookery Book* (London, 1958, repr. 1974) and Jon Solomon, *Ancient Roman Feasts and Recipes* (Miami, 1977). The *Excerpta* (*Apicii Excerpta a vinidario viro illustri*), clearly not by Apicius, is to be found in Milham 87-94. All citations in this chapter refer to the book, chapter, and recipe number of Milham's edition.

3. Unlike modern continental *haute cuisine* sauces, which often begin with the sautéing of onions in oil or butter or the melting of butter mixed with flour, and unlike Chinese and Indian cooking in which spices are heated in hot oil. Cf. 9.1.1, where onions are fried (if this is what *indura …cepam* implies; the passage is corrupt).

4. E.g. cumin, caraway, or fennel seed, or rue, dried onion, or bay leaf. The Romans knew how to add a bouquet of herbs, e.g. 6.2.1, which avoided the texture problem in stew and stock. Today most spices are purchased already pulver- ized, but this was rare in antiquity. Nonetheless, cf. J. Innes Miller, *The Spice Trade of the Roman Empire* (Oxford, 1969) 55, on ground ginger.

5. Apicius 9.10.10 (*salsum sine salso*).

6. A type of cumin: cf. Pliny *Natural History* 20.58 and Miller 105-106. Apicius does not use *ammi* in a sauce recipe: cf. 1.32. Pliny describes its uses in baking and for medicinal purposes, but perhaps Pliny's *condimentis interponitur* (it is included among the spices) refers to spices for (Alexandrian) sauces.

7. From Cyrenaica (7.1.1) and from Persia (1.30). The North African variety, celebrated in Catullus (7.4), was either

hurriedly harvested or exceedingly destructive to the soil; Pliny (*Natural History* 19.15.39) reports that it was no long- er available in his day. See also Theophrastos *Enquiry into Plants* 6.5; V. Vikentiev, 'Le Silphium et le rite du renou- vellement de la vigeur', *Bulletin de l'Institute d'Egypte* 37 (1954-55), 123-4; Flower and Rosenbaum, 28-9; and Miller 100. Flower and Rosenbaum needlessly wonder at the inability to identify an extinct species. Apicius (1.13) stows silphium with pine nuts in a glass jar and uses only the nuts. Flower and Rosenbaum rightly explain that this recipe is evidence of how high was the price for silphium, but it also shows how powerful its flavour was. In addition, it is evidence that the Romans were well aware of the value of glass (over ceramic or other fabrics) for preserving herbs and spices.

8. *Natural History* 19.44-56 and 20.44-98.

9. E.g. ginger, turmeric, sesame, and cinnamon. Conspicu- ously absent here are the capsicum peppers, allspice, and tarragon; cloves and nutmeg were brought from the Mo- luccas in the 4th century. For a complete discussion, see Pliny *Natural History* Books 19-20; Elisa Rose Graser, 'The Edict of Diocletian on Maximum Prices' in Tenny Frank, *An Economic Survey of Ancient Rome* (Baltimore, 1940), 305- 36 and 415-21; and the commentary on these by Miller *passim*. Not all the spices used in the *De re coquinaria* are to be found in the inventory listed in the *Excerpta* (Milham 87).

10. 6.6.2 and 10.1.14 respectively.

11. As our curry powder or five-spice powder. On the other hand, see also the *sinapis confectae* (made-up mustard) in Diocletian's price edict 1.35 (with Miller 24) and perhaps *condimentorum praemisquorum* (6.48 with Miller 24).

12. 3.2.2; 3.4.1, 2, 3, 7, and 8; 4.1; 4.3.5 and 6; 7.15; 7.16.3.

13. In 6.1.2 thyme and savory are interchangeable; such substi- tutions are not commonly called for.

14. For example 3.20.2 *coriandro viridi conciso* (with chopped green leaf of coriander), 5.2.1 *semen coriandri* (coriander seed), 7.6.7 *feniculum* (fennel), 8.1.3 *coriandrum* (coriander). In 7.6.7, *feniculum* is listed just following *apii semen*, celery seed, but it appears just before *mentam*, a leaf.

15. These are a substitute for filberts. For toasting the nuts before pounding, see 6.5.3. There are exceptions, of course,

such as hard-boiled egg whites (5.3.2. *ius candidum*).

16. Many recipes fail to distinguish nuts to be pounded from nuts to be added whole or merely chopped. In 6.5.3, for example, the nuts are listed between the pounded (pepper, lovage, cumin) and liquid (honey, *liquamen*, vinegar oil) ingredients. Chestnuts (5.2.2) and beechnuts (8.8.3) are whole or chopped in Roman cookery, but nowhere in the Apician corpus are they specifically to be pounded as a sauce ingredient. Walnuts (9.10.11) could be pounded with pepper and cumin and served in brine as a salt-fish substitute.

17. The actual instructions to pound (*teres*, e.g. 8.2.1; 8.6.2) seldom appear; cf. 9.1.6 *Aliter* [*ius*] *in locusta: piper, ligusticum, cuminum, mentam, rutam, nucleos, mel, acetum, liquamen et vinum* (Another method for cray fish: pepper, lovage, cumin, mint, rue, pine kernels, honey, vinegar, *liquamen*, wine). When the recipes do include the term, there is even more seldom an instruction to stop pounding and start mixing, e.g. 8.5.3 *Teres piper, ligusticum...suffundes mel, acetum...calefacies* (grind pepper, lovage...pour in honey, vinegar...heat) as opposed to 8.1.9 *Teres piper, ligusticum...rutam, liquamen, vinum, passum* (grind pepper, lovage...rue, *liquamen*, wine, *passum*).

18. As shown not only by the order in which they are listed (*teres piper...damascena enucleata, laseris modicum, vinum ...* [grind pepper, pitted damsons, a little silphium, wine]) but also by the fact that the plums have been pitted.

19. 10.1.1 for fish with dates, 6.6.1 for flamingo with dates, or perhaps 3.4.8 for peaches with squash. These fruits are cooked with the sauce.

20. Apicius never instructs the chef to strain a sauce; assuming the opposite viewpoint is Joan Liversidge, 'Roman Kitchens and Cooking Utensils', in Flower and Rosenbaum 35-8. Apicius at 3.13.1 presumably has the chef use a strainer for draining boiled turnips; cf. the non-boiling uses of the *colum* in Cato *On Agriculture* 11.2, Columella *On Agriculture* 11.2.70, 12.19.4, and Virgil *Georgics* 2.242.

21. Even in a non-cookbook description, Pliny (*Natural History* 23.12) offers the options of mixing, pounding, boiling, and chewing raisins, and only when they are pounded (for medicinal purposes) does he specify *sine nucleis* (pitted).

22. As well as *defrutum* of quince and fig (2.2.8); cf. also *decocti* (boiled down) (e.g. Diocletian's price edict 2.15).

23. Which many were. See below, on thickening agents.

24. Cf. 2.2.4, where the 11:2 ratio of water to *liquamen* and *caroenum* may be for the steaming liquid only.

25. Honey served a variety of purposes in antiquity, particularly for preserving fruits and meats (1.8, 17, 20); preparing *mulsum* (see below, n. 45); and, of course, for sweets, for which see Apicius 7.11.1-8; Cato *On Agriculture* 76-84; Varro *On the Latin Language* 5.22.106f.; Pollux *Onomasticon* 6.72f.; and Athenaeus *Deipnosophistae* 3.113a and 14.640a-f. Honey could also be mixed with water (*aqua mulsa*) and used to marinate liver (7.10.1). There were also various grades of honey: cf. Diocletian's price edict 3.10.12.

26. Pliny (*Natural History* 15.7), for example, lists, among others, wild olive, myrtle berry, laurel berry, cypress, walnuts, apples, cedar, chestnuts, rice, and rose; cf. Herodotos 1.193.

27. Again at 1.5, not specifically for a sauce, but for spiced oil, i.e. imitation Liburnian.

28. A little oil: 3.21.3 (*oleo modico*), 7.7.1. (*olei modicum*), and 7.14.3 (*oleum modice*). No added oil: 7.14.2; 8.5.4; 8.8.6; 10.1.10; 5.2.2; 6.5.5. The truffles in 7.14.2 are fried in oil with a honey, vinegar and *liquamen* (no oil) sauce; in 7.14.3 they are boiled and strained, then served with a honey, vinegar, *defrutum, liquamen* and oil sauce. Oil alone was used for frying; rendered fat could be browned and diced for sausage, e.g. 2.2.1 (pheasant fat), 2.4, and 2.5.3, but there is no recipe in Apicius in which animal fat is used for frying.

29. And perhaps in 6.9.13, although the text there seems to be corrupt.

30. Cf. Varro *On Agriculture* 2.11; Columella *On Agriculture* 7.2, 12.8; ancient commentator on Aristophanes, *Thesmophoriazusae* 506; Paximus *Geoponica* 18.21; and G. Herzog-Hauser, 'Milch', *Paulys Real-Encyclopädie der Classisischen Altertumswissencchaft* XV (1932), 1569-80.

31. The methods of preparation are in Columella *On Agriculture* 12.57 and Palladius 8.8. Pliny *Natural History* 19.54 adds that boiling the mustard will reduce its pungency.

32. E.g. 6.1.2 (boiled ostrich) and 9.1.1 (boiled prawns). Added to a sweet sauce: 6.2.4 (boiled crane); to neither 3.11.2. Mustard is also used in preserving turnips (1.24.2), and as a dressing for sausages (2.5.2).

33. E.g. 2.1.3 *liquamine optimo* and 2.2.4; cf. Diocletian's price edict 3.6.7.

34. *Geoponica* 20.46.1-6; Palladius 3.25.12 (*liquamen ex piris*); Flower and Rosenbaum 21-23; Pliny *Natural History* 31.95; Zahn, 'Garum', *Paulys Real-Encyclopädie der Classischen Altertumschaft* VII (1912), 841-9; and Robert I. Curtis *Garum and Salsamenta* (Leiden 1991).

35. At 3.10.1 leeks are cooked with a handful of salt, but then they are drained; at 4.4.1 salt is used in soup; cf. 5.1.3. At 5.3.4 it is added to a cold sauceless pea dish; at 6.2.1.3 and 6.8.13 it is used to pre-boil fowl; cf. 8.1.2 for boar boiled in sea water. More salt, of course, could be added at the table; cf. Horace *Satires* 1.6.11.

36. Flower and Rosenbaum (21) must be incorrect in comparing *liquamen* with Worcester (or A-1) sauce. *Liquamen* was a basic ingredient in almost every sauce. The closest analogy would be the various indispensible fish-derivative sauces and pastes used in Southeast Asia.

37. Amounts are given for the herbs and spices, but not for the *liquamen* and vinegar.

38. Which were at times forbidden or restricted for Roman parties in the cause of frugality: cf. Gellius *Attic Nights* 2.24.2, and Pliny *Natural History* 14.16.95.

39. Though Nasidienus (Horace *Satires* 2.8.48-9) insists that Chian is the only wine which boils correctly. The long lists can be compiled from Pliny *Natural History* Book 14, Martial 13.109-125, and Athenaeus *passim*.

40. For the method of preparation, see Columella *On Agriculture* 12.39; cf. Palladius 11.19. Pliny *Natural History* 14.19 describes the non-grape wines.

41. A stronger additive was *sapa*, must boiled down to one-third its original volume, but Apicius does not use it in any sauce recipes. For the various gradations, see Palladius 11.18, Columella *On Agriculture* 12.21f., and Pliny 14.11.20. The modern equivalent is not bottled grape juice (Flower and Rosenbaum 24) but Armenian *bekmez*.

42. For *mulsum*, see Pliny *Natural History* 14.20-21; Columella *On Agriculture* 12.41; *Geoponica* 8.25.1, 26; Varro *On Agriculture* 3.16; Petronius *Satyricon* 34; Horace *Satires* 2.4.24; and A. Hug, 'mulsum', *Paulys Real-Encyclopädie der classischen Altertumswissenschaft* XVI (1935), 513-14.

43. Cf. 8.7.17: *In porcello lactante: piperis unc. I, vini heminam, olei optimi acetabulum maius, liquaminis acetabulum, aceti acetabulum minus* (for a sucking pig: 1 oz. pepper, half a pint of wine, a generous eighth of a pint of best oil, one eighth of a pint of *liquamen*, a scant eighth of a pint of vinegar).

44. See Pliny *Natural History* 12.14 and Miller 14. Augustus fitted out a fleet to sail directly to Egypt and India to expedite the pepper and spice trade. Prices dropped, and pepper became the rage. This is the cause of Pliny's complaint.

45. The onions were pounded in the mortar either fresh (here) or dried (e.g. 9.2.1); only once in Apicius is an onion chopped and browned (9.1.1).

46. Oil, in fact, is generally the last additive, so Romans did not apparently make their sauces excessively fatty; somewhat frequently Apicius is careful to specify *oleum modice*, e.g. 10.1.12, 10.2.7; 10.2.8; 10.2.13. On the other hand, there are several recipes in which oil predominates, especially in sauces for poultry, e.g. 6.8.6 with only asafoetida, pepper, oil, *liquamen* and a little parsley.

47. It would be helpful if the proportioned recipes, even if from a different Apicius, showed that the first spice or herb and the first liquid were to be added in the greatest quantities, but in 2.2.5; 6.8.3, 6, and 11 the regular order of spices followed by liquids is not maintained, and 2.2.4 has the opposite of what is expected - one cup of *liquamen*, one of *caroenum*, and eleven of water; but this may be for steaming, not for a sauce.

48. Flower and Rosenbaum (65) correctly translate *piperis grana* as peppercorns, but this is a curious number; perhaps 31 peppercorns weighed the same as one *semiuncia*, *sicilius* or *sextula*, or filled one *coclear*.

49. Curiously in rissole (2.1.5) and sausage (2.5.3) recipes the number of eggs (5 or 3) is specified, but not the amount of brains, suet, or meat; perhaps the size of the *patina* (pan) was regular. Many *patina* recipes (4.2.4, 5, 8, 9, 29, 31, 33, and 36) have the proportions listed.

50. 7.5.2 *Petroselini scripulos sex, laser scripulos sex, gingeribus scripulos sex, lauri bacas quinque...liquaminis et olei quod sufficit* (6 scruples of parsley, 6 of silphium, 6 of ginger, 5 laurel berries,...and as much *liquamen* and oil as suffices).

51. A few proportioned recipes (not for sauces) are clearly from a medical (dietary) source, e.g. 1.27, 34 *Oxygarum digestibilem* and a rather unspecific 9.10.12 *Cuminum tantum quantum quinque digitis tollis...* If most modern cookbooks are designed for typical dinners for 4, 6 or 8 people, Apicius gives no hint of the size of the average Roman meal. The amount of meat is never specified, unless to say pork shoulder (7.9.3) which again is not specific and could serve 6 as well

as 23, depending on how many entrées were to be served. The evidence from Petronius and Horace (*Satires* 2.8) suggests that parties could be large or small, but that at each party a number of entrées and appetizers were served.

[52.] 4.5.4 *lento igni* (a low flame). A high flame for this recipe would destroy the texture of the apricots, reducing them to pulp.

[53.] For meats he once orders specifically that a fish be well done (9.1.2 – *quousque assantur bene*), but this is still a little vague.

[54.] With milk and crushed pine-nuts for *ius candidum*.

[55.] For a complete list of the sauces bound with *amulum*, see Jon Solomon, '*Tracta*: a versatile Roman pastry', *Hermes* 106 (1978), 544-55, note 69. See also Pliny *Natural History* 18.16.

[56.] I have discussed this use of *tracta* in Solomon (1978, 551-5). For a different view, see Bryer and Hill in this volume.

[57.] Again the amount of thickening agent is not given except in several *patina* recipes (4.2.4, 5, 8, 9, 31 and 36), but a *patina* is not a sauce; moreover, in each of these recipes it is only the number of eggs that is given. In a chicken recipe (6.8.11) the amount of *liquamen* is given precisely, but not the number of egg whites for binding.

[58.] At 9.3.2 (for stuffed squid) egg yolk is added to the other sauce ingredients, and then Apicius adds, *obligabis*. This could mean either to add another thickening agent, e.g. *amulum* as in 9.4.4, or to boil the sauce until the egg yolk does the thickening.

[59.] Other than this there are few examples of a sauce which contains both pounded dates and another thickener; cf. 9.2.10 (for tuna), which contains (pounded?) raisins and *amulum*, and 9.2.12 (for grilled dentex) which contains cooked quince (how much?) and *amulum*.

[60.] Cf. 8.4.1, where an unspecified amount of *passum* was added for an unspecified degree of colour.

[61.] As we commonly use lemon juice for the same purpose. The Romans had citrons, but not lemons: cf. 1.21 (and Pliny *Natural History* 16.25 on the lime).

[62.] Curiously by [adding?] raisins. The text as printed in Milham (82) has the incorrect punctuation; cf. Milham 78. Flower and Rosenbaum (209) assume hot raisins are to be added; this is possible, particularly since there is egg yolk in 9.2.2, which would change in thickness if heated over a flame. 10.1.2, however, does not contain egg yolk as a thickener; it contains pounded dates.

[63.] E.g. Horace *Satires* 2.8.42f.; Petronius *Satyricon* 66; Columella *On Agriculture* 12.42, 59; (and Greek recipes, e.g. Athenaeus 3.95c or 3.117d). Highly skilled techniques often look nonsensical, illogical, and unnecessarily elaborate to an outsider. When Horace complains about Nasidienus' excessive care for cookery, it is, of course, due to his general philosophy of simplicity; he eats beans and simple flour-water pancakes (*Satires* 1.6.115). But it is also due to his complete lack of knowledge of the intricacies of culinary arts.

❖ **10** ❖

EATING FISH
THE PARADOXES
OF SEAFOOD

Nicholas Purcell

Introduction

EATING fish is a difficult subject to address, as far as the Greeks and Romans were concerned, because, to a significant extent, fish were inedible. Bishop Synesius of Cyrene has an instructive tale on this subject (*Letter* 148). He and his companions, on a trip into the interior of Cyrenaica, were frying their fish for supper on the campfire, when some of the locals came up and peeping into the pan exclaimed with horror and disgust that the good bishop was cooking, and proposing to eat, snakes. Specific to a particular habitat in Nature, and one that was specially hostile to human life, fish were anatomically as hard to classify as any pangolin; wherever dietary prohibitions constituted a socially significant phenomenon, fish constituted a problematic case (Douglas 1966, 169-73; Wilkins 1993). Nor is that odd, when we remember that fish, alone of the animals eaten in the ancient Mediterranean, could and did eat people (a theme to which we shall return). Eating fish could be as morally ambiguous, therefore, as eating dog, as taxonomically disturbing as a diet of locusts, and as dissonant with the dispositions of Nature as a nice glass of sea-water (on undrinkable sea-water, see Wilkins (1993) and Strabo 6.1.1 (252), cf. Justin 43.3.5).

These negative connotations are reflected in the complexity of the cultural symbolism of fish in antiquity, a symbolism that has had a profound effect on main currents in the visual arts and in literature. Anyone who is inclined to doubt this complexity has only to spend a few minutes with one of the five volumes of Franz Joseph Dölger's *magnum opus* ICHTHYS (Dölger 1922-43). There are other symbol-rich species. But important as the eagle and the bee were in thought and art, neither remotely acquired the standing of aquatic life. The importance of fish as a sign is a direct reflection of the unpalatable fact that the inedible was frequently eaten by very many people in the coastlands of the Mediterranean. In this brief foray into a complex area, my aim is to try to explain the workings of this paradox a little, and to set them against a second and related dilemma: the more quantitative aspect of the problem.

The ancient evidence, as represented either by the analyses of Dölger or the more practical investigations into the pickling of fish of the contemporary expert on the subject, R.I. Curtis, can convey an exaggerated sense of the dietary contribution made by fish to Greek and Roman life.[1] Such a view has been sternly countered by Tom Gallant in his classic monograph *A Fisherman's Tale* (Gallant 1985, cf. Curtis 1991, 149). Using the reductionist-minimalist methodology of the Cambridge school he is able to prove that for the Athenian fleets of the 5th century BC to have been rowed by fish-eating oarsmen would have required a catch 34.7% larger than that of the whole Greek fishing fleet in 1938, preserved in nearly 8000 tonnes of salt. This paper does not aim to produce statistical *tours de force* of that kind, but rather to attempt to reconcile the abundance of the literary and artistic allusions to eating fish with Gallant's severe position – the quantitative paradox – and then attempt to relate that in turn to the sense of the inedibility of fish – the qualitative paradox.

On being eaten by fish: sea versus land[2]

'Lie there among the fish', says Achilles, heaving his fallen adversary into the river, 'who will heedlessly lick the gore off your wound. Your mother won't mourn you, laying you on the bier: Skamander will carry you off, whirling you down to the broad gulf of the sea. There, when it catches sight of you, some fish will dart over, beneath the dark and rippling surface of the waves, and eat Lykaon's glistening fat' (Homer *Iliad* 21.122-7).[3] This graphic passage stands at the head of a long and rather revolting progeny: the shipwreck scenes on early Greek pots which show drowned mariners being devoured; the epigram in the *Garland of Philip* on the drowned fisherman washed ashore with his hands missing because the fish have taken their revenge for the depredations of those hands in life (*Palatine Anthology* 7.294); Pliny the Elder on the horror of being attacked by giant squid when shipwrecked or diving (*Natural History* 9.91). This is the tradition that lies explicitly behind the religious prohibition, attributed to the Pythagoreans, against eating red mullet (Osborne 1990, 26-7, quoting Aelian *Natura Animalium* 24. 2).

This tradition is principally about the otherness of the sea, the hostility of the sea as an element, a different world.[4] This otherness is also the point of other cultural traditions, such as the long series of *topoi* about the Argo and how the first ship ended the Golden Age through the introduction of maritime communications; or the general hostility to the seaborne merchant and the world of risk that he inhabited, risk of death and risk of moral corruption operating hand-in-hand. Both of these parallel evocations of the world of the sea are actually structurally linked with the theme of the sea as the anti-human abode of fish.

The sea is poor. Wealth comes primarily from the land, from only some of it at that, and from the produce of agriculture. Wealth that lies hidden underground, like the pearls that come unexpectedly from the depths of the sea, is a morally ambiguous marvel.[5] Certain places are so poor that their inhabitants are reduced to dependence on the sea. The description of Anthedon in pseudo-Dikaiarchos makes the point in a colourful way:

> In size the city is not large, and lies on the sea towards Euboia. Its *agora*, enclosed by twin *stoas*, is totally shaded with trees. It is well-endowed with wine and *opson*, but lacks grain because of the poor quality of its territory. The inhabitants are nearly all fishermen, making their livelihood from hooks and fish, purple-dye and sponges, growing old in huts on the beaches amid the seaweed. Suffering the toils of the sea, they are reddened and thin in appearance, and their finger-nails are worn away: they are ferrymen and shipbuilders and not only do not work the land, but

scarcely have any, calling themselves descendants of marine Glaukos, who is agreed to have been a fisherman.

> (pseudo-Dikaiarchos, in *Geographi Graeci Minores* ed. Müller 1855, 104)

Phokaia is described in similar terms: it is specifically stated that it was through the badness of the land that the people were compelled 'to work the sea (*thalattourgein*), for the most part, and set up fish-pickling-works and other enterprises of that sort' (Strabo *Geography* 6.1.1 (252), cf. Justin 43.3.5).

This preconception can be reinforced from the perspective of 'actual' scientific ichthyology: the marine life of the Mediterranean is relatively poor compared with the great oceans, and that will have been a datum well-known to many seafarers. It was certainly familiar in the Islamic tradition. Al-Muqaddasi has a memorable account of the creation of the Mediterranean:

> When God created the Mediterranean he addressed it, saying: 'I have created thee and I shall send thee my servants, those who when they wish to ask some favour from me will say "Glory to God" or "God is very Great", or "There is no God but God". How wilt thou then treat these?'
>
> 'Well, Lord', replied the Mediterranean, 'I will drown them'.
>
> 'Away with thee, I curse thee: I will impoverish thy appearance and make thee less fishy!'
>
> (Al-Muqaddasi *Ahsan at-Taqasim fi ma'rifat al-aqalim*, 15-6)

The sea is therefore ugly and lonely, a desert in which the human is wholly out of place. Coastal villas for the Roman élite occupied the 'rocky and lonely seacoasts', *saxa et solitudo maris*, and the juxtaposition of the civilized with the wild sea was a more powerful romantic contrast than it is easy to imagine in our days of tamed and trivialized sea-beaches.[6]

Dependence on the desolate world of the sea is a potent sign of need, and in both Greek and Roman thought the fisherman is a classic type of poverty. Not only is he not engaged in the activities which provide normal food and the acceptable kind of wealth that derives from the soil; his work

On the value of fish: poor versus rich

consists of hunting and gathering and is more prone to chance than even the production of the semi-arid agriculturalist. The accidental gleanings of the sea-coast are akin to the returns of the hunter and the wildfowler, who are also inhabitants of wildernesses beyond the cultivated terrain of the territory of the city. Baked by the sun, semi-naked, emaciated, the fisherman lives in a hut and ekes out a precarious existence on his catch (Shaw 1982-3). Gallant has set out for us exactly how precarious that existence would have been, reminding us that the nutritional value of a kilo of fish in calories is only about ⅔ of that of a kilo of grain, and equally of how much energy had to be expended with relatively low-tech methods of fishing. Leake in the Peloponnese in the early 19th century observed how the villages near the coast supplemented their meagre reserves of agricultural produce during the long waterless summers by eating shellfish from the rocks; the consequence of desperation and the proximity of famine (Leake 1830 I, 258-9). From the stereotypes of Greek comedy to the statues of emaciated fisherfolk with which the Romans decorated their peristyles, it would be easy to compile a complete gallery of images of the destitute fisherman.

Equally, however, the tremendous value of fish as a symbol of wealth can be instantiated from all periods of antiquity. Again, this is not the place for a long recitation of instances of fish-luxury: the elder Pliny, and, more exhaustively, Athenaeus, produce just such lists, and they themselves were following in a long tradition which included Q. Ennius'*Hedyphagetica* ('Delikatessen'), and the whole literature of *truphe*, that luxurious excess that, while vicious, possessed a complex cultural ideology of its own in the Hellenistic and Roman worlds.[7] Fish takes its place in diet among the other tasty and nutritious complements to the staple, the *opsonemata*, but will eventually become the [o]*psari*[on] *par excellence*: the classical term for the 'relish' becomes the word for fish in medieval and modern Greek (*psari*). A taste for fish was something only affordable by the seriously well-to-do; the very wealthy went even further than eating them and reared them, nurturing them with personal attention while they appropriated for their own exquisite life-style other aspects of the destitution of the sea-shore.

Alongside the marble statues of worn-out fishermen, slave fishermen were deployed to give the air of a maritime location authenticity (the Digest tells of moving them around from one villa to another – *Digest* 33.7.27, Scaevola; cf. Varro *On Agriculture* 2.17.6). A villa which had a view of real fishermen at work was worth much more than one looking out onto unfished waters, as we discover from an anecdote in Cicero about a fraudulent sale by the Syracusan banker Pythius of a coastal estate in Sicily by means of a carefully laid on display of fishing out to sea at the crucial moment when the prospective purchaser was inspecting the property. When he subsequently arrived having spent his money and saw no fishing he at first thought that it must be because of a Fisherfolk's Festival, so thoroughly was he taken in! (Cicero *On Duties* 3. 58-60)

The taste for doing a little angling yourself was known; another of the chatty letters of Bishop Synesius shows him with his entourage in a small boat on a fishing excursion (*Letter* 5). Oppian of Korykos, in his poetic treatise on fish, pictures the fish of the imperial pond voluntarily giving themselves up to the ruler of the world (Oppian *Halieutica* 1.56-72). The most famous of all such scenes is Antony and Cleopatra out fishing together, with the Queen helping the Roman to catch his prey and likening it to the conquests that he is fated to make (Plutarch *Antony* 29.7). The point is significant: controlling the resources of the sea is a potent demonstration of power in general. The reason is that catching fish is a microcosm of luck in the wider world. 'On the shore at Baiae with a lucky reed, catching fishes'.[8] The inscription on a marble gaming-board from Rome (the letters marked the 36 places for moving counters) uses the imagery of fishing to evoke the chanciness of gambling, and, what is more, in the context of the life of luxury to which the fisherman ministers, and for which the gambler longs.

Now the first thing that should be said about this rather stark juxtaposition of contradictory images about the production of fish is that the second helps explain the difficulties of the first. The reason that a fisherman could in practice survive, despite the difficulty of catching enough fish to compensate for the energy expended in looking for them and catching them, is that he could usually sell them for enough money to buy a more than sufficient quantity of other foodstuffs.[9] Gallant sees this clearly (at least in places), and makes the telling and perceptive observation that as a productive activity, fishing resembles the growing of a cash-crop (Gallant

1985; cf. Estrada, Vives and Alcaraz 1985). In practice, in the ancient world we see a steady professionalization of the retail structures which distributed the fisherman's wares, parallel to some of the culturally complex developments which accompanied changes in the retailing of the produce of more normal cash-crops such as grapes and olives.[10] The gap between the picturesque images of the Roman peristyle and the realities of the sea-shore steadily widened: though as we shall see, there are some signs that the entrepreneurs who handled the redistribution of fish in the Roman Empire were conscious of the literary nuance of their activities. It probably helped in the process of marketing as much as bearded trawlermen in sou'westers do in the fish-marketing business today.

Ichthyology and opportunism: death versus survival

Reverting to 'reality' for a moment, Gallant's picture needs a little modification. The relative dearth of fish with which Allah cursed the Mediterranean reflects a general truth, but there are naturally variations in the distribution of what is to be found (even setting aside for the present lakes and rivers, often well-stocked with edible fish). The variations in salinity and temperature with depth and distance from the Strait of Gibraltar produce a huge variety of habitats which are exploited by a variety of migratory fish-species, and the observation of great shoals of fish like the tunny offers the coast dweller occasional opportunities of acquiring free food for relatively little effort on quite a large scale. Not all the coasts are well-endowed in this way, but the Sea of Marmara and its approaches, and the coasts and narrows in which Sicily sits dividing the eastern and western Mediterranean basins, are favoured, and here it is clear that fishing strategies rather more complex and organized than the hopeful solitary fisherman in his skiff have been practised since at least the classical Greek period.

The life-cycles of several prominent Mediterranean species such as the grey mullet, moreover, involve also the coastal lagoons of many of the Mediterranean wetlands. In these confined spaces sea-fishing can be controlled, and in fact the rudiments of systematic pisciculture were attributed to the exploitation of resources of this kind by the Carthaginians[11]. In historical times the deltaic lagoons of the Egyptian coast have likewise supported a fishery which does not suffer from the problem of low nutritional return per unit energy expended that Gallant so stresses (Brewer and Freedman 1989). His fisherman, whose tale is elucidated by the data of his work, is as Attic as so much of the ancient evidence. Had Athens controlled a major wetland, our picture would have been somewhat different.[12] The primary productivity of the lagoons of the western Mediterranean has been estimated to be twice that of the sea: when managed, they can produce up to 130 kg/ha/year, 20 times that of the open sea (Margalef 1985, 15).

Nonetheless, the chance element in the acquisition of nourishment from the sea remained a high one. When the people of Kerkyra (Corfu) enjoyed the experience of a particularly spectacular shoal of tunny, they dedicated a bronze bull to Apollo at Delphi out of a portion of their takings.[13] While this shows that the infrastructure was already in the early 5th century BC such that the extra quantum of food represented by the tunny was realizable, and not simply consumed opportunistically as a windfall, the incident highlights the extent to which a happening of this sort was rare and unpredictable, an occasion on which to invoke the divine in a special way.[14] Poor yields were equally the result of supernatural intervention: in Byzantine times empty nets throughout the Hellespontine area at tunny-time were the work of the devil (*Vita S. Parthenii* = *Paroemiographi Graeci* 114.1357).

This unpredictability of sea-food can be used to help resolve further the paradoxes with which this account began. This is the food that most strikingly stood for the precariousness of survival in the Mediterranean world; it could be used effectively as a symbol of the whole glut/dearth pendulum-swing experience of trying to provide against risk: the provision that was, as we now increasingly see, highly formative for the structure of ancient societies. This is confirmed by the link with luck that we have noticed; it is not any old luck, but a rather special sense of good fortune in the circumstances of the game of Mediterranean production.

Interspecific trophic exchanges

Interspecific trophic exchange is the name that ecologists give to the question of who eats whom, or in the case of plants, what. In ancient societies, provision of food was based on a complex and varying set of such exchanges, because of the presence of so many different kinds of animal husbandry in the repertoire of responses to variety in the environment and variability in weather conditions. Thus a highly diverse regime of possibilities in the layout of 'trophic exchanges' is one of the key background factors in the analysis of ancient cultural attitudes to the production and consumption of any foodstuff.

Where fish are concerned, however, the situation – the problem of being eaten by fish apart! – seems simpler. The fish, as we have seen, was thought to inhabit a world whose ecological interaction with the life of the land was considered minimal.[15] This point is the subject of those peculiar epigrams in the *Palatine Anthology* in which – for example – a fisherman hurls an octopus into the air, it catches a bird in mid-flight, and kills a hare as it falls to the ground (*Palatine Anthology* 9.14; 94; 227, etc.). In this plausible scenario, the improbable agency of one of the more characteristically odd denizens of the deep is imagined in spheres in which it does not belong. Normally the taking of marine fauna was seen as closely analogous to hunting on land, precisely because in the wild woods or mountains, as at sea, the action of pursuit and killing was not interdependent with any other human productive activity, and indeed took place, conceptually speaking, firmly outside the domain of such activity. It is this lack of contact with the range of possibilities of ordinary human control that made fish so strongly symbolic of chance in the business of procuring food. But it was, in its turn, because of the strength of that symbolism that the idea that you might, through power and skill, have an effect on the habitat even of maritime species had such an appeal to the members of the ancient élites. Just as hunting and fowling were improved and controlled in the *paradeisos* (the – originally Persian – pleasure-ground), the *vivarium* (game-reserve) and the aviary, so the sphere of activity of the fisherman could equally become the specialist interest of the proprietor of the luxury villa.

In the context of food and of the subject of trophic exchanges, then, we may highlight one or two instances of the way in which this development was reflected in the *feeding* of fish. This was after all, one of the aspects of pisciculture that needed to be understood if the practice was to succeed at all, and various stories of the more self-indulgent *piscinarii* focus on the personal role taken by the proprietor in the feeding of his favourite fish.[16]

The fish will in the end be eaten itself, but its status as food is dramatically increased by the personal attention to its diet of the lucky man who will eventually consume it.[17] In one case in particular, the practice of the fish-pond served to reinforce strongly the paradox of rich and poor in the fish business that we have already examined. One proprietor used to feed his specimen fish on the smaller fry that the local population of the coastline were wont to procure for their own sustenance. When the weather was too bad for the fishermen to put to sea, he and they found themselves in two different sorts of quandary. They had nothing to eat; he was threatened with the death of his pride and joy. The solution was relatively simple. He bought in jars of expensive preserved fish and fed his pets on that (Varro *On Agriculture* 3.17.7).

This disagreeable tale makes plain the role of *ichthyotrophia* ('the nurturing of fish', a significant term) in articulating the tiers into which ancient society was divided by its differential access to foodstuffs. In the much better-known story of the vile Vedius Pollio and the *murenae* to which he fed errant slaves, it is not just a question of depriving the poor of their food, but actually feeding the fish on the human resource itself (Seneca *De Ira* 3.40.2; *De Clementia* 1.18; Pliny *Natural History* 9.77; 167; Dio 54.23). The cruelty of death by fish and the shock of including people in the piscine food-chain are something that we have already considered, and the theme of *saevitia* (savagery) is undoubtedly central to this much told tale, but it is also connected more directly with the calibration of *truphe*, and excessive indulgence in the creation of conditions for the rearing of fish out of their natural element (Pliny *Natural History* 9.77 also stresses *saevitia*).

The phenomenon of considering people as fish is related. We have already seen (above) Antony fishing for kingdoms. The Persian practice of rounding up all the population of islands by the use of cordons was called *sageneia* or trawling by the Greeks (Herodotos 6.31, cf. 3.149). This, finally, was also the destiny of the Galilean fishermen who were impelled to become 'fishers of men' (Matthew 4.19; Mark 1.16).

Funny fish and fish to share

Because they expressed this gap between rich and poor and therefore formed a useful set of props for the demi-monde that inhabited the space between the two, and that provided the butt for much comic literature, fish were funny for the Greeks and Romans. This demi-monde included the purveyors of luxury produce and – especially – the hangers-on whose aim was to share in the leftovers – the parasites and toadies of so much of the comic and satiric tradition.[18] One aspect of this is clearly the ineluctable poverty of the fisherman who must eat his own produce; but another important angle is the central role of luck and chance in the acquisition of wealth, that we have already noticed in the context of the productive possibilities of Mediterranean life in general (Alkiphron 1.9, for fisherman as parasite). Ancient economic thought has more to do with the windfall and the treasure-trove than with investment planning or capital management. One form in which the fishy windfall appears is the miraculous draft of fishes; the other is the Big Fish.

There is a star in the outer fringes of the constellation Pisces, whose rising is the season of birth of those who will be fishermen, but specifically, the astrologer tells us, fishermen of big fish: 'these will take seals, sea-dogs, swordfish, tunny and "crocodiles"' (Firmicus Maternus 8.17.5). More mundanely, these are the people 'who will own establishments for salting or for the production of pickles or *liquamen*, and who will trade in these products'. The classification is important (we shall return to the equally interesting association of the Big Fish with the world of industrial fish-processing). The basic distinction of size in seafish was a fundamental one. The most valuable and exciting fish of all were singletons. Sometimes they took the form of a real monster, like the whale that was fought in a great set-piece Clash of the Titans by the emperor Claudius in the new harbour at Ostia, or the giant squid that wrought havoc in the fishponds of Baetican Carteia (Pliny *Natural History* 9.14-15, Ostia; 89-93, Carteia). In the latter case the great fish disturbing and feeding off the fisheries of human endeavour is an instance of the hierarchization of marine life that we have already met. The head was presented to Lucullus, the conquering general, just as the whale in the other incident made a worthy adversary for the *princeps* and his praetorian cohorts. In that case too we notice that it was the belief of the time that it had been a cargo of Gallic pearls capsized in the harbour that had lured the monster into shallow water: we witness the competition between the lords of the land and the great creatures of the sea for the luxury produce of the waters.[19]

The Big Fish is seen at its clearest in the tradition on the presentation of the singular specimen at the table of the great man (on fish for the king, see Wilkins 1993). No-one was more fortunate – in a sense – in this regard than Polykrates of Samos (Herodotos 3.41-3), but the idea of the special appeal of the outsize fish is one that was to have a long tradition thereafter. It is not surprising, given the size of the larger Mediterranean species, and the perishability of fish, that the point seems often to have concerned the delicate question of the choice of people with whom to share the windfall (Quintilian 6.3.90, on serving fish two days running). In this the rights of the powerful over the opportunities provided within the community by the accidents of chance is powerfully maintained, and with it the dependence of friends and assistants on the magnanimity of the great man.

To illustrate, an anecdote of Scipio Aemilianus. Scipio was at one of his country estates, at Lavernae near Formiae. A man called Pontius brought him that most special and highly admired of fish, an *acipenser qui admodum raro capitur*, 'which is quite a rare catch' (Macrobius *Saturnalia* 3.16.3; the identification of the fish remains uncertain). The occasion must have been the morning *salutatio* or greeting of clients, since, as more clients and friends came in to pay their respects, Scipio invited one after another to share it – until Pontius, appalled at his patron's splendid generosity, was impelled to whisper in his ear "the *acipenser* is a fish for a few" (*est paucorum hominum*). The joke seems to depend on the ambiguity between the rarity of the fish and the need not to share it with too many unworthy guests, or to be that Pontius was forced to admit that his splendid gift was not actually very large in comparison with the needs of a great patron like Scipio. The conceptual link between the significance of the special maritime delicacies and the tapering pyramid of the social hierarchy is clear.[20]

Turning this ideology on its head, the symbolism of sharing in fish in the New Testament and the eucharistic meaning that it very early acquired still draw strength from the accidental and unpredictable quantities in which fish turn up even in the sheltered waters of the Sea of Galilee. Although there are other explanations, I suspect that it is this that encourages the preoccupation with scale and detail witnessed in the number of fish caught by St Peter and the others in the miraculous draught – 153 fish, all specified as great.[21]

Realising the wealth of the sea: the thalassocracy of food

Over the Ionian billows, bringing it from Gades or from very holy Tarentum, some Bruttian or Campanian will bring the three-cornered pickled tunny-pieces that, with what is kept in bottles, will turn and turn about form our first course.

(Athenaeus 3.116 c)

Hexameters of epic tone of the later Hellenistic age celebrate the fisheries of the western Mediterranean. The loftiness of thought and allusion, in a mock-heroic style that itself has a very venerable pedigree, meets the banal reality of the dozens of fish-pickling sites that are known archaeologically around the coasts. The irony is real; the poor sea, the Mediterranean desert of the early tradition, had become the medium of enrichment and the purveyor of a wealth of its own. The elder Pliny expresses the same feeling in a different way; in speaking of the high-quality *garum* called *sociorum* (Pickle of the Associates), he sneers that in these decadent days even fish-pickles have acquired surnames (*cognomina*) (Pliny *Natural History* 9.66; Etienne 1970).

The development is relatively old. The foundation story of Phaselis in Pamphylia related how the territory of the city – a narrow strip between the Lycian mountains and the Gulf of Antalya – had been bought from a local shepherd called Kylabras in return for pickled fish (Philostephanos of Kyrene *De Asiae Civitatibus* fr. 1 Müller [*FHG* III 28] = Athenaeus 297 e-f, cf. Curtis 1990, 129). Part of the domain of the pastoralist had been alienated to the world of the sea in return for the latter's characteristic yield. The story is generically like several other toehold/beachhead anecdotes, such as the ox-hide story of the territory of Carthage, and presupposes a separate and distinctive maritime sphere, to which, in the Phaselis tale, the catching and processing of fish is central. In the 4th century a comic fragment has a scene in which the monster Geryon is planning to turn the whole sea into a great *bain-marie* in which to steam a fish the size of the island of Crete, a still more extreme approaching of the commonplaces of fishlore – how to cook the really special big one – to the geographical notion of the Mediterranean itself (Athenaeus 8.346f).

Now Curtis' book gives a splendid amount of detail about pickled fish, and dismisses Gallant in a rather terse footnote (Curtis 1990, 149). He never makes even a rough attempt to quantify the alimentary contribution of the fish products whose conceptual importance he so lavishly documents. I am inclined myself, on the basis of yields documented in other periods, which cannot be set out here in detail, to adopt a position which is substantially more optimistic than Gallant's, but which still agrees with it against Curtis' impression of superabundance.[22]

The states that grew rich on *salsamenta* were on this view *garum* republics in the same sense that we know some nations as banana republics: places enjoying a return from the nutritionally inexplicable tastes of more economically and politically powerful folk elsewhere. They were – on a larger scale – like the individual fishermen who could not have lived from hook-and-line fishing from their small skiffs, but who throve on sending their produce to the Athenian market. These people did indeed belong to the Mediterranean *koine*; it is in fact not too much to say that they were epiphenomena of it. Pontic fish at Athens are a yoke-fellow of the trade in Pontic cereals. The fisheries of the western Mediterranean are an adjunct of the redistribution networks that underpinned the late Carthaginian state. The late Hellenistic boom in evidence for fish is a reflection of the increasing unification of communications and interdependence which accompanied the dominion of Rome.

Curtis talks rather vaguely of the spread of technical knowledge about pickling, and, by implication, pisciculture (Curtis 1990, 178). But an explanation is needed rather than a description. It might be worth exploring further the ways in which local environmental opportunism could function in expressing hierarchies of wealth and power, and articulating those hierarchies in a Mediterranean-wide ambit.

The raw material for this social phenomenon lay in the dissonance between the squalor of the producer and the desirability of the product. This dissonance gave the circumstances of fishing and fish-processing a curious comic glamour and piquancy, which made it possible to address the organization of these economic processes with a visibility and a nuance that was not widespread in ancient economic ideology. The technicalities themselves were neither bland nor devoid of cultural meaning.

Fig. 10.1

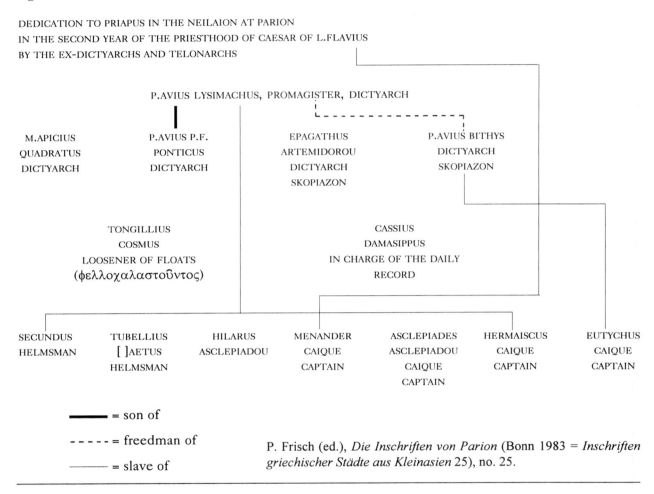

DEDICATION TO PRIAPUS IN THE NEILAION AT PARION
IN THE SECOND YEAR OF THE PRIESTHOOD OF CAESAR OF L.FLAVIUS
BY THE EX-DICTYARCHS AND TELONARCHS

P.AVIUS LYSIMACHUS, PROMAGISTER, DICTYARCH

M.APICIUS
QUADRATUS
DICTYARCH

P.AVIUS P.F.
PONTICUS
DICTYARCH

EPAGATHUS
ARTEMIDOROU
DICTYARCH
SKOPIAZON

P.AVIUS BITHYS
DICTYARCH
SKOPIAZON

TONGILLIUS
COSMUS
LOOSENER OF FLOATS
(φελλοχαλαστοῦντος)

CASSIUS
DAMASIPPUS
IN CHARGE OF THE DAILY
RECORD

SECUNDUS
HELMSMAN

TUBELLIUS
[ ]AETUS
HELMSMAN

HILARUS
ASCLEPIADOU

MENANDER
CAIQUE
CAPTAIN

ASCLEPIADES
ASCLEPIADOU
CAIQUE
CAPTAIN

HERMAISCUS
CAIQUE
CAPTAIN

EUTYCHUS
CAIQUE
CAPTAIN

———— = son of

- - - - - = freedman of

———— = slave of

P. Frisch (ed.), *Die Inschriften von Parion* (Bonn 1983 = *Inschriften griechischer Städte aus Kleinasien* 25), no. 25.

The high-falutin' description of the source in the west of pickled tunny with which this section began is part of the process. Another strange case comes from Parion on the Sea of Marmara. Here an inscription reveals an association of fisherfolk (the organisation is diagrammatically set out in fig.10.1; Frisch 1983, no. 5). Usually cited only in passing, it is actually a rich source for the atmosphere of the organisation of tunny-fishing at Parion. The association, built on a number of household-relationships, was highly stratified, the tiers of honour being apparent in the status of the holders of the offices, ranging from Roman citizen through local free man to freedman and slave. The economic and political relationship between Parion and the wider world is vividly expressed here. Even more striking is the self-consciousness of these people, in their formal collegial organization, and especially in the sonorous literary terms that they have chosen for their offices: *skopiazon*, look-out-man; 'loosener of floats'; *lembarch*, *dictyarch* and so on. They are using the mock-heroic mood (helped by the fact that the city-god of Parion, to whom they dedicate, was Priapos) with which fishing was regarded as a way of enhancing their social claims, and those of their community. What they are reaching out for, through all of these forms of self-presentation, is the analogy (seen in the fact that the boss is a *promagister*) with those most notorious and successful institutions of the regional and inter-regional economy, the associations of tax-farmers, who in turn did indeed manage the revenues of fisheries of this kind either for cities or for the Roman people.[23] Fish could indeed provide the *quaestus* (profit) which kept poverty at bay for the fishermen of Plautus' *Rudens*: Gripus' ambition is to 'fix up a farm and a house, with some slaves; I'll go for trade in big ships; I'll be a king among kings!' (Plautus *Rudens* 290-2, cf. 930-1)[24]

Conclusion: return to the paradoxes

The ecology of Mediterranean fishing involves two important facts: i) it provides a necessary, if precarious, resource in times of dearth, and ii) it offers intermittent and erratic but, in aggregate, significant possibilities of glut. Combine these two points with the physical realities of the sea and its centrality to communications, and the eating of fish becomes a potent sign of wealth and status, and the supporting of the eating of fish a remarkably complex aspect of the economic hierarchies of ancient society. The person who is the classic type of dependence on luck, the fisherman, has a special role in the economy of luck which is as based on the sea as his activities, for all its incomparably greater scale; and an economy of luck is what the ancient world knew. Given all of that, the literary, religious and other cultural ramifications of the fish as a dietary ingredient, which culminate in its near-identification with God, may surprise less than they do when seen from the viewpoint of a minimalist nutritional history.

Acknowledgements

I am grateful for the invitation to take part in the 1992 conference, for the contributions of the audience and the advice of the Editors.

Notes

1. It is a rather bizarre accident of the process of publication that Curtis' excellent work of economic and cultural history should appear in the series *Studies in Ancient Medicine*.
2. See further Wilkins (1993, 191-2), and especially note 3.
3. Compare the curse that the victim may be eaten by fish, attested at Smyrna (Watson 1991, 45).
4. Osborne (1990, 19-20) points out that sea-water is for Herakleitos both extremely pure and extremely impure (B 61 DK). For the horror of the sea, cf. Zug Tucci (1985).
5. Cf. Pliny *Natural History* 9.104, 'the devastation of our morals and luxurious excess come from no one source more than from the species of shells'; 105, 'What has the sea to do with clothing, or the waves and currents with wool?' (*quid mari cum vestibus, quid undis fluctibusque cum vellere?*).
6. Tacitus *Annals* 6.1, cf. 4.67. Cf. Columella 8.16.1 (the introduction to his section on pisciculture) 'What greater contrast is there than that between land and liquid?', *quid enim tam contrarium est, quam terrenum fluido?* He accepts that the profits of fisheries are about as alien as could be to the world of the farmer.
7. Apuleius *Apology* 39 shows that this work (dating probably from shortly after 189 BC) already referred to Cumae, Surrentum and Brundisium.
8. *Litore Baiano felici kalamo capere pisces*, *L'Année Epigraphique* 1949.80.
9. Pliny *Natural History* 9.104, 'so many different flavours of fish, valued because of the risks run by those who catch them', *tot piscium saporibus quis pretia capientium periculo fiunt*.
10. The capital cost of fishing-equipment is important: Bresc (1986, 262-3): three fine nets worth more than a tonne of fish.
11. Parain (1936, 56); Paskoff, Slim and Trousset (1991, 528-9) on the fisheries of the El Alia lagoon.
12. Gallant (1985, 24-5) similarly relies on the view that all ancient fishing with nets was carried out from the shore. The argument would have to be one *ex silentio*: but the silence is not in fact very deep (John 21: 6-8). His claim that the *madrague* or tunny-trap was unknown in antiquity is likewise unsound: Strabo *Geography* 12.3.11 on the marvellous *pelamudeia* of Sinope.
13. Pausanias 10.9.3-4; cf. *L'Antiquité Classique* 58 (1989), 32. For the social and economic significance of glut, Wylie (1993).
14. Variability of yield: Gallant (1985, 29-30); cf. Curtis (1990, 149 n. 3). The symbolism of fish-glut is therefore potent: Kleon and the tribute-tunny, Aristophanes *Knights* 312.
15. Wilkins (1993) on the social behaviour of fish as conceived by the ancients. Cf. Longo (1989).
16. Pliny *Natural History* 9.67, Asinius Celer's 8000 HS mullet and the relative prices of cooks, horses and fish.
17. Compare the symbolism, still more developed, of the preparation of *foie gras*. Here the force-feeding of the goose, well known in the lore of those who consume it, is a precursor of the greedy *truphe* with which it will itself be consumed.
18. Curtis (1990, 152-3), dishonesty of the fishmonger; Davidson (1993); Wilkins (1993).
19. This is perhaps also the background against which we should study the tales of the intelligence of dolphins.
20. The exclusive rarities served at the inaugural banquet by Metellus Pius, Macrobius 3.13.6-13, served to make the same kind of point. For the futher meaning of the distribution of different parts of the fish, Wilkins (1993).
21. John 21.11; eucharistic significance, Dölger (1922-43) vol. I.2, 120-42. The fate of the *silouros*, the 'Adonis of the river', in the new fragment of a comedy that may be Archippos' *Fishes*, is an interesting precursor: Willis (1993).

[22.] Gallant's estimates of fish-yields in Turkish waters derive from the period immediately after the relocation of the predominantly Greek fishing communities under the Treaty of Lausanne. For earlier data, see Lefebvre (1929); also Robert (1955, 272-4) on the 260 *voli* or fishing-districts of the Ottoman system. He also cites as pessimistic about the Adriatic fisheries of the 19th century the lavishly produced Faber (1883), which is clearly designed to celebrate their bounty (and which only refers to Austrian waters, as they then were, in any case).

[23.] For the association of fishermen and pickle-sellers at Ephesos, like the Parion association composed of locals and Roman citizens, and able to afford a very smart architectural design for their office from the duty on their wares, see Horsley (1989). See also Engelmann and Knibbe (1989) for the mood of the association collecting harbour-dues in western Anatolia.

[24.] At 978-9 he rejoices that fish are not common property like the sea.

Bibliography

Bayer, E. 1985 *Fischerbilder in der hellenistischer Plastik* (Bonn).

Bresc, H. 1986 *Un monde méditerranéen: économie et société en Sicile 1300-1450* (Rome).

Brewer D.J. & Friedman R.F. 1989 *Fish and fishing in ancient Egypt* (Warminster).

Curtis, R.I. 1991 *Garum and salsamenta* (Leiden: Studies in Ancient Medicine).

Davidson, J. 1993 'Fish, sex and revolution in classical Athens' *Classical Quarterly* 43, 53-66.

Dölger, F.J. 1922-43 ΙΧΘΥΣ: *das Fisch-Symbol in frühchristlicher Zeit*, 5 vols. (Münster).

Douglas, M. 1966 *Purity and Danger. An analysis of the concepts of pollution and taboo* (London).

Engelmann, H. & Knibbe, D. 1989 *Das Zollgesetz der Provinz Asia* (Bonn: Epigraphica Anatolica 14).

Estrada, M., Vives F. & Alcaraz M. 1985 'Life and the productiveness of the open sea', in Margalef (1985), 148-97.

Etienne, R. 1970 'A propos du *garum sociorum*', *Latomus* 29, 297-313.

Faber, G.L. 1883 *The fisheries of the Adriatic and the fish thereof* (London).

Frisch, P. (ed.) 1983 *Die Inschriften von Parion* (Bonn).

Gallant, T. 1985 *A Fisherman's Tale* (Ghent, Miscellanea Graeca 7).

Horsley, G.H.R. 1989 'A fishing cartel in first century Ephesus', *New Documents illustrating early Christianity* vol. 5, *Linguistic Essays* (Marrickville), 95-114.

Laubscher, H. 1982 *Fischer und Landleute* (Mainz).

Leake, Sir W. 1830 *Travels in the Morea* (London).

Lefebvre, Th. 1929 'La pêche en Turquie', *Annales de Géographie* 38, 470-9.

Longo, O. 1989 *Le forme della predazione: cacciatori e pescatori nella Grecia antica* (Naples).

Margalef, R. 1985 *The Western Mediterranean* (Oxford).

Osborne, C. 1990 'Boundaries in nature: eating with animals in the fifth century B.C.', *Bulletin of the Institute of Classical Studies* 37, 15-29.

Parain, C. 1936 *La Méditerranée: les hommes et leurs travaux* (Paris).

Paskoff R., Slim H. & Trousset P. 1991 'Le litoral de la Tunisie dans l'antiquité', *Comptes rendus de l'Académie des Inscriptions et Belles Lettres*, 515-46.

Ponsich, M. 1988 *Aceite de oliva y salazones de pescado* (Madrid).

Robert, L. 1955 'Inscriptions des Dardanelles', *Hellenica* 10 (Paris), 272-4.

Shaw, B.D. 1982-3 '"Eaters of flesh, drinkers of milk": the ancient Mediterranean ideology of the pastoral nomad', *Ancient Society* 26-31.

Watson, L. 1991 *Arae: the curse poetry of antiquity* (Leeds), 13-4, 6-31.

Wilkins J.M. 1993 'Social status and fish in Greece and Rome', in G. & V. Mars (eds) *Food, Culture and History* (London), 191-203.

Willis, W.H. 1993 'Comoedia Dukiana', *Greek, Roman and Byzantine Studies* 34, 331-53.

Wylie, J. 1993 'Crises of glut in the Faroe Islands and Dominica', *Comparative Stsdies in Society and History* 35, 353-9.

Zug Tucci, H. 1985 'Il mondo medievale dei pesci tra realtà e immaginazione' in *L'uomo di fronte al mondo animale nell'alto medioevo*, Spoleto. 31, 291-372 .

❖ 11 ❖

A PRETTY KETTLE OF FISH

Brian Sparkes

Iᴛ is now almost a decade since *La cité des images*[1] was published. The volume, mainly the work of French and Swiss scholars and with a preface by Jean-Pierre Vernant, has a subtitle 'Religion et Société en Grèce antique' and looks at the imagery of Athenian vase-painting from various anthropological angles which are not wholly unconnected with one another – such themes as the warrior, the huntsman, love, women, religious festivals and sacrifice. It was aimed at a wider audience than mere academics, and its publication in an English translation in 1989, under the title *A City of Images*[2], indicates that it was considered a successful venture.

1989 also saw the English publication of a slightly earlier book, *La cuisine du sacrifice en pays grec*,[3] originally issued in 1979 and edited by Marcel Detienne and (once again) Jean-Pierre Vernant; the translated title, *The Cuisine of Sacrifice among the Greeks*,[4] seems to me to have lost a little of its Gallic sparkle.

A contributor to both volumes was Jean-Louis Durand of the Centre National des Recherches Scientifiques in Paris. His theme in both was sacrifice, cooking and eating. In the *Cuisine* volume he wrote on 'Greek

animals: towards a topology of edible bodies'
(again not a very elegant English translation) and
also on 'Ritual as instrumentality'; in *A City of
Images* he wrote (with Alain Schnapp) on 'Sacrificial slaughter and initiatory hunt'. All the papers
drew extensively on Athenian vase-painting, and
many of the illustrated pieces were shared between the three articles. I wish to deal with one
of those illustrations (fig. 11.1) – it is the only one
concerned with fish, and I wish to argue that
Durand's interpretation is incorrect. But before
attempting that, let us stand back and look at the
way in which fish were shown on Greek vases.[5]

Fish as decoration is not my theme, important
though it is; I simply mention the well-known
6th-century BC Lakonian cup[6] with fish neatly
distributed round the inside of the bowl where
the presence of liquid would have given the
pretty conceit of a pool of fish, or those later Athenian and South Italian specialities of the late 5th
and 4th centuries, the fish-plates[7] which may
have mimicked the real fish that would have
been set upon the flat surface round the carefully
fashioned central concave dip to take the sauce.
Nor am I concerned with fish in myth or legend,
whether it is Herakles on a Caeretan *hydria* (water-
pot)[8] of *c.* 520 BC, facing up to a sea monster in the
presence of two dolphins, an octopus and an en-
trancing, if puzzled, seal, or a decade later the
Dionysos story of the transformation of the Tyrrhenian pirates into dolphins, shown in a most
unusual, not to say outlandish, Etruscan version.[9]

My theme is rather scenes of fish in narrative
contexts that belong to the real world – fishing,
transporting, selling, chopping, etc.[10] As far as I

Fig. 11.1

Fig. 11.2

know, these scenes were confined to Attic black-figure and red-figure and to South Italian red-figure vase-painting, and they were most popular in the late 6th century and the earlier decades of the 5th in Athens. There are not many that have survived, in whole or part. The subjects never constituted a major theme nor did they attract top-line artists, except that on occasion the paintings were poor work by artists who did better with other, more exalted themes. There is no real iconographical development, or at least only a glimmer of it.

Let us quickly run through the main examples in vase-painting. Scenes of actual fishing are rare. Best

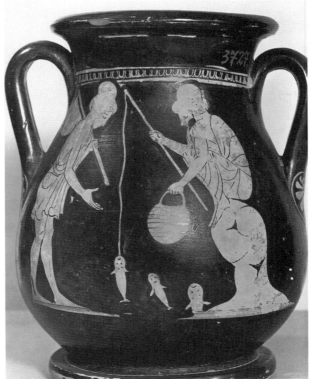

Fig. 11.3

known, and perhaps best loved, certainly most frequently reproduced, is the cup interior attributed to the Ambrosios Painter,[11] with a naked fisher boy perched on a convenient rock above a well-stocked pool (fig. 11.2). He dangles his line and hook to good effect, holds a creel and has lodged his fish-cage in the water below the rock. A generation later the Pan Painter decorated a *pelike*[12] (jug) with fisher folk in sheepskin hats and dressed in workmen's attire (fig. 11.3). The bearded fisherman, perched on another convenient rock and armed with another line and creel, is very much in luck with happy fish just aching to be caught; his young companion, with a pole and basket on his shoulder, waits for the second basket to be filled. It is not until nearly a century later that we meet the theme again, and this time it has been transported to the unlikely world of the satyr.[13] It makes one wonder whether we shall some day find the evidence for the continuity of the image in the intervening years.

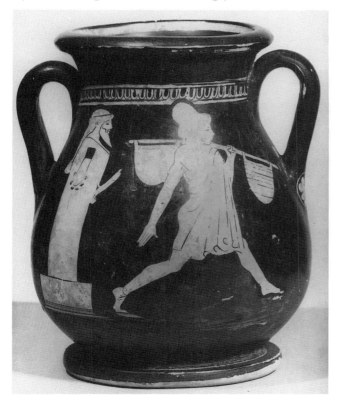

Fig. 11.4

Fig. 11.5

Fig. 11.6

On the back of the Pan Painter's *pelike* (fig. 11.4)[14] another youth, maybe thought to be the same as the young boy on the obverse, runs past a herm on his way to town with both baskets on a pole on his shoulder, doubtless in a hurry to get his fish to market while still fresh. The theme again is not common, but it is found earlier, in the late 6th century, that is, in the generation of the Ambrosios Painter, but this time on a black-figure *amphora* (wine-jar) of type B (fig. 11.5).[15] On one side a bearded man in a white hat carries two large tunny fish on a pole across his shoulder – a much more impressive catch than the ones we have seen earlier and than the catch on the other side of the same *amphora* (fig. 11.6). Two men, hatted again, busy themselves with fish: the one on the left has baskets of small fish hanging from the pole on his shoulder; the one kneeling on the right seems to be laying out

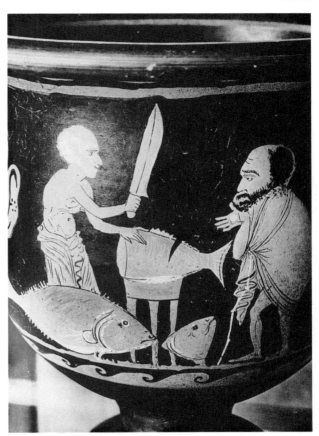

Fig. 11.7

Fig. 11.8

Fig. 11.9

even smaller fish on the ground. One must suppose that they have brought their catch to the market and are arranging the sprats for sale. Nearby a dog is on the scrounge.

Fish such as these small fry could be caught from the rocks, taken and sold in the nearby market, cooked and scoffed whole; big fish such as the tunny on the other side of the *amphora* (fig. 11.5) were much less resigned to being caught, had to be killed whilst struggling in the water and then had to be chopped into steaks before being sold, preserved, or cooked.

South Italian vase-painters furnish two scenes on the subject of the chopping up of fish. One is well known – the early 4th century Sicilian bell-*krater* (mixing-bowl) from the Lipari Islands in the Museo Mandralisca at Cefalù (fig.11.7).[16] An old customer, complete with coin in the palm of his hand, has come to purchase a tunny steak from a fishmonger. One fish is already in the process of being cut up, another lies on the ground, in line for similar treatment. The fishmonger brandishes a very large knife, perhaps known to the Greeks as a *kopis* (Pollux 10.104) as he stands before a three-legged block, doubtless of wood; again, if Greek names are to be given, it is most likely an *epixenon*.[17] The element of caricature in the scene, with large heads and spindly legs, has suggested connections with local Sicilian or South Italian farce.

Not very far removed in time from the Cefalù piece is another bell-*krater*, this time painted in an Apulian workshop (fig. 11.8).[18] It presents a similar scene with a fish, perhaps again intended for a tunny, on another three-legged block, certainly of wood as the grain has been picked out by the painter. This time however there is no doddery old customer, but a woman stands at the right pouring water over the fish, no doubt to rinse and clean it, while she steadies the tail of the fish with her left hand. Over on the left a naked satyr, complete with tail and pointed ears, touches the back fin of the tunny (if indeed that is what it is) to keep it upright, and holds a cleaver in his right hand. The satyr's tail and ears have transported us once again into a fantasy world, but the impedimenta are very much those of everyday life.

If we return to Athens and go back in time, we can point to a similar scene in Athenian red-figure. A *pelike* by the Syleus Painter (fig. 11.9)[19] shows a bald-headed man with a fish (it is suggested that it is intended for a mullet), and he is holding it by the tail. He stands at the now familiar three-legged block and wields a large knife by his right side. A young boy at the right looks as though he is disclaiming expertise in the matter; I would suggest he is learning the trade – I cannot see that this figure is a customer or even a slave sent to buy fish for his master. This is a unique scene in Athenian red-figure, but there is a parallel scene on another *pelike*[20] by the same painter which shows the chopping of meat – bald-headed man, three-legged block, cleaver, but this time the boy has a job to do, as he is helping the butcher to chop up the animal by spreading the carcass for ease of access. The date of these two *pelikai* is somewhere near 470 BC, much the same time as the Pan Painter was painting his fisher folk. It has been pointed out that the block used by the classical butchers and fishmongers can still be seen today in Greece and Sicily.[21]

Let us now go back earlier still, to the late 6th century, the period of the Ambrosios Painter's red-figure angler (fig. 11.2) and the black-figure *amphora* with tunny and small fry (figs 11.5 and 6). This brings us to the jug that Durand illustrated in the papers to which I referred at the beginning (fig. 11.1).[22] The jug is an *olpe* with decorated mouth; it is now in Berlin and has been placed in the Leagros Group. Two men tackle a tunny, while dogs wait in anticipation.

Let me quote a sentence from the English translation of Durand's paper in *A City of Images* (1989, 24):

> On a small vase (*olpe*) in Berlin…, one can see an unusual sacrifice victim, a tuna [now that word raises a different image in my English mind, but no matter], presented by an assistant on the right in the classic position for sacrificial killing. There is a table (*trapeza*) for the final blow, an altar to honor the gods, and a large receptacle to gather the blood destined for the gods alone, which the knife (*machaira*) will cause to flow.

Fish were rarely sacrificed, but of those that were, the tunny (or tuna, if you prefer) was the most important, as like all good sacrificial victims it bleeds.[23] But I am loath to accept this scene as a scene of sacrifice. Let us take some of Durand's points (he writes at greater length on the scene in the *Cuisine* book, 1989, 127-8 [178-9 in the French edition, 1979]). He says that the table, i.e. the structure with thin top and even thinner legs, is used for chopping. I suggest that he has mistaken the relationship of the figures to the setting, and the modern line drawing that illustrated the earlier paper was of little assistance. Such a table was surely not strong enough to receive the initial blow, though we do find sturdier tables used for the jointing of meat. Durand also speaks of the classic position for sacrificial killing. I would ask, if an assistant is going to hold a slippery fish for you to chop, how else is he to hold it? He would surely hesitate to place his hand on the top of the fish. Durand also mentions an altar, but the round upright block does not resemble any known shape of altar. Surely Durand's altar is the chopping block itself, and the man on the left is going to bring the cleaver down on the head of the fish which is held above the block. It is a variant or precursor of the three-legged block we saw before. In his *Cuisine* paper, Durand also adds to his *bomos*/altar and *trapeza*/table, the *sphageion*, what he calls 'le vase de la saignée' or what is translated as 'the blood vase', i.e. the bowl beneath the chopping block. I suggest that the receptacle is to receive the unwanted parts of the fish, and one notes the predatory dogs who know when they are on to a good thing. The bowl is one of the commonest household objects made in the Athenian pottery shops;[24] it is frequently to be seen in domestic scenes, never in scenes of sacrifice.

In line with his sacrificial interpretation, Durand also calls the men 'officiants' and speaks of their 'crowns', 'les couronnes des officiants'. Let us take two contemporary parallels. A black-figure *oinochoe*[25] (jug) of the late 6th century with a scene of the chopping of meat makes it plain that the table is at the back and is used as a surface on which to place the strips of cut meat, and also that a stand similar to the one we have just seen is the chopping block; there is also the large vessel below – this is certainly no sacrificial scene. And the well-known shoemaker *pelike* in Oxford[26] also sports a vessel below the table – surely not for catching the blood from the poor child's foot, more likely for softening the shoe leather the cobbler is soon to need. The shoemaker wears a crown or garland, but I doubt that this can signify any sacrificial context or any officiant's role for him. Such greenery was a popular space-filling decoration in late black-figure.

Both the eel and the tunny are cited in the context of sacrifice in classical literature (Athenaeus 7.297d, 303b), and there is no doubt that ritual killing of fish was on occasion carried out. However, I do not believe that the Berlin *olpe* can be brought into evidence as an image of such an act, and I would not wish it to be quoted as an agreed interpretation.[27] I prefer to understand the scene in the context of the other images I have shown, to disengage it from the world of altars, sacrifice and ritual slaughter, and place it in the more secular world of athletes at the gymnasium, musicians teaching pupils, carpenters, shoemakers and fishermen that in the late 6th century began to be chosen as themes by painters or their clients, and were considered as fit images for the decoration of pottery.

Acknowledgements

I wish to thank the museums and private collectors who have given me permission to illustrate this article with vases in their care and possession.

Postscript

A previously unpublished illustration has now appeared in *A Passion for Antiquities: Ancient Art from the Collection of Barbara and Lawrence Fleischman* (Malibu: the J. Paul Getty Museum in association with the Cleveland Museum of Art, 1994), cat. no. 38, pp. 92-4. The scenes are on either side of an Athenian black-figured cup (type C) of the late 6th century, in the Fleischman collection (New York). On one side there is a man carrying a tunny, on the other a man with a large knife cutting up a tunny at a tall block; on a long table are set fish steaks, and a fish head is on the floor.

Notes

1. Published by Fernard Nathan – L.E.P. (Lausanne and Paris, 1984).
2. Published by Princeton Univ. Press (1989), trans. by Deborah Lyons.
3. Published by Editions Gallimard (Paris, 1979).
4. Published by Chicago Univ. Press (1989), trans. by Paula Wissing.
5. For fish on Greek vases, see Davies (1978) and more generally Delorme and Roux (1987).
6. Taranto I.G. 4805, from Taranto: Stibbe (1972), no. 332.
7. For recent work on fish-plates, see McPhee and Trendall (1987); McPhee and Trendall (1990); Kunisch (1989); for an example, see the frontispiece to this volume, which is accompanied by a discussion of the genre.
8. Hirschmann Collection: Bloesch (1982, no. 10); Boardman (1987); Sparkes (1991a, colour pl.4B (reversed)).
9. Toledo Museum of Art 82.134: Boulter and Luckner (1984, pl. 90 (973)); Spivey (1987, 43, no. 3, attributed to the Painter of Vatican 238 = Kaineus Painter); Spivey and Stoddard (1991, 137 and fig. 91).
10. On fish and fishing, see Gow (1913, 215-17); Thompson (1947); Gallant (1985).

11. Boston Museum of Fine Arts 01.8024: Beazley (1963, 173, 9); Carpenter (1989, 184); Hurwit (1991, frontispiece and 50, fig. 19).

12. Vienna Kunsthistorisches Museum inv. 3727: Beazley (1963, 555, 88); Carpenter (1989, 258).

13. London, British Museum E 108: Beazley (1963, 1513, 43, attributed to the Jena Workshop); Carpenter (1989, 384); Brommer (1959, 59, fig. 58).

14. See note 12. For Athenian red-figure vases showing youths running to market with baskets (most likely full of fish), see a fragmentary plate, Athens, Acropolis 3: Beazley (1963, 109, 30, signed by Kachrylion as potter); a cup in Gela: Beazley (1963, 105, 7, attributed to the Group of Acropolis 96); a cup in Oxford, Ashmolean Museum 1919.26: Beazley (1963, 110, 6, attributed to the Hermaios Painter); a cup in Florence, Rome and Heidelberg: Beazley (1963, 134, top, said to recall the Group of London E 33). The Athenian red-figure cup with a youth with baskets (Copenhagen, Thorvaldsen Museum 105: Beazley (1963, 329, 131, attributed to Onesimos); Carpenter (1989, 217)) has been connected with fish but is likely to be an athlete in a sand pit (see Scholl 1986). Nor is the cup Geneva I 529 (Beazley (1963, 154, 7, attributed to the Painter of Berlin 2268) likely to be satyrs with fish in baskets; rather they are wineskins. I have not seen the Athenian red-figure cup Rome Villa Giulia 3575: Beazley (1963, 464, 72, attributed to Makron); there is a detail in Kunisch (1989, 68, fig. 12).

15. Berlin (E) inv. 4860, from Greece: Beazley (1971, 150, 4, addendum to Beazley 1956, 339, 4 and 694), attributed to the Hypobibazon Class; Carpenter (1989, 92). A strange Athenian red-figure *lekythos* (oil-flask) has a woman selling eels (?), Harvard Fogg Museum 2236: Chase and Pease (1942, pl. XVII (355) 5) and Beazley (1942, 99).

16. Cefalù, Museo Mandralisca 2, from Lipari: Trendall (1967a, 208, 54, attributed to the Tunny Seller Painter); Trendall (1967b, 83, 191); Chamay (1976, 284, fig. 4); Trendall (1983, 103, 89 (54)).

17. See Fraenkel (1950, 593 on v. 1277); Fraenkel (1960, 412-3); Sparkes (1975, 132).

18. Once private collection, Munich: Bielefeld (1966); Trendall (1967a, 207, n. 1); Trendall (1967b, 84); Chamay (1976, 285, fig. 5). I have not seen two Apulian vases which are said to have a fishing scene, Trendall (1978, 406, no. 57) and (1982, 951, no. 314).

19. Private collection: Chamay (1976, 282, fig. 2).

20. Erlangen, University inv. I. 486: Beazley (1963, 250, 21 and 1639); Chamay (1976, 286, fig. 7).

21. Chamay (1976, 286, fig. 6).

22. Berlin, Staatliche Museen, Charlottenburg 1915, from Vulci: Beazley (1956, 377, 247 and 382, attributed to the Leagros Group); Beazley (1971, 163); Carpenter (1989, 100); Chamay (1976, 283, fig. 3); Mommsen (1991, pl. 36). Compare a white-ground *lekythos* from Thasos, Thasos Museum: Beazley (1971, 262, middle).

23. See Burkert (1983, 204-12).

24. *Lekane*: Sparkes and Talcott (1970, 34); Sparkes (1991b, 73, 83, 90).

25. Boston Museum of Fine Arts 99.527: Beazley (1956, 430, 25, attributed to the Class of Vatican G 47); Beazley (1971, 184); Carpenter (1989, 111).

26. Oxford Ashmolean Museum G 247 (V. 563): Beazley (1956, 396, 21 and 696, attributed the Eucharides Painter); Beazley (1971, 173); Carpenter (1989, 104).

27. E.g. in Burkert (1983, 209, n. 21, 'a tuna sacrifice').

Bibliography

Beazley, J.D. 1942 Review of Chase and Pease (1942) *Journal of Hellenic Studies* 62, 99.

Beazley, J.D. 1956 *Attic Black-figure Vase-Painters* (Oxford).

Beazley, J.D. 1963 *Attic Red-figure Vase-Painters* 2nd ed. (Oxford).

Beazley, J.D. 1971 *Paralipomena, Additions to Attic Black-figure Vase-Painters and to Attic Red-figure Vase-Painters* (Oxford).

Bielefeld, E. 1966 'Ein unteritalische Vasenbild', *Pantheon* 24, 252-5.

Bloesch, H. (ed.) 1982 *Greek Vases from the Hirschmann Collection* (Zurich).

Boardman, J. 1987 'Very like a whale - classical sea monsters', in Farkas, Harper & Harrison (1987) 73-84.

Boulter, C.G. & Luckner, K.T. 1984 *Corpus Vasorum Antiquorum*, United States of America, Fasc. 20, The Toledo Museum of Art, Fasc. 2 (Toledo).

Brommer, F. 1959 *Satyrspiele* (*Bilder griechischer Vasen*) 2nd ed. (Berlin).

Buitron-Oliver, D. (ed.) 1991 *New Perspectives in Early Greek Art* (Washington).

Burkert, W. 1983 *Homo Necans, the Anthropology of Ancient Greek Sacrificial Ritual and Myth* (California).

Carpenter, T.H. 1989 *Beazley Addenda: Additional References to ABV, ARV² and Paralipomena* 2nd ed. (Oxford).

Chamay, J. 1976 'Une scène de la vie quotidienne sur une péliké du peintre de Sylée', *Genava* 24, 281-90.

Chase, G.H. & Pease, M.Z. 1942 *Corpus Vasorum Antiquorum*, United States of America, Fasc. 8, Fogg Museum and Gallatin Collections (Cambridge, Mass.).

Childs, W.A.P. (ed.) 1978 *Athens comes of Age: from Solon to Salamis* (Princeton).

Davies, M.I. 1978 'Sailing, rowing, and sporting in one's cups on the wine-dark sea', in Childs (1978) 72-95.

Delorme, J. & Roux, Ch. 1987 *Guide illustré de la faune aquatique dans l'art grec* (Juan-les-Pins).

Farkas, A.E., Harper, P.O. & Harrison, E.B. (eds) 1987 *Monsters and Demons in the Ancient and Medieval Worlds: Papers in honor of Edith Porada* (Mainz).

Fraenkel, E. 1950 *Aeschylus: Agamemnon* (Oxford).

Fraenkel, E. 1960 *Elementi Plautini in Plauto* (Florence).

Gallant, T.W. 1985 *A Fisherman's Tale* (Ghent, Miscellanea Graeca 7).

Gow, A.S.F. 1913 'The cup in the first idyll of Theocritus', *Journal of Hellenic Studies* 33, 207-22.

Hurwit, J.M. 1991 'The representation of nature in early Greek art', in Buitron-Oliver (1991) 33-62.

Kunisch, N. 1989 *Griechische Fischteller: Natur und Bild* (Berlin).

McPhee, I. & Trendall, A.D. 1987 *Greek Red-figured Fish-plates. Antike Kunst* Beiheft 14 (Basel).

McPhee, I. & Trendall, A.D. 1990 'Addenda to Greek Red-figured Fish-plates', *Antike Kunst* 33, 31-51.

Mommsen, H. 1991 *Corpus Vasorum Antiquorum*, Deutschland, Band 61, Berlin Antikenmuseum, Band 7 (Munich).

Scholl, R. 1986 'Sklaverei in der Arbeitswelt des Antike im Lichte der verschiedenen Quellenkategorien', *Gymnasium* 93, 476-96.

Sparkes, B.A. 1975 'Illustrating Aristophanes', *Journal of Hellenic Studies* 95, 122-35.

Sparkes, B.A. 1991a *Greek Art. Greece and Rome New Surveys in the Classics* no. 22 (Oxford).

Sparkes, B.A. 1991b *Greek Pottery: an introduction* (Manchester).

Sparkes, B.A. & Talcott, L. 1970 *Black and Plain Pottery of the 6th, 5th and 4th centuries BC.* The Athenian Agora XII (American School of Classical Studies, Athens).

Spivey, N.J. 1987 *The Micali Painter and his Followers* (Oxford).

Spivey, N.J. & Stoddard, S. 1991 *Etruscan Italy: an Archaeological History* (Batsford).

Stibbe, C.M. 1972 *Lakonische Vasenmaler des sechsten Jahrhunderts v. Chr* (Amsterdam).

Thompson, D'Arcy W. 1947 *A Glossary of Greek Fishes* (St Andrews University Publications no. 45) (Oxford).

Trendall, A.D. 1967a *The Red-figured Vases of Lucania, Campania and Sicily* (Oxford).

Trendall, A.D. 1967b *Phlyax Vases* 2nd ed. *Bulletin of the Institute of Classical Studies*, Supplement 19.

Trendall, A.D. 1978 *The Red-figured Vases of Apulia* I (Oxford).

Trendall, A.D. 1982 *The Red-figured Vases of Apulia* II (Oxford).

Trendall, A.D. 1983 *The Red-figured Vases of Lucania, Campania and Sicily*, Third Supplement (Consolidated). *Bulletin of the Institute of Classical Studies*, Supplement 41.

❖ 12 ❖

FISH FROM THE BLACK SEA
CLASSICAL BYZANTIUM AND THE GREEKNESS OF TRADE

David Braund

THIS chapter will argue that classical Byzantium is accorded undue prominence in our ancient evidence on the export of food from the Black Sea, primarily on account of its location and its Greekness. If this argument is accepted, a more nuanced assessment is required of exports from the Black Sea into the Aegean world, together with a reassessment of the role of Byzantium as a centre of production. Here it is argued that much of the fish that is said to have come into the Aegean world from Byzantium probably originated elsewhere around the Black Sea, and came not from but via Byzantium. Although fishing was no doubt important at Byzantium, it was rather less important than our sources might suggest and less of an 'industry' than some modern scholarship has argued.[1]

Polybios on the Black Sea trade

A single text dominates any consideration of Black Sea trade in general, and the role of Byzantium in particular, namely Polybios' explanation of the origins of the war fought by the Rhodians and the Byzantines at the end of the 3rd century BC:

> At the same time the Rhodians went to war with the Byzantines for the following reasons. With regard to the sea, the Byzantines inhabit a site that is the most favourable in our whole world both for security and for prosperity (*eudaimonia*). But with regard to the land, it is the most disadvantageous of all in both respects. For with regard to the sea they have so dominant a position at the mouth of the Black Sea that no merchant can sail either in or out without their assent. And whereas the Black Sea has much that is fine for the lives of other men, the Byzantines are lords of all these things. For as regards the necessities of life (*pros men gar tas anangkaias tou biou khreias*), both cattle and the multitude of people brought into slavery, the places on the Black Sea provide us with what is most abundant and what is most useful, as is generally agreed; while as regards their superfluities (*pros de periousian*[2]) they supply us with honey, wax and salted fish in abundance. They receive from the goods in surplus (*ton...peritteuonton*) in the places around us, olive-oil and wine of every type. And they exchange grain, sometimes giving it, when circumstance permits, and sometimes taking it...
>
> ...Accordingly, being, as it were, the common benefactors of all (viz. in ensuring Greek passage in the face of barbarian pressure), the Byzantines should meet not only with gratitude but also with joint assistance from the Greeks against the perils of the barbarians...[a long excursus on the Black Sea follows]...
>
> ...(45.9ff.) Even so, enduring warfare with the Thracians, as was their custom, they kept their ancient faith with the Greeks...(but the arrival of Gauls made the barbarians too strong; Byzantine appeals to the Greeks for help found scant response; so, to raise funds...)...[the Byzantines] were compelled to levy tolls on those sailing into the Black Sea. When all suffered great loss of profit and inconvenience through the Byzantine taxation on exports from [sic] the Black Sea, they took it badly. All the merchants appealed to the Rhodians as being the champions of maritime affairs. Thus began the war...
>
> (Polybios 4.37.8-47.2, excerpted)

The main thrust of Polybios' account is that the Byzantines deserved better from their fellow Greeks, so that the Rhodians are at best unsympathetic in going to war with them. The Greeks of Byzantium had made possible trade with the Black Sea region by warding off barbarians who, Polybios imagines, threatened to curtail the maritime link between the Black Sea and the Aegean.[3] When, through no fault of their own, the Byzantines could no longer hold back the growing barbarian threat without help from their fellow Greeks and that help was refused, the Byzantines turned to the taxation of Black Sea trade as a desperate last resort. However much one might question the justice of Polybios' judgment, his account is readily intelligible. And at the centre of that account stands trade between the Black Sea region and the Aegean world.

As usual, trade in food is not distinguished from trade in other goods: even individual cargoes were regularly composed of a plethora of different items. However, many of the goods which Polybios specifies are food-items: there was no 'food-trade', but trade in food was a large proportion of total trade, in the Black Sea region as elsewhere. Moreover, food was traded not only out of the Black Sea, as often imagined, but also into it. Even wheat was traded into the Black Sea as well as out of it, and Polybios' formulation suggests that such imports were no great rarity.[4]

Of course, Polybios does not set out to give a detailed or rounded account of Byzantium's economy, still less of the economy of the Black Sea region at large. His concern is with Byzantium's control of the sea-passage between the Black Sea and Aegean, for that was the locus of the conflict which he seeks to explain. He discusses the city's agriculture only to develop further his picture of a brave Greek community staving off the ravening barbarian. He compares the sufferings of the Byzantines to those of Tantalus, for as they see their crops ripening the Byzantines cannot gather and consume them because their crops are snatched away by the barbarians. However selective his concerns and presentation, Polybios makes it clear enough that Byzantium was a key point for the passage of goods between the worlds of the Black Sea and Aegean, in the Hellenistic period as in more recent centuries. It is crisis (at least on Polybios' account) that leads Byzantium to exploit that position through new taxation.

It is another crisis at Byzantium that leads the city to take desperate measures with regard to its economy, according to a very corrupt passage in pseudo-Aristotle *Oeconomica*:

> And the Byzantines, in need of money, sold off the dedicated lands owned by the state…[unsafe text: verb omitted – they sold?] the public lands which were around the gymnasium or the *agora* or the harbour, and the market-sites (*topous agoraious*) at which anyone sold anything, and the fishing of the sea (*kai tes thalattes ten halieian*), and the sale of salt and [verb and noun missing?] of professional wonder-workers and prophets and drug-sellers and other such of that sort. They levied a third of their profits in tax. And they sold the exchange of coins to one bank: no-one could buy from or sell to another, on pain of confiscation.
>
> Whereas they had a law under which a man was not a citizen unless his parents were both citizens, they voted, in their need for money, that the son of one citizen was a citizen once he had put down thirty *minae*.
>
> Suffering food-shortage and at a loss for money, they pulled in shipping from the Black Sea. In due course, in the face of merchants' protests, they exacted a 10% tax on them. And they imposed a 10% tax on all purchases, in addition to their price.
>
> (pseudo-Aristotle *Oeconomica* 1346b13-34)

The passage has been taken to support a characterization of Byzantine fishing in terms of a state-run fishing-industry: indeed, it constitutes the only potential evidence. However, given the corruption of the text, it is hardly evidence at all: it can hardly support so large a claim unaided.[5] All that is clear is that the state did something unusual with regard to a wide range of activities at Byzantium: not only fishing (or fish-selling?), but much else besides, apparently including wonder-workers, prophets and drug-sellers. It was crisis that led Byzantium not only to impose taxes, but even to plunder shipping. Quite apart from textual uncertainties, our passage can hardly be used to characterize fishing at Byzantium under normal circumstances. Rather, it presents a series of state measures which are evidently designed to meet a particular crisis. There is no reason to suppose that these measures, however we might imagine them, were anything other than temporary.

The dubious evidence of pseudo-Aristotle

Byzantine fish: an ideological distortion

However, there can be no doubt that Byzantium was renowned for its fish in antiquity. And, to an extent, that renown was deserved: fish were certainly caught at Byzantium, including fish of high quality and, periodically at least, good fish in quantity too.[6] Yet Byzantium's reputation requires critical analysis, nevertheless, for, as will be argued, it is an expression of a neglect, even contempt, that is profoundly ideological, in both political and ethnic terms.

Classical writers on Byzantium (notably Aristotle, Theopompos and Dio Chrysostom) present fishing at Byzantium as a principal feature of a matrix which also includes democracy and luxury. The three features are seen to have a mutually causal relationship. The existence of democracy at Byzantium is explained by the great numbers and prominence of fishermen there (and, it should be noted, traders). According to Theopompos, democracy generated excessive luxury (*truphe*) at Byzantium, while fishing too could be presented as a source of luxurious behaviour in that (by contrast with agriculture) it entailed gain without work (!). The apogee of that line of thought is Dio Chrysostom's claim that fish simply throw themselves on the shore at Byzantium. In that way, fishermen and fishing at Byzantium are key figures in an image of Byzantium as a democracy, living in luxury. Such political ramifications counsel caution in the interpretation of accounts of fishing at Byzantium, particularly when they are composed by authors who are particularly concerned to offer political and moral judgments.[7]

Fish are commonly said to have come from Byzantium, of course, but such statements can hardly be taken at face value. Slaves, for example, could be said to originate from a certain place, when they were simply bought at that place: they could even be named after their place of purchase.[8] One wonders, therefore, whether fish said to come from Byzantium or called Byzantine were caught and/or salted in the city, either always or even usually. The evidence of Athenaeus suggests that not all Byzantine fish originated in Byzantium. A computer search of his work and the wide range of Greek sources quoted therein reveals some twenty distinct allusions to fish (not least salted fish) from Byzantium. By remarkable contrast, there is nothing either in Athenaeus himself or in his many and various quotations about fish from any other specific point in the Black

Sea, save for a single allusion to mullet of Sinope.[9] Yet we know enough about fishing, salting and trading in the Black Sea region to be sure that fish from various locations there came into the Aegean. As we have seen, Polybios explicitly states as much: he mentions salted fish brought from "Pontic places" past Byzantium into the Aegean. This is not Byzantine production.[10]

We may wonder whether, for all his single-mindedness in explaining Rhodes' war with Byzantium, Polybios' lack of interest in the precise point of origin of goods from the Black Sea may also be typical of Greek writers in general. So much seems to have been the case with Athenaeus and his various sources. Fish were caught, salted and traded all over the Black Sea region, notably at Olbia, Chersonesos and Sinope, but our Greek sources seldom troubled to mention, let alone describe, those various activities in distant parts. Rare references to this activity in literary sources are confirmed and extended by the results of archaeology.[11] At Chersonesos, for example, in the western Crimea, both salt and fish were available in quantity: to date, some 100 fish-salting cisterns have been identified there from antiquity, with a total capacity of some 2000 m^3. Although these cisterns may not all have been in synchronous use, they constitute, nevertheless, a striking indication of the potential scale of fish-processing in the western Crimea.[12] It seems that, beyond Byzantium, our sources' familiar lack of concern with economic matters is compounded by the distance, obscurity and otherness of the Black Sea region in general, an obscurity which often, as in Polybios, encouraged no more than a geographical disquisition in outline.

It seems that Greek writers tended to describe the produce of a multiplicity of half-known locations around the Black Sea as 'Byzantine'. After all, fish were indeed caught at Byzantium and some may well have been traded-on there. In any event, they had all been shipped through Byzantine waters: to that extent, at least, they were indeed 'fish from Byzantium' for consumers in the Mediterranean. Only the most specialized discussion needed to enquire further. Euthydemos' *On Salted Fish* will have presented such knowledge as may have been available: there were many different fish and many different salts in the Black Sea as elsewhere, so that, for example, Olbian salt seems to have been valued in the Crimea for qualities not available in the salt gained more locally there.[13] But, on the whole, for less specialized writers such details were of scant concern.

Greeks versus Barbarians

Greek neglect of detail and satisfaction with 'Byzantine' for the goods of the Black Sea region may be explained not simply by ignorance but also by ethnic identity. In the passage quoted, for example, Polybios conceives barbarians as inimical to trade and Byzantium as a bulwark of Hellas, protecting trade. From a Greek perspective, trade itself was a Greek affair, albeit not to the exclusion of Phoenicians and some others. Dio Chrysostom, for example, claims that the Skythians needed a Greek presence in order to trade at Olbia, for 'the Skythians themselves had neither the ambition nor the knowledge to equip a trading-centre (*emporion*) of their own after the Greek manner'.[14] Through a sympathetic speaker, he proceeds to characterize the Greek traders who come to Olbia as really barbarous in that they do not engage in trade of a respectable type: indeed, it is 'improper' trade that renders Greek traders akin to barbarians. In similar vein, Oppian even characterizes barbarian fishing as particularly cruel and uncivilized.[15]

The Black Sea region was readily imagined as a barbarian world, relieved only by Greek settlements around its coast. Xenophon regarded the cities of the southern coast of the Black Sea as Greek, but, as Nussbaum puts it, 'only as oases in the barbarian desert'.[16] Xenophon could state, albeit for rhetorical effect, that Byzantium was the first Greek city which the Ten Thousand reached, having journeyed all along the south coast of the Black Sea west of Trapezous. Beyond Byzantium, the Thracian Chersonese was for him already part of Hellas.[17] Earlier, at Sinope, the Ten Thousand had been not in Hellas but near it: to the west of Sinope they were on the threshold of Hellas.[18] This was indeed the threshold between Greece and Barbary: Xenophon muses that to found a city in the Black Sea region would be to 'add territory and might to Hellas'.[19]

Xenophon's conception suggests that in describing fish from the Black Sea region simply as 'Byzantine' or 'from Byzantium', Greek writers were using the name of the first city in Hellas through and past which all fish from the Black Sea must come. After all, insofar as trade was a Greek affair, a Greek origin was perhaps preferable in itself. Moreover, fish from Byzantium were in a sense Greek fish. At the same time, no doubt, even at the level of the fishmonger there were good market reasons for designating fish as 'from Byzantium': the city was a familiar name and, in circular fashion, renowned for its fish. We can only speculate as to whether their supposed Greekness made Byzantine fish more marketable.

Of course, there is no doubt that fish were caught at Byzantium, though it remains unclear whether fish were salted there in any quantity. At times, fish were especially abundant there. And the *pelamys* (one of the tuna family), in particular, reached a good size as its journeying brought it to Byzantium.[20] Byzantine fishing was a hard reality. However, as we have seen, that is only part of the story. Realities aside, Byzantine fishing was not only the subject of political theorizing of a broadly negative kind, but also a substitute for enquiry beyond the bounds of Hellas. The export of fish from the Black Sea region is presented in our sources under the baleful influence of political and ethnocentric ideologies which grossly simplify and which locate the activity and produce of a whole region in one Greek city at the beginning of Hellas.

Notes

1. On this 'industry', see Dumont (1976/77), with the lengthy critique of Gallant (1985, esp. 37-8) on the notion of the 'professional' fisherman. On Gallant's statistical calculations, see Purcell in this volume.

2. *Periousia* is here rendered as 'superfluities', while Paton's Loeb translation has 'luxuries', a rather different meaning. The word seems to have no completely satisfactory counterpart in English: *LSJ* explain, 'that which is over and above necessary expenses, surplus, abundance, plenty'. Polybios is evidently contrasting necessities and non-necessities, which could (but need not) amount to luxuries. In any event, as his categories might suggest, definitions of 'necessity' and 'luxury' tend to be subjective and variable.

3. On this route, see now Malkin and Shmueli (1988), whose difficulties might be solved by a more critical approach to ancient traditions of foundation-dates: viz. can we be so sure that Chalkedon was founded before Byzantium? Indeed, what is meant by 'foundation'?

4. The Black Sea region was in no way immune from grain-shortage: see the neglected Stefan (1974). On grain-shortage in antiquity, see Garnsey (1988). For the Black Sea economy, see now Kadeyev and Sorochan (1989).

5. Dumont (1976/77) confidently dates this crisis to the middle of the 5th century BC, for reasons which are not apparent.

6. E.g. Pliny *Natural History* 9.49-53.

7. Aristotle *Politics* 1291b22-3; Athenaeus 526e (Theopompos); Dio Chrysostom 33.24-5, 35.25; cf. Athenaeus 116-17 (pseudo-Hesiod), 303e (Archestratus). On fishing as akin to piracy, see Braund (1993).

8. On slave-origins and the Black Sea trade, see Braund & Tsetskhladze (1989) and Braund (1994).

9. Athenaeus 307b.

10. Dumont (1976/77, 96-7) seems to claim it as such. A fine survey of fish-salting in the Black Sea is provided by Curtis (1991, 118-29).

11. Dumont himself acknowledges the point (1976/77, 109).

12. Kadeyev (1970, 12). On salting and salt-trade in this area, see also Braund (1991).

13. Dio Chrysostom 36.3; cf. Herodotos 4.53. Euthydemos of Athens is quoted by Athenaeus, for example at 307b.

14. Dio Chrysostom 36.5.

15. Dio Chrysostom 36.25; Oppian, *Halieutica* 4.531-61; cf. 5.519-23, on dolphins, including Byzantines in his strictures.

16. Nussbaum (1967, 149 n.4). Despite its title, Hirsch (1985), has little to say about the evidence of the *Anabasis*.

17. Xenophon *Anabasis* 7.1.29 (Byzantium); 5.6.25 (Chersonese: note that some of the Ten Thousand had been recruited there, *Anabasis* 1.1.9).

18. *Anabasis* 6.1.17; 6.5.23.

19. *Anabasis* 5.6.15.

20. According to Strabo, the *pelamys* was large enough to be worth catching first at Pharnakeia, it was larger at Sinope, and larger again at Byzantium: Strabo 12.3.11 (545); 12.3.19 (549); cf. 7.6.2 (320).

Bibliography

Braund, D.C. 1991 'Dion Khrisostom, torgivlya Ol'vii ta ol'viys'ka tavroskifs'ka viyna', *Arkheologiya* (Kiev) 3, 25-30 (in Ukrainian, with commentary by V.V. Krapivina *ibid.*, 31-3).

Braund, D.C. 1994 *Georgia in Antiquity* (Oxford).

Braund, D.C. 1993 'Piracy under the Principate: the myth of its elimination', in J. Rich & G. Shipley (eds) *War in the Ancient World: Rome* (London), 195-212.

Braund, D.C. & Tsetskhladze, G.R. 1989 'The export of slaves from Colchis', *Classical Quarterly* 39, 114-25.

Curtis, R.I. 1991 *Garum and Salsamenta* (Leiden).

Dumont, J.C. 1976/77 'La pêche du thon à Byzance à l'époque hellénistique', *Revue des Etudes Anciennes* 78/79, 96-119.

Gallant, T.W. 1985 *A Fisherman's Tale: an Analysis of the Potential Productivity of Fishing in the Ancient World* (Ghent).

Garnsey, P. 1988 *Famine and Food-supply in the Graeco-Roman World* (Cambridge).

Hirsch, S.W. 1985 *The Friendship of the Barbarians: Xenophon and the Persian Empire* (Hanover).

Kadeyev, V. 1970 *Ocherki istorii ekonomiki Khersonesa v I-II vv.n.e.* (Khar'kov).

Kadeyev, V.I. & Sorochan, S.B. 1989 *Ekonomicheskiye svyazi antichnykh gorodov Severnovo Prichernomor'ya* (Khar'kov).

Malkin, I. & Shmueli, N. 1988 'The "city of the blind" and the founding of Byzantium', in I. Malkin & R. Hohlfelder (eds) *Mediterranean Cities: Historical Perspectives* (London), 21-36.

Nussbaum, G.B. 1967 *The Ten Thousand: a Study in Social Organisation and Action in Xenophon's Anabasis* (Leiden).

Stefan, A. 1974 'Die Getreidekrisen in den Städten an den westlichen und nördlichen Küsten des Pontos Euxeinos in der hellenistischen Zeit', in E.C. Welskopf (ed.) *Hellenische Poleis* (Berlin) vol. 2, 648-63.

PART THREE

The Social and Religious Context of Food and Eating

Introduction ၛ
Part Three

Iₙ his poem *The Theogony*, Hesiod describes the generations of the gods in the early history of the world. A dispute arose between the Titan Prometheus and Zeus, king of the new Olympian gods:

> And when a settlement was made between the gods and mortal men at Mekone, then it was that Prometheus with his mind full of careful thought apportioned and served a great ox, deceiving the mind of Zeus. For him, he put in a hide meat and inner parts rich in fat, wrapped in an ox's stomach. For the men, on the other hand, he carefully arranged with cunning skill the white bones of the ox and put them down wrapped in white fat. Then the father of men and gods addressed him: 'Son of Iapetos, most glorious of all the gods, my gentle friend, in how partisan a way you have divided the portions!' So spoke Zeus who knows undying thoughts, rebuking him. Then in reply Prometheus of the crooked counsel addressed him, smiling gently, but not forgetting his cunning trick. 'Zeus, most glorious and greatest of the gods who live forever, choose whichever of the two the heart in your breast bids you.' He spoke with cunning purpose, but Zeus who knows undying thoughts recognized what was happening and was not unaware of the trick. He looked ahead in his heart to evils for mortal men, which he would put into action. In both hands he took up the white fat. He was angry in his breast and anger smote his heart when he saw the white bones of the ox arranged in the cunning plan. As a result of this, the tribes of men burn white bones for the immortals on altars smoking with incense.   (Hesiod *Theogony* 535-57)

This passage 'explains' why the Greeks offered sacrifice to the gods. In the ancient world, foods derived from plants were used extensively in sacrifice, but it was blood sacrifice that was the most important.

Meat was considered central to civilized life. There has been a particularly influential approach to the Prometheus myth in Hesiod by Jean-Pierre Vernant, which is broadly structuralist.[1] As a result of Prometheus' deception of Zeus, men are forced to show their inferiority to Zeus and the gods. They do this by offering a lesser being, an animal, in sacrifice to the greater being, the god, thereby affirming their intermediate position in the order of things, between divinity and bestiality. The animal, the domestic ox, is divided up so that the gods eat the divine parts of the animal where life was thought to reside (marrow bone and vital organs), and receive this tribute with incense in fragrant smoke, while the mortals eat the flesh and entrails – the mortal part – of the beast, boiled. The idea that the bones with their marrow are desirable (as containing life) is the reverse of the Hesiodic version where Zeus is angry to receive bones disguised: Hesiod's is a paradoxical account which stresses the unequal and unrelenting relationship between men and gods. In the mythical narrative, Zeus chooses the 'worse' portion, knowing full well what it is; in their daily rituals the true relationship between gods, humans and animals is played out, with the mortal part going to mortal, divine to divine.

In an alternative version of the myth in his *Works and Days* (42-105), Hesiod sets the dispute between Prometheus and Zeus within an agricultural context. Zeus in his anger withholds foods which grow spontaneously from men (in a Greek version of the myth of the Garden of Eden in *Genesis*), and obliges men to develop agriculture, with all the toil it entails, in order to survive. In both versions, Hesiod goes on to describe how, as a result of the trick of Prometheus, Zeus punishes men by withholding fire from them. Prometheus steals back the fire and gives it to men in a fennel stalk, thereby allowing them to keep warm, to smelt metals and to cook. Zeus retaliates further by instructing the craft gods to create the worst curse of all in Hesiod's terms, women. Men must either live with them and suffer all the torments of marriage or live without them and die childless. Women are like the ox's stomach which enclosed the thigh bones in a form of haggis in the myth above, in the sense (says Hesiod) that they look beautiful on the outside but are evil in their nature. At the same time, a woman's stomach (*gaster*) is of ambivalent value for men: it is greedy and eats him out of house and home, while on the positive side, when the *gaster* is considered as a womb, it prevents the man's line from extinction. This sexist approach is, again, not unlike that found in *Genesis*. The complexities of interpretation are developed with much subtlety in Vernant's excellent essay.

In the harsh post-Promethean system, men have fire, domesticated animals and agriculture, and marriage. This is civilization as conceived by the Greeks, and as it evolved into the classical city state. Vernant's system is not accepted by everyone, but the contention of *The Cuisine of Sacrifice among the Greeks* that all or nearly all meat was sacrificed, and that only domesticated animals were used, holds up. Wild animals and birds were hunted and eaten, but not in participation with the gods.

The myth in its own special way gives an account of the way the world is, an account overlaid with various Hesiodic glosses such as misogyny. This is not to say that meat-eating was more important than eating starch (there are a number of myths of the cereal goddess Demeter, one of which Gerhard Baudy examines in Chapter 13), but that the Prometheus myth is particularly striking. What a culture does with its animals is often of central importance. Readers will differ over how far and in what way they would like to interpret such systems.[2] There is a clear issue of gender in this high valuation of meat. Men control the meat; women (and slaves) control the laborious milling of the grain, the product of which is a much more widely-used food in Greek and most other peasant cultures. If that meat has a greater symbolic value, that may be in part because men have greater control of the symbolic.

Myth is important. For the Greeks, among other things, it explained the world as it was, it gave explanations for how certain things came into being and why certain rituals took the form that they did. This is clear whether or not a structuralist approach is adopted. To the 20 century observer, the ancient world appears strongly ritualized, perhaps because their rituals are different from ours. The consumption of foods often forms part of those rituals, particularly when exchanges are taking place. It was difficult to worship a god without offering him or her gifts of food and wine; when friends met, they ate together; when a stranger (a non-member of a group) was offered hospitality by the group, food and drink were the first consideration; when a city honoured one of its citizens or a friend from outside, the honoured person was feasted at the city's hearth.[3] Very often, these occasions were combined, with friends and neighbours sharing a meal in honour of a god in the locality and thereby confirming bonds both within the group and between the group and its divine protector. Where social and religious rituals are strong, they may be highlighted by disapproval of deviant behaviour. Thus in a context of eating, the glutton or the gate-crasher may be singled out as one who does not fit in. Such is the case in Chapters 14 and 15.

How the half of the community that was women organized their consumption of food in antiquity is much less clear. Texts, when they are not as misogynistic as Hesiod's, are often uninformative in this area. We know that women ate together at certain festivals, the most striking of which, the Thesmophoria, is described by Marcel Detienne in Chapter 6 of *The Cuisine of Sacrifice among the Greeks*.[4] In Greece citizen women did not attend the dinners of upper-class men, though *hetairai* (party girls a little like geishas) were there in plenty.[5] There were dinners for both sexes in Rome. To what extent women organized dinners among themselves is hard to say, because our sources are not interested in such matters. Some ancient attitudes towards women and eating are examined by Veronika Grimm in Chapter 17. She compares Jewish ideas about women starving themselves (broadly disapproving) with Christian ideas (strongly approving). These views are linked both with the expectation (or not) of the apocalypse and with eating disorders in women such as anorexia.

The chapters in Part 3 consider the social and religious structures lying behind or expressed by certain patterns of eating. Gerhard Baudy, in a striking interpretation, argues that the myths and rituals of harvest festivals, particularly at Eleusis, derive from the transition of the young from herding to the farming of adult life. Louise Bruit in Chapter 14 examines the ancient 'parasite' in the account in Athenaeus, Book 6. The word 'parasite', originally the term for a category of priest who dined in the company of a god, that is, in a special building in the precinct of his temple, later came to denote an inferior scrounger at a dinner. It is with the earlier sense of a diner in a religious context that this chapter is most concerned.

James Davidson in Chapter 15 takes up the matter of *sitos* and *opson*, showing that in many Athenian texts the associations of the latter have extended far beyond 'strong flavours', so that eating *opsa* may denote excessive desire, gluttony, and an inclination to corruption, criminality and even revolution.

Vegetarians had a special place in classical antiquity, as persons who did not share in the religious and political system of the city-state.[6] Those who refused to eat meat were thought to have opted out, not just as individuals but as citizens. They were a further group who confirmed the norm by dissension from it. We might note in addition that many peasants were vegetarians for much of the year, but though necessity, certainly not by choice. In Chapter 16, Catherine Osborne analyses the various motives which might define whether or not a person was a vegetarian.

J.W.

Notes

[1.] J-P. Vernant and M. Detienne *The Cuisine of Sacrifice among the Greeks* (Chicago, 1989) 21-86. This work is the basis for argument in Chapters 14 (Louise Bruit) and 26 (Helen King).

[2.] C. Lévi-Strauss's *The Raw and the Cooked* (Engl. trans. London, 1970), the inspiration for Vernant's and Detienne's work, is excessively schematized for some tastes.

[3.] Dining at the city's expense has been exhaustively investigated by P. Schmitt-Pantel *La Cité au Banquet* (Paris, 1992). She considers both the large-scale civic dining laid on by powerful cities such as Athens, and also much local detail revealed by civic inscriptions throughout the Greek world.

[4.] Robin Osborne ('Women and Sacrifice in ancient Greece', *Classical Quarterly* 43 (1993), 392-405) contests Detienne's view that women did not normally take part in animal sacrifice. He examines the implications for diet (if Detienne is right, did women eat less meat?) and also discusses what vase-painting can tell us about sacrificial practice, in a way similar to Brian Sparkes in Chapter 11.

[5.] For a feminist perspective on women in ancient Greece as material for male consumption along with their food see Madeleine Henry, 'The Edible Woman' in A. Richlin (ed.) *Pornography and Representation in Greece and Rome* (Oxford, 1992).

[6.] See M. Detienne *The Gardens of Adonis: Spices in Greek Mythology* (trans. Atlantic Highlands, 1977), C. Spencer *The Heretic's Feast* (London, 1993), and R. Sorabji *Animal Minds and Human Morals* (London, 1993). A version of Chapter 13 of Richard Sorabji's book was delivered at the *Food in Antiquity* conference in 1992.

CEREAL DIET AND THE ORIGINS OF MAN
MYTHS OF THE ELEUSINIA IN THE CONTEXT OF ANCIENT MEDITERRANEAN HARVEST FESTIVALS

Gerhard Baudy

The myths from the eastern Mediterranean which relate to harvest festivals[1] give a particular symbolic value to a cereal diet. I shall try to define this symbolic value by means of selected examples, and to determine its social function. My primary concern will be the religious tradition of Eleusis. I shall try to reconstruct the rites of the Eleusinian harvest festival from different mythical accounts, bringing in further eastern-Mediterranean traditions for the purpose of comparison.

Above all, I shall consider two interlocking mythologems (motifs). One of them signifies the way in which the first cereal harvest marked the end of uncivilized prehistory. At the same time, the consumption and cultivation of corn 'tamed' human nature,[2] so that every harvest was so to speak a re-enactment of the beginning of human history.

There are many local variants of the second motif, according to which mythical youths had once suffered a violent death at the moment of the cereal harvest. It was in their honour that ancient harvest festivals were

The Eleusinian harvest festival and myths of Demeter

held, and in doing so, celebrants imagined that the dead were identical with the grain.

Both *topoi* come together in a certain way in the myth of Demeter and Kore: Demeter's daughter who had been abducted into the underworld was identified with the seeding corn.[3] The story was also told that after the rape of Kore the agrarian cycle was either created[4] or at least – in the version of the Homeric *Hymn to Demeter* – re-established.[5] According to the Hellenistic version of the myth it was none other than Demeter who invented the cultivation of cereals and taught it to men.[6]

Heuresis, 'invention', means in this context above all quite literally the 'finding' of the grain still growing wild. Demeter first taught men to gather it in. Then she showed them how to use and to store it, and finally she told them how to sow.[7] Following this myth, the cultivation of grain started with the first harvest. So the annual harvest was a memory of the mythical primeval discovery of cereal food.[8]

Demeter's cultural performance could also be inserted into the paradigm of cosmogonic myth. The local tradition of the island of Corfu (Kerkyra) identified the sickle with which Kronos had castrated his father Ouranos with the first harvesting tool. With this instrument – so the story goes – Demeter taught the Titans how to reap the ears of cereals.[9] Consequently, the Titans represented primeval mankind: they were the golden genera-tion, living under Kronos, not yet separated from the gods.[10] As long as cereals were only cut and consumed, but not yet cultivated, early man continued to live in a primeval gathering paradise. It was not until they were constrained to store and to sow that men were alienated from their origins: together with the agrarian cycle civilization arose.

Many countries and places claimed to be the cradle of agriculture. In Attika alone three sacred plains were regarded as 'original fields': the Rharian Plain at Eleusis, the Bouzygian Plain below the acropolis at Athens, and a plain called Skiron halfway between them.[11] Ploughing and harvesting such sacred fields is to be interpreted as the signal which introduced the ploughing and harvesting season all over the country.

Eleusis: the myth

I would like to consider the mythical tradition of Eleusis, related to the Rharian Plain, for this tradition was the most famous in Greece. In Pausanias' time, visitors to the Rharian Plain were still shown the thresh-ing-floor of the hero Triptolemos. He was said to have used it when – instructed by Demeter – he was threshing the first cut grain, which he then in his serpent-drawn wagon carried all over the world to sow.[12] Indeed, corn from the sacred First Plain was taken to other parts of Greece. After the harvest, the Eleusinia (not to be confused with the Eleusinian Mysteries, celebrated later in the year) were celebrated at Eleusis.[13] Inter-regional Games were held at two- and four-year intervals. The young victors received ears of corn from the Sacred Field as prizes.[14] When they returned home, each was, as it were, a new Triptolemos. Or, vice-versa, we might say that the hero Triptolemos, Demeter's foster-son and first farmer, who once had brought seed-corn to mankind, was a mythical retrojection of those young *theoroi* (celebrants), who took corn from the Rharian Plain to their dwellings.[15]

According to the myth the Eleusinian Games were a commemoration not only of the first harvest, but also of the humanization of mankind: only by eating the hitherto unknown cereals would primeval men have become strong enough to lift the upper part of their bodies from the ground. That is to say, previously they had, because of their weakness, walked like animals on their four legs. In their overwhelming joy at their ability to walk upright, the myth continues, the men of that time organized a race to demonstrate their newly-won strength. That was how the Eleusinia were initiated.[16] So anthropogony was accomplished by consuming cereals.

Eleusis: the ritual

Because the myth seeks to explain the Eleusinian festival, it must have been based on customs there. So we can use it to reconstruct the ritual in the following way: it seems to be presupposed that, before the beginning of the Eleusinian Games, cereals from the Sacred Field had been eaten in a solemn meal. To mark its primeval character as First Corn, people perhaps ate it in its most simple form, as a mixed drink made of bruised barley grain – as it was also used during the mysteries celebrated later in the year, in autumn. The Homeric *Hymn to Demeter*, as is well known, refers the recipe for preparing such a mixed drink (*kykeon*) to the goddess herself. Accordingly, it was she who also drank first the *kykeon*, immediately after she had arrived at Eleusis.[17] According to Pausanias, the *oulai*, the barley corns thrown on the sacrificial cattle led to the altar, were taken from the Rharian Plain;[18] this sacrificial barley, according to Theophrastos, who probably followed Eleusinian cultic traditions in his *On Piety*,[19] represented the oldest form of corn suitable for human consumption.[20] But this corn from the sacred field could also be consumed in a more processed form. For it was used to bake special sacrificial cakes, *pemmata*.[21] By eating such cakes, the transition from the primitive mixed drink to the diet of bread could be shown in a ceremony. According to Theophrastos the sacrificial cakes thrown into fire represented the *alelemenos bios*, the 'ground [sc. 'civilized'] life', which dated from the invention of grinding tools.[22] The participle is deliberately ambiguous: 'ground life' in its first sense means the 'sacrificed' life of the grain-plants themselves; but metaphorically the *alelemenos bios* relates to human life. Eating refined flour caused so to speak a refinement of human nature analogous to the milling of corn.

As is well known, both language and ritual symbolically equated men and cultivated plants in many ways: *sperma* on the one hand meant the seed of corn out of which new ears grow up, and on the other hand the male seed engendering children. The plough symbolized the *phallos*, which impregnates the soil; likewise ploughing was a common metaphor for sexual intercourse.[23] The new-born child was treated like harvested grain: it was laid in a winnowing-basket (*liknon*), the prototype of the cradle.[24] More than that, the stages of human life were said to correspond to the annual cycle of cereal farming: the harvest was the symbolic equivalent of the first beard-shaving at the time when a youth became a man;[25] burying the dead in the earth corresponded to the autumn sowing.[26]

From the *aition* of the Eleusinia, the story told to explain its origins, we may now conclude that the young athletes before their meal of newly-harvested corn represented early man, uncultivated and not yet differing from beasts. Only the eating of cultivated plants, according to the ritual fiction, transformed them into cultivated or civilized human beings. For, as the myth tells us, the beginning of the games presupposed the transition from the *theriodes bios* to the *hemeros bios*.

Eating the sacred corn was, in other words, part of an initiation rite, which took place at harvest-time. It marked the close relationship of man and plant by enacting the dependence of the *bios* of man on the *bios* of the corn. The suggestion was that, by the act of eating, the life of the plant would be transferred to man, so constituting his historical identity as a 'cultivated' being.

But how did the young athletes enact the drama of 'becoming man' or 'becoming civilized'? We can form some conception of it if we assume that the Eleusinian Games were held in honour of Demophon, the foster-son of Demeter. For the Homeric *Hymn to Demeter* mentions annual games organized by the children (*paides*) of Eleusis in honour of Demophon.[27] These children are thought to be *kouroi*, youths. We know that the agonistic rites included stone-throwing, which gave the festival its name *Balletus*.[28] In my opinion we should probably take this local custom – following the suggestion of Otto Kern – as the historical origin of the Eleusinia,[29] because there were – as is natural for a harvest festival – also annual Eleusinian festivals. True, their annual sacrifice did not include the intra-regional games that were held at the two- and four-year-festivals;[30] but these games are best explained as an extension of local ephebic competitions, which had long been part of the annual harvest festivals at Eleusis.

This is supported by myth: the Eleusinia re-enacted the origins of civilized mankind, as set out above. It was precisely the ritual of stone-throwing which could enact anthropogony: according to a myth from the Parnassos area, post-diluvian mankind originated from the stones thrown by Deukalion and Pyrrha.[31] In the foundation myth of Thebes the city's first hoplites sprang from 'dragon's teeth': they were called Spartoi, 'sown men', because Kadmos had sown them like corn. According to the Theban myth, as soon as they appeared the Spartoi started fighting each other. Their death was a bloody 'harvest'.[32] Accordingly we could suppose that the *balletus* at Eleusis was the corresponding ritual signal for the contests of *ephebes* (young men) in honour of Demophon to begin. I propose the following reconstruction: stones were thrown before the Games to symbolize the sowing from which men grow, so that with the participating *ephebes* a 'new mankind' arose, following the model of the grain-plants.[33] But since the cereal diet alone was thought to have given men the ability to walk upright, the *ephebes* probably first lay on the ground, ritually identifying themselves with the thrown stones. Then they ate sacred corn. By this they were symbolically assimilated to the corn. When they rose up from the ground afterwards, they corresponded to growing ears of corn. The games that followed were structurally the same as the fratricidal combats of the Theban Spartoi.

The childhood of Demophon

I shall now attempt to interpret the story of Demophon's childhood as a mythical complement to these anthropogonic rites. There are two reasons for this: (a) this childhood-story forms the explicit *aition* (explanation of the origin) of the ephebic contests; and (b) there was a typological relationship between Triptolemos, the archetype of the *theoroi*, who took part in the Eleusinian festival and went home with the sacred ears of corn, and Demophon. For in Hellenistic times the myth of the childhood of Demophon, in whose honour the children of Eleusis held their annual games, was transferred to Triptolemos: both were boys fostered by Demeter after the abduction of her daughter. Both are new-born babies, and both are made to grow at miraculous speed by the goddess, who holds them in the fire at night to burn away the parts of them that are not immortal. In both cases she does not succeed, because their real mother intervenes, so that the heroes remain mortal.[34] In the Homeric Hymn, Demeter lays the child, after she has taken him from the fire, on the ground: a symbol that he now is doomed to death.[35] According to another version, the child burns directly in the fire of the hearth.[36]

Accordingly fire confers immortality only when correctly applied. Too much brings death. What is the real model for this motif in the myth? According to the Homeric *Hymn to Demeter* the goddess lays Demophon in the fire 'like a wooden log'.[37] Somebody who holds a piece of wood in the fire in such a way that it does not burn, is hardening it; he makes it immortal in a certain way. It now does not rot any more, but it does not produce roots and shoots any longer either. To remove the mortality of the wood means consequently to sterilize it. The premature interruption of this hardening by fire ensures in the case of Demophon that he personally stays mortal, but on the other hand continues to be able to propagate.

Now Demophon was the hero of the Eleusinian *paides* (children) or *kouroi* (youths), who acquired by ritual eating of cereals, harvested on the Rharian Plain, a *bios* corresponding to the cereal diet. This evokes and demands an understanding of the myth which relates it to the treating of cereals. The corn-goddess who, we are told, also taught men how to prepare and use the grain, treats the new-born child like the harvested seedcorns:[38] the barley first had to be roasted before it was ground.[39] The flour was kneaded with water into dough, which was then put back into the fire. Roasting the grain preserved it and improved its taste but at the same time destroyed its ability to germinate. An analogous myth puts it more plainly: Demeter grieved so much over the loss of her daughter that she 'burnt' the corn.[40] Similarly, in a Boiotian myth, Ino persuades the women of Thebes to roast the seedcorn; a famine results.[41] Such stories call attention to a danger which had to be averted after every harvest: in no circumstances must the gathered corn be completely consumed. One part of it must always be kept for seed. Only the grain destined for consumption should come into contact with fire.

If Demophon is now not completely roasted by Demeter, this means that mankind (like his mythical representative) clearly has a life (*bios*) analogous to that of the grain which is roasted and eaten, but contains nevertheless a residue of procreative seed not destroyed by the fire. That enables mankind to compensate for the mortality of the individual by the procreation of children. This is why Demeter lays Demophon finally on the ground: he represents the grain falling to the ground and 'dying' to produce new life. If this interpretation is right, then Demophon is incarnated and 'multiplied' in the persons of those *ephebes* who at the annual harvest festival rose from the ground, thus re-enacting the mythical origin of mankind.

Demophon's experience thus corresponds to the necessary separation of the seedcorn from grain that is to be eaten. The myth transfers the sparing of the procreative seed to the human level. That is why Demophon was a model for the Eleusinian *ephebes* who ate sacred corn at the harvest festival so as to assimilate themselves to the annual death and resurrection of the crop. The girls who took part in the festival had their own mythical paradigm in the figure of Kore, who, abducted to and released from the underworld, enacted the cyclic fate of the seed. In view of the combined myth of Kore and Demophon the ritual eating of cereals must have had a double sacramental connotation that was different for each sex.[42]

As for Demophon, the Homeric Hymn contains another image that reveals his agrarian significance: reared without nourishment, the boy grew during the day with miraculous speed (*prothales teletheske* 241). Whereas the child lying at night in the fire corresponds to the bread being baked, his amazing daytime growth corresponds to another model: Demophon resembles a sprouting plant.[43] This seems to refer to a custom which is not attested until the works of writers about agriculture in late antiquity: after the harvest, selected grains were put in vessels (pots or baskets) for a premature germination. At the hottest time of the year, at the early rising of Sirius which introduced the dog-days, the vessels were put open in the sun to see which seedlings could best bear the heat. This provided a criterion for the selection of the best seedcorn. (In modern seed-cultivation, incidentally, the vitality of the corn is tested by a similar procedure.) Because this test was executed in antiquity at the time of the early rising of Sirius, the dog-star was said to 'burn' the seed. For use as seedcorn, this sort of grain was preferable, the sort that did not 'burn' in its experimental bed on the vital day.[44]

Consequently the withering or metaphorical 'burning' of the seedlings in their experimental beds at these harvest festivals held during the dog-days (of which the Eleusinia was one) also pointed in another direction: it was a signal to release for human consumption the grain less suitable for sowing. This means that every time that the heavenly 'fire' of Sirius (together with the sun) effected a selection of the seed-corn, it was decided which part of the harvest would finally come to the fire of the hearth for processing into bread. It is precisely this combination of functions related to harvest-time which is, I think, evoked by the myth of Demophon: like the plants growing up in their experimental beds without nourishment, so Demophon grew in the care of Demeter.[45] And just as a part of them suffered a 'death by burning' – at first a representative sample in the experimental vessels, afterwards in the fire of the hearth – so Demophon (that is to say his mortal parts) died in the flames. But because one part of the harvest had to be preserved as seedcorn, analogously the fire destroyed Demophon's mortality only partially: like the seedcorn he was to die only apparently, and like the seedcorn he was to live on in his offspring.

It could be objected to this interpretation that the myth does not mention any vessel like those used for germination tests. It could further be objected that the sources which inform us about the custom in question – they are Palladius and Pseudo-Zoroaster – are comparatively late. The third and most important argument against my interpretation seems to be Palladius' designating the germination test as an Egyptian custom.

The gardens of Adonis

I would answer as follows: at least Palladius' statement makes it certain that this custom was very old in the eastern Mediterranean. For what Palladius describes, evidently, are the 'beds of Osiris', which can be traced back to Pharaonic times.[46] Until late antiquity the corpse of Osiris was represented by cereal grains put in certain receptacles or 'coffins' for premature germination.[47] Now, Osiris was honoured by the same rites as the Phoenician Adonis; that is why both were explicitly identified in antiquity. In the cult of Adonis analogous experimental vessels were called 'gardens of Adonis'. By this name they were also known to the Greeks who had taken over the cult of Adonis from the Phoenicians.[48] No *terminus post quem* for this borrowing can be found.

On Greek soil the custom of the gardens of Adonis is not attested before the 5th century BC. But did not similar germination tests exist much earlier in the context of the indigenous harvest festivals? One piece of evidence could be the Athenian myth of the earth-born king Erechtheus, attested already in the *Iliad*. In classical times the myth of the childhood of Erechtheus was transposed to Erichthonios, a figure who was split off from the former.[49] Athena lays the hero, born of the earth, into a chest and gives this to the daughters of king Kekrops. This story was the *aition* of a girls' ritual celebrated after the cereal harvest in the month of Skirophorion.[50] According to one version of the myth, Herse, one of the three princesses to whom Athena had entrusted the chest with the newborn baby, was the ancestress of the Phoenician Adonis.[51] There was a good reason for this story. The chest of Erichthonios, I suppose, must have had an agricultural function overlooked by earlier scholarship: it was in the official state cult the 'paradigm' of the private gardens of Adonis – those vessels wherein the Athenians allowed grains to germinate for a month after the harvest. So the mythical hero was not only incarnated in the 'earth-born' Athenians themselves, but also in the cereals of the experimental beds.[52] According to Athenian tradition, it was his foster-mother Athena who invented the plough and thereby agriculture; so she meant to Athens what Demeter meant to the Eleusinians.[53] This very same role of *kourotrophos* (nurse of children), played by Athena for the earth-born Erechtheus-Erichthonios, was taken over at Eleusis by Demeter for the new-born Demophon.[54]

This parallel is suggestive, I believe, for an interpretation of the myth of Demophon, too, as the reflex of a ritual germination test, although the Homeric *Hymn to Demeter* does not mention any chest of this sort. Indeed, the Hymn also conceals the famous *cista mystica* (chest of the mysteries) of Eleusis, but nobody would pretend it was missing in the cult of early times. I would suggest that the chest of the Eleusinian mysteries should be traced back to a practical function: to a basket with a lid, used for the purpose of germination tests, where the Attic farmers put grains for premature germination between the times of harvest and sowing.[55]

The *larnax* of Osiris

There is another important clue to the missing link we are looking for. It comes in a myth which enables us to compare the Eleusinian harvest-customs with other Mediterranean traditions. We find a mythical proto-type of the receptacle of an experimental seed in a narrative of late antiquity, which, by the way, is so similar to the Demophon episode that scholars very often take it for a late imitation of the Homeric *Hymn to Demeter*. In this case it is a matter of the *larnax*, that is the 'coffin', of Osiris which Plutarch describes in his *Isis and Osiris*. Let me remind you of the story:

> Isis, that is, the Egyptian Demeter, searching for the coffin of
> Osiris, comes to the Phoenician maritime town of Byblos. Here
> she becomes a servant as nurse of a new-born prince in the palace
> of the king Malkandros and of the queen Astarte. She treats the
> boy just as Demeter treated Demophon: she does not nourish
> him at all, and during the night she lays him in the fire to make
> him immortal. While the baby is lying in the flames, Isis changes
> into a swallow and is lamenting and circling round a pillar which
> contains the *larnax* with the corpse of Osiris. In this case, too, the
> real mother of the child wrecks the success of the enchantment
> by her intervention. Then Isis reveals herself and demands that
> the *larnax* of Osiris be taken out of the pillar and given to her.
> After this has happened, she throws herself over the re-found
> coffin, lamenting so grievously that the little prince dies because
> of her complaints. The goddess now loads the *larnax* onto a ship
> and departs. The elder brother of the dead prince accompanies
> her. In a desert region Isis opens the coffin to kiss the dead Osiris.
> When her young companion secretly watches her, he is stricken
> by the angry gaze of the goddess and killed immediately.
> (Plutarch *Isis and Osiris* 13-17=*Moralia* 356c-7f)

The story gives a key role to a mysterious coffin of a god. While the *larnax*
of Osiris is hidden in a cultic shrine, Isis fosters a little boy without
nourishment and burns his mortal parts in fire. The fetching of the *larnax*
out of the hiding-place coincides with the death of the foster-child. The
later opening of the *larnax* re-enacts this in a certain sense: now another
prince dies, the elder brother or double of the child.

The myth evidently has the function of producing an identificatory bond
between the god who lies dead in the coffin and the human princes. Both
royal sons represent male participants in a cult to whom the god's death is
transferred symbolically. When a child dies in myth, in the symbolic
language of ancient cult that always means the same thing: the child
represents in every case a neophyte who had to suffer a symbolic death
which marked the end of his life as an immature child and from which he
was resurrected as an adult able to procreate.

The *larnax* is to be interpreted as a mythical projection of the experimental
bed which contains the germinating corn. The dead god had been

transformed into this corn, according to the ritual fiction. It was in the form of this corn that the god became alive again and suffered at the end (on the day of the festival) a premature death once again. In Plutarch's narrative the baby fostered near the *larnax* and his elder brother superseding him both correspond to the phases of cereal growth in the experimental bed. In the reality of cult the 'dead' resurrected in the grain represented the mythic *alter ego* of the youth becoming adult.

The myth sets the story in Byblos, because the cult of Adonis there had the same form as the Egyptian cult of Osiris. We know from Lucian that the Egyptians living in Byblos took the Adonis honoured there to be Osiris. To bring the coffin of the dead into the open (in Plutarch's story the goddess Isis does this) symbolized at the annual Adonis-festival in Byblos the resurrection of the god.[56]

The cultic background of Plutarch's story about Isis makes me doubt whether we can adequately explain the convergences between this story and the Homeric *Hymn to Demeter* by the hypothesis of literary imitation.[57] For the main motif of the *larnax* of Osiris at least there was no explicit paradigm in the Eleusinian cultic myth. At most we could say that Plutarch transferred the episode of Demophon to the myth of Osiris because he saw reflected in the childhood story of Demophon a similar custom of germination tests. Thus he was able to insert the *larnax* of Osiris, that is, the mythical prototype of the experimental bed, into a story composed on the model of the Demophon episode.

The background to these mythic parallels seems to lie in harvest customs common to the peoples of the eastern Mediterranean. Fundamentally, Mannhardt and Frazer already recognized this.[58] But today we are no longer content to explain such rites and myths by means of an imaginary 'corn-spirit', a personalized growing-force of the grain, whose continuity had to be guaranteed over the critical periods of the agricultural year (harvest and sowing). The 'human', or, better, social dimensions of the myth are not fully understood in such theories. For not only did rites and myths lend the corn a symbolic value by deification or anthropomorphic representation; at the same time, language too transferred the cycles of corn-growing to the stages of human life.

Thus man and corn, which metaphorically could be called *bios*,[59] represented one another: they changed their marks of identity and thus defined one another by their symbiotic interchange. They were taken as it were as brothers, and that is what is meant by the mythical idea: a divine culture-hero had once changed into the nourishing plants and thus made agriculture possible.[60]

In Egypt this culture-hero was called Osiris. His death was re-enacted annually at the reaping of corn: that is why the harvesters struck up a ritual lament in front of the first sheaf.[61] The Greeks living in Egypt transferred to Osiris the myth of Triptolemos; they regarded him as the inventor of agriculture,[62] so he continued to live not only in the corn, but at the same time in the farmers who ate and cultivated it.

The death of Lityerses

A similar ritual mourning was part of the Phrygian harvest-festivals. This too, was in memory of an inventor of agriculture, namely the First Reaper, Lityerses. According to the myth Lityerses had entertained foreigners passing by during the harvest and then urged them to join with him in mowing the field. But during this first harvest in which they took part, the reapers were struck down by death: Lityerses wrapped their bodies in the sheaves and then cut off their heads with the sickle, just as if the human heads were identical to the ears of corn. In the end Lityerses died in the same way. In a drama by Sositheos, Herakles, who defeated him in a harvest competition, killed him. Herakles had accepted the challenge of Lityerses instead of the youth Daphnis whom he wanted to rescue from inevitable death.[63]

Mannhardt took this story as a 'historical' memory of former human sacrifices which represented the 'corn-spirit' dying during the harvest.[64] But there is no doubt that the function of this myth consisted in the expression of the symbiotic identity of the farmer and the harvested corn. The death of the first reaper Lityerses and the harvesters beheaded by him was symbolically reenacted at every harvest when young people participated for the first time. According to the ritual fiction the reapers died together with the harvested corn, because they took on a new social identity when they were inserted in the system of agriculture. The rites ensured that they were conscious of their responsibility in an impressive way, and that is why they interwove their lives symbolically with those of the cultivated plants. So Lityerses, ritually mourned during the harvest-festivals, is to be interpreted as a projection of adolescent reapers, who changed their social status at this time. The same is true for the Phoenician Adonis, lamented in a similar way, and for the Egyptian Osiris.[65] All over the eastern Mediterranean area the eating of the new crops during the harvest festival seems to have involved the idea of sacramental identification with a culture-hero or god, who was thought to live on in the nourishing plants as well as in the farmers.

From nomadism to agriculture

According to ancient myths the transition from the *theriodes bios* to the *hemeros bios*, effected by the cereal diet and re-enacted at the harvest festivals, had set an end to a former nomadic life. Being herdsmen, they had still been half-animals; men were even prepared to eat each other. It was not until Isis or Demeter brought to them the cereal diet that they were redeemed from cannibalism.[66]

The period of nomadism, when men were cannibals, existed only in ritual fiction. Its function was to stress the contrast between the herdsmen's life of youth and the agricultural life of adults. Being herdsmen young people were regarded so to speak as only half-men like the one-eyed Cyclopes, the mythical pastoralists who ate human flesh.[67] When therefore the initiates received at the harvest festivals the new food, which was bread, this was meant to re-enact a turning-point in the history of mankind: the turning away from the *allelophagia* (eating of each other) of the mythical time of nomadism.

There was an Orphic myth that portrayed the original inhabitants of Eleusis before the advent of Demeter as animal-herders. One of them was Triptolemos. In this version, he is not a newborn child, but a cowherd who becomes the first farmer and Demeter's missionary.[68] Similarly, Adonis was a young herdsman, representing the mythical age of nomads which gave way to the age of agriculture at his death and metamorphosis into grain.[69] A closely related figure was the herdsman Daphnis who died young and was ritually mourned.[70] In the play by Sositheos mentioned above he does not die but is saved by Herakles. So he marries and inherits the farm of Lityerses.[71] These myths show that the harvest festivals of the Eastern Mediterranean functioned as a turning-point in a man's lifetime: by participating in the harvest, young herdsmen left their duty of animal-herding to become adult farmers.

This reconstruction is supported to a certain degree by the theory of the stages of civilization proposed by Dikaiarchos. As in the myths mentioned above, he too assumes that the age of farming was preceded by a nomadic age.[72] He called the work in which he published his theory *Bios Hellados*, 'The Life-history of Greece'. The metaphorical title of this book tells us how he modelled the history of mankind: he takes the pattern directly from the life of the individual, in particular the life that was typical of societies of agricultural economy which included farming and animal-breeding. In the agricultural *oikos*-system (system of households), youths were usually used as herdsmen before they tilled the arable land as adults. Dikaiarchos, then, made out that all Greeks before the beginning of agriculture had been herdsmen.

Summary

To summarize: in my view, ancient harvest festivals ritually enacted the transition of youth from herding to farming. This was done in the following way: the rites endowed the eating of bread with a complex symbolic significance, represented on a mythical level. There are three points that I would particularly like to stress:

1. Because the bread represented the body of a mythical youth, specifically a herdsman, who was allegedly resurrected in the grain, the eating of grain was said to have superseded former cannibalistic food customs 'historically'.

2. At the harvest festivals, young herdsmen rejected the 'uncivilized' diet by eating the new grain. In this way they sacramentally assimilated themselves to the mythical culture-hero and transformed themselves in a complementary way into farming people. To express this, the Eleusinian initiates re-enacted anthropogony.

3. In order for herdsmen to become farmers, they received at harvest

festivals not only bread to eat, but also seedcorn, so that they could sow their own land. That is why seedcorn was given as a prize in the games at Eleusis. A mythical retrojection of the youthful participants of the festival were the herdsmen of the mythical past. They were said to have been transformed into farmers by Demeter's gift of corn.

Acknowledgements

I am grateful to Hazel Harvey, David Harvey, John Wilkins and Dorothea Baudy for translating successive versions of this chapter.

Notes

1. This chapter refers to ideas which I have put forward in the following three works: *Adonisgärten. Studien zur antiken Samensymbolik, Beiträge zur klassischen Philologie* 176 (1986); 'Das alexandrinische Erntefest', *Mitteilungen für Anthropologie und Religionsgeschichte* 6 (1991) 5-110; 'Der Heros in der Kiste. Der Erichthoniosmythos als Aition athenischer Erntefeste', *Antike und Abendland* 38 (1992) 1-47.

2. Compare for example Isokrates *Panegyricus* 28 ...τούς τε καρπούς, οἳ τοῦ μὴ θηριωδῶς ζῆν αἴτιοι γενόνασιν; Themistios *Orationes* 30 (= *Orphicorum Fragmenta* 112 Kern) ὑπὸ τῶν καρπῶν τῶν ἡμέρων ὧν γεωργία παρέχει πᾶσαν ἡμερῶσαι φύσιν καὶ θηρίων δίαιταν (sc. τὸν Ὀρφέα) κτλ. For further testimonies see A. Henrichs, 'Zwei Fragmente über die Erziehung (Antisthenes)', *Zeitschrift für Papyrologie und Epigraphik* 1 (1967) 45-53.

3. See Kleanthes *Stoicorum Veterum Fragmenta* I fr. 547 (=Plutarch *Isis and Osiris* 66 (*Moralia* 377d)); for Stoic theology in general, *SVF* II fr. 1093 (= Plutarch *Isis and Osiris* 40 (*Moralia* 367c)), Varro *Antiquitates Rerum Divinarum* fr. 167 Cardauns, Cicero *On the Nature of the Gods* 2.66. The sophist Prodikos already identified Demeter and bread (Diels - Kranz 84 B 5). On the problematic relation between mystery cult and ancient nature-allegorization see W. Burkert, *Ancient Mystery Cults* (Cambridge, Mass. 1987), 66-88 and especially 80-4.

4. For example Diodorus Siculus 5.4.3-4.

5. *Hymn to Demeter* 450-6.

6. A. Kleingünther (ΠΡΩΤΟΣ ΕΥΡΕΤΗΣ. *Untersuchungen zur Geschichte einer Fragestellung, Philologus* Suppl. 26 (1934) 6ff.) took the myth to be a creation of the 5th century. A. Henrichs traces it back to Prodikos ('The Sophists and Hellenistic Religion: Prodicus as the spiritual father of the Isis aretalogies', *Harvard Studies in Classical Philology* 38 (1984) 139-58 at 141-5). See further F. Graf, *Eleusis und die orphisische Dichtung Athens in vorhellenistischer Zeit, RGVV* 33 (1974) 35ff. – It is worth asking, though, whether the sophistic myth of the rise of culture is not already based on genuine cultic traditions.

7. Diodorus Siculus 5.68.1, in whose version this tuition precedes the rape of Kore. After her abduction, agriculture is destroyed by Demeter and later on newly founded (5.68.2).

8. At the same time the harvest festivals seem ritually to have enacted the abduction of Kore. Diodorus Siculus (5.4.6) attests a Kore-festival, celebrated after the cereal harvest, which was called 'Kore's *katagoge* (festival of return)'. In Egypt, 'Kore's Abduction' was celebrated when the sun was entering Leo (scholiast on Aratos 150). This, too, is a harvest festival. For more details see Baudy, 'Das alexandrinische Erntefest' (above note 1) 18ff.

9. Apollonios of Rhodes 4.984-92, with the ancient commentary; a different aetiology in Timaios, *FGH* 566 F 79. Compare the analagous foundation myth of Zankle: Kallimachos *Aetia* II fr. 43.69-71 Pfeiffer; Stephanus of Byzantium s.v. Ζάγκλη.

10. Hesiod *Works and Days* 111-20. As a king of paradise who had castrated his father with the sickle (Hesiod *Theogony* 178-91), Kronos was related to the Kronia, a harvest festival. The social hierarchy, once created and legitimated by Zeus, was now dissolved, as if the patriarchic governor of the cosmos was not yet in power. The landowners entertained their harvest-helpers (Philochoros *FGH* 328 F 97; L. Accius in Macrobius *Saturnalia* 1.7.37). Instructive parallels are found in northern European customs: see I. Weber-Kellermann *Erntebrauch in der ländlichen Arbeitswelt des 19. Jahrhunderts auf Grund der Mannhardtbefragung in Deutschland von 1865* (Marburg, 1965) 140, 147, 161, 217, 237. H.S. Versnel, 'Greek Myth and Ritual: The Case of Kronos', in J. Bremmer (ed.) *Interpretations of Greek Mythology* (1987) 121-152 (now in id. *Inconsistencies in Greek and Roman Religion*, vol. 2: *Transition and Reversal in Myth and Ritual* (Leiden, 1993) 89-135), places the Kronia among analogous festivals of the 'reversed-world' type, which were not harvest festivals. I doubt his statement (1993, 134-5) that the Kronia itself could not originally have been related only to the cereal harvest.

11. Plutarch *Advice to Bride and Groom* 43 (*Moralia* 144ab).

12. Pausanias 1.38.6. According to Kallimachos (*Hymn to Demeter* 19-21) Demeter taught agriculture to the hero Triptolemos by reaping ears, which she let cattle tread on the threshing floor. According to the Parian Marble (*FGH* 239 A 12 and 13) Demeter 'found' the corn at the time of king Erechtheus; Triptolemos reaped it and then sowed the Rharian Field. The literary and archaeological evidence for Triptolemos is collected by G. Schwarz *Triptolemos. Ikonographie einer Agrar- und Mysteriengottheit, Grazer Beiträge* Suppl. 2 (1987) 7ff.

13. The epigraphic and literary evidence for the Eleusinia is collected in A. Mommsen *Feste der Stadt Athen im Altertum* (1898) 179-204; A.P. Van der Loeff *De ludis Eleusiniis* (1903); P. Stengel, 'Eleusinia', *Paulys Real-Encyclopädie der classischen Altertumswissenschaft* 5.2 (1905) 2328-32; R.M. Simms, 'The Eleusinia in the Sixth to Fourth Centuries BC', *Greek, Roman and Byzantine Studies* 16 (1975) 269-79; K. Clinton, '*IG*² 5. The Eleusinia, and the Eleusinians', *American Journal of Philology* 100 (1979) 1-12; A. Ch. Brumfield *The Attic Festivals of Demeter and their Relation to the Agricultural Year* (1981) 182-91. – The calendaric *terminus ante quem* of the Eleusinia is the Panathenaia, following which they are mentioned in an inscription (*IG* II/III²

1496.129-30). – Since the Eleusinia was a harvest festival, it should not have been celebrated too long after the Panathenaia. So, rightly, Van der Loeff (80f.) against A. Mommsen, who dated the festival in the month Boedromion. See also Stengel (1905, 2332), Simms (1975, 270), Brumfield (1981, 183).

14. See *IG* II/III² 1672.252-5, scholiast on Pindar *Olympian* 9.150 Drachmann, Aristeides *Eleusinios* 257 (I p. 417 Dindorf), id., *Panathenaikos* 105 (I p. 168 Dindorf) with scholiast (III p. 55f Dindorf).

15. Compare Baudy, 'Das alexandrinische Erntefest' (above note 1) 23. According to a restored inscription, Triptolemos received a sacrifice at the Eleusinia: F. Sokolowski *Lois sacrées des cités grecques* (1969) no. 4.4. A ritual identification of the *theoroi* with the Triptolemos-role was also shown in their receiving prizes of seedcorn, as conversely in their voyaging with first-fruits of cereals to Attika (that is Eleusis), to thank the goddess for the seed once received from there: Aristeides *Eleusinios* 257 (I p. 417 Dindorf); id., *Panathenaikos* 105 (I p. 167f. Dindorf).

16. Scholiast on Pindar, *Olympian* 9.150 Drachmann; Aristeides *Eleusinios* 257 (I p. 417, 11ff. Dindorf). See also *Etymologicum Magnum* 743, 17ff. – According to Aristeides *Panathenaikos* 105 (I 168 Dindorf) the Attic (= Eleusinian) Games were for that reason the oldest ones of all.

17. Homeric *Hymn to Demeter* 208-11.

18. Pausanias 1.38.6. That the ephebes sacrificed cattle at the Eleusinia and that at this occasion a maiden took part as *kanephoros* (basket-bearer), is proved by inscription. See Mommsen (note 13) 191. *Kanephoroi* in the plural, going to the Eleusinia, are mentioned in the scholion to Aristophanes *Birds* 1508.

19. Compare A. Delatte, 'Le cycéon, breuvage rituel des mystères d'Eleusis', *Académie royale de Belgique, Bulletin de la classe des lettres et des sciences morales et politiques* 5e sér., 40 (1954) 690-752, 692ff.; W. Burkert *Homo Necans. Interpretationen altgriechischer Opferriten und Mythen, RGVV* 32 (1972) 300f. (English translation Berkeley 1983).

20. Theophrastos *On Piety* fr. 2 Pötscher = Porphyry *On Abstinence* 2.6.

21. Pausanias 1.38.6.

22. See note 20.

23. For references see A. Dieterich *Mutter Erde* (1925, reprint 1967) 47f.

24. See also W. Mannhardt, 'Kind und Korn', in id. *Mythologische Forschungen* (1884) 351-74.

25. Kallimachos *Hymn to Delos* 298 f. See also J.W. Fitton, 'The οὖλος/ἴουλος song', *Glotta* 53 (1975) 222-38 at 223.

26. The Athenians called their dead Demetrioi (Plutarch *The Face on the Moon* 28 (*Moralia* 943G)) and buried them together with seed-corn (Cicero *Laws* 2.25).

27. Homeric *Hymn to Demeter* 265-7.

28. Athenaeus 406 d; Hesychios s.v. Βαλλητύς: ἑορτὴ Ἀθήνησι ἐπὶ Δημοφῶντι τωι Κελεοῦ ἀγομένη, O. Kern, Βαλλητύς, *Paulys Real-Encyclopädie der classischen Altertumswissenschaft* 2 (1896) 2830f.

29. O. Kern, 'Mysterien', *Paulys Real-Encyclopädie der Classischen Altertumswissenschaft* 16 (1935) 1209-1314 at 1215. Following Kern, Brumfield (note 13) 183 f. proposes an identification of the *Balletus* with the Eleusinia. Conversely, N.J. Richardson *The Homeric Hymn to Demeter* (1974) 346 rejects Kern's thesis, for no cogent reason.

30. See Mommsen (note 13) 186ff. and Simms (note 13) 269.

31. Apollodoros *Library* 1.7.2. On this subject see G.A. Caduff, *Antike Sintflutsagen*, *Hypomnemata* 82 (1986) 228.

32. F. Vian (*Les origines de Thèbes. Cadmos et les Spartes* (1963), 171 also compares the men produced by Deukalion out of stones with the Theban Spartoi. He interprets (234-6) their combat as mythical retrojections of military initiation-rites. The agrarian symbolism of the motif points to a harvest festival (probably celebrated during the dog-days): see Baudy *Adonisgärten* (note 1) 30 ff.

33. Richard Seaford has called my attention to the aggressive connotations of the throwing of stones: presumably the initiands were (according to the ritual fiction) hit and killed by these stones, from which they were later resurrected with a new identity.

34. On Demophon see the Homeric *Hymn to Demeter* 221-54, on Triptolemos Ovid *Fasti* 4.529-60. Ovid took the story either from a Hellenistic source or directly - according to Timaios (so S. Hinds *The Metamorphoses of Persephone. Ovid and the self-conscious Muse* (1987) 51ff.). See also Hyginus *Astronomica* 2.14.

35. Homeric *Hymn to Demeter* 253.

36. See Apollodoros *Library* 1.5.1, Orphicorum Fragmenta 49, 100f. Kern.

37. Homeric *Hymn to Demeter* 239.

38. So already K. Kerényi, 'Kore. Zum Mythologem vom gött-
lichen Mädchen', *Paideuma* 1 (1938/40) 341-80, 351. See also W. Burkert (note 19) 321 with note 81. In a structuralist interpretation the Demophon episode seems to express generally the transition from the 'raw' to the 'cooked': P. Scarpi *Letture sulla religione classica: L'inno omerico di Demeter* (1976) 182ff. Furthermore, the myth of Demophon acted as an *aition* of a 'death by fire', which the initiate suffered symbolically during the Eleusinian consecration (see Burkert (note 19) 310, H.L. Jansen, 'Die eleusinische Weihe', in *Ex orbe Relgionum*, *Studia G. Widengren* I (1972) 287-98 at 294-8). In fact, a victim was substituted for him: see D. Furley, *Studies in the Use of Fire in Ancient Greek Religion* (1981) 84ff.

39. Pliny *Natural History* 18.72. According to Ovid (*Metamorphoses* 5.450) the corn used for the *kykeon* (mixed drink) too was roasted. See also K. Kerényi, *Eleusis. Archetypical Image of Mother and Daughter* (1967) 178.

40. Diodorus Siculus 5.68.2.

41. Apollodoros *Library* 1.9.1; Zenobios 4.38. The source is Euripides *Phrixos* (*Tragicorum Graecorum Fragmenta* 626-32 Nauck²). Ino instigated the roasting of the seed-corn in order that the Thebans should sacrifice Phrixos to make the earth fertile again. In this case also, therefore, the sacrifice of the life of a youth corresponds with the treatment of the seed-corn.

42. Related to this are some structural cross-relations which have been noted between the fates of Kore and Demophon: see N.F. Rubin and H.M. Deal, 'Some Functions of the Demophon Episode in the Homeric Hymn to Demeter', *Quaderni Urbinati di Cultura Classica* 34 (1980) 7-21.

43. On this and what follows see Baudy, 'Das alexandrinische Erntefest' (note 1) 31 ff.

44. See Palladius *On Husbandry* 7.9, Pseudo-Zoroaster in *Geoponica* 2.15, Baudy *Adonisgärten* (note 1) 13ff.

45. Homeric *Hymn to Demeter* 236 f.

46. See A. Scharff, 'Frühe Vorstufen zum 'Kornosiris'', *Forschungen und Fortschritte* 21/23 (1947) 38 f., Baudy, *Adonisgärten* (note 1) 14 and 38ff.

47. See also Firmicus Maternus *de errore profanarum religionum* 27.1.

48. B. Servais-Soyez, 'Lits d'Osiris et jardins d'Adonis', in *Vie et survie dans les civilisations orientales* (1983), 219-26; Baudy *Adonisgärten* (note 1), 9ff.; 'Das alexandrinische Erntefest' (note 1), 35ff.

[49] The collected sources can be found in B. Powell, *Erichthonios and the Three Daughters of Cecrops* (1906) 56 ff.

[50] See Pausanias 1.27.2-3. The story is rightly interpreted as an initiation rite, but without regard to its agrarian function, by W. Burkert, 'Kekropidensage und Arrhephoria. Vom Initiationsritus zum Panathenäenfest', *Hermes* 94 (1966) 1-25 (= id. *Wilder Ursprung. Opferritual und Mythos bei den Griechen* (1990) 40-59). Other sources are cited by Burkert and by Powell (note 49). See further D. Baudy, 'Ein Kultobjekt im Kontext: Der Erichthonios-Korb in Ovids Metamorphosen', *Wiener Studien* 106 (1993) 133-65.

[51] Apollodoros *Library* 3.14.3.

[52] A detailed argument is to be found in my article 'Der Heros in der Kiste' (note 1).

[53] See Servius auctus on Virgil *Aeneid* 5.402. At Athena's behest, the hero Buzyges performed the first ploughing: see Aristotle fr. 386 Rose, *Anecdota Graeca* I p. 221. 8 Bekker. See also Pliny *Natural History* 7.199, Aristeides *Athena* 13 (I p. 20 Dind.), Servius auctus on Virgil *Georgics* 1.19.

[54] On the typological relationship of both heroes see Richardson (note 29) 234f. Erichthonios with his snake-abdomen (Kekrops, Athens' first king, has the same) also represents, incidentally, the age of autochthony, like the primeval men of the Eleusinian myth who creep along the ground. That fits the thesis above: these primeval men would have been represented by ephebes, whose heroic representative was Demophon.

[55] See Baudy, 'Das alexandrinische Erntefest' (note 1) 49 ff.

[56] Lucian *On the Syrian Goddess* 6-7. On the ritual sequence see Baudy, *Adonisgärten* (note 1) 38ff.

[57] For a survey of scholarship in this area see Richardson (note 29), 238. Burkert (above note 3) 142, note 41, also supposes that Plutarch has transferred this from a Greek original, though because of other considerations he derives the myth of Demophon from the Egyptian tradition (20 f.).

[58] W. Mannhardt *Die Korndämonen* (1868), *Wald- und Feldkulte* 2 (1876, 1905²) 155 ff., *Mythologische Forschungen* (1884), J.G. Frazer, *The Golden Bough* (1913³, reprint 1980), especially part IV ('Adonis, Attis, Osiris') and part V ('Spirits of the Corn and the Wild'). – W. Berg's thesis, based on the Demeter-Kore myth, that Greek harvest-customs had a historic ('Indo-Germanic') root different from Mediterranean rites related to male gods ('Eleusinian and Mediterranean Harvest Myths', *Fabula* 15 (1974) 202-11), is in my view a failure, not least because there were also male representatives of the corn in the Eleusinian tradition.

[59] Hesiod *Works and Days* 31. See also the testimony of Theophrastos (note 20).

[60] This type of myth has been shown to belong to a common tradition of all plant-cultivating peoples by A.E. Jensen (most recently in *Die getötete Gottheit. Weltbild einer frühen Kultur* (1966)). E. de Martino ('La messe del dolore', *Studi e materiali di storia delle religioni* 28 (1957) 1-53) has already used Jensen's theory for the interpretation of ancient harvest-customs and their myths.

[61] Diodorus Siculus 1.14.2.

[62] Diodorus Siculus 1.14.1, 1.15.6, Tibullus 1.7.29-36, Servius auctus on Virgil *Georgics* 1.19. An integration of Triptolemos into the myth of Isis is to be found in the Isis-Enkomion from Maroneia, 36 ff.: text in Y. Grandjean *Une nouvelle arétalogie d'Isis à Maronée* (Leiden, 1975) 18 and M. Totti, *Ausgewählte Texte der Isis- und Sarapis-Religion* (1985) 61. See also Henrichs (note 6) 152-8.

[63] Sositheos *Daphnis or Lityerses* in *Tragicorum Graecorum Fragmenta* I 99 F 1-2 = scholiast to Theokritos *Idyll* 10.41f. Pollux 4. 54 parallels Lityerses with the Egyptian Maneros, whom he calls inventor of agriculture.

[64] W. Mannhardt 'Lityerses' in id. *Mythologische Forschungen* (1884) 1-57 at 50 ff.

[65] For further parallels see E. de Martino (note 60) 11 ff.

[66] For Demeter see Pausanias 8.42.6; see also Plato *Laws* 6.782bc with 3.677b and 680e. Like Demeter, Isis also sets an end to a former cannibalism: see Diodorus Siculus 1.14.1 and 'Isisaretalogien' §21 in M. Totti (note 62) 2. The novels of imperial times transpose the cannibalism of the precereal primeval period to herdsmen of the delta of the Nile. See also Baudy 'Das alexandrinische Erntefest' (note 1) 32 f. with note 182.

[67] See Homer *Odyssey* 9.287-98 and Euripides *Cyclops* 120-8.

[68] Clement of Alexandria *Protrepticus* 20.2.

[69] See also Baudy 'Adonisgärten' (note 1) 44ff.

[70] Theokritos *Idyll* 1.64-145.

[71] Servius auctus on Virgil *Eclogues* 8.68.

[72] Dikaiarchos *Bios Hellados* fr. 48 and 49 Wehrli.

❖ 14 ❖

RITUAL EATING IN ARCHAIC GREECE
PARASITES AND *PAREDROI*

Louise Bruit Zaidman

Introduction

THE need to eat is one of the ways in which the ancient Greeks defined humans in relation to gods, and is the basis of the radical division between man and god in the Hesiodic myth of Prometheus (*Theogony* 535-616, *Works and Days* 42-105). At the same time, food was still part of the sacred: the nature of what was eaten, the treatment of the food and the social and material circumstances of its consumption could be a mediation between the human and the divine as much as a statement of the rules that ordered them. There is what you eat, but there is also how you eat, on what occasion and with whom.

Parasites – a term whose meaning will emerge from our discussion – raise questions about the way the collective group expresses its relation with the gods in the consumption of sacrificial food. Further questions to arise will be: the place of food in the category of the sacred, the evolution of ritual eating in the city, and the evolution of the social image of food.

Parasites are a special case in ritual eating.[1] The term is made up from *sitos*, which signifies primarily cereals (grain, but also food in general), and is also associated with *sitesis*, a form of state dining in Athens; and *para*, suggesting proximity and attendance.

Parasites at Athens

The main source is Athenaeus Book 6 (the speaker in this section is Plutarch of Alexandria) and the texts and authorities he quotes. Here, the 'present-day' parasite is presented as comic, and this persona hinders our search for the earlier religious sense of parasite. The discussion on parasites is an answer to Ulpian, another speaker, who had said:

> Let us not drink and eat everything merely to satisfy the belly,
> like the persons whom we name parasites or flatterers.
> (Athenaeus 6.228d)

Athenaeus (234c) also works in the moralising *topos* of the comparison between the past and the present. The remarks of the antiquarians in Athenaeus suggest that at the end of the classical period it was not easy to reconstruct the precise function of the parasite. Polemon's definition is: 'something sacred, similar to a *sunthoinos* (fellow diner at a sacred banquet)' (quoted at Athenaeus 234d). *Sunthoinos* appears only here, though the related *sunthoinator* is found in Euripides *Electra* 638. *Thoine* signifies a religious feast. On the inscription of the Labyadai at Delphi[2], *thoinai* are the banquets which members of a *phratry* (kinship-group) are obliged to attend during major state festivals. The prefix *sun-* underlines the importance of commensality, and recalls another feature of parasites. In our texts they are always referred to in the plural, never singly. There are three at the Athenian deme of Pallene according to an inscription recorded by Athenaeus (234f); the Archon law cited by Krates specifies that they must be chosen in the demes, 'in line with the written statutes' (quoted at Athenaeus 235c). There is thus at least one per deme, probably more. The same text speaks of 'the parasites' of Acharnai, another Attic deme. Diodoros of Sinope refers to twelve parasites in the service of Herakles (fr. 2.23-30 KA, quoted at Athenaeus 239d).

Another word connected with parasites seems to recur in the text of the Archon law, and that is *dainusthai* (to feast), used of their participation in the ritual feast. Now *dais*, related to *daiein*, 'distribute', is a term belonging to the vocabulary of sacred meals, in particular to the division of sacrificial meat. The text is doubtful here. Gulick, the translator of Athenaeus in the Loeb series, believes that the grain distributed by the parasites is to be 'given as a meal to the Athenians in the sacred precinct'. Wilamowitz, defended by Schlaifer, argues that the parasites 'will share a meal in the sacred precinct after a preliminary offering to Athena'. Schlaifer remarks, and I agree with him, that the form *dainusthai* cannot mean 'give a meal', but only 'share a meal'.³

The other references are to *parasitein* ('to perform the office of parasite') without any more precise indication. That is the case in the Deliastai inscription concerning the Athenian citizens forming the city's annual delegation to the sanctuary of Apollo at Delphi: two members of the Kerykes clan must 'serve as parasites for a year in the sanctuary of Apollo' (Athenaeus 234f). That this function involved implicitly, besides the other duties mentioned in the texts, that of 'eating together' is what is suggested for example by Solon's use of the term *parasitein* when he obliged the Athenians to take turns in eating in the Prytaneion (the building containing the state hearth):

> An unusual law of Solon is the one concerning *sitesis* in the name of the *demos*, what he himself calls *parasitein*: he does not allow the same man to participate too often in the meal, and equally punishes him if he refuses to attend when required. He thought the first was inspired by greed, the second by scorn for the community. (Plutarch *Solon* 24.5; see below)

In addition to the shared meal, parasites participated in the sacrifice with the priest at Kynosarges (a precinct of Herakles at Athens), according to Polemon, quoted by Athenaeus at 234e; in the Archon law (235c) the parasites gathered, stored and distributed the sacred grain, like the *krithologoi* of Opous, the 'masters of the barley' attested in one of Plutarch's *Greek Questions* (= *Moralia* 292b-c).⁴ In fact, Krates almost seems to view '*attendant at* sacred *sitos*' as the true etymology of the word (235b).

In its archaic ritual dimension, the office is both a privilege and an obligation: a privilege shared with the priests, the old men and the women married for the first time, whereby they receive an honoured part of the meat (a third of the meat of two sacrificed animals during the festival of

Athena Pallenis is shared among the parasites, another third goes to the priest, the rest to the 'contest', according to the inscription from the Anakeion (shrine of the Dioskouroi) quoted by Athenaeus at 235b); and an unavoidable obligation, enforced by a court (see the inscription from the sanctuary of Herakles at Kynosarges quoted by Athenaeus at 234e).

All these references are to Attika, and concern four gods, Athena Pallenis, Apollo, Herakles and the Dioskouroi. Schlaifer (see note 3) uses Athenaeus' text to reconstitute the cult of Athena Pallenis, for which no further evidence survives. It appears to be a cult observed by an association of demes going back to the archaic period, which was from the seventh century placed under the control of the state and the *archon basileus* (the senior religious magistrate). Another deme cult going back to the archaic period before taking on some state control is that of Herakles at Kynosarges, participation in which is limited by law to 'bastard' parasites (in other words only their father must be Athenian; the inscription is quoted by Athenaeus at 234e). The reason for this provision is a matter for speculation: because the gymnasium was specially reserved for them (so Gulick)? Because they lived in large numbers in the deme Diomeia where the sanctuary was to be found?[5] The 'bastardy' of Herakles as an explanation seems to be secondary, despite Farnell, not least because Diodoros of Sinope insists on the quality of the parasites chosen by the city for the cult of Herakles which was celebrated on a great scale in all the demes: they were carefully selected as sons of two Athenians (Athenaeus 239d). As for the Dioskouroi, the parasites at the Anakeion, and the antiquity of the local festival, the Anakeia, whose cult was assimilated with that of the Dioskouroi, suggest a significant civic role for this cult in 6th century Athens.

The references in Athenaeus, then, suggest that parasites in the archaic period were citizens selected from aristocratic families, and their function was to accompany priests and assist at the sacrifice. They also collected contributions of corn and cattle. They had at their disposal in the sanctuary a building for storing the corn levied, called either the *archeion* or the *parasition* (Athenaeus 235b,d). The archaic character of the institution is implied by recruitment by election rather than by lot. That the number of parasites attached to Herakles was twelve may also imply an origin in Athens before the reorganization of Kleisthenes (508 BC).

The distinction surrounding their name in the aristocratic city, where the powerful families who controlled Athens gave themselves honours as priests and sanctuary administrators, was not the same in the post-Kleisthenic city where the state gradually took over deme cults. There was no longer a place, it seems, beside the new buildings for housing sacrificial banquets for the storage/dining halls of the parasites. It is not that commensality among small groups was declining: there are attestations all over Greece of many cult associations eating common meals, with various titles. But the delegation of a small number of its members by the deme or the city is now transferred to other kinds of religious and civic participation.[6] From the 6th century, Solon's imposition of *parasitein* on all citizens in turn perhaps indicates its antiquity and prestige at the same time as its obsolescence. Here *parasitein* is a synonym for *sussitein* (eating together), but it takes us half way towards the Spartan model of *sussitia* (messes) which combined compulsory dining with daily gathering of the citizens, thereby creating one of the institutions defining citizenship. In another way Solon's parasites link sacred function and civic commensality. The meal is taken not in a sanctuary but in the Prytaneion with its religious association as the city's hearth where Hestia's fire always burns. That too is where the city's permanent honoured guests will eat, the beneficiaries of *sitesis*, a privilege limited in the 5th century to a small number of citizens who embody all the values of the past aristocratic city.

Parasites outside Athens

Outside Athens, there are participants and assistants at sacrifices and banquets who are reminiscent of the Attic parasites of Athenaeus. At Tenos, inscriptions from the 2nd century BC[7] list chief magistrates and ten to twelve *paredroi* (people sitting together), believed by Robert to be table companions of the chief magistrates who perform daily sacrifice at the Prytaneion[8]. Kontoleon believes they assist at sacrifices in state festivals. At Astakos in Akarnania, a dedication (*IG* IX.1² 434, 2nd *c.* BC) is made by seven *hierapoloi* (sacred officials) of Zeus Karaios, which lists five *sunestai* (co-eaters at the banquet). Lists were also found at Olympia, Sparta, Delos, and Ephesos. To insist on the sacred over all forms of institutionalized commensality, either at festivals for gods at their sanctuary or at daily sacrifices where the Prytaneion is particularly important, seems to be the common element in the different forms of eating by parasites and *paredroi*. As for those officials mentioned by Klearchos of Soloi (quoted by Athenaeus at 235a) – 'in their old laws most cities even these days list parasites among their most honoured offices' – do they still have any sacred function, or are they not closer to those *paredroi* mentioned by Aristotle (*On the constitution of Methone* fr. 551 Rose, quoted by Athenaeus 235e) whose function is to assist magistrates and polemarchs, just like those others chosen by the Archons themselves to attend them and dine with them (Aristotle *Constitution of the Athenians* 56.1)?[9] It seems that, in moving amongst these texts of various dates assembled by Athenaeus, one proceeds gradually from a cult official reliably attested but maintained only as a survival, to a civic and political official with different functions but the same name.

The comic parasite

Diodoros of Sinope in his defence of the 'modern' parasite has a parasite call on Zeus himself as the inventor of *parasitein*. It is quite clear that the late sense of 'gross and abusive diner' is comically applied to the god, who, says Diodoros

> …enters our houses…and lies down with the guests decorously
> and feasts himself; and having eaten of this and drunk of that, he
> goes back home without paying his share.
> (fr. 2.7-13 KA, quoted by Athenaeus at 239b)

Diodoros plays on the two senses of the term to show that the profane and *private* parasite is sanctioned by his sacred and *public* predecessor whom he has simply copied. He playfully exploits the confusion between the two, whose differences are no longer understood. This is a literary model drawing on a modified social and religious phenomenon.

The comic version of the parasite as a person of low caste who eats at the expense of his host not only results from the obsolescence of the official parasite but also expresses a relationship other than commensality. In moving from one type of parasite to the other there is a shift from plural to singular. Now the parasite is an *individual* using all his talents to achieve acceptance at another individual's table, a rich or powerful patron who will 'nourish' (*trephein*) him (as the city 'nourished' its magistrates at the

Prytaneion). This is the individual as opposed to the communal. The condemnation by the comic poets tells us less about the reality of parasites than about the creation of a persona which can be used to denounce a relationship in eating that expresses a form of social organization. The parasite has declined from the representative civic eater to an eater who is a social perversion, a form of profiteer.[10] The character of the buffoon who offers foolery in exchange for a place at the meal is attested from the classical period: the *gelotopoios* (laughter-maker) Philip, for example, in Xenophon's *Symposion* 1.11-16. But buffoon and parasite are still distinct. Plato in the *Laches* (179b-c) speaks of *parasitein* without derision, using the verb of two boys who dine daily with their fathers (who *sussitousin* – take their meal together) and hear of ancestral deeds of honour. This is not official or religious, but it is traditional and aristocratic, and not unrelated to the Spartan system with its pedagogical purpose.

Conclusion

To conclude this survey of ancient parasites and what they can tell us about the place of food in the category of the sacred: the duty of parasites to eat sacrificial meat to one side in the sanctuary puts them, not in communion with the divine, but in a privileged relationship recalling the bond between men and gods. Representing the community, they call attention to the sacred importance of consuming sacrificial meat. They place a positive value on the ambivalence of the consumption of food, which is a human necessity and a sign of mortality. Parasites are at an intersection of two practices, commensality and ritual eating, which characterize the Greek notion of relations between gods and men. Sacrificial meat eaten in the sanctuary, far from being sacred, is in a sense desacralized by the division made between human and divine portions. The human portion of the beast, though, when consumed by representative humans with other food in the sanctuary, has a ritual value and special function. Because this space belongs to the god, it gives a sacred value and a positive symbolic significance to the meal. Such is the context in which, in the archaic city, certain citizens received from the community this special function which included the duty of eating together, in the name of all citizens, near to the gods.

Notes

1. See L. Ziehen 'Parasitoi', *Paulys Real-Encyclopädie der Classischen Altertumswissenschaft* 18 (1949) 1377-81.

2. G. Rougemont *Corpus des Inscriptions de Delphes* 1 (Paris, 1977) no. 9, side D.

3. See R. Schlaifer 'The Cult of Athena Pallenis', *Harvard Studies in Classical Philology* 54 (1943) 36-67, especially 58-9.

4. Schlaifer's conjecture (1943, 52) is that they had also to choose an ox from the sacred cattle.

5. See S. Woodford 'Cults of Herakles in Attica', in *Studies presented to George M.A. Hanfmann* (Cambridge, Mass. 1974), 211-25, particularly 216; L. Farnell *Greek Hero Cults and Ideas of Immortality* (Oxford, 1921) 164-5; further discussion in S.C. Humphreys, 'The *nothoi* of Kynosarges', *Journal of Hellenic Studies* 94 (1974) 88-95.

6. See P. Schmitt Pantel *La cité au banquet, histoire des repas publics dans les cités grecques* (Collection de l'Ecole française de Rome 157, 1992), especially 90-105, 'Rituels de commensalité'.

7. Published by N.M. Kontoleon, 'Inscriptions de Ténos', in *Geras Antoniou Keramopoulou* (Athens, 1953) 224-40; see L. Robert, 'Bulletin épigraphique' in *Revue des Etudes Greques* 68 (1955) 253-4 (no. 181) and 71 (1958) 257 (no. 274).

8. L. Robert *Revue des Etudes Grecques* Bulletin épigraphique 181 (1955) and 274 (1958).

9. See S. Dow 'Companionable Associates in the Athenian Government', *In Memoriam O. Brendel* (1976) 69-84, especially 80-4.

10. See Elisa Avezzù ('Il ventre del parassita: identità, spazio e tempo discontinuo', in O. Longo and P. Scarpi (eds) *Homo Edens* (Verona 1989) 235-40): 'il parassita è prodotto di un particolare momento storico,...là dove si manifesta un primo abbozzo di stato assistenziale...'. On the comic parasite, see now P.G. Mc C. Brown, 'Menander, fragments 745 and 746K-T, Menander's *Kolax*, and parasites and flatterers in Greek comedy', *Zeitschrift für Papyrologie und Epigraphik* 92 (1992) 91-107, especially 98-107.

❖ 15 ❖

OPSOPHAGIA
REVOLUTIONARY EATING
AT ATHENS

James Davidson

**What is
opsophagia?**

𝕀 wish to pursue a line of questioning initiated by a rather more distinguished mind some years ago, as described by Xenophon in his *Memorabilia* (3.14):

> On one occasion Socrates observed that one of the members of the dinner-party had stopped taking *sitos*, eating the *opson* itself on its own, and since the conversation was about names and the kind of action that gave rise to them he said 'Gentlemen, are we able to say for what kind of action a man is called *opsophagos*?'

Opsophagia is the key Greek term to describe some kind of problematic eating. Athenaeus provides a list of various characters, many of them politicians, who are caricatured as *opsophagoi* by comic playwrights, orators and collectors of anecdotes. Apart from Xenophon, we know of several other ancient discussions of the term and its proper usage: Chrysippos, Hegesander of Delphi, Athenaeus and Plutarch devoted time and space to the question, not all of them coming up with the same definition. The problems of definition continue today with different authorities translating *opsophagia* as gourmandise, greediness, and fondness for fish. This difficulty in defining the term is closely connected to the problematic of the activity the word describes, and constitutes an interesting topic in itself. For the moment I will confine myself to Xenophon's discussion and examine the nature of the fuss.

Greek victuals were regularly divided into three parts: *sitos* (the staple, usually bread), *opson* (whatever one eats with the staple) and *poton* (drink). This tripartite list occurs in numerous passages in ancient literature from Homer onwards, sometimes with *artos* (bread) substituted for *sitos*, and *oinos* (wine) for drink (see Liddell and Scott's *Greek-English Lexicon* s.v. *opson*). The most famous example is perhaps the passage where Thucydides describes how Themistokles, after having gone over to the Persians, was given three cities by the great King to meet his needs: Magnesia for his *artos*, Lampsakos for his *oinos*, and Myous for his *opson* (1.138.5). But on every occasion where the Greeks discussed diet, as a medical, political, economic or moral question, it was discussed under these three headings. If we put liquids on one side for the moment, what this meant was that solid food for the Greeks was fundamentally a binary system, an interplay of two quite different things. This binarism was not merely an intellectual reality, but continually figured *in practice*, inscribed in a personal geography in the form of a left-right distinction corresponding to the two categories in operation at meal-times. *Sitos* was taken with the left hand, *opson* with the right. Xenophon in the *Cyropaedia* (8.5.3) describes how Cyrus' tent was organised with the *opsopoioi* (*opson*-makers) on the right and the bakers on the left. Plutarch (*Moralia* 2.99d, cf. 1.5a) describes how children were castigated if they did it the wrong way round. Perhaps there were, as in India today, toilet habits which complemented these eating habits and helped to complete a system based on ideas of a clean hand, which can be used to dip into communal dishes, and a dirty hand which must not. But I know of no explicit references to such a complementary system in the classical period.

What is *opson*?

The explicit problematic about *opsophagia* found in texts from the 5th century onwards derives, I think, from a difficulty already inherent in this binary division of food. The status of the category *opson* is already ambivalent and fragile. It is a necessary element of the diet and yet somehow superfluous to it. It functions under a strange logic similar to that of Derrida's famous 'dangerous supplement', a term which covers what is necessary to complete something, and yet at the same time manages to be extraneous, threatening all the time to take it over.[1] In the same way *opson* is intrinsic to diet: it is what the right hand reaches out for to complement the bread in the left; it is one of the three pillars of existence, listed in numerous writings on diet. But at the same time it is an additional extra, a mere garnish. The first emphasis stressing the essential nature of *opson* is brought out in all those passages already referred to which discuss the tripartite division of foodstuffs, but also in those where the emphasis is on allowances, payments and earning a living in general. The chorus in Aristophanes' *Wasps* 300-1 complain that they already have to pay for barley, wood, and *opson* out of their *mistharion* (little fee). Diogeiton, according to the speaker of Lysias 32, had calculated as much as five obols per day for the *opson* for the children under his tutelage (section 20 – apparently a gross exaggeration), and it is from this emphasis that *opson* comes to give us *opsarion* – salary, which often seems to be a monetary payment in the papyri, to complement a wheat-ration (*sitesis* or *sitarion*).[2] The other side of *opson* is found in those places where it seems to mean no more than 'garnish'. This emphasis is found as early as Homer in *Iliad* 11.630, a passage well known to the Socratic circle since it was cited by both Plato and Xenophon. The same usage crops up, especially in metaphor, in Aristophanes (e.g. *Peace* 123).

The space of *opson* is therefore a very difficult one for the philosophers, intrinsically awkward to pin down. It cannot be done away with completely, only neglected, elided, or reduced to a negative space. A typical discussion in this regard is the treatment of pristine society in Plato's *Republic* (2.372).[3] Socrates is turning to the question of sustenance and daily necessities:

> 'They will produce *sitos* and wine and clothes and shoes. They will live off barley-meal or wheat-meal, …laid out on rushes or fresh leaves, and feast magnificently with their children around them, recumbent on couches of myrtle and bryony, drinking wine, wearing garlands and hymning the gods, enjoying each others' company…'

After this little excursus on an ancient idyll, Glaukon interrupts to point out the obvious omission:

> 'You're making these people dine without *opson*.'

> 'You're quite right', says Socrates, 'I forgot that they will have *opson* too: salt and oil and cheese and whatever vegetables are to be gathered from the fields for the kitchen...'

listing, amongst other things, acorns.[4] Glaukon is outraged and claims that Socrates has been describing a city of pigs. He demands:

> 'what is normal (*haper nomizetai*), including *opsa* that modern men have...' (*opsa haper hoi nun echousi...*)

The dialogue between Socrates and Glaukon illustrates perfectly the discursive disruption which accompanies the problematic about *opson*. It is a space the philosopher tries to ignore, or forget. When forced to address the omission, he fills the gap with the most perfunctory and ready-to-hand material. The dangerous supplement receives the same kind of limitations and depredations in Xenophon's *Cyropaedia*. In the old Persian system of education, we are told, boys up to sixteen or seventeen live off bread as *sitos*, water from a river as *poton*, and *kardamon* (a type of cress) as *opson*. The slightly older boys, whom Xenophon calls the *ephebes*, go hunting with one day's ration of bread, and no *opson* but what they manage to catch. The space of *opson* had at this point become a vacuum, a negative space, a neat and commonplace solution for the essential inessential. Socrates ate just sufficient food 'so that desire for *sitos* was its *opson*' claims Xenophon in the *Memorabilia* (1.3.5). The old saw, that hunger is the best *opson*, crops up twice in the *Cyropaedia* (1.5.12, 4.5.4; cf. 7.5.80, Cicero *de Finibus* 2.90).

Opsophagia

As I have already suggested, it is precisely the problematic inherent in the dangerous supplement, which threatens always to take over that which it is supposed to complete or embellish, that is represented in the discourse of *opsophagia*. The verb *opsophagein* and the noun *opsophagos* first occur in Aristophanes. In the *Clouds* (982-3), *opsophagein* is one of the activities which, according to Right Logic, were forbidden in the past, along with snatching herbs from elders, giggling, and fidgeting. The compound verb seems at first sight utterly transparent in meaning. Dover remarks in his commentary (Oxford, 1968) ad loc.: 'they are expected to be content with the staple diet of bread and wine, and not to be choosy over other foods', but in fact he is effectively conflating two separate approaches to translating the term *opson*, another example perhaps of mixing up etymological approaches to meaning and usage. On the one hand, by simple analysis, it should mean 'to eat *opson*' and here 'not to eat *opson*' i.e. 'to be content with the staple diet of bread and wine', but as Dover observes, no one would think that boys in the past really lived on a purely farinaceous diet. So to this sense he has added the common idea that *opsophagia* is dietary effeteness, gourmandise, choosiness, a meaning apparently much more in line with usage, and supported by another rendering of the word from the old obsolete lemmata of Passow and Liddell and Scott which translate *opson* as 'rich fare', 'dainties' and *opsophagia* as 'love of dainties', 'dainty living'.

But let us return to the scene described by Xenophon in the *Memorabilia*. We find that Socrates is already several steps ahead of us (and Sir Kenneth) in his discussion:

> 'Can we say, gentlemen, for what kind of action a man is called *opsophagos*? For, in fact, everyone eats *opson* on the *sitos*, whenever it is available; but I don't think they are called *opsophagoi* for this reason.' 'No, certainly not', said one of those present.
>
> 'What, then, if someone eats the *opson* itself, without the *sitos*, not because he is in training, but for the sake of pleasure, does he seem to be an *opsophagos* or not?'
>
> 'If not, it's hard to say who does', replied the other. And someone else said: 'What about the man who eats a large amount of *opson* on a bit of *sitos*?'
>
> 'He too seems to me to deserve the epithet', said Socrates.
>
> (Xenophon *Memorabilia* 3.14)

By this time the ears of the man whose eating habits started the discussion in the first place, a young man (*neaniskos*) as it happens, must have started to burn. He takes a piece of bread. Socrates notices this gesture, and not being a man to let things lie, calls on the man's neighbours 'to see whether he treats the *sitos* as *opson*, or the *opson* as *sitos*'.

Xenophon, then, has left us with an account of what kind of behaviour *opsophagia* could be thought to describe. How does this help us with the *opsophagoi* listed by Athenaeus' comic poets and anecdotalists and their feats of consumption? I quote a few examples. Antiphanes in *Rich Men* (fr.34.5-6 KA) talks of Phoinikides and dearest Taureas, 'two old *opsophagoi*, such men as gobble down fish slices in the agora'. The same Phoinikides is mentioned in Euphanes' *Muses* (fr. 1 KA). When he sees a boiling dish full of Nereus' offspring

> he restrained his hands, excited as they were with fury, and asked 'Who says that he has the skill to eat from the common table? Who has the skill to reach into the middle and snatch up the hot morsels? Where is Korydos (the Lark), or Phyromachos or mighty Nilos? Let him grapple with us and end up with nothing in no time at all.'

Another passage talks of one Diokles, who gobbled up his lands in *opsophagia*:

> On one occasion he gulped down a fish while still hot and said that it burnt the roof of his mouth [or as the Greeks said, 'the heavenly vault (*ouranos*)'] and Theokritos remarked 'The only thing you have left to swallow down is the sea and then you will have swallowed the three greatest elements, land, sea and sky'.
> (Athenaeus 8.344b)

But the comic passage that comes closest to Xenophon's/Socrates' discussion is from Axionikos' play *The Euripides Fanatic* (fr. 4 KA):

> Another fish, confident in its great size, has Glaukos caught in the deep net and brought to these parts, as *sitos* for *opsophagoi*.

These examples from Athenaeus, and Xenophon's discussion in the *Memorabilia*, although deriving from rather different kinds of discourse, can be interpreted as giving a consistent picture of *opsophagia*. There is no mention of these *opsophagoi* eating bread. Typically, they are shown snatching *opson* straight from the pan, so that it burns their fingers or their mouths. The kind of eating described often seems to take place outside a formal gathering like a *deipnon* (banquet), and is quite often solitary. This particular mode of consumption does not correspond exactly either to the gourmandise of epicures, nor to the greediness of gluttons, although it contains elements of both. It can only really be understood in the context of the fundamental *opson/sitos* structure of eating in ancient Greece, as a radical subversion of the normal order, the extra, additional and superfluous element taking over the necessary and substantial.

Opsophagia and revolution

This brings me to *opsophagia* and revolution. If *opsophagia* is simply a breaking of the rules of Greek table manners, something which Aristophanes can place alongside fidgeting and giggling, what's the big deal? Why go on about it? The key, I propose, lies in the precise kind of desire characterized by *opsophagia*. Many of the anecdotes in Athenaeus refer to gobbling food down (*katabrochthizein*), or to snatching food from the plate, or from a fellow-diner. Typical of the kind of eating involved, and clearly marking its distance from connoisseurship or gourmandise is a fragment of Anaxandrides' play *Odysseus* (fr. 34 KA). A fisherman is composing a eulogy of the fisherman's art:

> While the results of a painter's exquisite labours end up the object of admiration, hung on a wall, the fruit of our efforts is snatched from the dish without so much as a 'by your leave' and disappears directly from the pan. What other profession gets the lips of young men burning, gets their fingers pushing and shoving, gets their lungs gasping for air in their haste to swallow?

This incapacity of the *opsophagos* to resist, or even to have patience, is attested by several comic passages:

> I'd as soon give up my purpose as Kallimedon would the head of a *glaukos* [a type of fish]

is how a character in a play of Antiphanes (fr. 77 KA) illustrates his absolute determination. The image of a sizzling squid being snatched away from a drooling man at the last minute is the torture that accompanies the curse of the *Acharnians* 1156-61. The kind of desire associated with *opsophagia* is most comparable not to the refined palate of an epicure, nor to the guzzling of a Rabelaisian Hercules, but to the desperate and immediate need of a drug addict for a fix. And indeed *opsophagia* has many of the same automatic associations with criminal activity. A character in Diphilos' play

The Merchant (fr. 31.12-17 KA) suggests that if a man who in other regards is certainly short of money is seen buying eels, an *opsophagos*' delight, he should be arrested and carted off to prison

> because that man cannot live without some kind of criminal activity, you understand, but is bound to spend his nights as a cloak-snatcher, or a burglar, or as an accomplice of those who do such things, or he must play the sycophant in the *agora* or perjure himself for money.

Kleon

One of the earliest figures whose *opsophagia* is used to characterize his political corruption and criminality is Kleon in Aristophanes' *Knights*. At 353-5, the Paphlagonian (i.e. Kleon) boasts:

> 'Do you compare any man to me? I who can consume hot slices of tuna, drink a jugful of neat wine and then without a pause screw the generals at Pylos?'

Rather later, at 929-40, the connection with corruption is established in the curse of the Sausage-seller:

> 'May your skillet of squid be standing ready and sizzling; and may you be about to propose a motion concerning the Milesians, and make a talent if you carry it; and may you therefore make haste to fill yourself with the squid and still get to the Assembly in time and then, before you have eaten it may a man come for you, and may you in your eagerness to get the talent choke on the squid as you eat it.'

The curse implicitly links the desire for bribes with *opsophagia*, a link which is made explicit in other metaphors. In 313, for instance, Kleon is described as 'watching out for shoals of tribute, like a tunny-fisher.' In the pseudo-prophecy of 1030-4, Demos is advised to be wary of the dog Kerberos (Kleon again), who

> when thou dinest will wag his tail ingratiatingly, watch his opportunity, and eat up the *opson* when thou art looking in another direction; and he will go frequently to the kitchen and, dog-fashion, without thy being aware of it, will by night lick the plates and the islands clean.

In contrast, the Sausage-seller would not 'fall on the Milesian sea-bass, and devour them' (361). The imagery of *opsophagia* is being used by Aristophanes in these passages to characterize Kleon's greed for bribes as compelling, incessant and impossible to resist.

Timarchos

A similar discourse relating *opsophagia* to political malpractice and the betrayal or overthrow of the *demos* is found in descriptions of other politicians' eating habits, most frequently with regard to 4th century orators like Philokrates and Hypereides. The fullest and clearest account, however, of *opsophagia* and revolutionary desire which survives from the classical period is Aischines' depiction of Timarchos:

> 'Timarchos did not hesitate to submit to Misgolas' offer of money,' says the orator, 'although he had income enough. For his father had left him a very large property, which he has squandered, as I will show. But he behaved as he did, because he was a slave to the most shameful vices, *opsophagia*, expensive dinner parties, flute-girls, *hetairai*, dice and all those other things which a free and noble man should not allow to overwhelm him.'
>
> (1.42)

After leaving Misgolas and working through various other sugar-daddies, Timarchos ends up with Hegesander and together they proceed to work through money embezzled (of course) by the latter from the general Timomachos:

> 'but when these resources had been wasted away and diced away and eaten up in *opsophagia*, whilst at the same time his fading looks reduced the revenues from prostitution, and since he continued to be afflicted by the same desires, he turned his *akrasia* (lack of self-control) on his father's estates and not only gobbled them up but gulped them down, one could say. He couldn't wait for the best offer but let the property go for what it could fetch immediately, so urgently did he press on towards his pleasures.   (95-6)

In case we still haven't quite got the point, Aischines spells it all out in the peroration:

For he who despises the laws and decent behaviour (*sophrosune*) comes to be in a particular condition in his soul, which is plainly revealed by the disorderliness of his conduct... Many men of this sort you could find who have fallen into the greatest misfortunes themselves... The impetuous pleasures of the body are what fill the robbers' bands, and put men on board the pirates' boats. These pleasures are for each man his Fury, urging him to slay his fellow citizens, to serve the tyrant, to help overturn the democracy. (189-90)

The message is clear. If you want to avoid accusations of prostitution and fomenting revolution, you had better mind your table-manners.

Notes

1. See especially J. Derrida, '...That dangerous supplement...', in *Of Grammatology* (Baltimore, 1976) 141-64.

2. *Opson* cannot slip so easily as *sitos* and *poton* from the general to the specifics (bread and wine). On the contrary, it is that part of the diet associated with substitutions, variability and exchange.

3. This passage is also discussed by John Wilkins in the Introduction to Part One.

4. See Sarah Mason's contribution to this volume.

❖ 16 ❖

ANCIENT VEGETARIANISM

Catherine Osborne

Was there anything we should call vegetarianism in the ancient world?

A vegetarian, according to the *Concise Oxford Dictionary*, is:

> One who abstains from the use of flesh, fish and fowl as food, with or without the addition of eggs and dairy produce, and whose diet includes roots, leafy vegetables, cereals, seeds, fruit and nuts.

There are degrees of vegetarianism: some refuse only some kinds of meat, some are happy to eat fish but not flesh, some reject milk and eggs as well. Here I consider any kind of theory about abstaining from something that is animal in origin. This would apply to someone who refuses to eat butter, but has no objection to any other meat products, just as much as to someone who rejects the whole range.

I want to raise the issue of motives. The dictionary does not mention any specific motive for abstaining from animal products, and that is probably right, since in ordinary contexts we do not distinguish vegetarians on the basis of their reasons.

Nevertheless there are a variety of reasons for choosing such a diet. Take the person who eats *Flora*, the sunflower margarine, instead of butter. She might do so because her husband does the shopping and only buys *Flora*. But there are other reasons why she might actually choose *Flora*. There is the new puritanism, which makes her ashamed to choose butter in front of her disapproving colleagues. Or she might in fact prefer the taste of the margarine. Another possibility is that she believes that the *Flora* is better for her health. The *Flora* might be cheaper than butter. Yet another reason could be that *Flora* spreads more easily. This may not be an exhaustive list of the possible reasons.

We now have six explanations for using *Flora*:
1. Necessity, or restricted opportunity.
2. Convention, popular pressure.
3. Taste or pleasure.
4. Health.
5. Economy.
6. Convenience.

We would probably agree that none of these reasons makes the choice of *Flora* an instance of vegetarianism, although they all, as it happens, involve the use of a vegetable product in place of an animal product. Why in that case is it not strictly vegetarianism? Two things emerge from this example. One is that vegetarianism needs to be a conscious choice, not imposed by necessity or convention. Speaking generally we might say that a tribe whose diet was restricted to fruit and nuts, for want of any altern-ative, had a vegetarian diet, but we should probably not want to say that they practised vegetarianism. Vegetarianism implies that the diet is chosen deliberately and on principle.[1] But secondly we can see something about what the principle must be. Four of the six reasons for eating *Flora* seem to be matters that could be expressed as deliberate principles,[2] but they are not principles that belong to vegetarianism. They do not belong to vegetarianism because they do not invoke any issue specific to animal as opposed to vegetable products. To say that I choose *Flora* because it is cheaper is not to say that I choose it because it is of vegetable origin. The same principle might, on another occasion, lead me to choose liver rather than steak, or milk rather than whisky.

A vegetarian principle will be one that marks out animal products because they are animal products, or some animal products[3] because they are a particular kind of animal product. A principle that could include some vegetable products in certain circumstances would not be a vegetarian principle.

Now it might seem that the principle 'because it is healthy' might be a vegetarian principle in disguise. I might, for example, choose the *Flora* because it is healthy, on the grounds that vegetable fats are more healthy than animal fats. Spelt out fully then, the principle goes something like this:

> As regards the class of fats, I abstain from all animal fats on the grounds that they are animal fats (because animal fats are harmful to my health).

This seems to have the same form as a vegetarian principle such as:

> As regards proteins, I abstain from all animal protein on the grounds that it is animal (because, say, animals deserve to be treated with respect).

In both cases the principle marks out all and only animal products in the relevant class as forbidden. Applying such a principle seems to make me, in practice, a vegetarian in that respect.

Nevertheless there is a difference between the two principles and I want to pinpoint it by asking whether the principle is self-regarding or not. If I abstain from a particular item because it is not healthy for me, the consideration is not what the item is in itself, but how it affects me.[4] Thus we can classify the principles for choosing one's diet in two categories: considerations that are unrelated to who the consumer is, and considerations about the properties that the food exhibits in relation to the individual concerned. If we return to the sunflower margarine diet we can see that most of the rules involved are self-regarding rules: I reject the butter because

    (a)   it is not pleasant *to me*;
    (b)   it is not healthy *for me*;
    (c)   it is expensive *for me*;
    (d)   it is not convenient *for me*.

By contrast, other-regarding principles will be ones concerned with how my eating the food bears either on the source of nourishment itself, or on some other individual or group affected by the action. I reject the butter because

    (a)   it is not fair *on the cow* to take its milk;
    (b)   it is not fair *on the calf* to take its mother's milk;

(c)   the milk could be better used *for starving human babies*;

(d)   cattle are an inefficient use of the earth's resources which could be more fairly distributed *to other human beings*.

Among the other-regarding principles we might want to distinguish between those concerned with other human beings, and those concerning justice towards non-human nature.[5] But my present task is to look at the arguments for a vegetarian diet presented in antiquity. Were they based on self-regarding principles or on other-regarding principles?[6]

In the earliest period of Greek vegetarian thought, that is early Pythagoreanism and Empedokles, the chief motive behind the rejection of meat-eating seems to be symbolic. It concerns the status of the individual in relation to the gods and the beasts associated with sacrificial rituals. But while this motive may have been ultimately self-regarding – what I eat matters for how I stand in relation to the gods – the principles invoked to explain why this or that kind of food was ruled out for the true Pythagorean need not be self-regarding. They may include considerations about what is appropriate for the animals or plants involved. Thus when Empedokles cries out

> Alas that the pitiless day did not destroy me first, before I devised
> for my lips the cruel deed of eating flesh!
> (fr. B139, trans. Wright 1981)

he is acknowledging that the act of eating flesh has disastrous consequences for the meat-eater. But the reason why it has these disastrous consequences is because it is wrong, and it is wrong for other reasons. Although it may be harmful to me to do wrong, it does not follow that it was wrong *because* it was harmful to me.

What then, are the principles that determine why I ought not to eat certain kinds of food in Empedokles? In the case of beans and laurel leaves the reasons are far from clear and have been a subject of speculation since antiquity.[7] In the case of meat-eating or sacrifice we have a fair number of Empedokles' own lines which seem to indicate what the problem with killing or eating animals is, although the reasons are not spelt out formally. We find, for example, that we are 'devouring one another',[8] that we are slaughtering our own children, mothers or fathers, and serving them up as food,[9] and that in some golden age the taking of any life was considered an abomination.[10] What seems clear is that there is something about the identity of the victims of slaughter which makes it plainly wrong to kill them, that is that they are people ('one another') and even more emphatically that they are kin. Since it is plain that we do not kill and eat our kin, simply because of what they are, not (for example) because it would be uneconomical or harmful to our interests, it follows that Empedokles' reasons for abstaining from meat seem to be other-regarding principles (I do not kill or eat the sacrificial beasts because of what they are, my kin or my brethren).[11]

Porphyry, in his treatise *On Abstinence from Animal Food*, reviews the considerations in favour of a vegetarian diet put forward by philosophers up to his own day (the 3rd century AD). Among his predecessors in this field are not only Empedokles and Pythagoras from the very early period, but later thinkers too, most notably Theophrastos, pupil of Aristotle, and Plutarch, from the Platonist school. Given the range of philosophical schools involved it is not surprising that the considerations that lead to a vegetarian diet vary. While one may agree that the prevalent argument is that it is 'good for the soul',[12] we can now see that this formula is insufficiently precise. It fails to distinguish between the other-regarding principle that makes the health of my soul a secondary consideration ('animals ought not to be eaten, and to eat them is wrong and hence that would be bad for my soul') and on the other hand the self-regarding principle that makes the health of my soul the immediate concern ('my soul should be kept free of corruption, and enjoying a meat diet is corrupting or distracting to my soul and hence is wrong').

Can vegetarianism be defended on the grounds that eating meat is a luxury?

Among the reasons mentioned by Porphyry is the notion that eating a diet including meat is a luxury.[13] Much of what Porphyry has to say in his treatise amounts to a defence of a life of minimal necessities, free of the attachment to unnecessary pleasures and worldly concerns. Although various sections of the treatise focus on particular reasons why it might be just or unjust to kill animals, whether for sacrifice or food, the theme of the general exhortation to vegetarianism in Book 1 is the idea that abstaining from a meat-diet accords with the aims of the intellectual ascetic.[14] The main reason for choosing it is the desire to strip oneself of all superfluous pleasures and passions.[15] Porphyry observes that ideally we should like to abstain from all food. Hence vegetarianism is itself not an ideal, but only a poor substitute for total detachment.[16] In these circumstances we are not in the business of choosing what we should like to eat, but of making the best of a bad job.

We might question the detail of this reasoning. Why, we might ask, is it clear that meat is the only luxury or the only source of superfluous pleasure? It seems that there might be some kinds of vegetable food that are in themselves surplus to requirements and used purely for pleasure. But Porphyry's argument in this respect is backed up by the observations that meat-eating also involves injustice which adds to the problem. It is doubly corrupting because it is luxury procured at the expense of indefensible moral failure.

It seems clear from this strategy that Porphyry's interest in rejecting meat in his book *On Abstinence* is primarily focused on self-regarding principles. His view is, at its most basic, that the vegetarian diet is 'more healthy'.[17] An opposition to luxury can emerge as an other-regarding principle: one might refrain from over-indulgence or superfluous pleasures on the grounds that they were obtained at the expense of other human beings who were deprived of the bare necessities, or that they were obtained at the expense of the animals or the natural resources. In either of these cases we might hold that using such resources for our pleasure was not right, because it is damaging to others. Porphyry, however, is concerned that luxury is not right because it is damaging to ourselves.

The same is not strictly true of the argument that killing animals is unjust. While this argument may be subservient to the overall aim to show that meat-eating is bad *for us*, the immediate concern of the argument itself is to show that killing and eating animals is wrong and harmful *to animals*. It is for this reason that Porphyry rehearses the arguments to show that animals are intelligent or rational, for example. These issues are important in order to show that we ought not to kill them because of what they are.

There are, then, two halves to Porphyry's argument for vegetarianism: appeals to the self-regarding principle that we should avoid luxury, and a recognition of the status of animals as objects of justice and moral concern. Neither of these arguments seems to be sufficient on its own to lead to a properly vegetarian position. What seems clearest is that the condemnation of luxury alone cannot result in vegetarianism: we should need also to show that all and only animal products were excess to requirements, but there is no self-evident reason why this should be the case. Of course it may be true that it is possible, in certain circumstances, to live simply on a vegetarian diet, but it does not follow that that would always be the simplest or plainest way to obtain the essential nutrients we require.[18] If the concern were simply with procuring an adequate diet with minimal trouble, expense or pleasure, there seems no good reason to rule out animal products on principle.

The principle, then, is going to have to come from something about the animal products themselves, and that is where the second half of Porphyry's case comes in. Animal products are more objectionable than other kinds of nourishment because they depend upon the unjust treatment of the beasts. That does not make them a luxury, but it does make the use of such food, when it is a luxury, peculiarly unfortunate.

Perhaps it makes the use of such food unfortunate in any case, whether for luxury or not. Porphyry seems to suggest it would be:

> If it so happened that we needed animal-slaughter and meat-eating for our very subsistence, like we need air and water and vegetables and fruits, without which it is impossible to live, then our nature would have been inextricably bound up with this kind of injustice. (*On Abstinence* 3.18.3; my translation)

We are in fact physically capable of living without meat. But if we had not been physically capable of doing so, it would still have been unjust to kill and eat the beasts, but it would have been an unavoidable injustice, one we were condemned to perpetrate due to the exigencies of our nature. Porphyry does not distinguish here between the physical possibility (we can live without meat) and the practical possibility (whether we can live without meat depends on whether anything else is available), and hence he does not consider the possibility that one might have to choose between killing an animal and letting oneself or one's child starve.[19] But it seems clear from what he says that even if it were a necessity, the act would still be an injustice. The need for self-preservation may justify the act in one sense but it does not make it right.

With the combination of both halves of his argument, Porphyry can maintain the necessity of a vegetarian regime. Given that meat is, in theory for all and in practice for the audience Porphyry's treatise has in mind,[20] a dispensable part of the diet, it has the status of an optional extra, but showing that it is optional does not in itself show that it is undesirable. Showing that luxury is undesirable in itself is one move towards excluding it[21] but it will not pick out meat as more problematic than any other food that is not strictly necessary. Hence the argument that makes the objection to luxury into a strictly vegetarian thesis is the one that shows that meat-eating is morally wrong.

Would it be sufficient, then, simply to show that killing and eating is wrong, without also showing that it is luxurious? For Porphyry that is not sufficient, perhaps because his reader will want to know not only that it is harmful and unjust to the beasts, but also that it will be bad for her own soul. But it is also not sufficient, because although it may show that we *ought* not to kill and eat the beasts it will not show that we *can* avoid it and live.

Porphyry says that eating meat is a luxury. In terms of our physical nature this may invariably be true, but in terms of the practical possibilities for a particular culture meat may sometimes not be a luxury but an essential part of the diet. It is only if it is, in practice, a luxury that there can be a real choice between vegetarianism and meat-eating. Hence the question 'shall I be vegetarian?' presupposes a degree of affluence, a society or a class of society that can afford to *select* whether or not to indulge in more than the bare necessities, and to select which of a range of available sources of nutrition to employ.

Is vegetarianism a peculiarity of affluent societies with the luxury of choosing a diet?

I cannot claim to be an expert on how regularly meat was in practice eaten, or indeed available, in the ancient world. Indeed the dependence on meat, cereals, or fish probably varies according to the kind of terrain and quality of land in the vicinity, or the proximity to the sea. And *individuals* must have been in different degrees dependent on a market for meat, fish or vegetable products depending on where their main source of livelihood came from. Porphyry himself spent much of his life in Rome, but the predecessors whom he quotes were probably thinking of the cuisine of Greece in the Classical and Roman periods.

Now it may well be that the majority of the population were all but vegetarian in any case, that meat did not figure significantly in the daily fare of ordinary people, and that few of the population were heavily dependent upon livestock farmed for meat as opposed to dairy products or wool.[22] If so, then clearly the proposal that meat should be excluded altogether may indeed have been reasonably practical for the culture that Porphyry's text belongs to.[23] But Porphyry's point is not that the ordinary lifestyle is almost right already. The choice of vegetarianism has to be something that marks out the committed philosopher radically from the unthinking behaviour of his fellow human beings. This may be partly a symbolic identity: refusing meat may not be difficult in practical ways but yet profoundly cranky as regards the social, cultural and religious expectations of the community. Adopting vegetarianism is to be a result of reflection,[24] or (following an Epicurean argument) one should start with philosophy which will then give a basis for deciding about what nutrition is necessary and appropriate.[25]

All of this suggests to me that Porphyry is addressing a class of people who had the practical scope to choose their diet, and for whom the choice would be culturally significant. The resources available to them must have been such as to make the decision whether or not to eat meat a real one. His treatise was, it seems, addressed to those for whom it would be peculiar, but possible, not to kill or eat animals.

Porphyry is well aware that he is writing for philosophers, presumably largely from an affluent élite whose normal diet would almost certainly not be confined to simple necessities. The same recognition is not always so clear in modern discussions of vegetarianism, which rarely recognize that the arguments reflect a certain western 20th century Eurocentrism, in their assumption that one should choose not to eat meat because meat is not a requirement for human survival. Of course we may say to the Inuit or to a member of a hunter-gatherer tribe that it is unjust to kill animals for food; but if we do so we leave her with the uncomfortable option of choosing between being unjust to the prey they hunt, or being unjust to her children who will starve. In such a context we could hardly say that there is no justification for her to put the interests of one species above those of another. *We* appear to have a happier choice: we do not have to commit injustice against the animals because we have the choice of a meat-free diet. But that choice depends upon us living in a position of affluence, with a degree of luxury and surplus that is not available in the less-developed half of the world. And that very affluence, that allows us to congratulate ourselves on our 'justice', is surely a kind of injustice itself.[26]

Notes

1. There is an interesting issue here as to whether the vegetarian children of vegetarian parents are practising vegetarianism. If I am right it is only when they choose the diet for the right reason that they adopt vegetarianism. But can they be said to choose it from a real alternative when they have grown up with it as the norm? In this respect vegetarianism shares some of the puzzles of conventional religion.

2. E.g. I always eat what I like best. I ought to eat what is healthy. I do not believe in spending more than I need on food. I always go for convenience rather than appearance.

3. For example 'I do not eat battery hens' could be a vegetarian principle of a restricted sort, because although it does not exclude all animals, it does apply exclusively to animals and cannot be extended to vegetables.

4. This does not preclude the ultimate concern being not a matter of self-interest but altruistic: for example I choose the healthy diet not because I want to be healthy but so as not to be a burden to others in my old age. Nevertheless the relevance of the consideration of *this* food is how *this* food will affect *me*.

5. This roughly matches the distinction between deep ecology whose concern is for nature as valuable in itself, and shallow ecology whose concern is for nature as a resource of benefit to humankind.

6. To say that a principle is other-regarding does not necessarily imply that we must adhere to it for wholly un-self-interested reasons. My motive for treating another creature justly might be not, or not merely, for its sake, but instead (or also) for my own sake (that I should not be guilty of injustice, that I should be an upright and respectable citizen…). But this would be a secondary motive for pursuing a principle that respects the interests of another, just as preserving my health for the sake of those who will care for me later is a secondary (other-regarding) motive for pursuing a principle that respects my own interests.

7. See for example Diogenes Laertius 8.24; 8.34; Clement of Alexandria *Miscellanies (Stromateis)* 3.3, 24.1-2; Hippolytus *Refutation of all Heresies* 1.2.14; Plutarch *On the Education of Children* 12f. Of these the reasons canvassed in Diogenes Laertius 8.24 seem to be self-regarding reasons (beans cause flatulence and excessive dreaming or disturbed sleep), while the remainder depend upon a symbolic significance of the beans such that abstention from them is

to show a proper attitude to life, death or politics. In these cases it is wrong to touch them because of what they are (or mean) rather than because of what they will do to me (though of course touching them will do something to me).

8. Empedokles fr. B136.
9. Empedokles fr. B137.
10. Empedokles fr. B128.
11. On the irrelevance of looking for the reasons why we do not eat people see Diamond (1978).
12. Bouffartigue and Patillon (1977), introduction lxvii.
13. I am using the term luxury here to cover a range of ideas connected with the notion that meat is surplus to requirements, chosen for pleasure rather than need, a mark of worldly prosperity. Among the Greek terms that figure are *poikilia* and *poluteleia*, though the notion is more often conveyed by a contrast with what is simple, easily procured, minimal trouble and minimal expense.
14. Indeed Porphyry is careful to observe on a number of occasions that the meat-free diet may not be so appropriate to manual workers, athletes and the like: *On Abstinence* 1.27;2.3.
15. *On Abstinence* 1.31-38.
16. *On Abstinence* 1.38.
17. *On Abstinence* 1.52. This passage comes in a section based on Epicurean arguments, but Porphyry endorses the general implications concerning the benefits with regard to self-sufficiency and *ataraxia* gained from a simple diet.
18. Notice that Porphyry suggests that it is particularly for the city-dweller that animals are more difficult to procure than vegetables, *On Abstinence* 2.14.
19. He does make this point in other contexts, notably *On Abstinence* 2. 12 (a passage derived from Theophrastos).
20. The treatise is explicitly addressed to Firmus Castricius, who seems to have fallen from the ideal of philosophical vegetarianism, and is to be brought back to the fold.
21. It is not clear that Porphyry has established that meat is luxurious in the requisite sense. He has indeed asserted that it is physically possible to live without it, and in that sense it is surplus to requirements. But luxury is problematic in so far as it may mean that (a) we indulge in more than we require or (b) we indulge in passions or pleasure. It need not follow, however, that when meat is eaten it is eaten in addition to an otherwise adequate diet, nor that it is taken for the sake of pleasure. Porphyry has to suggest that there are certain particular physical and psychological disadvantages to the meat diet, 1.47.
22. Of course meat was not the only product of killing animals, and it is not clear whether it would be easy to survive in the ancient world without the use of leather, fleeces, bone, horn, tortoiseshell, gut and horsehair, of which the main supply would be from animals killed by man.
23. It is not quite clear what Porphyry's views on fish are. He makes a distinction between the method of killing fish and the method of killing animals (by implication) at *On Abstinence* 3.19.2, but he still regards it as unjust to kill the fish thus (apparently because it is not a natural but a forced death).
24. *On Abstinence* 1.27.
25. *On Abstinence* 1.50.
26. There is a similar difficulty over whether it could be right to harm animals that threaten us but are not for food. Again it is from the comfortable position of 20th century western affluence that it can be maintained that these creatures are really not enemies and have been maligned. At a more basic level of subsistence any natural competitor will be an enemy, whether it steals your lambs in winter, or eats your crops, so as to threaten the livelihood of your household.

Bibliography

Bouffartigue, J. & Patillon, M. 1977 *Porphyre De l'Abstinence* vol. 1 (Paris).

Diamond, C. 1978 'Eating meat and eating people', *Philosophy* 53, 465-79; reprinted in Diamond (1991).

Diamond, C. 1991 *The Realistic Spirit: Wittgenstein, philosophy and the mind* (Cambridge Mass.).

Wright, M.R. 1981 *Empedocles: the extant fragments* (New Haven).

❖ 17 ❖

FASTING WOMEN IN JUDAISM AND CHRISTIANITY IN LATE ANTIQUITY

Veronika Grimm

THE Judaism that is expressed in the written Torah tolerated with equanimity the human body with its fundamental biological requirements, including the need for food, drink and sex. The manner of the satisfaction of these needs, however, was subject to elaborate lists of restrictive rules and regulations. Holiness for the Jews consisted in observing strictly all of these, while sin was any transgression of the law.

In addition to restricting the range of foodstuffs, the law also ordained that Jews keep one day each year as a day of atonement on which they were to abstain completely from food and drink. Moreover, the Jews often turned to fasting spontaneously – in mourning or in times of disaster – aiming to catch their God's attention and pity. The purpose of fasting, just like that of the Temple sin-offering sacrifice, seems to have been to express repentance, remorse, submission and supplication for forgiveness. Fasting

Jewish attitudes to fasting

Spontaneous fasting

had the advantage over the sin-offering sacrifice in that it could be done by anyone in any place, while sacrifice was offered only in the Temple where it was carried out by the priests. Fasting seems to have been a rather conspicuous feature of Judaism in the Diaspora by the time of the Roman Empire. Many ancient authors when writing about Jews describe them as fasting, as if this were a peculiarly Jewish trait. They often claim that the Jewish Sabbath is a fast day, which is rather curious, since Jewish law expressly forbids fasting on the Sabbath. Jewish fasting is mentioned most notably by Tacitus (*Histories* 5.4), while Suetonius has Augustus say:

> 'Not even a Jew fasts so scrupulously on his Sabbaths as I have done today…for it was not until the first hour of the night that I ate two mouthfuls of bread in the bath…'
>
> (*Life of Augustus* 76.2)

Fronto writes:

> looking forward to the first of September as the superstitious look forward to the star, at the sight of which to break their fast.
>
> (*Letter to Marcus Aurelius* 2.7)

The fasting Jewish woman must have been a figure familiar enough amongst the readers of Martial for the poet to use it as a means of evoking a rather vivid, if unflattering, olfactory image: the odour of the breath of fasting Sabbath-keeping women (4.4).

The fact that many Greek and Roman writers found fasting to be one of the most salient characteristics of the Jews of the Diaspora suggests that the practice of fasting may have grown in importance among those who had no access to the Temple in Jerusalem, those in exile or in the Diaspora, and especially after the destruction of the Temple that put an end to sacrificial ritual.

Habitual fasting

In contrast to spontaneous fasting motivated by fear or disaster, habitual abstinence as an ascetic routine for the pious definitely seems to be a late development, attested only in the post-biblical, Second Temple period in the Apocrypha, Pseudepigrapha and Qumran literature.[1] Both the main Jewish writers of the 1st century AD, Philo of Alexandria and Josephus, describe ascetic Jewish groups, in the Land of Israel as well as outside it.[2]

The Essenes are characterized by sexual abstinence, but apparently ate a frugal but adequate diet, while Philo's Therapeutae of both sexes led virginal lives, ate only after sunset and practised abstinence also from meat and wine. Josephus describes the Pharisees, one of the major parties or trends in the Judaism of his contemporaries, as holding to a 'simplified standard of living and despising delicacies in diet' (*Jewish Antiquities* 18.3.12). In this the Gospels seem to support him, showing that ascetic fasting was practised and debated in some of the religious circles that Jesus encountered in his ministry:

> Then the disciples of John came to him saying, 'Why do we and the Pharisees fast but your disciples do not fast?'
> (*Matthew* 9.14)

The same sources attest even the existence of Jewish hermits living in the wilderness. Josephus claims to have been the apprentice of one Bannus,

> who dwelt in the wilderness, wearing only such clothing as trees provided, feeding on such things as grew of themselves, and using frequent ablutions of cold water by day and night for purity's sake.   (*Autobiography* 2.11-12)

And the Gospel says that John

> wore a garment of camel's hair and a leather girdle around his waist; and his food was locusts and wild honey.   (*Matthew* 3.4)

Abstaining from food and/or drink for a given number of hours daily, or from sunrise to sunset on particular days (usually Mondays and Thursdays) was practised for reasons of asceticism among some pious Jews, and especially among women. Judith

> wore sackcloth around her waist and dressed in widow's weeds. She fasted every day of her widowhood except the Sabbath Eve and the Sabbath itself, the Eve of New Moon, the feast of New Moon and the festival days of the House of Israel. (*Judith* 8.6)

The prophetess Anna never left the Temple, serving God night and day with fasting and prayer, according to the Gospel of Luke (2.37).

Rabbinic literature, collected between about 200 and 400 AD, in times when ascetic practices were increasingly highly valued in the gentile world, attests the extensive use of private fasts undertaken by extremely pious individuals for the atonement for sins. Some of these offences for which the pious rabbis fasted until their 'teeth were blackened' were so minor that the self-induced punishment for it seems out of proportion: for example, Rabbi Elazar ben Azariah for voicing a dissenting opinion (Jerusalem Talmud *Shabbath* 5.4.8e), Rabbi Joshua for using insulting words about an opinion of the school of Shammai (Babylonian Talmud *Hagigah* 22b), and Rabbi Shimon for making derogatory remarks about Rabbi Aqiba (Babylonian Talmud *Nazir* 52b) all fasted 'until their teeth were black.' But only in the story of Rab Hiyya ben Ashi do we meet a truly fully-fledged ascetic. Motivated by excessive piety, Rab Hiyya lived apart from his wife for years. Presumably to test his resolve, his wedded wife visited him one day, dressed as a harlot. Needless to say, she succeeded in seducing him. Even after realizing her identity, he was tormented by a sense of guilt and he repeated: 'But I intended to sin!' He starved himself to death, trying to expiate this sin (Babylonian Talmud *Kiddushin* 81b).

Jewish hostility towards fasting

Alongside the stories of extreme piety, there are strong objections in Jewish literature from Philo to the Talmud against fasting. Philo of Alexandria, himself a great advocate of self-restraint and enemy of gluttony, writes:

> If then thou observest anyone not taking food or drink when he should, or refusing to use bath and oil, or careless about his clothing, or sleeping on the ground, and occupying wretched lodgings, and then on the strength of all this fancying that he is practising self-control, take pity on his mistake, and show him the true method of self-control; for all these practices of his are fruitless and wearisome labours, prostrating soul and body by starving and in other ways maltreating them.
>
> (*The Worse Attacks the Better* 17-20)

The Talmud records the rabbis saying:

> Too many fasts trouble the community unduly...; whosoever fasts (for the sake of self-affliction) is termed a sinner...; how then could a man who fasts be called holy seeing that he humiliates God (who dwells within him) through fasting?
>
> (Babylonian Talmud *Taanith* 11a,b; 14b)

One should not fast, they argued, since fasting may cause illness and, in addition, one may become a public burden (*Tosefta Taanith* 2.12). Scholars, especially young ones, were denounced for fasting:

> The young scholar who would afflict himself by fasting, let a dog devour his meat!...; a scholar may not afflict himself by fasting because he lessens thereby his heavenly work.
> (Babylonian Talmud *Taanith* 11a)

Just like Judith and Esther in biblical literature, in Talmudic times too women seemed to have favoured the practice of fasting. Was this because fasting was the only cultic activity in which Jewish women were allowed to participate on equal footing with men? Or was fasting a pious excuse for reducing the work load or avoiding burdensome marital obligations? Whatever the reason for it may have been, the men did not favour female abstemiousness. From the time of the Mosaic Law, a Jewish woman's vows could be annulled by her father or, if she was married, by her husband (*Numbers* 30.3-9; Mishnah *Nedarim*). Since no abstention from food was considered a religious fast unless it was vowed, that is to say announced publicly beforehand, at least some of these women's vows must have concerned fasting.

The fasting of Judith and Esther was highly respected; however, the rabbis strongly disapproved of ascetic women of their time, condemning especially widows and 'fasting maids...a foolish saint, a smart knave, an abstemious woman, and the blows of the abstainers, lo, these wear out the world!' They added to the list 'the fasting virgin who fasts so strongly that she loses her virginity' (Jerusalem Talmud *Sotah* 3.4.12a; 13a). What the girl might actually lose by prolonged and severe fasting is of course not her virginity but her feminine shape, her menstrual periods, and her ability to conceive, i.e. her marriageability. Judging from the numerous injunctions against girls disfiguring themselves with fasting or extreme mourning, the rabbis seem to have been familiar with the problem of self-inflicted starvation in young women, and there is not one of them on record who would have found the practice praiseworthy. Female fasting and self-denial were regarded with considerable suspicion by the rabbis. The reason for this may be traced to their views concerning the nature of woman, a nature more closely tied to the body and its needs than that of the man. Men were generally instructed by the rabbis to honour their wives and to satisfy their needs within the well-regulated framework of marriage. Some went so far as to claim that the Biblical command to 'be fruitful and multiply' was addressed to men only, since women needed no inducement, their nature being coextensive with their appetite. 'A woman wants one *qab* (measure) of food with sexual satisfaction, more than nine *qabs* with abstinence!': Rabbi Joshua's pithy sentence (Jerusalem Talmud *Sotah* 3.4) sums up rabbinical opinion concerning female appetites. Consequently women who succeeded in overcoming their 'nature' by extreme piety may have been just as disturbing a phenomenon as those whose appetites were not amenable to control.

Early Christian attitudes to fasting

The early Christians took the notion of fasting as a religious practice from their Jewish background, often citing Old Testament passages to support their exhortations to fast.[3] But were Jewish and Christian fasts in fact comparable in practice, in purpose or in their underlying ideology as the two faiths went their separate ways?

Early Christian texts also reveal various and sometimes strongly opposing views on the practice of fasting. Some of the earliest extant texts appear to be clearly against fasting or against making food a religious concern:

> Food will not commend us to God. We are not worse off if we do not eat, and no better off if we do eat.   (*I Corinthians* 8.8)

> For the kingdom of God is not food and drink but righteousness and peace and joy in the Holy Spirit.   (*Romans* 14.17)

Christians should not abstain from food, since the urging of abstinence is one of the signs of heresy, as the apostle had forewarned:

> …(in) later times some will depart from the faith by giving heed to deceitful spirits and doctrines of daemons…who forbid marriage and enjoin abstinence from food which God created to be received with thanksgiving…for everything created by God is good, and nothing should be rejected...   (*I Timothy* 4.2-5)[4]

By the 3rd and 4th centuries fasting becomes even for orthodox Christian writers a highly praised form of behaviour, signifier of holiness and a challenge for those who aim to be perfect. The saying attributed to Antony, the famous model for the saintly eremitic life, gives expression to this other extreme view:

> Hate all peace that comes from the flesh. Renounce this life, so that you may be alive to God…Suffer hunger, thirst, nakedness, be watchful and sorrowful; weep and groan in your heart…despise the flesh, so that you may preserve your soul.
> (*Sayings of the Desert Fathers* 33)

Most of the texts that relate specifically to women fasting are the products of this latter period.

While some considered the act of abstaining from food and drink itself to be of no concern to God, most early Christian writers, like most philosophical pagans and pious Jews of the time, would set themselves squarely against greed, gluttony and drunkenness. The Christian Clement (died *c.* 220), echoing his fellow Alexandrian the Jewish Philo, insists that God demands strict temperance and self-control; food is to be taken only to keep the body alive, but all bodily pleasure ought to be denied; the philosophic Christian, just like the philosophic Jew, is

> 'to exercise control over the belly, and what is below the belly'
> (*Miscellanies* 2.20)[5]

Fasting and sexuality

By the 3rd and 4th centuries, however, the propaganda for the mortification of the flesh and the enthusiastic recommendation of various forms of self-torture, including fasting, deafen the ears against the voices of moderation. Christian advocates of fasting attribute a variety of advantages to the practice that range from strengthening prayer[6] and purification for worship[7] to impressing God with self-imposed penance, humiliation and suffering.[8] All of these were aims that Jewish fasters of the time also would hope to attain. However, the greatest benefit to be gained from fasting that was fervently hoped for by all its Christian advocates from the end of the 2nd century on, and what was, at least in its strongest form, a peculiarly Christian ideal, was the elimination of sexual desire. As Origen, Clement's heir as head of the Alexandrian Christian school, who considered fasting in itself irrelevant to God, stated unequivocally:

> We, however, when we abstain, do so because 'we keep our body
> under control and bring it into subjection' and desire to 'mortify
> our members that are upon the earth, and avoid fornication,
> uncleanness, inordinate affection, and evil concupiscence', and
> we use every effort to mortify the deeds of the flesh'.
>
> (*Against Celsus* 5.49)

For this reason the most severe fasting practices were urged on Christians
who aspired to be perfect, that is to say, on virgins and monks.[9]

As celibacy and virginity became more and more central to Christian
values, the difficulties inherent in overcoming the powerful biological
urges opposed to this ideal were becoming alarmingly clear. These urges
originated in the flesh, therefore the flesh was to be mortified. The
advocates of self-mortification, basing their argument on a rather fanciful
conception of the workings of the human body, urge fasting for fear that
a satisfied stomach will directly lead to sexual excesses.[10] Gluttony and lust
were said to be so united that

> had there been any possibility of disjoining them, the pudenda
> would not have been affixed to the belly itself rather than
> elsewhere...the order of vices is proportionate to the arrange-
> ment of the members.

declared Tertullian (*On Fasts* 1.1-2), and he added that fasting makes

> a mind more vigorous, a heart much more alive than when that
> whole habitation of our interior man is stuffed with meats,
> inundated with wines, fermenting for the purpose of excremental
> secretion...whereupon, plainly, nothing follows so closely as the
> savouring of lasciviousness.   (*On Fasts* 6.1)

Clement of Alexandria held similar views:

> Lusts are aroused when the excrement gathers around the
> organs of generation.   (*The Educator* 3.66)

These often repeated maxims of ancient biology had two advantages to
recommend them. They had a ring of medical expertise which may have
given these views added authority, and by connecting sexual desire with
the mental image of excrement they transferred the feeling of disgust that
was conjured up from one to the other. As eating was asserted to lead to
lust, so fasting was to promote continence, as Jerome holds:

by abstinence subjugate our refractory flesh that is eager to follow the allurements of lust. The eating of meat and the drinking of wine and the fullness of the stomach is the seed-plot of lust.   (*Against Jovinianus* 2.7)

A whole literary genre grew up idealizing extremely abstemious hermits, who waged unceasing battle against the devils of lust by heroic measures of self-starvation. Female ascetics, sometimes even more than the monks, were objects of wonder: according to John Chrysostom

> even at a tender age they go without food and sleep and drink, mortifying their bodies, crucifying their flesh, sleeping on the ground, wearing sackcloth, locked in narrow cells, sprinkling themselves with ashes and wearing chains.
> (John Chrysostom *On the Zeal of Those Who Are Present* 3 = *PG* 63.488)

Jerome: fasting to anorexia

One of the most energetic champions of virginity and the mortification of the flesh as a way of life for women was Jerome (345-420). Contemptuous of marriage, he waged a vigorous propaganda campaign in Rome to promote his ideal of the ascetic Christian woman

> who mourned and fasted, who was squalid with dirt, almost blinded by weeping,   (*Letter* 45)

a woman like his patroness and friend Paula whose whole life was a fast, whom Jerome claimed he never saw eating food!

Polemical treatises and letter after letter written mostly to women but meant for wide circulation show that virginity and sexual continence were central to Jerome's conception of the faith.[11] The problem of the young woman trying to maintain her chastity while 'her body is all on fire with rich food' (*Letter* 54.8) engaged Jerome in a number of his writings. In his letter to Furia, a young widow, he spells out explicitly the dietary regimen she should follow in order to maintain herself in virginal widowhood. In the first place, he advises her not to drink wine but to live on water, which cools the natural heat of the body:

> Secondly, in the way of food avoid all heating dishes. I do not speak of meat only...but with vegetables also anything that

creates wind or lies heavy on the stomach should be rejected.
You should know that nothing is so good for young Christians as
a diet of herbs...By cold food the heat of the body should be
tempered...This is the reason why some of those who aspire to
a life of chastity fall midway on the road. They think that they
need merely abstain from meat, and they load their stomach with
vegetables which are only harmless when taken sparingly and in
moderation. To give you my real opinion, I think that nothing so
inflames the body and titillates the organs of generation as
undigested food and convulsive belching...Regard as poison
anything that has within it the seeds of sensual pleasure. A frugal
diet which leaves you always hungry is to be preferred to a three
days' fast, and it is much better to go short every day than
occasionally to satisfy your appetite to the full.

(Letter 54.10)

Again and again as he advises young women on the rules according to
which virgins of the church ought to live, he urges extreme frugality in food
and the avoidance of wine. Even during early childhood,

Let her food be vegetables and wheaten bread and occasionally
a little fish...let her meals always leave her hungry.

(Letter 107.10)

In contrast to this severe regimen urged on virginal women, the Christian
morality preached for the benefit of the multitudes, reflected in various
canons of church councils of the period and in texts addressed by bishops
to their Christian flock, prescribed much less heroic measures. Moderation and frugality in food and drink was urged. Fasting meant giving up
meat and wine, and for the more devout, living on bread and water during
Lent. The main thrust of their exhortations was aimed against gluttony
and drunkenness rather than against eating and drinking. 'If you are not
able to keep a fast', asks Augustine, the bishop of Hippo, 'at least partake
of food with moderation!'[12] For the common Christian the picture of the
self-mortifying ascetic was held up as an ideal to admire; for the virgin it
was held up as an ideal to emulate.

For the virgin and for the monk, it was not enough to keep the body under
control by avoiding excess in rich food and drink; the flesh had to be
mortified. By a severely restricted diet the body had to be divested of its

natural impulses and be reduced to a sexless state. Fasting was not a value in itself, but was of importance only as a means for keeping one's chastity.

The recipients of the specific 'step-by-step' instructions concerning diet and fasting were women. Not only were women encouraged never to satisfy their hunger, they were also enjoined to separate themselves from society, where many women 'are intemperate as to the amount of food they take' (Jerome *Letter* 22.17), and where 'women care for nothing but their belly and its adjacent members' (*Letter* 22.29). The virgin is advised to keep to herself and if possible never to leave her room, to 'mortify and enslave her body', 'to blush at herself and be unable to look at her own nakedness', 'to quench the flame of lust and to check the hot desires of youth by cold chastity' (*Letter* 107.11).

The instructions Jerome gives to his various female readers concerning methods for the preservation of virginity bear a more than coincidental resemblance to the conditions that give rise to and are involved in anorexia nervosa. The diagnosis of this disease which is generally regarded today as a psychologically induced physical illness is based on the following manifestations: first, a self-induced weight loss of serious proportions, which would surely follow from living on bread and water and a meagre amount of vegetables and never satisfying one's hunger. Second, we find obsessional ideas about the body, about perfection and guilt and fear of eating, which provide the motivation for, and maintain the behaviour of self-starvation; the texts described above would have provided ample food for these obsessional thoughts. The third manifestation of anorexia comes as the result of the excessive weight loss, and this is indeed the loss of sexual interest together with loss of menstruation in women and loss of sexual potency in men. Anorectics today give various reasons for curtailing their food intake; most often they express a loathing for their own body, fear and guilt over eating, fear over losing control, obsessional aspirations to 'perfection' and an equally obsessional concern with the ugliness of fat.

Just as today not all those who identify with the cultural norms that equate thinness of body with beauty, health and power become anorectic, so in the time of Jerome too, not all those who equated emaciation with holiness became emaciated, and died from it; but some did. The story of Blaesilla, if told today, could easily enter medical textbooks as an example of that twenty-five per cent of cases of anorexia that end in death.

We learn about Blaesilla, the elder daughter of Jerome's patroness and friend Paula, from Jerome's *Letters* 38, 39. These letters aim to defend their writer from accusations of being responsible for the death of the young woman, or possibly, to defend him from his own guilt. What emerges is the following. Blaesilla, a happy, worldly young woman of about twenty, suddenly lost her husband after a short marriage. Jerome, her mother's spiritual mentor, probably in collaboration with Paula, instituted a vigorous campaign to oppose a possible second marriage for her, which was customary in wealthy Roman families but was frowned upon by Christian ascetics. The tragedy of her husband's death may have left her weak and vulnerable to disease, or maybe she succumbed to the same illness that killed her husband: we do not know. What is known is that she suffered from fever for nearly thirty days, during which time, it seems, her mother and self-appointed 'spiritual father' did all in their power to convince the young woman that all her suffering 'has been sent to teach her to renounce her overgreat attention to that body which the worms must shortly devour' (*Letter* 38.2), and that she should 'mourn the loss of her virginity more than the death of her husband' (*Letter* 39.1), and so on. When she was finally on the way to recovery from her illness, she was encouraged to exchange her involuntary abstinence from food that was due to fever for voluntary fasting, in order 'not to stimulate desire by bestowing care upon the flesh' (*Letter* 38.3). Jerome's efforts were crowned with success. 'Her steps tottered with weakness, her face was pale and quivering, her slender neck scarcely upheld her head', wrote her satisfied mentor (*Letters* 39.1, 38.4); thus Blaesilla was turned into a fasting, weeping, praying nun and in less than three months after her conversion she was dead. Her mother was so prostrated with guilt and grief that she was carried out fainting from the funeral procession while the assembled mourners murmured that Blaesilla was killed by fasting and pointed accusing fingers at the monks.

The contrast between rabbinical attitudes to female fasting and those expressed in Christian patristic literature is striking and merits further exploration. This contrast may reflect fundamental differences in the orientation of the two religions. The Christian longed for the 'end of this world' and for the 'kingdom of God' which the second coming of Jesus would herald. So, while living in this world, the Christian was only preparing himself for the other world to come. There was no need for marriage, none for children, since

> the world is already full and the population is too large for the soil.
> (Jerome *Against Helvidius* 23)

In contrast the Jew, living in this world, took his God's command 'be fruitful and multiply' seriously.[13] With the possible exception of some extremely ascetic sects like the Essenes or some of the Qumran communities, marriage was considered of the greatest importance, and children as God's blessing. Sexuality expressed within the bond of marriage was not only legitimate, but was regarded as a God-given joy. The marriage partners were encouraged to be attractive and pleasing to each other. Consequently, ascetic practices that would make the woman less pleasing were frowned upon.[14] To put it even more strongly, woman's sexuality, her ability to produce children, was regarded by Judaism as the main reason and justification for her being. The ideal woman among the Jews was a married woman, mother of many children. At the same time the ideal woman among the Christians was a virgin, a sexually abstaining wife or an old woman who ceased to be female.[15]

The emphasis on lifelong virginity among the Christians may also have been encouraged by a shift in the male/female ratio, and the special problems which this created. Jews and Christians equally regarded the exposing of infants as murder and as a pagan abomination. The practice of rearing all children may have resulted in an increased ratio of women to men. The Jews could, at least in principle, accommodate a larger number of women within the existing social framework by encouraging remarriage of the widowed or divorced of both sexes and by allowing polygyny. Among the Christians the problem of overabundance of women may have even been increased by a larger influx of female than male converts.[16] The solution to the problem that they proposed had to accommodate a diff-

Jewish and Christian attitudes: why did they diverge?

erent ideology, with its particular view of marriage. Marriage for the early Christians was necessary only for the weak, to keep them from the sin of fornication; but once marriage was contracted it was not to be dissolved. Multiple marriages were strongly disapproved of. These factors may have been responsible for Christian communities having to deal with significant numbers of unattached women. And since Christian moralists shared with the Jews and pagans a common fear and suspicion of female sexual appetites, the sight of these unattached women constituted for them a clear and ever-present danger. The solution that some of them proposed was to enforce lifelong chastity on the women fortified by solemn vows, to veil them completely, 'for her appearance will be dignified only when she cannot be seen', as Clement of Alexandria so succinctly declared (*The Educator* 3.79), and to separate them from the company of men as much as possible. Finally, an activity had to be found for them which would be beneficial for the church and at the same time would help to keep them chaste: fasting and prayer became the particular duty of the virgins and widows of the church.

Acknowledgement

The author wishes to express her gratitude to the Harry and Abe Sherman Foundation for their generous support of her research.

Notes

1. The Apocrypha consists of a collection of books written between 200 BC and about AD 100, which are not included in the Jewish canon of the Hebrew Bible; most of them, however, are a part of the Greek Old Testament known as the Septuagint. The Pseudepigrapha are a set of writings that date from 200 BC to AD 200; many of them have authors attributed to them who lived, or who were believed to have lived, long before this period. The Qumran literature was found on a number of scrolls in caves around the Dead Sea; archaeological evidence seems to date the occupation of the Qumran site to the period 140 BC - AD 68.

2. As Vermes and Goodman (1989, 34) point out, both Philo and Josephus desired to present a sympathetic picture of the Jews to a gentile audience. In attempting to demonstrate substantial similarities between Greek philosophy and Jewish doctrines they may have sacrificed strict accuracy by placing undue or misleading emphasis on those

aspects of Jewish civilization more easily assimilated to the culture of pagans.

3. Tertullian in his treatise *On Fasts* marshals all the evidence from the Old Testament that he could find to support his claim that God commands fasting, and calls 'a soul wholly shattered' (properly, of course, by stringent diet) a 'sacrifice' (*On Fasts* 3). Augustine in his struggle against his appetite reminds himself 'that Esau was defrauded by his greed for a dish of lentils; that David reproached himself for longing for a drink of water…' (*Confessions* 10.31(46)). And, of course, the example of the first man, obeying his belly rather than God, and as a consequence cast out from Paradise into this vale of tears, is a frequently repeated argument for fasting.

4. These trends soon appeared and had a long life both within orthodox Christianity and in various rigorist heretic groups. Irenaeus, bishop of Lyons (end of 2nd century AD), in his treatise *Against Heresies* characterizes the Encratites and the followers of Saturninus as heretics who preach against marriage and urge abstinence from meat. The council of Gangra (middle to late 4th century) anathemized the bishop Eustathius for similar offences.

5. This phrase is used and often repeated by Philo. The idea that this saying conjures up in so picturesque a fashion is that the stomach is directly connected to the sexual organs and that the filling of the stomach inevitably leads to the exercising of those organs.

> (They) begin with making themselves experts in dainty feeding, wine-bibbing and other pleasures of the belly and the parts below it. Then sated with these they reach such a pitch of wantonness, the natural offspring of satiety, that losing their senses they conceive a frantic passion… (*On the Special Laws* 3.43)

> …always and everywhere indeed he exhorted them to show this (self-restraint) in all the affairs of life, in controlling the tongue and the belly and the organs below the belly… (*On the Special Laws* 2.32)

6. As in the story of St. John and the robber:

> he then brought him back to the church. There he interceded for him with abundant prayers, and helped his struggles by continual fasting…
> (Clement of Alexandria
> *The Rich Man's Salvation* 960)

7. Let you, and me with you, fast this day along with her, and tomorrow she shall be baptized…Let us teach our

bodily senses, which are without us, to be in subjection to our inner senses; and not compel our inner senses, which savour the things that be of God, to follow the outer senses, which savour the things that be of the flesh… (*Clementine Recognitions* 7.37)

8. We, parched with fasting, pinched with every austerity, abstaining from all food that sustains life, wallowing in sackcloth and ashes, importune heaven with reproach, we touch God. (Tertullian *Apology* 40.15)

or

> The pitiable spectacle and humiliation of xerophagies expel fear and attract the ears of God…
> (*On Fasts* 9.4)

9. In his description of the Jewish ascetic sect, the Therapeutai, Philo of Alexandria claims a sexless virginal life for its members, together with an extremely frugal alimentary regime; however, the Therapeutai of either gender fast not in order to subdue their sexuality, but because they seem not to need much earthly food while living on the heavenly food of Holy Scripture and philosophy! (*On the Contemplative Life* 4.34-8).

10. Rousselle (1983) surveys Graeco-Roman attitudes to the body and to sexuality as these are reflected in medical writing, especially in the extant works of Soranos and Oribasios. The ancient physicians, while seldom agreeing among themselves on the useful or harmful effects of sexual behaviour, all tended to connect potency or desire with dietary factors. In Rousselle's opinion (171-8), ascetic self-discipline, or more accurately the texts that describe ascetic practices, were based on medical theories which held that sperm consists of the excess humours which result from absorbing too much food; the ascetic therefore must follow a diet which will dry out his body.

11. e.g. *Against Helvidius*, *Against Jovinianus*, *Letters* 45, 22, 107, 54, etc.

12. See the *Canons of the Synod of Gangra* (between 325 and 381), especially *Canons* II, XI, XV, XVIII; Augustine *On the Usefulness of Fasting* (*PL* 40); *Sermon* 198.2 (*PL* 38.1025); Basil of Caesarea *Response to a young man* 16.1 (*PG* 31.957B).

13. This is, of course, not to say that there were no voices in rabbinic Judaism urging an expectation of 'the world to come'. There were many like Rabbi Joshua of Beith Shammai who attributed to God the saying that "it is a good thing that I should impose extensive restrictions upon you in this world in order that your days may be prolonged in the world

to come" (Babylonian Talmud *Niddah* 16b). But the 'world to come' was not predicated on the imminent destruction of 'this world'.

14. E.g. 'A girl who has reached adolescence may not make herself unsightly during the days of mourning...' (Babylonian Talmud *Taanith* 13b)

15. A revealing example of this is the somewhat surprising greeting with which Origen addresses a pious lady friend:
    and you Tatiana, most modest and valiant lady (and I pray that as it had ceased to be with Sarah after the manner of women, so it may have ceased to be with you)...   (*On Prayer* 2)

16. Especially in the Roman upper classes for whom Jerome wrote (see Drijvers 1987). The problem of insufficient eligible marriage partners for Christian women goes back at least to the time of Pope Callistus (217-222 AD), who declared that marriages between free women and man of lower rank, not excluding slaves, were valid, although these were forbidden by Roman law (Baus 1980, vol. 1, 329).

Bibliography

Baus, K. 1980 *History of the Church, from the Apostolic Community to Constantine* (London).

Blok, J. & Mason, P. 1987 *Sexual Asymmetry: Studies in Ancient Society* (Amsterdam).

Danby, H. (trans.) 1933 *The Mishnah* (Oxford).

Drijvers, H.J.W. 1987 'Virginity and Asceticism in late Roman Western Elites', in Blok and Mason (1987), 241-73.

Epstein, I. (trans.) 1935 *The Babylonian Talmud* (London).

Neusner, J. (trans.) 1987 *The Talmud of the Land of Israel* (Chicago).

Neusner, J. (trans.) 1977-86 *The Tosefta* (New York).

Rousselle, A. 1983 *Porneia: on Desire and the Body in Antiquity* (Oxford).

Vermes, G. & Goodman, M. 1989 *The Essenes According to Classical Sources* (Sheffield).

Ward, B. (trans.) 1975 *The Sayings of the Desert Fathers: the Alphabetical Collection* (London and Oxford).

PART FOUR

Beyond the Greco-Roman World

Introduction ↷
Part Four

Poseidonios the Stoic philosopher (2nd *c.* BC) writes in his *Histories*, which are a review according to Stoic principles of the social practices and customs of many peoples:

> The Celts scatter hay underfoot before they present their food which is served on wooden tables raised only a little from the ground. As for the food itself, there are a few loaves of wheatbread and a great deal of meat either boiled or roasted over charcoal or on spits. They are clean and proper eaters but have appetites like lions, taking whole joints in both hands and biting the meat off the bone. If any meat is difficult to tear off, they slice it up with a little knife which lies at their side in a sheath in a special box. Celts who live by rivers and by the Mediterranean and Atlantic also eat fish which they bake with salt, vinegar and cummin. Cummin is also put into their wine. Olive oil is not used because of its rarity; they also think it unpleasant because it is unfamiliar.
>
> (part of fr. 67 Edelstein-Kidd = Athenaeus 4.151e-2a)

Poseidonios is describing a foreign people and is pointing out the ways in which they *differ* from an assumed and unstated norm. The hay is a rustic touch for the average Greek or Roman aristocrat, similar perhaps to the rustic couch mentioned by Plato (*Republic* 372b) and Dio Chrysostom (7.65). Tables are lower than expected. The balance between bread and meat is the reverse of the Mediterranean pattern with its large quantity of *sitos/puls* and its small element of tasty *opson/pulmentarium*. The references to their cleanliness and large appetites probably betray assumptions that foreign peoples such as these cannot as a rule be expected to be clean and that they are unlikely to be able to control their appetite, which was considered a moral failing. Meat takes precedence over fish, a feature that we have already discussed. The Celts use animal fats rather than olive oil: difference in product distinguishes difference in culture. The passage goes on to discuss hierarchies at the feast, drink (wine for the rich, beer for the poor) and drinking ritual.

'Posidonius (*c.* 135-50 BC), born at Apamea on the Orontes, after studying philosophy at Athens under Panaetius devoted several years of his life to scientific research in the western Mediterranean provinces and in North Africa. He then settled down at Rhodes, which became his adoptive country. Towards the end of 87 Posidonius was sent to Rome...In 78 Cicero attended the school of Posidonius...' (*Oxford Classical Dictionary* 2nd edition, 867-8). The brief details of this great polymath illustrate the extent of the Greco-Roman world at this date and the possibilities for travel throughout the Mediterranean. The Romans were the influential power in the region as a whole, but much of the eastern part of their empire retained the Greek influences put in place after Alexander the Great's conquest of the East in the years 334-323 BC. Poseidonios was a Syrian from a city on the Orontes river, but was as much at home in Greek culture as in a number of others.

Many people travelled widely in antiquity, for trade, on business public and private, in warfare; many people, equally, did not travel – the hundreds of thousands of peasant farmers for example. Writers were quite likely to travel – poets, historians, philosophers, doctors – and developed an international perspective. On the one hand they praised their own country, but on the other they profited from and were influenced by their extensive contacts. One effect of this was to distance them from their poorer fellow-citizens. So, in the area of food-consumption, we know at least as much about what and how Persians ate as what and how poor Athenians ate. Authors are liable, for example, to identify milk as a 'barbarian' (that is, non-Greek or non-Roman) drink (for example, Hippokrates *Airs, Waters, Places* 18, where cheese from mare's milk is also mentioned). Cheese is fine, but we might almost suppose that milk was unknown in the Greco-Roman world. This distinguishes the nomadic peoples of the steppes and the Libyan plains from the settled farmers of Greece and Italy. But it is very likely that Greek and Italian farmers did drink milk, particularly in upland areas (Hippokrates, again, says milk, wine and meat are beneficial or not according to location and custom, while cheese is beneficial or not according to digestion and metabolism (see Chapter 25, especially 346-7). In a sense, therefore, the upland peasant of Greece and Italy is as foreign to the wealthy writer in Athens or Rome as is a 'barbarian' from the plains of Russia or the Ukraine.

For large parts, if not all, of their history, both Greeks and Romans were actively engaged in exchanges with other peoples, with their neighbours and with those from further afield – the Greeks most notably with the

Persians, to take a clear example from the historical period, but also with Egyptians, Assyrians, Medes, Phoenicians, Phrygians and Lydians; the Romans with similar peoples of the East, but preeminently with the Greeks themselves, both from the Greek mainland and from the communities of southern Italy and Sicily, and to some extent with peoples from the African and northern and western European parts of their empire. Among the Greeks and Romans, the way foreigners were thought about varied according to location, the conditions of the time, and international affairs. So, in the 5th century BC, the Greeks divided themselves sharply from everybody else.[1] *They* are barbarians, *we* are Greeks (and therefore civilized). By this definition, civilization entailed living in a Greek culture. Anyone who did not could be identified by their language, social and political systems, and patterns of eating.

This kind of approach contrasts with that of Herodotos who in his *Histories* puts the conflict between the Greeks and Persians in the early 5th century BC into its cultural context with an ethnographical and historical survey of all the peoples under consideration. Herodotos is admirably even-handed in his approach. For others, who were less so, different meant worse. The Eastern cultures in particular were associated with luxury. So the king of the Assyrians, Sardanapalus (Ashurbanipal), brought ruin on his people by spending too much time at dinner and by being too effeminate; the Lydians introduced rich and 'luxurious' sauces into Greece (see p. 277); the Egyptians corrupted Julius Caesar and Mark Antony with their rich and soft living. Athenaeus is particularly concerned with such luxury among Greeks and other peoples in his Books 4 and 12.

In terms of eating, it was possible for the 'frugal' Athenians to construct themselves as a pure centre surrounded by excessive and indulgent eaters, the Lydians with their sauces, the Persians with their sweets and enormous ovens, the Thessalians and Boiotians with their huge appetites, the Sybarites and Syracusans with their luxurious eating (see Chapter 30). These stereotypes are plentifully evident in much of Greek comedy, in Athenaeus and elsewhere. Sybaris and Syracuse of course were Greek cities; founded in the 8th century BC, they had developed in ways that differed from those of their mother cities. Colonies of this kind were touched on by David Braund in Chapter 12. On several occasions,

Athenaeus refers to Sardanapalus, king of Assyria, as one who overindulged his senses in every way. Sardanapalus is important for his date (668-626) and his culture. Sybaris excepted, all the other states mentioned above were contemporary with 5th century Greece, our main point of reference. Sardanapalus is a representative of one of those older civilizations which predated Greek influence in the eastern Mediterranean and which in the form of Persia continued to threaten in the 5th and 4th centuries. It was possible for the Greeks to construct the Egyptians, Babylonians, Assyrians, Medes, Persians and Lydians as once-great civilizations which, rather like the Ottoman Empire in the minds of Western leaders in the 19th century, had traded military and administrative might for self indulgence, thereby becoming enfeebled and liable to be overthrown.

The East for the Greeks was always fascinating and yet suspect; they imitated and scorned. Thus wealthy Greeks and Romans reclined on couches, a style possibly inherited from the Assyrians, and absorbed eastern foods and techniques of preparation, and at the same time distanced themselves from them.

As far as influence is concerned, the peoples of the East were more important than the northern Europeans, at least until the Roman Empire. There was simply more contact and more influence. The Romans similarly distinguished themselves from foreigners, especially Greeks, and claimed a distinctive Roman diet at the same time as showing much interest in luxurious foods imported from abroad.[2]

But what were the perspectives of the peoples of the East or the Celts of northern Europe? According to Herodotos (1.133), the Persians thought the Greeks very poor eaters because they had not developed the Persian excellence in sweets and desserts (an excellence maintained in Turkey and other parts of the Middle East to the present day). Much of this book is written from the Greco-Roman perspective: in this section other cultures are considered in their own terms, though in most chapters some consideration is given to Greek or Roman – that is, outsiders' – assumptions.

Five of our seven chapters concern the Middle East.[3] In Chapter 18, Jean Bottéro examines some clay tablets from Babylonia that record recipes (a very small proportion of the whole collection). These are important for their great antiquity (17th century BC), for the fact that this category of information was stored in permanent form on tablets in this culture, for the kind of eating habits hereby attested for Babylonia, which involve a class of flavours that can be broadly identified with those of the Greeks.

Mario Lombardo takes us to the edge of the Greco-Roman world in Chapter 19, pursuing concepts of 'frontier history'. If a colony was successfully founded, there was always the question of how the new arrivals – Greeks in this case – blended with or removed the indigenous peoples – here Italians. The colonists brought familiar plants with them – the Greeks particularly brought the vine and the olive – and also their own social systems, to areas which as in the case of southern Italy were often more productive than the homeland. The new systems blended with the native but also took them over, and drove the natives to mountainous and wooded areas. Lombardo also puts charges of luxury against these southern Italian cities into their context: these are comments made by *outsiders*.

Next David Harvey considers Lydia, the kingdom between the Greek cities of the coast and the Anatolian interior, which flourished in the 7th and 6th centuries BC. The Lydians made a powerful impact on the neighbouring Greek cities, and were one of those peoples from the East whom the Greeks associated with luxurious living. Harvey looks at the contacts made between Lydia and Greece: Greeks who travelled to Lydia brought back various foods (once again we see the movement of foods west); the special dedication of a statue and the ritual sacrifice of dogs are also discussed.

In Chapter 21, Heleen Sancisi-Weerdenburg takes a Persian perspective. Persia was the dominant culture to the east of Greece after the defeat of the Lydians in the 540s BC, and its territory extended from Asia Minor to the Caspian Sea and south to the Iranian plateau with the Tigris on its West side and the Indus to the east. Sancisi-Weerdenburg maintains that when the Greeks spoke of the characteristic Persian foods, terebinth and cardomum, they were essentially correct on the product but uncomprehending as far as social context was concerned, since they were saying more about themselves than the Persians: foods in such cross-cultural contexts are rarely value-neutral. She also makes proposals, reached with the help of the carved reliefs from the palace at Persepolis, for interpreting the social significance of the meals of the great Persian king.

Peter Reynolds' chapter is the only one that looks outside Greco-Roman culture in Europe, and is based in part on his practical work at the Iron Age farm at Butser in Hampshire. His account of the Celts and their foods is written as a challenge to the cultural imperialism of the Romans and their apologists. In Chapter 23, Dorothy Thompson considers Egypt under the Ptolemies – the Greek kings who ruled the country from the end of the 4th century BC – with reference to the diet of minor temple officials working at a humble level in this Greco-Egyptian culture. The evidence suggests a pattern found in many other cultures, namely that at this level – as opposed to an upper-class level – new influences from outside came to Egypt only slowly. Shimon Dar compares the literary evidence of the Bible and Talmud for foods eaten in Palestine (compare Chapter 2) with archaeological evidence drawn from the period of Greco-Roman occupation, largely from the 1st century AD onwards.

J.W.

Notes

[1] For the influence of these ideas on Athenian literature, see E. Hall, *Inventing the Barbarian* (Oxford, 1989).

[2] On the complexities of Roman ideas about food see E. Gowers, *The Loaded Table* (Oxford, 1993).

[3] For the historical background see, in addition to the bibliographies for each chapter, *The Cambridge Ancient History* (2nd ed.), vols III.2 (1988), IV (1991) and V (1992).

❖ 18 ❖   THE MOST ANCIENT RECIPES OF ALL

Jean Bottéro

The new texts

Tʜᴇ subject of this study is three cuneiform tablets whose text was published in 1985/6 in volume eleven of *Babylonian Texts* (Yale University). They contain recipes which are the most ancient known, and which are also of surprising refinement.

Recipe books were written from the end of the 5th century BC until well into the Roman period. They took the form of collections of recipes. The Greeks of southern Italy first produced such works (see the chapters by Andrew Dalby, and John Wilkins and Shaun Hill in this volume), and the first was probably by Mithaikos of Syracuse. Often only a name survives, supported by a few quotations, notably in the precious work of Athenaeus, *The Deipnosophists* (2nd/3rd century AD). I am not aware of a more ancient collection of recipes surviving in the West than the famous *Art of Cooking* (*de re coquinaria*) attributed to Apicius, the celebrated Roman gourmet, gourmand and eccentricwhich was compiled *c.* 400 AD, there is a magisterial edition and translation of this work by J. André in the Budé series (Paris, 1974).

We do not know the provenance of the Yale tablets. They probably come from a clandestine find in Iraq over 50 years ago, site unknown, details of acquisition unknown. They are undated, but the copyist would have written the date in a colophon if they came from the 1st millennium BC. There are no allusions in the text to help with the date, but the writing style, orthography, language and vocabulary suggest southern Mesopotamia, probably in the area of Larsa, and a date in the 17th century BC (end of palaeo-Babylonian period), some 2000 years before 'Apicius'.

The tablets differ in character, and are not by the same hand.

1. *Yale Oriental Studies* (*YOS*) XI,25. Size 1180 x 1140 mm. Continuous script, no columns, recipes paragraphed, with horizontal line dividing them, and a double line to divide meat, vegetables, and a final résumé. The right side is damaged. There are 75 lines of text and 25 recipes, the first 21 meat, the others vegetable-based, but only the last one excluding meat.

2. *YOS* XI,26. Size 2230 x 1600 mm. The text is divided into two columns of 65 lines each on each face, making four columns and almost 250 lines. There are only seven recipes (all concerning birds), given in great detail, and separated by double horizontal strokes. At the end two lines written in reverse of which very little survives except at the beginning of the first line the first part of the name of the goddess Nisaba, patron of both cereals and writing. This is probably an invocation of the goddess, but nothing is clear. The text is damaged, especially on the reverse (cols III & IV), which obscures recipes four and six. Only one recipe can be read more or less in full, the first. For the others, there is enough to give the broad outline, with some details, and some gaps can be filled with prudent conjectures.

3. *YOS* XI,27. Smaller. 1370 x 890 mm. 53 lines. The most damaged, especially on the reverse. So much so that my colleague W.G. Farber, general collator of all the texts in *YOS* XI, and an experienced Assyrologist, has abandoned the attempt to read any of it. Still, if one knows the vocabulary well, and the style and the cooking terms of the other tablets, one can manage to read, with gaps, the general sense of the three recipes recopied here, the first two divided by a double horizontal stroke, the last by a single stroke.

Research on the texts

I was persuaded to work on these tablets fifteen years ago by Franz Kücher in Berlin, with whom I discussed recipes in preparation for a large article for the *Reallexikon der Assyriologie* on 'Küche'. The curator of the Babylonian collection at Yale, Prof. W.W. Hallo, and J. van Dijk, then at the Biblical Institute in Rome, entrusted me with the task of studying these three specialized texts, and offered me every assistance, so much so that I have not been to Yale to examine the precious tablets: this was done for me by Prof. W.G. Farber. I began this study in 1980, and only now is the MS of the edition and commentary complete. It is to be published in the USA by Eisenbrauns in the series *Mesopotamian Civilizations*, edited by my friend J.S. Cooper, Professor of Assyriology at Johns Hopkins University.

I have taken a long time not just because of other projects, but also because these are extremely difficult texts: they are unparalleled; they are technical documents; those techniques have not been practised for nearly 4000 years, and practice is vital for understanding manual crafts; the language itself is full of new and unknown terms intelligible only to professionals, as is the case in all crafts (even now, an outsider only partially understands a conversation between two chefs, two typographers, or two carpenters). The authors, writing for contemporary experts, write only the minimum needed for comprehension – by themselves, not by us. Long familiarity with the documents, frequent revisions and rereadings, coupled with efforts of the imagination to 'realize', as we say in English, what we are reading, have in part compensated for ignorance. I have moved very carefully and slowly.

Tablet 1
YOS XI,25

A concise style like that of some of 'Apicius' (e.g. 434ff). It lists ingredients and condiments, marking the essential preparation with a verb. The recipes are all for boiled dishes (*bouillons*). Each recipe has a title which may derive from its main component, e.g. 'bouillon of meat', no. 1, the simplest; 'bouillon of deer', of gazelle, of kid, of lamb, of rat? of spleen?, of pigeon, of francolin; bouillon of salt, of dodder; or simply by a term indicating foreign origin, 'Elamite', 'Assyrian'; or by a term difficult to understand, 'red bouillon', where nothing in the recipe suggests redness.

The instruction that follows is generally formulaic. You start with the meat of the title and with pieces of meat to be added, some mutton or beef, with other additions forbidden. Then the water and fat, which we have good reason to think is fresh sheep fat. Then condiments, for nutrition, taste and binding. Neither quantities nor cooking-time are given. These will depend on the cook's experience, the occasion etc. The recipe is then a kind of algebraic formula. Some condiments cook with the bouillon, others are added at the end, some certainly raw at the last minute. Apart from salt, these condiments are nearly all plants: oil, dodder, mint, coriander, cumin, cypress (if these are rightly translated); cereals in various forms (cakes and breads), for binding the liquid, as well as the blood and milk of animals. Some recipes have a dozen condiments, none less than three or four. The most widely used suggest if not a fashion at least a strong taste for the kind of flavour of the *alliacae*. There are five or six of these, of which half are not clearly identifiable. The most striking thing is that they are often used together, for these ancient gourmets liked the affinity of taste and the savoury combination of *alliacae*. This is the kind of finesse that characterizes *grande cuisine* and gastronomy. The *alliacae* that appear most often, sometimes more than once in the same recipe, and in different forms, for example crushed and puréed on the one hand, raw and whole on the other, are the leek and garlic. Added to these is a combination that even real southern Frenchmen would find fearsome: onion, *samidu*, *suhutinnu* (these are other *alliacae*) etc. They looked for dishes that were vigorous and, we might say, resolutely reinforced.

Four or five recipes:

Meat bouillon. You need meat. Place in water. Add fat, crushed leek and garlic and in proportion raw *suhutinnu*.

Lamb bouillon. You need other meat too. Place in water. Add fat, salt as you wish, crumbed cereal-cake, onion and *samidu*, coriander, cumin, leek and garlic. Serve.

Bouillon with dodder. No need for fresh meat, but salted. Place in water. Add dodder in sufficient quantity; some onion and *samidu*; coriander and cumin; leek and garlic. Serve.

Bouillon of pigeon. Open the pigeon in two. You need also some other meat. Place in water. Add fat, salt as you wish, cereal cake crumbed, onion and *samidu*; leek and garlic and 'herbs' (aromatics) earlier steeped in milk.

Vegetable recipes do not mention 'bouillon' in the title.

Cultivated turnips (and not wild or gathered). No meat. Place in water. Add fat, [...] onion, rocket, coriander, *samidu*, and the turnips. After first cooking add coriander, crumbed cereal cake, bind with blood, and crushed leek and garlic.

The tablet is a compendium, ultra-concise, leaving all detail to the cook.

Tablet 2
YOS XI,26

The recipes on the large tablet are quite different. If you leave to one side the inevitable onion, leek and garlic and several other ingredients, especially salt, vinegar (not mentioned on Tablet 1), mint, rue, and 'woods' (aromatics, cf. our *fines herbes*), and one or two others, there is less use of condiments, as though this came from a slightly different culinary tradition. There is none of the catalogue style, and much greater, if not complete, detail.

I publish here a translation of the first recipe only. No title. The end in view and the animal is normally specified (all birds): e.g. 'if you want to prepare such and such a bird for the pot...'. This is missing in the present recipe but can be reconstructed as something from the farmyard like 'ducklings' or young geese; not hens since we know from elsewhere that they were not known in Mesopotamia until centuries later.

...Remove the head, neck and feet. Open up the stomach to remove the innards and gizzard, which should be split and separated from its inner membrane. Wash the birds and cut up the innards.

In a scoured cauldron place birds' gizzards and entrails [for precooking, or sealing, perhaps dry]. After sufficient cooking, remove the meat and wash it in fresh water. Then wash well a large pot [note that cauldrons were of bronze, pots of earthenware for lengthy boiling in liquid] and add water, milk, and heat. Wipe dry birds, gizzards and entrails, sprinkle with salt, and put in the pot. Add fat with nerves removed [this is the evidence for fat from freshly killed animals, sheep or cattle], aromatic woods to choice, and de-leafed rue. When boiling add onion, but not excessively, and *samidu*; leeks and garlic crushed together, and a little clear water [to counter steam lost in cooking]. Leave to cook.

During cooking, soak properly cleaned *sasku*-semolina [coarse-grained?] in milk, and when it is damp enough, knead in *siqqu* [pickle of fish, shellfish and grasshoppers akin to *nuoc-nam*], and, all the time watching to ensure it stays supple, add to the kneading *samidu*, crushed leek and garlic, milk, and fat residue from the cooking. Make this mixture into two parts. Leave one to rise in a pot. Cook the other in small breads – *sebetu* [form and method unknown] – and when cooked remove from the wall of the oven [cf. modern cooking of flatbreads in hot pots].

Continue kneading the semolina dampened with milk, adding oil, crushed leek and garlic and *samidu*. Take a flat round vessel (*makaltu*) large enough to hold the birds and their garnish. Line it with the paste which must exceed the height of the rim.

Take up the dough already kneaded and placed to one side in a pot and spread it on another dish the same shape, chosen to cover the space with the birds and garnish. Sprinkle first with mint and then cover with the pastry to form the shape of a thin cover. Lift the front of the oven [...]

When cooked, remove the cover from its cooking vessel. Pass it through oil and leave to one side.

When the birds and their bouillon are done, crush and add leek, garlic and *andahsu* [*alliacae* again]. Just before eating, take the dish with pastry and place in the birds, adding the innards and gizzards taken from their cooking pot and the *sebetu* breads, leaving aside the fat cooking bouillon [which will be consumed separately. There is clearly too much of it to act as a sauce for the meat]. Cover it all with the pastry cover and send to table.

A cuisine which is refined and recherché, not only in its search for a rich and perfumed flavour but also in the preparation of a dish which is complex and nutritionally balanced, since the meat at the centre of the dish, made flavoursome in itself, is complemented by the cereal accompaniment and also pleases the eye. Like our own covered tarts.

The other recipes on the tablet have the same double aim, a taste intelligently achieved and a presentation both recherché and nutritionally rich. The last of the seven, some 63 lines long, features birds (francolins?) on a base in two parts and cooked separately, and around it a garnish of cereal porridge, of which we are given six or seven possible compositions.

Tablet 3
YOS XI,27

It is not possible to give the detailed recipes of the third tablet. The three recipes, for a bird, a green-wheat porridge and some other animal, could make a generous meal. It may also have been written for the moment, in haste.

Context and tradition

This cuisine, then is rich, for those with the skilled personnel, requisite cooking vessels and stoves, and money for expensive provisions. Mesopotamian society was one of those where the upper classes ate *better* than other classes, as opposed to societies where they eat the same but more. These are meals for the rich, and perhaps for kings and gods. The life of the gods was modelled on that of the kings, and they had similar needs, as seen in the myth of *Atrahasis* or Supersage. The aim was to work to offer the gods all that would ensure for them, as for the kings, a life of luxury and pleasure, beginning with copious and exquisite meals. The titles of the recipes, could imply acts of cult or of protocol in the preparation of meals for gods and kings.

This accounts for their being written down in a culture where writing was reserved for a select few. Kings and cooks were unlikely to be able to read. Further, cooks learnt their job by watching others and listening to them. The tablets thus have a normative, not a didactic purpose. This was a semi-ritual in which gradually improved recipes were preserved to ensure that no changes were made in them. They resemble in this way the thousands of therapeutic and exorcist tablets.

I must emphasize that these three tablets are the wreckage of a vast shipwreck. They imply a vast 'literary' tradition. They preserve for us only a small part of the large diet known to us in ancient Mesopotamia. All we have is meat, birds and a little vegetable. Where are the fish? The famous grasshoppers? The fruits? The roasts and grills they loved? The soups alluded to in an oneiromantic fragment?

The fragments imply different sources. For example the shift in the large tablet from second person address, 'you open up the gizzard and remove the inedible membrane', to first person, 'I open up the gizzard and remove the membrane' may imply different sources that were oral prior to being written down. There are many cases of this in the large tablet. 'Once *you* have plucked the pigeon, *you* wash it in fresh water and *I* will skin the body…*you* cut out the neck bones and the ribs. Then *I* open up the lower belly…and *you* moisten it in fresh water.' It is difficult to account for this in terms of a cook and assistant cook.

The tablets derive from a long tradition, oral and then written, and there was clearly a full cooking 'literature' in Mesopotamia. Comparable cases can be seen in beer-making, dyeing, perfumes.

There are traces of this culinary tradition here and there. Dating from 1780 BC there is an earlier reference in the archives of the kingdom of Mari to a sort of cake baked in the oven like bread, but with no recipe strictly speaking. It can be reconstructed, though, from administrative lists of ingredients for confectioners: flour, fat for kneading it, honey for sweetening it, dried fruits for garnishing it, condiments for perfuming it (garlic is included in this category!). There is also mention elsewhere of the vessel for preparing the dough, and the woman kneader (a woman is specified). In the same area a later recipe (*c.* 400 BC) for 'court bouillon' for cooking meat has been discovered. There is a long and continuous culinary tradition here.

These tablets bear witness to an original and striking tradition: the mania for washing meat after each cooking stage; the habit of one or two pre-cookings before the full cooking. It is possible – and other aspects would encourage this view, such as the passion for certain spices and condiments and the presentation of foods in tarts – that a similar ancient tradition lies behind more familiar cuisines today, that of Lebanon for example, or Turkey.

❖ 19 ❖

FOOD AND 'FRONTIER' IN THE GREEK COLONIES OF SOUTH ITALY

Mario Lombardo

Recent research on ancient food

Until a few decades ago the study of food in the ancient Greek world was essentially relegated to a marginal role. The way of looking at the subject was antiquarian rather than historical, focusing on the cataloguing of data, in the form of collections of ancient 'uses and customs', or trying to reconstruct a 'daily life' of the ancients.

This was a paradoxical situation, given the fact that ancient cultures, Greek especially, showed a constant awareness of the central place occupied by food in human life, and a considerable interest in the different activities connected with food: the means of producing and acquiring it, the ways of storing, accumulating, distributing, exchanging it, the ways of preparing, and of consuming it. Food is often seen as one of the main functions of a social system, or at least as an important indicator for the cultural identity and organization of a given society. This is the case, for example, with Herodotean ethnography – especially in those sections concerned with peoples living on the 'margins' of the inhabited world[1] – with Plato's discussion of the luxurious city in the second book of the *Republic* (372e-3d), or with the Aristotelian 'modes of production' (or better 'of subsistence') in the first book of the *Politics*.[2]

Recent research shows, on the whole, an increasing awareness of the central role which the subject of food should play in the study of ancient societies. Prominent here are the studies by Murray (1980, 197-203; 1983a; 1983b; 1986; 1988; 1990b) on the social and historical significance of the *symposion*, by Schmitt Pantel (1985; 1992) on forms of public commensality in the Greek world, Amouretti (1986) on bread and oil, Detienne and Vernant (1979; see also Berthiaume 1982) on the rituals of sacrifice, Bats (1988) on tableware, Gallo (1983; 1984) on food supply and demography, and Garnsey (1988) on famine and food supply. There have also been a number of recent conferences on themes variously related to food: at Oxford in 1984 (Murray 1990a), Verona in 1987 (Longo and Scarpi 1989) and Rome in 1991 (*In Vino Veritas* (forthcoming); on wine see also Dietler 1990). Such a wide range of subjects investigated and of approaches and methodologies employed shows clearly that, in the words of Michel Gras (1989, 68), 'l'étude de l'alimentation est au coeur de l'analyse des sociétés… Elle se relie à l'histoire de l'agriculture et donc du paysage, du climat, des famines, à la démographie mais aussi à l'histoire des mentalités'. And also, I would add, to the history of economy, trade and religion, of social structures, politics and institutions, and even to the history of warfare. The siege-strategy of the Spartans during the Peloponnesian War, for example, and Perikles' response, had considerable consequences for the ways in which food was produced, acquired, distributed and even consumed: see e.g. Hanson (1983, especially 109-43); Gallo (1989); Foxhall (1993).

In his recent book Robert Sallares (1991), with a diversity of arguments and analyses, calls for a comprehensive approach to questions connected with food, from a perspective that he himself rightly defines as 'ecological'. It is from this kind of perspective that I shall ask some questions in this chapter, and make some remarks on the relationship between food and colonization in the archaic Greek world, and more specifically on the role of food in the 'frontier history' of the Greek colonial world of South Italy. Established as 'new' settlements on non-Greek territory, the Greek colonies of South Italy became one of the 'frontiers' of the Greek world. Is it possible to identify some peculiarities in the role played by food in the socio-economic – I could say 'ecological'– processes which developed in

Food and the colonization of South Italy

the colonies themselves and in their relations with the local indigenous populations?

The legitimacy, and even necessity, of this kind of regional approach emerges clearly from the reflections made by Finley (1968), at the Congress at Taranto in 1967, on the historiographical notion of 'frontier history'. As he pointed out, this takes as its specific object of study the 'frontier', seen as contact, interaction and confrontation between different social and economic realities. In the case of Greek colonization, each of the areas affected by the Greek expansion in the Mediterranean should be studied in its own right, since, as he showed with a schematic comparison between South Italy, Sicily and the Black Sea region, in each instance the nature of the relationship and interaction between the Greek and the native elements can be very different. This is not only, according to Finley, because of differences in the Greek colonial experience, but also and especially because of differences in the respective indigenous contexts. Once we have accepted these methodological principles, we immediately discover that from many points of view the case of South Italy presents a variety of different features,[3] compelling us to adopt an approach gauged on a sub-regional scale.

The role of food in Greek colonization

However, to define in a wider and more correct historical perspective the problems relating to this Southern Italian colonial world, it seems to me necessary to mention, although very briefly, a number of questions about the role of food in the Greek colonial experience in general, and its consequences for the working of the ecosystem in Greece itself.

There is certainly little scope here for reviving an old, and on the whole quite sterile, discussion on whether land or trade should provide a single explanation for Greek colonization. Recent discoveries and discussions, e.g. Purcell (1990), Sherratt and Sherratt (1993) and Rihll (1993), suggest that colonization in the archaic period developed on a much wider Mediterranean scale and was characterized by much more 'mobility' ('physical' and economic, but also cultural, social and even institutional) than was previously admitted. Yet such experiences resulted, in most cases, in the establishment of independent and permanent colonial settlements abroad, in Greek terms of *apoikiai*, which showed – or developed with time, to various degrees – forms of cultural identity (in the broadest sense of the expression), especially *vis-à-vis* their native neighbours. And it is clear from works like those by Asheri (1966) on the distribution of land, or by Lepore (1968; 1973), Vallet (1968; 1983) and others[4] on 'city and territory' in Greek colonial areas, that the establishment of an *apoikia* regularly implied as its central feature the occupation of a territory which was to provide the economic basis for the survival and reproduction of the colonial settlement. Moreover, even if it is possible to conceive a sort of 'frontier history' centering around the contact and interaction between Greeks and natives, which developed in different and more 'mobile' forms, it is on the world of the *apoikiai* in particular (and more specifically the colonial territory) that we need to focus our attention, as the proper context for the dynamics of 'frontier history' in most Greek colonial areas. To this end, we shall first investigate the role played by problems connected with food in promoting the establishment of *apoikiai*.

Sallares (1991, 50-107, especially 90-3) persuasively suggests a link between the colonial movement which began in the second half of the 8th century BC and the transformations which, in the same period and immediately before, took place in the Greek food-supplying ecosystem in consequence of the introduction and diffusion of new varieties of crops, mainly from the Near East, and also in the social and demographic structures of the Greek communities.

It seems reasonable, taking into account also the geographical and environmental situation of the principal colonizing centres of the 8th century (Corinth, Megara, Chalkis, and the Achaian cities on the north-west coast of the Peloponnese), to understand the founding of colonies – as Sallares does – in terms of a typical response to demographic pressure and food shortage, or rather to conditions of serious stress created in the 'carrying capacity' of some areas by the new food-supplying practices and the social and demographic consequences which accompanied them. Elsewhere, as in the case of Attika, all this was to find a less traumatic response in the 'internal colonization' of a wide territory hitherto not much populated (Sallares 1991, 91). The notion of 'carrying capacity' appears to me to be of fundamental importance for the understanding of the Greek colonial experiences, including, as we shall see, the subsequent expansion of the colonies themselves. But this becomes even more true if we add to the concept a social significance. We may look at the food-supplying capacity of a given territory not only in relation to the technology for land-exploitation employed by its inhabitants, but also in relation to the ways in which a society living on that territory and interacting with its environment, organizes and reproduces itself: the social structures regulating the access to the means of production and the social modes in which these are exploited, as well as the social ways of distribution, disposal and consumption of products. With these social qualifications, our notion also comes to reflect more adequately the kind of indications provided by the ancient sources on the origins of *apoikiai*. Only very rarely, in fact, do they refer to overpopulation or famine in a strict sense, as originating from natural causes, brought about by pure demographic growth or by climatic or environmental factors, as for example in the case of Cyrene (Herodotos 4.151), while sometimes they rather underline situations of social (or socio-political) crisis, as for example, in the case of the Spartan colony of Taras (Tarentum).[5]

Clearly we cannot rule out the possibility that in some cases famines originating from natural circumstances might in themselves provide a sufficient explanation, as in the case of the exceptionally long drought at Thera. However, if we bear in mind the studies on famines in the ancient world by Jameson (1986) and Garnsey (1988), it does not seem reasonable to imagine phenomena of sufficient scale and frequency to provide an adequate explanation in themselves for the magnitude and recurrence of the Greek colonial experience. After all, a time of famine does not seem an ideal moment for organizing a colonial expedition, which had somehow to be provided with food supplies if it was to have any chance of success.

Colonization and the ecosystem

This brings us to what is perhaps the most important point about the role of food in colonizing enterprises, well described by Sallares. He observes (1991, 92), 'the Greeks were not merely exporting human beings. They also took with them the crops with which they were familiar. In other words they were not merely founding new colonies, but creating new ecosystems modelled as closely as possible on those at home'; and in the

8th century 'the olive tree, whose natural habitat was in coastal semi-arid regions, was becoming a fundamental component of the Greek crop complex. This explains' [I would rather say, helps to explain] 'why Greek colonization in the Mediterranean was confined to the coast', even if quite often the sites chosen by the colonists lacked good natural harbours, as for example in the cases of Sybaris, Metapontum and Selinous. All this, incidentally, contributes to a better understanding of the Greek colonial notion of 'empty land' (*eremos chora*) which we find applied to territories inhabited by natives but exploited in other, more or less different ways.

From this point of view, the question of the production and consumption of food in colonial frontier areas can to a large extent be seen as the problem of the actual ways in which Greek ecosystems are established and developed in the different colonial areas. Their relationship with the pre-existing indigenous ecosystems, differing, to a greater or lesser extent in each instance, from their Greek counterparts, can be one of competition, symbiotic interaction or, perhaps more frequently, aggressive expansion from the Greek side.

Thus colonization contributes to the diffusion on a Mediterranean scale of the Greek ecosystem, with typical cultivation based on the triad of cereals, vine and olive. From this point of view the colonies, not only at the moment of their foundation, but also afterwards, act in two ways. They introduce new cultivated plants and social practices related to food production, distribution and consumption in the regional areas they come directly to control. Secondly, they help to diffuse some of the crops which come with them (with or without the relative social practices) in areas occupied by the natives and not directly affected by colonization. It should be enough here to refer to the Greek origins, sometimes connected with Taras, attributed by the ancients themselves, with a good degree of probability, to various cultivated plants, especially arboreal, of the Italian peninsula (Nissen 1883, 135ff; Sallares 1991, 29-34, 423 n.30), or to the studies of Vallet (1962) on the introduction of olive-growing in archaic Etruria, and of Gras (1983) and others (e.g. Tchernia 1986) on vine-growing and wine-consumption in archaic Latium. On the other hand, it must be underlined that, unlike for example the modern colonization of the New World, Greek colonization does not seem to have had a significant feedback effect on the food-supplying ecosystem (or on the related social practices) of mainland Greece: no significant new crops or eating habits seem to have been borrowed from the colonial areas.

Colonization: its effects

Nonetheless, we can still say that colonization had several active and positive consequences on the overall working of the Greek ecosystem of food supply, offering not only a temporary, but a long-term solution to problems of recurrent imbalance in the (socially defined) carrying capacity of the regions of mainland and Aegean Greece. This happened in at least two ways. First, with the establishment of new settlements, often in the same regional areas which had already seen the foundation of colonies. We must remind ourselves that in South Italy colonies were founded not only in the 8th and 7th centuries, but also in the 6th (for example, Elea) and 5th (for example, Thourioi). The sending by (or simply the coming from) the mainland and Aegean city states (*poleis*) to the already existing colonies, of groups of colonists (*epoikoi*) of various kinds (among them guest-friends (*xenoi*), refugees and exiles (*phygades*), but also regular contingents of supplementary settlers) is a phenomenon difficult to quantify, but must have had a considerable incidence. Secondly, by expanding the ecosystem as a whole, and making it more various in its geographical and environmental features, colonization brought about some mechanisms of compensation which certainly worked in cases of local or regional crises (in the words of the *Constitution of Athens* attributed to Xenophon (2.6), 'the whole earth does not ail at the same time') but probably also in more regular and general ways. There emerges in fact, from the whole of the ancient sources, a specialized role for the colonies and more generally for colonial areas (some in particular, like Sicily and the Pontic region) in the production of food surplus, especially cereals, and its export to mainland and Aegean cities. It will be enough to mention the Herodotean passages on the ships carrying grain (*sitos*) from the Black Sea to Aigina and the Peloponnese in 480 BC (Herodotos 7.147), or on the great assistance and benefits (*megalai opheliai kai epaureseis*) that the mainland Greeks would have got, according to Gelon, from the Sicilian colonies, and on the offer by the same Gelon to supply food for the entire Greek army during the war against Xerxes (Herodotos 7.158-9); or else, the distribution of grain to various cities by Cyrene in the 4th century documented in *Supplementum*

Epigraphicum Graecum IX 2; or finally the interpretative model of the archaic 'colonial trade' (vases in exchange for grain) developed by Vallet and Villard (1961) on the basis of archaeological evidence.

Some sort of confirmation of this role for the colonies comes from the virtual absence of information about 'famines' affecting colonial areas (see Panessa 1991, 543ff and 626ff). The phenomenon as a whole, however, is difficult to evaluate exactly and must be properly qualified by specific chronological and historical frameworks. For the period between the 8th and the 6th centuries, for example, the hypothesis about 'colonial trade' appears too rigid and simplistic, while it is worth noticing that we have the evidence of many oil- and wine-jars (and unguent bottles) from the Greek mainland found in western colonial sites and areas, which bear witness to the export of such valuable commodities to colonial regions. They also testify, incidentally, to the role of colonization, and of colonial markets, in contributing to the development in mainland Greece of specialized agriculture and cash-crop farming. On the other hand, the evidence of an 'export role' for the colonies, at least in the case of valuable food commodities, cannot be easily dated before the 6th century, that is to say, a considerable time after the foundation of most colonies. In the case of South Italy and Sicily, for example, the oldest piece of evidence is perhaps the rather dubious tradition on Sybaritic pipelines carrying wine to the coast (Athenaeus 12.519d), while the sources on the massive export of oil from Akragas (Diodorus Siculus 13.81) certainly refer to the 5th century, and the same is true of the arrival in Athens of 'sweet things' (*hedysmata*) from Italy and Sicily attested by the *Constitution of Athens* attributed to Xenophon (2.11). It is not by chance that it is only from the 6th century onwards, and from Sybaris, as we shall see, that the western colonies emerge in ancient traditions as champions of prosperity (*eudaimonia*) and luxury (*truphe*) (Nenci 1983; Talamo 1987).

It is then possible to observe, albeit indistinctly, significant patterns of change in the relations between colonial and metropolitan areas, connected with different patterns of development in their respective food-producing capacities and food-consuming practices. This brings us nearer to our central question: the role played by food, when seen from an

Food and the colonies of South Italy

'ecological' perspective, in the colonial frontier world of South Italy. One of the most characteristic things about this area is indeed the emphasis placed by ancient sources on the expansion (*auxesis*) of the Greek cities in the region; see e.g. Maddoli (1982), Mele (1982) and Musti (1986). It is precisely to this 'growth' of the Greek archaic societies of South Italy, in its relationship with the native populations, that we should now turn, in order to point out some aspects directly relevant to our theme.

As I have already mentioned, both the literary and the archaeological evidence reveal a variety of features for each of the several sub-regional colonial contexts, which would require a separate approach and discussion; see n.3 and Lepore (1970; 1981). Reasons of space, however, make it obviously impossible to discuss more than one concrete example here, and in what follows I shall focus on the case of the Greeks of Sybaris and the native populations, mainly Oinotrians, with whom they came into contact. This is one of the better documented and studied cases, but also one which exemplifies, in an extreme form, some of the general dynamics intrinsically connected with the colonial frontier situation which can be observed in almost all of South Italy.

The fundamental factor characterizing the growth of archaic colonial societies is the trend for expansion which comes as a response to a lack of balance in the internal socio-economic organization, particularly in land ownership.[6] Equal shares (*isomoiria*) in the distribution of land remains essentially a merely ideological notion, and the distribution of the colonial land (*chora*) appears often to produce, in the words of Lepore (1981, 259) 'eterogeneità,…articolazioni e gerarchie sociali'. This happens first through the process of land division, which is affected by unavoidable disparities in the quality of the lots available, by the granting of privileges to certain categories of people, like founders, priests, first settlers, and by the alienation of property and inequalities caused by the inheritance system. But it also comes about through exploitation practices, concessions and other forms of appropriation and use of communal lands, or marginal areas, even when they are wooded and mountainous, since these are not necessarily of lesser value for the establishment of specialized cultivations or for activities connected with animal breeding and farming.

As a consequence, the way in which the division and exploitation of colonial territories is organized results in the emergence of a more or less rigid oligarchic society. And the process of social reproduction and of demographic growth – in the 'quasi-vacuum' of the colonial frontier area – produces a strong social demand for new land. This in turn leads to further territorial expansion, in the first instance along the coastline and the immediate hinterland, which is more suitable to the Greek ecosystem. All this culminates during the 6th century in a series of border wars between the various colonies: Metapontum against Taras, Achaian colonies against Siris, Kroton against Lokroi and then against Sybaris. The very occurrence of these wars reveals that the expansion of the colonies involved has reached its limit.

But the demand for new land produces also a territorial expansion towards the hills and mountains of the hinterland already occupied by the natives. This emerges quite clearly from both archaeological and historical sources, which provide evidence for the establishment of various types of sub-colonies on the other side of the mountains, along the Tyrrhenian coastline, and for the creation, on the edges of colonial territories, of a number of so-called 'frontier sanctuaries' (see Guzzo 1987a). These functioned as the proper places of contact and exchange with natives, and testify in their chronological and topographical distribution to the development of the exploitation of the indigenous hinterland with its peculiar ecosystem.

What finally results is a series of large colonial territories, to a great extent organized into middle-sized and large aristocratic estates, exploited through the employment of slave labour, probably provided mainly by natives, and of much larger colonial 'dominions' (or 'empires'), including native settlements and territories. Alongside the typical cultivations of the Greek ecosystem, we can notice here a strong incidence of animal husbandry, not only sheep-breeding, but also, and foremost, cattle- and horse-breeding (the latter – *hippotrophia* – is one of the principal features attributed by the sources to Southern Italian colonial aristocracies). In these territories, and near their borders, the exploitation of the forest and pastoral resources of the hinterland can take forms which, to Lepore (1981, 259), recalled the notion of 'frontier feudalism', in the sense in which the concept had been employed by Lattimore.

Sybaris

This model of interpretation and reconstruction of the phenomena and dynamics of colonial growth is particularly suited to the case of Sybaris, whose history is largely influenced by its geographical position. Lying in a broad and fertile coastal plain, at the estuary of the wide and ramifying fluvial system of the Crati-Coscile-Esaro, it occupies the natural outlet from which it is potentially possible to control this large geographical region (Osanna 1992, 115ff). This region had seen, during the 9th and 10th centuries, the flourishing of several native communities (Peroni 1987; Guzzo 1982a; Lombardo 1994, 68ff), occupying the top of hills near the coast and along the rivers, and taking advantage of the economic interdependence of mountain and plain and of coast and hinterland. With the foundation of Sybaris and the subsequent expansion of its territory, the existence of these communities comes to an end, not so much as a consequence of colonial conquest and destruction, but rather because the colony assumes the control and exploitation of the coastal plain and consequently of the mechanisms regulating the economic interdependence of coast and hinterland (Guzzo 1982a 1982b, 1987b; Osanna 1992, 118ff; Lombardo 1994, 70ff). Thus the territories previously exploited, in their individual ways, by the native communities, are reduced to the role of 'countryside' for the Greek city. As Guzzo (1982a, 242) puts it, 'dal punto di vista archeologico, per tutto il settimo secolo la Sibaritide interna è muta'. This points to a dismantling of the forms of social organization in place until then, with the possible survival only of loose and scattered production units, mainly relying, in all probability, on a pastoral and forest economy, and exploited in various ways by the colony. On the other hand, the northward expansion of Sybaris in the 6th century, with the conquest of Siris, brings into its orbit, if not exactly into the Sybaritic 'empire', a large area characterized by the presence of many flourishing native communities from Amendolara to those situated in the Sinni and Agri valleys, as well as in the Lao, Noce, and Bussento valleys on the Tyrrhenian side. It is not by chance that, as a result of the destruction of Sybaris, these communities, in most cases, suffer a crisis and disappear, thus confirming the vital role of their relationship with the colony (Lombardo 1994, 103ff).

It is against this background that we should place and evaluate a number of Greek traditions (Callaway 1950): on the empire (*arche*) exercised by Sybaris over four peoples (*ethne*) and 25 city states (*poleis*) (Strabo 6.1.13;

Greco 1990; Giangiulio 1991); on its exaggerated demographic growth, due to its unusual liberality in the concession of citizenship, according to Diodorus Siculus (12.9.2; Camassa 1989); and on the extraordinary scale of its horse-breeding. The city would have produced an aristocracy of five thousands knights, which included a group of five hundred extraordinarily wealthy individuals (Athenaeus 12.519c; Diodorus Siculus 12.9; de Sensi Sestito 1983; Lubtchansky 1993). The literary and documentary evidence (Aelian *On Animals* 6.44 or the *Lindian Chronicle* 26) points also to the importance of sheep- and cattle-breeding in the region of Sybaris, while great emphasis is placed on the exceptional fertility of its soil (e.g. Diodorus Siculus 12.9 and Varro *On Agriculture* 1.44.2, with reference to extraordinarily high cereal yields) and on vine-growing and wine-production (Callaway 1950), mentioned also in connection with the construction of the pipelines allegedly designed to convey wine from the countryside to the coast to be, at least in part, exported (Athenaeus 12.519d).

Sybaritic luxury

This finally brings us to the rich body of ancient traditions on the luxury of Sybaris.[7] I shall mention here only those aspects more directly connected with food: i) their exaggerated fondness for gourmet cuisine, leading to such extremes as the introduction of economic incentives among cooks to promote the invention of new recipes, or tax exemptions for eel-sellers (Athenaeus 12.521d, from Phylarchos); ii) their extravagant way of life (*diaita*) – significantly opposed to that of the Spartans (Athenaeus 4.138d and 12.518e, from Timaios) –, the most famous representative of which, Smindyrides, is described by Herodotos (6.127) as the man who reached the utmost limits of luxury (other sources inform us that he brought with him to Sikyon one thousand cooks and one thousand fishermen);[8] iii) the richness of their banquets, which rendered the 'Sybaritic table' (*Sybaritika trapeza*) and the Sybaritic feasts (*Sybaritikai euochiai*) the models par excellence of luxurious eating, later to become proverbial.[9]

These accounts surely derive mainly from hostile traditions, presenting an image of Sybaris as a paradigm of excess punished; see Nenci (1983), Talamo (1987) and Lubtchansky (1993). They may have originated with the victorious Krotonians, and more precisely from within the Pythagorean sect, whose ideology rejected a way of life like that of the Sybarites and the food-consuming practices that went with it (Talamo 1987), which was probably not so very different, except perhaps in scale, from that common to all archaic Greek aristocracies; see e.g. Lombardo (1983) and Ampolo (1984). In more general terms, these accounts probably reflect the crisis which during the 5th century, after Sybaris had already been destroyed, affected most of the Southern Italian archaic colonial societies, in their aristocratic socio-economic and political assets, as well as their cultural world (see e.g. Mele 1981; Lombardo 1987), and therefore cannot be taken at face value for the reconstruction of Sybarite society. However, if we look at them against the socio-economic and territorial situation mentioned above, taking into account, in particular, the position occupied by Sybaris in relation to a wide and articulated sub-regional ecosystem formed by the basin of the river Krathis, the picture they provide acquires some foundation. It seems to reflect, on the one hand, some common features of the 'frontier history' of Southern Italian colonies in the archaic period, and on the other, the peculiar outcome of that of Sybaris.

Of particular interest, in this respect, seems to me a fragment of the *Thouriopersians* of Metagenes (fr. 6 KA), an Athenian poet of the Old Comedy, quoted by Athenaeus (6.269f-70a). Following the vein of comedies on the Golden Age and the Land of Plenty (Baldry 1953), and alluding in his title to the *Persians* of Pherekrates, Metagenes had set the action of his comedy,[10] and consequently his Land of Plenty, in Thourioi.

> The river Krathis brings down for us huge barley-cakes which have kneaded themselves, while the other river [the Sybaris] thrusts its billow of cheese-cakes and meat and boiled rays wriggling to us here. These little rivulets flow on one side with baked cuttle-fish, braize, and crayfish, on the other side with sausages and hashed meat; here anchovies, yonder pancakes. And cutlets automatically stewed dart downwards into the mouth, others upwards at our very feet, while cakes of fine meal swim round us in a circle. (trans. Gulick)

Bearing in mind i) that the colony of Thourioi originated from an appeal to Athens by the surviving Sybarites for help in refounding their city; ii) that it was founded between 446/45 and 444/43 BC, on the same site as and as heir to ancient Sybaris;[11] iii) that another of the surviving fragments of the *Thouriopersians* seems to refer to the practices of the archaic Sybarite cavalry (see Lubtchansky 1993; Lombardo n.11), I think we should underline two elements in our fragment. First, the use of the present tense: whereas the tenses usually employed in the comic descriptions of the Golden Age and of the Land of Plenty are the past and the future (as in the *Persians* of Pherekrates), here the poet uses the present tense, as if to underline, even if from a concrete perspective, the contemporary and comic reality for his Thourian (or Sybarite?) characters. Second, and most important, there is the substantial correspondence, beyond the comic intentions of the poet, between the role he attributes to the rivers Krathis[12] and Sybaris in bringing about the fabulous wealth of his Land of Plenty/ Thourioi, and that emerging from the socio-archaeological, or better 'ecological', study of the region (cf. Osanna 1992, 134ff).

Notes

[1] Cf. Rosellini and Said (1978) and Redfield (1985). Herodotos regularly underlines, also when speaking of Lydians, Persians and Greeks (for example 1.70, 7.102, 9.122), the link between the food-supplying ecosystem on the one hand, and the social practices of food-consumption as well as the social, political and military structures on the other.

[2] See Wilkins (pp. 7-10 above) on Plato's luxurious city. A less obvious example is provided by Athenaeus' long and apparently casual list of different banquets in the fourth book of the *Deipnosophists* which, as Louise Bruit and Pauline Schmitt Pantel (1986) have shown, presupposes 'une réflexion sur les formes du pouvoir, sur les types d'organisation possibles de la vie en commun, sur le contexte en dehors duquel ces formes de repas ne sont que des pittoresque manières de table'.

[3] For the area of modern Calabria see Lombardo (1994); see also De Sensi Sestito (1984).

[4] For the Black Sea region see Vasowicz (1983); for Southern Italy, Osanna (1992).

[5] See Diodorus Siculus 8 fr. 21; Strabo 6.3.2-3, quoting long fragments from Antiochos (*FGH* 555 F13) and Ephorus (*FGH* 70 F216).

[6] I draw mainly on Lepore (1968; 1970; 1981), Vallet (1968), Osanna (1992). See also Lombardo (1987; 1994).

[7] The sources are collected by Callaway (1950, 72 ff.); cf. also Nenci (1983) and Talamo (1987). See also the discussion by C. Ampolo in the proceedings of the Congress at Taranto 1992 (forthcoming).

[8] Athenaeus 6.273b (from Chamaileon *On Pleasure*) and 12.541c (=Timaios *FGH* 566 F 9); Aelian *Varia Historia* 12.24. Cf. Rose (1966).

9 Cf. Zenobios 5.87; Apostolios 1.4; Athenaeus 1.25e; most important is the fragment from Aristophanes (225 KA) in Athenaeus 12.527c.

10 The play can perhaps be dated c.410 BC (cf. Baldry 1953) although, according to Athenaeus (6.270a), it was never produced.

11 Cf. e.g. Ehrenberg (1948) and Rutter (1973). See also my contribution to the Congress at Taranto 1992, forthcoming in the Proceedings with the title 'Da Sibari a Thurii'.

12 A similar, though not comically exaggerated, role is attributed to the same river in Euripides *Trojan Women* 228-9: 'Krathis with its wondrous water nourishes and makes prosper a land of vigorous men'.

Bibliography

Amouretti C., 1986 *Le pain et l'huile dans la Grèce antique* (Paris).

Ampolo C., 1984 'Il lusso nelle società arcaiche. Note preliminari sulla posizione del problema', *Opus* 3, 469ff.

Asheri D., 1966 *Distribuzioni di terre nell'Antica Grecia* (Torino).

Baldry H.C., 1953 'The Idler's Paradise in Attic Comedy', *Greece and Rome* 22, 49-60.

Bats M., 1988 *Vaisselle et alimentation à Olbia de Provence (v.350-v.50 a.C.). Modèles culturels et catégories ceramiques* (Paris).

Berthiaume G., 1982 *Les rôles du mageiros. Etude sur la boucherie, la cuisine et le sacrifice dans la Grèce ancienne* (Leiden).

Bruit L. & Schmitt Pantel P., 1986 'Citer, classer, penser: à propos des repas des Grecs et des repas des Autres dans le livre IV des *Deipnosophisthes* d'Athénée', *Annali dell' Istituto Universitario Orientale di Napoli (Archeologia)* 8, 203-21.

Callaway J.S., 1950 *Sybaris* (Baltimore).

Camassa G., 1989 'Sibari polyanthropos', *Serta historica antiqua* 3 (Roma), 1-9.

Detienne M. & Vernant J-P., 1979 *La cuisine du sacrifice en pays grec* (Paris).

Dietler M., 1990 'Driven by Drink: the Role of Drinking in the Political Economy and the case of Early Iron Age France', *Journal of Anthropological Archaeology* 9, 352-406.

Ehrenberg V., 1948 'The Foundation of Thurii', *American Journal of Philology* 69, 149-70 (=*Polis und Imperium* [Zurich-Stuttgart 1965], 298-315).

Finley M.I., 1968 'Intervention' in *La città e il suo territorio. Atti del VII Convegno di studi sulla Magna Grecia, Taranto, ottobre 1967* (Napoli), 186-8.

Foxhall L., 1993 'Farming and Fighting in the Greek World', in Rich and Shipley (1993), 134-45.

Gallo L., 1983 'Alimentazione e classi sociali: una nota su orzo e frumento in Grecia', *Opus* 4, 449-72.

Gallo L., 1984 *Alimentazione e demografia della Grecia antica* (Salerno).

Gallo L., 1989 'Alimentazione urbana e alimentazione contadina nell'Atene classica', in Longo and Scarpi (1989), 213-30.

Garnsey P.D.A., 1988 *Famine and Food-supply in the Graeco-Roman World: Response to Risk and Crisis* (Cambridge).

Giangiulio M., 1991 'Forme diplomatiche e realtà statuali. Un aspetto dele relazioni greco-indigene in Magna Grecia' in L. De Finis (ed.), *Civiltà classica e mondo dei barbari. Due modelli a confronto* (Trento), 137ff.

Gras M., 1983 'Vin et societé à Rome et dans le Latium à l'epoque archaique', in *Forme di contatto e processi di trasformazione nelle società antiche. Atti del Convegno di Cortona, 24-30 Maggio 1981* (Pisa-Roma), 1067-75.

Gras M., 1989 'De la céramique à la cuisine. Le mangeur d'Olbia', *Revue des Etudes Anciennes* 91, 65-71.

Greco E., 1990 'Serdaioi', *Annali dell' Istituto Universitario Orientale di Napoli (Archeologia)* 12, 39-57.

Guzzo P.G., 1982a 'La Sibaritide e Sibari nell'VIII e VII sec. a.C.', *Annuario della Scuola Archeologica di Atene e delle Missioni Italiane in Oriente* n.s. 44, 237-50.

Guzzo P.G., 1982b 'Modificazioni dell'ambiente e della cultura tra VIII e VII secolo sulla costa ionica d'Italia', *Dialoghi di Archeologia* n.s. 2, 146-51 .

Guzzo P.G., 1987a 'Schema per la categoria interpretativa del "Santuario di frontiera"', *Scienze dell'Antichità. Storia. Archeologia. Antropologia* 1, 373-9.

Guzzo P.G., 1987b 'L'archeologia dele colonie archaiche' in Settis (1987), 137ff.

Hanson V.D., 1983 *Warfare and Agriculture in Classical Greece* (Pisa).

Jameson M.H., 1986 'Famine in the Greek World', in P.D.A. Garnsey and C.R. Whittaker (eds), *Trade and Famine in classical Antiquity* (Cambridge), 6-16.

Lepore E., 1968 'Per una fenomenologia storica del rapporto città-territorio in Magna Grecia', in *La città e il suo territorio. Atti del VII Convegno di studi sulla Magna Grecia, Taranto, ottobre 1967* (Napoli), 29-62, 359-367 (= *Colonie greche dell'Occidente antico* [Roma 1989] 47-78).

Lepore E., 1970 'Classi e ordini in Magna Grecia' in *Recherches sur les structures sociales dans l'Antiquité classique, Caen 25-26 avril 1969* (Paris), 43-62 (= *Colonie greche dell'Occidente antico* [Roma 1989] 139-56).

Lepore E., 1973 'Problemi dell'organizzazione della chora coloniale', in M.I. Finley (ed.) *Problèmes de la terre en Grèce ancienne* (Paris-La Haye 1973) 15-47 (= *Colonie greche dell' Occidente antico* (Rome 1989), 79-110).

Lepore E., 1981 'I Greci in Italia', in *Storia della società italiana* 1 (Milano), 231-68.

Lombardo M., 1983 'Habrosyne e habrà nel mondo greco arcaico', in *Forme di contatto e processi di trasformazione nelle società antiche. Atti del Convegno di Cortona, 24-30 Maggio 1981* (Pisa-Roma), 1077-1103.

Lombardo M., 1987 'L'organizzazione militare degli Italioti', in G. Pugliese Carratelli (ed.), *Magna Grecia. Politica, economia, società* (Milano) 225-58, 301-3.

Lombardo M., 1993 'Greci e Indigeni in Calabria. Aspetti e problemi dei rapporti economici e sociali', in Settis (1994), 57-137.

Longo O. & Scarpi P., (eds) 1989 *Homo Edens. Regimi, riti e pratiche dell' alimentazione nelle civiltà del Mediterraneo* (Verona).

Lubtchansky N., 1993 'La valse tragique des cavaliers Sybarites selon Aristote', *Annali dell' Istituto Universitario Orientale di Napoli (Archeologia)* 15, 31-57.

Maddoli G., 1982 'Megale Hellas: genesi di un concetto e realtà storico-politiche', in *Megale Hellas: nome e immagine. Atti del XXI Convegno di studi sulla Magna Grecia, Taranto, 2-5 ottobre 1981* (Napoli), 9-33.

Mele A., 1981 'I Pitagorici e Archita', in *Storia della Società italiana* 1 (Milano), 271 ff.

Mele A., 1982 'La Megale Hellas pitagorica: aspetti politici, economici e sociali' in *Megale Hellas: nome e immagine. Atti del XXI Convegno di studi sulla Magna Grecia, Taranto, 2-5 ottobre 1981* (Napoli), 33-80.

Murray O., 1980 *Early Greece* (London).

Murray O., 1983a 'The symposion as social organization', in R. Hägg (ed.), *The Greek renaissance in the eighth century B.C. Tradition and Innovation. Proceedings of the 2nd international Symposion at the Swedish Institute in Athens, 1-5 June 1981* (Stockholm), 195-9.

Murray O., 1983b 'The Greek Symposion in History', in E. Gabba (ed.), *Tria Corda. Scritti in onore di Arnaldo Momigliano* (Como), 257-72.

Murray O., 1986 'Symposion und Männerbund' in *Actes de la Conférence Eirene Prague 1982* (Prague), 47-52.

Murray O., 1988 'Death and the symposion', *Annali dell' Istituto Universitario Orientale di Napoli (Archeologia)* 10, 239-57.

Murray O., (ed.) 1990a *Sympotica* (Oxford).

Murray O., 1990b 'War and the Symposion', in W.J. Slater (ed.), *Dining in a Classical Context* (Ann Arbor), 83-103.

Musti D., 1986 'Città di Magna Grecia II', *Rivista di Filologia e di Istruzione Classica* 114, 286-319.

Nenci G., 1983 'Tryphé e colonizzazione', in *Forme di contatto e processi di trasformazione nelle società antiche. Atti del Convegno di Cortona, 24-30 Maggio 1981* (Pisa-Roma), 1019-31.

Nissen H., 1883 *Italische Landeskunde* 1 (Berlin).

Osanna M., 1992 *Chorai coloniali da Taranto a Locri* (Roma).

Panessa G., 1991 *Fonti greche e latine per la storia dell'ambiente e del clima nel mondo greco* 2 vols (Pisa).

Peroni R., 1987 'La Protostoria', in Settis (1987), 112 ff.

Purcell N., 1990 'Mobility and the Polis', in O. Murray and S. Price (eds), *The Greek City from Homer to Alexander* (Oxford 1990), 29-58.

Redfield J., 1985 'Herodotus the Tourist', *Classical Philology* 80, 97-118.

Rich J. & Shipley G., (eds) 1993 *War and Society in the Greek World* (London-New York).

Rihll T., 1993 'War, Slavery and Settlements in Early Greece', in Rich and Shipley (1993), 77-107.

Rose K., 1966 'Smindyrides the Sybarite', *Classical Bulletin* 43, 27-8.

Rosellini M. and Said S., 1978 'Usages des femmes et autres nomoi chez les 'sauvages' d'Hérodote', *Annali della Scuola Normale Superiore di Pisa* series 3.8, 949-1005.

Rutter N.K., 1973 'Diodorus and the Foundation of Thurii', *Historia* 22, 155-76.

Sallares R., 1991 *The Ecology of the Ancient Greek World* (London).

Schmitt Pantel P., 1985 'Banquet et cité grecque. Quelques questions suscitées par les recherches récentes', *Mélanges d'Archéologie et d'Histoire de l'Ecole Française à Rome* 97, 135-58.

Schmitt Pantel P., 1992 *La cité au banquet: Histoire des repas publics dans les cités grecques* (Rome).

De Sensi Sestito G., 1983 'Gli oligarchici sibariti, Telys e la vittoria crotoniate sul Traente', in *Miscellanea di studi storici* 3, 37-56.

De Sensi Sestito G., 1984 *La Calabria in età arcaica e classica. Storia, economia, società* (Roma-Reggio Calabria).

Settis S., (ed.) 1987 & 1994 *Storia della Calabria* 2 vols (Roma-Reggio Calabria).

Sherratt S. & Sherratt A., 1993 'The Growth of the Mediterranean economy in the early first millennium B.C.', *World Archaeology* 24, 361-78 .

Talamo C., 1987 'Pitagora e la tryphé', *Rivista di Filologia e di Istruzione Classica* 115, 385-404.

Tchernia A., 1986 *Le vin dans l'Italie romaine* (Paris).

Vallet G., 1962 'L'introduction de l'olivier en Italie centrale d'après les données de la céramique', in M. Renard (ed.), *Hommages à Albert Grenier* 3 (Bruxelles), 1554-63.

Vallet G., 1968 'La cité et son territoire dans les colonies grecques d'Occident', in *La città e il suo territorio. Atti del VII Convegno di studi sulla Magna Grecia, Taranto, ottobre 1967* (Napoli), 67-142.

Vallet G., 1983 'Urbanisation et organisation de la chora coloniale grecque en Grande Grèce et en Sicile', in *Forme di contatto e processi di trasformazione nelle società antiche. Atti del Convegno di Cortona, 24-30 Maggio 1981* (Pisa-Roma), 937-56.

Vallet G. & Villard F., 1961 'Céramique et histoire grecque', *Revue Historique* 225, 295-318.

Vasowicz A., 1983 'Urbanisation et organisation de la chora coloniale grecque autour de la Mer Noire', in *Forme di contatto e processi di trasformazione nelle società antiche. Atti del Convegno di Cortona, 24-30 Maggio 1981* (Pisa-Roma), 911-35.

In Vino Veritas. An international Conference, Rome 19-22 March 1991 (forthcoming).

❖ 20 ❖ LYDIAN SPECIALITIES, CROESUS' GOLDEN BAKING-WOMAN, AND DOGS' DINNERS

David Harvey

In this chapter I shall discuss three disparate Lydian topics: Lydian specialities, and how they became known to the Greeks; the golden statue of his baking-woman that king Croesus is alleged to have dedicated at Delphi (Herodotos 1.51.5); and the ritual burials of puppies discovered at Sardis.

Lydia was a fertile land (Strabo 13.4.5 ['the best of all plains'], 13.4.8; Hanfmann 1983, 4-5, 219-20), and a number of its edible products were apparently well-known to the Greeks: we hear, for example, of Lydian bread, wine, chestnuts, figs, olives, onions and sauces.

Lydian specialities

The question arises: how did they come to know about them? Given that Athens and Persia were engaged in hostilities for much of the 5th and 4th centuries BC, and that Lydia was a Persian satrapy, how did Athenian comic poets and their audiences come to hear about Lydian specialities? – above all, their perishable foods: did Athenians travel across to Sardis to munch a Lydian onion, and come back home to tell their friends what colour it was? It seems unlikely.

There is no single answer: it varies according to the commodity.

WINE (Magie 1950, 809 n.58; Greenewalt 1976, 36 n.10) presents no problem at all. Several types are specifically named, of which the most interesting are the so-called 'nectar' produced near the Mysian Mount Olympus, a concoction of wine, honey and sweet-smelling flowers, which was both fragrant and sweet (Athenaeus 2.38f, quoting Ariston of Keos, head of the Lyceum, late 3rd *c*. BC), and the wine from the spectacularly volcanic Katakekaumene district just east of Sardis (Strabo 4.11), where no plant other than the vine would grow. It was said to be as good as the most famous varieties. These wines would of course have been transported in the normal way in amphorae, and there is no problem about how the Greeks knew what they were like. 'Nectar', admittedly, sounds like a local brew; maybe the Greeks in the cities of Ionia enjoyed it – and that is one very obvious way for knowledge of this and other Lydian specialities to spread to the Greek world.

The Gygean lake, later known as lake Koloe, just north of Sardis, is well stocked with FISH. Louis Robert (1982) cites the evidence of many travellers from 1765 onwards; one piscatorial expert singles out carp, pike and roach. A 30-pound carp was caught there in 1990. Until about 1890, the fishermen were Greek; then a colony of Russians, or 'Cossacks', took over, until 1963, when they left for Canada. These fish were not eaten locally: they were salted and sent off to Istanbul and Bulgaria.

Since the lake is so well stocked with fish, one would expect to find references to them in our ancient sources. The evidence is, in fact, surprisingly thin. 'Lovingly drawn fish' appear on goblets of *c*. 600 BC found near Sardis, which the excavators 'would like to think' were a local species (Hanfmann 1983, 6 with fig. 119). The comic poet Alexis (4th-3rd *c*. BC) includes salted fish among the ingredients of the Lydian sauce known as *kandaulos* (fr. 178.8, in Athenaeus 12.516d; comic fragments are cited from Kassel-Austin *Poetae Comici Graeci*.). An anonymous paradoxographer of uncertain date (Paradoxographus Florentinus 39, printed in Robert 1982, 344) seems to be the only ancient author to comment on the abundance of fish in the Gygean lake. Varro (3.17.4) says that shoals of fish in this lake come right up to the shore when they hear the music of the pipe-player, because no-one dares to catch them; that refers to a festival, but no doubt they were caught and eaten at other times. Pliny

(31.25) says that you will die immediately if you eat them, which would certainly make export unlikely and inadvisable; but, as Louis Robert has argued, this is probably to be interpreted as divine punishment for eating festival-fish.

Not much of a haul, then: apart from the stories about the festival, it amounts only to some drawings, one word in a comic poet, and a late paradoxographer. Perhaps we should conclude that the fish were eaten only locally, and not exported; or, more likely, it is just a fortuitous gap in our evidence. If they were exported, they would of course have been salted, as in modern times (see above).

BREAD is certainly not exportable: so how do we know that Lydian bread was particularly good? The answer is that we do not. Archestratos (4th *c.* BC; see Dalby, Chapter 30 below; advises us to get a Phoenician or a Lydian man in our house, who will prepare all different kinds of *sitos* – a versatile character (fr. 5 Brandt, in Athenaeus 3.112bc) . Athenaeus, in a moment of one-up-manship, says here that Archestratos did not realise that Kappadokian bakers are the best. So it was bakers, not bread, that the Lydians exported.

It is reasonable, though, to suppose that Lydian bread was good. After all, where did those Lydian bakers get their expertise in the first place? The plains of Lydia were fertile, and a large proportion of them seems to have been given over to the cultivation of cereals (Foss and Hanfmann 1975, 20; Hanfmann 1983, 217 n.9). A number of objects dating from the 7th and 6th centuries, interpreted as bread-trays, have been found at Sardis (Hanfmann 1983, 219 n.11). The remains of water-mills constitute good evidence for the production of cereals in later antiquity (Hanfmann 1983, 147, 276 n.106: inscription of 211 AD).

Xenophon (*Cyropaidia* 6.2.2) mentions Lydian FIGS; but then, he had been to the country, and he was by no means the only one: the march of the Ten Thousand started at Sardis (*Anabasis* 1.2.2-5) – one of the most famous occasions when plenty of Greeks could have seen the agricultural produce of Lydia. No doubt that is how Xenophon knows about Lydian OLIVES as well (*Cyropaidia* 6.2.22). But it is Varro who tells us exactly how Lydian figs became known throughout the ancient world:

We pass a piece of string through the figs when they are ripe, and after they have dried, they are tied up in bundles, and people can send them wherever they like; and on arrival they are planted in a nursery, and they reproduce. That is how the Lydian fig and other foreign varieties were imported into Italy.

(*On Agriculture* 1.41.5-6)

It is not often that an ancient text answers our questions so precisely. Varro's evidence also shows that there is no need to suppose that the Lydians exported *dried* figs. Pliny, too, refers to figs that have come to Italy from abroad, including the Lydian: these, he says, are purple (15.19.69) – indeed they were said to be similar to the blood-figs (*haimoniai*) of Paros (Athenaeus 3.76b). Columella (5.10.11, 10.418), however, describes their skin as *pictum*, dappled.

I turn now to the humble ONION. Onions from Sardis (Theophrastos *Enquiry into Plants* 7.4.7, 9; Pliny 19.32.104 [from Theophrastos]) were exceptionally white. If figs can be propagated in nurseries, so presumably can onions; perhaps seeds were exported. And of course the picture with which we began, of an enterprising Greek sailing across to Lydia, is a highly misleading caricature. We have only to think of Thucydides book 8 and the earlier books of Xenophon's *Hellenica* to realise how frequently Greek troops were fighting on Asiatic soil; and no doubt they had Lydian onions and figs among their rations. We might perhaps conclude that early references to Lydian perishables are to be explained by propagation; later ones by propagation or personal inspection.

We have detailed advice from the medical writer Diphilos (early 3rd *c*. BC) on how best to eat CHESTNUTS from Sardis, which are nourishing and have a good flavour: if you eat them raw, they are hard to digest; if you roast them, they are less filling, but more easily digested; it is best to boil them (Athenaeus 2.54c-d). Pliny (15.25.93) says that chestnuts first came to Italy from Sardis, and were subsequently improved by cultivation. So again, there is no need to think of Lydians exporting chestnuts, which would soon have rotted anyway. The Sardis chestnut tree flourished wherever the environment was favourable. (Cf. also Theophrastos *Enquiry into Plants* 4.5.4; Phylotimos [mid 3rd *c*. BC] in Athenaeus 2.53f; Pliny 15.25.93; Dioskourides *De materia medica* 1.106.3 Wellmann). Theophrastos (*En-*

quiry into Plants 4.5.4) mentions HAZEL-NUTS, APPLES and POMEGRANATES as well as chestnuts growing around Mount Tmolos and the Mysian Mount Olympus; this information presumably derives from personal observation by visitors.

Finally, two Lydian luxury sauces. The first is KARYKE, mentioned more frequently than any other Lydian speciality (Greenewalt 1976, 53 n.59 [sources], 52-4 [discussion]). This was certainly eaten in Greece: a character in a satyr-play by Achaios of Eretria (fr. 12 Snell, in Athenaeus 4.173c-d) says he loathes the men of Delphi because they pour *karyke* over the sacrificial meat; and Plutarch solemnly assures us (*Moralia* 2.644b) that the decline of Spartan power began when they began to indulge in *karyke* and *kandaulos*. There is no problem at all about how the recipe for this sauce spread throughout the Greek world: Athenaeus (12.516c) lists no less than eighteen cookery books in which the recipe was given.

The other gourmet Lydian sauce was KANDAULOS, KANDYLOS or KANDYLE; these seem to be alternative Greek spellings of the same Lydian word (Greenewalt 1976, 53 n.57 [sources], 52-4 [discussion]; Lydian origin: Athenaeus 12.516c-d; Eustathios on *Iliad* 18.291; earliest reference: Nikostratos [early 4th *c.* BC] fr. 16). Athenaeus (12.516c-d) tells us that there were three different varieties. Menander (fr. 397 Sandbach, in Athenaeus 4.132ef = 12.517a) associates it with aphrodisiacs, or more bluntly *hypobinetionta bromata*, literally 'food that makes one somewhat desirous of a screw'. The fact that it is sometimes linked with *karyke*, as we have seen, suggests that recipes for the two dishes might be found in the same cookery books; and sure enough, Athenaeus (12.516c-d) quotes the recipe given by Hegesippos of Tarentum (date unknown), one of the eighteen writers on cookery that he cites for *karyke*. So there is no problem: knowledge was circulated by cooks and by books. These methods should be added to those that we have already noted: propagation, autopsy, and contact with Ionian Greeks.

We have, I believe, dealt with all the major foods for which Lydia was famous. But it is difficult to resist mentioning one Lydian gustatory, or disgustatory, habit that fortunately did not catch on. We hear about it from the 5th century historian Xanthos of Lydia (*FGH* 765 F18 = Athenaeus 10.415c-d). King Kambles was such a glutton that one night he ate his own wife. In the morning, her hand was found sticking out of his mouth; it was obvious what he had been up to; the news flashed around Sardis, and the king committed suicide. This is not, I suspect, sensational history; it sounds more like a myth – we might compare the story of Kronos swallowing his children – that has been mistaken for history, a suggestion that has the support of Eustathios (on *Odyssey* 9.310), who arrived at much the same conclusion.

Croesus' golden baking-woman

In Book 1 Herodotos describes the lavish gifts that Croesus sent to Delphi, and amongst them (51.5) he mentions 'many other offerings without inscriptions'. These include 'a golden statue of a woman, three cubits high, which the people at Delphi say is an image of Croesus' baking woman', an *eikon* of his feminine *artokopou*. (Note *artos*, by the way: wheat-bread for a king.) Three cubits is four foot six: that is life-size – it corresponds exactly with the height of one of my former pupils. We should perhaps imagine a larger version of the little gold statuette from Ephesos illustrated in Bammer (1984, pl. 86).

Herodotos, with his usual caution, does not vouch for the story: it is 'what the men of Delphi say'. But what led them to believe that Croesus would have dedicated a golden statue of his baking-wench, of all people? Herodotos does not tell us, but Plutarch does: Croesus' stepmother attempted to poison him, and his baking-woman saved his life. I quote:

> 'There's one thing you've not mentioned', said the guide at Delphi: 'Croesus had a golden statue made of his baking-woman and dedicated it here'. 'Yes' replied Theon; 'but he didn't do it in order to insult the temple; he had a sound and proper reason. They say that Croesus' father Alyattes married a second wife, who bore him some more children; and this second wife plotted against Croesus and gave some poison to his baking-woman, with instructions to knead it into the bread and to give it to Croesus. But the baking-woman went and told Croesus about it, and gave the poisoned bread to his stepmother's children instead. So when Croesus became king, he rewarded her, and made Apollo a witness to her good deed.'
>
> (*Moralia* 401ef = *de Pythiae oraculis* 16)

This assassination attempt must surely belong in the context of the story that Herodotos tells a little later (1.92.2-4): before Croesus became king, some Lydians tried to get Pantaleon onto the throne instead. Both Croesus and Pantaleon were sons of the preceding king Alyattes, who had two wives: Croesus was the son of a Karian woman, Pantaleon of an Ionian. Croesus succeeded – in both senses – because he was Alyattes' choice; and he did some very nasty things indeed to the leader of the opposition. Since Pantaleon was his step-brother, Occam's law would lead us to suppose that the poison-plot of Croesus's stepmother – in other words, Pantaleon's mother – was part of the same constitutional crisis.

By Plutarch's time, the story has been 'improved': it is the stepmother's children who get poisoned instead of Croesus. Very neat, but we should not believe it. Herodotos liked stories of revenge, and he would surely have included this detail had he known it. It is a nice example of the way that an anecdote grows in the telling.

I have no idea whether there is any truth in Herodotos' story, or whether the Delphic guides elaborated the whole thing to explain the gold statue. The jealous stepmother is a standard character in folk-tale; and although Pantaleon is an ideal name for a Lydian – it means 'all-lion', and the lion was the Lydian national or royal symbol (Hanfmann and Ramage 1978, 20-22; Hanfmann 1983, 6, 184-5) – it is a *Greek* name, though of course it might be a Greek translation of a Lydian name.

On the other hand, there certainly was a life-sized gold statue of a woman at Delphi, and I see no reason to doubt that it was dedicated by Croesus. Diodorus mentions it (16.56.6): he says that Phayllos, the Phokian general, melted down quite a lot of the offerings at Delphi and turned them into coin to pay his mercenaries in his war against Philip II of Macedon. Diodorus then enumerates them: 120 golden bricks, 360 golden *phialai*, the golden lion (cf. Herodotos 1.50.3) and a woman – surely the baking-wench. This and other depredations, if we are to believe Diodorus, brought Phayllos the staggering sum of more than ten thousand talents, roughly equivalent to one man's wages for 200,000 years.

This also proves that the baking-woman was solid gold, not just gilded; and there are parallels for such extravagant dedications, as Sparkes has reminded me: for example, the fragments of a 6th century silver bull and chryselephantine images that have been found under the Sacred Way at Delphi (references in Hanfmann 1983, 222 n.16). But what I find difficult to swallow is that Croesus should have dedicated a sculpture of one of his servants, a *banausos* in Greek terms, even if she *had* saved his life. Could there be some other explanation?

Boardman has suggested to me that the sculpture might have looked something like the little ivory statuette from Ephesos illustrated in Boardman (1980, 89 fig. 99); she is a priestess holding a jug and a bowl, who might well be misunderstood by Greeks as someone who worked in the kitchen. (We might mentally fuse this ivory with the golden statuette that I mentioned at the beginning of this section to form a picture of Croesus's dedication.) But there is, of course, nothing to connect such a figure specifically with baking.

Surprisingly, hardly any commentator on Herodotos has expressed doubts about the Delphic identification of the statue. The exception is Sayce; and in my view he also came up with the key to a plausible explanation of the puzzle. 'It was probably an image of the Asiatic goddess', he writes (Sayce 1883, 28), by which he means Kybele. There is no reason to suppose that she was seated, as Sayce thought, and the Mycenaean parallel that he cites is worthless; but his suggestion points in an interesting direction. Kybele was, after all, one of the chief deities worshipped at Sardis (Hanfmann 1983, 460 [index] s.v. Cybele); and I think we can go further.

The musical instrument always associated with Kybele is the *tympanon*, the hand-drum (wrongly and indeed absurdly translated in Liddell and Scott as 'kettle-drum'; it is like a tambourine, except that it lacks that instrument's characteristic jangling metal plates: Meyers 1991, 18). There are several dozen references in Greek literature to the use of the *tympanon* in the rites of Kybele: for example, *Homeric Hymn* 14.1-3; Pindar *Dithyramb* fr. 61.6-10 Bowra; Herodotos 4.76.3-4; Euripides *Helen* 1339-49, *Bakchai* 58-9 with Dodds 1960 ad loc., and fr. 586 Nauck; for discussions, see Wegner 1964, 36-7, 52-3; Seaford 1984, 113, 143-4; West 1992, 124. I would like to suggest that the gold statue at Delphi represented a votary of Kybele playing, or holding, a *tympanon*. I illustrate (fig. 19.1) a row of terracotta figurines of the archaic period (7th-6th centuries BC) from Cyprus in Desmond Morris' collection who are surely playing *tympana*. Terracottas of this type have been discussed most recently by Meyers (1991), who provides a few illustrations and a bibliography; they appear to have originated in Phoenicia, and to have spread to Cyprus, where they are found in very large quantities (Meyers 1991, 19-21). I do not know of any examples from Lydia, so we must not think of them as direct models for the statue at Delphi; but representations of Kybele's female worshippers holding *tympana* must surely have been common at Sardis. Imagine one of them in gold, life-size, and there, I submit, we have Croesus' 'baking-woman': a misunderstood votary of Kybele.

As for the confusion at Delphi of a woman with a *tympanon* with a woman with a loaf of bread, I need only quote Desmond Morris' caption to this very illustration: 'it is possible that these figures are, in reality, carrying food offerings in the shape of circular loaves' (Morris 1985, 179).

Fig. 20.1 Archaic Cypriot terracotta figurines: women playing tympana. *Reproduced from Desmond Morris* The Art of Ancient Cyprus *(1985, 179 pl. 205), by permission of Phaidon Press Ltd (London).*

Dogs' dinners

My third and last topic is the ritual dinners discovered at Sardis in the 1960s, discussed by Greenewalt in his admirable monograph (Greenewalt 1976 *passim*; Hanfmann 1983, 64, 73, 79, 94, 96, 106). A typical 'assemblage' consisted of four pottery vessels: a one-handled cooking-pot (*chytra*), a small jug (*oinochoe*), a deep cup (*skyphos*) and a shallow dish, together with an iron knife. The cooking-pot contained the skeleton of a puppy (Greenewalt 1976, 1). No fewer than 26 virtually identical groups of this kind were discovered, together with 5 groups that are probably incomplete assemblages (ibid. 1-2, 56-78). Three were found in the area known as Paktolos North; all the rest about 300 metres away in the area known as the House of Bronzes (ibid. 4-5, plates II, III). The teeth of the skeletons have been examined by experts: they are all of puppies aged under 3 months; some were only a few weeks old (ibid. 19-23, plate XL).

Some have wondered whether a puppy could have been fitted into the cooking pot; the answer seems to be yes, if he had previously been skinned, gutted and jointed. It is possible, though, that they were cooked in a larger pot, and that their remains were packed into a smaller one before the assemblages were buried (ibid. 24-6).

Greenewalt argues, convincingly in my view, though not all agree, that these assemblages represent sacrifices to Kandaulas. Kandaules is best known to us as the name of a Lydian king, the one that Gyges murdered and succeeded (Herodotos 1.7-12). But the king bore the name of a Lydian god of the underworld. The sauce known as *kandaulos* (see above) must have some connection with this deity (Greenewalt 1976, 52-4). But what is significant in this context is that according to Hipponax (fr. 3 Masson; ibid. 45-54), Kandaulas' name means *kynanches*, 'dog-strangler'.

I would like to discuss two questions: whether the puppies were eaten by the sacrificers, and the historical context of the finds.

(a) Was the dogs' flesh eaten? The flesh was certainly removed, and we can even see the butcher's marks on the bones (ibid. 14, plate XLI); but of course that does not prove that it was eaten. Greenewalt brings forward a number of arguments which lead him to conclude that it was not.

First, he refers to 'the presence in the bone sets of very small bones from skeletal extremities [plates XXV-XXXIX], which implies that unedible parts had either been scrupulously saved and retained, or that the creatures had not been consumed' (ibid. 31). Let us look at Greek sacrificial practice. I quote from Burkert (1985, 57): 'The inedible remains are consecrated; the bones are laid on the pyre prepared on the altar in just order... The dismembered creature is to be reconstituted symbolically. Texts and paintings [later than Homer] emphasize the pelvic bones and the *tail*' [my italics]. The tail is singled out in, for example, the sacrifice scene in Aristophanes' *Peace* (1054-5; cf. Stengel 1920, 63, 114); and the feet or hooves in inscriptions regulating sacrificial procedure (e.g. Dittenberger 1915-21, no.1016 line 3 [Iasos, 4th *c.* BC]; no.1026 lines 18-19 [Kos, 4th-3rd *c.* BC]). Herodotos tells us (1.94.1) that Lydian customs were pretty much the same as Greek, and Greek practice suggests that the first of Greenewalt's alternatives is the right one: that the inedible parts had been scrupulously saved. And note the emphasis on the tail and feet, carefully preserved in the Sardis deposits.

Secondly, Greenewalt argues, 'no attempt was made, as it frequently was after ritual consumption, to destroy the containers' (ibid. 32). There appears to be no literary evidence for such a practice; it is presumably attested archaeologically. But the real give-away is the word 'frequently' – not *invariably*; which surely causes the argument to self-destruct.

The third argument is that the Greeks and Romans regarded the eating of dog-flesh as a strange and repugnant practice; yet no hint that the Lydians regularly indulged in it survives in any Greek account of Lydian *mores* or gastronomy (ibid. 31). Here the key word is 'regularly'. The burials belong to a brief period within the 6th *c.* BC. There is no reason why Greeks of the classical period or later should have known anything about a ritual that was practised for only a short time. More on this in a moment.

It seems to me, then, that none of Greenewalt's arguments against puppy-eating is water-tight. Dogs have certainly been eaten elsewhere, from China to the Canary Islands, and in both north and south America (ibid. 31-2 n.1). In the case of Sardis we can only say that we do not know; kynidiophagy certainly cannot be ruled out.

(b) I turn finally to chronology (ibid. 27-30). On the strength of the pottery, Greenewalt concludes: 'the termini of ca. 575 and 525 would represent the outside limits …[but the deposits] might have occupied a period of time appreciably shorter than fifty years' (30). A glance at his illustrations (ibid. pls. XVII-XXXII) will show that sizes differ, and shapes differ to a certain extent, but not much. As Greenewalt says, 'there is little stylistic evidence for chronological disparity…(and no suggestion of) developmental progression' (ibid. 27).

Greenewalt seems to envisage these assemblages as having been deposited over a period of time. I would like to put forward a different view, and I am emboldened to do so by the fact that similar ideas were held by George Hanfmann, Greenewalt's predecessor at Sardis. He seems not to have published his arguments in full, but alludes to the matter in passing in the invaluable volume on Sardis that he edited (Hanfmann 1983, 96). Might not all these burials have been deposited at the same time? – a time of unique danger? The context that immediately suggests itself is Cyrus' advance on Sardis in the 540s, which led to the capture of the city and consequently of its great empire by the Persians. (I incline towards a date *c.* 544 for this event, rather than the traditional 547 or 546: see Wade-Gery 1958, 166 n.3; Cargill 1977). If there were multiple sacrifices to Kandaulas on one single exceptional occasion, the Lydians will not have acquired a reputation for eating puppy-flesh.

Finally I would like to go one step further, and propose something that I do not quite believe myself. Herodotos knew four stories about the birth and upbringing of Cyrus (1.95.1); according to the version that he regards as most reliable, Cyrus was brought up by a herdsman called Mitradates and his wife Spako (1.110.1). For ten years (114.1), Spako was virtually Cyrus' mother. Now, as Herodotos tells us, the name Spako means *kyon*, 'bitch' (110.1). If Cyrus was thought of as the offspring of a canine (or a son of a bitch), then he will have been a puppy. What better method of averting the approaching king than by sacrificing puppies? And what god more suitable to sacrifice them to than Kandaulas the Dog-Strangler?

Acknowledgements

I am most grateful to Prof. Crawford H. Greenewalt, Jr., director of the Sardis excavations, for much information and friendly encouragement on Lydian matters over several years; I am not the only person to have benefitted from his willingness to share his unrivalled knowledge of Sardis. His *Ritual Dinners* (see below) contains the best account of Lydian food known to me, and is invaluable on many other matters, including Greek meals. In response to a request for one photograph to illustrate my lecture, he sent me no fewer than 18 colour slides. It seems churlish to repay such generosity with the bone-picking of my final section (which he did not see before publication); my intention, of course, is to explore alternative interpretations, not to indulge in acrimony.

My thanks also to Professors John Boardman and Brian Sparkes, for correspondence concerning the baking-woman; to Dr Richard Seaford for advice on ritual; to Dr Amélie Kuhrt for drawing my attention to Meyers (1991); and to Dr John Wilkins for constant cheerful encouragement.

Bibliography

Bammer, A., 1984 *Die Heiligtum der Artemis von Ephesos* (Graz).

Boardman, J., 1980 *The Greeks Overseas*, 3rd ed. (London).

Burkert, W., 1985 *Greek Religion* (English translation, Oxford).

Cargill, J., 1977 'The Nabonidus Chronicle and the fall of Lydia', *American Journal of Ancient History* 2, 97-116.

Dittenberger, W., 1915-21 *Sylloge Inscriptionum Graecarum*, 3rd ed. (Leipzig, 4 volumes).

Dodds, E.R., 1960 *Euripides: Bacchae*, 2nd ed. (Oxford).

Foss, C. & Hanfmann, G.M.A., 1975 'Regional setting and urban environment' in Hanfmann and Waldbaum (1975) 17-34, 170-5.

Greenewalt, C.H. Jr., 1976 *Ritual Dinners in Early Historic Sardis* (Berkeley).

Hanfmann, G.M.A. & Waldbaum, J.C., (eds) 1975 *A Survey of Sardis* (Cambridge Mass. and London).

Hanfmann, G.M.A. and Ramage, N.H., 1978 *Sculpture from Sardis* (Cambridge Mass. and London).

Hanfmann, G.M.A., (ed.) 1983 *Sardis from Prehistoric to Roman Times* (Cambridge Mass. and London).

Magie, D., 1950 *Roman Rule in Asia Minor* (Princeton).

Meyers, C.L., 1991 'Of drums and damsels', *Biblical Archaeologist* 54, 16-27.

Morris, D., 1985 *The Art of Ancient Cyprus* (London).

Robert, L., 1982 'Au nord de Sardes', *Bulletin de correspondance hellénique* 106, 334-52, reprinted in his *Documents de l'Asie Mineur* (Paris, 1987), 296-314.

Sayce, A.H., 1883 *The Ancient Empires of the East: Herodotus I-III* (London).

Seaford, R., 1984 *Euripides: Cyclops* (Oxford).

Stengel, P., 1920 *Die griechischen Kultusaltertümer*, 3rd ed. (Munich).

Wade-Gery, H.T., 1958 *Essays in Greek History* (Oxford).

Wegner, M., 1964 *Musikgeschichte in Bildern: Griechenland* (Leipzig).

West, M.L., 1992 *Ancient Greek Music* (Oxford).

❖ 21 ❖ PERSIAN FOOD
STEREOTYPES AND POLITICAL IDENTITY

Heleen Sancisi-Weerdenburg

In *Varia Historia* 3.39 Aelian states that the Persians eat terebinth and cardamum. Although Aelian says that they had it for a meal (*deipnon eichon*), this assertion need not be taken too literally. The whole section is a list of food-items typical of the peoples enumerated: the Arcadians eat acorns, the Argives eat pears, the Athenians figs, the people from Tiryns wild pears, the Indians reeds, the Carmanians dates, the Maiotians and the Sauromatians millet, the Persians have terebinth and cardamum. The whole passage is, of course, not so much a description of nutritional habits as an example of the recognized genre of food stereotypes. Both terebinth and cardamum are often mentioned in Greek accounts of Persian eating customs. As we shall see later, like any good stereotype, it is in part corroborated by Persian sources.

In 5th and 4th century Greek sources, however, both terebinth and cardamum are associated with frugal habits and associated with the good old times of Cyrus. It is remarkable that in Aelian's time precisely this stereotype was still current and had apparently maintained itself against a tradition dating from the 4th century BC in which Persian eating was seen as primarily luxurious and extravagant. I will discuss both the stereotypes and their relationship to the actual lifestyle of the Persians, as recorded in Persian sources. Although the Greek observations of Persians which resulted in these stereotypes were essentially correct, the implications of frugality in the one stereotype and of senseless and lavish indulgence in eating in the other are beside the mark. As so often in Greek descriptions of Persia and the Persians, it may legitimately be suspected that these statements do not serve to convey information on Persia, but rather serve as an implicit or explicit means of comparison with Greek customs (cf. Briant 1988, 10).

Terebinth

The earliest mention of terebinth-eating by the Persians probably goes back to Ktesias. Nicolaos of Damascus, who in this fragment (*FGH* 90 F66.34) seems to follow Ktesias rather closely, tells how, after the victory of the Persians over the Medes, the Median king Astyages shouted: 'Oh, how brave are those terebinth-eating (*terminthophagous*) Persians'. It may be doubted whether Median and Persian eating habits really differed as much as we are led to believe here, but the main point of the remark lies in the association between terebinth and bravery. The implied and alleged difference between the Medes and Persians fits well into the Greek framework whereby the wealthy Medes are juxtaposed with the early sober tastes of the Persians.

The terebinth-eating in Plutarch's description of the initiation of Persian kings (*Artaxerxes* 3.2) is associated with the good old times of Cyrus as well. In a sanctuary, the candidate for kingship must take off his clothes and put on the robe that Cyrus the elder wore before he became king. He must then eat a cake of figs (*sukon palathes*) and some terebinth (*terminthou katatragein*)[1], and drink a cup of sour milk (Sancisi-Weerdenburg 1983; Briant 1991, 7). It is generally thought that this initiation kept alive memories of the good old days, which were relatively sober and pastoral.[2] A similar connotation is to be found in Strabo's description of Persian educational practice (15.3.18): young boys are sent out to tend the flocks and to eat wild fruits, such as 'terebinth'[3], acorns and wild pears. When at home, however, their diet is different: it consists of bread, barley-cakes, cardamum, grains of salt and roasted or boiled meat. Terebinth-eating, therefore, is in the Greek evidence clearly associated with life in the wild, with austerity and with bravery.[4]

According to modern translators of the term *terminthos*, the prospective Persian king would be chewing turpentine-wood, and the young Persians would be eating pistachio-nuts. While the first item seems to have questionable nutritional value, eating pistachio-nuts for a diet is not appallingly unattractive. What exactly was 'terebinth' and how did the Persians use this obviously characteristic product in their diets? Marten Stol (1979) has made an exhaustive enquiry into what terebinth in antiquity was, where it occurred and how it was used. The following relies heavily on his conclusions. Terebinth is a species of the tree called the *Pistacia atlantica*. There are various subspecies, but that is hardly relevant here. One of the first things noted by Stol is that the terebinth was at one time almost ubiquitous in the ancient Near East. If it does occur now, it is usually a relic of destroyed forests (Stol 1979, 2). But even in recent times, it seems, one can find the fruits of the *Pistacia mutica* in markets in the Near East.[5] They are reddish and purplish, about the size of blackcurrants, and turn coppery-green on drying. The kernel of the stone is eaten. The tree is apparently still common on the mountain slopes of Kurdistan at altitudes between 500 and 1000 m., and it bears fruit between April and September (Guest 1933, 74, cited by Stol 1979, 3). It seems that especially in Mesopotamia the fruit of the terebinth is still eaten nowadays, and moreover it is renowned for its medical qualities. Although the Latin name *Pistacia* might suggest that the tree is the same as the one that gives us pistachio-nuts, this identification does not work. The *Pistacia vera* was brought from Bactria to the west only after the conquests of Alexander (Hehn 1902, 415-6, cited by Stol 1979, 5; cf. Theophrastos *Enquiry into Plants* 4.4.7). Terebinth fruit was a common commodity in the Near East: excavations have yielded large quantities of both charred fruits and nuts, although they are often called 'pistachio' by the excavators (van Zeist 1977, cited by Stol 1979, 13).

The word *pistakion* does not occur in Greek before Alexander. It seems to be a Persian word, and Hinz (1973, 84) has argued that Elamite *pi-is-TUK-ka*

(Hallock 1969, 6, 27 = PF) should be regarded as the Persian *pistaka. *Pistuka* occurs twice in this tablet, among other fruits, of which figs and dates are certainly identified, apples possibly.[6] Whether the fruits in the Persepolis Fortification Texts (PF) were cultivated or gathered in the wild is not clear. The occurrence of this word, however, is thus far limited to this one text, whereas other fruits such as dates and figs are very frequent. I take it, therefore, that terebinth-fruits were normally collected in the woods, as suggested by the text of Strabo (15.3.18). Terebinth can be used for more purposes: from its nuts good oil can be made: Xenophon has come across it (*Anabasis* 4.4.13) and, although Xenophon may have preferred olive-oil, we can be assured of its good quality since 'oil is made for the king from terebinth, the mastic tree, and what is called Persian nuts, all trees growing in mountains' (Amyntas *Persian Journeys*, in Athenaeus 2.67a). Although there is very little actual confirmation of the Greek references to terebinth in the Persian evidence, in view of its common occurrence in the ancient Near East, its use by the Persians is not at all unlikely. Its relative rarity compared with references to dates, apples and other culti-vated fruits in the Persepolis Fortification Texts published so far may point to its being gathered in the wild.

Cardamum

In the stereotypical Greek accounts of Persian food habits that I quoted above, terebinth is associated with 'nature,' life in the wild and manly virtues. How about cardamum? Here again, the path has been cleared by the exhaustive investigations of Stol (1985), who identifies cardamum with Babylonian *sahlu*. It is cress, and it is mainly used for its seeds that can be made into a mustard. The Greek word *kardamon* etymologically de-rives from the Assyrian *kuddimmu* (Stol 1985, 29; cf. Herzfeld 1968, 113). Cardamum is what Persian youths ate 'at home', according to Strabo (15.3.18): bread, barley cakes, a bit of salt and some cress, with cooked or roasted meat. Xenophon (*Cyropaedia* 1.2.8, 11) gives the same diet for young Persians, but he implies that this food is also taken along on hunting trips: if the elder boys fail to kill game, they have to content themselves with cress as the only relish with their bread. Xenophon does not make the distinction that Strabo makes: terebinth as a fruit gathered in the wild, cardamum as a cultivated product, eaten at home. He knows just one category: that of poor food suitable for a sober lifestyle. It is clear that for him cardamum is merely a poor condiment. He moralistically adds a variant of the saying with which most of us have been brought up: if you are hungry even plain bread and water taste marvellous. For Greeks cardamum (or cress) is very plain food. Plutarch describes in his treatise *On tranquillity of mind* how after an illness 'he who yesterday loathed eggs and delicate cakes and fine bread today eats eagerly and willingly of a coarse loaf with olives and water-cress' (*Moralia* 466d).

Cardamum, however, had other peculiar characteristics in the Greek view: it attracted moisture. So Aristophanes: 'for it is certain that the earth forcibly draws the moisture of thought to itself. Just the same thing happens to cress' (*Clouds* 234). The eating of cress apparently also served to keep moisture in the body: 'I urinate slowly; yesterday I ate some cress' says the Relative in Aristophanes' *Thesmophoriazousai* (616). According to Hesychios (s.v. *kardama*, ex v. *strangourio*), it stops urine and saliva, and he adds that this is the reason why the Persians were said to eat it, because they tried to refrain from spitting, urinating and wiping their noses frequently.

Besides these characteristics, the Greeks regarded cardamum as very pungent (cf. Aristophanes *Wasps* 455) and as of very little value.[7] Its worth in Greek eyes can be exactly measured by a comic fragment of the 4th century: 'as much as cardamum differs from figs' says Heniochos (fr. 4.2 KA), thereby apparently indicating two extremes. It is noticeable that on this scale of values, the Persians on Aelian's list are eating the poorest food, while the Athenians are associated with the best. In this context it is ironic that, according to Deinon, Xerxes attempted to conquer Greece in order to obtain a supply of Athenian figs (Athenaeus 14.652b-c; cf. Briant 1989b, 36). Athenian figs must have been particularly attractive in Greek eyes if they could serve as a metaphor or some sort of symbol for the presumed motives of Persian imperialism. Most certainly there was no dearth of figs in Persia according to the Persepolis Tablets, which frequently list this commodity (see Hallock 1969, 745 s.v. *pit*).

Cardamum quite clearly belonged to the staple foods of the Near East. It is not like terebinth, a fruit gathered in the wild. Although a minor crop, it is sowed and harvested (Ellis 1976, 133, 151; Stol 1985, 25f). It is not at all typical for the Persians, and one finds it frequently in Assyrian and Babylonian texts, although it seems to have gained in importance in Neo-Babylonian times.[8] Its use as a staple is confirmed by the royal menu preserved in Polyainos 4.3.32, which gives a list of commodities for the royal table, with quantities. The whole list can be divided into four categories: (a) various types of cereals and related items, (b) meat, (c) various condiments, wood for fuel, wine, and (d) food and related items to be distributed to the soldiers (cf. Lewis 1987, 82-7; Briant 1995 ch. 7.5). Cardamum is listed in the first and the fourth group. In the first group a figure for the amount is missing in the text, but among the items to be distributed (category d) one finds 30 *artaba* of cardamum. Cardamum is neither rare, nor precious.[9] If we may rely on the text of Polyainos, it is listed with the cereals and therefore probably also used in baking, as the Greek word *kardamale* (Tryphon in Athenaeus 3.114f) seems to suggest.

Stol (1985, 27 n.31) and Lewis (1987, 86) have suggested that cardamum occurs in the Persepolis Fortification Texts as a commodity under the name of *zali*. Both Hallock (1969, 772) and Hinz (1973, 85) thought that *zali* was some kind of grain (Hinz: 'Hirse?'). Its occurrence in PF 2076 (*passim*) and PF 1594 seems to corroborate the suggestion of Lewis and Stol: in PF 2076 it features along with barley; in PF 1594, 3½ BAR of *zali* is taken to Persepolis as rations for artisans, along with 4 BAR of grain and 80 BAR of flour. In Polyainos' list the king distributes 500 *artaba* of pure wheat-meal, 100 of pure barley-meal, and 1000 of second-class barley meal. There is, of course, no way of knowing whether the cardamum was to be used with all types of cereals, or only with one. In the latter case the ratio would be either 1:30 (barley) or 1:17 (wheat), whereas in PF 1596 the ratio of *zali* to grain is 1:24. There is a rough similarity in these ratios which lends some additional plausibility to the suggestion made by Stol and Lewis.

It is, on the whole, rather surprising that Aelian in his collection of stories uses cardamum and terebinth as the kinds of food that characterize national identity. Both commodities have very strong associations with

Aelian's stereotypes

simple and frugal life, and terebinth carries an unmistakable connotation of habits connected with nature and life in the wilds. That such a tradition had survived to the 2nd century AD, against currents which attributed far more luxurious habits to the Persians, seems confirmed by another remarkable passage, also in Aelian (*Varia Historia* 10.14): Sokrates is said to have called the Persians 'the bravest and the most free' (along with the Indians, by the way, who refrained from the type of commercial activities that made the Phrygians and the Lydians, the busiest peoples, into slaves (*douleuein*)). The reminiscence of Herodotos 1.153, which depicts Persian (i.e. Cyrus') contempt for people wheeling and dealing in markets, is clear.[10] It is impossible to trace Aelian's sources, and many of these stories will, by his time, have become detached from their original context and must have circulated independently in collections of rhetorical *exempla*. It seems clear that within their original context, i.e. Greek 5th and 4th century literature, they all referred to supposedly idyllic, early times when the Persians had not yet been spoiled by the results of their conquests (cf. Sancisi-Weerdenburg 1989a).

Oxen, camels and other cattle

The more common picture of Persian eating habits in Greek literature, however, is one of luxury and extravagance. Stories of elaborate food, specially prepared delicacies and enormous amounts of edible commodities circulate in Greek accounts (Briant 1989b, 36f). One of the more sober reports, that of Herodotos (1.133), tells us that, on their birthday, rich Persians served an ox, a horse or a camel or an ass roasted whole in large ovens; the poor make do with smaller beasts. They have a lot of side-dishes, which (still according to Herodotos) are served one after the other. They eat only once a day, but as Xenophon (*Cyropaedia* 8.8.9) acidly comments, their eating starts early in the morning and lasts till very late at night, so that this one meal takes all day.[11]

The Persian meal, as described by Herodotos, was often a matter of ridicule to the Greeks, who compared it with their own food-habits: they considered themselves 'small-table people' (*mikrotrapezoi*) and 'leaf-chewers' (*phullotroges*), implying that the Persians ate better food and in a grander way (Antiphanes in Athenaeus 4.130e-f). Persian dinner, according to the same comic fragment, included whole oxen, swine, deer and lambs and a whole roasted camel. Aristophanes (*Acharnians* 85-9, also cited by Athenaeus 4.131a) also mentions the whole ox, and 'a fowl three times as big as Kleonymos: its name was Cheat'. A more serious source, Herakleides of Kyme (ap. Athenaeus 4.145e), lists horses, camels, oxen, asses, deer, and most of the smaller animals; also many birds (cf. Briant 1989a, 39; Lewis 1987, 80), including Arabian ostriches, geese and cocks. The list of meat-supplies can be completed from Polyainos 4.3.32: in addition to the items mentioned above, it also comprises fatted geese, turtle-doves, various small birds, baby geese and gazelles. One of the most conspicuous features of the Persian table is the roasting of whole animals, considered an extravagance probably because of the inordinate amount of fuel needed to cook the meat.[12]

Herodotos' description applies to all Persian meals, those of the rich and those of the poor. Corroboration of this Greek information is relatively abundant. The Persepolis tablets give details of the rations provided to workers in the Fars area. Next to flour and wine, some fruit, dates or oil, workers sometimes receive parts of sheep. One sheep for ten persons seems to be a normal ration (PF 1793, 1794). On that basis, the stoneworkers (not further specified) of PF 1633 might well have been a group of 710 men, for they are receiving 71 sheep. In PF 1790, women chiefs of the Pasa [women] receive each 4 sheep for a whole year, and in PF 1791 the persons mentioned receive different proportions, from $^2/_3$ to $^1/_{15}$. Sheep-rations, however, are uncommon among this class of people. On the whole the picture is in agreement with the list of commodities distributed by the king in Polyainos 4.3.32: the soldiers receive grain, fodder for the horses, some oil and cardamum, but no meat. It may be surmised that the braver ones among them received some additional delicacies either from their commander's table or directly from the royal table. The tablets, however, strongly suggest that meat was a privilege of a higher social level, or else was reserved for festive occasions, as Herodotos says (1.133).

Sheep were issued at several occasions to the most important person mentioned on the tablets, Parnaka. In PF 654-663 he receives two sheep a day. Moreover, Parnaka also received large amounts of other food. It is a puzzle why Parnaka obtained these enormous quantities. It has been pointed out by Lewis (1987, 80) that these rations given to Parnaka cannot be explained by supposing that he had to feed his servants, since they received independent rations. Since Parnaka gets the food when travelling, too, I do not see why these generous portions should not have been used for wining and dining incidental visitors, or local authorities in the villages he visited. As I will argue below, there is more to a meal-table than just eating. Even if Parnaka's boys received their own rations to satisfy their needs, an additional helping or an extra portion of meat may well have been welcome.[13] For the duties of a rich Persian towards his dependants and friends and other people asking for his help or for favours, the comments by Pheraulas (Xenophon *Cyropaedia* 8.3.40) and his young Sakian friend (8.3.44) may be a good illustration: having much means being obliged to distribute more to other people. Herakleides (Athenaeus 4.145f) reports that the most honoured of the king's table-companions ate only their breakfast at court. At night they received their own *sundeipnoi* (fellow-diners) (cf. Briant 1995, ch. 7.5)

The larger cattle, cows, oxen, camels (PF 331) and asses (PF 289-291), are all mentioned in the tablets. Sometimes they appear in herds that need feeding or are the recipients of rations, sometimes as a commodity with the specification 'slaughtered' or 'alive.' Horses also feature in the texts, but so far there is no indication that they are intended for consumption. Lewis (1987, 85) concludes that all horses in the tablets were used for transport. However, it should not be doubted that horses were also used for consumption. We do not have to presume a Persepolis precinct for retired horses. As to the birds listed by Polyainos and Herakleides: PF 697-8 show birds as items 'dispensed on behalf of the king' – 134 and 432 fowls respectively. The various types of birds are specified, but the Elamite here is not fully understood (suggestions in Lewis 1987, 85). The *ippur* occurring in PF 1732-1744 receive the rather large amount of 1 *bar* of grain per month; some birds get half that amount. They may have been baby-*ippur* (PF 1736) or only fed for so many days until they arrived on somebody's table (cf. PF 1734: three days). In any case, the *ippur* is a large creature, and is found in the whole group of birds 'dispensed on behalf of the king' of PF 697-8, also a rare one. Hallock (1969, 48, 702) thinks that the *ippur* is similar to the Akkadian *kurka*, a goose. But its rarity (PF 2034:

17 *ippur* out of a total of 1333: all 'dispensed on behalf of the king'; PF 1743: 1 *ippur* among 181 fowls; PF 1744: 5 *ippur* among 79 fowls, as compared to the 400 geese and the 100 geese of Polyainos' text) makes me wonder if this *ippur* is not a candidate for the ostrich that Lewis (1987, 3) has been looking for. This, however, is sheer speculation and nothing more than a suggestion that Assyriologists may find useful.

In one other case, I have a more certain identification to offer. One type of animal Lewis was not able to hunt down in his 1987 article was the gazelle, which completed Polyainos' list. There is very clear evidence for the consumption of gazelles at the royal table, although not on the tablets. On the western stairway of Xerxes' palace at Persepolis, as on a number of other stairways (that of the Tripylon, the *tačara* and the much later palace of Artaxerxes), servants are ascending the stairs carrying food. They bear a large number of vessels, some covered, some open, the contents of which can only be guessed. There are also servants (always in the 'Persian' outfit) bringing in what must be wine in animal skins (cf. PF 58-72 for the collection of the hides of slaughtered animals, sheep, cattle and camels). It seems to be the exclusive prerogative of servants dressed in so-called 'Median' outfit to carry in small animals. Lamb and kid are the most frequent, but Schmidt (1957, 224, 240) also lists young gazelles and an antelope portrayed on the stairway of Xerxes' palace. On the stairway to Darius' palace, he has noticed a stag (perhaps the 'deer' of the fragment of Herakleides?)[14].

It is quite obvious, then, that the Greeks were not exaggerating when describing Persian royal meals. Almost all the items that excited so much surprise among the Greeks can be found in the contemporary Persian sources. Not even the enormous amounts listed by Polyainos should be doubted: already in antiquity they were compared to the cost of Alexander's more ceremonious meals, which cost 100 minas according to Ephippos (Athenaeus 4.146d), even though only sixty or seventy table-companions attended. Ktesias and Deinon estimated the number of those who feasted at a Persian banquet at 15,000 and the cost of the whole affair at 400 talents. Royal meals are rather large affairs. Even more telling is the text of the party given by Assurnasirpal for 70,000 guests, which lasted ten days (its expense-account contained seventeen overlaps with Polyainos' text, as

Lewis notes (1987, 79)). As he says, it is clear that these Greek observations are reliable, that they correctly observed and equally correctly reported on what they had seen or read. He contrasts this conclusion with the verdict of Momigliano (1975) who had accused Greek accounts, mostly those of the 4th century, of bias and distortion. It seems to me, however, that the two judgments rest on different grounds. Whereas Lewis looks for the corroboration of single facts and features, Momigliano discusses the interrelationship of these facts and features, the way these facts were incorporated into texts and the connotations and implications of the result. To return to our royal dinner: if the amounts and the specific items on the menu given in the Greek accounts of the Persian royal banquet are corroborated by Iranian sources, does that imply that the Greek narratives which suggest unlimited wealth, extravagant sumptuosity and boundless *truphe* (luxury) are equally true?

The economy of the royal table

There is more to a Persian royal dinner than meets the eye. In the fragment of Herakleides quoted above, the economy of the system is mentioned: at the dinner the king makes a redistribution to his table-companions and soldiers. How banqueting-procedures functioned within the tax- and tribute-system of the Persian empire has been elaborately discussed by Briant (1989a). As he argues (1989a, 42), the provisions of the King's table are an expression of tributary relations over the whole empire. The table is used as an illustration of a general system of alliances between the dynasty and the great aristocratic families. In the same volume, I have outlined the ideology of this system, which can be regarded as an exchange of services against honours, and for which, it seems, Herodotos (9.110.2) has preserved the Persian expression *tukta*: the banquet was the place where the king rewarded with gifts those that had served him well or outstandingly (Sancisi-Weerdenburg 1989b, 132ff). The emphasis in that paper was on the type of reciprocity involved: the king gave for what he got, although it should be noted that, by adding the lustre of a royal origin to those gifts, he made them worth more than their economic value alone. In that way, the profit was larger on the king's side (Sancisi-Weerdenburg 1989b, 131f): by inscribing the item, or just by presenting it himself, he added symbolical value to its economic worth and increased its ideological significance. It is remarkable that on the Persepolis reliefs, the so-called gift-bringing delegations carry exactly the same items that are handed out by the king in Greek stories (Sancisi-Weerdenburg 1989b, 166). The actual process of this sharing out is not recorded on the reliefs or anywhere else in the iconographic repertory of the Persian empire. But the Greek reports leave no doubt that much of this redistribution, if not all of it, took place during banquets.

A banquet is a very complicated 'social fact'. It has an ecological side to it, largely defined by what is available in given ecological (and economic) circumstances. There is an economic side to it: what it is feasible and affordable to bring to the table. There is a social side as well: certain foods, though available, are not eaten because the society has defined them as undesirable. To avoid the most obvious example, Jewish food proscriptions, here are some others: wild mushrooms, although abundant in the damp climate of Holland, were hardly ever eaten in the 17th century and do not feature in Northern Dutch still-life painting of that period. Combinations of certain foods and preparations may be undesirable for purely cultural reasons: the combination of fish and cheese in some classic Italian regional cuisines is still anathema.

There also is a political side to food and eating: politics can, even in a deliberate way, influence food habits. A nice case is the increase in the number of recipes for rabbit in Italian cooking books of the fascist period. Meat produced strong men, but was beyond the means of the poor. In such circumstances, the only accessible meat had to be produced in small gardens and on balconies. This was publicly encouraged: hence the need for more rabbit-recipes (Camporesi 1993, 159-61). But food is also a direct expression of political and economic relationships: our eating of fruits out of season throughout the year is an expression of Western economic, and by implication political, dominance. And last but not least, political relationships and social stratification can be furthered, strengthened and increased by eating habits: the term 'conspicuous consumption' is sufficient explanation (cf. Goody 1982, 98).

It has been suggested that ways of eating, meals and banquets, may be analysed in ways that are analogous to grammatical analyses. A meal is as complex as a sentence or a paragraph. It consists of various elements that have a provenance and carry a meaning. These separate elements can be joined in an infinite number of ways, and acquire as a whole yet another meaning. The organization of a meal is, in fact, not just a physical necessity or a pleasurable phenomenon, but a fact of communication, in which the underlying structure of the society can be read as clearly as in a written text (Douglas 1971). This does not necessarily entail analyses of a structuralist kind, in which choices of food-type or food preparation stand for something else and reveal the deep structure of a society; for criticism of the structuralist approach see Goody (1982, 17-29). Food is used to communicate, in much the same way as words or texts. Food carries messages in individual as well as in social or political relationships.

For political processes connected with food in the heartland of the Persian empire, the Persepolis Fortification Texts provide us with an archive which, although not unique, is still rare in the ancient world, and will be even more valuable once it has been completely published. It provides us with information on the types and amounts of food destined for different social levels in different situations: common workers, high officials, court and king. Because of the linguistic problems caused by the intractable Royal Elamite used on the tablets, a full analysis is an enormous and time-consuming task. In the preceding paragraphs some ways of linking these data to the more easily accessible Greek sources have been discussed. I want to conclude with some suggestions about the 'communicative' aspects of food at the summit of the Persian empire.

The political aspects of this process have been discussed in Briant's paper on the 'Table du Roi' (1989a) and in his paper on provisions of water for the king (1990). He has shown how the supply of food and drink from all over the empire highlighted and embodied the domination of the king over his subjects. A few points can be added. The Greeks considered the efforts to provide the king with the most delicate dishes as a sign of *truphe* (luxury) or even decadence, and narrate them with obvious disapproval. Prizes were even given to those who catered best to the royal pleasures.[15] Catering for the royal table was a system in which 'the regional food of peasants and the cooking of exotic foreigners' is incorporated and transformed (Goody 1982, 105) and leads to the creation of a *haute cuisine* dependent upon 'a variety of dishes which are largely the inventions of specialists' (Goody 1982, 104). In the same volume, Goody traces Arab cuisine back to the earlier cultures of Mesopotamia and the Persian empire and notes that in the latter part of the Sassanian period 'the empire expanded and the extravagance of the court reflected this imperial grandeur' (1982, 127). The Greek sources attest that this was already the case in the time of the Achaemenid empire, and that in this field too, the Sassanids continued earlier Persian practice. It is clear that the creation of a real cuisine is dependent on the development of a social and political hierarchy.

Culinary developments, however, are not merely a by-product of the growth of a central political system. They are also a component in its amplification. As Douglas phrases it: 'if food is treated as a code, the messages it encodes will be found in the pattern of social relations being expressed. The message is about different degrees of hierarchy, inclusion and exclusion, boundaries and transactions across the boundaries' (1971, 61). Food is one of the many codes used for communication within societies. It also serves as political (ideological, legitimizing) communication. Let us return to Persian practices.

Among the motifs on the Persepolis reliefs, that of servants bringing food to the royal table is very prominent. It is, however, rarely discussed.[16] It is apparently regarded as relevant only to the private sphere, not to the working of the empire as such. Three groups of servants are known, on the palaces of Darius (the Tačara), on the palace of Xerxes (the Hadiš) and on the destroyed palace of Artaxerxes I, in each case adorning the 'residential' palaces. Like all the other reliefs at Persepolis, the iconography does not change substantially from the first to the last example. The servants are all dressed in 'Median' or 'Persian' costume, but only 'Medes' are carrying animals. The purpose of this ceremony is quite clear. Food is being brought to the king's table. What happens next is not shown. The consumption of all these items is not recorded in stone.

In this respect these reliefs differ from the series of reliefs on the stairs of the Apadana, where delegations on the one side, guards and courtiers on the other, are shown as moving in the direction of the king, whose image once adorned the centre panel. There is no banqueting king on the reliefs of Persepolis. The absence of banqueting scenes at Persepolis is remarkable, since they were presumably known to the Achaemenids from Assyrian iconography. It also is a prominent motif in the 'Greco-Persian' stelae from Daskyleion. One reason for not portraying the king at dinner is possibly the belief that he should not be seen when eating. But another motive may well have been that there was no need to carve a stone image, since the real-life action was there to be seen by everybody who needed to see. Its not featuring at Persepolis may be explained by the reality of the ceremonies taking place there. These ceremonies, of which a banquet must have formed an important part,[17] were, like royal rituals elsewhere and everywhere, a visual encoding of what mattered in Achaemenid kingship. They not only gave expression to the relations between the king and his subjects, they also contributed to shaping them. The conspicuous consumption taking place at Persepolis, and wherever else the king happened to be, the concomitant bringing in of food in large quantities for the guests as well as in small but delicate amounts for the king, the redistribution of the royal meal and the tableware in which it was served,[18] both communicated and contributed to a political stratification in a language that in this multi-lingual empire must have been understandable to all.

Notes

1. Note that the Loeb translates 'chew turpentine-wood': there is no need to make the diet worse than it is. It is likely that here as in other cases either the fruits or the nuts of the tree are meant: see below.
2. Boyce (1982, 90, 209) thinks that this initiation was instituted by Darius, and that the ritual is characteristic of Zoroastrian observance, with two items coming from the vegetable, and one from the animal kingdom.

3. The Loeb translates here 'pistachio nuts', which is not correct but is preferable to the turpentine-wood translation of Plutarch *Artaxerxes* 3.2.
4. In the descriptions of Strabo and Plutarch there are probably some connotations of a *rite de passage*: cf. Widengren (1969, 83); Sancisi-Weerdenburg (1983, 147).
5. Stol (1979, 3f) with references to travellers' reports and floras of the region.

6. 'Trockenfrüchte' in all cases, according to Hinz (1973, 84).

7. *ti kardamizeis?* : 'what nonsense are you talking?', or maybe 'what peanuts are you discussing?', Aristophanes *Thesmophoriazousai* 617.

8. Stol (1985, 29f). Its importance can also be deduced from the fact that in the Astronomical Diaries (Stol ibid.) cress is very often given as one of the commodities that indicate the level of prices.

9. On the royal list one finds also *sinepuos spermatos*, mustard-seed. The small amount of this commodity (a third of an *artaba*) may well indicate that it is more precious than cardamum. The separate listing of the two items pleads against identifying *senape* with *sahlû*, or cress, as Stol (1985, 32) seems to do.

10. Cf. also Xenophon *Cyropaedia* 1.2.2: Persian education is conducted far away from the *agora*.

11. For the biased presentation in these concluding chapters of the *Cyropaedia* cf. Sancisi-Weerdenburg (1988).

12. Note that the list in Polyainos comprises 200 wagons of *xula* (timber) and 100 wagons of *hule* (wood).

13. Cf. Athenaeus 4.128d for a similar practice in Macedonia: guests at Karanos' wedding dinner distribute a part of the food served to the slaves waiting on them. For comments on this extremely interesting description see Dalby (1988); for its possible relevance to Persian redistributive customs see Sancisi-Weerdenburg (1993).

14. A unique item among those depicted on the banquet reliefs is discussed by Ann Tilia (1972, 281): a barrow carried by two Medes, with four lambs on it. The other side of the block is decorated with a piece that must belong to a tribute-procession, therefore the barrow-carriers in all likelihood were part of a group of food-carrying servants. It is the only example where these servants are clearly *not* ascending stairs.

15. The most interesting passages are: Xenophon *Agesilaos* 9; Athenaeus 12.529d, 12.539b, 545d. See the comments of Briant (1988, 37; 1989b; 1995 ch. 7.5).

16. It is not treated by Margaret Root in her book on Achaemenid reliefs (1979) in which she analyses the iconography of the reliefs and reconstructs the royal ideological programme. Is it because there are no very clear Near Eastern antecedents for this motif? Roaf (1974, 96) briefly comments that, since the animals that these servants bring in are live, they can hardly be food for the banquet, and suggests that they are perhaps bringing offerings for libations and sacrifices. Moorey (1979, 221 n.12) agrees with this suggestion and adds a comment by Boyce that these animals have been blessed earlier in the day and are now brought in for eating. If, however, meat has to be transported over some distance, the easiest way to do it is by letting the live animal walk. In my opinion, live animals on the reliefs should be seen as meat brought from far away. There is no need to interpret these food items as belonging to the ritual sphere: on the tablets most of the food carried around is just food and not sacrificial offerings.

17. Although it is no longer thought that the Persepolis reliefs give an accurate pictorial report on the protocol of these ceremonies – the so-called 'Nowruz'-hypothesis – it should still be clear that ceremonies were indeed taking place in this dynastic capital.

18. For a good analogy to this procedure, see the banquet organized by the Macedonian Karanos (who gives silver dishes and gold cups to all the guests) and described by Hippolochos (Athenaeus 4.128a-9e).

Bibliography

Boyce, M., 1982 *A History of Zoroastrianism* II (*Handbuch der Orientalistik* I Abteilung, Band 8, 1 Abschnitt 1, Lieferung 2, Heft 2A) (Leiden).

Briant, P., 1988 'Institutions perses et histoire comparatiste dans l'historiographie grecque', *Achaemenid History* 2, 1-10.

Briant, P., 1989a 'Table du roi. Tribut et redistribution chez les Achéménides,' in Briant and Herrenschmidt (1989), 35-44.

Briant, P., 1989b 'Histoire et idéologie: les Grecs et la "décadence perse,"' *Melanges P. Lévêque*, 33-47.

Briant, P., 1990 'L'eau du grand roi', *Convegno bere e bevande nella cultura alimentare dell' Oriente pre-classico* (Rome).

Briant, P., 1991 'Le roi est mort: vive le roi!', in *La religion iranienne á l'époque achéménide* (*Iranica Antiqua* suppl. 5) (Gent), 1-12.

Briant, P., 1995 *De Cyrus à Alexandre* (Leiden).

Briant, P. & Herrenschmidt, C., (eds) 1989 *Le Tribut dans l'empire perse* (Paris).

Camporesi, P., 1993 *The Magic Harvest. Food, Folklore and Society* (trans. Hall) (Cambridge).

Dalby, A., 1988 'The wedding feast of Caranus the Macedonian by Hippolochus', *Petits Propos Culinaires* 29, 37-45.

Douglas, M., 1971 'Deciphering a meal', in Geertz (1971), 61-82.

Geertz, C., (ed.) 1971 *Myth, symbol and culture* (New York).

Goody, J., 1982 *Cooking, Cuisine and Class. A study in comparative sociology* (Cambridge).

Guest, E., 1933 'Notes on plants and plant products with their colloquial names', *Iraq*, 74.

Hallock, R.T., 1969 *Persepolis Fortification Tablets* (Oriental Institute Publications 92) (Chicago).

Hehn, V., 1902 *Kulturpflanzen und Hausthiere*, 7th ed. (Berlin).

Herzfeld, E., 1968 *The Persian Empire. Studies in the Geography and Ethnography of the Ancient Near East* (Wiesbaden).

Hinz, W., 1973 *Neue Wege im Altpersischen* (Gottinger Orientforschungen III. Reihe: Iranica, Bd. 1) (Wiesbaden).

Lewis, D.M., 1987 'The King's Dinner', *Achaemenid History* 2, 79-87.

Lewis, D.M., 1990 'The Persepolis Fortification Texts', *Achaemenid History* 4, 1-6.

Momigliano, A., 1975 *Alien Wisdom* (Cambridge).

Moorey, R., 1976 'Aspects of worship and ritual on Achaemenid Seals', *Akten des VII. Internationalen Kongresses für Iranische Kunst und Archäologie, München 7-10 sept. 1976*, (Archäologische Mitteilungen aus Iran, Ergänzungsband 6) (Berlin), 218-26.

Roaf, M., 1974 'The subject peoples on the base of the statue of Darius,' *Cahiers de la Délegation Archéologique Française en Iran* 4, 73-160.

Root, M.C., 1979 The King and Kingship in Achaemenid Art (Acta Iranica 19) (Leiden).

Sancisi-Weerdenburg, H., 1983 'The Zendan and the Ka'abah', *Archäologische Mitteilungen aus Iran Ergänzungband* 10, 145-152.

Sancisi-Weerdenburg, H., 1988 'The fifth oriental monarchy and hellenocentrism', *Achaemenid History* 2, 117-31.

Sancisi-Weerdenburg, H., 1989a Review of S. Hirsch, *Friendship of the Barbarians, Mnemosyne* 4th series, 42, 186-90.

Sancisi-Weerdenburg, H., 1989b 'Gifts in the Persian empire,' in P. Briant and C. Herrenschmidt (1989), 129-46.

Sancisi-Weerdenburg, H., 1993 'Found: a gazelle!'; 'The effects of cardamum'; 'Caranus' distribution of tableware', *Data* 2, notes 8, 11, 13.

Schmidt, E.F., 1957 *Persepolis* I (Oriental Institute Publications 68) (Chicago).

Stol, M., 1979 *On trees, mountains, and millstones in the ancient Near East* (*MVEOL* 21) (Leiden).

Stol, M., 1985 'Cress and its mustard', *Jaarbericht van het Voorziatisch-Egyptisch Genootschap, 'Ex Oriente Lux'* 28 (1983-4) 1, 24-32.

Tilia, A.B., 1972 *Studies and restorations at Persepolis and other sites of Fars* (Rome).

van Zeist., 1977 *Natuur en Techniek* 45, 680f.

Widengren, C., 1969 *Der Feudalismus im alten Iran* (Wissenschaftliche Abhandlungen der Arbeitsgemeinschaft für Forschung des Landes Nordrhein-Westfalen 40) (Köln and Opladen).

❖ 22 ❖

THE FOOD OF THE PREHISTORIC CELTS

Peter Reynolds

Iɴ any discussion concerning the remote past, especially of people and places outside the classical world, there is a preconceived notion that a low subsistence regime existed until the gift of civilization was bestowed – a gift which in the case of the Celts took the form of conquest by the Romans. After this time, according to the prevailing notion, great strides were made in every aspect of life: statehood, social organization, economic strategy, technology and agriculture.

To a very large extent such a notion depends upon a preferred perception. It is quite true to say that the conquest of the Celts was achieved primarily because they had not achieved the state of a nation, and therefore fell piecemeal fashion. That they were on the threshold of nationhood in the middle of the 1st century BC was demonstrated by the combined forces led by Vercingetorix at the battle of Alesia. Had the result been different, the combination of all the different tribes into one Celtic nation would undoubtedly have followed. This notwithstanding, the conquest of Gaul by Caesar was not easily achieved, and Caesar's forays into Britain were in reality failures rather than successes, despite his political rewards for venturing beyond the Ocean into the unknown. He was effectively outmanoeuvred and outgeneralled by Cassivellaunus during the campaigns of 55 and 54 BC, and was fortunate to return to the continent relatively unscathed.

However, the fact that the Celts were ultimately defeated and subsequently Romanised, combined with the lack of any literary record from the Celtic side, has led to an overall perception of the history of the West as beginning with the Romans, and a belief that all that went before was significantly inferior. This is further compounded by selective quotations from the classical literature which make the Celt into some kind of swaggering ill-mannered unreliable boozy braggart. Undoubtedly there are such people in every nation in every period, but without media attention they are likely to be entirely unrepresentative. In terms of social organization in the first millennium BC the Celtic system was most probably some form of warrior aristocracy, perhaps akin to that of Homeric Greece at broadly the same time. For the Celts we have no real evidence of any major development in organization comparable to the emergence of the city-state. Nevertheless, a warrior aristocracy can equally well be described as a military oligarchy. What is of particular interest is the nature of the society that can sustain such a warrior aristocracy. Inevitably it is pyramidal in form, with a large base of a working population, slave and free, and with status limiting numbers in the upper layers up to the peak, the military itself. For the aristocracy to succeed in however small a unit area, the rest of the layered population must also be successful. In turn, the basic economy must also be sound and successful. In the context of all societies prior to the Industrial Revolution, with minor exceptions, the basic economy was agricultural. To consider the food of the prehistoric Celts it is therefore necessary to explore the nature of its agricultural economy both in the sense of its technology and its products. With only a few classical references, which necessarily refer to differences rather than similarities, the basic information is drawn from the archaeological data recovered by excavation.

Ploughs and ards

Central to the technology of agriculture is the plough or ard. The difference between the two lies in the mouldboard. The plough is fitted with a vertically set curved board in metal or wood, which turns the soil over and buries the surface debris. The ard simply stirs the soil in the horizontal dimension. In Britain the introduction of a mouldboard seems to be no earlier than the 10th century AD. Even today, the ard as the primary cultivation tool is more widespread globally than the turn-over plough. The advantages of the ard lie in its relatively limited depth of cultivation, *c.* 200 mm, its efficiency in stirring a good tilth without burying all the organic material which both holds the soil together, counteracting major erosion episodes, and provides steady release of nitrogen for plant take-up, given the presence of the right micro-organisms in the soil body. In Vergil's *Georgics* (1.162-75) there is a description of an ard, its beam bent by 'main force' as it grew in the woodlands, and fitted with two ears (*binae aures*) which push the soil away from the ard, forming furrows. These 'ears' are critical in shallow soils to increase the soil depth for better plant rooting. Such ards can be seen throughout Mediterranean countries to this day. For north-west Europe, however, the evidence for the ard shows no indication of these 'ears' at all.

The evidence comprises iconography in the form of rock carvings as well as actual ards recovered from peat bogs, mainly in Denmark. The major concentration of rock carvings is to be found in the region of Bohuslän in western Sweden. The carvings, undoubtedly ritual in inspiration, provide a quite remarkable insight both into the complexity of the ards themselves and into agricultural practice. The main representations depict the ard as a curved main beam with a share fitted through a joint in its foot, the end of the beam being attached to a yoke set across the horns of a pair of cattle, often cows, occasionally bulls. From Donneruplund in Denmark an actual ard was recovered from a peat bog which provided all the detail of the implement. The share arrangement comprised a pointed stick set upon a heart-shaped undershare and held in line with two vertical spigots set into the face of the undershare, and a handle or stilt, all of which passed through a mortice cut into the foot of the main beam and held in place by wedges. Its profile form agrees exactly with the rock carvings. Replicas of this ard constructed and tested by the writer have shown it to be an extremely efficient tool indeed, quite capable of dealing with both heavy and light soils. Some carvings show a vertical bar set between the beam and behind the main share, which in all probability is a coulter or vertical knife to cut through the vegetation in the soil, although it could also be a strengthening device or a method of altering the angle of penetration. The role of the pointed stick is simply to hold the ard in the soil matrix; the heart-shaped undershare lifts the soil which then flows past the foot of the main beam. It is unfortunate that these ards have been dubbed 'stick ploughs', a term which altogether belies their complexity and efficiency. A recently discovered rock carving in Krokholmen in Sweden dated to the early Iron Age shows a double span of cattle pulling such an ard. This idea of increasing the traction power by adding further spans of cattle is normally attributed to the early medieval period.

A second type of ard is also depicted in the rock carvings of Sweden, southern France and northern Italy. This type has a share set at a much steeper angle to the soil surface. Archaeological excavations of prehistoric field areas often reveal scores in the underlying rock surface which are commonly described as ard marks. Usually the scores are clearly defined and extend some three to four metres in length with an area of major disturbance at the end of the score. Repeated trials with the first type of ard that we discussed, the Donneruplund type, have failed to reproduce this or any other kind of mark in the underlying rock. It would be surprising if it did, since it is carefully designed to till just the soil body. This second type of ard, however, given its steeper angle of penetration, does reproduce these short scores. The explanation is offered in the rock carving of an agricultural scene in the Val Camonica in northern Italy. An ard of this type is depicted with a further figure following behind wielding a hoe as if breaking up clods of earth.

Furthermore, this type of ard was still in use in north-west Spain in this century. Called *el cambelo*, it is used specifically to bring into cultivation old fallow land or land never previously cultivated. Shaped in the form of a great hook jointed to a straight beam fitted with grab handles for the ploughman, it is attached to a pair of yoked bulls, the point of the hook being just set into the ground surface. Goads applied simultaneously to the bulls force them forward. The ploughman simply hangs on to the handles. The hook is driven deep into the soil and dragged forward, finally coming to a shuddering halt after two or three metres, blocked up with soil and matted vegetation. Then it is wrestled out of the ground and the process repeated, while labourers smash the uprooted soil behind with mattock hoes into a crude tilth ready to be ard-ploughed in the normal way. Examination of the trace evidence left by *el cambelo* show it to be exactly similar to the prehistoric 'ard marks' recovered by excavation.

A third type of ard is evidenced both in a rock carving from Litsleby in Sweden and by an actual ard recovered from a peat bog in Hvorslev in Denmark. It is perhaps the most significant agricultural scene of all, since it shows the ritual of spring sowing. The ard is made from the curving bough of a tree forming the beam, with the share fashioned from the trunk. A stilt or handle is fitted to the rear of the share, which is virtually horizontal. Beneath the scene are shown horizontal lines depicting seed drills, while the ploughman has what is thought to be a bag of seed in his left hand. Trials with a replica ard have demonstrated that all it can do is draw a shallow furrow or drill in a prepared tilth.

The implications of this carving and the ard are extremely significant for understanding the sowing process in north-west Europe. It would seem that seed was sown into seed drills and not broadcast in the traditionally accepted manner or according to Roman practice. This means that the germinability of the seed determines the potential output, rather than a standard loss of seventy-five per cent of the seed grain. In simple economic terms a reduced input will lead to an increased output. In practical terms it allows for crop management during the growing season, by hoeing the weeds between the drills, with the commensurate benefits of reduced competition for the seed.

The evidence, therefore, for the core agricultural technology of ploughing in the European Iron Age is complex. There was a panoply of plough types, the sod buster, the standard tilth ard and the seed drill ard. The efficiency of these tools, as demonstrated by empirical trials, indicates that all soil types were capable of cultivation. Indeed over the last thirty years archaeological survey and excavation have shown that by the Iron Age all soil types in Britain, including the heavy clays, were occupied and cultivated, and that by the end of the first millennium BC the population probably approached five million.

Plants

Our basic knowledge of Celtic agricultural products is derived from the recovery of carbonized seed, seed impressions accidentally fired into pottery, and pollen grains and berries from excavations. While the seed evidence can only tell part of the story, since the finds are invariably made within settlement areas and therefore relate only partially to the reality of the fields, the range of domestic products is not inconsiderable. For cereals there are four wheat types, four barley types, oats, rye and millet; for legumes beans, peas and vetch (table 1). In addition there is a range of plants now regarded as arable weeds which could also have been used as food plants. For example Fat Hen (*Chenopodium album*) was probably a crop plant: the young leaves were eaten like spinach, the mature plant cropped as winter animal fodder, and the seeds ground up into flour to be made into bread. Black bindweed (*Polygonum bilderdykia*) can similarly be dried, ground into flour and made into bread. Common orache (*Atriplex patula*), another typical weed of prehistoric fields, can also be treated just

TABLE 1

CEREALS

Wheat	Emmer	*Triticum dicoccum*
	Spelt	*Triticum spelta*
	Old Bread Wheat	*Triticum aestivum*
	Club Wheat	*Triticum aestivo-compactum*
Barley	Two-row hulled	*Hordeum distichum*
	Two-row naked	*Hordeum distichum var. nudum*
	Six-row hulled	*Hordeum hexastichum*
	Six-row naked	*Hordeum hexastichum var. nudum*
Oats		*Avena sativa*
Rye		*Secale cereale*
Millet		*Panicum miliaceum*

LEGUMES

Bean	*Vicia faba minor*
Pea	*Pisum sativum*
Vetch	*Vicia sativa*

like Fat Hen. The fact that carbonized seed of these and many other potential food plants is found within the settlement areas suggests their culinary use.

The bone evidence from the Celtic world indicates the presence of the full range of farm livestock plus the use of wild animals, birds and fish. The farm livestock comprised cattle, sheep, goats, pigs and chickens, although for the last there is very little evidence indeed.

The cattle, the Celtic shorthorn, were relatively small beasts, the direct modern equivalent being the medium-legged Dexter cattle. This, although a modern breed, has as its antecedents the Kerry cattle of Ireland and the Welsh Black, themselves probable direct descendants of the Celtic cattle. The Dexters are tough, thrifty animals capable of thriving on poorish pasture and well able to plough with the ard types discussed above. It is most likely that each farm would have had at least five cattle, most probably cows, two of which would have been trained to the yoke, the others as breeding and back-up stock. A stock bull would, most likely, be kept on one farm but used within the local area. For milk production a cow must have calved, which in turn allows regular slaughter of unwanted progeny at appropriate times. Given sufficient fodder to take cattle through the winter, the longer one can delay slaughter, the larger the beast and the greater the quantity of meat. The bone evidence suggests the slaughter of mature stock of three years of age or more and butchery marks are regularly found on the bones.

The typical sheep of the Iron Age are represented by the Soay, Manx Loaghtan and Hebridean breeds. Their bones correlate exactly with those found on Iron Age sites, and they are the direct descendants of the prehistoric breeds which have survived in discrete groups in remote areas, as their names indicate. Sheep, of course, provide wool as well as milk and meat. The meat from all these breeds is remarkably free of fat and extremely palatable. The goats were most probably like the Old English Goat and they, like the sheep, were kept for milk, meat and hide.

The pig was a special Celtic animal. The domestic pigs were undoubtedly bred from feral pigs, but precisely how they were kept is not clear. The

Livestock

wild boar which to this day abounds in the forests of France, Belgium and Germany, but sadly no longer in England, must have been hunted. Large numbers of small models of wild boar have been recovered from Iron Age sites and the emblem of a wild boar is attested as a shield design. The image of the Celtic farmer setting aside his toils to go boar hunting both for pleasure and for the pot has to be accurate.

Domestic fowl were almost certainly kept but the bone evidence is virtually non-existent. Caesar speaks of them keeping chickens and geese for pleasure but that they considered it wrong to eat them. One wonders what source Caesar used for his interpretation of Celtic beliefs. The chickens were, in all probability, a type which today we would recognize as the Old English Game Fowl, the cocks of which are naturally extremely aggressive and have been used for cock-fighting from time immemorial. This might just account for Caesar's observation that they were kept 'for pleasure' (*animi causa*), and also give an attractive interpretation for small stake-built round-houses which, unroofed, would have made admirable cock-pits. The geese were most likely a domesticated form of the Greylag goose. Again, as Roman history recorded, they make splendid sentinels and could have been kept for pleasure or even peace of mind. Whatever pleasures these fowl may have offered, there can be little doubt that their ultimate function was food.

Farm livestock aside, wild animals and birds also found their way into the cooking pot. The best-known resource was the wild boar – we hear of the thrill of the chase and the joy of the feast – but we must also include the traditional quarries of red and roe deer. Caesar's informant stated that the hare was regarded as taboo, but it is extremely unlikely that it escaped the chase. Unless all these were fair game there seems little point to the renowned British hunting dog. In viewing the remote past there has often been an unsceptical acceptance of doubtful documentary and icono-graphic evidence which has led to misleading 'definitive' statements. As with the hare, so with wild birds there is an anxiety to focus upon the magical and mystical. In excavations of the Glastonbury and Meare Lake Villages abundant evidence was found for the hunting of wild fowl, primarily ducks and geese, and for fishing and fish including the eel. It is not unreasonable to postulate that given edibility, wild animals, birds and fish were all exploited.

The wild, of course, also includes a great variety of plants and fruits which provide a seasonable harvest exploited from the time of the gatherer-hunter through, ironically, to the present day. The list of edible wild fruits, berries, roots and plants is formidable and ranges from the tubers of reeds and maces to blackberries and hazel nuts. When farming began in the Neolithic, the wealth of food-gathering knowledge would have persisted, ultimately becoming the country lore we recognize today.

From the above it can readily be concluded that a wide and varied range of food, grains, vegetables, plants, and meat, both domestic and wild, was not only available but also exploited. Exactly how is an altogether more complex problem. The archaeological data can offer a few indications, and perhaps the classic legends of the Celts written hundreds of years later provide echoes of prehistoric practice; but in the absence of records in the style of Apicius, knowledge of how food was actually prepared is denied to us.

Querns

One of the oldest artefacts from agricultural communities world-wide is the quern-stone. The earliest form is the saddle quern, a large gritty stone with a flat face and a small fist-sized rubber stone. The seed to be crushed into groats or flour is placed on the surface of the saddle stone, so called because the usual wear pattern marking it makes it look like a saddle, and then pounded and rubbed by a small hand-held stone. Saddle querns exactly similar to the prehistoric versions are in use today in many regions of the world. Present-day observations record the bouncing of the rubber stone on to the seed on the saddle stone, the movement being extremely rapid and efficient. The only rubbing done was to spread out the resultant flour to check for impurities. Sufficient flour per day for a family of six, well over two kilos, can be prepared in approximately a quarter of an hour, the flour being as fine as any machine-ground.

The successors to the saddle quern were the rotary and oscillatory querns. (For the use of the former in the Roman world, see the chapter by White in this volume.) These comprise a large round flat lower stone with a slightly raised conical surface, over which is placed a companion stone perforated with a central hole and with a prepared concave surface in the lower face to correspond with the lower stone's convex surface. A handle is fitted either into the side of the upper stone or in the top, a little way in from the edge. The grain is dribbled into the hole in the centre of the upper stone, which is then completely rotated on the lower stone, grinding the seed between the faces and filtering it out around the edges.

The oscillatory quern, usually with the handle set in the side of the upper stone, is moved back and forth through roughly a quarter of the circumference. The wear pattern on this type of quern is distinctly asymmetrical and totally different from the even wear of the rotary quern. One further alternative to the quern, for which there is a little evidence, is the wooden pestle and mortar. The mortar was fashioned by hollowing out a tree trunk about a metre long from one end.

Careful use of all these types of querns and the mortar and pestle can produce flour of all grades from cracked wheat to groats to fine flour. Undoubtedly the development of the rotary quern displaced the primary function of the saddle quern, but the latter continues into the later periods and could well have been used for specialist purposes such as preparing small quantities of herbs.

Ovens

The primary purpose of grinding grain into flour is for the making of bread. In fact a small carbonized leavened loaf has been found looking remarkably similar to a small Hovis loaf. The bread was a mixture of cracked groats and flour. It is often assumed that it was unleavened, but if the dough is left exposed to the air for just a few hours, sufficient yeasts will be collected from the atmosphere to make the bread 'rise'. The foundations of a number of ovens for cooking bread have been found on settlement sites. These seem to have been tandoori-like domed clay ovens which were pre-heated. Alternatively, unleavened bread like pitta and roti bread can be quickly baked on both the inner and outer surfaces of the oven. Like the tandoori oven, the prehistoric ovens can be used for cooking a great variety of different foods including meat.

The hearth and its equipment

Central to food preparation is the hearth itself and, indeed, in the circular houses of the prehistoric Celts the hearth was placed at the epicentre of the house. The principal cooking implements associated with the hearth which survive are the fire-dogs and the cauldrons. The fire-dogs are in practice a twofold device. The lower bar is used for supporting the logs in the hearth allowing a degree of heat control; the closer set the logs are to each other the greater the heat, the further apart the lower the heat. The upper bars are used for supporting the meat on the spits – one presumes whole carcasses at a time for feasting, perhaps just joints on less grand occasions. Quite a large number of fire-dogs have survived, some with relatively simple decoration, others with an intricate and complex design which displays the work and skills of the Celtic blacksmith. Fewer cauldrons have been recovered, but their purpose clearly is for boiling food over the hearth. It seems that they were suspended from an iron tripod, which allowed them to be raised or lowered according to the temperatures required by the cook.

These rather grand metal cooking implements were complemented by simple, often crudely manufactured, unglazed pottery vessels. Although earthenware is essentially porous it is relatively easy to seal using the fat from milk. Thereafter such pots can be used for boiling and simmering liquids without difficulty. Amongst the pottery fragments are a number which imply the making of cheese. There have even been suggestions that bees were kept in special pottery hives to ensure a regular supply of honey rather than relying upon the collection of wild honeycombs. Honey, of course, was the only sweetening agent available. Certainly both honey and cheese were important elements of diet.

Boiling

From the artefacts it can be seen that the Celts had all the facilities as well as the appropriate food materials for baking, roasting and boiling, although which came first or even which they preferred is almost impossible to tell. In all probability, simple roasting over an open hearth and baking in the ashes of a fire date from the gatherer-hunter days of the Mesolithic and early Neolithic. Only with the advent of farming in the late Neolithic and stable domestic housing did food preparation advance into wet cooking. The exploitation of metals further enhanced this latter method, since it was possible to make large durable utensils far beyond the capacity of an earthenware pot.

There is a growing body of evidence to suggest that boiling, especially of meat, could have been a very early process, certainly pre-Celtic in origin. These are the *Fulachta Fiadh* or cooking pits. Initially found in Ireland, they comprise a wooden lined pit set in a wet area beside a stream or spring where they can be filled easily with water. Next to them are found heaps of fire-reddened stones that are argued to be pot-boilers. Experiments have shown that it is a simple process to heat the stones in a bonfire, transfer them into the water and quickly bring the water to the boil and to maintain it at boiling temperature. Thereafter the meat, wrapped in a skein of straw, is introduced and cooked at a rate of twenty minutes to the pound plus a further twenty minutes. These timings are the result of empirical tests, but given the nature of cooking they have to be relatively accurate, since parboiled meat is inedible. The resultant cooked meat, whether beef or mutton, is particularly sweet and an entirely different gastronomic experience from spit-roasted meat. This is inevitably variable both in taste and texture. These cooking pits were thought at first to be peculiarly Irish, but mounds of burned stones unassociated with any settlement and generally any dating material have been found countrywide in Britain and Ireland. The absence of other evidence apart from the waste heaps of burned stones seems to enhance the traditional Irish idea that they were special feasting places set aside from normal life.

Feasting

The classical references to the eating habits of the Celts are few and limited. Strabo speaks of their banquets and the way in which strangers were welcomed: they were questioned only after the meal about their identity and needs. He also comments somewhat disparagingly on the large quantities of food eaten along with milk and all kinds of meat, especially fresh and salted pork. Tacitus, referring to the Germans specifically – whose life-style, however, was no doubt similar to that of the Celts on the other side of the Rhine – talks of their drinking a fermented liquor made from barley and wheat grains which bears a resemblance to, presumably, Roman wine. The food he describes as plain; it includes wild fruit, fresh game and curdled milk. Somewhat unfairly, if we bear in mind well-documented Roman indulgences, especially those railed against by Juvenal, Tacitus refers to their uncontrolled drinking habits, suggesting that alcohol would be as effective a conqueror as the force of arms.

This is not the place to discuss Celtic feasting habits other than to draw inferences regarding food preparation. The practice of salting meat, for example, is impossible to prove from the archaeological evidence but the implications are obvious. Similarly, the curdling of milk hints at the complex processing of dairy products. Would that there were more detailed descriptions.

The later legends of the Celts, especially *The Champion's Portion* or *Bricriu's Feast*, reinforce the hints to be found in Strabo, Tacitus, Diodorus Siculus and Posidonios. In this tale the champion's portion, traditionally the thigh-piece, was to come from the meat from a specially raised seven-year-old boar and a seven-year-old cow, for the gastronomic real pork and real beef, boiled in wine in a great bronze cauldron. To complement the meat, wheat cakes cooked in honey were provided. This was the main course and, naturally, the cause of the conflict between the champions. Within the story it was preceded by an unspecified first course. The implications of wealth and splendour for this aristocratic element of Celtic society in the prehistoric period are undeniable. For this to be the case, the lower echelons of that society doubtless enjoyed a less grand but equally satisfactory life-style. Their food resources as evidenced were wide and varied and, more importantly, commonly available.

Conclusion

In conclusion, one of the great disservices done to the Celtic world and our understanding of it was the televised recreation of a gruel based upon the evidence extracted from the bog body of Tollund man. This comprised a mixture of vegetable remains of a finely ground gruel prepared from barley, linseed, gold of pleasure, knotweed, black bindweed and arable weed seeds, which was universally condemned by those who ate it. This meal accords so badly with the wealth of alternative evidence that it can only be interpreted as a ritual last meal given to a condemned man. If only they had recreated a Celtic feast the media image of the remote past would have been entirely different and significantly more accurate.

❖ 23 ❖

FOOD FOR PTOLEMAIC TEMPLE WORKERS

Dorothy J. Thompson

Iɴ studies of food and foodways the realm of the Egyptian temple is standardly discussed in terms of food taboos. Herodotos' description of the limits on dietary freedom for Egyptian priests in Book Two of his *History* (37.5) may be filled out by later sources, particularly Plutarch in his work *On Isis and Osiris* (chapters 5-8 = *Moralia* 352f-354a). The concern of these authors, as of so many historians, is primarily with high level priests – the *wb* or 'purified' priests. The subject of this chapter in contrast is the temple workers of a more humble variety, the very many minor priests and others who lived, worked and functioned within the large temple enclosures of Ptolemaic as of Pharaonic or, later, Roman Egypt.

Minor priests in the Serapeum

These minor priests and workers included *pastophoroi* or priests of the forecourt, the locals taken on (on a temporary basis) to play the part of the deities in certain rituals, the servants, funerary workers, tradesmen, pilgrims and hangers-on of what were complex and multifaceted communities. In discussing their diet, a range of questions may be asked. There is the question of its quality – what did it consist of, how varied was it, how satisfactory was it in dietary terms and how did it compare with contemporary diets within Ptolemaic society? But there is also the question of whether the Macedonian conquest of Egypt by Alexander the Great in 332 BC brought with it changes to the traditional diet of Egypt. To what extent did the immigrant Greeks dietarily affect or change the people they had conquered,[1] how deep into society was that change felt and how far may Greeks and Egyptians be identified through the food they ate? Or to put it another way – how specifically Egyptian was an Egyptian temple when diet forms the focus of interest? Finally, and still in the context of food, I shall touch on a further result of the arrival of Greeks in Egypt – the monetarization of the economy as found in a temple context.

The questions are wide-ranging, but my search for answers here is more narrowly focused, concentrating on just one temple, the Serapeum at Memphis. Various archives (and indeed scattered documents) come from the area, documents which are written both in Greek and demotic (that is, the cursive Egyptian script). There have also been recent excavations at Memphis and soon we may expect seed studies to fill out the picture. One of the major archives of the Serapeum consists of the papers of two sons of a Macedonian soldier named Glaukias. Ptolemaios, the eldest son of Glaukias, and, more briefly, his younger brother Apollonios spent time in the Serapeum, in a position they describe as *katoche* or self-detention. During that period they were, to a limited degree, on the temple payroll and they moved within the primarily Egyptian community of this large, and nationally important, temple.[2] The brothers were marginally literate in Greek, and it is their draft letters and scrawled accounts which form the chief basis of the following reconstruction.

Closely connected with Ptolemaios and Apollonios, the two sons of Glaukias, were the Egyptian twins Taous and Thaues who played the parts of the twin goddesses Isis and Nephthys in the seventy-day funerary ritual for the Apis bull which died in April 164 BC. The brothers acted as scribes and protectors for these girls, and it is through their letters that we learn of the twins' difficulties with the temple authorities over the payment of the bread and oil allowances that were their due. Ptolemaios shared a room with an Egyptian, Harmais, and yet another Egyptian is part of the present cast of characters – Teebesis, described as a reed-merchant, who in addition served as priest to the children of Apis, the Apis calves. Teebesis thus enjoyed a double income, both as seller of reeds used for fuel and as priest in receipt of the incoming cult-revenues on certain specified occasions. For it is worth noting here the important role of temple-offerings in priestly diet. When, in Egypt, priesthoods were sold and ceded within the priestly caste it was in large part the edible revenues that formed the attraction of such posts.

The accounts

The roughly scrawled accounts of the two sons of Glaukias – full of arithmetical errors, duplications, emendations, redrafting, inconsistencies and illegibilities – provide a rich source of evidence for the nature and variety of diet within the temple. Leaving the staples to last, a brief survey of food items occurring in these accounts as objects of purchase shows the range of a regular diet. Besides water, beer (*zutos*),[3] the traditional drink of Egypt, is the beverage recorded; papyrus roots (*papuroi*) were regularly bought for food, to be eaten baked in the fire[4]; turnip (*gongulides*) was purchased and chick-peas (*arbia* = *orobia*?); vitamin C and other vitamins would come from lettuce (*thridakes*), from fennel (*marathron*) and radishes (*rhapania*), from green figs (*phoinikes chloroi*) and from dried figs (*eischades*), from walnuts (*karua*), pomegranate (*rhoia*) and mulberry (*sukaminon*); their food was flavoured with cumin (*melanthe* = *melanthion*?) and garlic (*skordon*), and a sauce made of brine and vinegar known as *exalme* (= *oxalme*?).[5] Salt too (*hals*) had to be bought. Protein might come from innards (an ancient form perhaps of *kokoretsi* named *splanchnides*), from goose-meat (*krea chenea*) and other unspecified fowl (*ornithes*, probably pigeon). Herodotos (2.37.4; 45) described the plentiful beef available to priests from sacrificial animals, but there is only one record of a *bous* in the personal accounts of the sons of Glaukias (*UPZ* I 67.4-5 [153/2 BC]); this was valued at 3½ talents (sufficient, that is, to provide a daily bread supply for a year and a half: see note 10 below).

As far as staples were concerned, cereals came in various forms. The most common form of bread was the rough *kyllestis*-bread, made of *olyra* and already described by Herodotos (2.77.4), that formed the staple food within the temple community. *Olyra*, an Egyptian form of husked tetraploid emmer-wheat, might also, as we shall see, be cooked up into a type of porridge. Special breads were made for temple festivals – a bread of Berenike is recorded in the Canopus Decree of 238 BC (*OGIS* 56.72, translated in Bagnall and Derow 1981, 226), and similarly an Apis bread is known (*PSI* 428.40). And the ancient Egyptians seem to have been as fond as are their present-day descendants of sweet-cakes – milk and milk-cakes (*gala*, *amptos*), honey and honey-cakes (*meli*, *melitomata*), sesame-cakes (*sesamina*) and pancakes (*lagania*) are all recorded in these accounts. The oils used were primarily sesame-oil (*sesaminos*) for food and castor-oil (*kiki*) for lighting. Indeed, as well as bread, those in temple employment received regular allowances of sesame- and *kiki*-oil.

Egyptian and Greek traditions

Such was the variety of the diet available for purchase by the twins and others living in the Serapeum. The regular bread and oil allowances that they received from the temple are also recorded in detail. These I have treated elsewhere (Thompson 1988, 222-3, 237-45). Here I shall concentrate on the questions of how traditional this temple diet may have been, and of how far it may have been affected by the arrival of the Greeks in Egypt some 150 years before.

The record of goose-meat in the Serapeum accounts has already been noted. The funerary art of Pharaonic Egypt displays geese as a standard constituent of feasting-scenes; gooseherds (*chenoboskoi*) were a familiar part of village life, raising their flocks beside the canals and along the river bank. It is interesting too that here in the temple community it is beer and not wine that is drunk. Brewing had long been a regular occupation of the Egyptian countryside, and was closely controlled and taxed by the new immigrant regime (Clarysse and Vandorpe 1990, 86-7, 98-100). The arrival of the Greeks in Egypt however appears to have had much the same effect on drinking practices as the EC on Britain; and, over three hundred years, wine consumption came gradually to overtake that of beer. Earlier wine had been a drink of status, consumed by purified priests or by guilds of undertakers and libation-pourers at their monthly get-togethers (Herodotos 2.37.4; de Cenival 1972), but under the Ptolemies wine consumption both increased and spread through society. And here in the Serapeum in the mid-2nd century BC the temple-workers, even the Greeks amongst them, still drank beer. *Olyra* too was the traditional Egyptian grain which, to judge from the papyri, had virtually (though not entirely) disappeared from cultivation in Egypt by the time the Romans came. Here it is staple.

Porridge-making

Two general observations may be made. First, on the evidence of the items recorded by the sons of Glaukias in these detailed accounts, the diet of temple-workers appears reasonably varied. The picture of Egypt as the land of plenty, a commonplace from *Exodus* to Napoleon, is supported by this evidence. And secondly, to judge from the record of their purchases alone, the diet of the sons of Glaukias remained the traditional one of temple-workers. In their record of purchases it is only the garlic which may be seen as an immigrant addition (Crawford 1973); other foodstuffs were those of Egypt.

The extent of Greek dietary innovation may be further investigated by looking in detail at two further accounts, *UPZ* I 98 (158 BC) and 94 (159/8 BC). *UPZ* I 98 is one of the most complex documents preserved in the archive. It is a muddled and repetitive account in which Ptolemaios son of Glaukias recorded the outlay and income involved in the provision of what is called *athera* for two groups of temple-workers – the mysteriously named *atatistai* and the *taplaeitai* – over the period 17 March to 6 April 158 BC (17 Mecheir to 7 Phamenoth, Year 23 of Ptolemy VI Philometor). *Athera*, used as a food both for cultic and regular purposes, was a form of porridge which is referred to by various authors. The late lexicographer Hesychios described it as a 'food made of grain and milk' which was porridge-like (*poltodes*) in substance'.[6] It was fed to the sacred serpents of Alexandria, the *Agathoi Daimones* (pseudo-Kallisthenes 1.32; cf. Aristophanes *Ploutos* 673), but also in Egypt served as a medicinal poultice (Pliny *Natural History* 22.121 and Dioskorides 2.91-2). Made up from pounded meal (*ereikte*) and liquid, mixed up and boiled (Suda s.v.*athera*), it was compared by Hellanikos to pease pottage (*etnos*).[7] Porridge-sellers, *atheropolai*, are recorded from Fayum villages,[8] where they took their place alongside other vendors of fast-food, of pumpkins, chickpeas and other cooked dishes sold on the street. Italian *polenta* or the Romanian *mammaligha* would be modern equivalents.

UPZ I 98 provides evidence both for the preparation of porridge in the Serapeum and for Ptolemaios' role in this process. For while the meal or *aleuron* was provided by the temple, its cooking required central organization; this is where Ptolemaios was involved. The porridge was cooked in great vats or *chalkia*, like those used for boiling out *kiki*-oil. (A contemporary papyrus records a shocking industrial accident when an unfortunate *kiki*-worker drowned in such a vat.[9]) Holding over 8.5 gallons, these kettles were fired with reeds purchased by Ptolemaios from the reed-seller Teebesis. Reeds came in units of 100 bundles (at 25 drachmas a hundred) and, on a direct division of the quantities recorded, one kettle needed 220 bundles to fire it. The boiler was stoked by a *hypokaustes*, but we do not know whether he was employed on a daily or piece-rate basis; his fee over the period was 405 drachmas. The two main ingredients, as already mentioned, were *olyra*-meal and water; salt is not specifically recorded. The meal was provided by the temple to those in its employment; Ptolemaios' clients, it would appear, came with their own meal for cooking. A water-carrier brought the water up from the valley and daily totals, for which Ptolemaios paid, range from 7 to 26 jars at an average price of 7.5 drachmas apiece. The simple recipe for *athera* might run as follows:

> Take 1 measure of *olyra*-meal and 9 jars of water. Place in a large copper kettle. Mix and cook, while stirring well.

Ptolemaios' function in this operation is not altogether clear. I do not believe it was Ptolemaios who wielded the great spoon which mixed these 8.5 gallon vats. He appears rather as middle-man, using cash coming in from the sale of this porridge to cushion the non-payment to him of other temple dues. For while the cost of the water and reeds might ultimately reach him from the temple authorities, in practice he was able to set the income from sales against other unpaid temple dues. *Athera* sold at 150 drachmas a kettle, with the volume of sales varying from one to three kettles a day. The profit margin was not large. Ptolemaios' accounts are far from ordered ones. The following tabulation of the information contained in *UPZ* I 98 should not therefore be understood as an accurate represen-

Account for 34½ pans of athera, 17 March - 6 April 158 BC

Expenditure

Meal provided by purchaser	from the temple
316 jars (*keramia*) of water @ 7.5 dr. each	2370 drachmas (to Petosor)
7,600 bundles of reed @ 25 dr. per 100	1900 drachmas (to Teebesis)
Payment to boiler-stoker	405 drachmas
Total	4675 drachmas

Income

34.5 pans of *athera* @ 150 dr. each	5175 drachmas

Profit to Ptolemaios   500 drachmas (of bronze)

---

tation of his accounting methods. It merely expresses the same information in a more comprehensible form.

Ptolemaios' sums are complex, the arithmetic sometimes wrong, but in spite of his untutored and near-illegible hand Glaukias' son comes through the complexity of his accounts as neurotic, but at the same time reasonably sophisticated in his calculations. He similarly records the incense and the wood-supplies that he organized for the temple of Astarte within the Serapeum. And when Ptolemaios used what writing skills he possessed to record these dealings with the temple, his accounts may be seen also as an individual Greek's attempt to check and control the Egyptian temple environment in which he had chosen to spend his life. The monetarization of the economy has here penetrated even the most traditional of Egyptian activities, the provision of food in the temple.

The food itself was a simple food, and throughout history porridge made of meal has been the simplest way of gaining nourishment from grain (see Bryer and Hill in this volume). *Olyra* remained the standard cereal in the temples of Egypt. Besides forming porridge-meal, it might, as already seen, be made up also into *kyllestis*-loaves, like those provided daily by the temple to Taous and Thaues, the Serapeum twins, when they played the roles of Isis and Nephthys in the mourning for the Apis bull. Their normal allowance was four loaves a day, but when they took on extra cultic duties for the temple of Asklepios/Imhotep this was raised to six – a generous allowance of approximately 2 kilograms a day and the equivalent of an *artaba* of unmilled *olyra* every five days, or 73 *artabai* a year[10].

The allowance of the twins was in theory a generous one; in practice it was rarely paid. This particular allowance was always one of *olyra*-loaves; others in the temple might get their cereals in different form. *UPZ* I 94, column ii 11-20, records the payment of Ptolemaios' personal cereal-allowance from the temple for the five-month period from 25 Thoth to 26 Mecheir of Year 23 (159/8 BC). That came as follows:[11]

PAYMENT OF PTOLEMAIOS' ALLOWANCE FROM THE TEMPLE

Date	Cereal	*artabai*	*choinikes*
Thoth (Oct. 159)	traditional grain (*palaios sitos*)		15
25 Thoth (27 Oct. 159)			5
2 Phaophi (2 Nov. 159)	spelt (*zenos*[12])	½	
6 Phaophi	wheat of Kalymnos		13
10 Phaophi	spelt		15
15 Phaophi			10
[20] Phaophi	spelt	1	4
	wheat of Kalymnos	1	
21 Phaophi	spelt	½	
24 Phaophi [*corrected from 14*]			14
2 Hathyr (2 Dec. 159)			16
20 Hathyr		[[½]]	
for the festival of Isis:	fine loaves		30
	personal loaves	½	
9 Choiakh (8 Jan. 158)			10
30 Choiakh			10
9 Tybi (7 Feb. 158)			10
10 Tybi			½
19 Tybi			15
28 Tybi			12 ½
4 Mecheir (4 Mar.)			10
[2]6 Mecheir (26 Mar.)			5
	athera		10

In this account we see the contrast made between traditional grain (i.e. *olyra*) and other cereals. The special loaves for instance (*artoi katharoi* in Greek) provided for the festival of Isis were probably made of naked *pyros-* or *durum*-wheat. That these loaves were for official dedication is suggested by the next item: loaves for Ptolemaios' personal consumption, presumably emmer-loaves. Wheat from the Aegean island of Kalymnos is also recorded here[13]. Ptolemy II Philadelphos is said to have introduced the strain to Egypt; it would seem to have become well-established.[14] Of particular interest in this account is the wide variety of cereals listed and the mixture here of the new and the old. In the temple community of the Serapeum, we may conclude, changes came, but they came only slowly. Greeks like Ptolemaios on the whole ate little differently from their Egyptian counterparts, and the traditional diet they enjoyed was a strikingly varied one.

Notes

1. See Sallares (1991, 359) on stimulus diffusion.
2. See further Thompson (1988, 212-65).
3. The original spellings have been preserved in transliterations; for references to foodstuffs see the indexes to Wilcken (1927 in 1957, 301-33).
4. Herodotos 2.92.5, in a *klibanos* described as *diaphanes* (with holes for steam?); Diodorus Siculus 1.80. See Chapter 5.
5. So Wilcken on *UPZ* 84.14; but *exalme* may rather signify salted fish, cf. Herodotos 1.77.4.
6. Hesychios, s.v. *athera*; cf. Dioskorides 2.92, 'like a wet porridge' (*hosper polarion hygron*); the Serapeum account shows that water might be used for milk.
7. Hellanikos *FGH* 4 F192; he also comments on the different forms of the word: *athare, athera, athara*.
8. *P.Sorb.inv*. 555 (2nd century BC); cf. *P.Oxy*. 1432.4-6 (AD 214) and 3138.2-3 (late 3rd to early 4th century AD), misleadingly translated as 'pulse-sellers'. See Perpillou-Thomas (1992).
9. *UPZ* 120. A *chalkion* or *metretes* equalled 80 Egyptian *hin*, 48 *choinikes*, 38.78 litres or 8.4 imperial gallons.
10. Loaves were termed 'cooked loaves', *artoi peptoi*, and four loaves a day was the standard allowance also in contemporary Egyptian marriage contracts. One *artaba* of *olyra* equalled 48 *choinikes* or 32.32 litres; it produced 30 *kyllestis*-loaves, reckoned as 15 pairs. The ratio of *olyra:durum* wheat stood at 5:2; an *artaba* of *olyra* cost 250-360 (bronze) drachmas (*UPZ* 91.7n.).
11. Compare *SB* 7617.91-103, monthly totals Pharmouthi-Epeiph implying an allowance which averaged one *artaba* a month, paid in differing grains.
12. This identification is adopted from Wilcken; it is far from certain.
13. Compare Syrian wheat known from the 3rd century BC Zenon archive (references in Pestman 1981, 498).
14. Suda, s.v. Kalymnos. For further innovations see Thompson (1984, 366-7).

Abbreviations

OGIS	W. Dittenberger *Orientis Graeci Inscriptiones Selectae* 2 vols (Leipzig, 1903).
P.Oxy.	*The Oxyrhynchus Papyri* (London, 1898-).
PSI	*Papiri greci e latini*. Pubblicazioni della Società Italiana per la ricerca dei papiri greci e latini in Egitto (Florence, 1912-).
P. Sorb. inv.	unpublished papyri of the Sorbonne, Paris.
SB	*Sammelbuch griechischer Urkunden aus Aegypten* (Strassburg and Berlin, now Wiesbaden, 1915-).
UPZ	*Urkunden der Ptolemäerzeit* I, ed. U. Wilcken (Berlin and Leipzig, 1927).

Bibliography

Bagnall, R.S. & Derow, P., 1981 *Greek Historical Documents: the Hellenistic Period* (Chico, C.A.).

Clarysse, W. & Vandorpe, K., 1990 *Zenon, een Grieks Manager in de Schaduw van de Piramiden* (Leuven).

Crawford, D.J., 1973 'Garlic-growing and agricultural specialization in Graeco-Roman Egypt', *Chronique d'Égypte* 48, 350-63.

de Cenival, F., 1972 *Les associations religieuses en Égypte d'après les documents démotiques* (Cairo).

Pestman, P.W., 1981 *A Guide to the Zenon Archive* 2 vols = *P.L.Bat.* 21 (Leiden).

Perpillou-Thomas, F., 1992 'Une bouillie de céréales: l'Athèra' *Aegyptus* 72, 103-110.

Sallares, J.R., 1991 *The ecology of the ancient Greek world* (London).

Thompson, D.J., 1984 'Agriculture', chapter 9c in *Cambridge Ancient History* VII.1², ed. F.W. Walbank, et al. (Cambridge).

Thompson, D.J., 1988 *Memphis under the Ptolemies* (Princeton).

Wilcken, U., 1927 *Urkunden der Ptolemäerzeit* I (Berlin and Leipzig).

_____ 1957 *Urkunden der Ptolemäerzeit* II (Berlin).

❖ 24 ❖

FOOD AND ARCHAEOLOGY IN ROMANO-BYZANTINE PALESTINE

Shimon Dar

Iɴ Biblical and Talmudic literature there are about five hundred kinds of vegetation, of which some one hundred and fifty types of cultured growth have been identified. These include three kinds of grains, about twenty kinds of legumes, twenty-four kinds of vegetables, sixteen kinds of spices, ten healing grasses and perfumes as well as eighteen types of industrial crops. In addition, some twenty-five fruit trees are listed (Feliks 1982, 419-41).

To attempt to reconstruct the diet in Palestine during the Romano-Byzantine period it is necessary to base ourselves on a combination of the written sources and the botanical, archaeological and osteologic-archaeological discoveries. In recent years the number of excavations in which ancient food remains have been investigated has increased, and it seems one can already present a picture of the situation which reflects the diets of the inhabitants of the country in ancient times. To complete the picture we are also aided by ancient production installations which were used to boost agricultural production (Frankel 1984; Dar 1986, 88-212) and by a variety of pottery from the excavations of the kitchens and storehouses of the buildings of the period (Zevulun and Olenik 1979). In the opinion of most researchers, the climate in Palestine has not changed fundamentally in the last two thousand years, and the flora and fauna still reflect what existed in ancient times, despite the intervention of man (Liphschitz 1988, 133-46).

Until the beginning of the 20th century the life-style of the rural Arab population in Israel had not changed qualitatively since the Byzantine period, and large portions of the rural Arab diets recorded in the 19th century and the beginning of the 20th century included ingredients comparable to those of ancient times (Guggenheim et al. 1991).

In the Mishnah *Ketubot* 5.8-9 we find the food ration which a woman receives from a husband who is far from home for the purposes of his work and business affairs:

> 8. If a husband maintained his wife at the hands of a third person, he may not grant her less than two *kabs* of wheat or four *kabs* of barley [every week]. R. Jose said: Only R. Ishmael provided her with barley [at such an estimation] because he lived near Edom. He must also give her half a *kab* of pulse and half a *log* of oil and a *kab* of dried figs or a *mina* of fig-cake; and if he has none of these he must provide her with other produce in their stead. He must also give her a bed and a bed-cover and if he has no bed-cover he must give her a rush mat. He must also give her a cap for her head and a girdle for her loins, and shoes at each of the [three] Feasts, and clothing to the value of fifty *zuz* every year. They may not give her new clothes for summer or worn-out clothes for winter; but he should give her clothes to the value of fifty *zuz* for winter, and she may clothe herself with the rags thereof in the summer time, and the discarded garments belong to her.

> 9. He must give her a silver *maah* for her needs, and she should eat with him on the night of every Sabbath. If he does not give her a silver *maah* for her needs, what she earns by her own work shall belong to herself. And how much work must she do for him? She must spin for him five *selas*' weight of warp in Judaea (which is ten *selas* in Galilee) or ten *selas*' weight of woof (which is twenty *selas* in Galilee); but if she was suckling a child they should lessen

Weekly and daily diet of a woman living alone in Roman Palestine

her handiwork and increase her maintenance. This applies to the poorest in Israel; but with folk of the better sort all should be according to the honour due to him.

The ration consists of wheat, legumes, olive oil and dried figs. The quantities of food are set out in measures of the *seah* and the *log*, and there are two systems of converting them into kilos (Feliks 1967, 185-6): a) 1 *seah* = 13 litres or b) 1 *seah* = 8.565 litres. The translation of the two systems into kilograms and calories gives us the following figures (Guggenheim 1964, 545-8; Broshi 1986; Safrai 1986, 113-6):

TABLE 1:   1 seah = 13 litres

Product	Weight in kilos	Calorific value
Wheat	3.3	10,000
Legumes		
(½ Chickpeas and		
½ Lentils)	0.92	3,139
Olive oil	0.229	2,061
Dried figs	1.1	2,992
Total		**18,192**

Thus theoretically the daily intake was 3,032 calories.

TABLE 2:   1 seah = 8.565 litres

Product	Weight in kilos	Calorific value
Wheat	2.037	6,111
Legumes	0.597	2,035
Olive oil	0.162	1,458
Dried figs	0.713	1,640
Total		**11,244**

Thus theoretically the daily intake was 1,874 calories.

If we take Table 2 with a daily consumption of 1,874 calories, we will approach the modern calculations of the recommendations of the United

Nations Organization regarding women of child-bearing age who need 2,000 to 2,200 calories per day. According to the Mishnaic source (*Ketubot* 5.9), women also received a weekly ration and could increase their food allocation by purchases, or the use of a vegetable garden beside their homes. It is interesting to note that a diet consisting of 2,500 calories was still normal for Arabs and Jews in Palestine during the British Mandate (Guggenheim et al. 1991, 149, 154).

Bread

According to the ration in the Mishnah (*Ketubot* 5.8), bread served as the major source of calories: more than 50% of the daily menu, i.e. a daily portion of 500 grams. Furthermore, there is no excavation in Palestine where various kinds of grains have not actually been discovered. The three principal kinds of grain discovered by archaeologists are wheat, barley and oats (see e.g. Kislev 1979; Meyers et al. 1981, 60-72, 273; Gal 1984; Kislev 1986; Kislev 1992a). In addition to the kinds of grain revealed in excavations, the threshing floors and various grinding stones served as concrete evidence of the growth of grains and preparation of bread in every settlement and in each home. Grinding stones and threshing floors are found from Mt. Hermon in the north to the Negev in the south (Avner 1990; Dar 1993).

Lehem or *path* – both of which are terms for bread – served in ancient Hebrew to describe food in general and a meal in particular. The importance of wheat as food was so great that the sages compared it to the Tree of Knowledge of which Adam and Eve partook (*Genesis Raba* 15.7). In the opinion of various researchers, throughout the last two thousand years the average person in Palestine consumed about 150-200 kilos of grain per year (Avitsur 1991). From 166 kilos of wheat per year one could bake 190 kilos of bread, i.e. a daily portion of 518 grams. The monks in the Judaean desert during the Byzantine period received a daily ration of 650 grains of bread, but the heads of the monasteries tried to reduce this quantity (Dorotheos of Gaza 1977, 38-9; Hirschfeld 1992, 82-6).

After the ripening and threshing, various porridges and flour for bread were prepared from the grain. The types of porridges depended on the way the seeds were broken and the type of processing, while the quality of the bread depended on the sifting of the floor. The lighter bread was considered better quality and was called 'a pure bread' while the black bread was called just that, 'black bread'. There were also various intermediate grades of bread that were baked from other grains (Krauss 1910, 92-106).

The bread eaten in Palestine was leavened, that is yeast was added to it; because of the climate flour could not be kept for a long time and the housewife and her daughters had to rise very early to grind the daily portion of bread and bake it in the oven. A family of six or seven persons ground for three to four hours every morning (Avitsur 1972, 247). Talmudic sources tell us that the girls who did the grinding of the flour in the villages from their youth had better developed breasts than the girls in the city who could buy flour and bread from the baker (*Tosefta Nida* 6.9 [Zuckermandel 648]).

Vegetables and legumes

After bread, legumes took a central place in the diet of Palestine: they could be eaten raw, cooked or dried. Moreover, in archaeological excavations it is common to discover different kinds of legumes, which were stored in clay jars in the houses of the inhabitants. It appears that the important kinds of legumes were lentils, broad beans, chickpeas, peas and lupins (Feliks 1982, 426).

The Mishnah *Baba Metzia* 5.1-5 states that the meal of hired agricultural workers consisted of bread and legumes which the owner supplied. It was also permitted to eat fruit, such as the figs and grapes which they were picking. Some workers ate their bread dipped in fish sauce (*garum*) in order to eat a lot of grapes. But the owners were allowed to give them wine to drink so that they would eat fewer grapes (*Tosefta Baba Metzia* 8.2-3 [Zuckermandel 387]).

Actual archaeological discoveries of vegetables have been few, and only garlic and onions were found in the hidden caves of the Judaean desert dating from the period of the Bar Kochba rebellion (132-135 AD) (Zaitschek 1962). The Talmudic sources abound with references to vegetables which were grown and consumed in Roman-Byzantine Palestine. The *Yerushalmi*

Talmud in *Kidushin* at the end of chapter 4 says: 'It is forbidden to dwell in a city where there are no vegetable gardens' (Krauss 1910, 116-9; Safrai 1981, 90-1). The inhabitants of Palestine during ancient times ate lettuce, spinach beets (mangold), kale, radishes, turnips, carrots, artichokes, black cala, leek, onion, garlic, cucumber, melon, watermelon and squash. Besides the cultured vegetables they ate wild plants as well as a great many spices from the *labiatae* family, such as various kinds of marjoram and mint (Feliks 1982, 430-2).

Fruit trees

As opposed to vegetables, which are not preserved on archaeological sites, fruit trees have fared better. Throughout the country remains of olive trees, vines, dates, figs, walnuts, almonds, pomegranates, peaches, a few carob trees, oaks and doum palms have been found. Also popular were the pistachio, apples and pears. A total of some twenty-five types of fruit trees were known in Roman Palestine (Feliks 1982, 433-4; Liphschitz 1987). Some of them were more important in the ancient diet and it appears that the olive and its oil, the vine and its wine, the dates and the fig were of prime importance. According to various calculations, every person consumed twenty kilos of olive oil per year as food, and an additional quantity for cosmetics and for illumination (Dar 1986, 165-90). (20 kg of olive oil per year for a person is still very common in many villages in Galilee and Samaria.) In every kilo of olive oil there are 9,000 calories, and it keeps very well in storage. There was no ancient settlement in Palestine that did not have its olive press to produce oil, and in areas where olives grew we found six or seven presses in every town and village of an area of 20-30 *dunams* (Dar, Safrai and Tepper 1986, 45, 131-2). The excess oil was sold in the market-places of the *poleis* and was even exported overseas.

The number of wine presses in Israel suggests that the ancients did not drink water but rather only wine (Broshi 1985). A medium-sized village like Horvat Sumaqa on the Carmel mountains possessed five large wine-presses with an estimated production of 250,000 litres per year (Dar 1988-9). From one Talmudic source one can reconstruct the minimum quantity of wine that a family in Palestine stored throughout a year: between 330 and 375 litres (*Yerushalmi Sheviit* 5.7.36). They used to mix the strong wine with water, half and half, or one-third to two-thirds (*Tosefta Baba Metzia* 3.27 [Zuckermandel 378]). In every litre of wine there are between 600 and 1,000 calories, and no doubt wine was one of the basic food elements in the ancient diet.

The dates from the Jordan Valley won international praise: Pliny (*Natural History* 13.26-48) referred to them with admiration. After they had been dried, the figs and dates served as food of high sugar concentrate which could be taken along when travelling and could be stored for years. They produced honey and even wine from dates and figs (Netzer 1987). In the papyrus archives of Babatha (from the period of the Bar-Kochba rebellion, 132-5 AD), three kinds of dates are mentioned: the Syrian, the split, and the Naarani, named after the settlement of Naaran in the Jordan Valley (Broshi 1990).

Meat

It used to be commonly thought that the inhabitants of the eastern Mediterranean basin did not eat much meat in ancient times (Safrai 1981, 90). But the most recent excavations do not support this theory. In a dozen digs where bones of animals were collected and examined by experts, a more balanced picture of the ancient diet emerges. In excavations of sites from the Hellenistic through to the Byzantine period, bones from caprovines, large cattle, swine, poultry and fish have been found. They also hunted rabbits, deer and songbirds for food. Caprovines (goats and sheep) constituted 65 to 75% of all the finds, and after them large cattle (10 to 15%), and swine, the breeding of which was not forbidden to Jews but only the eating (Horwitz, Tchernov and Dar 1990; Horwitz 1990; 1992a; 1992b; Kislev 1992b). In addition to the tame animals, some of which were slaughtered for food, there were also many kinds of poultry, especially hens, geese and ducks. Breeding pigeons in a *columbarium* (pigeon house) was common too in Israel, and today we know of some one thousand caves that were used for breeding pigeons (Tepper 1986).

Towards the Byzantine period the importance of fish and poultry in local diets increased, as the pig also became more important in non-Jewish settlements. This phenomenon was even observed in Transjordan, e.g. in Hesban (La Bianca 1990).

Dairy produce

Milk products from the caprovines – various types of cheese and butter – were common in the diet of Palestine and were mentioned a great deal in the Talmudic sources (Avitsur 1976, 64-7; Broshi 1986, 50-51). Olive oil, cheeses and dry cheese could be kept longer even in the warm climate of Israel. As for dessert, in the Talmudic sources some twenty kinds of sweets are mentioned. Most of them were made from flour, with wine, milk, honey, fruit and nuts, which were cooked or fried together (Krauss 1910, 106-8).

Summary

An analysis of the written sources from the Roman-Byzantine period, in addition to archaeological discoveries, teaches us about the varied and satisfying diet which the inhabitants of Palestine enjoyed in ancient times. It appears that the calorific value did not fall short of that of the present day.

Only in times of widespread starvation caused by a lengthy drought and wars did people die from lack of food in parts of Palestine and Syria. In the time of King Herod such a famine resulted from three years of drought. Josephus tells us that the problem was solved by importing grain from neighbouring Egypt (*Antiquities* 15.299-310). In that same period, Herod and his family enjoyed imports of fine Italian wine and apples, which were sent to him at his fortress at Masada (Cotton and Geiger 1989).

Acknowledgements

I would like to thank Prof. Nili Liphschitz of Tel Aviv University and Prof. M.E. Kislev of Bar-Ilan University for their generous advice in discussing the topics of this paper. Dr Liora Kolska-Horwitz of the Hebrew University in Jerusalem and the Antiquities Authority was also very kind in sending me her unpublished reports concerning animal bones from recent excavations in Israel.

Bibliography

Avitsur, S., 1972 *Daily Life in Eretz Israel in the Nineteenth Century* (Tel Aviv) (Hebrew).

Avitsur, S., 1976 *Man and his Work* (Jerusalem) (Hebrew).

Avitsur, S., 1991 'Bread consumption in time of abundance', in Y. Katz, Y. Ben Arieh, Y. Kaniel (eds), *Historical-Geographical Studies in the Settlement of Eretz-Israel* II (Jerusalem), 47-53 (Hebrew).

Avner, U., 1990 'Ancient agricultural settlement and religion in the Uvda Valley in southern Israel', *Biblical Archaeologist* 53.3, 125-41.

Broshi, M., 1985 *Wine in Ancient Palestine* (Haaretz Museum, Tel Aviv) (Hebrew).

Broshi, M., 1986 'The diet of Palestine in the Roman Period – Introductory Notes', *The Israel Museum Journal* 5, 41-56.

Broshi, M., 1990 'Agriculture and economy in Roman Palestine according to the Babatha papyri', *Zion* 55.3, 269-81 (Hebrew with English summary).

Cotton, H.M. & Geiger, Y., 1989 'Wine for Herod', *Cathedra* 55, 3-12 (Hebrew).

Dar, S., 1986 *Landscape and Pattern - an archaeological survey of Samaria 800 B.C.E.-636 C.E.*, British Archaeological Reports S308 (Oxford).

Dar, S., 1988-9 'Horvat Sumaqa: a settlement from the Roman and Byzantine periods in the Carmel', *Bulletin of the Anglo-Israel Archaeological Society* 8, 34-48.

Dar, S., 1993 *Settlements and Cult Sites on Mt. Hermon, Israel.* British Archaeological Reports S589 (Oxford).

Dar, S., Safrai, Z. & Tepper, Y., 1986 *Urn Rihan: a Village of the Mishnah* (Tel Aviv) (Hebrew).

Dorotheos of Gaza 1977 *Discourses and Sayings*, trans. E.P. Wheeler (Kalamazoo, Michigan).

Feliks, Y., 1967 *Mixed Sowing, Breeding and Grafting* (Tel Aviv) (Hebrew).

Feliks, Y., 1982 'The Jewish Agriculture in Palestine during the Mishna and Talmud Periods', in Z. Baras et al. (eds) *Eretz Israel from the Destruction of the Second Temple to the Muslim Conquest* I (Jerusalem) (Hebrew), 419-41.

Frankel, R., 1984 *The History of the Processing of Wine and Oil in Galilee in the Period of the Bible, the Mishna and the Talmud*, unpublished Ph.D. dissertation (Tel Aviv) (Hebrew).

Gal, Z., 1984 'Horvat Rosh Zayit - a Phoenician fort in Upper Galilee', *Qadmoniot* 66-67, 56-9.

Guggenheim, Y.K. 1964 *Human Nutrition* (Jerusalem: Hebrew).

Guggenheim, Y.K. et al., 1991 'The beginning of nutritional studies in Eretz-Israel', *Cathedra* 59, 144-60 (Hebrew).

Hirschfeld, Y., 1992 *The Judean Desert Monasteries in the Byzantine Period* (New Haven and London).

Horwitz, L.K., 1990 *Animal bones from Horvat Rimmon: Hellenistic to Byzantine periods*: unpublished report (Israel Antiquities Authority).

Horwitz, L.K., 1992a *Animal remains from excavations at the Third Wall (Jerusalem)*: unpublished report (Israel Antiquities Authority).

Horwitz, L.K., 1992b *The faunal remains from excavations at Mamilla – the Jaffa Gate (Jerusalem)*: unpublished report (Israel Antiquities Authority).

Horwitz, L.K., Tchernov, E. & Dar, S., 1990 'Subsistence and environment on Mt. Carmel in the Roman-Byzantine and Medieval periods: the evidence from Kh. Sumaqa', *Israel Exploration Journal* 40.4, 287-304.

Kislev, M.E., 1979-80 'Triticum parvicoccum Sp. Nov., the oldest naked wheat', *Israel Journal of Botany* 28, 95-107.

Kislev, M.E., 1986 'A barley store of the Bar-Kochba rebels (Roman period)', *Israel Journal of Botany* 35, 183-96.

Kislev, M.E., 1992a 'Vegetal food of Bar Kokhba rebels at Abi'or Cave near Jericho', *Review of Palaeobotany and Palynology* 73, 153-60.

Kislev, M.E., 1992b 'Hunting songbirds as a branch of the economy', in *New Discoveries in Ancient Agriculture and Economy. The 12th Congress*, ed. S. Dar (Ramat Gan), 52-9 (Hebrew).

Krauss, S., 1910 *Talmudische Archäologie* I (Leipzig).

La Bianca, P.S., 1990 *Sedentarization and Nomadization: Food System Cycles at Hesban and Vicinity in Transjordan: Hesban I* (Berrien Springs, Michigan, 197-200).

Liphschitz, N., 1987 'Fruit trees in ancient Israel', *Hassadeh* 67 (Hebrew with English summary), 492-7.

Liphschitz, N., 1988 'Dendrochronological and dendroarchaeological investigations in Israel as a means for the reconstruction of past vegetation and climate' in T. Hackens et al. (eds), *Wood and Archaeology* (Strasbourg), 133-46.

Meyers, E.M. et al., 1981 *Excavations at Ancient Meiron, Upper Galilee, Israel, 1971-72, 73-74, 79* (Cambridge, Mass.).

Netzer, E., 1987 'Water channels and a royal estate from the Hasmonean period in the western plains of Jericho' in D. Amit et al. (eds) *The Aqueducts of Ancient Palestine* (Jerusalem), 273-81 (Hebrew).

Safrai, S., 1981 *At the End of the Second Commonwealth and the Mishnaic Period* (Jerusalem).

Safrai, S., 1986 *The Galilee in the time of the Mishna and Talmud* (Ma'alot) (Hebrew).

Tepper, Y., 1986 'The rise and fall of dove-raising', in A. Kasher et al. (eds), *Man and Land in Eretz-Israel in Antiquity* (Jerusalem), 170-196 (Hebrew).

Zaitschek, D.V., 1962 'Remains of cultivated plants from the Cave of the Pool', *Yediot, Bulletin of the Israel Exploration Society* n.s. 26.3-4, 242-3 (Hebrew).

Zevulun, U. & Olenik, Y., 1979 *Function and Design in the Talmudic period*, Haaretz Museum (Tel Aviv).

PART FIVE

Food and Medicine

Diphilos of Siphnos says of figs that soft ones afford little nourishment and produce bad juices in the body, but are easily excreted, rise to the top of the stomach, and are more easy to assimilate than dry figs. Those that are forced to ripen at the onset of winter are worse, while those that are ripened at the height of their season by natural process are better. Those with a large amount of acidic juice and those with little water have a better flavour but are heavier. Figs from Tralles are similar to those from Rhodes, but those from Chios and elsewhere all produce worse juices in the body. Mnesitheos of Athens, in his book *On Foods*, says:

> In respect of those fruits that are eaten raw, such as pears, figs, Delphic apples and so on, care must be taken that the time is right, to ensure that they have juices that are neither 'uncooked' nor fermented nor dried up through ripeness.
>
> (Athenaeus 3.80b-d)

Introduction cs
Part Five

Athenaeus quotes two medical authorities from the 4th and 3rd centuries BC, whose works survive only here and in quotation in medical works such as those of Galen and Oribasios, both of whom are discussed in this section. Medical writing in antiquity depends on the appeal to such authorities ('X says such and such', 'Y says something else'). Thus not only writers such as Athenaeus, whose major value for us is in his preservation of lost authors, but also such influential figures as Galen call upon the words of Hippokrates and others. Athenaeus, as usual, has a particular importance for our purposes since he concentrates on foods. Dietetics were important in ancient medicine, much treatment being preventative (the eating of correctly-balanced foods) and corrective (the restoration of harmony to the body).[1] The theory of the humours was influential. The human body, composed largely of fluids ('humours') depended for its good health in the Hippokratic system on the right balance of the four humours (blood, phlegm, yellow bile and black bile) (Hippokrates *Nature of Man* 5-9) and on the right balance of the 'qualities' of those humours (hot, cool, moist, dry, and a number of others, some of which are discussed by Elizabeth Craik and Mark Grant). There were four humours just as there were four seasons and four elements (earth, air, fire and water). There might be an excess of one humour; a humour might have shifted its position, a humour might be too thick or too thin. Diseases could come from other causes, of course, but diet and style of life were of great importance: 'a man cannot enjoy good health just by eating; he must take exercise as well' (Hippokrates, *Regimen* 1.2: Elizabeth Craik has more to say on style of life [*diaita* in Greek]). Foods might be heating or cooling and generative of one humour or another; it was therefore important to understand the quality of the food. In the case above, figs produced some undesirable juices, and were particularly likely to do this if they were not in perfect condition for consumption, too ripe, under-ripe and so on. In addition, a food might have a predictable effect as it passed through the body – easy to assimilate, easily excreted, nourishing or not nourishing. There might also be other effects, such as the psychosomatic influences considered by Vivian Nutton below in the case of Galen himself.

In a sense, the food experienced some processes analogous to those suffered by the body. Thus the fig might be 'uncooked', that is under-ripened by the sun, just as the body's processing of the food with heat may be successful or unsuccessful 'cooking', that is digestion. If a food was not in the appropriate state for assimilation into the body, disease and disorders might ensue. A Hippokratic writer alludes to such an idea in the treatise *On Ancient Medicine*. In chapter 3 he speaks of the sufferings of prehistoric peoples:

> Many and terrible were their sufferings from their strong and bestial way of life. They ate foods which were raw, unmixed and with very strong properties... Most of them probably died... They seem to me consequently to have sought a diet that was in harmony with their body, and to have discovered what is our present diet. So from wheat, they soaked the grain, winnowed, ground, sifted, mixed and baked it to produce bread, while from barley they made barley cake (*maza*).

Mark Grant has more to say on the subject in Chapter 28.

Similarly, the Hippokratic author of *Airs, Waters and Places* considers the importance of place and climate for the human body just as Diphilos considers the influence of place on varieties of fig: 'anyone who wishes to pursue the science of medicine correctly' should take account of season, winds, qualities of the water and soil, and also 'the way of life that the local people find pleasing, whether they love their drink, whether they have two full meals a day (compare 431), whether they lack exercise or are athletic, whether they work hard, are enthusiastic eaters, and do not drink (chapter 1). *Airs, Waters and Places* distinguishes peoples by their location: so 'Europeans' may be distinguished from 'Asians' and 'Scythians' from the Russian steppes in physique and medical constitution as well as in the ways discussed in the introduction to Part Four. 'Europeans', not surprisingly perhaps given the nationality of the author, come out of the comparison as best and toughest.

Within the Hippokratic system, special consideration is given by Helen King to the nature of women, who were considered moister than men and sometimes hotter, sometimes cooler according to context. Women are particularly interesting in the system because of their liability to an excess in one of the humours, blood. While blood is a form that food takes once it has been assimilated by the body, in excess it provokes various disorders. The beliefs held about women in this connection may be compared with those examined by Veronika Grimm in Chapter 17.

The works attributed to Hippokrates form a corpus – much of it written in the late 5th and 4th centuries, some time after his death – which naturally addresses far more branches of medicine than the dietetics which are our concern here. Few if any works may be ascribed to Hippokrates himself (see the discussion of Edelstein (n. 5), 133-44); nor was their authenticity above doubt in antiquity. There is much internal inconsistency in the corpus, but in some works there is a clear searching for rational and scientific method, as in *On Ancient Medicine*, for example. At all periods the practitioners of such methods were in contention with others, and all competed with the local experts in towns and villages who trusted in experience and traditional wisdom. A striking work in the corpus is the *Epidemics*, in which the physician travels from place to place recording in strict detail his observations on the progress of various disorders. This is part of the first case in Book 1:

> Severe chill of the extremities which were only warmed up with difficulty. Bowels disordered, the stools mixed with bile, scanty, unmixed, thin and smarting. They often made the patient get up. Urine either thin, colourless, uncooked and scanty or thick with a light deposit, not forming well, but with a crude [lit. raw] and untimely deposit.

This use of observation may be compared with Thucydides' famous description of a plague in Athens in 430 BC (*Histories* 2.47-54), which considers social effects as well as symptoms.

Medical schools grew up, notably at Kos (the base of Hippokrates), Alexandria and Kroton in southern Italy. Doctors travelled as much as other professionals (see the introduction to Part Four) and a big name could make a large impact. At an early date (6th century BC), Demokedes from Kroton travelled to Aigina, Athens, and then to the court of the tyrant Polykrates on Samos, whence he was taken as a captive to Persia. There he outshone the doctors of the much more ancient Egyptian system[2] who were trying to cure the king (Herodotos 3.125-36). Another example, from the 2nd century AD, is Galen, who went from his home of Pergamon in western Asia Minor to Rome, where he treated the emperor Marcus Aurelius. Clearly, the famous names and the conflicting theory were for the rich who could afford to select their physician. For most people, doctors were simply skilled people of the village, male or female, who were known by reputation to be effective. In the case of the Romans, when Greek doctors first made an impact there in the late 3rd/early 2nd centuries BC, they were treated with distrust by traditionalists who preferred the local folk remedies.

At an earlier date, there were the mythological doctors Podaleirios and Machaon in Homer's *Iliad*, who treated the wounds of warriors. Elsewhere, there was a supernatural element in medicine; Apollo was the god of healing and of plague; in mythological healing, he was joined by Cheiron the centaur; and in mythological and cult healing his son Asklepios, who appears to have come from Thessaly in northern Greece, has a special importance. Under his protection, healing included incubation in temples, such as those in the complex at Epidauros, which supplied gymnasia, baths and the theatre for the healing of the whole person. Incubation entailed sleeping in the temple and receiving healing dreams. When cured, thankful worshippers dedicated models of the affected parts, as do the pious in the modern world. Gods of the underworld played a part as well as the gods of Olympus: Asklepios himself came partly into this category, hence his association with snakes, the creatures of the earth.

There is a comic description of the experience of incubation in the *Wealth* of Aristophanes (lines 647-770).

Herbs and potions, locally gathered by village experts or prescribed by the great doctors, were clearly related to the normal diet of the people in a way that many modern drugs are not. There is much on the medical uses of plants and animals in Pliny's *Natural History*.

While Hippokrates is a somewhat shadowy figure, Galen is totally different. Vivian Nutton, drawing on an extensive acquaintance with his works, writes here and elsewhere on personal opinions which Galen offers at length with much detail and anecdote. Galen influenced medical thought well beyond the Middle Ages.[3] While famous for his dissections – often performed in public – and views on anatomy and organs, he also entered philosophical debate. I mention only a small instance here, which is redolent of Plato, and is echoed at a somewhat lower level in Athenaeus, in whose book Galen is almost certainly a character.[4]

In the early 4th century, Plato's character Socrates is made to say that there are various intellectual skills which excel corresponding skills relating to the body. In each category, 'Socrates' continues, there may be a further division into skills which are genuine and skills which are meretricious. In the case of the body, if any disorder is to be corrected, the genuine skill is that of the doctor, who will effect a cure, however unpleasant, while the meretricious is that of the cook, a mere flatterer, who will produce something that tastes good but does no good to the body.[5] In the 2nd century AD, Galen, in his *On the Therapeutic Method* 1.3-4, denounced the luxurious lives of the rich who disported themselves in public places with gambling, sex, bathing, drinking and profligate celebrations at *symposia*. Such people when well, let alone ill, were incapable of selecting the best doctor, says Galen; instead, they chose fawning flatterers who prescribed cold drinks, baths, and anything to please.[6]

This moralising tone is found in some of Galen's polemic, but is by no means a universal feature. Elizabeth Craik notes that the Hippokratics considered taste and enjoyment in food irrelevant (Chapter 25). Galen, however, has no objection to saying that the *skaros* (the parrotfish) is considered the best of the rockfish 'for pleasure', i.e. for taste (6.718 Kühn), though in other passages nutrition is preferred over pleasure.

Other important medical authors were Celsus (1st century AD, writing in Latin), Dioskorides (1st century AD, writing in Greek) and Soranos (2nd century AD, writing in Greek). Like Galen, they brought Greek medicine to the city of Rome which received them with both adulation and suspicion. Oribasios (4th century AD, writing in Greek) has little to contribute beyond the (valuable) quotation of earlier authorities.[7]

J.W.

Notes

1. For broad treatments of ancient medicine see L. Edelstein *Ancient Medicine* (Baltimore, 1967); J. Scarborough *Roman Medicine* (London, 1969); E.D. Phillips *Greek Medicine* (London, 1973). Diet plays a small part in the last two. Edelstein discusses dietetics at 303-16. On the contribution of Diphilos of Siphnos to dietetics see J. Scarborough 'Diphilus of Siphnos and Hellenistic Medical Dietetics', *Journal of the History of Medicine and Allied Sciences* 25 (1970), 194-201.

2. For a comparison between the Egyptian, Babylonian and Greek systems, see 'The Distinctive Hellenism of Greek Medicine', in Edelstein (n. 1), 367-97.

3. See V. Nutton *From Democedes to Harvey* (London, 1988, chapters 1-3).

4. Nutton (n. 3), 317-8.

5. Plato *Gorgias* 463e-66a.

6. This work is available in a translation and commentary by R.J. Hankinson as *Galen: On the Therapeutic Method, Books I and II* (Oxford, 1991). On philosophy in medicine see further Edelstein (n. 1), 349-66.

7. Many of the Hippokratic works are available in English in the Loeb edition (ed. W.H.S. Jones, E.T. Withington, P. Potter (Cambridge Mass. and London, 1923)) but Galen is not. See also G.E.R. Lloyd (ed.), *Hippocratic Writings* (Penguin, Harmondsworth, 1978), which includes a lengthy introduction.

❖ 25 ❖

HIPPOKRATIC DIAITA

Elizabeth Craik

It may be appropriate to begin by explaining that my interest in Greek diet has a personal as well as a professional source. The personal source is this: first, when my children embraced vegetarianism, I found that many passages in Greek literature, especially Aristophanic comedy, were illumined by an unexpected new light: I now knew just what chickpeas were, and various ways of cooking them. And secondly, when I moved with my family to a house previously occupied by a homeopathic doctor, who grew many of his own medicinal specifics, I found that herbs such as lovage and hyssop, previously mere names of esoteric items known to Hippokrates and Theophrastos, became a familiar part of my own culinary repertoire. The professional source is that I have long had an interest in Hippokrates, stemming from my work on the island of Kos; that I more recently supervised the dissertation of Mark Grant (another contributor to this volume) on Oribasios; and that I am currently preparing a chapter on diet and dietetics for a general history of the Greek world (Routledge).

Diaita and terminology

To the Hippokratic writers, diet is an important part of regimen *diaita*. Several treatises investigate matters of *diaita* – in general, in health, or in acute illness (*Vict.* 1-4, *Acut.*, *Salubr.* – Hippokratic works are cited by abbreviated titles, translations of which are given at the end of this chapter). One of these treatises (*Vict.* 4) deals with dreams. A quotation will indicate its tenor:

> If [in dreams] trees are shedding their leaves, there is damage [in the body] from moist and cold causes; if they are leafy but without fruit, from hot and dry causes. In the former case, one must promote hotness and dryness by types of regimen; in the latter, coldness and wetness... When rivers are unusual, they indicate an abnormal state in the blood: high water an excess, low water a deficiency. One must seek increase in the case of the latter, and decrease in the case of the former... Springs and cisterns indicate a problem relating to the bladder: it should be purged by diuretics. A troubled sea indicates disease in the stomach; it should be purged by light, soft aperients...
>
> (*Vict.* 4.90).

From this, the character of the work is evident. The idea of four qualities – hot, cold, wet, dry – is pervasive; and sympathetic magic is not far away in a scheme where the condition of sea, stream and other natural waters is supposed to reflect the condition of body fluids and physical functions. Here and elsewhere, *diaita* as regimen, way of life, embraces diet, exercise, baths and emetics. Hippokratic medical *diaita* is envisaged as bringing health, security and nourishment to replace the primitive conditions of trouble, disease and death (*VM* 3 *fin.*). But medical regimen brings its own suffering: exercise is regularly *ponos*, 'ordeal' or physical hardship; and the systematic purging of the bowels by emetics could hardly have been comfortable.

Diaita then is diet, but not just diet. The word for nourishment, *trophe*, is more specific to food. Any expression linking the two words (as in *VM* 3) is not a hendiadys, but involves two ideas, related but distinct. (This passage occurs in an excursus on the evolution of human diet, and its differentiation from animal fodder: originally, in the days of food gathering, before the advent of agricultural cultivation, the human diet was subject to the casual availability of 'fruit, bark, and grass' – a description of an unusually inglorious Golden Age.) The Hippokratic treatise entitled 'On Food' (*Alim.*) resembles the Hippokratic aphorisms, containing a series of pithy and inconsequential maxims, incorporating many commonsense observations, alongside various crude notions. One sentence from the end of that treatise expresses the common Hippokratic faith in the value of moist food: 'moisture is the vehicle of food' – 'gravy makes the food go down' (*Alim.* 54). The treatise 'On the Use of the Moist' (*Liqu.*) deals at length with external application of different fluids to the body.

Hippokrates and modern ideas

The idea that health, diet and physical fitness are allied is prevalent in the late 20th century. In antiquity, it is not peculiar to the Hippokratics, though it receives its fullest expression in them. Plato commonly makes an association between the practice of medicine and activities of the gymnasium. Other Hippokratic ideas with a modern air are: the value of preventive medicine (that one ought to have examined the patient in health before treating him in sickness – see especially the treatises on regimen); the importance of environmental health (that a study of local conditions is a prerequisite for medical treatment of the populace – see especially the treatise on 'Airs, Waters and Places' – *Aer.*); the exigencies of medical ethics (see especially the doctors' oath – *Jusj.*, and the treatises on the surgery and medical decorum – *Medic.*, *Decent.*); and, finally, the validity of homeopathic principles.

The last is not surprising, in that these principles were formulated (by Hahnemann (1939) in 1835) on the basis of a reading of Hippokrates. The most important elements, apart from the core belief that 'like cures like', are these: first, the patient is an individual made up of body, mind and spirit; secondly, disease is literally dis-ease, or physical disharmony, rather than being a matter of clinical findings; thirdly, drugs and medical intervention must aim to restore harmony, rather than act as lethal weapons against disease; fourthly, the body can mount its own defence against infections, withstanding them by its own vital force.

But we must not exaggerate the modernity of the Hippokratics, and the ensuing sections have more to say on differences from than on similarities with modern views on diet.

Hippokratic balance

(a) *Balance for the individual.* The idea that we are what we eat, or rather that what we are conditions what we ought to eat, and that what we eat affects how we function, is much in evidence. The Hippokratic writers concern themselves with the right balance for the individual. All qualities in foods as in other things are relative. Good things are not absolutely good, but good for the individual's condition. Young people have different needs from the old (*Alim.* 40); men different needs from women. This is an aspect of the view that different qualities are inherent in different individuals:

> A child is made up of moist and warm elements, because he is composed of these and developed in them... The males of all species are warmer and drier and the females moister and colder for these reasons: originally each sex came from this state and took increase from it; but after birth men use a more strenuous regimen so that they are warmed and dried, whereas women use a more moist and relaxed regimen...   (*Vict.* 1.33-34)

Customary practice too determines the appropriate balance: it is important to maintain a regular routine, for instance not varying the number of meals regularly taken each day:

> Some people, taking lunch when the practice does not agree with them, at once become heavy and sluggish physically and mentally, beset by yawning, drowsiness and thirst... On the other hand, if someone who has adopted the practice of lunching – and it does agree with him – doesn't get his lunch, as soon as the time passes he at once suffers terrible weakness, trembling and faintness...   (*VM* 10)

The seasons have a crucial effect on the requisite balance: in winter, to secure a dry and hot body it is better to eat wheaten bread, roast meat and few vegetables; whereas in summer it is appropriate to eat barley cake, boiled meat and softer foods (*Vict.* 3.58). And location plays an important part: southern countries have dry and hot inhabitants, who must eat correspondingly.

So, in *On Nourishment*, milk, wine and meat are sometimes beneficial, sometimes not, 'according to location and custom' (*Alim.* 32). And cheese is described as beneficial or harmful, according to the individual's digestion and metabolism:

Cheese does not harm all people alike, and there are some people who can eat as much of it as they like without the slightest adverse effects; indeed it is a wonderfully nourishing food for the people it agrees with. But others suffer dreadfully... (*VM* 20)

(b) *Balance in physical condition.* To achieve physical equilibrium, according to the Hippokratics, different functions of the body had to be carefully balanced. Most strikingly, surfeit and abstinence or repletion and depletion had to be kept in equipoise:

All diseases which are generated by repletion are cured by depletion, and all which arise from depletion are cured by repletion; all which arise from exertion are cured by inactivity, and all which arise from inactivity are cured by exertion...

(*Nat. Hom.* 9)

(c) *Balance of elements in diaita.* The balance of food with exercise, bathing and emetics was crucially important:

A regime of this sort is bad – when one gives the body more food, whether solid or liquid, than the body can bear; and fails to balance the large quantity of food with any exercise...

(*Flat.* 7)

I have discovered ways to diagnose what is the dominant element in the body: if exercise predominates over food, or food over exercise; how to put each situation right and to ensure health...   (*Vict.* 3 *init.*)

(d) *Balance in food.* The question of balance, harmony and mixture in food specifically is vital. Food contains qualities (such as bitterness) which if presented 'unadulterated and strong' are bad. Cooking mingles these elements and so helps break down bad qualities.

From such foods, ingested in quantity by a person, there arises no upset...but strength, growth and nourishment, for no other reason than that they are well mingled and have nothing in them that is unmixed and strong, but are a single unified whole...

(*Vict.*1.2)

Qualities in foods are analogous to humours in the body: too much of any single one is bad, and a good mix is essential. 'Strong' food is to be avoided;

'soft' food is to be preferred. The 'power' of foods and drinks must be monitored:

> One must have knowledge of how to reduce the power of those foods which are intrinsically strong, and skilfully to add strength to the weak, as the opportunity presents itself in each case...
>
> (*Vict.* 1.2)

It has been seen that the Hippokratics were consistently concerned with balance. But this balance was rather theoretical. Whereas there is much about dietary theory, there is little about dietary practice. The Hippokratic idea of a 'balanced diet' bears no resemblance to what we understand by that phrase today. And yet the actual diet regularly followed seems to have been balanced in the modern sense, achieving – more by accident than design, in the absence of any knowledge of food groups and food values – a good combination of proteins (especially pulses, fish and cheese), carbohydrates (especially filling wholemeal bread) and fats (without too much animal fat), and an adequate supply of minerals and vitamins (especially from fresh and dried fruit).

Hippokratic attitudes to eating

(a) *Digestion.* The Hippokratic doctors took a great interest in the digestive process, which they aided and abetted, or subverted, by constant use of emetics and purges. Such systematic purging had a similar vogue earlier in this century, when inner cleanliness came first, and many medicine chests contained a constant supply of such violently effective purges as 'Gregory's Mixture'. The Hippokratics were equally concerned with drugs to achieve the opposite effect, that is with loosening as well as bind-ing agents: 'medicines which purge and medicines which bind' (*de Arte* 6).

In the case of foods, as in the case of drugs, the main classification was into those with a binding and those with a laxative effect. Lists of foods for the table (*Vict.* 2.45-55) and ingredients in recipe cures (*Morb.* 3.17) alike lay emphasis on diuretic, laxative or other digestive virtues. One may suspect that digestive upsets stemming from poor personal and domestic hygiene, or inadequate facilities for food storage and preparation, were more common than those resulting from eating the 'wrong' foods. The

Hippokratics advocated cleanliness in the medical person and surgery, but of course without awareness of the bacteriological reasons for it; and did not extend the recommendation of hygiene beyond their own immediate professional requirements and standards.

The preoccupation with the digestive process was not accompanied by any sophisticated physiological understanding of it. Jouanna reasonably writes of the '*limites de la physiologie hippocratique*' and comments on the vague and metaphorical language applied to digestion.

(b) *Taste and enjoyment.* To the Hippokratics, this was totally irrelevant. A glance at the descriptive words applied to the nouns *diaita, diaitema* (regimen) and to the verb *diaitao* (to follow a regimen) in Kühn and Fleischer (1986-9) shows no hint that a chosen regime might be enjoyable: such words as 'hot', 'cold', 'for summer', 'for winter' predominate; a regime might be 'weak' or 'strong', 'studied' or 'careless'; but never, it seems, pleasurable.

In the case of particular foods, such comparisons as are made are between foods of similar type: cereals such as wheat and barley (wheat being stronger and more nourishing); or animal flesh such as pork and goat meat; or different cuts of fish (*Vict.* 2.52).

(c) *Preparation and cooking.* Despite an evident awareness of the desirability of exercising choice in eating habits (as seen in all the stress, noted earlier, on achieving the right balance of foodstuffs for the individual's inherent condition and current situation; on preparing food in an appropriate fashion for the season etc.), there is very little practical information on cooking methods. The doctors have clearly no first-hand knowledge of this. Fresh foodstuffs are preferred, but for aridly theoretical reasons:

> All fresh foods provide more strength than the alternatives, for
> this reason, that they are closer to the living creature...
> (Vict. 2.56)

They are aware in the broadest terms of differences between different methods of baking bread: 'in open or closed ovens' *Vict.* 3.79); and of the differences between food prepared in a rich sauce, or in vinegar.

On the whole, their approach is austere: foods which are fancy and not homogeneous in character are castigated: 'Dissimilar foods disagree' (*Flat.*7). 'Strong' food is harmful, whereas food which is 'sloppy' (*VM* 5-6) and where the elements are 'cooked and mixed' (*VM* 18) is beneficial in health and, especially, in sickness. Barley gruels and porridges serve as an ubiquitous standby and panacea.

It is fair to say that Hippokrates was a theoretical dietician; an armchair menu-maker who knew nothing of the kitchen. But no doubt he would have agreed with Plato in regarding cooking as a mere 'knack' (*tribe*), whereas medicine of course was a supreme 'craft' (*techne* : *VM* 1 etc.).

Abbreviations

Full, translated titles of the Hippokratic treatises are as follows:

Acut.	Regimen in Acute Illness		*Liqu.*	On the Moist
Aer.	Airs, Waters and Places		*Medic.*	On the Surgery
Alim.	On Food		*Morb.*	On Diseases
de Arte	On the Art		*Nat. Hom.*	On the Nature of Man
Decent.	On Decorum		*Salubr.*	On Health
Flat.	On Winds		*VM*	On Ancient Medicine
Jusj.	Oath		*Vict.*	On Regimen

Bibliography

Editions and translations of the Hippokratic writings:

Complete works:
ed. with French trans. E. Littré (Paris, 1839-61);
ed. with Latin trans. F.Z. Ermerins (Leipzig and Paris, 1859-64).

Selections:
ed. with English trans. W.H.S. Jones, E.T. Withington et al. (London and Cambridge Mass., 1923-).

Selections in English trans.:
G.E. Lloyd *Hippocratic Writings* (Harmondsworth, 1978).

VM ed. A.J. Festugière (Paris, 1948).

Secondary works:

Craik E.M., 1980 *The Dorian Aegean* (London), ch. 6.

Craik E.M., (forthcoming) 'Diet, *diaita* and dietetics', in C.A. Powell (ed.) *The Greek World* (London).

Edelstein L., 1967 *Ancient Medicine* (Baltimore).

Hahnemann, S.C.F., 1939 *The Chronic Diseases: their peculiar nature and their homoeopathic cure* (1835, trans. L.H. Tafel, Calcutta, 1939).

Joly R., 1966 *Le niveau de la science hippocratique* (Paris).

Jouanna J., 1992 *Hippocrate* (Paris).

Kühn J-H. & Fleischer U., 1986-89 *Index Hippocraticus* (Göttingen).

❖ 26 ❖

FOOD AND BLOOD IN HIPPOKRATIC GYNAECOLOGY

Helen King

Mᴇᴅɪᴄᴀʟ texts form one of the many areas of ancient culture within which the position of mankind, both within the world and over time, is discussed. Baudy in Chapter 13 demonstrates how a cereal diet came to be opposed to primitive patterns of food consumption, taking on a range of symbolic associations. When medical texts discuss diet, it is within this wider context of food as an indicator of social and cultural status. If agriculture and a cereal diet characterize civilized humanity, how should diet be altered in different types of disease? Should men's diet differ from that appropriate to women?

In the Hippokratic texts, and in more general defences of medicine as a *techne* that date from the 5th century BC,[1] medicine becomes an indicator of civilization, as it moves into a position analogous to that of agriculture in the ongoing process by which the position of mankind is raised above that of the beasts, coming to approach that of the gods themselves. The culture-hero Prometheus, in Aeschylus' play of that title, describes how medicine is the greatest of the *technai*, and how he himself taught men how 'to drive away savage diseases'.[2] An inscription of the early 4th century BC

Medicine and Civilization

brings the deities of healing and agriculture, Asklepios and Demeter, into conjunction, stating that the god's first residence in Athens was the Eleusinion.[3] It was Demeter who was supposed to have brought to Athens the fruits which inaugurated man's separation from the life of the beasts.[4] Increasingly complex variations on this analogy endure in the classical world; thus Celsus, a writer of the 1st century AD, says that agriculture provides food for the healthy, medicine health for the sick.[5]

Another aspect of the analogy is that corn 'tames' human nature, and agriculture 'tames' corn,[6] while medicine 'tames' savage diseases. In the Hippokratic *Pseudepigrapha*, Hippokrates, as founder of the medical *techne*, 'purges the earth and the sea, not of the race of beasts, but of bestial and savage diseases, scattering the aid of Asclepios just as Triptolemos scattered the seeds of Demeter.'[7] This passage recalls how the dying Herakles in Sophokles' play *Trachiniai* claims to have worn himself out purging the sea and the woods of wild beasts, on behalf of the Greeks. The sons of Asklepios, Machaon and Podaleirios, later thought to specialize respectively in wounds and diet, are also described as 'healers of savage diseases.'[8] It is of course a 'savage disease' which attacks Herakles in the *Trachiniai*; Herakles encapsulates in his person the point that, even after the beasts have been tamed, bestial disease continues to threaten mankind.[9]

The healer thus becomes a culture-hero in the mould of Herakles, bringing mankind to civilization through the defeat of the bestial. Disease is assimilated to the beasts, and vanquished by the sons of Asklepios, by Hippokrates and by Prometheus.

Medicine, like agriculture, tames, civilizes, raises man above the beasts; both use food to improve the lot of mankind. In the Hippokratic text *On Ancient Medicine*, which Craik also discusses in Chapter 25, it is argued that men and beasts used to share a diet of raw fruit, vegetables and grass. This savage and unsuitable diet of raw, unmixed foods led to disease, until it was gradually abandoned and a 'human' diet established.[10]

In Greek thought, the normal human diet is closely tied to the normal human experience: illness, ageing, death. Outside medical literature, particularly in accounts of the customs of geographically or historically distant peoples, we find examples of groups who manipulate their diet in an attempt to change their human nature; from the Fish-Eaters of Diodorus Siculus, whose simple diet is supposed to protect them from disease, to Herodotos' long-lived Ethiopians who avoid agricultural products and wine, but eat meat spontaneously produced from the table of the sun.[11] In medical texts, dietary variation aims merely to restore the normal human experience when it is disrupted by disease. The doctor does not simply specify foods to be eaten and foods to be avoided; he gives detailed advice on the preparation of foods.

Women and blood

Where women are concerned, the most significant point for Hippokratic medicine is their preponderance of blood. Elizabeth Craik describes in her chapter how, medically, women are often thought to be moist and cold; in the group of three Hippokratic texts known as the *Diseases of Women*, they are more often seen as moist and hot. All the Hippokratic writers would, however, agree that they are moist, dominated by blood. Aristotle describes how blood is the final form taken by food; blood, he also says, is the food of the body.[12] Blood is thus essential to life, but only to mortal life. The Homeric gods neither eat *sitos* nor drink wine, so they are bloodless and immortal. When a god's flesh is cut, it is *ichor*, described only as 'immortal blood,' which flows.[13] From the same diet as that of men, women produce more blood because of the nature of their flesh, softer and more spongy in texture than that of a man, which absorbs more moisture.[14]

The three books of the *Diseases of Women* contain the bulk of the recipes known to us from Hippokratic medicine; sections read so much like a recipe book that it has been argued – for example, by Aline Rousselle – that they derive from a female tradition of home remedies handed down from mother to daughter.[15] Diet is far from being the only method of treatment; in one long section, fourteen expulsive pessaries and two drinks to expel the afterbirth are followed by, 'Another expulsive. Hold the woman under her armpits and shake her vigorously.'[16] Nevertheless, a formidable battery of recipes lies at the centre of the treatment, the form of these ranging from brief lists of ingredients for a drink, to highly detailed descriptions of preparing, mixing and cooking. As in the recipes in Apicius, quantities are rarely specified; although sometimes dry or liquid measures, or proportions, are given – for example, four parts of narcissus oil to one part of each of the other ingredients[17] – and sometimes the amounts of certain ingredients are clearly stated, such as 'take five beetles and fifteen cuttlefish eggs.'[18] I would argue that the reason why it is in gynaecology that 'dietary prescriptions' are most utilized derives from Hippokratic theories about the origin of blood in general, and the amount of blood in the female body in particular.[19] Many of women's health problems are presented as the result of excess blood which, for a variety of reasons, is unable to leave the body; such problems are particularly amenable to treatment which restricts or controls the food intake, thus influencing the amount of blood produced in the body.

Eating and blood production in the female body are explicitly linked in theory, prescription and case history. Where a woman's menstrual periods are heavier and thicker than they should be, this will be made worse by a bout of heavy feasting.[20] At menarche, the combination of 'food and the growth of the body' leads to the first production of excess, menstrual blood.[21] The daughter of Philon, in a case history in the *Epidemics*, had a beneficial nosebleed which removed her excess blood, but then died after 'dining inopportunely' overloaded her system with blood once more.[22]

Corrective recipes

The dominant oppositions in the gynaecological texts are wet versus dry, hot versus cold and, in the case of the recipes, gentle or mild versus sharp, pungent or salty.[23] If a woman is too dry, she is given baths, boiled food, and watered wine: if too wet, 'the opposites.'[24] In one chapter of the *Diseases of Women* a drying diet is prescribed for a woman who is too wet, a condition revealed not only by phlegmatic menses but also by copious and sticky saliva. She is given vapour baths – aromatic substances thrown on hot ashes under a cloth – and emetics, while her womb is purged with pessaries and her diet kept as dry as possible, with very little to drink. Frequent exercise contributes to the removal of the excess fluid.[25] After a menstrual period successfully free of phlegm, she is instructed to sleep with her husband and have plenty of aromatic, astringent fumigations to her womb. If the seed does not fall out, she is to cross her legs and stay still, and not eat that day. If the seed stays in place for two more days, she must abstain from solid foods and baths, but can drink unsalted barley water two or three times a day. This regimen can be followed for up to six or seven days after intercourse. When solid food is reintroduced, the only *sitos* allowed is wheat bread or barley bread. For meats, she is permitted pigeon, roast not boiled and domesticated not wild. As for fish, she is allowed only that which settles the stomach, while bitter vegetables are forbidden. This is an interesting set of prescriptions. Roast meat is seen as 'dry' and, in view of the role of medicine and agriculture in the conquest of the beasts, the use of domesticated birds is perhaps significant. Furthermore, pigeon is the second 'driest' bird in the foods listed in the Hippokratic text *Regimen*.[26] This is not only a 'dry' diet, but also a 'tame' one.

Barley water, the first item of 'food' to be introduced after the fast, is one of the mildest foods in the repertoire; it also features in a fever after childbirth in which the finest flour of pearl barley is given in a drink, it being specified that if the woman is very weak indeed then she should take it in cold water.[27] The diet for this fever is not, however, a totally 'cold' one; the main element is a mixture of pomegranate juice mixed with lentil flour, then cooked with cumin, salt, oil and vinegar and given to the patient when cold. Lentils are regarded as a food which heats the body[28] while pomegranates may operate at a symbolic level, their many seeds promoting future fertility. A recipe explicitly to promote conception consists of juice of pomegranate seeds mixed with the milk of a woman suckling a male child.[29]

Drugs

Only occasionally are these recipes explicitly called *pharmaka*, drugs. For example, the *pharmakon*-elements for ulceration of the womb after childbirth involve not only pork fat applied to the womb by finger, but also lint seed grilled and chopped, with white poppy chopped up with barley flour. The patient is also given 'goat's cheese from which you have scraped off the dirt and the salt,' mixed with butter and fine barley flour.[30] The text then instructs the doctor to take an equal amount of the *pharmakon*, the cheese and the flour, and give it to the fasting patient to drink, in wine. The pork fat ointment is regarded as a *pharmakon*; so is the lint seed with poppy;

but the cheese, butter and barley flour mixture is not. This text is also of interest for the way in which the author regards 'women's remedies' – *gynaikeia* – for the same condition; at the end of the chapter, we read, 'and amongst the *gynaikeia*, give whatever works best'. This appears to suggest that the male author, rather than taking over and repeating women's remedies, is trying to create something new and different in his *pharmakon*; however, he does not go so far as to deny the efficacy of the traditional female cures.

For ulceration of the womb, the remedies are explicitly described here and elsewhere as *malthakos*, soft and gentle, a quality which is also that of the normal, healthy female flesh.[31] What is to be avoided is anything *drimus*: sharp, stinging, pungent. The softest meats are described as being fish, birds and hare.[32] Where the aim is to expel unwanted matter, however, the pungent category comes into use. Pessaries to expel retained blood are 'stinging,' being made of beetles, myrrh and rose oil.[33] The main role of beef in these texts is, incidentally, when it is inserted as a pessary for ulceration.[34] Beef is not recommended as a food for women; according to *Regimen*, it is strong, drying, and hard to digest, because it has thick, plentiful blood.[35] Women, full of blood by their very nature, would thus be unwise to eat such food.

Diet can also be used on a principle akin to that of 'sympathetic magic'. One way of encouraging conception is to give both the woman and her husband the same diet as a woman in childbed, with the exception of garlic, onion, pea soup (*etnos*) and asafoetida, all of which are wind-producing expulsives appropriate to a woman who is still expelling her lochial flow, but not to one who needs to retain her husband's seed.[36]

Finally, it is worth mentioning that the culinary vocabulary is used, by analogy, of abnormal manifestations of the female body. A discharge can be 'like raw egg' or 'like the juices of cooked meat,'[37] while abnormal lochia or menses are 'like water in which bloody meat has been washed.'[38] The mouth of the womb, when closed, feels hard, 'like a wild fig.'[39] Not only are women what they eat; they are themselves commodified as food, of a very specific kind.

Notes

1. A good definition of a *techne* is that given by Ferrari and Vegetti (1983, 202): 'any practical activity that required intellectual competence as well as manual dexterity, was based on scientific knowledge, produced results that it was possible to verify, and was governed by well-defined rules that could be transmitted through teaching.' The Hippokratic text *Lex* 1 (Littré 4.638) claims that medicine is the most distinguished of the *technai*.
2. Aeschylus *Prometheus* 478-483.
3. IG II² 4960a.
4. Isokrates *Panegyricus* 28.
5. Celsus *De medicina*, preface, 1. See in general King (1986).
6. Detienne (1972, 29-35); Vernant (1979, 62 and 69).
7. Littré 9.314.
8. Sophokles *Trachiniai* 1011-12; Eustathius' commentary on the *Iliad* 463.26 ff and 859.42 ff. On the sons of Asklepios, see for example Herodas, *Mimes* 4.8.
9. Sophokles *Tr.* 975 and 1030.
10. For discussions of *On Ancient Medicine* (*VM*; Littré 1.570-637), see Lain Entralgo (1944); Miller (1949) and (1955); Herter (1963); Dierauer (1977, 28).
11. Diodorus Siculus 3.17.5; Herodotos *Histories* 3.16-26. Cf. Pausanias 6.26.2; see also Rosellini and Said (1978); Hartog (1980).
12. Aristotle *De partibus animalium* 651a 14-15; 650a 34-5; Byl (1980, 41).
13. Homer *Iliad* 5.339-342.
14. *Diseases of women* (hereafter *Mul.*) 1.1 (Littré 8.10-12); Hanson (1990).
15. Rousselle (1980).
16. *Mul.* 1.78 (Littré 8.180).
17. *Mul.* 1.84 (Littré 8.204).
18. *Mul.* 1.84 (Littré 8.208-210); see also 1.78 (Littré 8.182).
19. King (1987).
20. *Mul.* 1.5 (Littré 8.28).
21. *Diseases of young girls* (*Virg.*, Littré 8.466).
22. *Epidemics* 1.2.9 (Littré 2.658); King (1989).
23. *Mul.* 2.119 (Littré 8.260). On polarities in Greek medical and philosophical thought, see Lloyd (1966).
24. *Mul.* 1.16 (Littré 8.54).
25. *Mul.* 1.11 (Littré 8.44-48).
26. *Regimen* (hereafter *Vict.*) 2.47 (Littré 6.544).
27. *Mul.* 1.52 (Littré 8.112).
28. *Vict.* 2.45 (Littré 6.544).
29. *Mul.* 1.75 (Littré 8.166).
30. *Mul.* 1.64 (Littré 8.132).
31. *Mul.* 1.1 (Littré 8.10); 1.66 (Littré 8.140).
32. *Mul.* 2.119 (Littré 8.260).
33. *Mul.* 1.74 (Littré 8.158).
34. *Mul.* 1.90 (Littré 8.214-6); 2.173 (Littré 8.354).
35. *Vict.* 2.46 (Littré 6.544).
36. *Mul.* 1.75 (Littré 8.164). It is instructive here to compare the belief, in Ayurvedic medicine, that wind-producing foods cause miscarriage by disturbing the baby's security in the womb; see Homas (1983).
37. *Mul.* 2.119 (Littré 8.260); 2.115 (Littré 8.248); 2.121 (Littré 8.262); 2.122 (Littré 8.264).
38. *Mul.* 1.30 (Littré 8.74); 1.61 (Littré 8.124).
39. *Mul.* 2.163 (Littré 8.342).

Bibliography

Byl, S., 1980 *Recherches sur les grands traités biologiques d'Aristote* (Brussels).

Cameron, A., 1989 *History as Text* (London).

Corsi, P. & Weindling, P., 1983 *Information Sources in the History of Science and Medicine* (London).

Detienne, M., 1972 *Les jardins d'Adonis* (Paris).

Detienne, M. & Vernant, J.-P., 1979 *La cuisine du sacrifice en pays grec* (Paris).

Dierauer, U. 1977 *Tier und Mensch im Denken der Antike* (Amsterdam).

Ferrari, G.A. & Vegetti, M., 1983 'Science, technology and medicine in the classical tradition', in Corsi and Weindling (1983), 197-220.

Halperin, D. et al., (eds) 1990 *Before Sexuality* (Princeton).

Hanson, A.E., 1990 'The medical writers' woman' in Halperin et al. (1990), 309-337.

Hartog, F., 1980 *Le miroir d'Herodote* (Paris).

Herter, H., 1963 'Die kulturhistorische Theorie der Hippokratic Schrift von den alten Medizin', *Maia* 15, 464-83.

Homas, H., 1983 'A question of balance: Asian and British women's perceptions of food during pregnancy', in Murcott (1983), 73-83.

King, H., 1986 'Food as symbol in classical Greece', *History Today* 36 (ix), 35-9.

King, H., 1987 'Sacrificial blood: the role of the *amnion* in ancient gynecology', *Helios* 13, 117-26.

King, H., 1988 'The daughter of Leonides: reading the Hippocratic corpus', in Cameron (1988), 11-32.

Lain Entralgo, P., 1944 'El escrito 'de prisca medicina' y su valor historiografico', *Emerita* 12, 1-28.

Littré, E. 1839-61 *Les oeuvres completes d'Hippocrate*, 10 vols (Paris; reprinted 1961, Amsterdam).

Lloyd, G.E.R., 1966 *Polarity and Analogy* (Cambridge).

Miller, H.W., 1949 '"On Ancient Medicine" and the origin of medicine', *Transactions of the American Philological Association* 80, 187-202.

Miller, H.W. 1955 'Techne and discovery in "On Ancient Medicine"', *Transactions of the American Philological Association* 86, 51-62.

Murcott, A., (ed.) 1983 *The Sociology of Food and Eating* (Aldershot).

Rosellini, M. & Said, S. 1978 'Usages de femmes et autres 'nomoi' chez les 'sauvages' d'Herodote: essai de lecture structurale', *Annuario Scuola Normale Superiore di Pisa* 8, 949-1005.

Rousselle, A. 1980 'Observation féminine et idéologie masculine: le corps de la femme d'apres les médecins grecs', *Annales E.S.C.* 35, 1089-1115.

Vernant, J.-P., 1979 'A la table des hommes', in Detienne and Vernant (1979), 37-132.

GALEN AND THE TRAVELLER'S FARE

Vivian Nutton

Galen on diet

GALEN of Pergamon (129-199/216 AD) was a great traveller. Between 150 and the end of his life his wanderings took him from his home in Pergamon up the Nile, to the Dead Sea, to Cyprus, Greece, the Balkans, and finally to Italy. It was Galen, particularly in his *Hygiene*, known in Latin as *De sanitate tuenda*, who formulated what were to be the rules for healthy diet for the Middle Ages and beyond, and whose superabundant verbosity has handicapped all who have sought to understand the complexities of his argument and his character.[1] This chapter represents a series of questions and footnotes rather than a general exposition of Galen's views on diet, in which in general he followed a typical Hippokratic line. Food and diet mattered to him: it was in one sense true that one was what one ate – those who consumed the flesh of foxes, dogs, or even lions were likely to become like them, and he saw nothing incongruous in both writing sympathetically of peasants in Asia Minor forced for lack of anything better to eat horse and donkey meat, and, in more than one passage, dismissing them as being asses, thoroughly brutish in their nature.[2] It is diet, in the widest sense, that will determine whether one's healthy state turns into the praeternatural one of illness. A proper diet will keep one healthy into old age, like Telephos the grammarian, who lived almost to a hundred, or Dr Antiochos, who walked the half mile or so from his house to the Roman forum daily and visited his patients on foot or, if they resided some way off, in a litter or a chariot, even though he was well past eighty.[3] It is not only in times of famine, when the countryside was plundered by the more powerful officials from the city and its inhabitants were forced to eat grass and shrubs, that serious illnesses were liable to break out through malnutrition.[4] One has only to look at the Alexandrians' diet of pulses, lentils, and shellfish, even donkey meat – all washed down with barley beer – and their hot climate to see why one can find there enormous numbers of sufferers from skin diseases. By contrast, there are few such cases among the Germans or the Mysians, and almost none at all among the milk-drinking Scythians.[5] Diet encompasses both food and medicine; drink supplies nutriment in sickness and in health; and by regulating diet the physician can control his patient's propensity to illness.

Galen and the tradition

None of this is particularly new or striking, and the concentration on categorizing foodstuffs according to their effect on bodily humours, and using such terms as sharp or binding, goes back centuries before Galen. One has only to turn to the fragments of Rufus of Ephesos, active two or three generations before Galen, to see how an earlier Hippokratic could make use of exactly the same schema of explanation and of many of the same data. If one reads Rufus on how the eating of lettuce or poppy seed can reduce the brain's capacity for memory and swift thought, and then compares it with Galen's own example of taking lettuce at night to combat the multitude of thoughts that disturbed his sleep and prevented him from studying properly, one can then see how the two men are operating within the same Hippokratic tradition and using the same sort of remedies, diets, and explanations.[6] Nor should we be surprised to find Rufus writing on dietetics for the old and for the young, as well as composing a huge work, full of dietetic information, entitled *For the layman* or *For those who have no doctor*, or that in so much of his work he prefigures what Galen has to say in his more extensive dietetic writings.[7]

His own contribution

What then, apart from bulk, does Galen contribute to our understanding of ancient foods as part of diet? In the first place, Galen is, of course, a prime source of information. His dietetic writings, in the sixth volume of Kühn's edition, cover some four hundred pages of Greek, to which one can add the little tract *On slimming diets*, first printed in Greek in 1898, although available in a good Latin translation in print since 1490, and the very many comments he makes throughout his writings on pharmacology, on Hippokratic texts, and on medical therapeutics in general.[8] There may well be more to come, not least in the three books of commentary on Hippokrates, *Airs, waters, and places*, at present being edited for publication.[9] But what were Galen's sources for all this? He was, as is well known, a deeply learned man, with a wide range of interests, medical and non-medical alike. He had a particular interest in Attic comedy, writing a series of tracts specifically on the vocabulary of the comic poets, including the words they used to describe everyday life. Traces of this philological learning are scattered throughout his works – not only can he quote a dozen or so lines from Aristophanes' *Birds* and then Theokritos to illustrate what these authors meant by a lark, or offer a rare line from Aristophanes' *Freighters* (*Holkades*) to justify the spelling of *arakos*, perhaps a form of chickpea, with a kappa, but he takes considerable pains to explain how the terms for foods in the older Attic writers differ from those of modern Athenians or modern Greeks.[10] He is particularly precise about spelling, and the various changes in it over time, but that, as he says, is really of importance only to the etymologist, not to the physician. But, since words matter, the physician at least ought to be aware of the possible confusion of terms over the centuries. Here is Galen using his academic learning as a source for his medical writings.

His sources

Among his dietetic sources, it is, naturally enough, the Hippokratic Corpus that provides him with his main proof texts, but beyond that there are surprises. His main authorities for dietetics are four, Diokles of Karystos, especially his *Hygiene* ; Mnesitheos of Athens, especially his *On Foodstuffs*; Praxagoras of Kos; and his pupil Phylotimos, *On diet*, all authors writing around 300 BC. After this there is a black hole: no author is cited at length, and only four mentioned in passing, until we come to the 2nd century AD, where we have a reminiscence of professor Quintus, snide remarks about the neoterics, and a detailed refutation of the dietetic views of Theon, a gymnastic trainer from Alexandria.[11] What has happened to Hellenistic dietetics? Where, for example, is Diphilos of Siphnos, known to us through Athenaeus, and credited, though for no good reason, with doing for dietetics what his Hellenistic contemporaries did for anatomy and physiology?[12] To those who believe in the authority of Diphilos, or the omniscience of Galen, this omission might seem puzzling. But this pattern of apparent ignorance is not confined to Galen or to his dietetics. It is found in Rufus, in such collections of earlier information as the so-called *Anonymous Parisinus*, the pseudo-Galenic *Introduction to Medicine*, and some papyrus fragments of medical questions and answers. Together they suggest that by about 250 BC, almost certainly in Alexandria, a canon of medical authors had been drawn up that effectively separated the sheep from the goats. Those who passed the test survived; their opinions were recorded in medical doxographies and catechisms, and some of their books, like those quoted by Galen and, later, by Oribasios, continued to circulate. Mnesitheos is still being cited for his views of food and in passages that are not reported in any earlier author by medical scholars in 6th century Alexandria, although whether they took their information directly from him or from an intermediate source is not clear.[13] Those medical writers who failed to gain this classic status, such as Diphilos, had a much harder time of it. Authors would thus in general be aware only of the classics and the writings of contemporaries or near contemporaries, and they had little chance of filling in the gaps in their knowledge. Hellenistic dietetics seem destined, alas, to remain a medical mystery.

His observations

If Galen's written sources turn out to be disappointing, the reverse is true of his own observations. More and more in working on him one is impressed with his ability to see and to notice things: the behaviour of animals, the names of months in Macedonia, and, of course, food habits.[14] It is Galen who tells us about the making of quince jam or of quince tarts exported from Spain to Rome – quince jam, as he says in passing, will keep well.[15] He notes the local varieties of foods – the rye-bread of Thrace and Macedonia, the *melka* of Lombardy, the honey from near the tomb of

Protesilaos outside Troy that crystallized and thickened with keeping — and the ingenious ways in which Egyptian peasants keep their water from becoming quickly tepid as well as improve on the actual quality of the original Nile water.[16] He tells about the olive oil he tasted at Aulon by the Strymon, which was, he remarks, so like the more common Spanish oil he knew from Rome. One would love him to have said more about the local varieties of wine that he knew, and on which he comments that they were totally unknown outside their area, being either all consumed locally or, if exported, failing to travel well and hence giving a false impression of their quality.[17]

Peasant life

Above all, he displays an unusual interest in the food of the peasantry and carefully distinguishes between the peasants in different regions and, secondly, between life in town and country. No other medical, and few agricultural, authors talk about the peasantry to this extent, and the daily life of a subsistence farmer in Thrace is some way beneath the vision of an Athenaeus.[18] In part this is because Galen was a countryman himself. His father owned at least two estates near Pergamon, and Arabic biographers – on what grounds is unclear – say that his ancestors had been land-surveyors in the area.[19] His father had himself carried out experiments with plant-breeding, with plant-selection, and with the adulteration of wine with sulphur to see if it would keep better. Galen had the same experimental attitude, once keeping honey for half a century to see whether it thickened with age (it did), and became bitter (it did not). He talks of going out with his friends on picnics into the countryside of Mysia, and of travelling in Bithynia in search of unusual herbs and even more unusual herbalists.[20] He is aware of the difficulties of life in the country, with the inhabitants reduced in times of famine to eating the oats that they would otherwise have fed to their animals, or even worse, preyed upon by the powerful inhabitants of the towns who made sure that *their* granaries were well stocked.[21] But the fault was not always on one side – when delivering up their corn to town bakers, they would often wet it to increase its weight and their profits; a few hours in the warm sun would soon dry out the corn, but the culprits were usually away before their crimes could be detected.[22]

Town and country

Galen uses the opposition between town and country in two ways. The first is as a counterweight to life in the city. Whether in Rome or Alexandria the result is the same – illness. In Alexandria, the food is bad; a diet of salt fish, beans, lentils and pulses, supplemented by the flesh of vipers, camels, and donkeys; their wine is too thin and watery for the climate; their dates quickly go bad; their pistachio nuts have little nutritional value, however nice they might taste; and as for Egyptian beans, these are best avoided, being indigestible and of no therapeutic value. Those commentators who believed that Hippokrates recommended Egyptian beans and caraway seeds in *Epidemics* II might get away with such nonsense in Asia Minor where such foods are not eaten; the slightest acquaintance with an Alexandrian bean would make that explanation appear ludicrous. In short, says Galen, the text in question must be a forgery, for Hippokrates would not have committed such a prime error of dietetics.[23]

Rome was almost as dangerous: the poor live like peasants, feeding off unleavened bread onto which, the moment it comes out of the oven, they pour honey to make it soft and sweet. Their cheap wine, kept in large amphorae, is awful; and improves only a little if it is decanted quickly into small carafes.[24] The rich suffer the pains of over-indulgence; and their passion for snow-cooled drinks can almost kill them, particularly if they take no exercise. But a drink of wine kept cool by having the flask immersed in cold water is very refreshing, and Galen recommends this for those on military campaign, long journeys, or engaged in public business, governors of cities and provinces – or, still more, their officials, who are the ones who really do the work.[25] City life is a hazard to health – that had been known already to Celsus - not least if one likes fish. The channels that pour away the scourings of fullers, cookshops, baths, and lavatories pollute the river Tiber, as one can see at a glance. One has only to compare the sort of fish caught from the Tiber in Rome with that from the estuary, and with that from a little out to sea, and the difference becomes obvious – and still more so, if one puts a fish from the Nar, a swift-flowing clear stream flowing into the Tiber thirty miles to the North, alongside one from the filthy Tiber in Rome. In size, shape, and savour, there is no need to waste time in judging which is the best, but newcomers to Rome or those who know little about fish should beware of the health hazards. One might be tempted by the very cheapness of the Tiber fish on sale to believe that one had a bargain. Besides, if in a sea like the Pontus, the coastal waters are not always as productive of good fish as one might think, they are still far better than the marshy lagoons of Tuscany, let alone the filthy scourings of the Tiber estuary.[26]

Home and abroad

The contrast between town and country is superimposed on one between home and abroad, between Pergamon and Asia Minor (for that is what Galen, with one possible exception, means when he talks about 'at home') and Rome.[27] Life in Rome has many advantages, not least its water supply, brought in stone aqueducts from the hills around Tivoli, swift flowing, free from all impurities, never too hot or too cold – and just like those back in Pergamon.[28] In general, though, the air in Rome is worse than back home; the food is worse; and although some of the wines are good, they cannot really compare with those of Asia Minor, from Tmolos, Titacaza, Mysian Aigeai, and Perperene.[29] He talks of the experience he had in the hills around Pergamon where, one summer morning, the trees and shrubs were covered with honeydew, Zeus's rain, as the peasants called it. This was a rarity in Mysia, unlike the mountains of the Lebanon, where it was allegedly collected in large amounts on skins and in pots by the natives.[30] The local honey around Pergamon was, for Galen, unsurpassed, even if also unsung. Near the village of Britton a rocky outcrop produced a honey of exquisite sweetness, but too much would induce vomiting. He knew another bank where the wild thyme grew, a hillock to the left of the road from Pergamon to Elea, which produced scented honey far surpassing that of Thasos or Hymettos.[31]

In a sense Galen took his environment with him to Rome – his friends came from his part of the world, like Protas the rhetor, 'our fellow-citizen', who fell ill after eating unripe apples and pears, or the man from Keramos who told him of the beans that were sown there, or Primigenes of Mytilene, the rectification of whose diet forms the crowning exemplum to Book V of the *Hygiene* and proves, to Galen's satisfaction, the practical value of Hippokratic dietetic theory.[32] One might also imagine that this long semi-exile from home also sharpened his memories of the foods, the smells, and the savours of his youth, the crunchy taste of the nuts from Mt. Ida contrasted with the sweeter pistachios from Beroia in Syria, or the noise of the Pergamon hunt as they set off in autumn in search of foxes.[33]

Does Galen generalize from his own experience?

But these intensely personal experiences raise a problem for the historian of food. How far is Galen generalizing from his own experience to refute or reject the ideas of others, or to set up his own guidelines for proper diet? This is a major problem, if not *the* major one. Sometimes Galen plays fair. He notes, for instance, that many doctors have prescribed the eating of raw radishes, citing their own experiences – but he finds them indigestible even when boiled, and lacking in nutritive value. Besides, all those who have laid down these rules for radishes have suffered for it.[34] Galen is equally definite that pork, not roast beef, is the best meat – witness athletes who become noticeably weaker if the pork in their diet is replaced by another meat even for a day. This is because pork is most like human flesh, as anyone will know who has been served in some remote and scandalous hostelry with a pork soup containing human bones.[35]

Wheaten porridge he would have thought totally inedible, had he not had the misfortune to come with two other lads, at the end of the day and after a long journey, on a group of peasants having their meal. They generously offered them some boiled wheat porridge (prepared by the women on the spot), and moderately salted. The result was flatulence, constipation, headache, and eye disturbances. But, says Galen, the peasants said that in similar circumstances they regularly ate this wheaten porridge, even though, when prepared in this way, it was, they admitted, rather heavy and indigestible – as any one can see, says Galen scathingly, even without having to eat it.[36]

But what of his notorious rejection of fresh fruit, which he believes produce bad humours?[37] Only very occasionally, as on a long journey in high summer, are their cooling and moistening properties of any use. Even figs can cause flatulence, and, when eaten dried in large quantities, they can give rise to lice (almost certainly a reference to the problems involved in storing even dried fruit).[38] Apples allowed to ripen and then stored, if baked or steamed, may benefit the sick, but Galen shows no surprise at the practice of Asian peasants in feeding their pigs on apples. Apricots, peaches, nectarines are all liable to rot quickly.[39] Why this denunciation of fruit? Galen is not entirely alone in this, for the poor keeping qualities of some fruit are regularly noted elsewhere. But it is his own personal experience that is crucial. His father had been strongly against fresh fruit, but when he was eighteen, during his father's absence, he allowed himself to be led astray by friends into eating a large quantity of autumnal fresh fruits. The result (not surprisingly, one might think) was an acute illness, cured only by venesection. The next year, returning to eating fruit only in moderation, Galen was free from illness, but the next year, following his father's death, and almost every year for the next eight years, the same pains returned. Only when, at twenty eight, Galen decided to abstain from all fruit save small amounts of figs and grapes, did the illness cease. Therefore, he concludes, eating fruit is dangerous; and he gives examples of other friends who had enjoyed a long period of good health simply as a result of abstaining from fruit.[40] Galen's observations may be right, but his logic is wrong. The year's remission and the curious 'almost every year' appear to a modern clinician to exclude allergies or some digestive insufficiency; to Grmek, Galen was suffering from amoebic dysentery, picked up in the course of his travels.[41] But a more likely explanation is that this is a psychosomatic disorder, linked first to his breaking of his father's taboo and, secondly, after his father's death, to disobeying him while in the course of a very unusual eight-year-long period of study away from home. Only when Galen returns home to Pergamon and resumes his family duties there, does the condition cease. But whatever the cause – and one might also adduce other examples of various types of ailments brought on by ingesting unripe or over-ripe fruits – this is a good example of the way in which Galen jumps to conclusions. It is true, as some have said, that he never lets the facts get in the way of a good theory, but, in his defence, he is also prepared, more than most, to give us the facts that do not always fit his preconceptions.

His influence

His dietetics gradually came to dominate subsequent medical thinking. One can trace the gradual elimination of non-Galenic texts from medical encyclopaedias: the 9th century Arabic translators possessed still large portions of Rufus' dietetics that by the 12th century were to be lost in Greek; and the schema of dietetics set forth in the *Articella*, the bible of medieval Western medicine, owed far more to Galen's interpretation of Hippokrates than to the text *On diet in acute diseases* that by 1200 was included in it.[42] Thanks to their Galenist forbears and teachers, western physicians already knew how to interpret Hippokratic dietetics well before they came to read the Hippokratic text itself in translation. In Latin, Galen was cited for remedies in Gargilius Martialis, *On gardens*, a text traditionally assigned to around 250 AD, little more than a generation after Galen's death, an unusually swift transition from Greek to Latin culture.[43]

Galen in Athenaeus

Notoriously, Galen also appears as one of the interlocutors in Athenaeus, a work that may have been composed even in his own lifetime.[44] He is praised as one who has produced more books on philosophy and medicine than all his predecessors, and is given two long interjections. At I 26c-27d, Galen mentions thirty two varieties of wine; at III 115c-116a five varieties of bread. Unlike the Galenic quotations in Gargilius, most of which can be identified easily, none of those in Athenaeus fits with anything else surviving in Galen. There is even a learned reference to Diphilos of Siphnos, who is otherwise not mentioned in the Galenic corpus. Some have alleged that Athenaeus' Galen is a purely fictional creation and that the initial comment on Galen's publication record is a later addition, betraying the hand of a later epitomator – but this seems an odd addition for an epitomator, and one cannot easily determine the extent to which Book I has been cut down.[45] Others have supposed that we are dealing with lost fragments of Galen or with one of the forgeries he himself records as circulating under his name. A third explanation would centre on Athenaeus' method of citation from prose medical authors: a glimpse at the fragments of Mnesitheos, collected by Janine Bertier, will show how inaccurate Athenaeus is in his quotations as compared with Galen and Aulus Gellius.[46] Is Athenaeus then 'paraphrasing Galen' – for none of his statements contradicts a known Galenic opinion – and adding his own learned touches like the quotation from Diphilos, in order to build up his own literary picture of Galen the deipnosophist? The answer is not at all clear, although it is perhaps easier to believe in Athenaeus' literary imagination than in the chance survival of a substantial amount of material omitted by Galen from relevant treatises. At all events, whether we are dealing with a literary phantom or the homage of one contemporary to another, one point is clear. Galen is already being regarded in Alexandria by 210 as a weighty authority on food and diet. Athenaeus' interest, if not his investigative methods, could be profitably pursued by modern historians of ancient food.

Notes

1. References in this chapter to Galen are given by volume and page in the standard edition of C.G. Kühn (Leipzig, 1821-32). Most of Galen's dietetic writings were reedited in the Berlin *Corpus Medicorum Graecorum* series, Vol. V 4, 2 (1923), with considerable improvement. Where possible I have followed this edition, which prints the Kühn page references in the margin. For *A diet for slimmers* (*De subtiliante diaeta*), which is not in Kühn, I follow the pagination in the edition of N. Marinone (Turin, 1973).

2. Galen 6.486, 664 and *De subtil. diaet.* 84.

3. 6.333-4, 332-3, and for the centenarian peasant, 6.343.

4. 6.686, 749.

5. 6.486, 539-40, 668, 11.142.

6. Rufus of Ephesos, fr. 129 Daremberg-Ruelle, and Galen 6.626.

7. Rufus has been edited by C. Daremberg and Ruelle (Paris, 1879). New material, from the Arabic, on his dietetics is given by Ullmann (1974), (1975).

8. Details are given by Marinone in his 1973 edition; and in the preface to the edition of Kalbfleisch et al. in *Corpus Medicorum Graecorum* V 4,2.

9. Preliminary details in Ullmann (1977). A Hebrew summary of the text, which is preserved in full in Arabic, was published by Wasserstein (1982).

10. 12.360, 6.541, 6.700 and *De subtil. diaet.* 54.

11. For the modern authors, 6.228, 330, 96-119, 182, 206-15.

12. Thus Scarborough (1970).

13. Mnesitheos, frag. 11 Bertier. The interesting point here is that the Alexandrian commentator is expanding a quotation from Mnesitheos deliberately abbreviated by Galen in his *Method of healing, for Glaucon* (11.3). To the same period may be dated the scholium, frag. 20 Bertier, which supplies information not in the earlier Oribasios.

14. Animals, Stern (1956); months, 17A 20-21.

15. 6.602 ff.

16. Respectively, 6.514, 10.468 and 6.811, 14.22, 17A.155, 161, 163, 182.

17. 6.196 (Aulon), 806 (for wines).

18. Cf. 6.514, 518, 540, 782.

19. Rosenthal (1965) 55.

20. Respectively, 6.783, 755, 546, 552, 11.21, 6.499, 11.336.

21. 6.523, 551, 749.

22. 1.55 (a passage rarely cited by historians of the corn supply).

23. Nutton (1993).

24. 6.491, 802.

25. 6.813. Cf. 6.507, for comments on a change in army diet.

26. 6.795, 709, 711, 721-2, 727 (price).

27. The exception to the rule enunciated by Schöne (1917) is 6.424, where Galen contrasts the source of the Allia 'at home' with a spring at Prusa in Bithynia, and that of the

Liketos (?) 'at home' with another Bithynian spring. The first certainly and the second possibly refers to Italy.

28. 17B.159, cf. 182.
29. 6.800-4.
30. 6.738-40.
31. 14.21-3.
32. Respectively, 6.598, 547, 365-71.
33. 6.778, 612, 665.
34. 6.658.
35. 6.661-3, 12.254.
36. 6.498-9; cf. 507 for Galen's views on the eating habits of peasants in Cyprus.

37. 6.755-6.
38. 6.791-3; cf. 785-6.
39. 6.596-8; cf. 11.367-8, 6.602-4.
40. 6.756-7.
41. Grmek, in Moraux (1985) 179.
42. For Rufus' dietetics under the Arabs, see above, n. 6; for the *Articella*, see Kristeller (1986).
43. Riddle (1992), ch. X.
44. For the date of Galen's death, see Nutton (1988), ch. 3.
45. So Scarborough (1981), 19-21.
46. Bertier (1972).

Bibliography

Bertier, J., 1972 *Mnésithée et Dieuchès* (Leiden).

Joly, R., (ed.) 1977 *Corpus Hippocraticum. Actes du Colloque hippocratique de Mons (22-26 septembre 1975)* (Paris).

Kollesch, J., (ed.) 1993 *Proceedings of the fourth International Galen Symposium, Berlin, Sudhoffs Archiv*, Beiheft 40.

Kristeller, P.O., 1986 *Studi sulla Scuola medica salernitana* (Naples).

Moraux, P., 1985 *Galien de Pergame* (Paris).

Nutton, V., 1988 *From Democedes to Harvey. Studies in the History of Medicine* (London).

Nutton, V., 1993 'Galen and Egypt', in Kollesch (1993).

Riddle, J., 1992 *Quid pro Quo. Studies in the History of Drugs* (Aldershot).

Rosenthal, F., 1965 *Das Fortleben der Antike im Islam* (Zurich).

Scarborough, J., 1970 'Diphilus of Siphnos and Hellenistic medical dietetics', *Journal of the History of Medicine and Allied Sciences* 25, 194-201.

Scarborough, J., 1981 'The Galenic question', *Sudhoffs Archiv* 65, 1-31.

Schöne, H., 1917 '*To tou Traianou gumnasion* bei Galen', *Hermes* 52, 105-11.

Stern, S.M., 1956 'Some fragments of Galen's *On dispositions* in Arabic', *Classical Quarterly* 6, 91-7.

Ullmann, M., 1974 'Neues zu den diätetischen Schriften des Rufus von Ephesos', *Medizinhistorisches Journal* 9, 23-40.

Ullmann, M., 1975 'Die Schrift des Rufus *De infantium curatione* und das Problem der Autorenlemmata in den *Collectiones Medicae* des Oreibasios', *Medizinhistorisches Journal* 10, 165-90.

Ullmann, M., 1977 'Galens Kommentar zu der Schrift *De aerae aquis locis*', in Joly (1977), 353-65.

Wasserstein, A., 1982 *Galen's Commentary on the Hippocratic Treatise Airs, Waters, Places in the Hebrew Translation of Solomon ha-Me'ati* (Jerusalem).

❖ 28 ❖ ORIBASIOS AND MEDICAL DIETETICS OR THE THREE Ps

Mark Grant

Monsieur Homais, the chemist of Yonville l'Abbaye in Flaubert's *Madame Bovary*,[1] discusses the dangers of countryfolk moving to Paris and exposing themselves to changes in diet. He stresses the dubious qualities of the water and the heating of the blood by highly-seasoned restaurant dishes. The so-called *Salerno Scheme of Health*, translated by the Elizabethan poet Sir John Harington in 1607,[2] remarks that those who eat garlic:

> May drinke, and care not who their drink do brew:
> May walke in aires infected every houre.
> Sith Garlicke then hath powers to save from death,
> Bear with it though it make unsavory breath:
> And scorne not *Garlicke*, like to some that thinke,
> It only makes men winke, and drinke, and stinke.

Oribasios, who published his work in the mid 4th century AD, begins his excerpts with a note by Galen on the caution required when eating on arrival in a foreign country.[3] Similarly Anthimus,[4] writing in Gaul sometime after 511, advises taking garlic against the vicissitudes of unfamiliar water. This historical continuity is an aspect of dietetics that has been examined in detail by Riddle in his excellent book on Dioskorides.[5] Yet

Continuity in dietetics

there is scope for further work: for example on the relationship between some seemingly ineffectual ancient remedies and specific modern homeopathic medicines, and between overall views of courses of treatment in Galen or Soranos and such modern schemes as the Bristol diet. Rainforest tribes dubbed primitive by the western world often are found to have a deep knowledge of curative plants and herbal preparations. The skilled physician in the ancient world had access not only to centuries of trial and error, but presumably also to folk heritage unmarked by the scientific theories of the day.

Oribasios and his works

Oribasios is not one of the most widely-read of classical authors[6] and his *Medical Compilations* are unlikely ever to reach the exalted status of an A-level set text. He was born some time in the early 320s either at Pergamon or Sardis.[7] The future emperor Julian was studying at Pergamon in 351 under the Neoplatonist Aidesios. It was perhaps then that the two men met. Julian was in 355 appointed Caesar in Gaul and Britain by the Augustus Constantine II. Pens were busy, and during this term of office Oribasios presented Julian with an abridged version of Galen. Julian commended this literary endeavour and asked his friend to add extracts from other medical writers to form a proper encyclopaedia. The preface of the *Medical Compilations* is addressed to Julian but refers to the residence in Gaul in the past tense. So a date of publication can be fixed tentatively between the departure from Gaul in 360 and Julian's death in 363.

The only part of the seventy books of the *Medical Compilations* that Oribasios wrote himself seems to have been the preface. Otherwise the work is divided into five sections of excerpts: food and drink, nature and constitution of man, treatment and restoration of health, diagnostic and prognostic theories, and the treatment of illnesses and their symptoms. The extracts from Galen are sometimes interesting textually, but do not add to our knowledge of that prolific writer. However, following Julian's suggestion, Oribasios added excerpts from twenty-six other medical authors. These are invaluable: next to nothing would be known about Philagrios or Antyllos or Athenaios of Attaleia without Oribasios' industry. Books 1 to 5 of the *Medical Compilations* are concerned with diet in the narrow sense of food and drink.

Provenance of foods

Ancient medical writers examined foods and their effect on the human body in three ways: provenance, preparation and pepsis. Provenance can be divided into two areas: the first, knowledge of where foods came from, was of paramount importance. Athenaios of Attaleia, who lived under the emperors Claudius and Nero, stresses that:

> The wheats differ according to locality, those which grow in dry and poor lands differing from those which flourish in good rich soils: for the former, being composed of an inferior, lighter and thinner material are easily worked up for food and are easy of digestion, but they afford less nourishment, as do those wheats sown in what are called 'burnt fields'; this is because when stuff is burnt in these fields, the wheats become white and spongy and like spring wheats because of the meagreness of the ash which is without nutritives. The cereals grown on rich land with good soil, because they are fed by plentiful and solid material, are dense, heavy, and very nutritious.[8]

Part of what Athenaios writes is popular wisdom. That wheat was believed to grow better in damp conditions since it required more nutrients, whilst barley was best planted in poorer soils because it could not assimilate much, is supported by a farming aphorism quoted by Plutarch and Cato: 'Wheat grows in heavy soil, barley in light soil'.[9] The technique of burning-off stubble in fields was widely applied in the ancient world, both to incinerate the seeds of weeds as Pliny says in his *Natural History*[10] and to fertilize as Virgil remarks in his *Georgics*.[11] Too much ash with its excessive alkalinity could inhibit germination and growth. Athenaios is no doubt referring to this when he warns that wheat sown on 'burnt ground' afforded 'poorer nourishment'. The second area under the heading of provenance was that of time.

> Sheep are worst in winter, but after the equinox they grow fat until the summer solstice; cows grow fat when the grass seeds as spring is ending and for the whole summer. As for birds, those that appear in winter – such as the blackbird, thrush, and wood-pigeon – are best during this season; francolins are fattest in autumn as are the black-headed titmice, the fig-pecker, green-finch, and quails.[12]

Galen and other writers also noted that sheep are better in spring and summer than in winter,[13] a tradition continued in both Greece and Spain today where young lambs are an Easter speciality, roasted on a spit or in the oven. Palladius[14] and Columella[15] argued that cows were hardy enough to endure a winter under the open sky, but added that a chilly weather made them grow thin. Their blunt jaw and thick lips were considered to be inadequate at tackling short herbage. Again Athenaios is relying on farming knowledge and commonsense. According to other ancient writers, the birds listed are all at their edible best precisely when Athenaios says they are.

Preparation of foods

From ancient references, particularly in Galen, Rufus of Ephesos cannot have lived before the second half of the 1st century AD, although his exact floruit is still open to debate. In Book 4 of the *Medical Compilations* there is a chapter by Rufus on the preparation of foods. Having located a supply of wholesome ingredients, the cook and dietician had to ensure that the maximum benefit was derived from the meats, vegetables, pulses and grains. In his *On the Natural Faculties*[16] Galen mentions the qualities:

> Of all those known to us who have been both physicians and philosophers, Hippokrates was the first who took in hand to demonstrate that there are, in all, four interacting qualities, and that to the operation of these is due the genesis and destruction of all things that come into and pass out of being.

Galen considered that diseases arose sometimes only from an immoderate increase of the hot or of the cold, or from some opposition of one of these things with another such as between the dry and the moist, and sometimes because of some combination of these things which increased excessively so as to become a disease, that is hot at the same time as dry, or cold and dry, or hot and moist, or cold and moist. Rufus seems to be concurring with this view at the start of his chapter:

> Everything we eat that has been roasted is dry; and everything that has been boiled is moist, even if it happens that each of the foods concerned are by their nature different.

Celsus[17] argued that food cooked in a sauce nourished more than plain roasted food, whilst what had been roasted was more nourishing than foods boiled on their own. There is nothing remarkable in this statement:

roast or fried chicken seems to most people more satisfying than boiled chicken soup; whilst a chicken oven-roasted in a red-wine and herb sauce provides a satisfying gourmet experience. Rufus advises against excessive seasoning since this burdens the stomach. Herbs and spices should be added at the start of the preparation of a meal to allow for even cooking. Only in the case of strongly-flavoured foods – presumably hung meats and salted fish – could the later addition of seasonings be justified, the reason being that the herbs and spices would be absorbed by the foods. The herbs and spices so typical of the Apician kitchen are listed: coriander, dill, cumin, leeks, asafoetida, mint, celery, thyme and marjoram. Other details about preparation include: beating octopus to tenderize the meat, hanging game-birds and animals, and cooking fish (preferably in hot embers) while they are still quivering. The chapter following that of Rufus features an extract from Diokles of Karystos, the 4th century BC physician whom the Athenians called 'the second Hippokrates'. He adds further information about good cooking practice: making foods wholesome by boiling, soaking, washing, and removal of extraneous matter such as leaves or fat. Anything with a sharp taste was to be boiled in fresh water; anything with a bitter taste was to be boiled in water and vinegar. Looking at Apicius and the fragments of other ancient cookery books, these instructions by Rufus and Diokles were no more than what a proficient cook was supposed to do.

One sentence is worth considering in detail to emphasize the problematic nature of some of the medical texts. The style of most ancient medical writers can hardly be said to be elegant. Hence it is difficult to decide whether, on hitting awkward syntax or outrageous advice, the obscurity is due to obtuseness on the part of the writer or manuscript error. Rufus appears to have written: 'As for chickens, one must chase (*diokein*) them, and pour over them some vinegar: the chase is worth it. The reason for this is that if you were to cook some wild game immediately after a hunt, no great harm would come to you'. The two previous translations of Oribasios, Rasario's Latin version in the 16th century and Daremberg's French version of the 19th century, offer for *diokein asservare* and *fatiguer* respectively. Yet *diokein* cannot mean 'to preserve' (although vinegar was of course used as a preservative), and the idea of *tiring* is not contained in the Greek.

Diokein must mean 'chase', and the suggestion that it means 'seek after' or 'procure' seems lame considering that chickens were not rare creatures in the ancient world. Chasing would have the effect of producing lactic acid which supposedly gives meat a superior flavour, and certainly Celsus[18] mentions that the least flatulence came from whatever was got by hunting, and Galen even suggests mountain-roaming chickens in an attenuating diet.[19] Aretaios (a medical writer of the 2nd century AD) considered chickens best when eaten freshly-slaughtered[20] which underlines the comment made by Rufus about eating wild creatures immediately after the hunt. Birds were sometimes cooked in vinegar as Apicius,[21] Theodorus Priscus[22] and pseudo- Pliny[23] describe, and the general toughness of free-range chickens would have necessitated some sort of marinating. Laurens van der Post says that chicken, the favourite delicacy of the West African table, is rarely tender enough for roasting or grilling straight away, but has to be marinated not for flavour so much as to make it tender enough for real enjoyment.[24]

Pepsis

Finally *pepsis*. An article in *The Guardian* for July 16th 1992[25] reported that seven patients using the weight-loss herb germander developed hepatitis and that the liver disease, disappearing when the patients stopped using the herb, recurred in three who started taking it again. The article concluded by saying that bergamot, rosemary, mint, nutmeg and cloves can also be toxic in certain amounts. In his *On Humours*[26] Galen stated:

> It seems that health is characterized by the equality and symmetry of these humours. When they are deficient or increasing contrary to what is necessary either as regards quantity, quality, shifting of position, irregular combination, or putrefaction of things that have been spoilt, diseases occur. Just as it has been said that diseases happen as a result of an excess of the humours, so health returns by the removal and by the addition, and by the thinness and thickness of the humours, and generally through their mildness and symmetry.

Physicians could attempt this symmetry of the humours either by drugs, such as scammony and safflower which drew yellow bile from the body; or by food, beef, camel and goat meat, snails, cabbage, and soft cheeses producing black bile; brains, fungi, lamb, and hard apples causing phlegm; with bitter almonds and garlic on the other hand reducing phlegm. In his *On Prognosis*[27] Galen paints an intriguing vignette of an examination and diagnosis he performed on the emperor Marcus Aurelius. The latter thought that his stomach, on becoming overloaded, had converted the ingested food into phlegm, and since phlegm was cold and moist his body temperature had been lowered and fever had struck. Food therefore had to be prepared in such a way as to maintain the good order of the humours and the health of the diner. Many of the recipes given in the *Medical Compilations* appear quite effective. For example, Dieuches, who lived at the beginning of the 3rd century BC, gives a recipe for a sleeping draught:[28]

> It is sufficient to put into a pint and a half of the finest and ripest barley four and a half pints of milk and water, in the proportion of two-thirds of milk to one-third of water, and the head of a poppy that has been toasted; and, after mixing in by the fire one tenth of an ounce of pounded figs, boil the ingredients together, and serve after cooking to the consistency of soup; it provides some respite and also sleep for those who are convalescent.

The ancient physicians knew about the soporific and cooling effect of poppies, which is why the gods Sleep, Night and Death are represented in ancient art as garlanded with or holding poppies. Hippokrates gives a similar recipe for the displacement of the womb, the ingredients being barley, cheese and poppy-seeds.[29] Antyllos, a medical writer of the 2nd century AD, gives a recipe for mallows in *garum* and olive-oil and adds that they are the most useful of all the vegetables. Plutarch[30] says that the leaves, roots and flowers of the mallow can be eaten, and modern research has shown the plant to have demulcent and emollient properties that make it useful in inflammation and irritation of the alimentary canal, and of the urinary and respiratory organs.[31] However, there are also seeming discrepancies between modern and ancient ideas. When discussing *asa-foetida* Dieuches[32] says that only the whitest, most fragrant and most sharp should be used 'if perhaps it is needed'. If this last phrase is taken as a caveat ('if it is needed to some degree'), this would coincide with other ancient medical statements – ranging from Hippokrates to Dioskorides and Galen – about its flatulent and dyspeptic effects.[33] Modern pharma-ceutical ideas about *asafoetida* suggest that the plant does in fact act as a carminative in flatulent colic and as a stimulant to the alimentary tract.[34] Either the phrase means something other than a warning or Dieuches is describing an effect that modern herbals have not taken into account. The following sentence militates against the former suggestion: Dieuches asks people to avoid dishes containing too much cheese, sesame-seeds and *asafoetida* because they 'cause trouble'.

The ancient medical writers contain a wealth of information about diet and food. As Scribonius Largus says in his preface,[35] diet was ranked alongside medicines as one of the main weapons that Greek and Roman physicians possessed for combatting ill health. There were dishes for healthy people, people suffering from illness, convalescents. Some of the medical recipes are tasty enough to be served as a meal, designed to tempt a reluctant patient; other recipes are utterly foul, as the millet and pennyroyal concoction for throat complaints that I have cooked and tasted. The details about cooking techniques perhaps fill a gap in treatises such as the *De Re Coquinaria* of Apicius, whilst future research may reveal further sophistication in the area of homeopathic treatment.

Notes

1. G. Hopkins (trans.) (Oxford, 1981, 115).
2. J. Harington (trans.) (1953, 29).
3. *Compilationes Medicae* 1.1.
4. *Epistulae* 61.
5. Riddle (1985).
6. Jones (1931) 198.
7. Eunapios *Vitae Sophistarum* 21.1.1; Philostorgius *Historia Ecclesiastica* 7.15.
8. See Oribasios *Compilationes Medicae* 1.2.4-5.
9. Plutarch *Moralia* 915e; cf. Cato *De Agricultura* 34.2.
10. *Natural History* 18.300.
11. *Georgics* 1.84; cf. Columella 2.14.5; *Corpus Inscriptionum Latinarum* 6.2305.
12. Oribasios 1.3.3-4.
13. *De alimentorum facultatibus* 3.1.13=6.665-666 Kühn, Ananios, quoted by Athenaeus 7.282b.
14. 4.11.8.
15. 6.22.2.
16. *De naturalibus facultatibus* 1.2=2.5 Kühn.
17. 2.18.10.
18. 2.26.2.
19. *De victu attenuente* 8.69.
20. Aretaios *De chronicis morbis* 1.2.16=24A.300 Kühn.
21. 6.9.3.
22. *Logicus* 101.
23. *Medica* 2.6.

[24.] Van der Post (1977, 51-2).
[25.] *The Guardian* 6.
[26.] 19.491 Kühn.
[27.] 11.1-9=14.658-660 Kühn.
[28.] Oribasios 4.3.7.
[29.] Hippokrates *Muliebria* 2.149=8.324 Littré.
[30.] *Moralia* 158e.

[31.] Grieve (1976, 506-8).
[32.] Oribasios 4.6.2.
[33.] Galen *De simplici medica* 8.18.6=12.123 Kühn; Pliny *Natural History* 22.100; Hippokrates *De morbis acutis* 10.298 Littré; Dioskorides *De materia medica* 3.80.1.
[34.] E.g. Grieve (1977, 62-3).
[35.] Preface, 1-2.

Bibliography

Grieve, M., 1931 *A Modern Herbal* (London).

Harington, Sir J., 1953 *The School of Salernum* (Rome).

Jones, W.H.S., 1931 'Review of Raeder's edition of Oribasios', *Classical Review* 45, 198.

Riddle, J.M., 1985 *Dioscorides on Pharmacy and Medicine* (Austin, Texas).

van der Post, L., 1977 *First Catch Your Eland: A Taste Of Africa* (London).

PART SIX

Food and Literature

'Since, then', said Eryximachos, 'we have agreed that everyone will drink as much as he likes, and there will be no compulsory drinking, the next thing I propose is that we let the girl piper who has just come in go away again: she can play to herself or, if she prefers, to the women inside. We meanwhile will enjoy each other's company today in conversation. And if you like, I wish to propose what our topic should be.'

(Plato *Symposium* 176e-177a)

Introduction ↶ Part Six

Doctor Eryximachos, one of the diners at Plato's imagined dinner and symposium, proposes the rules for the drinking once the eating is completed.[1] It is established just before this passage that the drinking will not be excessive. On this kind of occasion, all had to agree on what form the drinking should take (what proportion of water to wine in the mixing bowl, how the drinking cups should be passed round, and how often) and on what the entertainment should be. Pipers, singers, dancers and recitations were common: there are professional performers, for example, in the *Symposium* of Xenophon. Here, conversation is chosen, which allows Plato to develop the social form into a philosophical discussion on the nature of love. Eryximachos is tentative in his proposals, being careful to secure the willing agreement of all. It is characteristic of this form of upper-class gathering that a light and playful atmosphere is the rule unless things get out of hand with too much drinking or other physical pleasures such as sexual encounters. The latter is common, and indeed is alluded to in Eryximachos' proposal that the conversation will be about love – words only on this occasion.[2] Note that the girl piper might go and play to the women of the household: they do not attend the men's dinner and symposium, and almost certainly are not enjoying an all-women symposium of their own.

Plato thus set his dialogue within the context of social eating and drinking. His *Symposium* was a classic in antiquity and was often alluded to or imitated: to take two examples, in Greek, Athenaeus' *Deipnosophists* is modelled on it (1.2a) and praises it (e.g. 5.186e); in Latin, 'Trimalchio's Feast' in the *Satyricon* of Petronius appears to borrow features from it. This literary form is only one of many which derive from a social context based on eating and drinking. Lyric poetry is another example, as perhaps are the Homeric epics: once the eating and drinking were complete, the Homeric bard entertained the company with his songs about the heroes of old (this at least is the practice in *Odyssey* 7).[3]

There is also much food in the *content* of literature: in the literary symposium food (as opposed to wine) is often in the background. This is not always the case: in the *Deipnosophists*, eating is followed by drinking, as expected, but the banter and conversation continue at all stages. The prominent role that food plays in ancient literature has not always been recognized, despite the fact that the foods that people eat and the social context within which they eat it can be very expressive, and are often drawn upon by writers either consciously or unconsciously. As we have seen (above), Homer's heroes in the *Iliad* ate a disproportionate amount of beef, apparently oblivious of all the fish in the Hellespont, while in the *Odyssey*, almost every strange being that Odysseus visits consumes a correspondingly strange food. In tragedy, where eating is surprisingly rare and when it is referred to, the allusion is sometimes to the cannibalistic eating of kinsmen, eating brings out the unnatural and disordered world in which the characters suffer. In comedy, conversely, there is a celebration of eating: at the beginning of a play, there is often an absence of eating, or appalling eating (the dung beetle eats cakes of excrement at the beginning of Aristophanes' *Peace*), while at the end of the play, the restoration of order is demonstrated in festive or nuptial eating. Eating is closely related to human and plant reproduction in cultures (such as that of the Greeks) that are close to the agricultural world.

Eating is both essential and too trivial to mention. Without nourishment we die; we rarely eat merely for fuel – many other associations and values make us choose one food over another. At the same time food is not considered by many people (now or in antiquity) to be as important as say politics or art or literature – except in emergencies such as famine. This is why it is particularly appropriate to comedy, the playful form of literature. Three of the four chapters in this section are about comedy or the related genre of parody (on which Degani has much to say in Chapter 31), that is, poetry in epic style but with non-epic content.

All four chapters in this final part derive from the *Deipnosophists* of Athenaeus. This is an encyclopaedic work whose literary pretentions are, for most readers, unfulfilled. It is written in the form of the symposium, as dinner conversation between witty and learned men who, like Plato's symposiasts, preferred to talk rather than get drunk or play games; in this case the learning is directed not to elegant or complex argument but to quotation from thousands of works, many of which would otherwise be lost. In the words of Vivian Nutton, Athenaeus's work is a 'compendium of all that you need to know for health, wealth and word-power'.[4] He is thus a gold mine for ancient authors – such as Poseidonios quoted in the introduction to Part Four and Diphilos in that to Part Five. His general theme is the dinner and the symposium at which his characters are enjoying themselves, but the dinner is introduced with very broad criteria, and therefore much grammatical, zoological, botanical, medical and ethnographic material is also brought in, as well as the lists of vegetables, fruits, fish, meats, drinking cups, garlands, party girls (*hetairai*) and so on. Athenaeus' work has been used in a number of chapters in this book (for example Louise Bruit on parasites and David Harvey on Lydia); there is a speculative note at the end of Vivian Nutton's chapter on Athenaeus' use of Galen.

Athenaeus was an Egyptian Greek born in Naukratis in the 2nd century AD. Naukratis, in the Nile delta, had been a Greek city since the 7th century BC. He is thought to have travelled to Rome (at least the book is set in Rome at the house of a minor official for whom there is inscriptional attestation). If he did travel to Rome, Athenaeus resembles many other literary and philosophical writers under the Roman Empire. Plutarch went to Rome for a while from his native Greece; Galen, as we have seen, travelled from Pergamon to Rome. Rome attracted many: despite excellent facilities in the library at Alexandria or at Pergamon for those with an interest in learning, Rome was still at the centre of the world.

Just as Plato has Aristophanes, Socrates, the tragic poet Agathon and other historical personages in his *Symposium*, so Athenaeus has Ulpian the lawyer, Galen the doctor and the minor official, P. Livius Larensis among the guests at his party.

Athenaeus sometimes distances himself from authors he quotes: he criticises Archestratos, for example, for his encouragement of luxury.[5]

Much of the work is influenced by a philosophical tradition stretching back to Plato. Athenaeus concentrates heavily on comedy. This may partly be explained because the subject matter of comedy was, as we have seen, particularly suitable for his themes of eating and dining. While we know little about Athenaeus himself, he tells us that he had written two other works, one of which (7.329c) was on the comedy *The Fishes* by the dramatist Archippos (5th century BC).[6] The context suggests this may have been a work about fish rather than about comedy, but if this is so, then the use of comedy as a source of information is significant. Although distorting, it is considered to have evidential value for this kind of author. Comedy had acquired an additional status by this period, which was to last well into the Byzantine age. For example, the encyclopedia of the 10th century AD known as the *Suda* which gives explanations of how things were in earlier ages draws heavily on Aristophanes for its quotations. In quoting from comedy to illustrate a particular kind of fish, Athenaeus may also illustrate a grammatical oddity – the use of the dative case or a rare ending – or particularly pleasing stylistic features, as he notes in the cases of Aristophanes and Pherekrates (6.268e, 269e).

Athenaeus is one of a number of authors in the Imperial period in Rome who produced anthologies or compendia of earlier works. The *Attic Nights* of Aulus Gellius is a similar work. Both are to be contrasted with those works that cite earlier authors only in passing, such as Plutarch's essays in his *Moralia*. These authors drew on Greek and Latin authors with ease (though the latter are a small minority in Athenaeus).

The text of Athenaeus lacks the first two and part of the third books, which survive only in summary form (the 'epitome'). We know of fifteen books, but the whole work may have contained thirty.[7] It is not easy to assess how Athenaeus amassed all his information, either directly from some sources or indirectly from others.[8]

In Chapter 29, Dwora Gilula examines themes relating to food in Greek comedies, in particular those which date to the 5th and 4th centuries BC. Here are jokes about food that were written for audiences of fifteen to twenty thousand. Chapters 30 and 31 concern parodic poems on food written for select groups enjoying recitations while they drank wine at the symposium. In Chapter 30, Andrew Dalby examines the historicity and cultural context of *The Life of Luxury* of Archestratos, most of which concerns the selection and cooking of fish, in contrast to the *Attic Dinner* of Matro, Enzo Degani's subject in Chapter 31. Matro's purpose is to imitate the language of Homer as closely as possible while describing a decidedly non-Homeric banquet. In Chapter 32, John Wilkins and Shaun Hill consider Athenaeus' attitudes towards cookery books, and the class of flavours displayed by the books preserved in the *Deipnosophists*.[9]

J.W.

Notes

1. On the qualities of Eryximachos as a doctor see L. Edelstein, *Greek Medicine* (Baltimore, 1967, 153-72).

2. For sex at the symposium see e.g. E. Keuls *The Reign of the Phallus* (Berkeley, 1985), in which many scenes on vases are presented.

3. See further O. Murray 'Sympotic History', *Sympotica* (ed. O. Murray, Oxford, 1990, 3-14).

4. For an assessment of the *literary* qualities of Athenaeus, see A. Lukinovich in Murray (n. 3, 263-71). The reference for Vivian Nutton's observation is *From Democedes to Harvey* (London, 1978, 317).

5. See J. Wilkins and S. Hill *Archestratus: The Life of Luxury* (Totnes, 1994, 25-8).

6. The other was on the kings of Syria (5.211a).

7. The most accessible text is *Athenaeus: The Deipnosophists*, trans. C.B. Gulick (Loeb Classical Library: Cambridge, Mass. and London, 1927-41; seven volumes).

8. On sources, see G. Wentzel 'Athenaios', *Paulys Real-Encyclopädie der classischen Altertumswissenschaft*, ed. G. Wissowa, II.2 (1896, 2025-33).

9. For further studies of food in literature, see, on the chef in comedy, H. Dohm *Mageiros* (Munich, 1964); on Roman literature, N. Hudson 'Food in Roman Satire', in *Satire and Society in Ancient Rome* ed. S.H. Braund (Exeter, 1989, 69-88), and on the ambivalence of the Romans to food in literature, E. Gowers *The Loaded Table* (Oxford, 1993).

❖ 29 ❖

COMIC FOOD
AND FOOD FOR
COMEDY

Dwora Gilula

Greedy Thebans and abstemious Athenians

Iɴ Euboulos' *Antiope* (fr. 10; fragments of the comic poets are numbered according to the edition of R. Kassel and C. Austin *Poetae Comici Graeci* (Berlin and New York, 1983-)), Amphion and Zethos, the two sons of the heroine, are not both sent to Thebes, as was undoubtedly expected by those in the audience who were familiar with the myth and with Euripides' tragedy. Only Zethos the glutton is told to go to Thebes where, joining the self-indulgent Boiotians, he himself can be self-indulgent at bargain prices. His brother, Amphion the musician, in what may be an innovation of Euboulos, is most surprisingly dispatched to glorious Athens where the citizens starve, swallowing air and feeding on hopes, and in whose company he can pursue his aesthetic interests. 'The Athenians eat little', says Euboulos, 'the Thebans a lot' (fr. 11).[1]

The self-image of the Athenians, as presented by Euboulos and also found elsewhere in comedy, is one of frugality, of small eaters satisfied with simple, moderate, and sometimes even poor fare, following mainly intellectual pursuits, while the thick-witted Boiotians, with Herakles their most notorious food-consuming champion, are depicted as their gluttonous other. The Boiotians eat all day long (Euboulos fr. 33); they cannot get enough of stuffing themselves, even though they dine all through the night and into the following day (fr. 38). Considering their eating habits, it is their great luck and luxury to have a private toilet by the door (frs 52, 66); they are unmoved by reason and know only how to shout, drink and dine (Alexis fr. 239). This depiction of the Boiotians emphasizes by contrast the opposite characteristics of the Athenians: the typical Boiotian eats a great deal and talks very little (Mnesimachos fr. 2), while the typical Athenian talks a great deal and eats very little.[2] But side by side with this picture of Athenian intellectuality and frugality, comedy, especially Middle and New Comedy, also reflects another image, that of Athenian luxury (*truphe*), abundance, refinement and even ostentation. The Athenians, to use Luigi Gallo's term, underwent a 'gastronomic revolution', already reflected in the comedies of Aristophanes, in which a rural diet based on essentially local products gave way to an urban way of life based on an abundance of imported foods. Even Dikaiopolis, who at the beginning of the *Acharnians* longs to leave the city and contrasts its noisy markets with the blessing of country life, which is not dominated by greedy, plotting, astute and dishonest peddlers, is at the end won over to 'the market economy'.[3]

It is true, of course, that comedy, and already Old Comedy, does indeed describe different diets, but it focuses chiefly on luxurious eating, partly because luxury is more interesting than penury, especially to the poor, and affords richer dramatic possibilities, but mainly because the plots of Middle and New Comedy deal with social classes that are economically more than comfortably off, and show a preference for foods which because of their price are not accessible to those who practice frugality for other than ideological reasons. Frugality in comedy often takes the form of ridicule of the archaic past, as Gallo says, or an idealization of it and a longing for it. Sometimes, however, it is a device used to present a cultural contrast and to symbolize different social classes. It is also used, as befits comedy, to satirize those who practise *truphe* but wish to be seen and considered frugal. It is when the Athenians began to eat like the Boiotians but continued to idealize frugality and to preach it that comedy started to ridicule their tendency to emphasize their wish to project such a contradictory self-image of frugality.

Comedy and the comic fragments

The majority of passages in comedy dealing with food are fragments from lost Middle and New Comedy plays, cited selectively by Athenaeus. This preponderance sometimes overshadows the centrality of food and matters related to food in Aristophanes' plays and in the fragments of Old Comedy of the last decades of the 5th century BC (from which most of them come). These already contain, *in nucleo*, almost all the themes elaborated by later comedy, and even some which are abandoned, such as the centrality of food in the descriptions of the Golden Age, and the colourful metaphorical use of food and eating as sexual innuendoes that Henderson (1975, 47-8, 142-4) has so conveniently catalogued. In addition to this, the extant comedies of Aristophanes provide something that it is almost impossible to deduce with certainty from fragments, that is, the context in which the various comic and dramatic functions of food are incorporated into the stage action, and especially the use of food as an element in the organization of the plot.

Perhaps the most obvious use of food for this purpose is the role of feasting and eating in the happy endings of the comedies. Food is presented as an indispensable ingredient of the achievement of the good life, and banquets appear in the happy endings of the majority of the extant comedies of Aristophanes. This frequency, and the later transformation in New Comedy of public banquets into private family affairs, especially wedding dinners, indicates that such a closure was felt to be appropriate for comedies. A particularly fine example of an Aristophanic dinner as a finale is the double-edged ending of the *Acharnians*, in which a banquet is prepared for some characters and not for others, and food or its absence is used thematically as a tangible illustration of the two antithetical poles of the play: the hardships of war as contrasted with the pleasures of peace. If, as Oswyn Murray suggests, the *symposion* of pleasure evolved from what was once an exclusive gathering of warriors, in the *Acharnians* it has come to be a gathering from which the warriors were excluded.[4]

Focal as food and feasts are for comedies, they contain no *Tom Jones*-style scenes. Actual feasting and preparation of food were not usually shown on stage, though drinking occasionally was. Such activities belonged indoors, that is to off-stage scenes, which as a rule were reported and not enacted.[5] Usually food is introduced into the stage action through narrative descriptions, which in the course of time tend to become variations on limited and recurring themes, usually cast in the form of catalogues of shopping lists, food marketing, invitations for dinner, food preparations, and descriptions of meals or of the pleasures of a meal just finished. These descriptions, so popular with the audiences, did not please the spectators physically, for even the Athenians could not be satisfied for ever with the gulping of air. But, as Athenaeus (402d) puts it: 'The dinners spoken of in the comic poets afford very pleasant hearing to the ear, rather than delight to the gullet'.[6]

Middle and New Comedy tend to put such descriptions into the mouths of two increasingly ubiquitous stock characters, the parasite and the cook, usually in the form of a monologue which becomes increasingly lengthy; these monologues strive to display linguistic virtuosity but inescapably verge dangerously on the brink of repetition, boasting slight thematic innovations as their claim to originality. 'My good sir,' someone says to a cook in Hegesippos (fr. 1), 'much has been said by many men on the subject of cookery. Do you either prove that you can do something novel (as compared with your predecessors), or else stop butchering me'. And Xenarchos (fr. 7) introduces someone who, before adding his bit on the subject of fishmongers (see below), says that 'the poets are rubbish, for they invent not a single thing that is new, but every one of the them just shifts the same topics back and forth'.

Themes and motifs

Let us look now at a few examples of themes and motifs found in Old Comedy and developed later in Middle and New. We may begin by taking again the Boiotians and Herakles, their gluttonous representative. He appears as such in the *Birds* (1565-1692) and *Frogs* (62-65, 107), is mentioned in *Peace* (741-743), *Wasps* (60) and *Lysistrata* (928); there is evidence that he was not absent from the comedies of Eupolis and Kratinos (*Peace* 741; cf. Athenaeus 411b-12b). It is clearly not by chance that Aristophanes choses a bun-eating Boiotian (*Acharnians* 872) to bring fish, flesh and fowl to Dikaiopolis' private market.[7] This Boiotian is not suffering from starvation, nor does he have to sell his starving daughters as the Megarian does, but is so overburdened with Boiotia's merchandise and produce that he has developed a porter's hump (860) and needs a slave to help him carry it all. The most valued item of his fare is definitely the Kopaic eel.

The eel

Aristophanes' comic personification of the Kopaic eel – a star of many comedies to come – is worthy of attention. The scene is a parody of a reunion scene in tragedy. Dikaiopolis greets the eel lovingly as a longed-for mistress (*enchelus* is feminine) from whom he has been separated for years on end, to be precise from the beginning of the war (881-94), and the Boiotian bids the 'mistress' to be nice, that is to grant sexual favours (*kepicharittoi* 884) to Dikaiopolis. Aristophanes repeats the device in the *Lysistrata* (701-3):

> I invited my chum from next door – a fine girl and one I was fond
> of, an eel from Boiotia; but they say they wouldn't let her come,
> because of your decrees.   (trans. Sommerstein)

In *Clouds* 559, Aristophanes complains that other writers of comedy steal his similes about the eels. Commentators as a rule follow the ancient commentator on *Clouds* 559, where *Knights* 864ff., is mentioned. Dover (1968) on *Clouds* 559, overlooking the two personifications of eels in *Acharnians* and *Lysistrata*, even goes as far as to state that in the extant plays of Aristophanes a simile with eels can only be found in *Knights* 864ff., 'where Cleon is compared with an eel-fisher who stirs up the mud'. No plagiarism of this comparison survives in Old Comedy, nor in Middle or New. Evidently Aristophanes in *Clouds* 559 is complaining not about the plundering of his simile in the *Knights*, but about the plundering of his personifications of the eel in *Acharnians* (and *Lysistrata*), for, although no plagiarism of this personification in Old Comedy survives, it does appear in Middle Comedy, for Euboulos (fr. 34) clearly followed Aristophanes' lead and even carried the personification of the eel a step further. Using the traditional language of the wedding song, he describes it as a bride suddenly making her almost divine appearance, white-skinned and dressed in purple dress – the beetroot covering of the white flesh of the eel – the traditional way of serving eels.[8] Elsewhere Euboulos even elevates Boiotian eels to the status of goddesses (frs 36, 64). The Middle Comedy playwright

Antiphanes (fr. 145) gives the divine aspect of the eels an additional twist:

> They say that the Egyptians are clever in other ways too, but
> especially in recognizing the eel as equal to the gods. For merely
> by offering prayers we may reach the gods, but to get just a smell
> of eels we must spend at the least a dozen drachmas or more. So
> altogether sacred is the beast.[9]

Fish

These divine creatures, as Antiphanes implies, were divinely expensive.
A passage from Aristophanes' *Frogs* 1068 may serve as an early illustration
of the theme of the high price of fish. In it, a wealthy man tries to evade
the trierarchy by pleading poverty, and 'if he gets away with it, he pops up
in the fish market' – the very place where the conspicuous consumption
of the rich is ostentatiously displayed. Fish were many times more
expensive than cereals, and some types of fish were luxury items aimed at
a very restricted market, certainly not the food of the masses. Alexis (fr. 78)
says that a poor man who is rich enough to buy fish often is obviously a
thief, especially if he is young. Antiphanes (fr. 69) calls large fish man-
eaters (*anthropophagoi*), for their high cost consumes a man's estate; Alexis
(fr. 76) refers to the high price of fish in a paradoxical passage: 'These fish
are held for sale at the price of our estates, and he who buys, straightway
ambles home a beggar',[10] immediately swelling the ranks of the parasites.
Fish, then, are man's enemies, for at sea they eat the shipwrecked (see
Purcell in this volume) and when they are caught and killed they ruin their
buyers. The Old Comedy poet Archippos, in *The Fishes*, a comedy produced at the end of the 5th century BC (after 403), satirizes the fondness
of the Athenians for sea food. He humorously describes this situation as a
state of war between the polis of the Athenians and the polis of Fishes, who
hold assemblies and are addressed by speakers as 'fish-citizens', (fr. 30).
Under the treaty of peace some Athenians are handed over to the fish for
punishment, among them Melanthios, the tragic poet, known for his
luxurious eating habits (fr. 28).[11]

Some rich fish-lovers became sufficiently notorious to merit satiric mention in Middle Comedy as men who storm the fish market like a hurricane,
buying whatever there is at high prices and forcing others to eat vegeta-

bles. Some even buy the fishermen's entire catch and then no fish reach the market.[12] Thus Antiphanes (fr. 50) ridicules two rich men who clash over buying fish:

> Menelaus fought ten years against the Trojans for the sake of a woman of lovely countenance, but Phoinikides fights with Taureas for the sake of an eel.

Diphilos (fr. 31.19-23), explaining the laws of Corinth which regulate marketing, describes the plight of those who cannot engage in such expensive fights:

> You have forced our city on to vegetables. We fight for parsley as if it were the Isthmian games.
>
> (trans. Webster: see Webster 1970,
> 158; cf. also Diphilos fr. 32).

Fishmongers, prominent in jocular descriptions in Middle and New Comedy, make an early appearance in Aristophanes, *Wasps* 493-5, where an outspoken fishmonger, who does not make a sale, attacks an extravagant buyer: 'This man seems to be buying fish like a would-be dictator!'; and in *Islands*, Aristophanes includes among the good things that peace provides the pleasure of not having to be kept waiting by a fishmonger in the *agora* and then finally being forced to buy an overpriced, manhandled two-day-old fish (fr. 402). Fishmongers do not appear on stage in the extant plays and fragments, but their customs and manners are frequently described humorously and even sarcastically by other characters. Someone in Antiphanes (fr. 164) compares them to Gorgons, since one is forced to avert one's glance when one talks to them, for seeing what they charge for a small-sized fish immediately turns the buyer into stone. When they laugh and joke with a customer, you may be sure that the fish they offer for sale is rotten (Alexis fr. 217); when their fare is fresh they behave like generals, proudly lifting their eyebrows and disdaining the buyers. If anyone tries to bargain with them, they send him off with insolent repartee (Alexis fr. 16); it is easier to be received by a general than to approach a fishmonger and get a straight answer from him, not one couched in jargon or clipped, half-pronounced words (Amphis fr. 30). Xenarchos (fr. 7) relates how fishermen circumvent the law which forbids them to rinse their fish in order to create the false impression that they had just been caught. They cleverly start a fight among themselves: one of them pretends to have received a mortal blow and collapses onto the fish, another yells 'Water! Water!' and immediately water is poured generously over the fish, and just a tiny drop lands on the fishmonger who has allegedly been mortally wounded. Antiphanes (fr. 123) makes fun of the way fishmongers advertise their wares:

> One man was just now loudly bawling that he had *membrades* to sell sweeter than honey. If that is so, there is nothing to prevent the honey-dealers in their turn from saying and shouting that the honey they have to sell is rottener than *membrades*.

Feasting

Two varieties of fish are included in the menus of Dikaiopolis and Lamachos in the *Acharnians*. A messenger from Dionysos' priest invites Dikaiopolis to dinner: he urges him to come quickly with his lunch-box of food and his pitcher of wine. The host provides the venue with the necessary accessories, the dessert and the entertainment. The messenger recites a short catalogue of what awaits the guests (1089-92):

> Everything is ready, couches, tables, cushions, covers, garlands, unguents, sweetmeats; the whores are there; sponge-cakes, flatcakes, sesame-cakes, wafer-cakes; and dancing girls, 'Harmodios' beloved', lovely ones.   (trans. Sommerstein)[13]

Similar invitations to dinner, describing the preparations and the kinds of food being prepared, are also found in the *Frogs* (503-418) and the *Ecclesiazousai* (834-52). In the *Acharnians*, however, it seems that Aristophanes is handling a familiar *topos* in a novel way by incorporating it in an unusual context. The dinner invitation is juxtaposed with another type of invitation, or rather with an order to Lamachos to prepare for a military campaign. The two invitations are set one against the other, leading to a comic scene of antithetical preparations for two contrasting events.

Not much food is available to Lamachos, who did not have the benefit of access to Dikaiopolis' private market. The provisions that he takes with him (*Ach.* 1097ff.) consist of a dried, rotten salted fish – the cheapest imaginable and most ordinary food (see *Wasps* 491-2) – wrapped in a fig leaf, some salt flavoured with thyme to make the fish more palatable, and onions, the garnish of the poor man or the soldier (cf. also *Peace* 1129). When the little he takes with him runs out, he will, if he is lucky, catch some locusts on arriving at his post.[14]

As against the salted, rotten fish wrapped in a fig leaf, Dikaiopolis is taking slices of fresh fish to the feast, freshly prepared for immediate consumption. The fig leaf, which serves as a mere wrapper for Lamachos' rations, diversifies into a separate appetizing dish, 'a fig-leaf of fat', which is explained in the ancient commentator as 'a dish comprising pig's or kid's fat, fine flour, milk, and egg yolk for stiffening, wrapped in a fig-leaf.' All the rest of Dikaiopolis' food consists of luxuries that have no parallel in Lamachos' ration box: a pigeon, a thrush (an uncommon and desirable dish), a bowl containing hare's meat – a delicacy not easily obtainable in Attika, especially in wartime, a jugged hare, which Dikaiopolis contemplates eating on the spot before dinner, and sausages. To wash down this rich menu, Dikaiopolis brings along a pitcher full of wine. Nor is that all. When he finishes stuffing himself with his own food, he will be served dessert prepared by his host as promised.

Sex at dinner

With the dessert come the girls as well. They are not to be found, of course, where Lamachos is heading. Therefore he can take onions to his post. That is why Dikaiopolis is made to say that he hates onions, for he is heading for a dinner where there are girls waiting, and from which he returns tipsy, supported by two of them, with whom he takes it in turn to exchange deep kisses. In *Lysistrata* 798, when the half-chorus of old men say that they want to kiss the half-chorus of women, the women respond: 'In that case you won't be eating onions,' that is, eating onions will spoil your chances of getting a kiss.[15]

A banquet was a place where sex was an appropriate ingredient of the meal, and vice versa, where food provided the necessary condition for sex. *Sine Cerere et Libero friget Venus* wrote Terence (*Eun.* 732), and Antiphanes (fr. 238) expresses the same idea: 'Love dwells where plenty is, but among those who are hard up Aphrodite will not stay.'[16] Female dancers and musicians, hired by the host to provide entertainment, also performed sexual services for the male participants. Murray calls it 'the creation of a type of "free love" associated with the *hetaira* and the other attendants or entertainers in the *symposion*.'[17] Theirs was bought love, on the same footing as the food, and supplied together with it. Love not bought, however, that is the love of boys associated with the *symposion*, this had to be won. Instead of resorting to the rhetoric of seduction, food could be, and indeed was, used as a powerful and effective tool of amatory persuasion for the enticement and seduction of beautiful and desirable boys. A meal with fish on its menu was a sure way of achieving just that. In his *Odysseus* (fr. 34.12-18), Anaxandrides introduces a fisherman who says:

> By what enchantments or eloquence can a beautiful lad be seduced, tell me, if one abolishes the fisherman's art? This it is which goes on its conquering way, subduing with the cheerful aspect of stewed fish, luring their very bodies to the gates of luncheon, and forces their natures to succumb without receiving a fee.

Athenaeus, when discussing the dog-fish (*galeos*) 295b), quotes Lynkeus of Samos, who says in his *Letter to Diagoras* that Archestratos rightly urges anyone unable to pay the price of the fish to win it by other ways, and that 'When Theseus grew to be handsome, he yielded his favours because Tlepolemos gave him this fish.'

The boldest attempt at seducing a large number of desirable youths at one go by a vast assortment of exquisite foods is presented by Mnesimachos in *Hippotrophos* (fr. 4). A master orders his slave to invite all the boys of the right age (*horaioi*) who are exercising their equestrian skills in the *agora* to a feast at his house. It is the longest extant description of a menu in comedy: the fragment runs to 65 lines. After some starters such as bulbs and olives, stuffed fig- and vine-leaves, comes a long, seemingly endless catalogue of every imaginable fish, some common, such as sprats and mackerels, most rare and expensive. The latter are the most effective substitute for the rhetoric of persuasion and may be taken as the equivalent of a hyperbole: tunny, dogfish, eel, conger eel, electric ray, perch, red mullet, grey mullet, murry, cuttlefish, sea perch, sole, octopus, squid, shrimp and crayfish. Men would fight fiercely for the privilege of buying and consuming many of these (see above). And this is not all, for after the fish comes a catalogue of all sorts of meat in great quantities. It is clearly not the kind of dinner to which the guests bring their own lunch-box. Everything is provided by the host and cooked by his gourmet chef, whom the guests are asked not to insult by turning up late. It is definitely a ruinously expensive dinner. Some of the fish on the menu could eat up an entire estate or two just by themselves. The catalogue is composed in such a way that its very exhaustiveness is a pointer to its fantastic character, thus helping the audience to realise that it is a comic device and to undermine any attempt to refer what they hear to reality. Not only do the mountains of food seem unreal, but it is hardly imaginable that a single cook could have orchestrated such a lavish spread in a single day. Maritime folk would also be aware that this variety of fishes, which came from different places and were caught at different seasons, could not have been caught and brought to market at one time.[18] As Athenaeus says:

> It is not, to be sure, feasible to serve all things at the same time,
> yet it is easy to talk about them.   (5a)

It is therefore quite apparent that this lengthy description of a menu is to be taken with a grain of salt. It is intended to entertain the spectators not just by the enumeration of food, but also by making it perfectly clear to them that it is not a description of an actual meal but a means of seduction. An inherent part of the entertainment-value of this fragment is the perception that the host does not conceal his intentions and his aim is immediately transparent. The culinary gratification of the boys is to pave the way for the erotic gratification of the host and his guests. There is a subtext to this enumeration of foods: the longer the list, the greater the erotic ardour it represents, and it grows with the addition of each item.

'The sensible man should collect pleasures,' says Alexis (fr. 273). 'These are three, the genuine factors in life: drinking, eating, sexual indulgence. All the rest must be called appendages.' (trans. Norwood). All three pleasures are there, combined in the *symposion* of pleasure.

Notes

1. 'Feeding on hopes' is a commonplace. See for example Aristophanes fr. 121.7 and Fraenkel (1950) on Aeschylus *Agamemnon* 1668; Borthwick (1966, 110): 'The neglect by intellectuals of basic things like eating and drinking is a common joke in comedy'. In Homer (*Odyss.* 11.262-3), Zethos as well as Amphion founded and fortified Thebes; both brothers go to Thebes also in Euripides: see Hunter (1983, 96-9, 101-2); Egan (1985). See also Plato *Gorgias* 485e ff. with Dodds (1959) *ad loc.*; on Antiope see Nesselrath (1990, 223-7).

2. See also Demonikos (Middle Comedy) fr. 1 and Diphilos fr. 22. The image of the thick-witted Boiotian persisted, and not only in comedy. Plutarch *Moralia* 995e writes that 'the Athenians used to call us Boiotians dense and insensitive and witless, mainly because of our big appetites. It was also they who named us pigs. And Menander called us "The men with the jaws"'; and see Roberts (1895, 1-9); the opinion attributed by Herodotos 1. 133 to the Persians is that 'the Greeks when they eat, leave off hungry, having nothing worth mention served up to them after the meats; whereas if they had more put before them, they would not stop eating' (trans. Rawlinson), a passage quoted by Athenaeus 144a. For ridicule of an Attic dinner, see Lynkeus (IV/IIIc.) fr. 1; Alexis fr. 216: a man about to entertain a Thessalian (who are also depicted as big eaters) intends to hire two cooks, the most professional in town, to prepare a meal not in any Attic fashion: not everybody likes an Attic meal. See also Diphilos fr. 17; Antiphanes fr. 170

3. On the proliferation of peddlers we have this catalogue by Nicophon, fr. 10: Anchovy-peddlers, charcoal-peddlers, dried-fig-peddlers, hide-peddlers, barley-peddlers, spoon-peddlers, book-peddlers, sieve-peddlers, sweet-cake-peddlers, seed-peddlers; see also Euboulos, fr. 74. On the contrast between frugality and luxury in Athens, see Gallo (1989, 213-30).

4. See Murray (1990a, 3-13), and the literature cited there; also Bremmer (1990). On the contrast betwen war and feasting, see also the scene with Lamachos' son, *Peace* 1270 ff. and especially 1284: 'they were sated with war and then they began eating' (trans. Sommerstein); in *Peace* 775ff. the Muse is asked to sing of feasting rather than war: see Sommerstein *ad loc.* and Richardson (1981).

5. In Aristophanes' comedies there are several instances of cooking on stage: in *Birds* 1579ff. Peisetairos and his slaves cook the oligarchic birds (see Rogers (1906) on 1579, who assumes that an *ekkyklema* (stage trolley) was used); in *Peace* 1016-1135 there is an on-stage presentation of a sacrificial ceremony of a sheep butchered off-stage; Sommerstein (1985) on *Peace* 1197 sees no sign of Trygaios cooking on stage, but believes that Dikaiopolis in *Acharnians* 1003ff. does so, but clearly the food for Dikaiopolis' banquet is brought from inside the house (*Ach.* 1096ff.). There are several instances of the drinking of wine on stage. Philokleon is apparently to sip some soup in *Wasps* 906ff. Among the props of this scene are a chamber-pot (807), a fire in a brazier (811), and a bowl of soup (811) with two cups (855, 906); Sommerstein (1984, 148, 152 n.36), following Landfester (1977, 184), entertained the notion for a while that in *Peace* 'the chorus after singing helped themselves to the food which had been brought out at 1195-6.' Later, in his edition of *Peace* (1985), he retracted this position and offered another explanation (see his remarks on *Peace* 1315). It is indeed difficult to believe that the entire chorus of singers and dancers would actually indulge in unrestrained feasting (while most probably facing a hungry audience), and subsequently continue their singing and dancing with full bellies. The only example that Webster (1970a), 112 cites for the enaction of feasting on stage in Middle Comedy, which he claims 'audiences evidently greatly enjoyed', is the end of Plautus' *Stichus*. But see Prehn (1916, 7): 'neque vero est iusta cena sed magis potatio, quam agitant Sangarinus et Stichus'; for other episodes see Prehn 5ff. His conclusion (8ff.) – which is adopted by Webster – is that episodes of drinking, singing and dancing had been popular in Old and Middle Comedy and in the plays of Diphilos, but that Philemon and Menander (at least in his later comedies) had avoided such scenes. On Menander's *Synaristosai* see the discussion in Turner (1970, 35-9); also Brown (1992, 95); on banquets out of doors in Roman comedy, Duckworth (1952, 126-7).

6. All translations of Athenaeus and of comic fragments cited by him are from the Loeb version by C.B. Gulick.

7. See also Ephippos fr. 1; Arist. fr. 380; Gallo (1983, 456-7).

8. See Aristophanes *Acharnians* 894; *Peace* 1014; Athenaeus

297c-300d; Antiphanes fr. 216; Hunter (1983, 126-7); also Philetairos fr. 13: 'All mortals who live unhappily when they have abundant substance I for one count as despicable. For surely when you're dead you never have eels to eat, and they don't bake wedding-cake in the land of the dead' (trans. Sommerstein).

9. See Herodotos 2.72: 'Only two sorts of fish are venerated, that called Roman *lepidotus* and the eel. These are regarded sacred to the Nile' (trans. Rawlinson). Other fish elevated by comic writers to the status of gods are the red mullet (*trigle*), sea lizard (*glaukiskos*, diminutive of *glaukos*) and conger eel (*gongros*) (Nausikrates fr. 1). See also Archippos fr. 18. Athenaeus (337f-8a) quotes Hegesander, who says in his *Commentaries* that Dorion, the piper, told his slave to recite the names of the best fishes, and when he enumerated the sea perch, sea lizard, conger eel and others of that sort, Dorion said to him: 'I told you to recite the names of fish, not gods.' Other 'gods' connected with feasting: Amphis fr. 9 names white bread (*ametes*), good wine (*oinos hedus*), eggs (*oia*), sesame seeds (*sesamai*), perfume (*muron*), a wreath (*stephanos*), and a flutegirl (*auletris*), and makes someone exclaim that these are the names of the Twelve Gods (*onoma ton dodeka theon*). See also Dumont (1988).

10. Diphilos fr. 32 describes a man who bought a conger eel weighed in gold, just as Priam bought the body of Hector; and Antiphanes (fr. 27) says that Kallisthenes is consuming his estate for the sake of one red mullet (*trigle* – most probably the nickname of a hetaira); see also Timokles fr. 4.8, who relates that Hypereides took bribes from Harpalos and that 'he will make our fishmongers rich'; for fish that only the rich can afford see Eriphos fr. 3; Aristophanes fr. 380; Gallant (1985, 40); Curtis (1991, 4, 6-8, 113-131, 149 n.3); Schaps (1985/88).

11. On Melanthios' eating habits, see Aristophanes *Peace* 804 ff.; Leukon fr. 3; Pherekrates fr. 148; on Archippos *The Fishes*, see Kaibel (1889).

12. Alexis frs. 47, 249; Antiphanes fr. 188. For an early example of fighting over fish in the market, see Aristophanes *Peace* 999-1015.

13. For what the host provides, see for example Xenophon *Symposium* 3.2: Kallias has hired the Syracusan owner of a performing troupe of slaves, a boy and two girls. They entertain the guests with music, singing, dancing, acrobatics and mime; on the *akletoi* (uninvited guests) as entertainers, see Fehr (1990): 'The most important variants of the *akletos* in later literature are the *kolax* ['flatterer'], and close to him, the *parasitos* ['parasite']' (186). See also 185 n.2 (Philippos at Kallias' banquet), 187-8, 193-4. When guests brought their own home-cooked food to a dinner, there was no emphasis on cookery as art. But when hosts also provided the food and cooks were hired for such special occasions as, for example, the wedding-feasts of Middle and New Comedy, the cook became a prominent character. The boasting that characterizes this stock character in comedy perhaps reflects commercially oriented self-advertisement in real life.

14. On locusts, see Davies and Kathirithamby (1986, 141-2); Beavis (1988, 76); the former do not believe that Greeks ate them. On salted fish, imported and cheap, see Gallo (1989, 223 n.8, 229 n.56).

15. See also *Peace* 1138, where Thratta is kissed at an onionless dinner, and *Peace* 529, where the smell that comes from the soldier's ration-bag is the smell of onions and indigestion (*krommuoxuregmias*); in Xenophon *Symposium* 4.9 we read: 'I grant that when a man is setting out for battle, it is well for him to nibble an onion… as for us, however, our plans look more to getting a kiss from someone than to fighting' (trans. Todd); and see also Plutarch *Quaestiones conviviales* 4.4 = *Moralia* 669b. In Aristophanes *Thesmophoriazousae* 494-6 an adulterous wife chews garlic before her husband returns home.

16. Euripides expresses a similar idea: 'You will find Aphrodite when people have plenty of recourses, but not among the poor' (*en plesmosyne toi Kupris, en peinosi d' ou*, fr. 895N).

17. See Murray (1990a, 7); Pellizer (1990, 181); Halperin (1990, 110); on one of the services usually required of the girls at symposia see Aristophanes *Wasps* 1345-50 and Jocelyn (1980, 25-6).

18. Gallant (1985, 43-44).

Bibliography

Beavis, I.C., 1988 *Insects and other Invertebrates in Classical Antiquity* (Exeter).

Bodson, L., 1988 *L'animal dans l'alimentation humaine: les critères de choix* (Actes du colloque international de Liège 26-29 novembre 1986 = *Anthropozoologica* 2.

Borthwick, E.K., 1966 'A grasshopper's diet: notes on an epigram of Meleager and a fragment of Eubulus', *Classical Quarterly* 16, 107-12.

Bremmer, J., 1990 'Adolescents, *symposion* and pederasty' in Murray (1990), 135-46.

Brown, P.G.McC., 1992 'Menander frr. 745 and 746 K-T: kolax and parasites and flatterers', *Zeitschrift für Papyrologie und Epigrafik* 92, 91-107.

Curtis, R.I., 1991 *Garum and Salsamenta* (Leiden, New York, Copenhagen, Cologne).

Davies, M. & Kathirithamby, J., 1986 *Greek Insects* (London).

Dodds, E.R., 1959 *Plato: Gorgias* (Oxford).

Dover, K.J., 1968 *Aristophanes: Clouds* (Oxford).

Duckworth, G.E., 1952 *The Nature of Roman Comedy* (Princeton).

Dumont, J., 1988 'Les critères culturels du choix des poissons dans l'alimentation grecque antique: le cas d'Athénée de Naucratis', in Bodson (1988), 99-113.

Egan, R.B., 1985 'Cecropids in Eubulus (fr. 10) and Satyrus (*A.P.* 10.6)', *Classical Quarterly* 35, 523-5.

Fehr, B., 1990 'Entertainers at the symposion', in Murray (1990), 185-95.

Fraenkel, E., 1950 *Aeschylus: Agamemnon* (Oxford).

Gallant, T.W., 1985 *A Fisherman's Tale* (Gent).

Gallo. L., 1983 'Alimentazione e classi sociali: una nota su orro e frumento in Grecia', *Opus* 2, 449-472, and especially 456-7.

Gallo, L., 1989 'Alimentazione urbana e alimentazione contadina nell' Atene classica', in Longo and Scarpi (1989), 213-30.

Halperin, D.M., 1990 *One Hundred Years of Homosexuality* (London).

Henderson, J., 1975 *The Maculate Muse* (New Haven and London).

Hunter, R.L., 1983 *Eubulus: the Fragments* (Cambridge).

Jocelyn, H.D., 1980 'A Greek indecency and its students', *Proceedings of the Cambridge Philological Society* 26, 12-66.

Kaibel, G., 1889 'Zur attischen Komödie, *Hermes* 24, 35-66 and 49-54.

Landfester, M., 1977 *Handlungsverlauf und Komik in den frühen Komödien des Aristophanes* (Berlin and New York).

Longo, O. & Scarpi, P., (eds) 1989 *Homo Edens* (Verona).

MacDowell, D.M., 1971 *Aristophanes: Wasps* (Oxford).

Murray, O., (ed.) 1990 *Sympotica* (Oxford).

Murray, O., 1990a 'Sympotic history', in Murray (1990), 3-13.

Nesselrath, H.-G., 1990 *Die attische mittlere Komödie* (Berlin and New York) .

Pellizer, E., 1990 'Outlines of a morphology of sympotic entertainment' in Murray (1990), 177-84.

Prehn, B., 1916 *Quaestiones Plautinae* (Breslau).

Richardson, N.J., 1981 'The contest of Homer and Hesiod and Alcidamas' *Mouseion*', *Classical Quarterly* 31, 1-3 .

Roberts, W.R., 1895 *The Ancient Boeotians* (Cambridge).

Rogers, B.B., 1906 *Aristophanes: Birds* (London).

Schaps, D.M., 1985/88 'Comic inflation in the market place', *Scripta Classica Israelica* 8-9, 66-73.

Sommerstein, A.H., 1984 'Act division in Old Comedy', *Bulletin of the Institute of Classical Studies* 31, 139-52.

Sommerstein, A.H., 1985 *Aristophanes: Peace* (Warminster).

Turner, E.G., 1970 *Ménandre* (Entretiens sur l'Antiquité Classique XVI) (Vandoevres-Geneva).

Webster, T.B.L., 1970a *Studies in Menander*[2] (Manchester).

Webster, T.B.L., 1970b *Studies in Later Greek Comedy*[2] (Manchester).

❖ 30 ❖   ARCHESTRATOS
WHERE AND WHEN?

Andrew Dalby

The threatened world

Gᴿᴇᴇᴋs of the middle Mediterranean, in 350 BC, faced a terrifying future: and some of them, at least, were aware of it.

In eastern Sicily and southern Italy, two of the wealthiest regions ever settled by Greeks, irresponsible power and ambition had brought warfare, destruction and wholesale uprooting of populations. Dionysios I of Syracuse had swept out the inhabitants from seven cities or more, selling some as slaves, forcibly resettling others in his chaotic capital. He had fought four useless and exhausting wars with the Carthaginians who ruled western Sicily. The Carthaginians had ravaged most of the island at some stage, and had destroyed at least six cities, killing and enslaving, leaving a few to survive in the ruins. Oscan-speaking mercenaries from central Italy, employed by both sides, had decided to stay on and had already seized at least four cities for themselves.

As Greeks fought over the remains of Dionysios' fragmented kingdom, more mercenaries were still being commissioned; and the Carthaginians were watching for their opportunity. The Mediterranean here is at its narrowest: just across the water lay Phoenician-speaking Carthage itself, vast, prosperous, powerful.

The philosopher Plato, who had visited the Syracusan court twice and knew the power of the rowdy mercenaries (*Letter* 7.348a), saw ahead clearly:

> I pray it will not happen but I fear it will: all of Sicily, practically, will lose the Greek tongue and will fall to some Phoenician or Oscan government and power.   (*Letter* 8.353f)[1]

In Greece itself warfare between tiny cities was a way of life, but the long Peloponnesian War had drawn many into a cycle of long-term, vendetta-like mutual destruction which no one seemed to be able to stop. Spartan troops, long thought invincible, had been brought low by Thebans in 371; Thebes was soon to fall. The Athenians' tyranny over the coasts and islands of the Aegean, once unchallengeable, was faltering. The real threat here was coming from north and east.

The King of Macedon had begun to show his strength. Philip II, a 'nomadic shepherd' according to one supercilious Athenian, was acquisitive rather than destructive. Macedonia was not above destroying cities, as Olynthos and Thebes were to find; but many – Torone and Abdera and Maroneia incorporated in 358, Ainos by 350 – retained prosperity for the time being under a power which would soon reach to Byzantium and to central Greece.

Meanwhile the Greek-speaking cities on the eastern coast of the Aegean, once dominated by the Athenian fleet, had nearly all submitted once again in 387 BC to the 'King' as Greeks unambiguously called him, the King of the Persians who now controlled all the coasts of the eastern Mediterranean. Many Greeks had found employment under the King – as mercenaries, in particular. Greeks had learned to live on Persian fringes.

This was all very well; but some already saw that Macedonians would challenge Persians for the empire. Any who thought about the subject could see both the growth of Macedon and the remaining might of Persia and knew that there was reason to fear for the future.

The single-minded gastronome

One Greek who must have travelled from end to end of this terrifying world wrote, at precisely this time, a book unlike any before[2] (and we know of only one later imitation, Ennius' early Latin *Hedyphagetica*): a poetic catalogue of seaside cities and their gastronomic specialities.

Archestratos's poem cannot any longer be read in its entirety. It was already surely a very rare work in the 3rd century AD when, luckily, Athenaeus came across it and quoted extensively from it in *The Deipnosophists*. No manuscript survived the Middle Ages: all that is now known of *The Experience of Pleasure* are the lines that Athenaeus selected.[3]

Archestratos was linked by later scholars with two Sicilian cities, Syracuse and Gela (Athenaeus *Epitome* 4e): at any rate he would have been a subject of Dionysios and of that monarch's unattractive successors. Later scholars argued too over the title of the book, though the majority settled on *Hedypatheia*, 'The Experience of Pleasure.'[4]

It is a vague enough title, and gave some excuse for Athenaeus to speak of 'Archestratos, who circumnavigated the world for the sake of the stomach and what lies below the stomach'.[5] Even so, to modern readers of Archestratos's verses, it does seem unfair that writers of only fifty years later should already be wilfully confusing the gastronomic poet's subject-matter with quite a different kind of pleasure. Klearchos, a student of Aristotle, never happier than when going into detail on other people's sexual depravity, criticised 'those people nowadays who start conversations at parties like which sexual posture is the most enjoyable, or which fish, or how cooked; or which is in season now, or which is best to eat after Arcturus or after the Pleiades or after Sirius… This is typical of a man who is at home with the works of Philaenis and Archestratos' (Klearchos fr.63 Wehrli, quoted by Athenaeus 457c-e), Philaenis being the authoress of the first known sex manual (*Oxyrhynchus Papyrus* 2891).

But the coupling of gastronomy and sex in these philosophers' strictures is natural enough.[6] Dinner parties for men were all-round entertainments, designed to please every fleshly sense. With the taste of food and wine came the scents of perfumes and wreaths, the sounds of song and music and the sight of musicians and dancers; and the female performers, and other women who were present, were in general not untouchable.[7]

Moreover, the symposium itself was a performance, and in these terms it was one that allowed no audience but only actors.[8] Men who disapproved of sensual indulgence (in shorthand, 'philosophers') might well wonder what part in the entertainment they themselves should be playing. Should they be the impassive observer, or the observer who succumbs to temptation,[9] or the guest who leaves early? Or, since all these roles were open to ridicule,[10] should they not be there at all?

These are important topics in analysing the response to Archestratos, but not, from all that we can judge, in analysing Archestratos's actual work. Archestratos concentrated on food. He knew what fish to buy on the seafront at Carthage,[11] and in the market at Pella (fr.30 [328a]). He knew of the industrial bread ovens of Athens and of the 'clay ovens' or *klibanoi* of Persian-dominated Erythrai (fr.4 [111f]; cf. Cubberley in this volume). People traded with Oscan-lettered coins at Hipponion, with Phoenician at Selinous:[12] at Iasos the current coins named Mausolos, hereditary Persian governor; at Maroneia and Abdera they named Philip. Archestratos could have written of the politics of all these places, but he stuck to their food.

Only once, perhaps unconsciously, he allowed the nightmare through which he and his contemporaries lived to break the surface of his poem:

> All to dine at one hospitable table: there shall be three or four
> altogether or at most five, or you would have a tentful of plun-
> dering mercenaries.   (fr.61 [Athenaeus *Epitome* 4d])

There, in a throwaway phrase, was the single greatest threat to the stability and prosperity of his native Sicily.

When did Archestratos write?

Modern scholars have tried several ways of pinning *The Experience of Pleasure* to a date. Archestratos has to be early enough for Klearchos to drop his name: Klearchos was born about 342 BC. He has to be early enough for the comic playwright Antiphanes and his Athenian audience to know of him – if it is true that Antiphanes' play title *Archestrate* is a reference to Archestratos (the title would mean something like *Archestratos' Sister, The Female Gourmet*): Antiphanes died about 330 BC.[13] Two other cross-references might in theory be useful for dating but are not much use in practice.[14]

It is time for a different approach. This is provided by the particular combination of places of which Archestratos wrote. First we must work forwards. As a starting point, he could not have advised anyone to buy food in Tyndaris (fr.34 [301f]) before that city was founded in 396 BC.[15] But then in 396 BC the Carthaginians destroyed Messana, and a few years later Dionysios wiped Hipponion and Rhegion off the traveller's itinerary: Hipponion was deserted from 389 to 379 (when the Carthaginians re-established it), Rhegion from 387 onwards. It was probably only some time after Dionysios' death in 367 that people went back to Messana and Rhegion.[16] Only then would it have made sense for Archestratos to advise his readers – as he does five times – to look to the towns on the Straits of Messina for fine food (see for example fr.8 [298e]).

Now we can work backwards. Archestratos never mentions any town, or any food, that became accessible to Greeks after Alexander's conquest of Persia. He recommends (mildly) the barley of 'seven-gated Thebes' (fr.4 [111e]): the phrase is a poets' cliché,[17] but to use it would have been a joke in poor taste after Thebes and all its gates had been flattened by Alexander's army in 335 (it was refounded only in 315). And the clinching detail is this brief instruction:

> But for my sake go shopping for the head of a *glaukos* at Olynthos
> and Megara, for it is caught in the shallows…   (fr.20 [295c])

Whatever kind of fish a *glaukos* may be – a bluefish, possibly, *Pomatomus saltator*[18] – you could not have gone shopping at Olynthos after 348 BC when Philip of Macedon destroyed the city. Its fate was felt as a wound to Greece; and it was not rebuilt.

These are the arguments that justify my opening survey of central Mediterranean politics around 350 BC. Between about 360 and 348 Archestratos completed and circulated his remarkable poem.

Real traveller or armchair littérateur?

Classicists are becoming sophisticated. One must ask, nowadays, a sophisticated question or two. Had Archestratos really been to any of these places? – as is claimed by himself[19] and on his behalf, more repetitively, by Athenaeus's speakers (116f, 278d, 294a). Is his advice really meant to be taken as gastronomic advice? Or is its apparent meaning negated by some secret, subtle, satirical sub-text?

The answer must be worked through in stages. First: some of the advice *agrees* with received gastronomic opinion of Archestratos's own time. Since most of the relevant surviving literature of the period is Athenian (references in the following footnotes), these points of agreement can now be recognised most often when they concern food and wine available in Athens. Archestratos approved of the bread baked for sale in the Athenian market place,[20] of cakes either made in Athens or soaked in Attic honey,[21] and of the anchovy fry available there:

> Shit on small fry except the Athenian…and choose for preference
> what is caught in the holy straits of motherly Phaleron.
>
> (fr.9 [285b])[22]

And he praised the eels of Lake Kopais that Boiotia exported to Athens.[23] In his approval of these delicacies Archestratos was not alone.

Just so with wine. Archestratos, while he appreciated Thasian wine, so widely praised by earlier generations,[24] really preferred Lesbian (fr.59 [Athenaeus *Epitome* 29b]); and other sources confirm that it was Lesbian which became widely popular in the 4th century and after.[25]

Only two of Archestratos' place-names are in the Peloponnese. Archestratos approved the bread of Tegea, baked under ashes, and the conger eels of Sikyon[26] – and that is all. In his silence, too, Archestratos agrees with other 4th century opinions. Greeks of the Peloponnese had certainly had their own favourite foods and wines, especially the latter: after Alkman (quoted in Athenaeus *Epitome* 31c) the author of one of the Theognis poems (879-84) named a good wine from the foothills of Taygetos; and a *vin cotto* was produced in Sparta (Demokritos in *Geoponica* 7.4). But from outside one hears only of the wine of Phleious and the fish of Sikyon.

Gastronomically speaking, the Peloponnese had almost ceased to belong to the Greek world: this seems true even of the Corinthians. Although the mother city of Syracuse, Corinth is never mentioned in the surviving fragments of Archestratos. The food market at Corinth in the 4th century was said by Athenians, perhaps inconsistently, to be a place where natives looked for expensive foreign wine in preference to their own, yet where lavish spending attracted investigation and punishment.[27]

Secondly: in spite of these agreements, the poem is far from being a string of gastronomic commonplaces already expressed by others. Archestratos disapproved, it seems, of the culinary elaboration which the Sokrates of Plato's *Republic* identified with 'Syracusan tables',[28] and he had no good word for the average 'Sicilian cook':

> Let no Syracusan and no Italiot come near you when you make this dish: they do not know how to prepare good fish, but wickedly spoil it by cheesing everything and dousing it with watery vinegar and pickled silphium.   (fr.45.10-14 [311a])[29]

Archestratos had nothing good to say either, so far as we know, for the way Sicilians arranged their meals:

> And as you imbibe, have served some such relish as this: tripe or boiled sow's womb marinated in cumin and sharp vinegar and silphium, and the tender tribe of birds, such as are in season. But have nothing to do with those Syracusans who simply drink, like frogs, without eating anything. You must not give in to them: eat the food I tell you to.   (fr.62 [101c])

Thirdly (for the argument is still incomplete) Archestratos did far more than to take existing opinions and build on them, agreeing or disagreeing as he chose. No work now known, and no lost work whose subject can now be reconstructed, took on the judging of such a range of foodstuffs or combined it with such an exploration of the smaller Greek harbours and markets. We can best complete this examination of Archestratos with a study of the places named in the poem.

Why Archestratos travelled

If Archestratos appears to have said little about the Peloponnese, it is unlikely to have been for any political reason. Nor does anything political link the places that he named in the Mediterranean world in general. All, probably, had Greek-speaking communities[30] – nearly all had Greek-speaking majorities – but by no means all were ruled by Greeks. We have seen already the extent of Persian, Macedonian and Carthaginian rule in about 350.

But there is a link between most or all of these places: simply that they were of a certain size and a certain prosperity at that precise time. They were worth stopping at 'on business', whatever the business. It is indicative, for example, that no place-names crop up so often in the fragments as Ambrakia and Byzantium (six times each). Ambrakia, though not one of the most talked-of cities in the Greek world, was a regular port of call for Sicilians and Italians sailing east:[31] if he indeed researched in person, Archestratos had sufficient opportunities as he went to and from Sicily to sample all that Ambrakia had to offer gastronomically. Byzantium, an important city, an unavoidable stopping place on the route to the Black Sea (cf. Braund in this volume) and a prolific source of foodstuffs, likewise had every reason to recur in the notebook of a frequent traveller. I suggest that the very fact that these two places recur so frequently shows that we have a reasonable sample of the whole of the original poem.

Nearly all of these places issued coins in the 4th century BC (though Philip of Macedon was against local coinages, and shut down the mints he took over). Those that happen not to have issued coins at this period can still be shown to have been important in trade: they include Carthage, centre of a great trading network; Kalydon, a very important geographical location and according to Strabo's official Roman geography, written in Augustus's time, 'once a showpiece of Greece' (*Geography* 10.2.3); Torone, a significant exporter of wine; Delos, an Athenian dependency of which Strabo (10.5.4) said, 'The festival is a commercial affair…when the Athenians took over the island they took equal care of the religious rites and of the businessmen'; Dion, centre of Macedonian religious festivity and games.

I will at this point suggest a hypothesis. Archestratos did go to the places he named, or to most of them. He travelled on business; he travelled cheaply enough – as most people do – to take a close personal interest in his daily food, its purchase and preparation. But whether he was a ship's captain, a tradesman, a sophist or a rhapsode, I will not presume to guess. He was probably not a mercenary soldier!

Étapes
gastronomiques

Finally let us look at the exceptional places, those about which the attentive reader will now be ready to ask: 'Why on earth would such a traveller go *there*?'

Anthedon was not an important place: it issued no coins. Why would Archestratos have bothered with Anthedon (fr.14 [316a])? This is how Herakleides Kritikos, perhaps a century later, described the place:

> Thebes to Anthedon twenty miles, winding road among the fields but fit for carts. It is not a big city, lying right on the Straits of Euboia. The *agora* is all tree-shaded, with two covered markets, one on each side. There is good wine and good food though a shortage of bread because the farmland is poor. The inhabitants are almost all fishermen, living off hooks and fish and purple-shells and sponges, growing old among beaches and seaweed and fishing-huts, ruddy-faced and agile, their fingernails worn down by the labours of the sea.
>
> (*On the Cities of Greece* 23-4)

I take it there is no further need to ask why Archestratos was interested in Anthedon. It was a place conveniently close to Thebes and noted for its wine and its seafood: in fact Archestratos singles out its cod, saying that he does not like it but others do.

Iasos might also be considered of doubtful interest to the traveller, though it was important enough in its own estimation to correspond with Alexander's court in due course. Strabo's description of the place will prove helpful:

> The people gain most of their living from the sea: there are lots of fish but the land is pretty poor. This is the kind of story they make up about Iasos: a lyre player was performing and everyone was listening to him, when suddenly the fish-market bell sounded and the whole lot went off to market except one deaf man. So the lyre player went up to him and said, 'Sir, I am very grateful to you for the honour you have done me and for your love of music: the others have all gone the moment the bell went.' 'What's that you say? Was that the bell already?' said the deaf man; 'well, goodbye', and he got up and went away as well.   (*Geography* 14.2.21)

Iasos lived for its fish market, and its interest in seafood was almost the only thing about it that Strabo thought worth noting. It was a short sea journey from Miletos; what more natural than for a traveller interested in food, such as Archestratos, to test its reputation? He chooses to comment on the prawns of Iasos – their size and their low price (fr.25 [105e]).

Again, Peloron or Pelorias, the long sandy spit stretching ten miles north of Messana, 'offers equal pleasure in fishing and in hunting,' according to the late Latin author Solinus (5.3) at any rate. Archestratos praises its swordfish (fr.40 [314e]).

There is really only one more place on Archestratos's map that seems to require justification: 'sandy Teichioussa, village of the Milesians', a harbour town – facing south towards Halicarnassos – where good red mullet was to be found (fr.41 [320a]). May we conjecture, given the foregoing precedents, that Teichioussa really was habitually visited by those frequenting the great shrine of Didyma, just five miles away, who were connoisseurs of fish?

Archestratos and the gastronomic tradition

To sum up: most places discussed by Archestratos – and visited by him, I think we should suppose – were worth visiting for several reasons, and were fairly prosperous and active in trade at the time. The smaller the place, the more likely it seems to be that its one notable feature, in other sources as well as in Archestratos's poem, will be its food.

This may be thought, after all, too obvious to have been worth saying. But it suggests further reflection. Most of what any food writer writes comes not from his *unaided* research but also from all the clues he can pick up. He has not tasted everything that a particular place supplies. He has taken advice; he tastes the things that local people are proud of; in most cases he writes to confirm their opinion. It must have been so with Archestratos too: he cannot have tasted, scientifically, everything that all these sixty places had to offer. There were received opinions for him too to build on. How many centuries of unknown gastronomy led up to Archestratos?

Notes

1. Written to advise friends in Syracusan politics in about 352 BC, if it is genuinely by Plato: this proviso has to be made about all personal letters attributed to classical Greek authors.

2. Athenaeus 337b puts it thus: "Klearchos in *On Proverbs* says that Terpsion had been the teacher of Archestratos, being the first to have written a 'Gastrology' telling learners what not to eat; Terpsion having improvised the following about tortoise: 'Eat up, or don't eat, the tortoise's meat'". Gulick, in his translation of Athenaeus (see n. 3), understands this to mean that it was Terpsion who was the first to write a 'Gastrology'. And, yes, that is the grammatically preferable sense of Athenaeus's sentence. But the context, especially the word *apeschediakenai* 'improvised', suggests Klearchos may have meant that *Archestratos* was the first to write a 'Gastrology', an alimentary poem, the germ of the idea having come from the one-line hexameter proverb on food avoidance that was attributed to Terpsion.

3. For an English translation and commentary see Wilkins and Hill (1994). Translations of all passages can be found via the index of Gulick's 7-volume bilingual edition of Athenaeus (Gulick 1927-41). Archestratos in Greek, with textual notes, can be found separated out from Athenaeus in collections by Brandt (1888) and by Lloyd-Jones and Parsons (1983); there is also a separate edition of the Greek text by Montanari (1983) (which I have not worked with). Most current texts, and therefore Gulick's translation too, mislead the unwary by incorporating too many emendations by a succession of scholars.

4. In fact it was probably best known by the name of its author. It was known as *Hedypatheia* to Lynkeus and Kalli-machos, the least obvious word, the best authenticated and so perhaps the most likely to be authoritative; as *Gastronomia* 'The Rules of Eating', *Deipnologia* 'The Science of Dining' and *Opsopoiia* 'Cookery' to others. So we are told in the *Epitome* of Athenaeus 4e. The epitomator is certainly compressing *something* that Athenaeus said, but the statement has to be evaluated sceptically.

He ascribes the title *Gastronomia* to Chrysippos: the evidence, clearly, was in the quotations from Chrysippos actually given later at length by Athenaeus, 335de (and partly translated in n.6 below), and no one can say whether Chrysippos would have troubled, in these dismissive references, to get right the actual title of Archestratos' work. The title *Deipnologia* ascribed to Klearchos may be a mistake for the 'gastrology', *gastrologia* which Klearchos uses as a similarly dismissive generic term in a passage also later quoted by Athenaeus 337b (translated in n.2 above).

No corroboration is available for *Opsopoiia* (or for the alternative *Opsologia* 'Science of Cookery' found in its place in the other witness to Athenaeus's text at this point, the Byzantine dictionary *Suda* at its entry for 'Athenaeus'). But, after all, such names were applied indiscriminately to books about food.

The word ἡδυπάθεια had been used earlier by Xenophon, *Cyropaideia* 7.5.74; there was also a verb ἡδυπαθεῖν 'enjoy oneself', Xen.*Symposium* 4.41 etc.; and 'squander', Xen. *Anabasis* 1.3.3. The word seems to have been a favourite of Xenophon, the Athenian author of the early 4th century BC. Later, in the 2nd century AD, Lucian would refer to the philosopher Aristippos as σοφιστὴς ἡδυπαθείας, 'professor of pleasure'. Later still the word crops up in the scholia on *Odyssey* 8.267, where the subject of the tale of Ares and Aphrodite's adultery is characterised as ἡδυπαθῆ, 'pleasures'.

5. Athenaeus 116f: the remark is put in the mouth of Daphnos, Athenaeus's fictional doctor.

6. Before Klearchos, Plato, in disapproval of the luxury he had found in Sicily, had linked the "tables of the Italiots and Syracusans" with "never sleeping alone at night" (*Letter* 7.326b). And Klearchos's comment in turn was read by Chrysippos of Soloi, who later in the 3rd century coupled gastronomy with sexual experimentation in very similar terms: "...and books like Philaenis's, and the *Gastronomy* of Archestratos, and stimulants to love and sexual intercourse, and then again slave girls practised in such movements and postures...to study all this and to get the books about it by Philaenis and Archestratos and the other writers of such things...likewise not to study Philaenis, or the *Gastronomy* of Archestratos, with the expectation of improving one's life!" (quoted by Athenaeus 335de).

7. Hence all these topics are appropriately dealt with by Athenaeus in his *Deipnosophists*.

8. On the *symposion* seen as a performance, with the guests

among the actors, see Martin (1931), Rossi (1983), Lissarrague (1987).

9. For amusing examples see Persaios of Kition 584 F4 quoted by Athenaeus 607a-e; Antigonos of Karystos quoted by Athenaeus 607e.

10. Plutarch, *Symposium Questions* 7.7: the work is an enjoyable discussion of Greek symposia (as still practised in his time) by the 2nd century AD biographer and essayist. For a view of philosophers as 'parasites' see Timon of Phleious quoted in Athenaeus *Epitome* 22d.

11. Fr. 13 (320a). Archestratos will be cited in this article by Brandt's fragment numbering (the reader can add 131 to arrive at Lloyd-Jones and Parsons' numbering) followed in brackets by a reference to Athenaeus.
Printed texts of this fragment say 'Kalchedon' (opposite Byzantium), but the manuscript of Athenaeus has 'Carthage'. The names differ by only one letter in Greek.

12. Probably the Punic Ras Melkarth, according to Kraay (1976, 234).

13. Antiphanes fr.43 Kock quoted by Athenaeus 322c. Note also Dionysios of Sinope fr.2.24 Kock quoted by Athenaeus 405b.
The poem (or at least its title) was also known to Lynkeus of Samos, student of Theophrastos – see Dalby (1991), to Lykophron of Chalkis, to Klearchos of Soloi, to Kallimachos (Alexandrian poet, died *c.* 240 BC) and to Chrysippos of Soloi (Stoic philosopher – died *c.* 206 BC). References: Klearchos, Kallimachos fr.436 Pfeiffer, Chrysippos and Lynkeus, all cited in Athenaeus *Epitome* 4e; Lynkeus, *Shopping for Food* quoted by Athenaeus 313f; Lykophron, *On Comedy* 19 quoted by Athenaeus 278a.
Already to Klearchos, indeed, Archestratus seemed so well known that gourmets could be described superciliously as οἱ περὶ Ἀρχέστρατον "the people round Archestratos", (quoted by Athenaeus 285d), while Lynkeus expected a correspondent to understand his allusion to ὁ τὴν Ἡδυπαθείαν γράψας "the author of the *Experience of Pleasure*", (quoted by Athenaeus 286a, 294e). Ulpian, a participant in Athenaeus's fictional dialogue, says that Archestratos had "shown Epicurus the way" (Athenaeus 101f).

14. Archestratos refers to two contemporaries: Diodoros of Aspendos, the vegetarian philosopher, fr. 23.19 (163c), but his date is as vague as Archestratos's own; Agathon, 'herald' at Lesbos, otherwise unknown: fr. 56.9 (92d).

15. It was founded by Dionysios I of Syracuse for exiled Messenians, who chose the name (Diodorus Siculus 14.78.5-6).

16. Rhegion was re-founded by Dionysios II before 356 BC (Strabo 6.1.6; Diodorus Siculus 16.16.1).

17. E.g. Homer, *Iliad* 4.406; Anaxandrides fr.41 Kock quoted by Athenaeus 131c.

18. A good food fish, matching some of the features of the ancient γλαῦκος, and one for which no ancient Greek name is known. It is an open sea fish but comes close inshore in summer (Davidson 1981, 100). The translators' usual 'grey-fish' is a literal rendering of the Greek term but is not the name of any fish.

19. Understanding ἱστορίη as 'personal enquiry' (fr.1 (Athenaeus *Epitome* 4e).

20. Fr. 4 (111e). See Athenaeus's neighbouring citations for contemporary support.

21. Fr. 62 (101c). For Attic cakes see also Hippolochos's letter to Lynkeus quoted by Athenaeus 130d: a translation and commentary on this early 3rd century BC letter will be found in Dalby (1988). On Attic honey see Antiphanes fr. 179 Kock quoted by Athenaeus 74e; Phoinikides fr. 2 Kock quoted by Athenaeus 652d.

22. In the 3rd century Chrysippos of Soloi, quoted by Athenaeus 285d, observed that the best anchovy fry were caught at Athens but were not prized by the Athenians themselves. Phaleron is named as the source for Athenian anchovies at least three times in comedies by Aristophanes, *Acharnians* 901, *Birds* 76, and fr. 507 Kock quoted by Athenaeus 285e – as well as by several later sources. Aristotle in his *Study of Animals* 569b10-14 names the best sources for small fry around Athens as Salamis, Marathon and near Themistocles' tomb (which was at the Peiraieus, not at Phaleron).

23. Fr.8 (298e). For contemporary Athenian praise of Kopaic eels see Aristoph., *Peace* 1005, *Acharn.* 880, *Lysistrata* 36, 702, etc.; Antiphanes fr.236 Kock quoted in the Athenaeus *Epitome* 27d.

24. Hermippus fr.82 Kock quoted in Athenaeus *Epitome* 29e; Epilykos fr.6 Kock quoted in Athenaeus *Epitome* 28d; Aristoph., *Assemblywomen* 1119-39; Aristoph. fr.317 Kock

quoted in Athenaeus *Epitome* 29a: the speaker of this last considers 'Pramnian', Thasian, Chian and Peparethan equally arousing. These texts all emphasise the strength, rather than the flavour, of Thasian. There is a great deal to read on Thasos and its wine in the collection edited by Empereur and Garlan (1986).

25. First, around 400 BC, a speaker in Philyllios fr.24 Kock quoted in Athenaeus *Epitome* 31a; then a speaker in Alexis frr.276-8 Kock quoted in Athenaeus *Epitome* 28e. By the 1st century BC it was being said that Sappho's brother Charaxos (Herodotus 2.135 could already tell a romantic tale about his trip to Egypt) had been a dealer in Lesbian wine (Strabo 17.1.33). Ephippos fr.28 Kock quoted in Athenaeus *Epitome* 28f wrote of πράμνιον οἶνον Λέσβιον, 'Pramnian wine of Lesbos': but that's another story.

26. Fr.18 (293f). This is supported by Antiphanes fr.236 Kock quoted in Athenaeus *Epitome* 27d; Eudoxos quoted by Athenaeus 288c; Philemon fr.79 Kock quoted by Athenaeus 288c.

27. Alexis fr.290 Kock quoted in Athenaeus *Epitome* 30f (the context is unknown); Diphilos of Sinope fr.32 Kock quoted by Athenaeus 227d.

28. Of which (understanding the phrase literally) Sokrates knew nothing, though Plato did: Plato, *Republic* 404d.

29. A recipe for bass. For the choice between 'Sicilian baking' and a simpler method for fish, see Ephippos fr.22 Kock quoted by Athenaeus 286e.

30. This may be thought doubtful in the case of the Sicilian and Italian towns recently re-founded by Carthaginians and Oscans. Carthage itself certainly had a Greek-speaking community.

31. Strabo 7.7.5; Dionysios son of Kalliphon, *Description of Greece* 24. Note also the plentiful coinage of Ambrakia – most specimens being found in southern Italy and Sicily.

Bibliography

Brandt, P. (ed.) 1888 *Corpusculum poesis epicae Graecae ludibundae* vol. 1 (Leipzig).

Dalby, A. (trs.) 1988 'The wedding feast of Caranus the Macedonian by Hippolochus', *Petits propos culinaires* 29: 37-45.

Dalby, A. 1991 'The curriculum vitae of Duris of Samos', *Classical Quarterly* n.s. 41: 539-541.

Davidson, A. 1981 *Mediterranean Seafood* 2nd ed., (Harmondsworth).

Empereur, J.-Y. and Garlan, Y. (eds) 1986 *Recherches sur les amphores grecques* (*BCH* suppl. 13) (Athens).

Gulick, C.B. (ed.) 1927-41 Athenaeus, *The Deipnosophists* (Cambridge, Mass.).

Kraay, C. 1976 *Archaic and Classical Greek Coins* (London).

Lissarrague, F. 1987 *Un flot d'images: une esthétique du banquet grec* (Paris).

Lloyd-Jones, H. and Parsons, P. (eds) 1983 *Supplementum Hellenisticum* (Berlin).

Martin, J. 1931 *Symposion* (Paderborn).

Montanari, O. (ed.) 1983 *Archestrato di Gela*, vol. 1. (Bologna).

Rossi, L.E. (ed.) 1983 'Il simposio greco arcaico e classico come spettacolo a se stesso' in *Spettacoli conviviali dall' antichità classica alle corte italiane del '400: atti del VII convegno di studio, Viterbo, maggio 1983* (Viterbo), 41-50.

Wilkins, J., & Hill, S., 1994 *Archestratus: The Life of Luxury* (Totnes).

PROBLEMS IN GREEK GASTRONOMIC POETRY
ON MATRO'S *ATTIKON DEIPNON*

Enzo Degani

Born in Pitane, an Aeolic town on the western coast of Asia Minor, close to Lesbos, Matro produced his best work at the end of the 4th century BC. Athenaeus has handed down six short fragments of his (Lloyd-Jones and Parsons 1983, nos. 535-540), as well as his *Attic Banquet* (Lloyd-Jones and Parsons 1983, no. 534) that has probably come down to us almost unabridged. Our source (represented as a table companion of Athenaeus) states that he wishes to quote Matro's short poem in its entirety, 'because of its rarity' (4.134d). However, scholars have found more than one gap among the surviving 122 hexameters. These could well be ascribed to inaccuracies in textual transmission or to intervention by epitomators, rather than to carelessness on the part of Athenaeus. However, it is probable that not many verses have been lost.

Unlike Archestratos, Matro was a professional parodist (παρωιδος). For some years, in Greece, parody had all the characteristic features of an autonomous literary genre, with its own contests: I think it worth outlining its history, before analysing Matro's *Attic Banquet*. As Aristotle affirms

Matro and Greek parody

(*Poetics* 1448a12-13), with support from Polemon (fr. 40 Preller), Hegemon initiated the parodic genre in Athens in the final decades of the 5th century BC, and his prize-winning composition, the *Gigantomachia* (Battle of the Giants), was probably performed at the time of the Athenian defeat in Sicily in 413 BC. Some years before, probably between 430 and 425,[1] the poet had emigrated from his native island (Thasos) to Athens. Hegemon himself tells us this in the only parodic fragment of his that has come down to us (42-44 Brandt). It consists of a score of hexameters, in which the parodist humorously recalls the hard times at the start of his career: his poverty, hunger and his nickname the Lentil (Φακῆ) which he used to refer to in jest; the unpleasant reception (with balls of dung), which awaited him on his return to Thasos; his moderate successes in Athens; then, Athena's intervention when she roused him from his meditation by touching him with her golden wand and showing him the way to the contests.

Euboios of Paros and Boiotos of Syracuse lived in the second half of the 4th century. Few traces of their work remain – only the echoes of their reputation. Yet, despite this, they were probably very famous among the parodists (especially Euboios, whom Polemon called the best-known of them). There is evidence to suggest that Matro's *Attic Banquet* was composed at the end of the century, between 305 and 300 BC, but then nothing more is heard of parodists until the Roman period. Two of the anonymous fragments collected by Brandt (96-111) are worthy of note. The first is the work of a parodist, a contemporary of Dio Chrysostom (1st-2nd century AD), the second of a contemporary of Galen the physician (2nd century AD). The former poet mocks the craze for chariot races (fr. 8a) and circus performances (fr. 8b), the latter scorns athleticism. The contribution of inscriptions concerning literary contests should be added to this documentary evidence. The earliest inscription (*IG* XII 9, 189) which comes from Eretria, is dated around 340 BC and con-cerns the institution of a musical contest at the festival of Artemis.

Rhapsodes, *aulos*-players, lyre-players and even parodists took part in it. The inscription lists the prizes, in drachmas, that were awarded in each category and it is worth noting that the lowest went to the parodists.[2] It seems that they were considered to hold the lowest rank among the artists. Another inscription, from Delos (*IG* XII 2, 120, 48), mentions that there was even a parodist among the artists who gave free performances at the festival of Apollo in 236 BC (*kitharodes*, comic poets, harpists, workers of wonders etc.).

Scholars once thought that these were the only inscriptions that mention parodists and therefore drew the logical conclusion that the parodic contests did not continue beyond the 3rd century BC.[3] This, however, is wrong, because a fragmentary Attic inscription, dated at around the 2nd-3rd century AD (*IG* II² 2153), contains a list of artists that explicitly includes a π]αρῳιδός in line 9.[4] This clearly reflects what Dio and Galen have told us and shows, beyond all doubt, that parodic contests were still taking place in the Roman period, even though they were probably not a regular event because references to parodists are very few and far between in the numerous inscriptions for festivals that have come down to us. Clearly parody, although it was no longer a regular feature of contests, did appear occasionally and was an appendix to performances by rhapsodes just as a satyr play was to tragedy.[5]

In general parodists were not highly paid professionals. Perhaps Hegemon in Athens was an exception to the rule. But even he, when he set sail from Thasos for the first time, chasing the mirage of one mina (the first prize) or, if he had to, willing to accept only half that (fifty drachmas), was certainly never dealing with large sums of money.[6] And, as we shall see, the hard life led by these itinerant artists is mentioned even at Matro's opulent banquet.

The *Attic Banquet*

Every respectable epic poem opens with an invocation to the Muse: 'Sing to me, Muse, of the versatile and much-wandering man…', sang Homer in the *Odyssey* (1.1 ἄνδρα μοι ἔννεπε, Μοῦσα, πολύτροπον, ὃς μάλα πολλὰ | πλάγχθη…). And Matro begins, 'Sing to me, Muse, of the dinners, plenteous and many, which Xenocles the orator offered us in Athens…(1-2 δεῖπνά μοι ἔννεπε, Μοῦσα, πολύτροφα καὶ μάλα πολλά, | ἃ Ξενοκλῆς ῥήτωρ ἐν Ἀθήναις δείπνισεν ἡμᾶς). And he continues, 'Even I went thither, and a great hunger followed me' (ἦλθον γὰρ ἐκεῖσε, πολὺς δέ μοι ἕσπετο λιμός). This line reflects *Odyssey* 6.164, when Odysseus was recalling his voyage to Delos: 'Even I went thither, and a great army (λαός) came with me'. And, Matro goes on, at Xenokles' house 'I beheld fair, large loaves, whiter than snow, like ἄμυλοι in their flavour', that is like the bread of the finest meal (οὗ δὴ καλλίστους ἄρτους ἴδον ἠδὲ μεγίστους, | λευκοτέρους χιόνος, ἔσθειν δ' ἀμύλοισι ὁμοίους). This image is drawn from *Iliad* 10.436-7, where Rhesos' famous mares are said to be 'like the winds in their running' (θείειν δ' ἀνέμοισι ὁμοῖοι). And, as Homer says of the no less renowned foals of Erichthonios, 'even Boreas yearned for them when they were grazing' (τάων καὶ Βορέης ἠράσσατο βοσκομενάων: *Iliad* 20.223), so Matro speaks of his perfect white loaves saying, 'even Boreas yearned for them when they were baking' (πεσσομενάων: 6).

The dinner, or, perhaps one should say, the battle begins. Gastronomic poetry is often full of military images, but Matro's *Banquet* is particularly rich in them: the food almost seems to be the enemy that has to be attacked and conquered, the cooks and the host are the strategists reviewing the troops, and the guests compete to see who will cover themselves with glory, while the food shares in the epic ideal of being the very best (πρωτιστεύειν) and seems to be a hero too. Now, just as Agamemnon, 'reviewed the ranks of soldiers' (*Iliad* 4.231) escorted by the squire Eurymedon, so Xenokles 'reviews the ranks of his valiant table companions' (αὐτὸς δὲ Χενοκλῆς ἐπεπωλεῖτο στίχας ἀνδρῶν: 7), escorted by the parasite Chaerephon, who looks like a hungry seagull (πεινῶντι λάρωι ὄρνιθι ἐοικώς: 9). Naturally he is 'empty' (νήστης: 10) and 'well acquainted with other people's banquets' (ἀλλοτρίων εὖ εἰδὼς δειπνοσυνάων: 10). Here the translation, though not incorrect, nonetheless does not render the subtleties of the original Greek text. The phrase is a parody of *Odyssey* 5.250 where Odysseus, who is building his raft, is compared to a craftsman 'well acquainted with the art of architecture' (εὖ εἰδὼς τεκτοσυνάων). Matro's surprising δειπνοσύνη is a new coinage and unique, a rewriting of Homer's τεκτοσύνη. If we wish to reveal the hidden subtlety, the wit, in the Greek text we might translate, 'well acquainted with the art of *lunchi*tecture'.

In the meantime the cooks begin serving the food and the table companions immediately throw themselves upon the vegetables (λαχάνοις: 14). But the poet has other preferences: bulbs and asparagus, and then the 'marrowy oysters' (ὄστρεα μυελόεντα: 16, a rewriting of *Odyssey* 9.293

ὀστέα μυελόεντα = 'marrowy bones'). He avoids the marinated tuna (ὠμοτάριχον) and in 17 tells it, idiomatically, to 'ὠμοτάριχον ἐῶν χαίρειν' (from the expression of farewell, χαίρειν = goodbye) which could be translated 'gastronomically' as 'telling it to go and get…fried!' The poet turns his attention to sea-urchins (ἐχίνους) 'with their high head-dress of spines' (καρηκομόωντας ἀκάνθαις, 18), which is a pun on *Iliad* 2.11 καρηκομόωντας Ἀχαιούς) but he throws them down as soon as he sees the more appetising Phaleric anchovy, 'Triton's true mistress'. The anchovy appears to be as modest as the Homeric Penelope who appears 'holding a bright veil before her face' (ἄντα παρειάων σχομένη λιπαρὰ κρήδεμνα: *Odyssey* 1.334), but with the difference that the veil of this fish is not bright but, rather, is 'clouded', almost 'soiled', as befits its oily, strong-smelling nature. Now come the pinnas: big oysters 'in their ringing bowls', which white salt water[7] has nourished 'on the rocks crowned with seaweed' (κατὰ φυκότριχος πέτρης, 26); here come the cartilaginous sole and the 'red-cheeked mullet' (τρίγλη μιλτοπάρηιος: 27). The poet voraciously stretches out his hand 'with grasping talons' (κρατερώνυχα χεῖρα: 28) at once, to take the latter delicacy, but in vain, for Phoebus Apollo stops him: another guest, Stratokles, 'stern master of the rout' (30 κρατερὸν μήστωρα φόβοιο = *Iliad* 6.97, where it refers to Diomedes) has got there before him and already 'holds the head of the noble[8] mullet in his hands' (τρίγλης ἱπποδάμοιο κάρη μετὰ χερσὶν ἔχοντα: 31). This line parodies the image of the desperate Andromache (Ἕκτορος ἱπποδάμοιο κάρη μετὰ χερσὶν ἔχουσα: *Iliad* 24.724). But the intrepid Matro throws himself upon Stratokles: 'then I recovered it in the fray and tore its insatiable throat' (ἂψ δ' ἑλόμην χάρμηι, λαιμὸν δ' ἄπληστον ἄμυξα: 32). And here is the daughter of Nereus, silver-footed (ἀργυρόπεζα), the fair-tressed cuttle, dread goddess with the voice of a mortal (34: σηπίη εὐπλόκαμος, δεινὴ θεὸς αὐδήεσσα: derived from *Odyssey* 10.136, with σηπίη replacing Κίρκη). 'Of all fish,[9] she alone knows the difference between black and white' (ἡ μόνη, ἰχθὺς ἐοῦσα τὸ λευκὸν καὶ μέλαν οἶδε: 35).

The muster of fishes, tastily stuffed with Homeric formulae ably transformed, goes on to list other fish: indeed this short poem has justifiably been called 'The Catalogue of Fish', written on the lines of the more famous 'Catalogue of Ships' in *Iliad* 2.[10] Now comes the conger-eel as huge as Homer's Tityos (*Odyssey* 11.576) and following in its footsteps comes 'the white-armed, goddess fish, the eel', who even 'boasts that she has lain in Zeus' embrace' (ἔγχελυς, ἡ Διὸς εὔχετ' ἐν ἀγκοίνῃσι μιγῆναι: 39). Then the 'fleet squid' (ὠκέα τευθίς) enters, likened to Iris, the windswift messenger of the gods (50); then the variegated perch (πέρκη τ' ἀνθεσίχρως: 51) and the plebeian black-tail. Now comes the tuna, 'son of Lurkhole' (53 θαλαμηιάδαο: note the amusing patronymic, which is derived from θαλάμη = 'a lurking place'), whose bare head[11] stood, frowning, at a distance, as angry at the loss of his armour as the Homeric Ajax had been at the lost of that of Achilles (*Odyssey* 11.543-6). Here comes the monkfish, or 'file fish', which carpenters love so much (ῥίνη θ' ἣν φιλέουσι περισσῶς τέκτονες ἄνδρες: 56); then a gigantic grey mullet (κεστρεύς: 59) – 'a doughty knight' (πελώριος ἱππότα) who arrives, roasted, in the company of a dozen white bream (σαργοί); then a sky-blue *amias*: 61), razor shells and mantis shrimps (καρῖδες), which, strangely, are called the 'songsters of Olympic Zeus' (Ζηνὸς Ὀλυμπίοιο...ἀοιδοί: 63). Here comes the gilthead (χρύσοφρυς), the most beautiful of all the fish, then the lobster (κάραβος: 66) and the crayfish, 'eager to show off their armour' (θωρήσσασθαι: but the context of this phrase also points to the second meaning of this verb – to get drunk) in 'the banquets of the blessed' (ἐν μακάρων δείπνοις: 67). That phrase is an exception and echoes Hesiod, *Works and Days* 171 ἐν μακάρων νήσοισι). Now it is the turn of the *elops* or swordfish (69), mighty in battle with his glorious sword, who seems to the poet 'to be like the ambrosia that the blessed gods who live for ever eat' (72). In the meantime, the cook, a new Achilles, goes back and forth all over the room 'epically balancing the platters covered with delicacies on his right shoulder' (σείων ὀψοφόρους πίνακας κατὰ δεξιὸν ὦμον: 47). This is based on *Iliad* 22.133 (σείων Πηλιάδα μελίην κατὰ δεξιὸν ὦμον), which is said of Achilles balancing his beech spear from Mount Pelion on his mighty shoulder. The chef is followed by fifty-odd black saucepans and about the same number of frying pans. Now the cooks bring an enormous moray, that covers the table (73), then some plaice or flounders (σάνδαλα: 76), a *buglossus* (= 'sole': 77), some wrasse and a variety of other fish.

At last, something other than sea food is served. Here comes a ham and when he sees it, the poet, perhaps thinking of Sappho[12] feels himself tremble: κωλῆν δ᾿ ὡς εἶδον, ὡς ἔτρεμον: 89). Then, with a pot of delicious mustard in front of him, he can no longer keep back…his tears, as he wittily adds, when he thinks of tomorrow when, after all this plenty, he will have to content himself with the usual cheese and the 'hasty roll' (μάζηι ὀτρηρῆι: 92). Matro's stomach can take no more, but a boy from Salamis, a second Philippides, brings in thirteen fat ducks (νήσσας: 95), and so the gorging goes on. Chairephon devours everything like a lion, but never forgets to put something aside for his dinner (100-1).

And now the drinking begins in earnest: chaplets are given to the guests and they start. They compete to see who can drink the most of the fine wine from Lesbos and, in the meanwhile, fruit is brought in: pears, 'plump apples' (πίονα μῆλα = *Iliad* 12.319 and elsewhere, always in reference to plump livestock); pomegranates and bunches of grapes, 'the nurses of divine Bacchus'. However, Matro does not eat anything more: 'I lay back, too full' (μεστὸς δ᾿ ἀνακείμην: 115), but his inertia does not last very long. A peerless cake enters: 'blonde, sweet, big, round, gentlemen![13] A true child of Demeter, perfumed: however could I not partake of such a divine thing as this?' And the poem ends with the arrival of a couple of young girls, brought there by Stratokles; they come swiftly, they look like birds (ὄρνιθας ὥς: 122, cf. *Iliad* 2.764), and they guarantee a fitting end to this Pantagruelian banquet, for, as the poet uncompromisingly assures us, they are 'capable of working wonders'.[14]

Judgments on Matro

The ancients approved of Matro's short poem: before declaiming it, Athenaeus' table-companion affirmed that our parodist had produced a 'not unpleasing description' of the banquet (οὐκ ἀχαρίτως διαγράφει). And we have to admit that Matro may well have influenced some Greek and perhaps even Latin poets, especially humorous poets.[15] Modern scholars are more divided in their opinions. The American Shero wrote that Matro's parodies have 'an exceptionally amusing effect',[16] and forty years before him, an Englishman, Mackail, when reviewing Brandt's *Corpusculum Poesis Graecae Ludibundae*, extolled Matro's 'great spirit and humour', adding that 'nothing could be happier for instance than the mock heroic descriptions of the cook' (11-13, 46-9) and that the final description of the dessert (104-122) 'is the best and most vivid we possess'.[17] However, the Germans did not agree. Maas, for instance, defines the *Attic Banquet* as *ein erbärmliches Machwerk* (a wretched confection).[18] A judgment like this, with no appeal allowed is, we think, the result of Wilamowitz's sharp opinion on Matro's *Banquet* some seventy years ago. He contemptuously defined this short poem as the work of 'a rather wretched journeyman'.[19]

The extremes of disagreement reflect personal tastes and artistic likes and dislikes. However, it is also true that gastronomic poetry is little known and poorly studied. Scholars have, in general, paid little attention to it, have examined it hastily or carelessly and have taken a rather snobbish attitude to it, tending to dismiss the genre as mere buffoonery or even a 'mental aberration'. This is certainly true as regards the work of Philoxenos and Archestratos,[20] and it is very true for the author of the *Attic Banquet*. Matro's only aim was to entertain his audience, and there is a tendency to dismiss the 'comic' as being less valid, therefore trivial, when compared with the serious.[21] Furthermore, Matro was a gastronomic poet, and there has always been prejudice against this genre.[22] Lastly, he was a parodist, and parody was seen as a 'parasitic' genre living off its more noble companions;[23] thus parody had a hard time, both in Greece and elsewhere.

Wilamowitz' Criticisms

But Wilamowitz's judgement is not *a priori*. Commenting on some inconsistencies and obscurities in the *Attic Banquet*, he sees some of the comparisons between fish and gods as far-fetched and eccentric. 'The art of parody,' he writes, 'is rather cheap (*sehr billig*). We cannot judge Matro to be more astute (*klüger*) than he really was, which is often the case in the *Corpusculum* of Brandt. For a start, all of us would expect there to be more witticisms (*Pointen*), but his audience was happy just as long as the phrases and Homeric verses, which they knew very well, appeared in a context that was as different as possible from their true epic dignity. They did not worry if some of it was nonsense, because they could always laugh at nonsense too.' For example, why is the mullet called ἱππόδαμος (31)? For no other reason 'than that it then takes the place Hector has in *Iliad* 24.724'. And the puzzling statement that the eel boasts that she has lain in Zeus' arms (39)? 'Of course it does not mean anything other than that she is highly prized (*sehr vornehm*). In 50, we read 'Iris the messenger came, wind-footed' (Ἶρις δ' ἄγγελος ἦλθε ποδήνεμος). It is Homeric. If it is about a squid (τευθις), that is amusing enough: no one really asks whether the fish does resemble a goddess; it is brought to the table and has no message to offer'. Can the cuttle-fish really be called 'silver-footed Thetis (Θέτις ἀρψυρόπεζα) and 'the goddess who speaks' (θεὸς αὐδήεσσα: 33)? If we do not want to spoil Matro's joke, then we must say that 'any learned comment that seeks to find a resemblance between the two, and asks what the polyp's voice really was like, is quite simply out of place'. Thus, in Wilamowitz's view,[24] such examples of nonsense, and especially such strange matchings of gods and fishes, should be enough to prove beyond all reasonable doubt how low the level of Matro's parodies is.

A basis for reassessment

Undoubtedly Matro is not a crystal-clear, polished poet like Archestratos. This can in part be explained by the different audiences they wrote for. Archestratos wrote for a narrow circle of learned dining companions, who would have been able to appreciate his more subtle parodies, while Matro's work – like that of Hegemon which, according to Chamaeleon, had the Athenians running to hear it (fr. 43 St) – had to address his audience more directly, and he had to base himself on a more accessible, more easily understood code, that is, on Homer, which most of his public would have studied and learned by heart at school. In fact, there is no verse of the *Attic Banquet* that does not follow a precise epic model and does not transform one or more of Homer's verses.

Sometimes, this complex and variegated mosaic is similar to a cento: thus, when Eustathius (1665, 33) called Matro's short poem a 'cento' (κέντρων) it was not by chance, and he was not far wrong. Of course, when we judge a poet we cannot ignore his own personal style of composition. We must also be aware of the problems of writing a poem as a cento: overabundance, repetitions, logical inconsistencies, anomalous metre and prosody and so on,[25] problems that no poet has ever been entirely able to avoid, not even if his skill, as for example that of Ausonius, is a miracle in itself.

On the other hand a poet who set out to compose a cento rarely had very ambitious goals: it was enough to reduce the contradictions to a minimum, eliminate the most glaring absurdities, and give a certain logic to the discourse, without worrying overmuch about any secondary details. We must remember this and make allowances for it when we study a short poem that seems to lie half way between a parody and a cento; and when we study a poet who adheres almost entirely to Homer – with the exception of the names of the foods, but little else – and seeks only to draw out every possible linguistic and expressive ingredient he can from the Homeric model.

It is clear that if we attempt to study Matro using the same criteria we would use to examine any other epic, we will find obscurities, incoherencies and anomalies. For example, at 41-5, after he has talked about an eel that is so big that 'not even two wrestlers like Astynanax and Antenor, would have been able to lift it onto a cart very easily', he adds, rather incongruously, that '*they* were nine cubits and three spans in length and *they both* were three fathoms high' (τρισπίθαμοι γὰρ ταί γε καὶ ἐννεαπήχεες ἦσαν | εὖρος, ἀτὰρ μῆκός γε γενέσθην ἐννεόργυιοι (44-5), obviously copied from *Odyssey* 11.311-2, where the giants Otos and Ephialtes ἐννέωροι γὰρ τοί γε καὶ ἐννεαπήχεες ἦσαν | εὖρος, ἀτὰρ μῆκός γε γενέσθην ἐννεόργυιοι). This abrupt shift from singular (41) to plural (44), and then to dual (45) is forced on the poet by the Homeric phrase he wants to use. Such anomalies are not uncommon,[26] and perhaps it was precisely because of this that we can find a reason, just as Wilamowitz wished, for purely 'ornamental' epithets, that is to say, with no real or true semantic function, the first being the 'horse-breaking mullet' quoted above (31). The mullet is called a horse breaker, meaning, of course, that it is a 'noble' fish,[27] only because it takes the place of the Homeric Hector in the parodic variation.[28] A similar explanation can be offered for the eel 'with its white arms' in 38, an adjective that should be the same as the simple 'white',[29] and for the cuttle fish too, defined as the 'dread goddess who speaks', and so called because of the same mechanical transposition of the famous phrase 'the dread goddess who speaks' (δεινὴ θεὸς αὐδήεσσα) at *Odyssey* 10.136, 11.8, 12.150 and 449).[30] As for 'Zeus' songsters', the razor shells (63), the idiom 'the singers of Olympian Zeus' (Ζηνὸς Ὀλυμπίου...ἀοιδοί) in the identical position in the verse appears in *Homeric Hymn* 17.2), and is thought to derive from a lost epic poem.[31]

Matro's rigid adherence to epic models almost inevitably – and perhaps fatally – forced him to use a variety of inconsequentialities which are not very important, and against which the rationalistic preoccupations of modern scholars are rather ineffectual. Nevertheless, we do feel that when Matro was not bound by such constraints he was not as careless (*unsorgfältig*) as Wilamowitz thought. He must have had his reasons, probably perfectly valid, for matching a specific fish with a specific god. Nowadays his jokey comparisons may not be clear, but before we accuse him of sloppiness, we should perhaps ask ourselves if they might not be based on myths, beliefs and superstitions that we do not know of today, but that his public, his audience, would have been well acquainted with.

First, there was a close resemblance between Iris and the squid, based not on the unlikely messages that the squid brought, nor because the squid is distinguished from the other fish 'on account of its splendid coloration, particularly in the purples' (Brandt), but rather, on the fact that both of them are characterized by the lightning speed which is the distinguishing feature and the true similarity between these two winged beings. Iris is always represented with wings (χρυσόπτερος, 'with golden wings':*Iliad* 8.398, 11.185), and speed is her main attribute. She is the swiftest of all the gods, and Homer calls her 'storm-footed' (ἀέλλοπος, *Iliad* 8.409, 24.77, 159), 'wind-footed' (ποδήνεμος, *Iliad* 2.786, 5.368, 11.195, 15.168), 'fast' (ταχεῖα 8.399, 15.158, 24.144) and 'swift' (ὠκέα, 2.786, 790, 795, 3.129, 5.368, etc.). On the other hand, the squids can easily shoot up out of the water by using their peculiar 'little wing' (πτερύγιον = 'fin') – cf. Aristotle *History of Animals* 523b29-524a2. They often fly in flocks like birds (they were even thought to be able to sink ships): thus Epicharmos was quite right to call them 'winged' (ποταναί, fr. 61 Kaibel). Other fish, such as ἱέρακες (flying gurnards?) and χελιδόνες πελάγιαι (flying fish?) can do this too, but the squids are far superior to them.[32] Above all they are so swift because of their tapering body: as Pliny says 'the squid even flies out of the water, shooting itself out like an arrow' (*lolligo etiam volitat extra aquam se efferens...sagittae modo*, *Natural History* 9.84).

The squid, the eel and the cuttlefish

Now we come to the eel. As has already been suggested, this fish's sexual intercourse with Zeus (39), relates it to the Homeric Antiope (*Odyssey* 11.261) and Alkmene (11.268), and it involves the belief, widespread in ancient times, that the eel had no genitals and reproduced itself with the help of rain-water (cf. Aristotle *History of Animals* 570a6-24). It was equally well-known, and Matro himself states it (Lloyd-Jones and Parsons 1983, no. 536,4), that rainwater was a direct emanation from Zeus. This hypothesis, which was often put forward in the last century,[33] is, in my opinion, well worth looking into. While not denying that this could be a witty reference to the eel's asexuality, I think it quite likely that the idea of sexual intercourse was also suggested to Matro by the previous 'the fish goddess with the white arms', which was obviously copied from the famous 'Hera, the goddess with the white arms' (θεὰ λευκώλενος Ἥρη), which appears at least twenty times in the *Iliad* (1.55, 195, 208, 595, etc.). In other words, the eel is implicitly compared to Zeus' august consort and the comparison is easy to explain. If the former was the queen of the gods (cf. *Homeric Hymn* 12.2), the latter was no doubt the queen of fish (cf. Archestratos *Life of Luxury* 8.7). Indeed the excellence of her flesh was such that the comic poets too did not hesitate to call the eel a goddess, as did the ancient Egyptians, who believed her to be divine.[34] Three fragments of the comic poet Eubulos express this very well [cf. Chapter 29]. In these fragments, this heavenly creature, robed in beets (τεῦτλον) ennobles a memorable banquet. In the first fragment (fr. 43 KA) 'the unwedded nymph, the eel with the white skin' enters. In the second (fr. 36.2-4) we can admire the most precious 'Boiotian eels, goddesses with white fair bodies'.[35] In the third (fr. 64) 'the Boiotian virgin of the Kopaic Lake' enters again, that 'goddess' whom the amazed poet – imitating Euripides (*Orestes* 37 'I dread to name the goddesses', which was said of the terrible Erinyes) – confesses he 'thinks twice before calling her by her name'. If the terms 'unwedded nymph' and 'virgin' take for granted the belief in the eel's asexuality cited above, then the variants 'with white skin' and 'with white fair bodies' are connected to Matro's 'with the white arms'. Duly skinned and robed in her inevitable trousseau of beets (cf. Aristophanes *Acharnians* 864, *Peace* 1013-4 etc.) that make her immaculate whiteness stand out all the more, the queen of the table makes her solemn entrance into the room where the guests are, just as the venerated consort of Zeus, with her fair white arms, entered the meeting of the immortal gods.

Lastly, there is a very close affinity between the cuttlefish and Thetis, whose traditional epithet 'silver-footed' (ἀργυρόπεζα, *Iliad* 16.222, 574, 18.369, etc.), happily recalls the 'feet' of the mollusc, which is famous for its whiteness.[36] A thick bunch of feet frame the head (cf. Aristotle *History of Animals* 523b22-32, etc.). Two long tentacles, which Oppian compares to 'tresses' or 'plaits' (*Halieutica* 2.122) are attached to it. Because of this, the cuttlefish is called 'of the fair tresses (εὐπλόκαμος), a name that brings to mind Thetis' flowing locks (*Iliad* 4.512, 16.860, 18.407 etc.). But most of all, these two marine beings (*Thetis* is constantly called 'of the salt sea', 'of the sea', etc.) have cunning intelligence (μῆτις) in common, their *intelligenza dell'evento* in the words of Diano: their capacity to adapt quickly to any situation, and also their cunning, their fraudulence, their camouflage, their polymorphism. As for the cuttlefish, she was a relative of the octopus, whose mimetic skill was proverbial and well known. Suffice it to say that Aristotle calls her 'the most cunning of the molluscs' because of her remarkable skill in using her 'ink to conceal herself', not only to counter dangers (as octopuses and squids do), but even to capture fish that are far bigger than she is (*History of Animals* 621b28-35; cf. Plutarch *Moralia* 978 a-b). Oppian too defines her with such epithets as 'with cunning mind', 'with cunning intelligence', 'crafty' (*Halieutica* 1.312, 3.156, 2.120, 4.160). As for Thetis, it is hard to forget the many and various metamorphoses she undergoes in order to escape from the desires of Peleus, to whom Zeus had given her against her will (cf. *Iliad* 6.434). The goddess who is 'able to take on any shape', is how Sophocles defined her (fr. 618.2 Radt) and she became fire, water, a plant, then a beast: a bird, a tiger, a lion, a snake, and, lastly...the cuttle, and in this shape, the persevering hero finally succeeds in taking her.[37] See especially the ancient commentator on Lykophron's *Alexandra* 175 (p. 85, 2-6 Scheer), who is probably discussing Euripides, fr. 1093 N². The commentator says that it was in the place where afterwards the precinct of Thetis came to be that 'she, pursued by Peleus, changed herself into various forms... There he secured her when she was in the shape of a cuttle and made love with her, as a result of which this part of Thessalian Magnesia is called Sepias (the place of the cuttle)'.

This is Cape Sepias, now on the side of Mount Pelion, on the peninsula of Magnesia. In these waters, which Athenaeus tells us abound in cuttles (1.30d), Xerxes' fleet was hit by a very violent storm and decimated which, Herodotos says, 'induced the Persians to make sacrifices and offerings in honour of Thetis, because they learned from the Ionians it was in this precise place that Thetis had been raped by Peleus and now this promontory belonged to her and the Nereids' (7.191.2). Thus, this myth was already well-known in the time of Herodotos and Euripides. As regards the latter, it is possible that, as Scheer believed, the commentary on Lykophron contained only a simple reference to *Andromache* 1265-72., in which Thetis asks the ageing Peleus to wait for her in the hollow gorge of the ancient cliff of Sepias, the place where, as Euripides emphasises (1276-83, cf. also *Iphigenia in Aulis* 700-7), they first made love.

Notes

For the philological background which lies behind this work, I refer to my works: Degani 1975, 1982a, 1982b, 1985;. For Archestratos, I refer to Montanari (1983); for Matro, to Lloyd-Jones and Parsons (1983) nos 534-540, = pages 259-268: henceforth *SH*. For the other parodic poets, see Brandt (1888).

1. Cf. Schachermeyr (1965).
2. A third prize was not even foreseen (rhapsodists: 110/50/20; *aulos*-players: 50/30/20; *kitharistai*: 110/70/55; *rhapsoidoi*: 200/150/100; *paroidoi*: 50/10).
3. Cf. Wilamowitz-Moellendorff (1905), Shroeter (1967), Poehlmann (1972).
4. This was proved by Robert (1936).
5. The first to state this was Scaliger (1561), followed - among others – by Householder (1944) and Maas (1949).
6. This was pointed out by Wilamowitz (1905, 174).
7. I would read λεπτόν instead of λευκόν: cf. Degani (1975, 171ff.).
8. Literally, 'tamer of horses' (ἱπποδάμοιο). This unexpected epithet will be re-examined below. On the textual problems presented by 27-50, cf. Degani (1985, 48ff.).
9. The latest editors print ἰχθὺς ἐοῦσα with cruces, but I believe this is wrong: cf. Degani (1985, 50).
10. Shero (1929).
11. Being scaled and boned, the tunny is deprived of its 'armour': τευχέων (54) is referring to the 'scales' of the fish, unless it is hinting at its precious 'collarbones' (κλεῖδες), on which see Athenaeus 7.303a-b. So Brandt thought, though his correction of τευχέων into κλειδῶν is needless. Following Wilamowitz, the editors of *SH* interpret it otherwise (*submovitur thynni caput, ingustatum, molesteque fert a fictilibus segregari*).
12. Cf. Sappho 31.6 and 13 V. However, the schema ὡς...ὥς (with ἰδεῖν or similar verb in the first member of the sequence) already occurs in *Iliad* 14.294, 19.16 (note ἔτρεσαν at line 16), 20.424. After Matro, it can be found in Kallimachos fr. 260.2 Pfeiffer, *Hymn* 4 (*On Delos*) 200. In an erotic framework (such as in Sappho and *Iliad* 14.294) it recurs in Theokritos 2.82 and 3.47, Moschos *Europa* 74, Oppian *Halieutica* 4.47, Kollouthos 255 (on a different level: Bion 1.40, Apollonios of Rhodes 4.1392, Quintus of Smyrna 12.120 and Nonnos *Dionysiaca* 47.158ff.). For the Latin parallel *ut...ut*, cf. Timpanaro (1978) 219-287.
13. The text of the codices ἄνδρες (116) has been rightly defended by Wilamowitz (1905: 75). Other conjectures are many and uncalled for, see Montanari (1980/82)

[14.] Male and female θαυματοποιοί were similar to conjurors and prestidigitators, much in demand at the end of the banquet: cf. Xenophon *Symposium* 2.1 and generally Martin (1931, 53). In Matro – as is to be inferred from the cruder πόρναι (prostitutes, 121) – this term includes a salacious *double entendre*.

[15.] This has often been pointed out of Archestratos. In particular Shero (1929) would connect Lucilius' *Cena rustica* with Matro's frr. 2-3 Brandt (= *SH* 536-537). He also provides a list of Greek comic passages, where some 'mock-heroic tone' after the fashion of Matro might be found (68ff.). The parodic ichthyomorphism of lines 36ff. (namely the gigantic conger-eel compared with Homeric Tityos, for which compare *Odyssey* 11.576f.) recurs again in Horace (*Satires* 2.2.39), as A. Traina (1989) pointed out.

[16.] Shero (1929, 65).

[17.] Mackail (1899).

[18.] Maas (1949, 1685).

[19.] Wilamowitz-Moellendorff (1923): this definition is at 73.

[20.] Documentary evidence of this assertion may be found in Degani (1982b, 31ff.).

[21.] Cf. Ferroni (1974 1), Bachtin (1979, 423).

[22.] See for instance Giannini (1956), who speaks of '*aberrazioni…nel campo della letteratura*'.

[23.] Cf. Poehlmann (1972 152), Koller (1956); even the definition '*furti genus*' (a form of theft) - already found in Estienne (1573, 71) – is quite common.

[24.] Wilamowitz-Moellendorff (1923, 75 = 331ff.).

[25.] Cf. Salannitro (1981, 17).

[26.] Apart from the prosodic licence at 35 (see n. 9), suffice it to mention the surprising τάων of line 6 (referring to the former ἄρτους, in spite of the feminine gender): regarding this compare Montanari (1978/79).

[27.] Note that Archestratos is glad to dignify the 'nobility' of some of the most precious fish with the epithet γενναῖος (frs 9.5 and 34.5), and also of the wine of Thasos (fr. 60.1).

[28.] Some scholars supposed that this unexpected epithet is explained by the bravery shown by the mullet, the only fish able to destroy the poisonous *aplysia* (sea-hare): see Peltzer (1855, 53) and Paessens (1856, 22); on this property of the mullet, cf. Thompson (1947, 267). But such a supposition seems to me rather fanciful. Maybe it is worthwhile mentioning the 'salacious' interpretation that was suggested by a student of mine some years ago (Rossi 1980-81, 113ff.).

[29.] According to him, ἱππόδαμος (= 'tamer of the penis') would hint at the well-known property of the mullet, namely to inhibit virility: cf. Degani (1985 49, 64 n.8).

[30.] With the skin removed, the eel looks like a white arm – as Brandt thought (79). I once thought the term suggested that this fish has got two fins (πτερύγια), while other fish have got four fins – or none, like the moray (Degani 1975, 173). But now I am doubtful about such a rationalistic exegesis.

[31.] Or rather, as it seems, 'with human voice' (cf. Chantraine 1968-, 137). For the editors of *SH*, Matro's, αὐδήεσσα = 'with human voice' is plainly absurd unless it meant 'famous' or 'worthy of note'. Now, the ancient exegetes of Homer hesitated between the 'active' meaning (= 'talking'), supported by Aristophanes of Byzantium (197 Sl.), and the passive meaning (= 'renowned'), supported by Apion (fr. 25 Neitz.). Aristotle (fr. 171 R.) - followed by Chamaeleon (fr. 20 St.) – even wanted to correct it into οὐδήεσσα ('terrestrial') or αὐλήεσσα ('secluded'). However, it is doubtful that Matro would have foreseen the lucubrations of Hellenistic scholars. On the other hand, Brandt thought that αὐδήεσσα hints at the sound the cuttlefish emits when caught (78). I believe that this interpretation must not be forgotten, because this fact seems well-known (Brehm spoke of 'a most noticeable grinding of the teeth'), and because Aristotle himself admitted a sort of 'voice' – made by particular noises and grindings in certain fish, with the exception of molluscs (*History of Animals* 535b12). As for δεινή (dread), both Peltzer and Paessens thought it hinted at the aggressiveness of the cuttle-fish, capable of overwhelming with her slyness even fish whose size is far bigger (Aristotle *History of Animals* 590b33 – 591a1; 622a1). In spite of the scholars' scepticism about this weak explanation, we could add that δεινή too is an epithet of Thetis in *Iliad* 18.394.

[31.] So thought Wilomowitz-Moellendorff (1923, 76). Apart from καρῖδες, the idiom is used by the poet of bolbinai, a sort of leek (*SH* 536, 3 βολβῖνας θ᾽ ἃι Ζηνὸς Ὀλυμπίου εἰσὶν ἀοιδοί). On this, an indecent but not unlikely hypothesis has been put forward. According to various scholars (Schweighäuser 1801, 432; Paessens 1856, 35; Brandt 84), both καρῖδες and βολβῖναι were 'flatulent foods which produce noises of the stomach'.

[32.] Cf. Aelian *History of Animals* 9.52, Oppian *Halieutica* 1.427ff.;

further documentary evidence on the squid may be found in Thompson (1947, 260-1).

[33.] Peltzer (1855, 55); Paessens (1856, 25); Brandt 79. On the eel, see Thompson (1947, 59).

[34.] Compare the various comic fragments quoted by Athenaeus 7.299e-f, and wittily referring to this belief. Even in some Greek localities, the eel was connected with various rites and cults: cf. Thompson (1947, 60).

[35.] We could read λευκοσώματοι as Lorenzoni (1980/81) in-stead of the impossible λιμνοσώματοι given by the codices.

[36.] 35 recalls the whiteness of the cuttle-fish, and it also notes her skill playfully, reusing the proverbial 'to distinguish between black and white' (cf. Peltzer 1855, 54). On the goddess, cf. Roscher (1884-1937, II I 324-; on the fish, Thompson (1947, 231-3).

[37.] Documentary evidence in Roscher (1884-1937, V c. 787, 25ff.); cf. Detienne & Vernant (1991, 131-74).

Bibliography

Bachtin, M., 1979 *Estetica e romanzo* (It. trans., Torino).

Brandt, P., 1888 *Corpusculum poesis epicae Graecae ludibundae, I. Parodorum epicorum Graecorum et Archestrati reliquiae* (Leipzig).

Chantraine, P., 1968- *Dictionnaire étymologique de la langue grecque* (Paris).

Degani, E. 1975 'Note ai parodi greci', *Sileno* 1, 157-74.

Degani, E. 1982a *Poesia parodica greca²* (Bologna).

Degani, E., 1982b 'Appunti di poesia gastronomica greca', in *AA.VV.*, *Prosimetrum e spoudogeloion* (Genova), 29-54.

Degani, E., 1985 'Problemas de poesia gastronomica griega', in *AA.VV.*, *Miscelanea humanistica: Sofocles - Matròn - Leopardi, Cuadernos de la Fundacion Pastor de Estudios Clasicos* 33, 41-66.

Detienne, M. & Vernant, J.-P., 1991 *Cunning Intelligence in Greek Culture and Society* (1974, Eng. trans. 1978, Chicago).

Estienne, H., 1573 *Homeri et Hesiodi certamen, Matronis et aliorum parodiae...* (Paris).

Ferroni, G., 1974 *Il comico nelle teorie contemporanee* (Roma).

Giannini, A., 1956 *Dioniso* 19, 239.

Householder, P.W. 1944 *Classical Philology* 39, 8.

Koller, H., 1956 *Glotta* 35, 17-32.

Lloyd-Jones, H. & Parsons, P., 1983 *Supplementum Hellenisticum* (Berlin-New York).

Lorenzoni, A., 1980/81 *AION* 1-2, 67-70.

Maas, P., 1949 *Paulys Reallexicon der classischen Altertumswissenschaft*, ed. G. Wissowa and W. Kroll, 18, 1684-6.

Mackail, J.W., 1899 *Classical Review* 3, 204.

Martin, J., 1931 *Symposion. Die Geschichte einer literarischen Form* (Paderborn).

Montanari, O. 1978/79 *Museum Criticum* 12/14, 309ff.

Montanari, O., 1980/82 *Museum Criticum* 15-17, 127ff.

Montanari, O., 1983 *Archestrato di Gela. I Testimonianze e frammenti* (Bologna).

Paessens, H.G., 1856 *De Matronis parodiarum reliquiis* (Diss. Monasterii).

Peltzer, B.J., 1855 *De paroedica Graecorum poesi et de Hipponactis, Hegemonis, Matronis parodiarum fragmentis* (Diss. Monasterii).

Poehlmann, E., 1972 *Glotta* 50, 144-56.

Robert, L., 1936 *Revue des Etudes Grecques* 49, 251-4.

Roscher, W., 1884-1937 *Ausfürlicher Lexikon der griechischen und römisches Mythologie* (Leipzig).

Rossi, R., 1980/81 *Il Faone di Platone comico* (Diss. Bologna, A.A.).

Salanitro, G., 1981 *Osidio Geta. Medea* (Roma).

Scaliger, J.C., 1561 *Poetices libri septem* (Lyons), 46.

Schachermeyr, F., 1965 *Sitzungsberichte der Oesterreicheischen Akademie der Wissenschaft in Wien* 247, 7ff.

Schweighäuser, J., 1801 *Animadversiones in Athenaeum* I (Strasbourg).

Shero, L., 1929 'Lucilius' Cena Rustica', *American Journal of Philology* 50, 64-70.

Shroeter, R., 1967 *Poetica* I, 13.

Thompson, D'Arcy W. 1947 *A Glossary of Greek Fishes* (Oxford).

Timpanaro, S. 1978 *Contributi di filologia e di storia della lingua latina* (Roma).

Traina, A., 1989 *Materiali e discussioni per l'analisi dei testi classici* 13, 145-50.

Wilamowitz-Moellendorff, U. von 1905 *Hermes* 40, 174ff. (= *Kleine Shriften* 4, 220ff.).

Wilamowitz-Moellendorff, U. von 1923 *Hermes* 58, 73-79 (= *Kleine Schriften* 4, 330-35).

❖ 32 ❖

THE SOURCES AND SAUCES OF ATHENAEUS

John Wilkins and Shaun Hill

This chapter differs from Degani's and most of the others on food and literature in being concerned not with food in literature – about which we may ask the kind of question, What is the significance of the reference to black pudding in the *Knights* of Aristophanes? – but with literature on food – about which we may ask the questions, What sort of food is this? What does it taste like? Is it nourishing? What happens if we cook it as instructed? We have taken one of the most important Greek authorities on food, Athenaeus of Naukratis and his book *Deipnosophistai* (*Philosophers at Dinner*), and try first to illustrate the kind of evidence that he draws on and transmits, and then to reconstruct some of the dishes from his descriptions, which are very different from the modern recipe. This chapter does not attempt to investigate the sources of Athenaeus fully: this is not formal source criticism but a preliminary account of the type and quality of information Athenaeus supplies to the historian of food. We are further-more only concerned with the preparation of foodstuffs and not with the myriad other associations of the banquet in Athenaeus' work. Nor do we consider the way early sources such as cookery books from the 4th century BC were transmitted to Athenaeus, who was writing in some cases over 500 years later.[1]

Athenaeus and his sources

At 1.78f, Athenaeus quotes a fragment of the 6th century BC poet, Ananios (fr. 3 West):

> If a man were to lock up in his house a large amount of gold, a few figs and two or three men, he would find out how much better figs are than gold.

The fragment, reversing the normal order of values in a way reminiscent of the myth of King Midas, is from an iambic poem. It is *literature*. The paradoxical valuation of figs over gold is characteristic of Greek literature on food, which is surprising, comic, irreverent, the other side of the tracks as it were from more conventional literature. This is one of only six fragments surviving from antiquity of the fragments of Ananios the iambic poet. Four are preserved by Athenaeus, and in this sense he is a connoisseur of the unusual. Athenaeus tells us, further, that not much is known of the life of Ananios, but that it was one based on pleasure (12.511c). We shall consider this life of pleasure further below.

We began with Ananios because he is a source for Athenaeus, one in a list of 'authorities' on figs. Athenaeus, writing about 200 AD, has found this rare book and adds it to his list. It tells us nothing about figs as a foodstuff that is to be cooked or consumed.

In Book 7, Athenaeus gives a long list of fish, in a variant of alphabetical order, and illustrates each with quotation from poetry, comedy,[2] zoological works, medical works, and cookery books. Ananios is quoted again under the entry for the *anthias* or 'beauty-fish':

> In spring the *chromios* is best, in winter the *anthias*. The best of fine delicacies (*opsa*) is the shrimp cooked in a fig leaf. It is sweet to eat in autumn the flesh of the nanny goat, and of the adult pig, when they turn and tread the vintage. Then is the season of dogs and hares and foxes. The season for sheep is the summer when the cicadas chirp. Then from the sea comes the tuna, no mean food that, but outstanding among all fish in a sharp sauce [herb and cheese, like pesto]. The fat ox, it seems to me, is sweet in the middle of the night and in the day.   (Ananios fr. 5 West)

Here we have Athenaeus the lexicographer at work, running a word-search through Greek literature, and arriving at a citation which in fact tells us almost nothing about the *anthias*. Scientific authors writing in prose, such as Hikesios the medical author, Aristotle on animals and Dorion *On Fish* are called upon to help with the nature and classification of the fish. But pride of place in this representative entry on the *anthias* goes to Epicharmos, the comic poet from Syracuse, and Ananios the poet.

There is also the provenance of Ananios to be considered. He was a western Greek, probably from southern Italy. It was in the Greek communities of Sicily and southern Italy that the most rapid developments in cuisine and writing about cuisine were seen. Plato refers with disgust to these developments in a number of passages, the most striking of which Athenaeus quotes at 12.527c-d (= Plato *Epistle* 7.326b):

> It was with this intention, accordingly, that I went to Italy and Sicily on the occasion of my first visit. But when I arrived, the life there satisfied me in no way or manner; think of a life stuffing twice a day, and never being able to sleep alone at night, to say nothing of all the practices that accompany that mode of living!

We have singled out Ananios because in his treatment of food-preparation and cooking Athenaeus favours poetry, and on occasion gives special attention to rare books.[3] Beside Ananios we may set Mithaikos, who also comes from the Greek West, Sicily, and who is also cited only four times by Athenaeus, though almost never *verbatim*. Because Mithaikos wrote one of Europe's earliest cookery books we would have hoped that Athenaeus might preserve some of his prose, indeed some of his recipes at length, if only in fragments like those of Ananios. He does not. The four references to Mithaikos are: at 7.282a, 'Mithaikos mentions *alphestai* (a species of wrasse)'; at 7.325a, 'Mithaikos in his cookery book says "cut off the head and remove the guts from the ribbon fish, wash and cut into slices, and pour on cheese and oil"; at 12.516c, 'the Lydians first invented *karuke*,[4] concerning the preparation of which the compilers of cookery books (*hoi ta opsartutika sunthentes*) have spoken: Glaukos of Lokroi, Mithaikos, Dionysios, Herakleides of Syracuse, Agis of Syracuse, Epainetos, Dionysios, and also Hegesippos and Erasistratos and Euthydemos and Krito; and in addition to these Stephanos, Archytas, Akestios, Akesias, Diokles and Philistion'. The last passage is a list of what we have lost. Cookery books are ephemeral in world history. All of these authors who wrote on the *karuke* sauce were accessible to Athenaeus in most cases, we

may be fairly certain, in prose works. Included are medical writers[5] –
Erasistratos, Euthydemos, Akesias, Diokles and Philistion. It is not that
Athenaeus fails to quote from prose authors; rather he is less likely to quote
if they are writing of the *preparation* and *consumption* of food.

The fourth fragment of Mithaikos in Athenaeus is a quotation of Plato,
Gorgias 518b:

> When I asked you what men have been good or are good at caring
> for men's bodies, you answered me with the utmost seriousness,
> Thearion the baker [in Athens], Mithaikos, who wrote the
> treatise on Sicilian cookery, and Sarambos the wine merchant.

So much for the recipe book of Mithaikos, now lost. Most references to it
in the ancient world simply echo this passage of Plato, which is hostile to
cooks and cookery books.

The art of writing about cooking, as opposed to farming, botany or zoology,
originated, then, or was at least strong, in southern Italy and Sicily.
Athenaeus read most of these books on food, but rarely quotes them. Of
the list of authors who mention *karuke*, those most cited in the whole of
Athenaeus are Epainetos, Herakleides of Syracuse and Euthydemos, but
rarely does a citation refer to more than the food product *tout court*.

Athenaeus was more disposed to quote poetry, wit, and the results of the
filtering and selection processes of the philosophical tradition within
which his scholarship works. All of these can be seen in his most important
source for our studies, Archestratos of Gela. The recipes of Mithaikos were
dull to Athenaeus beside the pseudo-Hesiodic hexameters of Archestratos,[6]
though both Archestratos and Mithaikos offer the titillation of forbidden
fruit. Just as Mithaikos was largely known to Athenaeus through the
censures of Plato, so Archestratos was probably mediated to him through
the philosophical categories of the Stoic school.

The recipes of Archestratos are most impressive, but Athenaeus might not
have preserved them had they been in prose. Certainly Athenaeus recog-
nizes the importance of Archestratos and draws attention to him in his
proemium (1.4e). He also quotes a staggering sixty-two fragments. What
about his cooking? It is the cooking of food for the secular setting of the

banquet,[7] after all, that distinguishes Archestratos from scientific and respectable authors.

> Bake the great parrotfish at Chalkedon by the sea after rinsing it well. You will see a good and large one in Byzantium, carrying a body resembling a circling shield. Prepare it whole as follows:

> Cover completely with cheese and oil and hang in a hot oven. Then bake well. Sprinkle with salt mixed with cumin and yellow-grey oil, pouring down from your hand the god-given stream.   (Archestratos fr. 13 Brandt)

> You have the head of the conger, friend, in Sikyon, a fat and strong and large head, and all the belly parts. Then boil it for a long time in salt water, sprinkled with green herbs.
>   (Archestratos fr. 18 Brandt)

These cooking instructions are clear and they place emphasis on produce from a location where it is at its best: there are no better recipes in Athenaeus. He read them though through the hostile filter of the Stoic Chrysippos. What we find in Athenaeus' treatment of Archestratos is the quotation – and thus preservation – of the recipe, along with the occasional mocking introduction, such as 'the glutton Archestratos advises...' (3.112b). Archestratos is honoured but also mocked in ways that writers of comedy and others are not.[8] This tells us much about Athenaeus. We have at once the excellent source on food, and a moralising context in which to locate him. That context exerts a powerful influence on Athenaeus' work. Archestratos may have been well known, even if only preserved *verbatim* in Athenaeus, because of his being held up as a terrible example of luxury by Klearchos the historian and Chrysippos the Stoic philosopher. Athenaeus quotes both authors as linking Archestratos with another famous purveyor of immorality, Philaenis, alleged author of a sex manual (10.457c, 8.335d-e), and adds that Archestratos tried to emulate the fabulous luxury of the Assyrian potentate Sardanapalus (8.335e-f). These are important associations,[9] but they probably tell us more about Athenaeus than about Archestratos. Compare the attestation of Athenaeus to the luxury of Ananios, mentioned above: Ananios may indeed have lived a life of luxury, but he may simply have written about food regularly in his poetry.

Athenaeus reflects a mainstream, in which Plato and Aristotle and the Stoic philosophers figure largely, and which is heavily based on Athens as the cultural centre of the world. That mainstream in Athenaeus is under pressure from two very interesting quarters. The first is the influence of the East and the West, the Lydians, the Persians, the Assyrians and the Phoenicians; and the Greeks of southern Italy. These are exotic and attractive areas for the Greek palate, and food books also often came from these places. Many writers came from the West, Matro from the eastern Aegean. These were areas associated with luxury, Assyria with her King Sardanapalus in particular. Food and foodwriters from the West were also associated with luxury, as we have seen in the cases of Mithaikos, Ananios and Archestratos. These associations sometimes get in the way of the clear information on cooking which we would like.

The second influence on Athenaeus is his curiosity and breadth. More than Pollux and the lexicographers, he quotes and refers widely, and often *verbatim*. Unfortunately for the purposes of this investigation, Athenaeus does not quote as much as we would like, nor does he quote as much as we would wish from surviving authors that we can check on: Theophrastos, for example, on silphium. Zoological details of fish in Aristotle's works on animals are also not quoted in full.

Athenaeus then, who was no original thinker, is strong on many aspects of Greek culture and literature but fragmentary on food and on the reconstruction of diet and tastes. That reconstruction can however be attempted.

Towards a reconstruction of the foods in Athenaeus

Making sense of the tantalisingly brief references to his sources in order to reconstruct dishes and tastes requires rather wider investigation than may initially appear necessary. Food is not an academic exercise; it is the daily experience, necessity, and occasionally pleasure, of each and every person. Once the basic needs of refuelling have been met, there is an element of choice, especially in areas such as flavourings and texture. These will give good indications of the taste and lifestyle of an era.

The starch element of a meal, that which provides comfort rather than excitement, is normally decided by factors such as climate and soil conditions. Whether this starch is cereal or vegetable and whether it is eaten as porridge or baked as bread is a question of convenience and custom. The function performed will be the same, that of rice in Asia, pasta in Italy or potatoes in Ireland – filler.

Similarly, sweetened starch products such as cakes and biscuits will be made from whatever is freely available. Lesser qualities of wheat may not be suitable for transformation into pastry but will still make creditable bread as well as thickening liquids or combining with honey and nuts to make good milk cake.

The following recipe, *staititas*, derives from the description by Athenaeus at 14.646b:

> Batter: ½ oz fresh yeast, 1 teaspoon honey, ³/₄ pint lukewarm water, 2 cups of plain flour.
>
> Topping: feta cheese, honey, sesame seeds.
>
> Method: mix yeast, honey and half the water; leave for 10 minutes until the yeast bubbles; add mixture to the flour and stir in remaining water; leave dough in a warm draught-free place for an hour to prove; heat a pan or griddle, lightly oil, and pour on the dough/batter, half a ladleful at a time; cook on both sides; spread with cheese, honey and sesame and eat warm.

Athenaeus wrote baldly: 'the dough is poured on a frying-pan and honey, sesame and cheese are added'. The reconstructed dish is similar to *ataifi*, an Arab pancake popular in the Middle East since medieval times. While yeast was certainly known in the 4th century BC, there is little evidence of any widespread popularity or use. Flatbreads, which are firmer, may have been more practical in transporting morsels of food from table to mouth. It is possible to reconstruct the dish, albeit with less enjoyable results to our modern palates, without yeast. The resulting soft dough will produce a conventional pancake if good quality flour is used and something like a chapati with coarser flours.

Breads and doughs are, in fact, the easiest to reconstruct even from such vague and fleeting references. These mixtures simply fail to work if the ratios of liquid to flour are incorrect, especially where yeast is used. The scientific rules which dictate what happens in breadmaking and the relative quantities of grain to liquid needed to set any polenta or milk cake will be the same now as then.

It is also reasonable to assume that the fish described by writers like Archestratos will not have evolved appreciably in the last two thousand years. Making any such assumptions about cultivated plants or domesticated livestock is quite a different matter. It is also unsafe to assume that translations of terms used for herbs and vegetables are equivalent to their modern counterparts.

The major flavourings of the time are no longer fashionable in Europe and there is much consternation at salt fish sauces such as *garum*.[10] The idea of dipping food into a preparation made from fermented fish and guts is unappetising. Of course this is absurd. The cuisine of S.E. Asia uses and prizes many of the flavours enjoyed in Classical Greece and Rome. Nam Pla which is produced in the same way as garum and from the same kind of ingredients does not taste of fish at all – the fermentation process changes that – and can be compared to a mild version of soy sauce. The favoured herb is silphium, said by Pliny (*Natural History* 19.38-46) to be related in flavour to asafoetida, which is still used in Indian vegetarian cookery and is one of the principal flavourings, along with fermented fish, of Worcestershire sauce.

One of the most detailed descriptions given by Athenaeus outside the fragments of Archestratos is for the Lydian dish *kandaulos*.[11] The text, which follows the passage on *karuke* cited above, says (12.516d): Hegesippos of Tarentum says that it was made of boiled meat, breadcrumbs, Phrygian cheese, dill and fatty meat stock.

The amount of breadcrumb used to thicken the dish determines whether it is in fact a soup or a stew but not the overall style or taste. If the word translated as dill – *anethon* – does refer to dill, then there is an unusual if recognizable combination of flavours that produces a tasty and interesting dish. If anise seeds are used a rather stranger and less familiar flavour, not unlike liquorice, is produced.

In either case, sophisticated and complex tastes are being called for, treatments which indicate a discerning palate, not a diet of porridge and salt fish. The food references in the *Deipnosophistai* must of course be treated with the same caution as food-writing and criticism today, namely that the comment and opinion will tell as much about the reviewer as the subject under review. The prejudices and fashions of the writer and his period, through which everything must filter, must always be taken into account.

Archestratos is derided but his outlook on food is very sympathetic to the most modern views. His emphasis on finding the best produce and then treating it simply is completely in tune with our own. His advocacy of strong treatments, cheese and vinegar sauces, only for inferior fish or meat dishes is sensible and unpretentious. Athenaeus does not see it that way: he both identifies Archestratos' simple style with the supposed oriental luxury of Sardanapalus, and fails to distinguish this simplicity from the richness of *karuke* sauce. For this most important of writers on the history of food, food is of great cultural interest, but to be viewed as something immoral rather than as raw material for the skills of the cook.

Notes

1. On the transmission of Archestratos, see for example Brandt (1888, 114-39).
2. Comedy is a class of evidence used extensively by Athenaeus: we have discussed the implications in Wilkins and Hill (1992).
3. A striking example of this is the *Attic Dinner* of Matro the parodist, quoted 'because of its rarity' (4.134d).
4. Greek culture identified sauces with luxurious eating. Foreign sauces such as this *karuke* from Lydia in Asia Minor set off a frisson in the Greek breast similar to that aroused by an hollandaise in an old fashioned Briton, on which see Mennell (1985, 72, 96-7).
5. Cookery books were closely related to medical books in antiquity. Plato, ever hostile to the pleasures of eating, implies as much in his *Gorgias* when he sets the doctor who heals, albeit with unpleasant medicines, in contrast with the cook who gives food that tastes good but in no way improves the patient's health.
6. In many ways Archestratos is a literary writer, a parodist, though in a different way from Matro (n.3). Both authors have been studied impressively by Degani in his chapter here, and in Degani (1982; 1990; 1991).
7. The cooking associated with animal sacrifices belongs to a different category in Greek culture: see Vernant and Detienne (1989).
8. This phenomenon is discussed in Wilkins and Hill (1994, 25-8).
9. For a discussion of the connection between sex and eating in Athenaeus see Henry (1992).
10. See for example Mary Beard *TLS* 26.11.92.
11. For full references on the Lydian sauces *kandaulos* and *karuke* see Chapter 19, 'Lydian Specialities'.

Bibliography

Brandt P., 1888 *Corpusculum Poesis Epicae Graecae Ludibundae I* (Leipzig).

Degani E., 1982 'Appunti di poesia gastronomica greca', *AA.VV, Prosimetrum e Spoudogeloion* (Genova) 29-54.

Degani E., 1990 *Alma Mater Studiorum* I (Bologna) 51-63.

Degabi E., 1991 *Alma Mater Studiorum* II (Bologna) 164-75.

Henry, M., 1992 'The Edible Woman: Athenaeus' Concept of the Pornographic', in A. Richlin (ed.) *Pornography and Representation in Greece and Rome* (Oxford), 250-68.

Mennell S., 1985 *All Manners of Food* (Oxford).

Vernant, J.-P. & M. Detienne, M., 1989 *The Cuisine of Sacrifice among the Greeks* (1979, English trans., Chicago).

Wilkins J. & Hill S., 1992 'The Flavours of Ancient Greece', *Spicing Up The Palate: Studies of Flavourings – Ancient and Modern. Proceedings of the Oxford Symposium on Food and Cookery 1992* (London) 275-9.

Wilkins J. & Hill S., 1994 *Archestratus: The Life of Luxury* (Totnes).

INDEX OF PASSAGES DISCUSSED

This index will guide the reader to the most substantial discussions of ancient texts in this volume, and to passages quoted verbatim. The numerous passages simply cited as evidence, or mentioned in passing, are not listed.

GENERAL INDEX

The names of modern scholars have not been indexed, nor has any attempt been made to index all the ingredients mentioned in the notes to Chapter 9.

Dionysos 151
Dioskorides 15, 36, 52, 58
Dioskouroi 199
dip 205
Diphilos (comic writer) 210-11; of Siphnos 32, 276, 362, 368
dirt 205, 233
disease 236, 345, 351-3, 360; identification 93; diseases of cereals 26, 35
disguised food see deception, culinary
disgust 232
dish 112, 126, 253, 282
distribution of acorn species 16-19; of food 256, 260; of sacrificial meat 197-8; distribution of food 70, 84, 145; of grain 33, 83, 198, 262; of land 259, 264
diuretics 348
diving 134
divorce 237-8
DNA ch.7
documentary evidence, bias in 21-3
dodder 250-1
dogs 156-8, 211, 310, 359; eaten? 282-4; dog-days 184
dokane 51
dole, corn 83
dolphin 148, 151, 170
domestic pottery ch.5; production 48; domesticated animals 97, 104, 173-4
donkey 40, 120, 292-4, 359, 360, 364
Dorians 91
Dougga 109
dough 41, 43, 45-8, 50, 61, 67, 97, 183, 253, 255
drachma 81
dreams 255, 344
dried fruit 255, 276
drink, drinking 1, 7-9, 174, 179-80, 205-6, 225, 228, 230, 242; abstention from 227, 231, 233; ritual 242; drunkenness 231, 234; see also water, wine
drooling 210
drought 260
drowning 134-5

drug-sellers 165
drums 280-1
dry conditions 89; drying of grain 36
duck 310
duckling 252
dung-cake 51; death by 51
durum wheat 95-7
'dust', wheat-flour 31
dyeing 255

early man ch.13; earliest food 12
earning a living 206
earthenware 252
East, the 3, 5, 243; Near 288
eating and blood production 354; in bath, Augustan/top-level? 226; better/more 254; clean 242; collective ch.14; habits, Celtic 242; Greek 262; kin 217-8; repugnant practices 283; revolutionary 204; ritual ch.14; sacred ch.14; solitary 209
ecology 147, 223, 257, 263-4, 269; see also ecosystems
economics chs 6, 12, 296-300; Greek lack of interest in 167; strategies 71; aspects of diet 205; basis of colonies 259; exemptions 267; hierarchies 147; ideology, thought 142, 145; interaction 258; interdependence 266; links 147; organization 264; economy of Black Sea 163; of Byzantium 163, 165; of Sybaris 266-7; history of 257
ecosystems, colonial 258-62; competition 261; expansion 261, 262; Greek 258-62, 265; indigenous 261, 265 [with colonial?]; interaction 261; Sybarite 266-9; variety 262
Eden, Garden of 173
education 202, 287
eels 159, 160, 211, 267, 310, 390-1, 405, 418, 421-2, 424, 427; -sellers, tax-free 267
eggs 41, 125, 126, 214, 290; egg white 125; egg yolk 125, 131

Egypt 25, 27, 33-7, 52, 93, 138, 185-90, 195, 320, 363, 391, 424, (Ptolemaic) ch. 23
einkorn 14
elaborate food 123; culinary techniques 131
Elamite 250, 288-9, 294
Elea 262
election 199
Eleusis 26, ch.13; Eleusinia ch.13
élite 83-4, 222
emaciation 235
embezzlement 212
emergencies 13, 73
emmer ch. 2, 46-8, 76, 94-5, 97
Empedokles 217-8, 223
Emperor, Roman 51, 84, 137, 142
enclosures for beasts 114
endogamy/exogamy 92
energy 136, 139
English farms 73; Oak 18; pottery 64-7; prejudice 106; shepherds 49; words 56, 62
enhancement of food 127
Ennius 39, 136, 148, 402
entertainment, Greek-style 56, 398
entrails see innards
environment 1, 93, 98, 140, 145, 260, 276 see also ecosystem
ephebes 181-4, 195, 207
Ephesos 31, 33, 149, 200, 278, 280
epicures 105, 209-10
Epicurus, Epicureans 222, 224
Epidamnos 91
epigrams 134, 140
epigraphic evidence 72, 81-2, 109, 110, 112, 137, 197-200, 262-3
Erechtheus 185-6; Erichthonios 185-6, 195
Eresos 30
Erotianos 30
Erythrae 403
escalope 111
Esquiline 109